Intersections of Aging

Readings in Social Gerontology

Elizabeth W. Markson
Boston University

Lisa A. Hollis-Sawyer
Northeastern Illinois University

Foreword by
Jon Hendricks
Oregon State University

Roxbury Publishing Company
Los Angeles, California

Library of Congress Cataloging-in-Publication Data

Intersections of aging: readings in social gerontology [edited by] Elizabeth W.
  Markson, Lisa A. Hollis-Sawyer.
    p. cm.
    Includes bibliographical references.
    ISBN 1-891487-06-X
  1. Aging—Social aspects. 2. Aging—Psychological aspects.
  3. Aging—Government policy. I. Markson, Elizabeth Warren.
  II. Hollis-Sawyer, Lisa A., 1963–
  HQ1061.A468 2000   98-17848
    305.26—dc21   CIP

Intersections of Aging: Readings in Social Gerontology

Publisher and Editor: Claude Teweles
Managing Editor: Dawn VanDercreek
Production Editor: Carla Max-Ryan
Copy Editor: Susan Converse Winslow
Production Assistant: Mike Sametz
Typography: Rebecca Evans & Associates
Cover Design: Marnie Kenney

Printed on acid-free paper in the United States of America. This paper meets the standards
for recycling of the Environmental Protection Agency.

ISBN: 1-891487-06-X

ROXBURY PUBLISHING COMPANY
P.O. Box 491044
Los Angeles, California 90049-9044
Tel.: (310) 473-3312 • Fax: (310) 473-4490
E-mail: roxbury@roxbury.net
Website: www.roxbury.net

*To Alison and David, who are
very different young adults and one
day will be very different elders*

The trouble is that old age is not interesting
until one gets there, a foreign country with
an unknown language to the young,
and even to the middle-aged.

—May Sarton, *As We Are Now*

Our culture is not much interested in *why* we grow old, or how we *ought* to grow old, or what it *means* to grow old. . . . Focusing narrowly on a reified "problem of old age," apart from the actual lives and cultural representations of people growing older, the scientific management of aging (gerontology and geriatrics) denies our universal participation and solidarity in this most human experience.

—Thomas R. Cole, "Oedipus and the Meaning of Aging:
Personal Reflections and Historical Perspectives"

Contents

Section I: Cultural Constructions of Later Life

     Jay Sokolovsky

     Sokolovsky discusses the importance of culture in understanding how old age and gender are defined and how these designations affect people's options in later life.

     James S. O'Leary

     O'Leary describes how industrialization and urbanization are changing the norms of filial piety in Japan.

     Mike Hepworth

     Hepworth contends that younger people's anxiety about so-called "childish" behavior in old age can free older people from constraining social norms.

     Carole Haber

     Haber, a historian, shows how old age in nineteenth-century America became defined as a medical condition without a cure.

     Benjamin Schlesinger

     Schlesinger details how the concept of older people as asexual results in negative psychological and physical effects and gives others control over their lives and well-being.

Section II: Social Contexts of Aging

Section III: Work, Retirement, and Income Security

Section IV: Family, Social Relationships, and Intergenerational Reciprocity

Section V: Health and Illness in Later Life

Section VI: Future Directions for Older Americans and for Gerontology

In this concluding selection, Riley discusses the mismatch between diverse individuals and the social structures that influence the course of aging ("structural lag")—noting the many ways in which policies can be redirected to minimize the lag.

Foreword
Diversity is the Name of the Game

Jon Hendricks
Oregon State University

What will happen tomorrow, or the day after? Those questions may sound like insecurity talking to some; to others they are exactly the questions we should be asking. Not knowing history may increase the likelihood of repeating it, but not anticipating the future is unlikely to lead to any Elysian field either. In this volume, Markson, Hollis-Sawyer and the scholars they have brought together come to grips with the causes as well as the consequences of inequalities across the life course.

Perhaps it is part of our ideology, or a consequence of the scientific method as it has taken root in social gerontology, but the overriding interpretation has been that, except for a few hardship cases, people pretty much create their own futures. No doubt that is true, in part—but only in part. Domestic policies, in their many guises, circumscribe options and frequently affect access to opportunity. To make the case as simply as possible: definitions of old age have traditionally derived from legal mandates that age 65 is the eligibility threshold for most entitlement benefits. That age has been "reified," as the social scientists among us say when speaking of something that is taken as factual and concrete, even if it exists only by consensus. Anything thought to be characteristic of old age that occurs prior to this chronological portal is often described as premature, and anything later is characterized as delayed. With all the baggage surrounding age 65, we have created a social category that is then put to use for explanatory purposes, plain and simple.

When the world left the twentieth century behind, it did so with some three times the number of people who entered it. Within the next dozen years, another billion will be added, bringing the total to seven billion. Without delving into the details, suffice it to say that is an exponential rate of growth unprecedented in human history. It is also important to point out that demography in and of itself is not destiny, nor is its meaning automatically apocalyptic. The numbers mean what we say—they mean nothing more and nothing less. What the demographics do tell us is that people are living longer and remaining vital well past the age when in times past they would have one or both feet in the grave. They tell us that public policies, ranging from public health measures to employment policies and old age assurances, are part of the fabric of the human condition. You cannot speak of the one without acknowledging the role of the others.

It is one thing to debate whether integration or segregation of the elderly is in their best interests, quite another to contemplate the factors facilitating one or another pattern. What the authors represented in this volume contend is that no single recommendation is appropriate for all older persons, and whatever promotes well-being of one group likely varies for another group. Why is this so? Imagine two walkers who set off in different directions and encounter distinct topographies, people, languages, cultures, circumstances, and hurdles. When they come back together, the factors underpinning their descriptions of what they came across along the way would be very different too. Only a moment is required to realize the two walkers would gain very disparate world views based on the dissimilarity of their experience and would encounter new situations differentially equipped to deal with them. "But of course" is the appropriate response. So why is it so much more difficult to comprehend that the complexities of life are going to lead to diverse old ages? After all, malleability is as much a part of the human condition as is eye color, hair color, or skin color; how much significance we attach to any attribute is up to us.

From time to time one hears of older people who rail against the tides and are determined to grow old by their own design, not according to what social categories prescribe. The late Maggie Kuhn, founder of the grassroots organization Gray Panthers, was one such person. In talking with her one could never be certain which comments were intended to tweak the listener and which were heartfelt; either way she was determined to seize the initiative and not be one of those "poor dears" peopling the scholarly and popular opinion of the era. As she said, policy is personal, and Kuhn was the personification of exactly the type of older person driving the focus in this book.

Reading closely the essays and reports found in *Intersections of Aging: Readings in Social Gerontology* will improve our acuity as we gaze into the crystal ball looking for life's lessons. To the extent we have comparable experiences we may have comparable old ages, but the converse is just as likely the case. As T. M. Calasanti points out, utilizing one group to establish a norm and then contrasting another group to that norm is not a method likely to provide much insight into the condition of either. In every instance, the social resources upon which a person draws will differ according to race, gender, ethnicity, social class, age, educational, and occupational background. What is important to remember is that the effects of each are not merely additive, regardless of the order in which they are considered. These and other factors establish life styles, the quality of life experience, and, as the editors point out, they contour the pathways to and through old age. Regardless of critical and countervailing points of view, we do grow old no matter what. The point is to do it optimally, as Baltes and Carstensen make clear, for to do so within the bounds of our own lives is to ensure that we live successfully.

Markson and Hollis-Sawyer are quick to point out that variability and social contexts go hand-in-hand. The meaning we attach to personal attributes within those contexts is what gives meaning to life; there is no getting around it. Gender is a case in point. As I have said elsewhere: sex is easy, one X chromosome or two about settles it. Gender is more difficult; it is the social meaning that attaches to chromosomes. The same process accompanies many other biological attributes as well and is incorporated into public identities and self-concepts. The feeling of what happens is largely determined by the relativity of social prescriptions and expectations.

Beyond essential ascribed characteristics are a host of achieved characteristics. Among the latter are work and occupational background, which contribute directly to patterns of retirement and income security. As we wend our way along the sometimes-circuitous path of earning a living, we simultaneously create our autobiography. It is too bad that we have to consider one factor after another as we attempt to examine their impact, for doing so tends to create conceptual gaps about the relevance of their interdependence. In spite of the fact that we concentrate on human capital, there is no denying that social capital is equally germane to what becomes of us—although the effects of the latter are more difficult to ascertain. It can be done, but it requires a sophisticated conceptual lens. Fortunately, the editors bring together a corps of experts willing to take on the challenge and to share the results of their insights. No one who reads the contributions herein will look at life the same way again, nor will they be able to speak of "productive aging" with quite the same myopic sense of assurance that the facts are quite as they seem at first glance.

Personal and fiduciary resources are central to the aging experience. The first includes both physiological and psychological resources facilitating environmental mastery and the imposition of will over the flow of events. The second revolves around ability to barter in whatever the currency of exchange. Beyond those lies another resource, one that is embedded in family and social networks or connections. These latter are equally germane and cannot be considered apart from the first two, for together they circumscribe social life space.

In the entries Markson and Hollis-Sawyer compile in Section IV, the relevance of these ties of later life emerges in bold relief and provides ample testimony as to their importance in contouring life's trajectories. Once again the relevance of gender, race, ethnicity, socioeconomic status, and so on is pervasive and inexorably linked to the shape of relationships. These also color the meaning of health and of ill-health, flip sides of a single coin and one whose purchasing power is inevitably part of the cultural milieu.

What is clear is that even the experienced gerontologist has something to learn from *Intersections of Aging*. I can only imagine the thrill of discovery for novitiates negotiating their way through this new terrain. I envy you. The journey will be worth the effort, and it will alter the way you think of aging and of yourself.

Preface

The focus in this book is on the many faces of aging. To provide a glimpse of these, we have drawn primarily upon qualitative research articles in the social sciences and from literature. The volume is divided into six sections, each dealing with a broad aspect of later life. Some articles were especially commissioned for this volume; others have been selected from published sources. All are intended to provide views of the aging experience through multiple lenses.

Not since the early years of the twentieth century has the American population been as diverse as it will be in the twenty-first century. We as social scientists can predict with relative certainty that, as a group, the baby boomers will enter old age as a more educated (and probably more affluent) cohort than today's elderly. Yet pockets of poverty and gender, racial or ethnic, and social inequality continue to exist among today's elderly and are likely to continue in the next few decades.

What are the many experiences of growing old? There is, as we know, no one pattern of aging, for all of us age at different rates with different social and personal characteristics. Clearly, the increasing heterogeneity of individual aging experiences and the diversity of broader social factors such as family structure, race and ethnicity, social class, gender, and relative power within the society are shaping the ways in which people age.

Incorporating both heterogeneity and diversity into our study of aging involves paying attention to comparison of similarities and differences across and within groups. Too, it is important that we understand the social arrangements that shape the social reality of groups regardless of race, ethnicity, social class, or gender.

The course of individual lives remains inextricably connected with social institutions. As we live longer, family structures and relationships, living arrangements, housing design, entitlement programs, health care, retirement, and the methods by which we die are but a few of the arenas that will become critically important in the years ahead.

We hope that you will enjoy reading this book as much as we enjoyed putting it together. We also hope that you will find the selections useful in illuminating both the variations in individual aging and the role of social hierarchies—gender, race or ethnicity, and social class—in shaping later life.

Acknowledgments

Many people have made this book possible. Special thanks go to Beth B. Hess for her assistance, generous friendship, and moral support, without which this book would not have become a reality. She has been friend and colleague for more than 20 years; for those who know her and her work, her influence will be apparent throughout the anthology. Karen Johnston worked diligently, thoughtfully, and cheerfully on permissions, scanning, and a multitude of other tasks and offered enthusiastic, good-humored, and sustaining support throughout this project. Yahminah Dean and Jenny Rogers performed the laborious and time-consuming tasks of correcting and retyping many of the selections. Our husbands, Ralph Markson and Thomas Sawyer, provided moral support and empathy throughout.

At Boston University, Melissa Amick, Nancy Capobianco Boyer, Kathleen Jordan, Julie Plaut Mahoney, and Faith Little contributed thoughtful and helpful feedback on many of the portions of the volume. Claude Teweles, our publisher, provided both inspiration for the creation of this collection and amazing faith and composure during its preparation. We would especially like to thank the following people who reviewed an earlier draft of this book for their careful and constructive input and guidance: Toni Calasanti (Virginia Polytechnical University); Carol A. Gaetjens (Northwestern University); Deborah Gold (Duke University); Roma Hanks (University of South Alabama); Dale J. Jaffe (University of Wisconsin, Milwaukee); Paul C. Luken (Arkansas State University); Charles McGehee (Central Washington University); Robin D. Moreman (Northern Illinois University); and Mary Ellen Yates. And last, but not least, we should like to thank the authors whose contributions are included. We only regret that we were not able to include all the numerous excellent pieces that we read and enjoyed, which expand upon the themes in this volume.

About the Contributors[*]

Hiroko Akiyama is Associate Research Scientist, the Institute for Social Research, University of Michigan, Ann Arbor. Author of numerous articles, including publications in *Sex Roles* and *Journal of Gerontology*, she is interested in social supports and social networks in later life.

Katherine R. Allen is Associate Professor of Family Studies at Virginia Polytechnic Institute and State University, Blacksburg. Her research reported in this volume was supported by a grant from the National Institutes of Health through the American Nurses' Association.

Toni Antonucci is Program Director in the Life Course Development Program, Institute for Social Research, and Professor of Psychology, University of Michigan, Ann Arbor. Her research interests have focused on social relationships across the life span, most recently on comparative life-span studies of social relationships in the United States and Japan. Her numerous publications include articles in *Journal of Gerontology, Developmental Psychology, Journal of Marriage and the Family*, and *Psychology of Women*.

María P. Aranda is Assistant Professor at the School of Social Work, University of Southern California. Her research centers on health and functional disability, psychiatric disorders, service utilization among middle-aged and older Latinos, and the influence of ethnicity on the health of those receiving rehabilitation and long-term care.

Margret M. Baltes was a psychologist at the Department of Gerontopsychiatry, Free University of Berlin, where she conducted research on the description, explanation, and modification of aging processes from a life-span perspective, until her recent death.

Patricia P. Barry, former President of the American Geriatrics Society and former Chair of the Board of Directors of the American Geriatrics Society, is Director of the Geriatrics Service, Boston Medical Center, and Professor of Medicine, Boston University, where she also directs the Center of Excellence in Geriatrics, funded by the John A. Hartford Foundation. Her research focuses on health, home care, and functioning in later life.

Robert H. Binstock, Professor of Aging, Health, and Society at the School of Medicine, Case Western Reserve University, has written and published extensively on aging and social policy, including the volume *The Future of Long-Term Care: Social and Policy Issues* (co-edited with Leighton E. Cluff and Otto Von Mering). He is currently Book Editor of *The Gerontologist*.

Toni M. Calasanti is Associate Professor of Sociology, Virginia Polytechnic Institute and State University, Blacksburg. Author of numerous articles on aging, she is currently interested in diversity and aging, economic restructuring, and retirement experiences.

Daniel Callahan is Director of the Hastings Center and has written many books and articles on medical ethics and health policy, including *Setting Limits: Medical Goals in an Aging Society* and *What Kind of Life?: The Limits of Medical Progress*.

Laura L. Carstensen is Professor of Psychology, Stanford University, and a fellow of the American Psychological Association, the American Psychological Society, and the Gerontological Society of America. Among her numerous publications is *Handbook of Clinical Gerontology* (co-edited with B. A. Edelstein).

Diana Chang, born in the United States to a Eurasian mother and Chinese father, grew up in the United States and China. Her fiction and poetry have been published in numerous literary magazines; among her novels is *Frontiers of Love*, first published in 1956 and reissued in 1994. She is also a painter whose work has been exhibited in numerous one-person shows.

Victoria Chin-Sang is Associate Chief of Nursing Education at the Hampton Veterans' Administration Medical Center, Hampton, Virginia. Her research reported in this volume was supported by a grant from the National Institutes of

Health through the American Nurses' Association.

William H. Crown is Director of Outcomes Research and Econometrics, the MEDSTAT Group, Cambridge, Massachusetts, and author of *Handbook on Employment and the Elderly*.

Stephen J. Cutler is Professor of Sociology and the Bishop Robert F. Joyce Distinguished University Professor of Gerontology, University of Vermont, and past President of the Gerontological Society of America. Among his many books and journal articles is *Promoting Successful and Productive Aging* (co-edited with Lynne Bond and Armin Grams).

A. Elizabeth Delany was the younger of the two Delany sisters, both of whom lived to be over 100 years old and died in the 1990s. A former dentist, she was a member of one of the most eminent African-American families in North Carolina and Harlem.

Sarah Delany was a high school teacher and, with her sister, one of the oldest known surviving members of one of the most eminent African-American families in North Carolina and Harlem. Their life stories, from which the selection in this volume is excerpted, were not only published as the book *Having Our Say: The Delany Sisters' First One Hundred Years* but also rewritten as a play and performed on the New York stage.

J. Kevin Eckert is Professor of Sociology and Anthropology at the University of Maryland. Dr. Eckert's specializations are social-cultural gerontology, urban and medical anthropology, and living and care environments for dependent adults. Current research includes projects studying residential care environments for the frail elderly, family caregiving for elders with dementia, and home- and community-based care alternatives.

Kathryn Elliott is Director of the Gerontology Program/Center on Aging and Assistant Professor of Gerontology at Minnesota State University, Mankato. Her research interests include cross-cultural aging; aging and culture among ethnic minorities in the United States; cultural awareness in providing services to both mainstream and ethnic minority elders in the United States; culture, aging, and health, including dementia and chronic illness; culture and elder caregiving; and rural aging.

Morris Friedell is Professor Emeritus, Department of Sociology, University of California, Santa Barbara. Diagnosed with Alzheimer's disease, he currently resides in Ventura, California, where he is actively engaged with others who have Alzheimer's.

Marcene Goodman, now Marcene Nodine, is retired and lives in Philadelphia, where she is a community leader and activist for a cleaner city.

Carole Haber, Professor and Chair, Department of History, University of Delaware, has written extensively about the history of aging in America. She is currently working on a new project on the medicalization of death in the late nineteenth and early twentieth centuries.

Gunhild O. Hagestad, of the Institute for Social Research, Oslo, Norway, and Northwestern University, Chicago, has published numerous articles on family relationships in later life. Research for the selection in this volume was supported by a Research Career Development Award from the National Institute on Aging.

Jennifer Hand is currently on the faculty of the Department of Community Health, University of Auckland, and is conducting research on the developmentally disabled in New Zealand as well as on health promotion in later life.

Amy Hill Hearth, a freelance writer for the *New York Times*, collaborated with the Delany sisters on the book, *Having Our Say*.

Marilyn Helterline is Professor of Sociology and Women's Studies and Chair, Sociology Department, State University of New York College, Oneota. Her current research focuses on the changing concepts of gender in the nineteenth century.

Mike Hepworth, Reader in Sociology at the University of Aberdeen, has published extensively on visual and literary images of aging in the construction of the aging experience.

Lynne Gershenson Hodgson is Chair, Department of Sociology, Quinnipiac College, Hamden, Connecticut, and member of the Executive Committee, Association for Gerontology in Higher Education. Her research in recent years has centered on the relationships between grandparents and adult grandchildren and the social-psychological concerns of families dealing with Alzheimer's disease.

Lisa A. Hollis-Sawyer is Assistant Professor of Psychology and Gerontology, Northeastern Illinois University, Chicago. She received her doctorate in Industrial Gerontology and Psychology from the University of Akron and was a National Institute on Aging Post-Doctoral Trainee in research on the aging at Boston University.

Margaret Hellie Huyck is Professor, Institute of Psychology, Illinois Institute of Technology, Chicago, and a Fellow of the Gerontological Society of America. The author of *Growing Older* and (with W. Hoyer) *Adult Development and Aging*, as well as chapters on gender and family relationships during midlife, she has (funded by the National Health Institute of Mental Health) focused on young-adult children and their parents in Parkville, Illinois.

Colleen L. Johnson is Professor of Medical Anthropology at the University of California, San Francisco. She has conducted research on ethnicity, the family, aging, and adaptation of the oldest old.

Katrina W. Johnson, formerly on the staff of the Behavioral and Social Sciences Division of the National Institute on Aging, is a family and medical sociologist with ongoing interests in aging, minority health, and family-based interventions. After 18 years at the National Institutes of Health, she teaches sociology at Shepherd College, West Virginia.

Eric R. Kingson is Professor of Social Work at Syracuse University's School of Social Work. His research examines the politics and economics of population aging, including Social Security policy, the aging of the baby boom cohorts, and cross-generational obligations.

Bob G. Knight is the Merle H. Bensinger Professor of Gerontology at the University of Southern California Andrus Gerontology Center.

Charles F. Longino, Jr., Professor of Sociology and Professor of Public Health Sciences, Associate Director of Sticht Center on Aging and Rehabilitation, Bowman Gray School of Medicine, Wake Forest University, North Carolina, is a demographer with strong theoretical and policy interests. His many publications include *The Oldest Americans: State Profiles for Data-based Planning*.

Elizabeth W. Markson is Academic Director of the Gerontology Center, Professor of Socio-Medical Sciences and Community Medicine, Research Professor, Department of Medicine, and Adjunct Professor, Department of Sociology at Boston University. With Beth B. Hess, she co-edited several editions of *Growing Old in America*. Her current research focuses on two areas: older women and health care in later life.

William J. McAuley, Co-chair and Director of Research, Oklahoma Center on Aging, Oklahoma City, is conducting research on the experiences of white elders and elders descended from "Indian freedmen" in rural Oklahoma. He is also investigating the demography of long-term care, including nursing-home admission migration patterns.

Kathleen McInnis-Dittrich, Associate Professor, Graduate School of Social Work, Boston College, has conducted research on aging and poverty in Appalachia.

Lydia Minatoya is a psychologist and author of *Talking With Monks in High Places*.

Meredith Minkler is Professor and Chair of Health and Social Behavior in the School of Public Health, University of California, Berkeley. Her publications include the co-authored book *Grandmothers as Caregivers: Raising Children of the Crack Cocaine Epidemic*, the edited volume *Community Organizing and Community Building for Health*, and a co-edited book, *Critical Perspectives on Aging: The Political and Moral Economy of Growing Old* (with Carroll L. Estes).

Leslie A. Morgan, Professor and Chair of the Department of Sociology and Anthropology, University of Maryland, has published numerous articles in reviewed journals and, with Suzanne Kunkel, is author of *Aging: The Social Context*. She is currently conducting research on residential-care alternatives for frail elders and the financial impact of caregiving by kin for elders with dementia.

Philip R. Muskin is a psychiatrist in the Department of Psychiatry, Columbia-Presbyterian Medical Center, Columbia University, College of Physicians and Surgeons, and Columbia University Psychoanalytic Center for Training and Research, New York.

Marilyn Nouri, Associate Professor of Sociology at the State University of New York, Oneota, is also Director of the Center for Life Course Studies. Her present research focuses on themes of the life course as well as applications to local, community-action agencies.

James S. O'Leary is Senior Analyst for the Blue Cross Blue Shield Association. He received his Ph.D. in sociology from the University of Wisconsin-Madison. The contents of his study were supported by an educational grant from the Japanese Ministry of Education.

Pedro Pietri is a Puerto Rican poet who ironically details the everyday life and vicissitudes of Puerto Ricans living in the mainland United States.

Rachel Pruchno is Research Professor at the Center for Child, Family, and Community Partnerships at Boston College, Chestnut Hill, Massachusetts. Principal investigator of ongoing funded research at the center, she studies grandparenting and developmental disabilities.

Patricia Reid is currently Research Coordinator, Faculty of Humanities, Nelson Polytechnic, Nelson, New Zealand.

Matilda White Riley, Professor Emeritus of Sociology, Rutgers University, is the author of numerous books and monographs on aging, including *Age and Structural Lag* (with Robert L. Kahn and Anne Foner).

Jack Rosenthal is the editor of the *Sunday New York Times Magazine*.

Philip Roth is a novelist whose numerous books include *Goodbye Columbus*, *Portnoy's Complaint*, and *Patrimony*.

Robert L. Rubinstein is Professor of Anthropology at the University of Maryland. He has done fieldwork in Vanuatu in the South Pacific and among older persons in the United States.

Joel Savishinsky is Charles A. Dana Professor in the Social Sciences, Department of Anthropology, Ithaca College, and author of *The Ends of Time: Life and Work in a Nursing Home*.

Benjamin Schlesinger is Professor Emeritus, School of Social Work, University of Toronto.

Judith Bunnell Sellers is Associate Professor in the Department of Nursing, Northern Arizona University. She was assisted with the data collection for her research in this volume by her students who are Navajo speakers.

Susan R. Sherman is Professor of Social Welfare, State University of New York at Albany, former president of the Association for Gerontology in Higher Education, and the author of numerous articles and monographs on aging.

Laurie Shields, co-founder (with Tish Sommers) of the Older Women's League, was also a founder and the first Executive Director of the Alliance for Displaced Homemakers, now called Women Work! National Network for Women's Employment.

Priyanthi Silva is a research analyst at Westat in Rockville, Maryland. She received her doctorate in Gerontology from the University of Massachusetts, Boston.

Jay Sokolovsky, Professor of Anthropology, University of South Florida, St. Petersburg, has conducted research on aging in Croatia, England, a village in Mexico, New York's inner city, Colombia, and the Tampa Bay area. His recent publications include *The Cultural Context of Aging: World-Wide Perspectives*.

Tish Sommers was a co-founder of the Older Women's League (OWL) and an activist for displaced homemakers. With Laurie Shields, she drafted the first displaced homemakers' legislation, initially introduced in California and later in the U.S. Congress.

Studs Terkel is a Chicago-based journalist whose countless interviews encompass a former Ku Klux Klan member as well as salespeople, artists, writers, congressmen, and labor organizers. His books include *Chicago*, *Division Street: America*, and *Hard Times* as well as *Coming of Age*.

Edward H. Thompson, Jr. is Professor of Sociology at Holy Cross College, Worcester, Massachusetts, where he also directs the Gerontology Studies Program. He is the author of *Older Men's Lives: Research on Men and Masculinities*.

Barbara Formaniak Turner is Professor of Gerontology at the University of Massachusetts, Boston, and a fellow of the American Psychological Association, the Gerontological Society of America, and the American Psychological Society. Co-editor (with Lillian E. Troll) of *Women Growing Older: Psychological Perspectives*, she focuses on the intersection of gender and aging.

Helena Maria Viramontes, a writer with a special interest in the lives of Chicanas in the United States, is the author of *The Moths and Other Stories*.

Joan Weibel-Orlando, an anthropologist whose research focuses on the experiences of Native Americans, is on the faculty of the University of Southern California.

Note: Biographical information has been included as available.

About the Selections

In choosing a general approach for the volume, we—Markson, a sociologist, and Hollis-Sawyer, a psychologist—chose to use the concept of the life course. We made this choice deliberately because we felt that it provided a framework within which to consider both individual lives and their heterogeneity and the diversity of these individuals as aggregate members of a particular social category who were positioned within the social hierarchies of class, gender, race, and ethnicity. Guiding our selections were several criteria: representation of different social classes, ethnic and racial groups, gender, and birth cohorts; timelessness of the concepts or material presented; and relevance to an understanding of the life course, its heterogeneity and diversity, and the relationship of private troubles to public issues.

We also chose selections that we felt would be of interest to a broad audience: undergraduate and graduate students, practitioners, and a general audience interested in exploring the many facets of aging and old age yesterday, today, and tomorrow. Qualitative research studies are emphasized, but we also deliberately drew upon selections from a variety of disciplines and perspectives: anthropology, autobiography, economics, fiction, history, journalism, nursing, medicine, poetry, political and social theory, psychology, social work, and sociology.

Some of the topics discussed are familiar to everyone through personal experience: work, retirement, and income security, family and social relationships (Section IV: Family, Social Relationships, and Intergenerational Reciprocity), and health (Section V: Health and Illness in Later Life). The topics with which the book opens may be less within our immediate experience. Few of us think about the sociocultural construction of aging and old age (Section I: Cultural Constructions of Later Life); we tend to take our assumptions about aging for granted. Nor do we think about the differences in the ways each birth cohort is likely to age in a particular socio-historical and cultural context. Yet there are marked cross-cultural, historical, social class, and gender differences in how old age is defined, and many views of old age as a period of asexual decrepitude stem from earlier (and inaccurate) medical and psychiatric definitions of later life. Successful aging may, as selections in this section show, have many definitions. Indeed, some of the unconventional conduct or eccentricity often ascribed to the elderly can be a conscious revolt against cultural definitions of old age that limit social behavior in later life.

Also less familiar to most of us is the terrain of life traveled by different birth cohorts. The pecking order of social hierarchies of gender, race, ethnicity, and social class not only contour the lives and opportunities of each of us born in a specific time period but also our self-concepts and senses of self-esteem (Section II: Social Contexts of Aging). How, for example, do people define themselves as "masculine" or "feminine," and are there differences between parents and children in such self-designations? In what ways are social class, gender, racial, and ethnic identities sources of strength, social support, and pride in old age? How do adverse experiences associated with membership in one or more of these social hierarchies impact one's life? To explore these themes, selections have been included that draw upon the experiences of European Americans, African Americans, Native Americans, and Asian Americans to illuminate the many meanings of participation in various social hierarchies.

All of us have knowledge of work, retirement, and income security (Section III: Work, Retirement, and Income Security), whether from our own participation in the labor force or the experience of parents, grandparents, or relatives and friends. Selections on work, retirement, and income explore this wide area by examining labor force trends for older workers and policies affecting older workers, such as the Age Discrimination and Employment Act and the Americans with Disabilities Act. In the future, the labor force will also be more ethnically and racially diverse with Latino Americans, Asian Americans, African Americans, and females representing a larger proportion than ever before. However, age discrimination continues, reducing both incomes and life chances of millions of Americans. It is difficult to predict if in the future older workers will be encouraged to continue in their current jobs, retrain for new jobs, seek part-time employment, or retire. Others have been trapped in dead-end jobs without opportunities to learn new skills or to use what they know, clearly affecting their income and opportunities in retirement. And what is retirement like anyway? Is retirement the golden opportunity to enjoy a life of leisure or is it an opportunity to give to others? An opportunity to work for social change? How do life-long poverty, prior work history, gender and race/ethnicity interweave with power inequalities to shape work, retirement, and income? Voices from whites of different ethnic backgrounds, African-Americans, and Latinos address these questions in Section III.

All of us, too, have been involved in family and social relationships in one form or another from birth, and the selections in Section IV elaborate upon current familial and social relationships in old age, cohort differences in such relationships, and giving and receiving care. Contrary to popular belief, caregiving is not a one-way street; rather, it is a multi-faceted process, influenced not only by individual needs but by social class, ethnicity and race, and gender. Women—often at great personal cost—are traditionally the caregivers. Are the contributions of men ignored, and, if so, what effect does defining caregiving as "women's work" have on both men and women? In what ways do culture and ethnicity hinder or enhance caregiving? Are some recipients of care "hand-me-down people," passed from one family member to another? What are the many roles of grandparents and how do these vary according to membership in the social hierarchies of race and ethnicity, gender, and social class? Through fiction, biographical accounts, and psychological and

sociological research, these themes are explored in Section IV.

Health, too, is a common concern to most of us. Section V explores the many dimensions of health, including the ways that, due to ageist views, old age itself can be a barrier to care. Cultural and racial/ethnic differences in beliefs about health also are barriers; for example, treatment approaches that are successful with native-born whites are likely to be unsuccessful with another ethnic group such as the Navajo. The basic assessments of health to be undertaken in a medical evaluation of an elder are another significant issue. Two additional emerging issues are dementia and end-of-life care. Many people today are concerned about the probability of Alzheimer's Disease, whether for themselves or their family members. What is it like to discover you have early-onset Alzheimer's? And what kinds of psychological and social impacts do having a family member with Alzheimer's have upon the lives of their younger relatives?

End-of-life care, living wills, and the death of a parent may also intertwine, interweaving ethnicity, religion, and social class. Allied to end-of- life care is the topic of assisted suicide. Should one be permitted to commit assisted suicide, and, if so, in what circumstances and with what precautions against abuse? Costs of health care are also an issue of widespread concern. Is aging a fiscal black hole where resources should be reallocated to enable the needs of the young to take precedence over the old? Are American health care costs spent on elders higher than in other nations? These are questions addressed in Section V from the viewpoints of social work, medicine and nursing, ethics, political science, sociology, and individuals reflecting upon their own experience.

The volume concludes with Section VI: Future Directions for Older Americans and for Gerontology, which examines numerous issues including the influence the aging of the baby boomers will have on the future of Social Security, patterns of medical care and possible directions for improvement in the health care for future older Americans, and the ways in which gerontology and the education of future gerontologists need to change if we are to understand the heterogeneity and diversity of the aging experience. The section concludes with a discussion of the misalignment between individuals and the social structures influencing the course of aging and suggests directions that policies might take to address this misalignment.

To help you identify specific topics of interest, the following table provides a brief overview of selections by issues, such as gender, social class, race and ethnicity, birth cohort, successful aging, etc. The table is intended as a general rather than an all-inclusive guide, as many of the selections deal with more than one topic, emphasizing the many facets of growing older.

Table 1

Brief Outline of Topical Coverage by Author of Selection and Chapter Number

Author(s) of Selection	Chapter Number	age and aging as status	cultural construction	cohort	diversity	heterogeneity	social class	race/ethnicity	gender	successful aging	life styles
Sokolovsky	1	X	X		X			X	X		X
O'Leary	2	X	X					X			
Hepworth	3	X	X			X					
Haber	4	X	X			X					
Schlesinger	5	X	X			X			X		
Rosenthal	6		X	X		X					X
Baltes and Carstensen	7		X	X		X				X	
Huyck	8			X		X	X		X		
Turner	9			X		X			X		
Nouri and Helterline	10					X	X		X	X	X
Minatoya	11			X	X		X	X	X	X	X
Johnson	12				X		X	X		X	X
McAuley	13				X		X	X		X	X
Weibel-Orlando	14	X			X			X	X	X	
Chang	15				X	X	X	X	X	X	X
Delany and Delany	16	X		X	X		X	X	X	X	X
Calasanti	17	X		X	X	X	X	X	X	X	X
Crown and Longino	18										
Hollis-Sawyer	19	X									
Pietri	20				X		X	X			X
Savishinsky	21					X	X			X	X
Terkel	22				X	X	X	X	X	X	
Allen and Chin-Sang	23				X	X	X	X		X	X

(continued)

Table 1 (continued)

Brief Outline of Topical Coverage by Author of Selection and Chapter Number

Author(s) of Selection	Chapter Number	age and aging		cohort	diversity	hetero-geneity	social class	race/ethnicity	gender	success-ful aging	life styles
		cultural construc-tion	as status								
McInnis-Dittrich	24			x	x		x	x			
Akiyama, Elliott and Antonucci	25							x	x		x
Hagestad	26			x						x	
Goodman and Rubinstein	27			x					x		x
Sherman	28					x	x				
Viramontes	29			x		x		x	x		x
Pruchno and Johnson	30			x	x						
Aranda and Knight	31			x	x		x	x			
Sommers and Shields	32			x					x		
Thompson	33								x		
Hand and Reid	34			x							x
Grant	35	x	x								
Sellers	36		x	x	x	x		x		x	
Barry	37									x	
Friedell	38					x			x		
Hodgson and Cutler	39	x		x							
Morgan and Eckert	40										
Roth	41			x				x	x		x
Mushkin	42										
Callahan	43	x									
Binstock	44										
Kingson	45			x							
Longino	46			x							
Minkler	47	x	x	x	x					x	
Riley	48	x	x	x					x	x	

Introduction

Perspectives on the Diversity of the Life Course

When we are young, few of us spend much time thinking about old age and the ways in which Western and other cultures have defined it. Why should we? All of us are preoccupied with thoughts about our current lives and our plans for the future: education, friends, romance, careers, and other marks of adulthood. Yet all cultures convey explicit or tacit views, and sometimes fears, about what old age is. Aging is a biological event that begins at birth and ends at death. Old age, however, is a concept we invent—a social construction. At any point in the life course, one's age simultaneously denotes not only a number of years and a physiological state but a set of guidelines (norms) for everyday behavior, specific to a given society at a particular point in history. Every culture has norms about what is appropriate behavior at various stages in the life course and defines the usual set of entrances, changes, or exits from one age to another (Neugarten, Moore, and Lowe 1965).

A basic concern of this book is how older people's lives are patterned and why groups and individuals differ from one another in later life. For example, very old African-American women who live alone are more likely to be poor than their white counterparts and also than very old African-American or white men. What social structural arrangements bring about this difference? Fundamental to disentangling the answer to this and other questions about later life are two concepts. The first is hierarchy: the ranking of people with certain innate or acquired characteristics from highest to lowest. When people with certain characteristics are evaluated differently by others, a social hierarchy is formed. The second concept, allied to the first, is diversity: that is, the unique characteristics of a particular category of people, whether very old African-American women or middle-class white men, within the matrices of power hierarchies (Calasanti 1996).

This introduction presents several key concepts in understanding the many faces of old age. It begins with a discussion of age as a status. Next follows a review of the concepts of birth cohorts and the life course, both significant factors in understanding the opportunities and barriers that individuals and groups face as they age in different ways. Then comes an examination of the social hierarchies of race or ethnicity, gender, and class as they affect different life courses to account for much of the diversity in aging experiences. The introduction concludes with a discussion of various social theories that have guided both popular views and scholarly research on old age.

Age as a Status

Although age has been used systematically to distinguish and categorize people, age itself explains very little. As L. Hazelrigg has pointed out:

> Like gender or height or the presence/absence of earlobes, age itself is not the cause of anything. Rather it is properly regarded as a classification variable, the title of a set of categories in a particular classification system. . . . This is surely not to say that titles lack social significance nor even that titles cannot be causally significant . . . causal force is contributed by the selection process and resulting discriminatory behavior or action, not the state title. (1997, p. 96)

What is important about age is how a specific society or culture uses it to classify entry into and exit from different statuses. As a status, age is important in three ways. First, like sex, age is an ascribed characteristic. At any moment, everyone is a specific age. All societies use age to organize social and economic life. For example, 6-year-olds are not expected to do some of the things that their parents do. In American society, children usually are not expected to be full-time workers, nor are parents expected to attend first grade.

Second, unlike sex, age is always a transitional state. We are constantly moving from one age to another. Everyone begins life at age zero and ends with a certain number of hours, days, or years at death (Hazelrigg 1997). Age provides a kind of road map of our lives: where we have been, where we should be going, and how we should get there at particular points in our lives (Neugarten, Moore, and Lowe 1965). Moving from one age group to another is regulated by socialization to age-appropriate behavior. Conformity to the norms for age-appropriate behavior is rewarded; violation of these norms is disapproved. For example, in American society, 12-year-olds and 80-year-olds who suck pacifiers are both violating age norms for appropriate social behavior.

Third, although in every society some age groups are richer, more powerful, and more respected than others, the unique aspect of age as a status is that throughout our lives we can expect to occupy positions of various leadership based on our age. All of us were once helpless infants; and for most of us, our power and influence are likely to change as we move from one age status to another, although our progress is affected by a variety of other characteristics, such as gender, race, ethnicity, and social class, that affect our life opportunities.

Thus, although every society regulates the flow of people into and out of valued statuses on the basis of age, definitions of appropriate ages for specific statuses and behaviors are socially constructed and not biologically given. The notion of being old or elderly is especially fluid, defined by a particular culture during a specific historical period. In in-dustrialized societies such as the United States, age is associated with a particular number of years as well as with specific behaviors and social roles. The significance of age as a number is relatively new. In Northern Europe, for example, it was not until the mid-sixteenth century that numerical age had any social significance. Indeed, few people knew how old they were (Cole 1993). In other societies where life expectancy at birth is short and physical conditions are hard, a person may be defined as an "elder" in what Americans consider midlife: age 40 or 45.

There is, of course, no one way to age, for individuals age at different rates with different social and personal characteristics in different socio-structural and historical contexts. The increasing heterogeneity both of individual aging experiences and broader social structural factors, such as race and ethnicity, gender, social class, and relative power within the society, clearly will shape how people age now and in the future. Today's elderly are pioneering the new frontiers of demographic changes and are growing old in ways that are both qualitatively and quantitatively different from the ways of their parents and grandparents. And this generation will grow old in ways different from those of our parents.

Cohorts and the Life Course

Important in understanding the ways in which people age are the concepts of birth cohort and life course. A birth cohort comprises people born during a specific time, such as 1925 to 1930. The life course is the sequence of stages that people move through as they mature. Individuals within a birth cohort assess and react to events in different ways that are connected to their personal biographies. Just as everyone's personal biography and life course is unique, so is every birth cohort different from any other. Members of a birth cohort, the size of which is determined by birth rates and death rates associated with social class, gender, and race or ethnicity, and by in- and out-migration, encounter historically grounded opportunities and obstacles to fulfill social roles as they move through the life course. For example, many more people were born during the baby boom years of 1947 to 1967 than during the Great Depression of the 1930s. The large number of baby boom cohorts compared to the smaller number of Depression cohorts will clearly influence the number of elderly people in U.S. society by 2020, when the population age 65 and over is expected to increase from about 13 percent to 20 percent.

The size of a birth cohort affects opportunities and lifestyles. For example, members of the large baby boom cohort faced greater competition for jobs and education than the small Depression cohort; they also comprised a larger luxury market for goods and services. The shared history of one birth cohort is likely to shape the experiences and aging of its members very differently from the ways the members of another birth cohort are shaped. An individual's location in a specific birth cohort determines his or her social roles and forms his or her attitudes or actions. Thus, some of the presumably fixed, built-in life stages that have been proposed by social scientists and physicians alike reflect the experiences of a particular cohort rather than a specific stage of life (Riley, Foner, and Johnson 1972).

All members of a birth cohort age through a particular historical period during which they share common experiences. Although cohort members encounter the same major events in an era, whether an economic depression, a war, or even the popularity of particular rock and film stars, the meaning of these happenings varies for each person. Influenced by their race or ethnicity, social class, and gender, members of a birth cohort construct individual biographies in assorted ways throughout the life course. Individual life courses are also shaped by social class, gender, and race or ethnicity. As G. H. Elder and J. K. Liker (1982) have shown, living through the Great Depression not only differed for middle-class and working-class women but also affected their subsequent old age. Although women of both social classes were hampered by their status as females in a male-dominated society and both suffered economic losses, women of higher status were less vulnerable to setbacks. In their old age, feelings of mastery and assertiveness characterized those middle-class women, while feelings of passivity and helplessness were more typical among working-class women. Elder's and Liker's research emphasizes both the importance of birth cohort and the intertwining of gender, social class, and historical events.

The Hierarchies of Social Class, Race, Ethnicity, and Gender

In all societies, three resources are valued: power, or the ability to impose one's will on others; prestige, or respect from others; and property, whether knowledge, money, or goods. Social class reflects the unequal distribution of power, prestige, and property within a society. In all but the simplest societies, a hierarchy, based on the ability to control power, prestige, and property, is constructed by its members. American society is no exception, for although we value egalitarianism, in fact we allocate power, prestige, and property unequally.

Like age and social class, race and ethnicity are social constructs, rather than essential properties of an individual. Consider the many meanings of the word *race* over time. In scientific terms, race is almost impossible to define because human populations are so intermixed that no pure racial types exist today and perhaps never did. As M. Omi and H. Winant observed, race is a powerful social construction, a complex of ever-changing meanings that is "defined and contested throughout society in both collective action and personal practice . . . racial categories themselves are formed, transformed, destroyed and reformed" (1987, p. 61). It is the social meaning attached to race that gives it power. For example, throughout much of the history of the United States, drawing a line between "black" and "white" was important in maintaining the dominance of one category of people over another. Although decades of racial mixing obscured differences, the "one drop" rule, by which one drop of "black" blood caused people to be considered nonwhite, has been an excuse for unequal treatment. Similarly, ethnicity is a constructed reality, designating variously one's initial national origin, such as Irish American, Mexican American, or Chinese American; one's original language, such as Spanish; or one's religion, such as Jewish American. More fluid than race, ethnic identification may vary over one's life span owing to personal changes or changes in the circumstances of the group; one may choose to become "more Irish," or "less Polish" as one ages. The option to recreate one's ethnic identity is, however, not open to all; in American society, only white people have this opportunity (Waters 1990). Both race and ethnicity thus may be used within a society to rank people into groups according to certain ascribed characteristics.

Gender, too, is a social construct. Gendered inequality is produced by different social evaluations of people's worth on the basis of biological sex. The result is a social hierarchy where men have higher status than women. As B. B. Hess has pointed out: "Layers of meaning have been wrapped around the distinguishing feature of biological sex. . . . Thus rather than being a property of the individual, maleness and femaleness are products of the operation of social systems on both the variability and similarities provided by nature" (1990, p. 83).

The social constructs of race or ethnicity and gender convey public messages used to categorize people into hierarchies where, as on George Orwell's *Animal Farm* (1946), all are equal but some are more equal than others. Ignoring the ways in which these hierarchies intertwine obscures the structural patterns of society and the power relationships and material inequalities that affect the life chances of individuals and groups.

Incorporating into the study of aging the awareness of diversity produced by hierarchies is important, for it not only calls attention to comparison of similarities and differences across and within groups but also concentrates on uncovering the social arrangements that construct and shape the social reality of groups—whether European American, African American, Latino, Native American, or Asian American; male or female; rich or poor; gay or straight (Calasanti 1996). At the individual level, health or sickness, employment or retirement, and interaction with friends, family, and acquaintances affect one's conception of oneself as

"elderly": the notion that "you are only as old or as young as you feel." But being elderly also acquires meaning through the social structural arrangements that pattern one's life course. Consider J. Nelson's account of her father's old age:

> It was not enough for my father to succeed in the black world that slavery created and segregation maintained, he wanted more, a bigger palette than one reduced to black and white. . . . He did not want to be white, but to live as white, to have all that white folks had, including the luxury of being oblivious to color—without having to abandon his race. . . . He became a dentist, was the most successful of his siblings, made it into the upper middle class. But for him and many fathers of his generation, the price of navigating the segregated road to success in the 1940s and 1950s was defensiveness, a constant, smoldering rage. . . . In his eighth decade, long retired from a career . . . that provided an income that enabled him to retire before he was sixty, that currently finances a spiritual quest . . . my father would be defined by anyone's standards as "A Success." Yet it was never enough. (1997, pp. 62–63, 67)

Compare this account with M. Meigs' (1991) description of her elderly friend, Catherine, a white, well-educated musician, teacher, and nun with a doctorate, with whom Meigs appeared in a semi-documentary film:

> She speaks her mind; she has a tone of authority and the evident habit of being listened to. . . . She is still entirely her own woman. . . . Catherine, at one with her Walkman, thinking in sound, excited now at the prospect of "going back into the educational world at Stockton." . . . Now she is preparing herself again, in training for "the most complete thing to teach," a fresh career in music that will make use of all her faculties and beliefs. "I just have to know . . . keep on learning," she says. (1991, pp. 141–142)

As Max Weber (1978) pointed out, people's life chances contour both their social circumstances and their satisfaction with life. Although Nelson's father's life chances were improved in two hierarchies—social class and gender—he was at a disadvantage because of his color. Both his opportunities and his life contentment were limited despite his achievements. In contrast, Catherine was at a disadvantage because of her gender but was privileged by her color and social class. Clearly, their experiences throughout the life course and their enjoyment in old age were shaped by their positions in the social hierarchies of race, gender, and class.

Social Theories of Aging

T. M. Calasanti (1996) has argued that most gerontological theories are based on the experiences of white, middle-class men, with the result that only selected 'male facts,' are produced that have little relevance to the lives of all people. Similarly, P. Dressler, M. Minkler, and I. Yen (1997) have pointed out that issues of gender, race or ethnicity, and social class in theories of aging have been present but were implicitly based on comparisons to the dominant group of Euro-white, middle-class males. This section reviews briefly a set of paradigms about aging, that is, "a basic set of beliefs that guides action, whether of the everyday garden variety or action taken in connection with a disciplined inquiry" (Guba 1990, p. 17) and the ways these paradigms guiding social research on old age have changed in the past century. Two general types of theories have been proposed: theories examining old age at the micro, or individual, level and those focusing on the macro, or societal, level.

Paradigm One: Old Age Is
Need and Dependence

Like most disciplines concerned with aspects of human aging, early social scientists associated old age with some sort of need or dependence. The nineteenth-century Belgian statistician, L. A. Quetelet (1842), for example, called attention to the life course by dividing large numbers of people according to age, and he concluded that in old age, both intellect and moral sense declined. Old age was a twilight journey to the grave. Social scientists such as the Englishman Charles Booth, writing in the 1890s, called attention to poverty as an almost inevitable consequence of aging. In one-third of all poverty

cases he studied, he concluded that old age was the major cause of poverty; the old were unnecessary in an industrialized society and were cast aside to go on the dole or enter an almshouse (Haber 1983). During the early twentieth century, American social scientists depicted the elderly as discarded upon the scrap heap of industrial society. As one social scientist described the lives of the elderly:

> The transition from non-dependence to dependence is an easy stage—property gone, friends passed away or removed, relatives become few, ambition collapsed, only a few years left to live, with death a final and welcome end to it all—such conclusions inevitably sweep the wage-earner from the class of hopeful independent citizens into that of the helpless poor. (Squier 1912, pp. 28–29)

Most social inquiries about old age during the first half of the twentieth century accepted the premise that old age was a condition explicitly or tacitly undesirable in an individualistic, instrumental, activist society such as the United States.

Paradigm Two: Old Age Is Undesirable but Requires Individual Adjustment

According to this micro-level approach, social isolation, declining health, poverty, and retirement are highly probable in old age but can be overcome by individual efforts. L. Cottrell (1942), for example, called attention to individual "adjustment" to age and sex roles. "Adjustment" referred primarily to the congruence between the perceived needs of old people and the extent to which they were able to fulfill these needs. Work by such social researchers as R. Cavan, R. J. Havighurst, and E. Burgess (1949), based on the Kansas City Studies of Adult Life, emphasized activity and individual life satisfaction as hallmarks of normal (versus pathological) old age. That old age was best handled through remaining as middle-aged as possible was the tacit assumption.

Another theorist, B. Phillips (1957), also taking a micro-level perspective, echoed the theme that people who identify themselves as elderly or old were far more likely to be maladjusted than those identifying themselves as middle aged. Involvement in fantasy, absentmindedness, daydreaming about the past, and thoughts of death were not part of "adjustment" to old age. Moreover, retirement, death of a spouse, and reaching the age of 70 were all weighted equally as negative role changes associated with maladjustment. Individual theories such as those just described were based upon white, middle-class, male experiences and ignored differences associated with gender, class, and race or ethnicity. Recent, more sophisticated theories of adjustment to aging have focused on the concept of "successful aging," discussed more fully in the selection by M. Baltes and L. L. Carstensen later in this volume.

Paradigm Three: Old Age Occurs in a Social System

The year 1961 marked the appearance of a different, macro-level perspective: the controversial theory of disengagement. Proposed by sociologist Elaine Cumming, a former student of Talcott Parsons, and psychologist William Henry, it argued that aging must be understood *within* the social system. Although they, like Cavan, Havighurst, and Burgess, based their work on the Kansas City studies, they emphasized not the individual's adjustment but the needs of a society to maintain equilibrium. As originally stated, disengagement may be summarized by its first two postulates:

1. Although individuals differ, the expectation of death is universal and decrement of ability is probable. Therefore, a mutual severing of ties will take place between a person and others in that society.

2. Because interactions create and reaffirm norms, a reduction in the number or variety of interactions leads to an increased freedom from the control of the norms governing everyday behavior. Consequently, once begun, disengagement becomes a circular or self-perpetuating process. (Cumming and Cumming 1961, p. 211)

Like Parsons, Cumming and Cumming were interested in the functioning of social structures rather than individual adjustment or attitudes. Although they called attention to the obvious—but largely neglected point that none of us grows old in a vacuum but rather in a social context, they nonetheless accepted the premise that old age is inevitably associated with mental and physical decline. It is precisely this inevitable decline that creates a social imperative for societies to oust the elderly from vital roles. Simply put, as people age, they become less competent and would weigh the society down unless they disengaged from vital social roles. Societies deal with this fact by institutionalizing disengagement, "an inevitable mutual withdrawal" between the aged person and social institutions.

Without dwelling on the numerous criticisms and debates to which the disengagement theory gave rise, its importance is fourfold. First, it called attention to aging not as an individual phenomenon but as a socially governed occurrence within a social structure. Morally sanctioned norms dictate withdrawal of the elderly from vital social roles in order to maintain social order. Second, it challenged a major premise of activity theory—that successful old age was a continuation of middle age—by proposing that it was a distinct life stage characterized by activities different in quantity and quality than those of earlier life. Third, disengagement made perhaps the first explicit recognition of gender differences in aging. Whether, as Cumming (1963) later proposed, growing old is easier for men than for women remains debatable, but clearly gender differences structure how old age is experienced. Lastly, and most important, disengagement theory stimulated the development of social theories about old age during the next decade or so—A. M. Rose's (1965) subculture of aging, J. J. Dowd's (1975) exchange theory, D. Cowgill's (1974) modernization theory examining aging in cross-cultural perspective, and M. W. Riley's (1972) age stratification approach are but a few.

Paradigm Four: The Elderly Are Excluded From Social Life

Several approaches during the 1960s and 1970s explored macro-level social forces sociated with the relatively disadvant position of the elderly in industrialized society and emphasized the concept of "age as leveler", that is, elders have a uniform experience because of their age (Kent 1971). Rose proposed that a subculture of aging develops when elders have common backgrounds and interests or are excluded from interaction with other groups in the society, or both. As a result, many older Americans, he contended, acquire diminished self-concepts as they age because of the high value placed on youth in American society. Older people may, however, offset their negative self-concepts through exerting political power as a voting bloc (an option that to date has rarely occurred).

Exclusion of the elderly from the society's mainstream was also advanced by Cowgill. In his modernization theory, the transition from a rural, nontechnological society characterized by traditional values to a primarily urban one characterized by highly developed scientific technology and highly differentiated social institutions has reduced the status of the elderly with respect to leadership roles, power, and influence, as well as increasing their disengagement from community life.

Still another theory emphasizing the segregation of elders from mainstream social life is Dowd's exchange theory, which argues that the problems of the aged in twentieth-century industrial societies are problems of decreased bargaining power. Workers who once exchanged skills for wages lose their power to exchange goods and services upon their retirement and thus become objects of benevolence rather than achievers of equality in social exchange.

Riley's age stratification theory points out that it is theoretically and practically useful to think of members of a society as stratified along the dimension of age as well as social class. As discussed earlier in this introduction, membership in specific strata becomes a basis for control over resources through age-linked statuses. Inequality among age strata occurs because age is used as a criterion of entry or exit from potentially powerful statuses. Children and the elderly are least likely to be in statuses where they control goods, knowledge, and resources, with the result that their power is likely to be acquired informally. For example, children may gain limited power through demands upon their parents; elders may gain limited authority through demands for respect. Both, however, remain in age strata where their command is less than those in more powerful statuses.

Riley also emphasized that the so-called generation gap is probably a function of differences in cohort experiences and changing age norms for appropriate role behavior. Since the experience of each cohort differs, great caution must be observed in making broad generalizations about old age. Age stratification also alerted sociologists to the ways in which age strata influence and are influenced by the social, political, and economic fabric of a society. Consider, for example, current debates about the impact of the large boomer cohorts on Medicare and Social Security.

A Paradigmatic Shift: Growing Awareness of Diversity

During the past few decades a paradigm shift has occurred, setting new directions for examining old age. In this shift, social theorists turned their critical lenses inward, examining previous assumptions about aging. Rather than focusing on how birth cohorts, life stages, or the needs of the social system organize the experience of growing old, theorists challenged the so-called facts of aging to criticize the concept of "age as leveler." Interest in the interplay between race, social class, gender, and ethnicity was in part a response to the assumption that elders have a uniform experience because of their age. Much initial research on aging, race, and ethnicity has been built on the premise that old age is characterized by physical health and economic problems. When the dual disadvantages of old age and minority group membership are combined, "double jeopardy" results (Talley and Kaplan 1956).

The concept of double jeopardy initially applied to the odds faced by elderly African Americans as members of an oppressed minority group: and old was subsequently expanded to focus attention on problems faced by other elders such as women, gays, lesbians, and ethnic groups discriminated against by the more powerful. Nonetheless, as

Dressler, Minkler, and Yen point out, focus on social disadvantage has inadvertently contributed to a "deficit thinking mentality" that once again portrays disadvantaged elders as victims, ignoring the strengths that disadvantaged groups possess. By emphasizing differences *between* groups, the meaning and dynamics of aging *within* groups are ignored.

Increased attention to the political economy of aging has enlarged awareness of the importance of social hierarchies. Implicit—and sometimes explicit—in this approach is concern about whether capitalism as a productive social system can be reconciled with the needs of the elderly. The British sociologist Chris Phillipson (1982) argues that the priorities of capitalism almost always subordinate social and individual needs to the search for profits; he concludes that the elderly are likely to be caught between the need for better services and the steady decline of facilities and increase in cuts in the standard of living imposed by the most powerful social classes. A leading American proponent of the political economy approach to aging has been Carroll Estes, who, with her associates (1984) proposed that the course of the aging process is conditioned by each individual's location in the social structure and the economic and social factors that affect that position. Clearly, gender, race or ethnicity, and social class are intrinsic to the political economy approach.

In the last few years, critical theory, stressing the need for theories of aging to be self-reflective and to consider how they are constructed, interpreted, and applied in real life, has also challenged older theories and assumptions in social gerontology. Of particular interest to critical theory is how theories of aging have divorced elders' lives from those actively living, with the result that the elderly become "the other," objects rather than subjects of study. As H. R. Moody, an outstanding spokesperson for the critical approach in theories about aging, has emphasized, "Above all, critical gerontology is concerned with the problem of emancipation from all forms of domination . . . identifying possibilities for emancipatory social change, including positive ideals for later life" (1993, p. xv).

The nineteenth-century Russian nove Leo Tolstoy is credited with saying, "Scien is meaningless because it gives no answer our question, the only question important to us, 'what shall we do and how shall we live?' " (Cole 1995). Future social theories of old age need to respond to this question by attention to issues of social class, gender, and race or ethnicity that affect elders' lives as well as our own. Private troubles are, after all, related to public issues—or phrased differently, like it or not, our individual lives are inextricably interwoven with the social structure of which we are a part throughout the life course (Mills 1959). As you read the selections in this volume, keep in mind the many ways in which old age is affected by the interplay of social class, race or ethnicity, gender, and individual biography during a particular slice of history. Also, consider ways that gerontology may help promote a positive vision of old age as part of the life course. It is impossible to foresee what the old of future generations will be like, but we can reliably predict that their experiences will be shaped by the historical periods, social hierarchies, and political contexts in which they live. How will your experiences, fashioned by these same variables, shape your old age?

References

Calasanti, T. M. 1996. "Incorporating Diversity: Meaning, Levels of Research, and Implications for Theory." *Gerontologist* 36(2): 147–156.

Cavan, R., Havighurst, R. J., and Burgess, E. 1949. *Personal Adjustment in Old Age*. Chicago: Science Research Associates.

Cole, T. R. 1993. *The Journey of Life: A Cultural History of Aging in America*. New York: Cambridge University Press.

Cole, T. R. 1995. "What Have We 'Made' of Aging?" *Journal of Gerontology: Social Sciences* 50B(6): S341–S343.

Cole, Thomas R. 1991. "Oedipus and the Meaning of Aging: Personal Reflections and Historical Perspectives." In Nancy S. Jeeker, ed., *Aging and Ethics: Philosophical Problems in Gerontology*. Clifton, NJ: Humana Press.

Cottrell, L. 1942. "The Adjustment of the Individual to His Age and Sex Roles." *American Sociological Review* 7: 617–620.

Cowgill, D. 1974. "Aging and Modernization: Revision of the Theory." In J. Gubrium

...ate Life: Communities and Environmental Policy. Springfield, IL: Charles C. Thomas.

...umming, E. 1963. "Engagement With an Old Theory." International Social Science Journal 15: 377–393.

Cumming E., and Cumming, Henry W. 1961. Growing Old. New York: Basic Books.

Dowd, J. J. 1975. "Aging as Exchange: A Preface to Theory." Journal of Gerontology 30: 585–594.

Dressler, P., Minkler, M., and Yen, I. 1997. "Gender, Race, Class, and Aging: Advances and Opportunities." International Journal of Health Services 27 (4): 579–600.

Elder, G. H., Jr., and Liker, J. K. 1982. "Hard Times in Women's Lives: Historical Influences Across Forty Years." American Journal of Sociology 88 (2): 241–269.

Estes, C., Swan, J. H., and Gerard, L. E. 1984. "Dominant and Competing Paradigms in Gerontology: Toward a Political Economy of Aging." In M. Minkler and C. L. Estes, eds., Readings in the Political Economy of Aging. Farmingdale, NY: Baywood.

Guba, E. G., ed. 1990. The Paradigm Dialogue. Newbury Park, CA: Sage.

Haber, C. 1983. Beyond Sixty-Five. New York: Cambridge University Press.

Hazelrigg, L. 1997. "On the Importance of Age." In M. A. Hardy, ed., Studying Aging and Social Change. Thousand Oaks, CA: Sage.

Hess, B. B. 1990. "Beyond Dichotomy: Drawing Distinctions and Embracing Differences." Sociological Forum 5 (1): 75–93.

Kent, D. P. 1971. "The Negro Aged." The Gerontologist 11: 48–51.

Meigs, M. 1991. In the Company of Strangers. Vancouver, British Columbia: Talonbooks.

Mills, C. W. 1959. The Sociological Imagination. Greenwich, CT: Greenwood Press.

Moody, H. R. 1993. "Overview: What Is Critical Gerontology and Why Is It Important?" In T. R. Cole, W. A. Achenbaum, P. L. Jakobi, and R.

Kastenbaum, eds., Voices and Visions of Aging: Toward a Critical Gerontology. New York: Springer.

Nelson, J. 1997. Straight, No Chaser: How I Became a Grown-up Black Woman. New York: Penguin Books.

Neugarten, B. L., Moore, J. W., and Lowe, J. C. 1965. "Age Norms, Age Constraints, Adult Socialization." In B. L. Neugarten, ed., Middle Age and Aging, pp. 22–28. Chicago: University of Chicago Press.

Omi, M., and Winant, H. 1987. Racial Formation in the United States From the 1960s to the 1980s. New York: Routledge & Kegan Paul.

Orwell, G. 1946. Animal Farm. New York: Harcourt Brace and Co.

Phillips B. 1957. "A Role Theory Approach to Adjustment in Old Age." American Sociological Review 22: 212–217.

Phillipson, C. 1982. Capitalism and the Construction of Old Age. London: Macmillan.

Quetelet, L. A. [1842] 1983. "A Treatise on Man and the Development of His Faculties." Cited in C. Haber, Beyond Sixty-Five, pp. 42–44. New York: Cambridge University Press.

Riley, M. W., Foner, A., and Johnson, M. E. 1972. Aging and Society, Vol. 3: A Sociology of Age Stratification. New York: Russell Sage Foundation.

Rose, A. M. 1965. "The Subculture of the Aging: A Framework for Research in Social Gerontology." In A. M. Rose and W. A. Peterson, eds., Older People and Their Social Worlds. Philadelphia: F. A. Davis.

Squier, L. W. 1912. Old Age Dependency in the United States. New York: Macmillan.

Talley, T., and Kaplan, J. 1956. "The Negro Aged." December Newsletter. Gerontological Society, Vol. 6.

Waters, M. 1990. Ethnic Options: Choosing Identities in America. Berkeley: University of California Press.

Weber, M. 1978. Economy and Society. Berkeley: University of California Press.

Section I

Cultural Constructions of Later Life

What are appropriate norms for behavior in old age? And when is an individual "elderly"? Expectations about how people should behave and the kinds of social roles they should occupy because of their age make social behavior predictable. Yet expectations about old age may lead to ageism, that is, the systematic stereotyping and discrimination against people because they are old (Butler 1989). Ageism, like racism and sexism, perpetuates inequalities. These inequalities will ultimately affect younger people, for they, too, will grow old. Biologist Alex Comfort drew an ironic parallel between ageist beliefs and other forms of bigotry, alluding to the television character Archie Bunker, known for his discrimination against women, people of color, immigrants, and ethnic groups other than his own:

> One wonders what Archie Bunker would feel about immigrants if he knew that on his sixty-fifth birthday he would turn into a Puerto Rican. white racists don't turn black, black racists don't become white, male chauvinists don't become women, anti-Semites don't wake up and find themselves Jewish—but we have a lifetime of indoctrination with the idea of the difference and inferiority of the old. (1976, p. 4)

The readings in this section discuss various ways in which old age has been socially constructed to establish a framework for considering myths and realities about later life. Through these readings, we see that old age is not a steady state; its definitions unfold in a cultural, social, and historical context. A selection by Jay Sokolovsky introduces this section. As he aptly points out, cultural definitions of old age and the status accorded to the elderly have varied widely from culture to culture and have dramatic implications for the way people in a society think about its elderly. There is no simple association, however, between pre-industrial and simple societies and a specific view of aging. Even within a specific sociocultural system, images of aging are variable and complex, influenced by degree of family support, gender, class position, and infirmity. There has probably never been a "golden age" in which elders were automatically respected or loved (Nydegger 1985). Rather, respect for the elderly reflected their ability to control valued goods and resources (including knowledge) or to fulfill mythologic roles in which they inhabited a close-by nether world from which they supervised human activities. Nor is there evidence that younger members in any society welcomed being powerless any more than they would in the United States today. Although there is a common belief that somewhere in some far-distant land—China, Japan, and India are frequently mentioned—there were societies dominated by respect for elders, what is ignored is that such honor was often bought at a dear price paid by younger relatives. As R. Gallin has pointed out:

Filial piety and veneration of age buttressed a status system that defined authority and fostered control of the young by the old. Within this rigid hierarchy, daughters-in-law were subjugated by mothers-in-law to ensure the stability of the family and security in old age. Such stability and security, however, were achieved at the price of the immeasurable repression of daughters-in-law. (1998, p. 4)

And, as one older Taiwanese woman summarized her earlier life:

When we were married we cried because we belonged to another family. We had to cook and to serve others. We used to worry would they like our cooking. If they didn't, your mother-in-law beat you. (1998, p. 1)

Nor were elders exempt from age norms even in societies such as pre-World War II Japan; misfits could pay with their lives. Often forgotten in discussion of respect for elders is that, until the twentieth century, few people survived into old age. High mortality rates in the past meant that the percentage of the population reaching old age was relatively small. This situation is changing rapidly; for example, the number of older people being supported by their children in Japan is expected to more than double between 1998 and 2025 (Velkoff and Lawson 1998). Examining contemporary Japanese culture, in the second selection James O'Leary expands upon the concept of respect for the elderly in Japanese society. The often praised concept of Asian filial obligation has altered as the proportion of elders in the population, industrialization, and urbanization have increased. He describes how definitions of old age, population characteristics, and organization of social and economic life are inherently linked and how traditional patterns of family structure no longer fit much of Japan today. Declines in family size coupled with increased life expectancy and rapid urbanization are redefining the status of the elderly in ways that may create new problems for a society unprepared to provide nonfamily-based care for the very old and frail.

Although historians such as David Fischer (1978) have argued that a firmly established (and male) gerontocracy existed in colonial America, other historians such as Demos (1986) have noted that any high status enjoyed by the elderly resulted from their control of resources. Economic power outweighed chronological age (Haber and Gratton 1994) and even gender (Cole 1993). Impoverished older men and women, dependent upon the good will of their relatives and the community, did not, however, enjoy high status (Haber and Gratton 1994).

This approach to the status of the elderly is an illustration of exchange theory, an approach first developed by George Homans (1974). Applying this theory to the status of the elderly in present-day society, J. J. Dowd has argued that "the problems of aging are essentially problems of decreasing power resources" (1975, p. 590). As people age, both the value and amount of resources they have available for exchange dwindle. As the elderly gradually lose resources, such as money, skills, and physical strength, that are valued by the society, their power also diminishes. Simply put, they have fewer chips with which to bargain in the game of life. The worker who once exchanged skill for wages loses this bargaining power upon retirement and becomes the object of charity rather than an agent able to achieve proportionality in social exchange. Widespread social and economic changes in the United States and other industrialized nations have reduced the ability of older workers to control resources. During the nineteenth century, craft shops began to be replaced by large-scale industries where younger workers and new immigrants who were willing to work for lower wages competed for the new jobs. Accompanying these economic changes affecting older workers was a growing social antipathy toward old age (Cole 1993). By 1851, according to one commentator: "It would seem as if the national youthfulness had expressed itself in the maxims of social life, making it, by a supreme law of fashion, un-American to be anything but young" (Kirkland 1851, cited in Cole 1993).

By the end of the nineteenth century, old age was defined by social reformers as a social problem, directly linked to poverty and ill health. The connection between dependent old age and almshouse residency was clear: "Generations grew up with 'a reverence for God, the hope of heaven, and the fear of the poorhouse' " (Haber and Gratton 1994, p. 122).

Deficit models of aging, such as those advanced by physicians during the nineteenth and early twentieth centuries, continue to influence numerous practices as well as portrayals of old age even today. The belief that older people are "senile" or childish enables us to view elders as "the other," distinct from ourselves, thus alleviating our own fears of aging and finitude. In his selection Mike Hepworth addresses the notion of old age as a second childhood and proposes that situations exist where "acting childish" in later life may at times be beneficial, permitting elders to challenge stereotypical beliefs about later life. By casting off norms for expected behavior as old persons, elders may both gain a self-esteem and challenge ageist beliefs about their capacities through doing the unexpected. As Karl Marx once observed: "A man cannot become a child again, or he becomes childish. But does he not find joy in the child's naivete, and must he himself not strive to reproduce its truth at a higher stage?" (1973, p. 111).

The development of science and scientific medicine in the nineteenth century also contributed to negative views of old age as physicians became increasingly interested in old age as a disease. The selection by Carole Haber describes the ways in which old age became medicalized and designated as an accumulation of pathological processes in the United States. Medicalization describes the use of a medical diagnosis to label individual behavior, such as hyperactivity among children, or a particular social problem or concern such as drug addiction. Although medicalizing a condition may remove it from its previous state as a moral flaw or sin and provide for its treatment, it is also a powerful tool for social control.

Medical labels not only influence the way the condition is handled but also affect other spheres of life, such as job opportunities, family life, legal privileges, social entitlements, social attitudes, and self-definitions. Haber investigates how physicians contributed to the definition of old age as synonymous with physical and mental decrepitude and a disease without a cure that nonetheless required scientific management—an attitude that persists even today.

Part of the medicalization of old age encompassed the belief that the elderly were incapable of sexual activity but prone to depraved sexual desires, giving force to the image of a "dirty old man" and "dirty old woman." The selection by Benjamin Schlesinger examines the cultural and personal consequences of this concept and stipulates how the desexualization of old age has both negative social consequences and adverse physical and mental health results for older people. He provides a striking description of how long-term-care settings prohibit and penalize expression of sexuality in old age and suggests ways in which these policies should be changed.

Medicalization of old age also emphasized the inevitability of mental decline and loss of reasoning and judgment. In the early twentieth century, physician William Osler (1979, cited in Cole 1993, pp. 170–174) commented on the comparative uselessness of those over the age of 40, a worthlessness of the elderly reiterated by another physician, I. L. Nascher (who coined the term *geriatrics*): "We realize that for all practical purposes the lives of the aged are useless, that they are often a burden to themselves, their family, and the community at large" (Nascher 1909, cited in Cole 1993, p. 202).

As a result of improved public health measures and medical advances, more and more people can expect to live longer and often healthier lives. As L. Burton, P. Dilworth-Anderson, and V. Bengston have pointed out:

Current and future generations of the elderly are part of a quiet revolution—a revolution of older individuals representing the broadest range of ethnic, racial . . . [and] regional diversity ever witnessed. . . . This diversity challenges us to evaluate the applicability of existing research, policy and programs to emerging elderly populations. And more important, it prods us to reassess the relevance of gerontological theories and perspectives. (1992, p. 129)

Old age, rather than a period of decline and incapacity, is emerging as a new stage of life with innovative lifestyles that counter unfavorable perspectives on later life. Disability, depression, and decline are not part of normal aging but rather hallmarks of disease and despair (Rowe and Kahn 1998). The selection by Jack Rosenthal expands upon elders' "quiet revolution," exploring ways that the meaning and experience of later life is changing rapidly in American society.

Searches for "successful aging" (Rowe and Kahn 1998) and "productive aging" (Bass, Caro, and Chen 1992) are replacing the quest for the fountain of youth. What precisely is successful (or productive) aging? Is there a single definition? The selection by Margret Baltes and Laura Carstensen examines various theoretical images of successful aging and discards a "one size fits all" concept. Suggesting that later life encompasses a sequence of simultaneous gains and losses in capacity and performance, the authors call attention to the importance of individual and personal definitions of successful old age. Throughout the life course, people select their own specific goals and ways to achieve them, often focusing on one life domain in which they believe success is attainable. For example, after the actor Christopher Reeve, known for his numerous movie appearances including the *Superman* films, was thrown from his horse in 1995, he sustained massive spinal cord injuries. Paralyzed and dependent on others for his basic physical functions, he nonetheless exercises with the help of others:

> Apart from the physical benefits, I have found that exercising the body helps me focus on the future. No matter what kind of mood I'm in, I always make myself do something that will help prevent my physical condition from deteriorating. It's just like the first few months of 1977, when I was training for *Superman* and told my driver to take me to the gym even if I said I wanted to go home. (Reeve 1998, p. 266)

Exercising is one way that Reeve maintains self-mastery and self-respect; his work

on behalf of the disabled is another. Despite profound physical handicaps, he is "successful"—no longer as a film star but as an individual challenging disability and working for the disabled. His definition of "success" has changed due to life circumstances. In old age, too, one individual's definition of "successful aging" may not only change but differ markedly from another's. "Success" in aging—and in living—is influenced by life experiences, personal preferences, and physical capacities.

As we consider the social constructions of old age and the potentials or hazards of later life, we need to give thought to the complexities of both. We need also to remember the webs of connection, discrimination, and conflict that affect individuals, social contexts, and societies as people age. Race and ethnicity, gender, and social class shape all of us throughout the life course and are integral to the ways that we regard ourselves and are regarded by others as we grow old. Attempts to give global definitions of "old age" and "aging" raise concern, for both heterogeneity and diversity are the most outstanding hallmarks of later life.

References

Bass, S., Caro, F., and Chen, Y. P. 1992. *Achieving a Productive Aging Society*. Westport, CT: Auburn House.

Burton, L., Dilworth-Anderson, P., and Bengston, V. 1992. "Creating Culturally Relevant Ways of Thinking About Aging and Diversity: Theoretical Challenges for the 21st Century." In E. P. Stanford and F. M. Torres-Gill, eds., *Diversity: New Approaches to Ethnic Minority Aging*. New York: Amityville.

Butler, R. N. 1989. "Dispelling Ageism: The Cross-cutting Intervention." *Annals of the American Academy of Political and Social Sciences*, 503: 138–147.

Cole, T. R. 1993. *The Journey of Life: A Cultural History of Aging in America*. New York: Cambridge University Press.

Comfort, A. 1976. "Age Prejudice in America." *Social Policy*, 7(3): 3–8.

Demos, J. 1986. *Past, Present, and Personal*. New York: Oxford University Press.

Dowd, J. J. 1975. "Aging as Exchange: A Preface to Theory." *Journal of Gerontology*, 30: 585–594.

Fischer, D. H. 1978. *Growing Old in America*, expanded edition. New York: Oxford University Press.

Gallin, R. 1998. "The Intersection of Class and Age: Mother-in-law/Daughter-in-law Relations in Rural Taiwan." In J. Dickerson-Putnam and J. K. Brown, eds., *Women Among Women*, pp. 1–14. Urbana: University of Illinois Press.

Haber, C., and Gratton, B. 1994. *Old Age and the Search for Security*. Indiana University Press.

Homans, G. C. 1974. *Social Behavior: Its Elementary Forms*. New York: Harcourt Brace Jovanovich.

Kirkland, C. M. 1851. "Growing Old Gracefully." *The Evening Book.* New York: Scribner. Cited in Cole, T. R. 1993. *The Journey of Life: A Cultural History of Aging in America*, p. 48. New York: Cambridge University Press.

Marx, K. 1973. *Grundrisse: Foundations of the Critique of Political Economy*, translated by M. Nicolaus. New York: Vintage.

Nydegger, C. N. 1985. "Family Ties of the Aged in Cross-cultural Perspective." In B. B. Hess and E. W. Markson, eds., *Growing Old in America*. New Brunswick, NJ: Transaction.

Reeve, C. 1998. *Still Me.* New York: Random House.

Rowe, J. W., and Kahn, R. L. 1998. *Successful Aging.* New York: Pantheon.

Velkoff, V. A., and Lawson, V. A. 1998. International Brief. *Gender and Aging: Caregiving.* Washington, DC: U.S. Dept. of Commerce, Bureau of the Census.

Chapter 1
Images of Aging

Jay Sokolovsky

Unlike becoming a teenager, there is no specific age at which one becomes old. How people view old age is a "social construction," that is, a set of commonly accepted cultural beliefs about the elderly. The American choice of age 65 as "old" was adapted from General Otto von Bismarck, chancellor of Germany, who in the nineteenth century declared pension eligibility to begin at that age. Bismarck's selection of age 65 was both politically popular and cost-effective. Workers were ensured a pension, but since average life expectancy at that time was only 47, relatively few workers lived to collect these benefits. Indeed a very economical pension policy for the nation!

In the following selection, Jay Sokolovsky explores the ways in which old age is delineated in various cultures other than our own. In some cultures, the old are regarded as valuable resources; other societies may consider the elderly to be unproductive social burdens. These differences in the social construction of old age in turn affect the influence and power older adults have in a specific society at a particular point in its history. Sokolovsky points out that changes in social and economic roles are the most common marks of becoming old; changes in physical and mental health are the least common. Gender is also important in cultural definitions of old age. There are diverse stereotypes about the characteristics of older women, ranging from "Dear Old Thing" to "Scheming Old Hag." As you read the following selection, pay attention to the interplay among culture, gender, and images of old age, and their relationship to perceptions of time, aging, generation, and cherished cultural myths. Notice the use of social roles to define old age. Think about the concept of "over aged" and the ways in which this concept changes attitudes and treatment of the elderly. Consider how our social constructs of old age affect not only our thinking but also shed light on particular social and public policies affecting the lives of older adults in the United States.

Even a cursory look at global and historical data on the aging process provides testimony to the great variety and complexity of the ways in which images of aging are formed and reflected in the realities of a citizen's life. While for classical Greek culture, aging was deemed an unmitigated misfortune, among the Samoans being a healthy old person was the pinnacle of life (Holmes and Rhoads, 1987). Whereas the Greeks not only said, "Whom the gods love, die young," and invented various myths to support this notion (Slater, 1964), Samoan adults could not fully enter many of the most important realms of their culture until the fifth and sixth decades of life.

As revealed by the cross-cultural examination of imagery connected to aging, the non-Western vision of the aging process and old people not only indicates the divergence from our own perceptions of aging but points to critical intrasocietal distinctions based on gender and perceived phases of late adulthood. It is becoming clear that culturally constructed perceptions of becoming old, being old, and fading into a stage of nonfunctioning senescence can have dramatic implications for how a given society metaphorically thinks about its elders. In exploring these issues, I will first examine how cultural variation relates to created images of aging and the aged and then consider how images of the culturally nonfunctional aged interact with societal reaction to such persons.

Culture, Image, Context, and Aging

A growing body of research highlights the importance of understanding the nature of the aging experience within an appropriate cultural context. There is no simple association between preindustrial/premodern societies and a particular image of aging. Each cultural system acts as a set of symbolic constructs through which a particular version of reality is perceived. In this way any sociocultural system establishes the collective representations and values that shape, and in turn are shaped by, distinct patterns of political economy, kinship, and ritual behavior. Also at work are contextual factors that can alter how cultures transform people's lives. Therefore, one must always be cognizant of how such variables as degree of family support, gender, or class position might alter the images associated with aging in a single society.

The basis for culturally constructing images of aging stems from the dependence of human communities on high levels of prolonged material and social interdependence among generations. This connection of people in different parts of the life cycle is universally recognized by age-linked language categories, such as child, adult, and old person. The variable definitions of when and how persons move through such markers of age-based status strongly shape the culturally differentiated perceptions of time, aging, and generation and are vitally linked to the cherished myths each culture possesses (Fry and Keith, 1982; Kertzer, 1982; Foner, 1984; Kertzer and Schaie, 1989; Fry, 1990).

Social boundaries associated with age-based statuses show great variation in the degree to which they allot power and create images invoking separation among the differently named categories of persons. For example, the Mbuti pygmy hunter-gatherers of Zaire have four loosely defined age grades (categories): children, youths, adults, and older persons (Turnbull, 1965). No elaborate rituals mark the passage from one grade to another and no barriers prevent easy interaction between those in different age categories. Still, well-known norms do shape the behavior and responsibility assumed to be the preserve of a given grade. The Mbuti have created a potent, positive, but *nonhierarchical image* of the aged, who as a category of person are called *mangese*—"the great ones." Their culture contains one of the most balanced, egalitarian systems for linking generations that is known in the ethnographic literature.

In contrast, one can find societies where age grades are transformed into sharply ascribed age sets. Here different spans along the life cycle are sharply set apart by highly managed images involving spectacular ritual, distinct dress, and specialized tasks, modes of speech, comportment, and deferential gestures. Persons move through the life cycle collectively and form tightly bound groups performing specific tasks. The most elaborated forms of such cultural systems are found among East African nomadic herders, such as the Samburu of Kenya (Spencer, 1965). Here age sets of males initiated together move through the life cycle collectively. Over time and through elaborate ritual, they progressively take on, as a group, age-bounded roles of herders, warriors, and various grades of elders. Male elders in their fifth and sixth decades gain substantial power through maintaining large polygynous households, holding wealth in their numerous cattle, and having a ritual link to the ancestors, whom they can call upon to supernaturally curse younger persons who misbehave. As is the case for most such age-based societies, Samburu women's societal maturation is accomplished through individual life-cycle rituals, and their status is much more tied to their place in family units (see Kertzer and Madison, 1981, for the rarer case of women's age sets).

All too often, such cultures have been held up as exemplars of places where a strong positive image of the elderly reaches its zenith. It is important to note that this is frequently accomplished at the expense of intense intergenerational conflict, exploiting and repressing the young, and preventing women from gaining an equitable place in the community. Among the Samburu, older women in fact do not share the very powerful image as associated with old men. When they are widowed, women are not permitted to marry again and suffer both materially and socially. Elder widows are more apt to be characterized as "old donkeys" rather than as paragons of moral strength and virtue (Fratkin, 1983, personal communications).

The Image of the Old

The conception of being "old" is almost universal and is culturally constructed by a variety of measures. Only one study to date has systematically used worldwide data, contained in the Human Relations Area Rules, to examine this issue. In this study, anthropologists Anthony Glascock and Susan Feinman

(1981) found that in a random sample of 60 societies there were three basic means of identifying a category of "old": change of social/economic role, chronology, and change in physical characteristics. Particularly striking in this work are the following conclusions:

1. A change in social/economic role is by far the most common marker of becoming old. This can include one's children becoming parents, general shifts in the types of productive activities one engages in, or beginning to receive more goods and services than one produces.

2. A change in capabilities is the least common marker. Factors such as invalid status and senility are quite rare as primary indicators of a general designation of old. This seems to be the case because societies frequently create a category of old that begins before many people encounter such radical signs of physical decline.

3. Almost a majority of societies in the sample have multiple definitions of being aged. These varied definitions of aging are commonly applied to distinct categories of "old," which include a phase of aging linked to movement toward the loss of normal functioning and death.

This last item seems to add a component of both complexity and ambiguity to how societies fully flesh out their images of aging. As we will see later on, confronting an image of the old tilted to the dimensions of incapacity and death can initiate drastic changes in the attitudes and behavior exhibited toward those so labeled.

Mythic Images of the Elderly

In preindustrial societies, where people existed without situation comedies or Pepsi commercials, orally conveyed folktales often transmitted complex symbolic messages about different parts of the life cycle. Not infrequently, the mythic images of the elderly were of sacred personages who inhabit a close-by nether world and who watch over human endeavors. For example, the hunting/gathering Inuit of arctic North America not only tended to glorify elders in folktales, but the majority of gods, heroes, and demons depicted were prototypically ancient adults. The polar Eskimo, for example, believed an old woman named Nerivik to be a goddess who lives beneath the water. She would thwart the efforts of the young seal hunters until the village shaman made a cosmic voyage to visit her and comb her matted hair. Only then could the seals swim through her sacred hairdo and be caught (Holmes 1983, p. 89). Another myth of a related Inuit people tells of an old man who was transfigured into a luminous body and shot up into the sky, where he then existed as a bright guiding star to hunters. Of course, such mythic images of aged figures much be balanced against the overall Inuit cultural context in which it is actually the virile, young adult male hunter who is the object of social cynosure and against whom ultimate prestige is measured (Guemple, 1987).

In his study of the Qigiktamuit Inuit of Labrador, Guemple found that while the aged in general were viewed as resources for extra labor, repositories of valuable knowledge, and means of social control, the transition, especially for males, to being regarded as old (*ituk*) took place early (late 40s to early 50s) and was resisted with a variety of "renewal" activities. This package of "image management" ranged from ostentatious generosity with hunted game to the taking of a young wife. Adult females tended not to be called old woman (*ningui*) until they were past ages 55–60 and seemed to have a longer transition to being so labeled. Not so burdened with the comparison to the ideal male mode, older females appeared less apt to pursue renewal activities; if they did, these most typically involved the adoption of children. While many older women were seen as having garnered special esoteric powers, especially for curing, when things went wrong in the village it was such aged females who were most likely to be blamed for the misfortune.

It is noteworthy that in societies such as the Mbuti or pre-1960s Japan, where the general image of the aged was about as positive as one finds in the range of human societies, myths and folktales existed that projected dire consequences for straying from age norms. In the Mbuti case there is a tale of a misfit elder who is buried alive. Among the Japanese there is the story of Old Rin, made famous by the Japanese novel, *The Oak Mountain Song*. In the folktale, people in the poor isolated rural area are required at age 70 to go to Old Mountain to await death. Old Rin is only 69 and very healthy, but her son thinks she is a burden and urges her to make the suicidal pilgrimage. To look the part of the very old, Rin knocks out some teeth and trudges up the mountain to die. Interestingly, this tale has various endings: (1) the son suffers remorse and rescues Rin; (2) the son arrives too late and finds Rin dead; and (3) the son hides Rin and uses her knowledge to solve a problem of a king, who then grants his wish to end abandonment of the elderly (Plath, 1972).

The Feminine Triaxial Mystique

One of the critical issues to consider in a cross-cultural look at images of aging is the divergent metaphors created on the basis of gender. Predominant in many societies is the hydra-headed perception of older women. Within one society, they may be viewed in a variety of seemingly contradictory ways, with images that range from the positive, nurturing matriarch/granny to a mystical shamaness and finally to the feared evil witch. Such variant depictions of female elderhood seem most glaring in patrilineal societies, especially those that fuse a public image for older males to the cultural heights of prestige and respect. A number of authors have commented on patterns of gender role reversal that originate when women enter their postreproductive phase and culminate when mastery of the domestic sphere is complete. This is typically marked by control of the daughter-in-law and other adult female kin. It is further enhanced by influence over married sons and their children, greater authority over rituals regulating social ties (especially life cycle events), and the gradual movement of a woman's spouse out of his public domain and into her hearth-centered life (see especially Kerns and Brown, 1992; Cool and McCabe, 1987; Gutmann, 1987). This can be coupled with selective forays into public arenas, previously off limits to these women as premenopausal females. As Silverman notes, "even in male dominated societies, like the Comanche in North America, the Mundurucu of South America and the Ewe of West Africa, women who have reached menopause fill important decision-roles otherwise restricted to men" (Silverman, 1987, p. 335). A classic description of this process is provided by Kayberry (1939) in an early anthropological study of Australian aboriginal women. Here she observed how as women become senior adults, they often assume greater authority within and outside their own extended kin network. They were observed functioning as arbiters of tribal law and taking the initiative in establishing order when community disputes raged out of control.

A dramatic alteration between images projecting a "Dear Old Thing" versus the "Scheming Hag" now abounds in the ethnographic literature (Cool and McCabe, 1987). Public metaphors depicting aging women seem to be more divergent and dramatic than the cultural images created for men. This is likely related to the preponderance of male-dominated societies and the consequent greater ability of males to manipulate public images. A graphic example of this was the disproportionate projection of an image of "witch" on middle-aged and older women during the Middle Ages (Bever, 1982).

The 'Near Dead'—Image Management's Ultimate Challenge

Leo Simmons, in his opus on global patterns of aging, states the following:

> Among all peoples a point is reached in aging at which any further usefulness appears to be over, and the incumbent is regarded as a living liability. "Senility" may be a suitable label for this. Other terms among primitive peoples are the "over aged," the "useless stage," the "sleeping period," "the age grade of the dying," and the "already dead." (1960, p. 87)

Worldwide comparative studies have corroborated the commonality of such distinctions (Maxwell and Maxwell, 1980; Maxwell, Silverman and Maxwell, 1982; Glascock, 1990). This research has also demonstrated a potent connection between such altered images of aging and dramatically changed attitudes toward individuals. Even societies that give high praise for the general concept of aging and provide valued roles for the active, healthy elders may not only quickly withdraw cultural forms of esteem for the "over aged" but even direct forms of contempt and "death-hastening" measures toward such elderly. In a crucial comparative study of the reasons for showing contempt toward the elderly, Maxwell and Maxwell (1980) isolated eight types of complaints leveled against the aged as rationales for the display of negative treatment. While physical deterioration was a significant variable in explaining the variance in expressed contempt, it lagged behind "loss of family support system" and "devalued appearance" in accounting for the vagaries of negative behavior shown in the elderly. The authors suggest that a negatively altered physical image of the old may be a far more important factor than has been expected in understanding the construction and deconstruction of personhood in later life (see also Barker, 1990).

Conclusions

This article has suggested how culture and context can serve to transform the societally construed image of the aged. It has shown that consideration of certain variables is critical in any analysis of how the elderly are portrayed. These crucial variables have to do with the ways in which cultures (1) create social boundaries between generations, (2) distribute power between genders over the life cycle, and (3) use mythology. Finally, this article has suggested that one of the most difficult dilemmas any society must deal with is how to manage the image of the frail, very old individual. Image management of this category of person has perhaps the most potential for producing harm to those least able to cope with psychological threats to their personhood.

Discussion Questions

1. Describe the ways in which different cultures create social boundaries between generations and the variables involved.

2. Explain how elaborate rituals may or may not mark the passage from one age grade to another.

3. What are the three most common ways found in cross-cultural research of categorizing someone as old?

4. Define the feminine triaxial mystique.

5. How may a negative physical image of the elderly be an important factor in understanding the deconstruction of personhood in later life?

References

Barker, J., 1990. "Between Humans and Ghosts: The Decrepit Elderly in a Polynesian Society." In J. Sokolovsky, ed., *The Cultural Context of Old Age: World-Wide Perspectives*. New York: Bergin and Garvey.

Bever, E., 1982. "Old Age and Witchcraft in Early Modern Europe." In P. Sterns, ed., *Old Age in Preindustrial Society*. New York: Homes and Meier.

Cool, L., and McCabe, J., 1987. "The 'Scheming Hag' and the 'Dear Old Thing': The Anthropology of Aging Women." In J. Sokolovsky, ed., *Growing Old in Different Societies*. Acton, Mass.: Copley.

Foner, N., 1984. *Ages in Conflict: A Cross-Cultural Perspective on Inequality Between Old and Young*. New York: Columbia Press.

Fry, C., 1990. "The Life Course in Context: Implications of Research." In R. Rubinstein, ed., *Anthropology and Aging: Comprehensive Reviews*. Dordrecht, Netherlands: Kluwer.

Fry, C., and Keith, J., 1982. "The Life Course as a Cultural Unit." In M. Riley, ed., *Aging from Birth to Death: Interdisciplinary Perspectives*, vol. 2. Boulder, Colo.: Westview Press.

Glascock, A., 1990. "By Any Other Name It Is Still Killing: A Comparison of the Treatment of the Elderly in America and Other Societies." In J. Sokolovsky, ed., *The Cultural Context of Old Age: World-Wide Perspectives*. New York: Bergin and Garvey.

Glascock, A., and Feinman, S., 1981. "Social Asset or Social Burden: An Analysis of the Treatment of the Aged in Non-Industrial Societies." In C. Fry, ed., *Dimensions: Aging, Culture and Health*. New York: Praeger.

Guemple, D., 1987. "Growing Old in Inuit Society." In J. Sokolovsky, ed., *Growing Old in Different Societies*. Acton, Mass.: Copley.

Gutmann, D., 1987. *Reclaimed Powers: Toward a New Psychology of Men and Women in Later Life*. New York: Basic Books.

Holmes, L., 1983. *Other Cultures' Elder Years: An Introduction to Cultural Gerontology*. Minneapolis. Minn.: Burgess.

Holmes, L., and Rhoads, E., 1987. "Aging and Change in Samoa." In J. Sokolovsky, ed., *Growing Old in Different Societies*. Acton, Mass.: Copley

Kayberry, P., 1939. *Aboriginal Women: Sacred and Profane*. London: Rutledge and Sons.

Kerns, B., and Brown, J., 1992. *In Her Prime: New Views of Middle-Aged Women*. Urbana, Ill.: University of Illinois Press.

Kertzer, D., 1982. "Generation and Age in Cross-Cultural Perspective." In M. Riley, ed., *Aging From Birth to Death*, vol. 2. Boulder, Colo.: Westview Press.

Kertzer, D., and Madison, O.B.B., 1981. "Women's Age-Set Systems in Africa: The Latuka of Southern Sudan." In C. Fry, ed., *Dimensions: Aging, Culture and Health*. Brooklyn, N.Y.: Praeger.

Kertzer, D., and Schaie, K. W., 1989. *Age Structuring in Comparative Perspective*. Hillsdale, N.J.: Lawrence Erlbaum.

Maxwell, E., and Maxwell, R., 1980. "Contempt for the Elderly: A Cross-Cultural Analysis." *Current Anthropology* 24: 569–70.

Maxwell, R., Silverman, P., and Maxwell, E., 1982. "The Motive for Gerontocide." In J. Sokolovsky, ed., *Aging and the Aged in the Third World: Part I Studies in Third World Societies*, No. 22. Williamsburg, Va.: College of William and Mary.

Plath, D., 1972. "Japan: The After Years." In D. Cowgill and L. Holmes, eds., *Aging and Modernization*. New York: Appleton-Century-Crofts.

Silverman, P., ed., 1987. *The Elderly as Modern Pioneers*. Bloomington and Indianapolis, Ind., Indiana University Press.

Simmons, L., 1945. *The Role of the Aged in Primitive Society*. New Haven, Conn.: Yale University Press.

Simmons, L., 1960. "Aging in Primitive Societies: A Comparative Survey of Family Life and Relationships." In C. Tibbetts, ed., *Handbook of Social Gerontology: Societal Aspects of Aging*. Chicago, Ill.: University of Chicago Press.

Slater, P., 1964. "Cross-Cultural Views of the Aged." In R. Kastenbaum, ed., *New Thoughts on Old Age*. New York: Springer.

Spencer, P., 1965. *The Samburu: A Study of Gerontocracy in a Nomadic Tribe*. Berkeley, Calif.: University of California Press.

Turnbull, C., 1965. *Wayward Servants*. New York: Natural History Press.

Reprinted from: Jay Sokolovsky, "Images of Aging: A Cross-Cultural Perspective." In *Generations*, 17:2 Spring/Summer 1993, pp. 51–54. Copyright © 1993. The American Society on Aging, San Francisco, CA. Reprinted by permission.

Chapter 2

Japan's Honorable Elders

James S. O'Leary

The preceding selection emphasizes the importance of culture in determining the status of the elderly. Americans often cite Japanese culture as an outstanding example of veneration and respect for old people. To what extent is the belief that Japanese elders maintain high social status and positive regard accurate today? Not only is Japan the world's most rapidly aging society, but its nonstop economic expansion during the past 50 years has transformed almost every aspect of daily living. As part of this industrial expansion, younger people have migrated from rural to urban areas, thus changing the pattern of the extended family. Life expectancy has also increased in Japan, where average life expectancy at birth is higher than in the United States.

*James O'Leary's selection suggests that these changes in lifestyle have influenced traditional Japanese cultural values toward the family in general and toward the elderly in particular. As Japan has become a highly industrialized, capitalist economy, the concept of Ie, the traditional belief that family blood lines and family relationships are more important than all other human relationships, has become less important. O'Leary provides important insights about dynamic interplay of changing population characteristics, rapid social change, and attitudes toward the elderly. As you read, pay attention to the impact of increasing life span and migration of younger people to urban areas on the traditional family structure and its implications for elders' quality of life. Think also about the role of the Japanese government in the provision of services for the old-old and whether the government should furnish services for the infirm elderly. Consider what the role of governments in industri-*alized nations, such as Japan, the United States, and elsewhere, should be in ensuring quality of life in very old age.*

Introduction

An increase in the percentage of the population over age 65 is occurring in all developed countries and has stimulated a rapid growth in the study of comparative social gerontology. Of particular interest has been the relationship between modernization and the changing social status of the elderly in Japan. There are two major reasons for this special interest. First, since "age" is both a socially and culturally created construct, a universally valid theory of social gerontology requires us to "consider the meaning of age from a more open, comparative stance" (Keith 1990). By studying the first non-Western country to industrialize, social gerontology in Japan can offer a comparative case controlling for overlapping historical, social, and cultural factors that make most Western countries "Western." Second, Japan is the world's most rapidly aging society; aging at a rate twice as fast as Finland, its nearest rival. These two factors have combined to provoke speculation as to how this major demographic transition will affect Japanese social, cultural, and political institutions. Despite this interest, the literature on Japanese gerontology is relatively small. A majority of studies in English have examined the extent to which traditional Japanese norms of respect for the aged have been preserved in modern Japanese society. It is assumed that such norms mitigate the negative effects modernization has on the social status of the aged in the West.

In this article I examine this assumption in light of the expanding literature on social gerontology written in Japanese. This literature presents a description of current changes in the age structure of the Japanese population and reviews theoretical discussions of relationships between aging and modernization in Japan. I then review recent studies of the image that young Japanese hold of the aged in general, and the attitudes of both aged and non-aged Japanese towards living in traditional three generation families in particular. The review will suggest that much of the literature in English suffers from an exclusive focus on the sustaining impact of cultural norms and ignores important attitudinal changes towards the elderly that have occurred in Japan.

Demographic Profile of Japan's Elderly

The rapid expansion of Japan's post-war economy has produced a tremendous change in the structure of the Japanese society, transforming almost every aspect of daily life. The Japanese cohort in their 60s and 70s have witnessed a profound nonrevolutionary continuous social transformation. The same cohort that was raised in isolated village hamlets without cars or bicycles and supplied with none or only minimal electrical power now routinely finds itself caught in massive traffic jams, riding high speed bullet trains, and often having to make calls to their sons or daughters overseas (Dore 1978). Although the outward transformation of the lifestyle and physical environment is most apparent, the change in the social fabric of the society has been just as dramatic, producing a shift in values and attitudes (Ike 1973).

The fruits of economic growth have manifested themselves clearly in improvement in infant mortality rates and medical services. In the West an increase in the average lifespan began to appear in the early 1900s, but in Japan the average lifespan changed little between the start of the Meiji period (1867) and the end of the Pacific War. With the start of the postwar recovery period and the onset of a period of high economic growth, the length of the average Japanese lifespan soared. Japanese currently enjoy a longer average lifespan than any other nationality. Simultaneous with the lengthening of the average lifespan, the birthrate, which also skyrocketed in the immediate postwar period, has since dropped off precipitously. Japan's current birthrate (1.69) is lower than the United States and every European country except West Germany and Italy (Kosei Hakusho, 1990). The combination of these changes has contributed to an especially rapid increase in the aging of its population.[1]

Heightened concern about the aging of the population and the problems of the aged first appeared in Japan in the mid 1970s. The percentage of the Japanese population over 65 reached 7 percent in 1970 which, by the United Nations definition, moved it into the "aged society" category. The 1973 oil crisis that marked the start of an era of moderate growth for the Japanese economy led to concerns that recent expansions in the social welfare system would result in higher than expected government expenditures. Presently, the Japanese elderly are still a smaller portion of the population than in the U.S. or most Western European nations, but their numbers are projected to grow at a rate high enough to pass all other industrialized countries. To indicate the speed of this increase, it took 50 years, from 1935 to 1985, for the percentage of the population over age 65 in Japan to double from 4.7 percent to 10.3 percent but it is forecasted that this percentage will once again double within the next 25 years. By comparison, in Sweden, which presently has a greater percentage of its population over 65 (17.4 percent) than Japan (10.6 percent), a period of eighty years passed for the percentage of its aged population to double from 7 percent to 14 percent. Japan will make the same demographic transition in the more compressed period of 24 years (Miura 1990). It is estimated that by the time the majority of the postwar baby boom generation reaches the age of 65, 22 percent of Japan's population will be over 65.

In addition to the speed at which Japan's population is aging, the government[2] has identified two other distinct aspects of this demographic transition adding to its complexity: the increasing percentage of the elderly considered "old-old" (i.e., those individuals 75 years or older) and the different pace at which some areas of the country are aging. In 1940 only 1.2 percent of the population was over age 75. By 1985 the percentage had tripled to 3.9 percent. It is estimated that at least until the year 2010, this section of the elderly population will increase at a faster rate than the rate for the "young-old" (ages 65–74). To put this more concretely, the Japanese government estimates that within the next 25 years, the percentage of the "young-old" will increase 70 percent from 6.4 percent to 10.8 percent, while the percentage of the "old-old" will increase by 140 percent, from 3.9 percent to 9.2 percent. Thus, as a percentage of all individuals over 65, those 75 and over will increase from 37.8 percent in 1985 to 46.0 percent in 2010; by 2023 it is estimated that the "old-old" will constitute over 50 percent of the elderly population.

The significance of this change is that not only are there more people over age 65 but also that these people are living longer than before. Only recently have social gerontologists begun to examine the distinctive needs of this "old-old" population and the impact the increase in the size of this subset of the aged will have on public expenditures (Habib 1990). Japanese government statistics . . . indicate that this subsection of the elderly tends to be more female, unemployed, and more likely to be suffering from some disabling physical ailment.

From the standpoint of utilization of social resources, the most distinctive characteristic of the "old-old" is that they are five times more likely to be bedridden than their "young-old" counterparts. It is estimated that the number of bedridden elderly will increase from 600,000 to 1,400,000 within the next 25 years, and the number of elderly with some form of mental or physical impairment living at home will increase from 600,000 to 1,600,0000. This increase is expected to put a tremendous burden on Japan's already overloaded and inadequate nursing facilities and personnel (Zenrosai Kyokai 1990). In order to meet the demand for nursing home services the Japanese government recently announced that it will be necessary to increase the number of home helpers from the present (1989) nationwide number of 31,405 to 100,000 within 10 years. Two years previously a similar government report had estimated that Japan would need only half as many home helpers.[3] Even the current report may be too optimistic. Ogawa Naohiro has estimated that unless the number of nursing homes is dramatically increased the percentage of women in their 40s [who] will have to assume responsibility for the care of an elderly patient in their homes will increase from the 1987 figure of 8 percent to almost

50 percent by the year 2025 (Ogawa 1989). The low percentage of elderly institutionalized has often been cited as evidence that they prefer to live with their children (Anderson 1990), but the present percentage may be less due to the low demand for such institutions and more influenced by the low supply. Existing facilities are now at 90 percent capacity with waiting periods of several years[4] not unusual. This shortage of [facilities] has prompted political groups among the elderly in Japan to call for a dramatic increase in the number of nursing homes (Zenkoku Koreisha Daikai 1990).

The third distinctive characteristic of Japan's aging population is the unevenness of the aging pattern within the country. For example, in the majority of municipal/regional units (*Shikuchoson*), 74 percent have an elderly population that constitutes between 10 percent to 20 percent of their population thus conforming to the national norm. [And] 17.5 percent have an elderly population of less than 10 percent while 9 percent have a concentration of over 20 percent. The major cause of this unevenness in the geographical distribution of the elderly is that during the period of rapid economic growth there was a tremendous outflow of young people from rural areas into urban centers seeking employment in the expanding industrial sectors. While in more recently urbanized areas such as the suburbs of Tokyo in Chiba prefecture, the elderly population represent a low of 4 percent of the population, in some rural areas of Yamaguchi prefecture it is as high as 35 percent.

This disproportional rate of growth has important implications for understanding and interpreting the current status of Japan's elders. Japan presently has two distinctly separate aging groups: the rural elderly and the urban elderly, each with special needs (Sato 1981; Okayama 1981). Despite the population shift from rural to urban areas during the immediate postwar period, the vast majority of Japan's elderly continue to live in rural areas, owning their own homes,[5] and highly integrated into traditional village networks. The percentage of elderly in urban areas is still relatively small and of these urban elderly a large number are not part of the postwar migration; in fact, they have lived at their present location for most, if not all of their lives. Most of these urban elders are well integrated into local community networks (Kaneko 1988). However, as more of the younger generation *sarariman*[6] retire and are separated from their primary job-related social network, they may have difficulty integrating themselves into locally based networks. Young and middle-aged men report low levels of association with their neighbors (Urata 1990). This postwar urban migration cohort, who in their late teens or early 20s moved into urban areas during the period of rapid industrialization, are only now beginning to retire. As one Japanese social gerontologist has said: "When the problem of the elderly comes, it will be greatest in the cities" (Ogawa 1990).

The increased concentration of elderly in rural officially designated "depopulated areas" has resulted in difficulties for the aged.[7] The major problem is that it has increased the burden of caring for the elderly since it is in the rural areas where the shortage of trained medical and nursing personnel is most apparent. This is considered one of the most difficult complications during the development of adequate social services for the aged (Maeda and Asano 1978). Conversely, in urban areas where there is a more sufficient supply of trained personnel, high land prices have hampered efforts to construct nursing homes and other social services for the elderly (Tabata 1990).

This uneven growth in the number of elderly persons in a country that has traditionally delegated responsibility for the care of such persons to family or community social support circles has placed a great deal of pressure on both Japan's private informal and public welfare system (Soeda 1987). How the government will respond to this change has become the number one domestic concern of the Japanese people.[8] The potential burden that the increase in the percentage of elderly can place on a nation's economy has been summed up in the "dependency ratio" equation which is computed by dividing the number of persons of working age (15–64 years of age) by the number of elderly persons (65 years and older). Although there

are problems with this ratio such as its assumption that everyone under 64 is working (i.e., no unemployment, complete female labor participation, etc.) and that everyone over 64 is not working, it still provides a gross estimation of how many individuals within the traditional working ages are supporting each senior citizen. When one examines the figures for Japan, one can understand the concern on the part of the Japanese. In 1987 this ratio stood at 6.3; by the year 2013 it is expected to decrease to 2.8 and hit a low point in 2021 at 2.5. In terms of the financial burden of supporting this elderly population, a government report estimated that to keep the Government pension system solvent, the joint employer/employee contribution would have to increase from the 1986 levels of 10.6 percent to 38.7 percent by the year 2025.[9]

Because the family structure of Japan is influenced by traditional preindustrial Confucian values which are cited as explaining the large number of elderly persons who live in three generation families, it has been argued that this ratio has less relevancy in the case of Japan. Care provided in these families reduces the social responsibility and fiscal burden on the state thus making the impact of dependency ratios less significant to social policy. Also, it is widely accepted that these extended family structures accord older people high prestige and provide them with greater psychological security.

Economic Development and Status Change Among the Elderly

The idea that despite its modernization, Japan's elders have maintained a high degree of prestige and social integration challenges perhaps the best scrutinized and hotly debated hypothesis concerning the relationship between aging and modernization. According to this hypothesis, modernization of the economy and the resulting changes in occupational, residential, and familial structures have a negative effect on the status of the aged (Houser 1976). In an early review of the cross-cultural research, Cowgill concluded, "As a general principle, it may be affirmed that the status of the aged in a community is inversely proportional to the degree of modernization of the society" (Cowgill 1972). The underlying premise of this view is that both social and economic changes create a process where previously powerful roles held by the aged, both within the context of the family and the economy, are taken over by the young. Modernization alters the ground rules of economic interdependence among generations. No longer is the younger generation's livelihood dependent upon the anticipated inheritance of the older generation's property which provided "both a carrot for the young and a surety (of support) for the old" (Goody 1976). This negative relationship between economic development and the status of the old has been supported by empirical evidence and has been generally accepted by social gerontologists (Cohn 1982; Palmore and Manton 1974).

A more recent restatement of this hypothesis is that the relationship is actually curvilinear, beginning with relatively low status for the aged in hunting and gathering societies, reaching a peak in settled agricultural societies, and then declining with industrialization (Williamson, Evans, and Powell 1982). Even with this refinement, modernization theory has been criticized for not taking the variations within societies in the status of the aged into account (Dowd 1980), idealizing a presumed "Golden Age" for the elderly in pre-industrialized societies (Laslett 1976; Quadagno 1982), and for mistaking "ritual deference" for actual esteem (Lipman 1970). Cowgill (1986) has responded to these criticisms by acknowledging the theory needs to be further refined to take into account such factors as social class or sex, but cautions a broad theory, by definition, is forced to overlook variations in details. He stands by his original theses that modernization results in a decline in the "relative status" of the aged.

Whether one chooses to accept an industrial or a political economic explanation (Phillipson 1982) for the loss of status among elderly persons, one would argue that there should be a corresponding lowering of the status of the aged in Japan. As a capitalist industrialized country, Japan's economy is second in size only to the United States. It has a highly urbanized population, with less than 10 percent of its population working in the

primary sector, and has a social welfare system that in many respects predates that of the United States (Ishida 1984). Yet, much of the social gerontology literature on Japan has questioned the universality of this process. Both Japanese and Western researchers have suggested that the influence of cultural values that emphasize respect for the elderly mitigates the relationship between industrialization and the status of the aged in Japanese society. This line of thinking is based on more general analyses that have suggested that the industrialization process in Japan has resulted in less social discontinuity from the preindustrial agrarian structure (Dore 1973; Vogal 1963). Certain Japanese cultural values, such as filial piety and "familyism," are viewed as pervasive and providing a favorable cultural environment for preserving a high status and active roles for elderly persons. Unlike in the West, Japanese people are taught to accept the Confucian ethic of "filial piety and respect for the elderly" (Maeda et al. 1989). This ethic emphasizes that personal preference and ambition should be subordinated to the common good of the family and that all members of the family should respect and obey the elderly family members. These values have helped promote the continued high status of the elderly in Japan and appear to inhibit the erosive impact of modernization. This impression has found acceptance not only among Western academics in the field but also among the general public in the United States (Tobin 1987).

Most authors commenting on the strength of traditional Japanese cultural values towards the family have cited the uniqueness of the concept of *Ie* (Kumagai 1986). This word is composed of the Chinese character for house and is often directly translated to mean family but in fact has a much broader meaning (Mitsuyoshi 1986). The concept of the *Ie* above all else represents the embodiment of a direct genealogical continuity or blood line. It is interpreted as symbolizing a continuing entity, that transcends any one individual or even any one present generation. The uniqueness of the Japanese concept of the *Ie* has been described as "penetrating every nook and cranny of Japanese society" (Nakane 1970) forming the basis of Japanese group

consciousness and even forming the foundation of a distinctive social order (Murakami
1981). The most important element of the *Ie*
is that human relationships within the *Ie* take
precedence over all other human relationships. The result is the development of an "*Ie*
consciousness" which emphasizes the careful
preservation of family property, maintenance
of ancestral graves, and seeing to the health
of older family members who represent the
closest historical linkage to past *Ie* members
(Fukutake 1967).

In prewar Japan the *Ie* was more than an
abstract notion of what the proper family
structure should be. It was concretely reinforced as having a legal status under the
civil code. When the civil code was revised in
the postwar period, the Occupation authorities deliberately eliminated the legality of the
Ie system which they viewed as an ideological
prop of the prewar regime (Steiner 1987).
However, looking at the current family structure in Japan, many authors have concluded
that the *Ie* system did not break down in the
wake of Occupation reforms (Rosenmayr
1987).

The lingering influence of the concept of
the *Ie* is cited as a major influence on Japanese family structure and attitudes towards
the aged, and has formed the rationale for
arguing that despite its highly industrialized,
advanced capitalist economy, Japan differs
from other industrialized countries in maintaining respect and a high social status
among the aged. The first and probably most
influential statement on the relationship between Japanese culture and greater respect
for the aged is Ruth Benedict's often cited
description of the Japanese arc of life.

> The arc of life in Japan is plotted in oppo-
> site fashion to that in the United States. It
> is a great shallow U-curve with maximum
> freedom and indulgence allowed to babies
> and to the old. Restrictions are slowly in-
> creased after babyhood till having one's
> own way reaches a low just before and
> after marriage. This low line continues
> many years during the prime of life, but
> the arc gradually ascends again until after
> the age of sixty, men and women are al-
> most as unhampered by shame as little
> children are. (Benedict 1946)

Perhaps the best known attempt to document
this relationship and determine if it still applies to current Japanese social conditions is
the work of Erdman Palmore who has concluded that Japan's unique cultural tradition
has preserved the social status of the aged
despite the country's rapid industrial transformation (Palmore 1975). Palmore bases his
conclusion on two main factors: the strong
tradition of vertical social relations and the
Confucian emphasis on filial piety. The former establishes the right of all aged to general
respect from younger persons. The latter attributes a cultural observance to honor one's
own parents and grandparents. Palmore concludes that Japan's "social system and culture
have distinctive elements which have helped
maintain the relatively high status and integration of older Japanese." To support this
conclusion Palmore cites statistics that, when
compared to the West, indicate that the Japanese elderly have a longer life span, are less
likely to be institutionalized, and are often
likely to either be living with their children or
live close enough to visit them almost daily.
Japan's elders are also more likely to continue working in their later years than their
counterparts in the West. Not only is there
less discrimination against the aged in the
work place, according to Palmore, but there
are also more opportunities to work. In a ten
year follow-up to his original research he reaffirmed his initial hypothesis that, "compared to other industrialized countries Japan
continues to provide higher integration and
status for its elders . . . (and that despite a
recent decline in status, when compared to
the West) . . . these large differences will persist for the foreseeable future" (Palmore and
Maeda 1985).

There exists a wide range of opinion
among Japanese scholars and social policy
makers on their evaluation of the strength
and influence of these norms. For example,
in an attempt to argue that Japan's public
welfare system and social norms provide the
elderly with an amenable environment far
superior to anything found in the West, Nagakawa states in no uncertain terms that,
"Welfare for the aged in Japan is so very well
established that it simply cannot be compared with what exists along these lines in

any other nation in the world" (Nagakawa 1979). Unfortunately he provides absolutely no adequate empirical data to back up this conclusion other than that the rise in the value of the yen has increased the value of Japanese pensions when compared to pensions in other countries. Furusa Toori (1989), a professor at one of Japan's major social research institutes, follows similar lines, stating that, "It is incorrect to say that the average Japanese has a dark (*kurai*) view of aging and the prospect of growing old. Rather they feel that the more one ages the greater wisdom and respect one acquires." Recently a school of thought has formed in Japan that argues that Japan should avoid creating a welfare system similar to the West that "overrationalizes the interpersonal relations and the family structure and thus weakens international competitiveness" (Maruo 1989). This argument, known as *Nihongata Fukushi Seido*, has stated that Japan can create a welfare system superior to the West by reinforcing the traditional family structure and the culturally instilled willingness of the Japanese people to honor and take care of their elders.

In direct contrast to this view Kamitsubo Hikari has sharply criticized the treatment of the elderly in Japan and believes they get less respect than the elderly living in the West. He has stated that the Japanese government, in order to pursue its own policy of reducing welfare expenditures, has publicly abused elderly people and made them a scapegoat for the projected problems associated with Japan's aging society. He cites as an example of the government's negative attitude towards the aged, the case of the Ministry of Welfare's Social Service Chief in 1986 who during an interview concerning the Ministry's budget allocations stated that, "no matter how much money you spend on the elderly in the end it's like giving water to an already withered tree" (Kamitsubo 1988).

These statements present opposite interpretations of the status of Japan's elders reflecting a diversity of opinion that exists within Japan. Such statements by themselves however, can provide no more of an accurate assessment of the current status of Japan's elders than can a reading of Confucian texts.

What is needed to provide such an assessment is a more systematic and analytical exploration of major factors affecting the evolution of Japan's view of elderly people.

Changes in the Structure of the Japanese Family

Although it is widely believed in the West that the percentage of three generation extended families in Japan has been maintained at a high level (with one article even erroneously reporting that this percentage has increased since 1975) (Morgan and Hirosima 1983), the industrialization and urbanization that has occurred in Japan has drastically affected the family structure. While it is true that when compared to the West, there is a higher percentage of three generation families, this percentage has been steadily decreasing throughout the postwar period. As a percentage of total households, the percentage of three generation extended family households has declined from 38 percent in 1960 to 15 percent in 1987. In contrast to this, the percentage of individual households and nuclear family households (married couple only, married couple and children, single parent and children) has continued to increase and now represents 18 percent and 62 percent respectively of total households in 1986.

If only the structure of households including an elderly member is examined, however, it is possible to see the lingering effects of a more traditional family structure. In 1970, 55 percent of all households with an elderly member were three generation households. . . . This percentage has decreased to 40 percent while the percentage of single individual elderly households increased from 7.4 percent to 13.2 percent. The percentage of elderly households composed of just an elderly couple almost doubled from 11.5 percent to 20.7 percent (Miura 1990). The trend in these data clearly indicates that an increasing number of elderly are living by themselves or as a couple. Because the percentage of single generation elderly households is increasing at the same time the total number of elderly persons is increasing, it is producing a rapid rise in the number of elderly only households. The number of these households was 5,200,00 in 1985 but is expected to increase by 270 percent by 2025 (Miura 1990).

Extended family households however, are a distinguishing feature of Japanese society and have been praised for the role they play in providing economic and social support across generations. Their continued existence has been used by Japanese politicians such as former prime minister Takashita Noboru, to suggest the creation of a "Japanese style welfare system" based on greater reliance on the family for providing support for the elderly in their later years (Takeshita 1988). Recently, however, reflecting the changes in household structure, attitudes towards the importance of maintaining extended households have been changing. A recent government report indicates that there are sharp differences between age groups in the desire to live in an extended family (Urata 1990). . . . [The] younger the age group the greater the percentage of respondents who report that it is better for parents to live apart from their children . . . . At all age levels, women are more likely than men to report a preference for parents living apart from their children. Among respondents between 30 to 40 years old, the percentage of men who report it's better to live together is only 36.7 percent and the percentage of women is even less at 26.0 percent. The most revealing percentage is that almost 50 percent of women between 30 to 40 years old believe it is better to live apart. The extended family in Japan primarily relies on women between 30 and 50 years old to provide the bulk of the care to elder family members living in the same household. It is significant that women in this age group are least interested in continuing to live in an extended household.[10] This data directly contradicts Palmore's assertion in his revised edition of *Honorable Elders* that "the youngest generation was even more favorable toward joint households than the middle-aged generation" (Palmore and Maeda 1985, p. 47).

The distribution of three generation families is also highly influenced by area with a higher percentage of old people living separately from their children in big cities which, ironically, are the very areas facing a severe housing shortage. For example, in rural Yamagata prefecture's Obanazawa city, the percentage of elderly living in extended families is 90 percent but in highly urbanized Yokohama, it is only 28 percent (Sakata 1988). Even in rural areas, however, Miura Furnio has hypothesized that the number of elderly only households will increase due to a continuing outflow of the younger population into more urban areas (Miura 1981). This hypothesis has been challenged by a Ministry of Welfare research report which has shown that there is no relationship between an increase in the elderly population in an area and an increase in the percentage of elderly only households (Koseisho 1988). As a result of this research, the population research center at the Ministry of Welfare has suggested that neither an interpretation of Japan's family structure as homogenous (*doshitsuron*) or changing (*henshitsuron*) can adequately account for the present distribution of three generation households and instead they suggest that Japan has a heterogen[eity] (*ishitsuron*) that includes both stability and change. The increase in the number of nuclear families will proceed in urban areas but the rural areas will continue to maintain a high level of three generation households. In other words, although the family structure is changing and the percentage of third generation households decreasing, because Japan's family structure is still influenced by traditional values this percentage will stabilize at a level higher than that found in the West. But Sakata Shyuichi has criticized the Ministry of Welfare's report for being based on a faulty calculation of urbanization and has concluded that the distribution of third generation households will become roughly equal and that in every region there will be a rapid decrease in the number of these households (Sakata 1988).

The vast majority of studies on changes in Japanese family structure, in both Japanese and English, have primarily focused on change or continuity in cultural norms regarding the traditional three generation family. Very few studies have attempted to understand how such factors as sex, occupation, education, or living conditions influence the desire to continue to live with one's parents. One of the few exceptions has been a study carried out by the Tokyo Metropolitan Institute of Gerontology among male residents between the ages of 60 to 64 in two Tokyo wards (Takahashi 1989). Takahashi's basic hypothesis is that the decision to live together with children, especially married children, is not decided by social norms but rather by individual living conditions, and that this is especially true in the case of larger cities. In addition to economic factors such as the amount of living space available and income level, the strength of the cultural norm of living together also varies depending on: (1) occupation—it is strongest among farmers and independent business men; (2) age—individuals educated during the prewar period are more willing to support the *Ie* system than those educated during the postwar period; and (3) education—it is weaker among the more highly educated who are critical of traditional customs. Of the 472 respondents who had children, 50.4 percent reported living with an unmarried child, 33.7 percent were not living with any of their children, and 15.9 percent were living with a married child.

When respondents in Takahashi's study were requested to express their intentions to either live with or separately from their children in the future, there is no clearly discernible preference for wanting to live with one's children. . . . Almost 90 percent of those respondents living with a married child express a desire to continue to live together while only 8 percent want to live separately and another 2.7 percent are not sure. The more interesting categories are those respondents either living with an unmarried child or living separately. The largest percentage (43 percent) of those living separately from their children have apparently already made the decision not to live with their children either at the present time or in the future while another 25 percent are not sure. Only 30.8 percent desire to change their present separate living situation and move in with their children in the future. Among those respondents presently living with an unmarried child, presumably some decision will have to made as to whether to continue to live together after the child is married. Among these respondents, their intentions are more or less evenly split between wanting to continue to live together, not wanting to continue, and not knowing for

sure with a slightly higher percentage (39.1 percent) reporting wanting to continue to live with their children.

In North America and Western Europe it is very common to be living separately from one's children or for an unmarried child to live with his or her parents until marriage, but the uniqueness of Japanese family structure is the large percentage of parents who continue to live with a married son or daughter. Because of the uniqueness of this group, Takahashi selected out all respondents who had married children to do a discriminant analysis in order to determine what variables might explain the decision to continue to live with a married child or not. He then conducted discriminant analyses on both actual living conditions and respondent's expressed intentions about wanting to live with their children. The results indicated that the most important factor in determining both present living situations and expressed intentions is the size of the parent's dwelling. A parent who is living in a dwelling of 20 *tsubo* or more[11] is much more likely to be living with a married child and also much more likely to express a desire to want to live with one of their children. On the other hand, if the parent lives in a dwelling with less than 19 *tsubo* they are much more likely to both not be living with their children and not wanting to live with their children in the future. This conclusion is supported by a government survey of three generation homes that showed that 98.2 percent of all three generation families were living in households whose total area exceeded 70 square meters and of this group, 71.4 percent were living in households with a total area of over 100 square meters (Somucho 1985).

In the occupation category, those most likely to be either living with their children or expressing a desire to want to live with their children were respondents whose longest period of employment was as a blue collar worker doing either manual labor or manufacturing related jobs. The effect of education showed a clear pattern; the more educated the respondent the less likely they were to report a desire to live with one of their married children. What is also interesting about Takahashi's results is that there is a very clear pattern in the effect of retirement annuity on the desire to live with one's children which may suggest that some respondents with a sizable retirement annuity are unable to change or freely choose their living situation.

What this data suggests, and what Takahashi has concluded is that the culturally embodied norm of the extended family has been dramatically altered by Japan's modernization process. Not only do the majority of young and middle-aged adults express a desire not to want to live with their parents, but elder Japanese themselves also indicate an ambivalent attitude. As Takahashi's study clearly demonstrates, current social changes, such as dwelling size, occupation, and education levels appear to be playing a much more important role in determining the structure of the Japanese family than the filial obligations of Confucian tenets.

Japanese Attitudes Towards the Elderly

At the heart of the perception that the Japanese elderly have maintained a high social status despite the modernization of the economy is the belief that the Confucian tradition evokes a stronger disposition of respect towards the elderly. In examining or making judgments about Japanese attitudes and behavior towards the elderly however, one should not interpret official statements or traditional verbal usages as representing actual attitudes or behaviors. Soeda Yoshida has described the difference between the two by utilizing the Japanese concepts of *tatemae* and *hone*. *Tatemae* represents outward socially or culturally acceptable attitudes while *hone* represents hidden actual feelings. In his view, the public statements about respect for elderly persons should be interpreted as *tatemae* in contrast to *hone*, actual widely accepted attitudes that the elderly are slow witted and often a cumbersome burden (Soeda 1978). Although Soeda utilizes the Japanese concepts of *hone* and *tatemae* to call attention to the discrepancy between norms of respect for the elderly and actual attitudes and beliefs, it's a discrepancy not confined to Japan. The need to distinguish between status and actual attitudes has been brought to light by

analyses from information contained in the Human Relations Area Files which indicated that high status of the elderly is not incompatible with nonsupportive treatment, even abandonment and killing (Glascock and Feinman 1981; Glascock and Feinman 1986). Glascock and Feinman have developed the hypothesis that societies make a distinction between healthy functional and decrepit care-needing aged. Prestige and support is extended to those elderly whose cognitive and physical abilities are still intact but is withdrawn when physical or mental impairment occurs and caregiving needs arise.

In a review of studies on attitudes toward elderly persons in Japan, Koyano Wataru concluded that many of these studies indicated the presence of strong negative "hone" attitudes which "were usually masked with rituals of respect for the elderly" (Koyano 1989). . . . In almost all of the studies the respondents were more prone to indicate a larger number and range of negative characteristics than positive characteristics. The list of adjectives listed by the various studies does not constitute the universe of all possible attitudes towards the elderly held by young Japanese but rather indicates that their attitudes are highly ambivalent and that this ambivalence appears to be a constant theme running through all studies that have attempted to gauge attitudes towards the elderly.

To obtain a better understanding of what are the principal components of university students' attitude towards elderly persons and the basic factors influencing these attitudes, Hosaka Kumiko and Sodei Takako performed a factor analysis on 50 adjectives offered by respondents to describe their attitude towards the elderly. From these 50 adjectives they produced six main factors: ability, independence/activity, happiness, cooperativeness, pacifistic, sociability (Hosaka and Sodei 1986). They then examined what kind of personal experiences are related to either a negative or positive attitude towards these six factors. Their most significant finding was that the experience of living with one's grandparents does not necessarily improve one's image of the elderly. What is more important than the actual experience is the content of that experience. In other words, the nature of the relationship with one's grandparents and also, between one's parents and grandparents determines if living with one's grandparents improved or lowered respondents' image of the elderly. The most important experiences contributing to a positive image were: (1) interest in the problem of the aged; (2) conversations with one's grandparents; (3) memories of one's grandparents; and (4) interaction with other old people.

This finding that having the experience of living with one's grandparents does not necessarily improve one's image of the elderly is echoed in other research efforts on Japanese attitudes towards elderly persons. For example, Sato and Nagashima concluded that the major difference in attitudes towards the old that separates college students who have or have not lived with their grandparents is that those who have are more likely to describe the old as warm but bothersome while those who haven't are more likely to use the term impudent (*Zuuzuushii*) (Sato and Nagashima 1976). Makizono found that Japanese college students had a greater negative image than positive image of the old and that those who had lived with their grandparents were more likely to attribute a greater number of faults to the old. Also, having lived with one's grandparents has no impact on the degree to which a student reports that he or she has something to learn from the old. She concluded that it's very difficult to determine the effect that living with one's elders has on the younger generation and that until more research is done it would be incorrect to conclude that the experience instills greater filial piety (Makizono 1986). These findings indicate [that] more attention needs to be devoted to the many dimensions of interpersonal relations besides care and comfort occurring within three generational families. Role expectations within traditional Japanese families can be rigid, heavy, and burdensome (Kiefer 1990).

Discussion

In presenting this review of recent Japanese social gerontology studies, I have sought to correct the predominant view in the Eng-

lish literature that modernization has had a less deleterious impact on the social integration of elderly persons in Japan than in the West. Taken together the studies presented in this review suggest that the commitment to traditional extended families in Japan is decreasing and the desire to live in such a family structure is affected by education, income, and housing size. They also suggest that it is incorrect to assume that either living now, or having experienced living in a three generation family, directly contributes to giving greater social status or respect to the elderly. It would be incorrect, however, to draw the conclusion by extension that traditional cultural norms are of no significance to understanding Japanese attitudes towards the elderly, or that the social status of the elderly suffers from modernization. The status and social well-being of the elderly in Japan today, similar to any other advanced industrial nation, is affected by a myriad of factors all of which have a differential impact depending on the individual's socioeconomic status. What needs to be emphasized from this review is that an analysis based on cultural norms alone, especially one based on a static isolated conception of these norms, is insufficient to understand the complex and changing role of the elderly in Japan today. Reflecting the greater complexity of the society as a whole, the role of elderly persons in Japan is changing, affected by factors other than preexisting norms.

Disagreements on whether the status of the elderly in Japan has been differentially affected by modernization is one part of the larger debate on efforts to extend social scientific theories based on Western experience to rapidly industrialized non-Western nations. A fair amount of effort has been expended examining the tenacity of traditional cultural values in the face of modern social change. The conventional wisdom has been to consider the two as mutually exclusive; the more modern the society the weaker the strength of traditional values. Recent examinations of Japan's modernization process has challenged this conventional wisdom and introduced some uncertainty on the antagonistic nature of traditional and modern values. In examining Japanese and German development, Reinhard Bendix concluded that, "Every industrial country retains features of its preindustrial society, and the forms of industrial societies are likely to differ widely depending on their earlier traditions" (Bendix 1967). Even though industrial countries may all face similar problems, he argued, the persistence of social, cultural, and ideological differences are likely to result in different responses to these problems.

While there may indeed be a great variation in industrial development, with each country preserving some of its preindustrial features, it's hard to imagine traditional features or cultural norms that survive intact the onslaught of a rapid transition to a modern economy. Even if some feature of the country's preindustrial stage does survive industrialization, the underlying motives that supported it during the preindustrial stage may not remain constant. For example, Morgan and Hirosima have concluded that the continued existence of traditional extended families in Japan is not an anachronism supported by norms from the preindustrial past but instead, given the scarcity of quality child care programs in Japan, the care giving advantages of such a family structure are being utilized by young dual income families in Japan to "adapt old institutional structures to address a new set of exigencies."[12] Toshitani (1984) also has analyzed how the current Japanese family structure is influenced by the undeveloped nature of the public pension system and Japanese family law which gives extraordinary legal precedence to the right of the aged parent to demand and receive care from their children.

From the very beginning of its development as an independent field, social gerontology has attempted to establish that there is no one rigidly set aging process but that aging is greatly influenced by the social environment. As each new cohort of individuals moves along its own axis of historical time, it has unique characteristics formed by the particular historical events they have experienced (Neugarten et al. 1965). Matilda Riley has attempted to conceptualize this process by developing an age stratification model (Riley 1985) which identifies three underlying processes: (1) historical change and the flow of cohorts through various age groups; (2) social changes coming from outside the boundaries of the age stratification system; and (3) allocation and socialization processes that attempt to articulate the dual structures of people and of roles. The third process is the outcome of the interaction between the first two. Thus, the essence of the model is the continuing interplay between social change and the aging of individuals. Although Riley's model does not specifically address how to incorporate the tension between slowly evolving cultural values and rapidly changing economic and social changes, she does state that there exists a "dialectical tension" since individual aging and social change tend to be poorly synchronized. Modernization is believed to intensify this dialectical tension since the transmission of values from one generation to another is much more distorted in modern industrial societies as the amount of change, the density of historical events, during any one period of time becomes more compressed.

The density of historical change has been especially marked in Japan where there have been two major transformations in economic and political structure in the postwar period. The Occupation brought about an end to the imperial system and the creation of democratic institutions. The second, equally profound change, was the period of rapid economic growth between 1960 and 1973. The first of these transformations eliminated the educational curriculum based on the ideology of the *Ie* system and the legal basis of primogeniture. The second altered the economic basis of the traditional three generation family creating both the demand and the opportunity for alternative family structures. These two changes fundamentally altered the ideological control mechanisms that reinforced norms of filial piety and undermined the head of the family's control of the economic resources of its members. Family structure in Japan has now become more diverse, influenced by fluctuating economic circumstances and changing state policies (Harada 1988). Similar to the dramatic changes that have occurred in China, the relationship between the socioeconomic context and the social status of the elderly in Japan is influenced by a complex interaction among economic development, traditional cultural patterns, and social control mechanisms (Streib 1987). The interaction among these three factors makes the relationship between different age cohorts in general, and the social status of the aged in particular, highly dependent on temporal developments.

It is worth noting that the postwar changes have occurred relatively recently in terms of generational change. As Ogawa Naohiro and Robert D. Rutherford (1990) have suggested, cultural norms adjust to underlying socioeconomic changes but the process of change is not necessarily gradual. It may come in abrupt changes. They speculate that these "spurts" in normative change can be sparked by several different factors, including changes in social legislation or the formation of organized advocacy movements and that when they do change, in a homogeneous country like Japan, they tend to change much more quickly throughout the population. As normative and socioeconomic change continues to occur in Japan, it will be more prudent for social gerontologists to investigate how various aspects of social deference (Silverman and Maxwell 1983) are affected rather than concentrate on a difficult to operationalize global measure of respect.

It may be a bit early to determine the full impact that recent socioeconomic changes that have occurred in Japan will have on the structure of the Japanese family and attitudes towards the elderly. The present elderly cohort in Japan (65–95 yrs) was born during the prewar period. The full effects of Japan's postwar changes will be felt when the cohorts of *sarariman* born and raised after the war retire. Given the large numbers of women who have entered the workforce and their desire to stay there, it is likely that there will be a continued shift in the burden of caring from the private family sector to the public. The cultural values and attitudes towards the aged of the younger generation represented in the studies cited above will determine the degree to which Japan will prove to be an exception to the [expected] relationship between modernization and the social status of the old and whether the Japanese govern-

ment will be able successfully to establish its own unique Japanese style welfare system.

Discussion Questions

1. What is the concept of *Ie*? What evidence does O'Leary present to indicate changes in "*Ie* consciousness"?

2. O'Leary makes a distinction between *tatemae* and *hone* in Japanese statements about the elderly, especially among young people. Do you think that similar differences about old people exist in American society?

3. Given the rapid social change in Japan, what public governmental action would be useful to ensure a "good old age" for the increasing proportions of female, unemployed, and disabled elderly? Why?

4. In the United States, how is awareness of the probable care needs for the "old-old" population affecting our cultural perceptions of aging?

Notes

1. Although the increase in the average lifespan and the decrease in the birth rate are usually cited in government publications as the primary contributors to Japan's aging society, an often unmentioned ancillary reason why Japan will soon be aging at a faster rate than any other country is due to a military-related government policy during the 1920s and 30s to increase the size of the population. This policy kept birthrates well above those of Italy, the European country with the largest birth rate during the same period.

2. The data presented in the following section, unless otherwise noted, were gathered from the 1988 edition of the *Kosei Hakusho*.

3. The two reports in question are the *Fukushi Vision*, published in October, 1988 and the *Koreisha Hoken Fukushi Suishin Jukanen Senryaku*, published in December, 1990. The first report also estimated that the number of nursing homes (*Tokubetsu yogo rojin homu* and *Rojin Hoken shisetsu*) would have to be expanded from the present combined total of 189,820 to 500,000 by the year 2000 while the second report has increased the number expected to be needed to 520,000.

4. Public nursing home facilities for the elderly in Japan are divided into three categories based on the intensity of care provided. Those facilities that offer the most intense care, the special care nursing homes were operating at 99 percent capacity in 1984. Comparable figures for regular nursing homes were 94 percent and for the low cost nursing homes 93.5 percent. The results of a national survey conducted by the Japanese government (Urata 1990) indicated an increase in the number of facilities for the elderly was the second most desired improvement in social welfare reform reported by a national sample of adult Japanese (increase in the public pension system was identified as the most desired improvement).

5. Due to often over sensationalized reports in the West of the high costs of housing in Japan's large metropolitan areas, there is a widespread belief that most Japanese cannot afford their own homes and are forced to live in "rabbit hutch" sized apartments. While this may be true of the Tokyo and Osaka areas, the percentage of Japanese living in their own homes is over 60 percent, only a few percentage points lower than the U.S. and higher than either Germany or Great Britain. A national sample of 3,000 age 25–74 Japanese indicated that over 80 percent of respondents age 55 and over were living in their own homes (*Keizai Kikakucho* 1986, p. 151).

6. A Japanese term referring to blue and white collar workers who are receiving a salary.

7. According to new law passed in 1988, designated depopulated villages (*kasoshitei shicho son*) are defined as any village that experienced a 20 percent reduction in its population between the 1960 and 1975 census and has also suffered a yearly decrease in public revenues of more than 0.4 percent every year between 1976 and 1978. As of April 1988, there were 1,157 such areas extending throughout the length of the Japanese Archipelago with an average 17 percent of their population over 65 (Hoshino 1989).

8. In response to the question of "What would you like the government to devote more effort to?," a national sample of adult Japanese most frequent response was "an adequate social security and welfare program." This response out polled its nearest rival—"The problem of Taxes," by 11 percentage points (*Gekkan Seron Chosa* Oct. 1991, p. 57).

9. This figure was calculated on the basis of no reforms being made in the eligibility and computation of pension benefits. The pension system was revised however in 1986 and based on these reforms this figure is expected to increase to only 29 percent. If the eligibility age, as proposed by the government, is raised from 60 to 65, it will further be lowered to 24 percent (Ito 1987).

10. Over 80 percent of individuals taking care of an incapacitated elderly family member in their own home are women and less than 7 percent of caregivers are under 40 years old (Miura 1990, p. 47).

11. A *tsubo* is the traditional Japanese measure of land area and is roughly equivalent to 4 sq. yds. Thus 20 *tsubo* would be equivalent to 720 sq. ft.

12. Phillip Morgan and Kiyosi Hirosima, "The Persistence of Extended Family Residence in Japan: Anachronism or Alternative Strategy?" *American Sociological Review* Vol. 48, April 1983, pps. 269–271. Although Morgan and Hirosima conclude that the traditional extended family structure represents a functional adaptation that allows the mother to more successfully manage the conflicting roles of mother and outside wage earner, their analysis is biased in favor of such a conclusion since it is based on a subsample of three generation families with preschool age children. This selection process produces not only their intended young couple sample (20–30 yrs.) that would most likely be feeling the pressure of employment versus child care but also by extension a relatively young grandparent cohort (40–60 yrs) capable of providing the necessary child care service. The inclusion of three generation families with older children would boost the age of the grandparent cohort which would have a greater probability of not only less capacity to take care of the children but also a higher possibility of needing care themselves thus reducing the functional attractiveness of the family structure to the working wife. This sample selection bias does not, however, invalidate the conclusions they make for the subsample of traditional families that they studied nor the point made in this paper that the underlying factors supporting any one particular family structure can change over time.

References

Anderson, S. 1990. "The Political Economy of Japanese Saving: How Postal Savings and Public Pensions Support High Rates of Household Saving in Japan." *Journal of Japanese Studies* 16:61–92.

Bendix, R. 1967. "Preconditions of Development: A Comparison of Japan and Germany." In *Aspects of Social Change in Modern Japan*, edited by R. Dore. Princeton, NJ: Princeton University Press.

Benedict, R. 1946. *The Chrysanthemum and the Sword*. New York: Houghton Mifflin.

Cohn, R. 1982. "Economic Development and Status Change of the Aged." *American Journal of Sociology* 87:1150–1161.

Cowgill, D. 1972. "A Theory of Aging in Cross-Cultural Perspective." In *Aging and Modernization*, edited by D. Cowgill and L. Holmes. New York: Appleton-Century-Crofts.

——. 1986. *Aging Around the World*. Belmont, CA: Wadsworth Publishing Co.

Dore, R. 1973. *Japanese Factory, British Factory*. Berkeley: University of California Press.

——. 1978. *Shinohata*. New York: Pantheon Books.

Dowd, J. 1980. *Stratification Among the Aged*. Monterey, CA: Brooks/Cole.

Fukutake, T. 1967. *Japanese Rural Society*. Ithaca, NY: Cornell University Press.

Furusa, T. 1989. "Akuruku seikatsu aru choju shakai ni mukete." In *Koreisha 21 Seki e no Cho sen*. Tokyo: Government Printing Office.

Gekkan Seron Chosa. 1991. October.

Glascock, A. and S. Feinman. 1981. "Social Asset or Social Burden: An Analysis of the Treatment for the Aged in Non-Industrial Societies." in *Dimensions: Aging, Culture and Health*, edited by C. Fry. New York: Praeger.

——. 1986. "Toward a Comparative Framework: Propositions Concerning the Treatment for the Aged in Non-Industrial Societies." In *New Methods for Old Age Research: Strategies for Studying Diversity*, edited by C. Fry and J. Keith. South Hadley, MA: Bergin & Garvey.

Goody, J. 1976. "Aging in Nonindustrial Societies." Pp. 117–129 in *Handbook of Aging and the Social Sciences*, edited by R. Binstock and E. Shanas. New York: Van Nostrand Reinhold.

Habib, J. 1990. "Population Aging and the Economy." Pp. 328–345 in *Handbook of Aging and the Social Sciences*, third edition, edited by R. H. Binstock and L. K. George. New York: Academic Press.

Harada, S. 1988. "Nihongata fukushi shakailron to Kazokusho." Pp. 303–368 in *Tenkanki no Fukushi Kokka*, edited by Tokyo Daigaku Shakaigaku Kenkyujo. Tokyo: Tokyo University Publishers.

Hosaka K. and T. Sodei. 1986. "Daigakusei no ronin imagji." *Shakai Ronengaku* 27:22–33.

Hoshino, S. 1989. "Kaso Chiiki ni okeru Rojin Mondai." *Kikan-Shakai Hosho Kenkyu*, 25(3): 244–262.

Houser, P. 1976. "Aging and World–Wide Population Change." Pp. 58–86. In *Handbook of Aging and the Social Sciences*, edited by R. H. Binstock and E. Shanas. New York: Van Nostrand.

Ike, N. 1973. "Economic Growth and Intergenerational Change in Japan." *The American Political Science Review* 67:1194–1203.

Ishida, T. 1984. "Nihon ni okeru Fukushi Gannen no tokushitsu." Pp. 3–59 in *Fukushi Kokka: Nihon no Ho to Fukushi*, edited by Daigaku Shakaikagaku Kenkyujo. Tokyo: Tokyo: Daigaku Shuppankai.

Ito, M. 1987. "Oi no seiji keizaigaku." Pp. 11–52 in *Oi no Hatsugen 5: Oi to Shakai Shisutemu*, edited by M. Ito et al. Tokyo: Iwanami Shoten.

Kamitsubo, H. 1988. *Koreisha Undo Sengen*. Tokyo: Jichitai Kenkysha.

Kaneko, I. 1988. "Toshi Koreisha no nettwaku kozo." *Shakaigaku Hyoron* 32: 336–350.

Keith, J. 1990. "Age in Social and Cultural Context: Anthropological Perspectives." Pp. 91–111 in *Handbook of Aging and the Social Sciences*, third edition, edited by R. H. Binstock and L. K. George. New York: Academic Press.

Keizai Kikakucho Kokumin Seikatsukyoku. 1986. *Choju Shakai e mukete no Seikatsu Sentaku*. Tokyo: Okurasho Insatsukyoku.

Kerr, C. and J. Dunlop. 1964. *Industrialism and Industrial Man*. New York: Oxford University Press.

Kiefer, C. 1990. "Aging and the Elderly in Japan." Pp. 153–171 in *Anthropology and Aging*, edited by R. Rubinstein. Dordrecht, Netherlands: Kluwer Academic Publishers.

Koseisho. 1988. *Showa 61–63 Nendo Tokubetsu Kenkyu: Koreika Shakai niokeru Setai Keisei no Chiikisa ni Kan suru Jinkogakuteki Kenkyu*. Tokyo: Ministry of Welfare Population Research Center Publication.

Kosei Hakusho. 1988. Tokyo: Ministry of Finance Publication.

——. 1990. Tokyo: Ministry of Finance Publication.

Koyano. W. 1989. "Japanese Attitudes Toward the Elderly: A Review of Research Findings." *Journal of Cross-Cultural Gerontology* 4:335–345.

Kumagai, F. 1986. "Modernization and the Family in Japan." *Journal of Family History* 11(4):371–382.

Laslett, P. 1976. "Societal Development and Aging." Pp. 87–116 in *Handbook of Aging and the Social Sciences*, edited by R. Binstock and E. Shanas. New York: Van Nostrand Reinhold.

Lipman, A. 1970. "Prestige of the Aged in Portual: Realistic Appraisal and Ritualistic Deference." *The International Journal of Aging and Human Development* 1: 127–136.

Maeda, D. and H. Asano. 1978. "Public Policies for the Aged." Pp. 115–138 in *Aging in Japan*, edited by D. Maeda. Tokyo: Tokyo Metropolitan Institute of Gerontology.

Maeda, D., K. Teshima, H. Sugisawa, and Y. Asakura. 1989. "Aging and Health in Japan." *Journal of Cross-Cultural Gerontology* 4:143–162.

Makizono, K. 1986. "Gendai seinen no ronenkan." *Seishonen Mondai* 33:4–13.

Maruo, N. 1989. *Nihongata Fukushi Shakai*. Tokyo: NHK Publications.

Miura, F. 1981. *Koreika to chiikishakai. 21 Seki e no Sentaku: Koreika Shakai to Chiiki Seisaku. Tokyo: Government Publication. 1990*.

——. 1990. *Koreisha Hakusho*. Tokyo: Zenkoku Shakai Fukushi Kyogikai.

Mitsuyoshi, T. 1986. *Redeingusu Nihon no Shakaigaku: Dento Kazoku*. Tokyo: University of Tokyo Press.

Morgan, P. and K. Hirosima. 1983. "The Persistence of Extended Family Residence in Japan: Anachronism or Alternative Strategy?" *American Sociological Review* 48:269–281.

Moriya, K. 1974. "Joshi Tandaisei no Ronenzo." *Meijiro Gakuen Joshi Tandaigaku Kiyo* 11:83–90.

Murakami, Y. 1981. "*Ie* Society as a Pattern of Civilization" *Journal of Japanese Studies* 7:281–334.

Nagakawa, T. 1979. "Japan, the Welfare Super-Power." *Journal of Japanese Studies* 5:5–51.

Nakane, C. 1970. *Japanese Society*. London: Weidenfeld and Nicholson.

Neugarten, B., J. Moore, and J. Lowe. 1965. "Age Norms, Age Constraints, and Adult Socialization." *American Journal of Sociology* 70:710–717.

Ogawa, N. 1989. "Population Aging and Its Impact upon Health Resource Requirements at Government and Familial Levels in Japan." *Ageing and Society* 9:383–405.

Ogawa, N. and R. Rutherford. 1990. "Changing Norms and Expectations about Care of the Elderly in Japan." Unpublished manuscript.

Ogawa, Z. 1990. "Kaso chiiki ni okeru koreisha mondai." Pp. 120–139 in *Koreisha Hakusho*, edited by F. Miura. Tokyo: Zenkoku Shakai Fukushi Kyogikai.

Okayama, S. 1981. "Noka koreisha no shuro to kazoku seikatsu." Pp. 401–426 in *Ronen Shakaigaku: 1*, edited by Y. Soeda. Tokyo: Tannai.

Palmore, E. 1975, *The Honorable Elders: A Cross-Cultural Analysis of Aging in Japan*. Durham, NC: Duke University Press.

Palmore, E. and D. Maeda. 1985. *The Honorable Elders Revisited*. Durham, NC: Duke University Press.

Palmore, E. and K. Manton. 1974. "Modernization and the Status of the Aged: International Correlations." *Journal of Gerontology* 29:205–210.

Phillipson, C. 1982. *Capitalism and the Construction of Old Age*. London: Macmillan Press Ltd.

Quadagno, J. 1982. *Aging in Elderly Industrial Society: Work, Family, and Social Policy in Nineteenth-Century England*. New York: Academic Press.

Riley, M. 1985. "Age Strata in Social Systems." Pp. 369-411 in *Handbook of Aging & Social Sciences*, second edition, edited by R. Binstock and E. Shanas. New York: Van Nostrand Reinhold.

Rosenmayr, L. 1987. "Is the Japanese Family Really Different?" *Shakai Ronengaku* 16:61–69.

Sakata, S. 1988. "Chiiki jinko no koreika to rojin Dokyoritsu no niju kozo-Dokyoritsu no kenkyu 2." *Shakai Ronengaku* 28:46–57.

Sato, Y. 1981. "Toshi ronin no seikatsu to hinan." Pp. 347–400 in *Ronin Shakaigaku: 1*, edited by Y. Soeda. Tokyo: Tannai.

Sato, Y. and S. Nagashima. 1976. "Roka imeji (4) - Daigakusei ni yoru rojin no imeji." *Yokufukai Chosa Kenkyu Kiyo* 60:63–76.

Silverman, P. and R. J. Maxwell. 1983. "The Significance of Information and Power in the Comparative Study of the Aged." In *Growing Old in Different Societies: Cross-Cultural Perspectives*, edited by J. Sokolovsky. Belmont, CA: Wadsworth Publishing.

Soeda, Y. 1978. "Shutaitekina ronenzo o matomete." *Gendai no Esprit* 126:5–24.

——. 1981. "Ronen shakaigaku no kadai to hoho." Pp. 1–101 in *Ronen Shakaigaku: 1*, edited by Y. Soeda. Tokyo: Tannai.

——. 1987. "Rojin Fukushi no Kozo Genri." Pp. 53–79 in *Oi to Shakai Shisutemu (5): Oi to Hatsugen*, edited by I. Mitsuharu. Tokyo: Iwanami Shoten.

Somucho. 1985. *Katei Seikatsu ni okeru Rojin no Chii to Yakuwari ni kan suru Chosa Kekka-Oya no Fuyo suru Tachiba ni aru mono kara mita rojin no Chii to Yakuwari*. Tokyo: Okurasho Insatsukyoku.

Streib, G. 1987. "Old Age in Sociocultural Context: China and the United States." *Journal of Aging Studies* 1:95–112.

Steiner, K. 1987. "The Occupation and the Reform of the Japanese Civil Code." Pp. 188–252.

In *The Allied Occupation*, edited by R. Ward and Y. Sakamoto. Honolulu: University of Hawaii Press.

Tabata, M. 1990. *Zaitaku Fukushi Sabisu no Minimamu Sakutei no tame ni*. Tokyo: Tokyoto Shakai Fukushi Sogo Centa.

Tachibana, K. 1971. "Seishin Shobo." *Ronengaku* 3:59–71.

Takahashi, M. 1989. "Karoki ni okeru dokyo-betsukyo to ishiki." *Shakai Ronengaku* 25:19–29.

Takeshita, N. 1988. "Nihongata fukushi shakai no kochiku." In *Watashi no Kangaeru Choju Shakai*. Tokyo: Jiminshuto Shuppansha.

Tobin, J. 1987. "The American Idealization of Old Age in Japan." *Gerontology* 27:35–52.

Toshitani, Y. 1984. "Fukushi to kazoku-rooya fuyo to chushin to shite." Pp. 183–248 in *Fukushi Kokka: 4*, edited by Tokyo Daigaku Shakaikagaku Kenkyujo. Tokyo: Tokyo University Press.

Urata, N. 1990. *choju Shakai to Danja no Yakuwari-Ishiki*. Tokyo: Ministry of Finance Publications.

Vogal, E. 1963. *Japan's New Middle Class: The Salaryman and His Family in a Tokyo Suburb*, second edition. Berkeley, CA: University of California Press.

Williamson, J., L. Evans, and L. Powell. 1982. *The Politics of Aging: Power and Policy*. Springfield, IL: Thomas.

Yokoyama, K. 1985. "Sengo Nihon no Shakai Hosho no Tenkai." Pp. 3–48 in *Fukushi Kokka [5]: Nihon no Keizai to Fukushi*, edited by Daigaku Shakaikagaku Kenkyujo. Tokyo: University of Tokyo.

Zenkoku Koreisha Daikai. 1990. *Hokokushu*. Final report of the National Association of Senior Citizens annual convention.

Zenrosai Kyokai. 1990. *Yutakana Nihon, Mazushii Kaigo*. Final report on the national nursing care problem sponsored by Zenrosai Kyokai.

Chapter 3
'William' and the Old Folks[1]

Mike Hepworth

The tendency to treat old people as if they are slow-witted, dependent children is not uncommon among many younger people. As noted in the previous selections, the ageist assumption that older people are of low social value infantilizes them, portraying old age as a second childhood. Infantilizing old age usually has negative consequences because it undermines elders' status as mature adults who are capable of rational action. Infantilizing the elderly not only erodes their own sense of self-esteem but is a self-fulfilling prophecy, increasing their dependence on others. But there may also be situations where "acting childish" may actually allow the elderly to resist both social and physical constraints and attempts to deconstruct their personhood in later life. In the following selection, Mike Hepworth examines "positive infantilisation" in a set of fictional short stories about an 11-year-old boy, William, that remains popular in England even today. William and his friends, the Outlaws, live in an English village where they make mischief, take risks, and frustrate most adults. In his encounters with old people, however, William finds allies. Both young and old rebel against the social brakes placed upon them by parents, relatives, and well-meaning middle-aged adults. The old and young jointly conspire against social norms. Hepworth argues that the ability of the older characters in the William stories to abandon their adult dignity is an example of temporary liberation from the negative stereotypes of the dignified and stuffy or decrepit older adult. Rather than descending into childish irresponsibility and dependency, elders who cast off their stereotypical roles as old persons gain a sense of self through playfulness. As you read the following selection, evaluate the ways in which the older people portrayed in these stories challenge age norms for behavior. Think about the ways in which these contradictions to expected role behavior by an older person may contribute to that person's self-esteem and refute or confirm social norms for elders' conduct.

The concern in social gerontology to expose the detrimental consequences which follow from the tendency in western culture to treat older people, and particularly those with some degree of age-related dependency, as if they are children has very properly demonstrated the role of infantilisation practices in the social construction of dependency in later life. In, for example, her observations of 'Parkview' residential home, Johnson, has recorded the frequency with which infantilisation was accomplished through naming practices:

> Pet names, other names of endearment and infantilising words were sometimes employed. One resident was observed requesting, and being rewarded with a sweet for "being a good girl." They were often treated, and behaved, like children and frequently resorted to staff to resolve arguments with other residents.[2]

In institutional settings such naming practices work towards the public minimisation of the adult dignity of residents and are therefore often described as a form of stigmatisation. Muriel Spark provides a sardonic fictional example of the implications of these practices for those who are bedridden in her references to the use of the label 'granny' (an ambiguous mode of address indicating the cultural association of older women with children) on the 'Maud Long Medical Ward':

> There were twelve occupants of the Maud Long Medical Ward (aged people, female) . . . These twelve old women were known variously as Granny Roberts, Granny Duncan, Granny Taylor, Grannies Barnacle, Trotsky, Green, Valvona, and so on.
> Sometimes, on first being received into her bed, the patient would be shocked and feel rather let down by being called Granny. Miss or Mrs. Reeves Duncan threatened for a whole week to report anyone who called her Granny Duncan. She

threatened to cut them out of her will and to write to her M.P. . . . However, she changed her mind about informing her M.P. when they promised not to call her Granny any more. 'But,' she said, 'you shall never go back into my will.'[3]

Moving from the literary to the gerontological sphere, further evidence of the damaging effects of 'infantilising words', or 'babytalk', can be found in Coupland *et al.*'s analyses of the role of language in constructing what they describe as 'societal ageism'.[4] The use of babytalk by carers is not only an indication of some pre-existing state of physical and/or psychological dependency but also plays a significant role in cultivating dependency. They refer to research which shows that whilst babytalk may have a 'nurturing effect if used with patients of lower functional ability,' it is 'more likely to create self-fulfilling prophecies by promoting learned dependency if used more consistently to all patients and residents.'[5] Talk thus *embodies* critical aspects of caring itself and plays a part in the construction of caring norms and ideologies.[6] Language, in other words, is the medium of infantilisation. To borrow from Green's analysis of gerontology as a discursive practice, infantilising talk can be regarded as a 'linguistic field of discourse defined by certain practices of literary production.'[7]

The dependencies associated with ageing into old age are thus constituted through a reflexive repertoire of verbal and visual images governed, as Green has argued, by specific conventions. And, as far as infantilisation is concerned, the key cultural resource, or what Hockey and James have referred to as the 'root metaphor', is that of the dependent child. In their theoretical analysis of the metaphorical structure of infantilisation Hockey and James have defined a metaphor 'as making one thing, one stage, one condition knowable through reference to another.'[8] Infantilisation is conceptualised as a process of drawing on the dominant image in western culture of children as dependent and socially unfinished creatures who are not yet fully mature in order to comprehend and accommodate the socially disturbing decrements of later life. Most importantly, the use of metaphor can be seen as a 'creative process whereby that which is familiar provides the metaphoric grounding for knowledge of that which is less familiar.'[9] In order to understand the unknown we move from our existing stock of interrelated shared language categories and visual images to that which is the subject of our curiosity. In the case of old age, childhood offers a particularly rich source of metaphors for the conceptual ordering and comprehension of the decrements of old age because of the tendency since the nineteenth century to define childhood as a progressive though potentially disruptive growth process requiring the constant guidance and discipline of mature adult persons. This process involves a supervised transition to the peak of mature adulthood followed by a gradual yet inevitable decline into the dependency of old age.

Historically, the social construction of childhood as an extended stage of growth and development is framed within the traditional model of 'Ages of Man'/'Ages of Woman.' Western images of the ageing process have for several centuries been ordered and categorized in terms of a 'U' curve towards the high point of middle-aged maturity and thence downwards to old age, death, and ultimately to the life beyond the tomb. As Cole notes:

> By depicting the appropriate appearance and behavior for each stage of life the motif taught that *each* age has its necessary place in the order of things. To submit to the physical exigencies of the ageing process was to acquiesce in divine purpose. Thus the motif attempted to restore or create order, and especially *religious order*, by focussing on a newly imagined course of life. This new cultural ideal of a long, orderly, and secure lifetime would not become a social and demographic reality for 300 years.[10]

Although in the west much of the original theological underpinning of the ages-of-life model no longer predominates, the belief that life can be differentiated into a number of phases, each with its own definitive characteristics interconnected by appropriate transitions or status passages,[11] continues to structure our thinking about the ageing process even in a social climate of postmodern ferment.[12]

Metaphorical understanding is thus relational. Our knowledge of old age, and particularly the decrements of old age is an elaboration of socially prescribed knowledge of what it is to be a child in western culture: in other words, images, both verbal and visual, of childhood. Hockey and James take the line that the tendency to treat old age as what we so often describe as a 'second childhood' is in essence a technique for managing our deep fear of old age by transforming it into an infantile state. They argue that the decrements, physical or psychological, typically associated with what are now known increasingly as 'the old old' become easier to handle when any dependency which may ensue is defined as a return to the original (and more socially acceptable) dependency of early infancy. It is precisely because infancy and childhood have, since Victorian times, been socially constructed as stages of legitimately innocent and beguiling dependency that this metaphorical transformation is an effective technique for containing and dispersing the fears of deep old age which is endemic in western culture.

For Hockey and James and other students of infantilisation[13] the status of childishness is imposed on older people by those who regard themselves as mature adults, often within an institutional setting. These enforced affinities are achieved through social practices epitomised in the linguistic construct 'young at heart'. The label 'young at heart' imposes on older people the idea that children and they themselves are existentially related. For the older person such a return to childhood's state is inevitably to be viewed as undermining legitimate claims to mature personhood. Much the same view can be found in Elias's sociological analysis of the shifting balances of power in later life.[14] And the metaphoric transformation of the physical dependencies of old age into the signs of a 'second childhood' has an ironic effect: the achievement of a form of rejuvenation which is produced by a shift from the associations of old age with autumn and winter to the associations of childhood with spring and summer. Associations which are, on the evidence, of great comfort to carers but arguably less consoling to older individuals themselves

as the short excerpt from Muriel Spark's novel reproduced above implies.

Yet at the same time the prospect is not entirely one of gloom and doom. Whilst the negative implications of infantilisation practices must not be ignored there is also a positive image to be added to the overall picture. There are occasions when, from the perspective of the older person, infantilisation may be regarded as a mode of resistance to the impositions of later life and identification with the world of childhood perceived as a way of recovering or sustaining an essential sense of enduring personal identity. Infantilisation, in other words, as a mode of resistance which is adopted by an older person and not imposed from outside. In his study of the consciousness of the individual self Cohen draws attention to empirical evidence of the resilience of people in later life. Studies of the techniques older people adopt in order to cope with the decrements of later life (his examples include the work of Hazan, Myerhoff, and Jerrome) remind us of the 'authorial power of agency, the capacity to be self-directing.'[15] In our zeal to record the constraining influences of social structures and institutions we overestimate their power to restrain both the experience and expression of the individual self. We must never forget the reflexive powers of individuals and be alert to the danger of confusing the loss of the physical capacity to control one's life with the loss of the capacity to control one's self. Institutions may, intentionally or otherwise, attempt to subvert the self but we cannot be sure that this is in fact their ultimate achievement. The spirit of older people may well be much more resilient than is sometimes believed. One of the conclusions to emerge from ethnographic studies of old age is 'that the reassertion or selfhood against its social subversion is an essential element of the life work of the elderly, the labor which Myerhoff, among others, refers to as the "aging career." '[16]

In what follows I wish to pursue images of the 'reassertion of selfhood' in later life as illustrated in one particular series of literary constructions: the popular 'William' stories of Richmal Crompton. I wish to argue that in certain of the adventures and encounters of

Crompton's fictional boy hero with older men and women we are offered a vivid example of the emergence of an independent selfhood in later life in the face of the inflated sense of self-importance and misperception of the 'mature' adult world. In doing so I focus directly on those stories which specifically involve encounters between William, his trusty companions 'the Outlaws', and characters who are often described in the stories as 'elderly'. My intention is to offer further illustrative material of the personal spaces surrounding infantilisation processes and thus to highlight through reference to fictional examples opportunities for what may reasonably be labeled 'positive infantilisation'. Positive infantilisation can therefore be interpreted, in this version, as the personal exploitation of opportunities for virtuoso resistance to the stereotypes of dependent old age.

Richmal Crompton's 'William' Stories

Richmal Crompton was born in Bury in Lancashire in 1890 and died in 1969. She took a degree in classics at Royal Holloway College in 1914, and became a girls' teacher until 1924 when she contracted polio and turned to full-time writing. She was a regular church attender, a staunch supporter of the Conservative Party, and a prolific writer of fiction for adults—40 adult novels all of which have been largely forgotten. Her claim to international fame, therefore, rests on her series of William stories, the first being published in 1919 and the last in 1970.[17]

William, the leader of Douglas, Henry, and Ginger, collectively and significantly known as 'the Outlaws', is the hero of hundreds of short stories collected into thirty-eight books and translated into several languages. He is eleven years old and lives in an un-named village somewhere in the Home Counties of England, a location which Mary Cadogan has described as a

> quintessentially English village, where, over the years William tangled with edgy dyspeptic ex-military men, stuffy spinsters, nervous clerics, "self-made" social climbers, and batty aesthetes authors and artists.[18]

William's family can be described as upper middle class. There is no shortage of money, their house and its surrounding garden is large, and there are servants with whom William has often hostile relations, especially the gardener. His father works somewhere in London ('town') and he has a grown-up brother and sister and a long-suffering mother. In sharp contrast to his socially advantaged background, William is scruffy, anarchic, loquacious—refusing to be 'seen and not heard'. But he is also honest, loyal, generous and courageous with a basic faith in his fellow humans often evident in his dealings with 'the elderly'. Through his eyes readers are given what can be considered to be a fascinating perspective on English social history but more importantly with regard to infantilisation, a view of the errors of judgement concerning individual identity in later life to which 'mature' adult humans are prone.

Although over the years the William stories have become classified as children's fiction it is important to note that between 1919 and 1954 a large number were first published in what were essentially family magazines or magazines for women: namely the *Home Magazine, Ladies' Home Magazine, The Happy Mag, Tit-Bits; Modern Woman, Homes and Gardens, Home Notes*, and *Woman's Own*. As the title of these magazines indicate, William stories are not simply stories for children. An editorial in *Home Notes* described their appeal as being to all ages, including significantly, 'the young in heart, if not in years.'[19] To be young in heart was to combine William's qualities of mischief, risk-taking, courage and idealism. In other words, to resist Outlaw-like the dispiriting forces of the adult world and civilisation. In this respect, Richmal Crompton is on the side of boyhood as she conceives it and her vision is one unswervingly opposed to both stuffy convention and thoughtless sentimentality. Mary Cadogan, her biographer, tells us that Crompton made a collection of quotations on boyhood, one of her favourites in later life being taken in 1959 from the *New York Times*. This contained a reference to a book with the title 'And To Be A Boy Eternal,' a collection of comments on boyhood, inspired by letters of Mark Twain.

In 1968, after she had given a radio broadcast about William a friend wrote to her and said:

> What you said about William made me think he is a sort of "prodigal Son," I mean, he is the primitive, natural, spontaneous, adventurous part of ourselves which we all have to repress in order to fit into conventional society. But he is capable of re-birth, like the Prodigal Son.[20]

Richmal Crompton's stories are of interest to students of ageing and infantilisation because they reflect the deep interest she maintained right until the end of her life in idealized boyhood (I should really say, British boyhood). She was still writing William stories to the day before she died and it is typical that her last book published posthumously in 1970, should have been given the title 'William the Lawless.'

Boyhood and Old Age

As the title 'William the Lawless' implies William is no angel and it has to be said that he derives a great deal of pleasure in disguising himself as an old man and simulating the physical decrements of later life. There are, however, few if any signs of mockery in his masquerades. In one of the earlier stories 'William and Uncle George'[21] William buys a pair of horn-rimmed spectacles which had originally belonged to someone's grandfather. The Outlaws discover by chance an empty bath-chair containing a rug and scarf and William arranges himself in the chair and is pushed along the way:

> William tucked in his rug and adjusted his spectacles again.
>
> 'Do I look like a pore old man?' he said proudly.
>
> Ginger gave a scornful laugh.
>
> 'No, you don't. You've gotter boy's face. You've got no lines nor whiskers nor screwdupness like an old man.'
>
> William drew his mouth down and screwed up his eyes into a hideous contortion.
>
> 'Do I now?' he said as clearly as he could through his distorted mask of twisted muscles.

> Ginger looked at him dispassionately.
>
> 'You look like a kinder monkey now,' he said.

William took the long knitted scarf that was at the bottom of the bath-chair and wound it round and round his head till only his horn-rimmed spectacles could be seen.

> 'Do I now?' he said in a muffled voice.

> Ginger stared at him in critical silence for a minute and said: 'Yes, you do now. At least you look's as if you might be *anything* now.'

> 'All right,' said William in his far-away muffled voice. Pretend I'm an old man. Wheel me back now . . . *slowly* mind! 'cause I'm an old man.'[22]

Thus disguised William is mistaken by a short sighted middle-aged woman (another stock Crompton character whom William regularly encounters) for her Uncle George. Taken aback, William goes along with the masquerade, his muffled features and silence amongst Uncle George's relatives (who have not seen him for ten years) as confirmation of his invalidity and deafness.

The masquerade comes to an end, predictably enough, when the real Uncle George makes an unexpected and extremely active and irate appearance: running up the driveway 'purple with anger' over the theft of his bath-chair.

In 'William Goes Shopping'[23] a more mutually respectful form of interaction between William and an older character, reflecting a closer affinity between boyhood and old age, comes to the fore. William, who is engrossed in trying to carve himself a whistle has his concentration disturbed by an old man sitting outside the door of a cottage:

> Suddenly he heard a voice behind him.
>
> 'An' what are ye tryin' to do, young sir?'
>
> He turned round.
>
> An old man sat on a chair outside a cottage door. So intent had William been upon putty and his whistle that he had not noticed him before.

'Make a whistle,' he said shortly and returned to his attempts.

'It's the wrong way,' quavered the old man 'Ye'll never make a whistle that way.'

William wheeled around, open-mouthed. 'D'you know how to make a whistle?' he said breathlessly.

'Ay. Course I do,' said the old man. 'Course I do. I were the best hand at makin' a whistle for miles when I were your age. Let's look at it now . . . let's look at it.'[24]

The old man shows William how to carve a whistle with the desired ear-shattering pitch and, overcome with gratitude, William reciprocates by recovering for the old man a penknife which had been wrongfully appropriated years before by his brother. The only discordant note in this encounter is a middle-aged woman, presumably the old man's daughter but certainly his carer, who has been drawn out of the cottage by the piercing sound of the whistle and who addresses William with considerable irritation:

'I'm sick of that noise,' she said. 'Get off with you! he's trouble enough alone, but when he gets with the likes of you . . .

The old man chuckled.

'You'd better be goin',' he said to William.[25]

Infantilisation has a double twist in this incident because it is simultaneously expressed as the mutual identification of the old man and the child through the pleasures of boyhood, and in terms of the irritable reaction of the woman who deplores this interaction as further evidence of her aged father's inappropriate behavior:

'I'm sick of hearing about the penknife,' said the woman. 'What do you want with penknives at your age?'

'What's age got to do with it? You tell me any age a man doesn't want a good penknife while he's above ground!'[26]

The old man wishes to recapture his boyhood when he was adept at making whistles, and his carer wishes to treat him as a stereotypical old man who has set aside his boyish enthusiasms. But for William and the old

man the encounter is mutually rewarding because it dispenses with the mask of age the old man is in effect expected to wear. Because he has an old body he is expected to behave as if he has an old self.[27]

A strong theme in those William stories which highlight encounters with sympathetic older characters is that of infantilisation as a rejuvenating and sometimes death-defying force. Under William's benign, if not always intentional influence, one bedridden old person, Great-Aunt Jane, is stimulated back to life.

In this story Great-Aunt Jane[28] is believed to be dying and William's mother asks Uncle John how she is:

'Sinking', said Uncle John in a voice of deepest gloom.

'Sinking fast—sinking fast.'

William's expression grew animated.

'Where is she? he said. 'Is she out in the sea?'[29]

But Great-Aunt Jane asks to see William in preference to his cousin Francis who is fat and spoiled. When she drifts into a sleep the two boys start to fight and, wakened by the noise, Great-Aunt Jane begins to brighten considerably:

Great-Aunt Jane was sitting up in bed, her checks flushed, her eyes bright.

'Go it, William!' she said 'Get one in on his nose. That's right, Fatty, well fended! Go on, William. Another, Another! No biting, Fatty. Go————— Oh, dear!'

'Quick!' said Great-Aunt Jane.

They darted to their seats, smoothing their hair as they went. The nurse entered.

'Whatever ————-' she began, then looked round the peaceful room.

'Oh, it must have been in the street!'

Great-Aunt Jane opened her eyes.

'I feel much better,' she said. '*Ever* so much better.'

'You *look* better,' said the nurse. 'I hope the children were good.'

'Good as gold!' said Great-Aunt Jane, with the ghost of a wink at William . . .

. . . Downstairs Uncle John was standing, gloomy as ever, by the fireplace.

'How is she?' he said, as they entered.

'I think she's risin' a bit,' said William.[30]

Needless to say, Great-Aunt Jane makes a complete recovery.

William is also related to yet another Aunt Jane who is unexpectedly given a new lease of life when she visits his family at Christmas.[31] Unlike Great Aunt Jane, Aunt Jane is not bedridden but one of the walking wounded: 'tall, angular, and precise.'[32] In spite of these deficiencies she overcomes William's initial resistance to maiden aunts of depressing appearance by offering him a seasonal treat although she stipulates that it should be 'quiet and orderly—as I don't approve of merry-making':

William looked at her kind, weak face with the spectacles and scraped back hair and sighed. He thought that Aunt Jane would be enough to dispel the hilarity of any treat. Great-Aunt Jane's father had been a Plymouth Brother, and Great-Aunt Jane had been brought up to disbelieve in pleasure except as a potent aid to the devil.[33]

Aunt Jane is herself filled with trepidation on the night before the treat:

'I do hope,' she murmured on the threshold, holding William firmly by the hand, 'that there's nothing really *wrong* in it.'[34]

Once inside the fair Aunt Jane is literally transformed by the sights and sounds, vigorously throwing balls at coconuts and participating enthusiastically in the rides, incongruous in her 'long and voluminous black coat, and a small black hat, adorned with black ears of wheat, perched upon her prim little head.'[35] So complete is the transformation that Great-Aunt Jane's eyes seem to be drawn 'out of her sockets and through her large, round spectacles.'[36] In the end Great Aunt Jane exhibits much greater stamina than the Outlaws who are forced to retire defeated from the field. Control of the situation thus passes out of their hands.

'There's something quite rejuvenating about it all, William,' she murmured.

'She went again on the Roundabout, she had another coconut-shy, she went on the Switchback, the Fairy Boat and the Wild Sea Waves. William trailed along behind her. He refused to venture on the Wild Sea Waves, and watched her on them with a certain grudging admiration.

'Crumbs!' he murmured 'she must have gotter inside of *iron*!'[37]

The circus has arrived in the neighborhood and Grandfather Moore has come to stay:

William had never met his grandfather before, and he gazed in astonishment at him. He had met old people before, but he had not thought that anything quite so old as grandfather Moore had ever existed or ever could exist. He was little and wrinkled and shriveled and bald. His face was yellow, with tiny little lines running crisscross all over it; his bright little eyes seemed to have sunk right back. When he smiled he revealed a large expanse of bare gum, with three lonely-looking teeth at intervals. He had a few hairs, just above his neck at the back, otherwise his head was like a shining new egg. William was fascinated. He could hardly keep his eyes off him all tea-time.[38]

Grandfather Moore is accompanied by a full time carer in the shape of Aunt Lilian. Aunt Lilian believes he is becoming simple but an unspoken sympathy develops between him and William during the afternoon. Later that evening William decides to sneak out of the house to make a forbidden visit to the circus. As he passes Grandfather Moore's room he is surprised to see the old man sitting up and fully dressed. William is persuaded to take Grandfather Moore along and they sneak out of the house and find seats in the circus where Grandfather Moore is ecstatic:

'That *was* a circus William! I saw a fine one when I was a boy too. I didn't care what I did to get to a circus.'

William felt he had found a kindred spirit.[39]

The following morning at breakfast, Aunt Lilian enthuses over Grandfather Moore's appearance of well-being:

'Doesn't he look well this morning. I don't know *when* I remember him looking so well. A good long night does him no end of good. I'm so glad I persuaded him to go to bed directly after tea.'

William's eyes and Grandfather Moore's eyes met for a second across the table.[40]

Conclusion

Richmal Crompton herself described William as part savage and part hero. A character whose attraction lay in his combination of mischief-making, risk-taking, courage and idealism. In her fictional representations of rapport between boyhood and old age the willingness of older characters to abandon adult dignity and gravitas is not represented as a loss of essential personhood through a descent into childish irresponsibility and dependency. Quite the contrary: in these stories the older characters are liberated, albeit sometimes only temporarily, from the negative stereotyping and thus depersonalisation of the mature adult world. And it is William, the incorrigible conspirator against fustiness and convention, who is the agent of their personalisation.

Another interesting example of this rejuvenating rapport between old age and boyhood can be found in 'Violet Elizabeth's Party' first published in 1964, when Richmal Crompton was aged 74.[41] William and the Outlaws have been instructed by their parents to attend Violet Elizabeth Bott's party where old fashioned party games, like Postman's Knock (involving the dreaded and unmanly kissing) are to be played in honour of Aunt Jo who is Violet Elizabeth's mother's godmother. Determined to avoid the party, the Outlaws make a detour into the woods where their peaceful retreat is disturbed by 'an elderly woman, wearing boots, a pork-pie hat and a large tweed overcoat.'[42] She has 'a small wizened face, bright blue eyes and a long humourous mouth'[43] and asks them what they are doing. In reply to their reluctant response that they are just 'sittin' and 'restin' she informs the Outlaws she is running away from a children's party which, of course, turns out to be the one the Outlaws are also avoiding. Coincidentally it is, she asserts, the thought of playing the kiss-ing games she remembers with such aversion from her childhood which turn her blood.

A bond of companionship is sealed and the conspirators, seeking to evade the search party that has been dispatched by Mrs. Bott to find Aunt Jo, conceal themselves upstairs in an empty house. The search party gather on the lawn below and are overheard by the Outlaws and Aunt Jo. Mrs Bott, much given to hysteria, has become convinced Aunt Jo has been kidnapped by a murderous gang. Her tearful demands that her husband ('Botty') intervene are overheard by the conspirators:

'Oh, Botty, *do* something,' said Mrs Bott hysterically. 'They mayn't have finished doin' away with her yet. There may be time to stop 'em. I can't go down to me grave with Auntie Jo's death on me 'ands. A poor helpless old woman like that!'

Aunt Jo had been listening with mild amusement, but at the words 'poor helpless old woman' the smile dropped from her face. 'Poor helpless old woman,' she echoed indignantly. 'I'll show her!'

She seized one of the rotten apples and flung it with unerring aim out of the window. It burst with a plop! full in Mrs Bott's face.[44]

In this story Aunt Jo conspires with boyhood against the sentimental attitude of the mature adult world towards both older women and children. She, like the Outlaws, literally occupies a space between the two socially constructed worlds (and it is worthwhile speculating on the physical resemblance between photographs of the author as she grew older and the image of Aunt Jo as she appears in the Thomas Henry's illustration). In their encounters with William those of her older characters who are treated sympathetically (for there are some who are not, but that's another story) lose nothing of their personal dignity from their vigorous interaction with William and the Outlaws. It is only the staid, the pretentious and the self-important who lose face. Infantilisation is thus experienced as a process of mutual liberation through resistance: in this case the public triumph of private self-consciousness over prescriptive social categorisation.

Discussion Questions

1. How is language used to "infantilise" the elderly? What are the effects on their status and treatment in American society?

2. According to Hepworth, what purposes does the social construction of old age as a second childhood play in relieving our own anxieties about growing old?

3. What are some strategies of "positive infantilisation used by characters in the William stories?

4. Are there any potential problems with this concept of "positive infantilisation" as a strategy by older adults? If so, what are they?

Notes

1. The author gratefully acknowledges permission from Macmillan Children's Books to reproduce passages from stories by Richmal Crompton (c Richmal C. Ashbee) and illustrations to these stories by Thomas Henry (c Thomas Henry Fisher Estate). Specific textual references are given in the notes below. The first publication dates of these stories are cited in the references below.

2. Johnson, J. 1993. Does group living work?, in Johnson, J. and Slater, R. (eds), *Aging and Later Life*. Sage in Association with the Open University, London, Thousand Oaks, New Delhi, p. 124.

3. Spark, M. 1993 (1959). *Memento Mori*. Penguin, Harmondsworth.

4. Coupland, N., Coupland, J. and Giles, H. 1991. *Language, Society and The Elderly: Discourse, Identity and Aging.* Blackwell, Oxford UK & Cambridge USA, p. 13.

5. Ibid. p. 176.

6. Ibid. p. 177.

7. Green, B. S. 1993. *Gerontology and The Construction of Old Age: A Study in Discourse Analysis*. Aldine de Gruyter, New York, p. 1.

8. Hockey, and James, A. 1993. *Growing Up and Growing Old: Aging and Dependency in The Life Course*. Sage, London, Newbury Park, New Delhi, p. 39.

9. Ibid. p. 39.

10. Cole, T. R. 1992. *The Journey of Life: A Cultural History of Aging in America*. Cambridge University Press, Cambridge, New York, Poll Chester, Melbourne, Sydney, p. 28.

11. Mclsaac, S. J. 1993. How nursing home residents live while in the sub-passage of confusion: the battle of dignity and respect versus deterioration and decline. Unpub. PhD, Department of Sociology, University of Aberdeen.

12. Featherstone, M. and Hepworth, M. 1989. Aging and old age: reflections on the post-modern life course. In Bytheway, B., Keil, T., Allatt, P. and Bryman, A. (eds), *Becoming and Being Old: Sociological Approaches to Later Life*. Sage, London, Newbury Park, New Delhi.

13. Of particular relevance is Kitwood's work on the role of social interaction in the dementing process: Kitwood, T. 1990. The dialectics of dementia: with particular reference to Alzheimer's Disease. *Ageing and Society*, **10**, 177–196; Kitwood, T. 1993. Towards a theory of dementia care: the interpersonal process. *Ageing and Society*, **13**, 51–67.

14. Elias, N. 1985. *The Loneliness of The Dying*. Basil Blackwell, Oxford, New York.

15. Cohen, A. P. 1994. *Self-Consciousness: An Alternative Anthropology of Identity*. Routledge, London and New York, p. 99.

16. Ibid. p. 105

17. The standard references on the life and work of Richmal Crompton are Mary Cadogan's biography (1986), *Richmal Crompton: The Woman Behind William*. Allen & Unwin, London, Boston, Sydney, Wellington, and her reference book (with David Schutte) 1990. *The William Companion*, Allen & Unwin, London, Boston Sydney, Wellington. These works are indispensable for any student of 'William' and I am particularly indebted to Cadogan's description and discussion of three of the stories discussed in this paper: 'The Cure' (Great-Aunt Jane), 'Aunt Jane's Treat' (Aunt Jane), and 'The Circus' (Grandfather Moore). These accounts are found respectively in pp. 140–142 and pp. 151–152 of her biography.

18. Cadogan M. *The William Companion*, p. 2.

19. Ibid. p. 118.

20. Cadogan, M. *Richmal Crompton*, pp. 152–153.

21. Crompton, R. 1984. (first published 1925). William and Uncle George, in *Still William*. Macmillan Children's Books, London.

22. Ibid. pp. 222–223.

23. Crompton, R. 1984. (first published 1930). William Goes Shopping, in *William's Happy Days*. Macmillan, Children's Books, London.

24. Ibid. pp. 7–8.

25. Ibid. pp. 9–10.

26. Ibid. p. 12.

27. Hepworth, M. 1991. Positive ageing and the mask of age. *Journal of Educational Gerontology*, **6**, 93û101.

28. Crompton, R. 1983. (first published 1923). The Cure, in *William Again*. Macmillan Children's Books, London.

29. Ibid. p. 29.

30. Ibid. pp 31–33.

31. Crompton, R. 1983. (first published 1924). Aunt Jane's Treat, in *William The Fourth*. Macmillan Children's Books, London.

32. Ibid. p. 65.

33. Ibid. p. 66.

34. Ibid. p. 68.

35. Ibid. p. 78.

36. Ibid. p. 68.

37. Ibid. p. 76.

38. Crompton R. 1983. (first published 1923). The Circus, in *William Again*. Macmillan Children's Books, London, pp. 176–177.

39. Ibid. p. 184.

40. Ibid. p. 185.

41. Crompton, R. 1992. (first published 1964,). Violet Elizabeth's Party, in *William and The Witch*. Macmillan Children's Book, London.

42. Ibid. p. 50.

43. Ibid. pp. 50–51.

44. Ibid p. 59.

Chapter 4

Old Age as a Time of Decay

Carole Haber

A preceding selection pointed out that younger people in Japan have increasingly negative views of older people. This perspective is shared by many Americans. How did old age become viewed as a period of physical and mental decline? In the following selection, Carole Haber critically examines the role of American medicine during the past two centuries in defining this last stage of life. By the end of the nineteenth century, physicians viewed most elders, regardless of their actual health, as patients in need of constant, if fruitless, medical care. Old age was transformed into a pathological condition that robbed elders of both body and mind. Because few doctors or students of medicine saw healthy older people in their practices, their definitions of the last stage of life were formed by their experience with older people as sick patients and as dead bodies upon whom they performed autopsies. It is perhaps not surprising that physicians concluded that disease in later life is inevitable and fundamentally different from illnesses among other age groups. According to this view, the old are unable to adapt to new circumstances; they are unproductive and lose not only their physical health and reason but their sexual capacity. They are likely to turn into "dirty old men" (and women) and even child molesters. Haber points out that the nineteenth- and early twentieth-century model of aging developed by physicians contributed to the exclusion of elders from social life. Consider the assumptions made by physicians in this selection and their impact on popular impressions of aging that persist even today. Think about the implications of these beliefs for the treatment of chronic diseases in later life.

. . . As demographic and economic changes in society caused the increasing isolation of the elderly, doctors endorsed an age-based regimen that justified their seclusion and retirement. By the early twentieth century, as we shall see, American physicians had developed a conception of old age that legitimated the complete separation of the aged from the rest of society. . . . Unlike many French or German physicians, few mid-nineteenth-century American physicians would have extensive clinical training, study degenerated tissue, or view the "senile cell" under the microscope. The primary source of information about senescence remained their experience in treating the old. Most, therefore, continued to characterize senescence in general, descriptive terms. "Old age," according to one mid-century physician, was "that stage of life in which the vital forces show unequivocal marks of languishment and decline, where the elasticity of youth and vigor of mankind are followed by a condition in which are manifest symptoms of decay in all parts, both in body and mind."[1]

Most English-language physicians would have agreed. Consensus on such a definition was possible because most practitioners still relied implicitly upon the vitality model of growing old. As we have seen, the studies of the clinicians and pathologists did not really invalidate traditional notions of how the body aged. Although these scientists questioned the plausibility of particular theories of aging, their work produced no firm conclusion; the mechanism that controlled aging remained unexplained and ill-defined. Although pathological studies could be interpreted as replacing vital energy with mechanical or chemical processes, most English and American medical writers seemed to find no conflict between the clinical-pathological views and the age-old metaphoric model of aging.[2] In their texts, the two theories were neatly combined: The tissue or cell degenerated while the organism systemically wasted away.

In accepting this synthesis, American physicians slightly recast the traditional notion of vital energy. Once French clinical studies became publicized, the concept had to be made consistent with both the visible evidence and the postmortem findings. Loss of energy not only resulted in a worn exterior appearance but accounted for physiological and anatomical alterations as well. When the patient's resources were depleted, the body underwent numerous pathological changes: The lesions, the calcareous deposits, and the fibrous tissues were all the result of rapidly dissipating strength. Once the waning of vital energy could be made to explain the discrete lesions and other degenerative changes found in the elderly, the physician could easily link the orthodox model of aging with more novel ideas. In 1859, for example, James Copland summarized the organic transformations discovered in the elderly organism. In part, he believed that these alterations were caused by peculiarities of food, constitution, employment, acquired habits, and indulgences. "But," he concluded:

> We are not altogether justified in considering the contingencies as the primary cause of the changes now described. We are rather to view them as more or less remote effects of the failure of vital endowment of the frame manifesting itself first in the less perfect performance of the different functions and subsequently in the modifications of structure, and ultimately in the very obvious lesions of both function and structure.[3]

Throughout the nineteenth century, the notion of vital energy remained an essential aspect of the American view of aging. . . . If there were cause for disagreement at all, it concerned the process through which vital energy worked, rather than its existence. Why, some doctors asked, if vital power was endowed at birth, were young adults more energetic than infants? Why were athletes likely to outlive the totally inactive? These inconsistencies, however, did not cause medical authorities to abandon the notion. They merely reshaped the hypothetical mechanics of its operation. In the new interpretation, an individual's vital energy first increased to adulthood and then began its slow decline. "It cannot really be debated," argued one physician, "that the functions of life as they may be observed in any specialized organism increase for a time in strength, range and

complexity, pass through a period of comparative repose, and finally break up and disappear."[4]

This reformulation was necessary because the theory had to correspond to observation. Vital energy remained a popular concept precisely because it provided visibly—and emotionally—satisfying rationales for a process over which the physician had little control. As doctors showed increased skill in fighting the diseases of women, children, and the middle-aged of both sexes, only the illnesses of the old seemed generally impervious to modern therapeutics. Death, once feared by all individuals, gradually became thought of as the sole province of the old.[5] Vital energy explained this close relationship in a way more recent scientific hypotheses could not. In addition, before the germ theory, the traditional model of vitality could be employed to justify the high morbidity among the elderly from very contagious diseases. George E. Day, for example, despite his clinical pathological approach to the illnesses of the old, relied upon the notion of vital energy to explain senile influenza. The disease was devastating to the aged, he believed, because "it extinguishes the vital force in old age and in persons suffering from chronic diseases."[6] Even after the introduction of the germ theory, vital energy played a central role in the physician's explanation of the ailments of the elderly. According to one doctor, it was precisely the lack of energy of the aged that caused them to be susceptible to infection; they no longer had the strength to resist the onset of the illness.[7]. . .

Any one of a number of illnesses could then destroy the old. Throughout the nineteenth century, the physician's enumeration of such potentially fatal diseases grew steadily. This list of ailments was the result both of a new interest in the illnesses of the old and of a more general trend in defining age-related diseases. . . .

[P]rior to the nineteenth century, the death of an elderly person caused little surprise. Merely by surviving to old age, the individual was already considered to have escaped the most commonly fatal diseases. No one, after all, was expected to triumph in the battle against time. A rising professionalism and interest in specific disease entities, however, caused several physicians to question the validity of such an attitude. "The diseases and infirmities [of the aged]," wrote Daniel Maclachlan in 1863, "have been too much regarded as inescapable concomitants in advancing years, the inevitable consequences of the progressive, natural decay of the organism and decline of the vital function generally, and therefore but little if at all within the reach of the physician."[8]

At last, Maclachlan believed, this attitude was beginning to change. In growing numbers, physicians were attempting to isolate and identify the primary reasons for their elderly patients' deaths. With an ever-increasing list of possible causes, they needed to rely upon the prognosis "decay" or "mere old age" far less often; any one of a number of diseases was believed capable of terminating the patient's life. Some illnesses were merely old ailments in modern dress. "Decay from old age," for example, became "senile maramus." Yet the theory behind the disease had not changed: The body, drained of its energy, simply wasted away as the years progressed. Other illnesses were of more recent origin, the result of the physician's attempt to link the patient's exterior symptoms to subsequent pathological discoveries . . . the fits and fevers of the old had once been characterized as a general disease state. With the gradual acceptance of disease specificity, such symptoms were redefined as an ailment particular to the elderly, caused, perhaps, by an age-related heart or vascular condition.[9] The pathological alterations of the body were responsible for a number of such specific ailments. Prostatic malfunctions, apoplexy, and Bright's disease were only a few of the many organic difficulties that could present problems in old age.

European and American practitioners generally agreed in their list of age-related ailments. In this area, English-language physicians were often content to repeat the findings of their predecessors. American and English doctors, however, recognized one disease that was usually ignored by the French. This was climacteric illness, a disease believed to occur in women between forty-five and fifty-five and in men between

fifty and seventy-five. As defined by one physician, climacteric disease was:

> That extraordinary decline of the corporeal powers which, before the system falls prey to confirmed old age, sometimes makes its appearance in advanced age without any sufficient ostensible cause, and is occasionally succeeded by a renovation of health and vigor though it more generally precipitates the patient into the grave.[10]

Few prominent pathologists would take great note of this ailment; no organ showed sudden signs of deterioration, nor were characteristic lesions discovered through autopsies.[11] American physicians were content to link the illness directly to the waning of vital energy. The ailment marked the point at which "the body had run its course"[12] and had irreversibly begun its final decline. For these physicians, the proof of the disease could be found not through postmortem studies but in the patient's appearance. All at once, an individual looked old: The backbone stooped, the muscles sagged, and the mind grew dim. No one factor was believed to be the source of the problem. Physicians listed accidents, overwork, anxiety, and even the common cold as possible initiating causes. Once afflicted, however, the individual could expect little real relief from the practitioner. Even in those who seemed fully recovered, their energy was spent. They now looked, acted, and felt as if they had entered the final phase of existence.

The notion of the climacteric period mirrored ideas current in classic antiquity. As we have seen, one ancient view of the body had identified key points in the individual's life. Age sixty-three, the grand climacteric, was believed to designate the start of old age. In the early nineteenth century, physicians gave new meaning to the concept. Although the climacteric retained its connotation as the start of senescence, it became designated as well as an unavoidable disease. . . .

Practitioners usually believed that this visible transformation could affect both men and women. Some cited the cessation of the menses as part of the illness; others said that menopause preceded the broader, more obvious ailment. Most agreed, however, that climacteric disease was far more severe in men than in women;[13] the well-marked periodicity of the female cushioned her decline into senescence. Over an extended time span, her body could adjust to the new stage of life. In men, though, the alteration was instantly apparent; their weight, facial appearance, and temperament all changed. The entire organism suddenly and obviously seemed to age.

By far the most serious sign of climacteric disease was the tendency toward insanity. The sudden loss of vital energy caused a rapid transformation of the entire system. The brain, as well as the body, was likely to suffer severe and permanent damage. The confident person lost assuredness, the diligent individual self-control. Unfounded fears, delusions, and even kleptomania could be linked to this fundamental physiological alteration.[14] "The epoch of reconstruction," wrote Dr. W. Bevan Lewis in 1890:

is one of peril to the mind. . . . Reflection wants the calm essential to its orderly operation, and judgment is liable to be warped and one-sided; hence, also it is that this age of life is one prone to bigotry, to religious fanaticism, or to conduct based upon dogmatic and immature beliefs. An unusual inordinate religious zeal is, indeed, a most frequent expression of this transition period in mental life; and this is of interest viewed in connection with the insanity of this age.[15]

During the second half of the nineteenth century, American physicians referred to this transition less often as a disease and more often as a normal—though painful—stage of existence. . . . The climacteric period was an abrupt change rather than a slow decline. Yet, "the turning point towards the downhill course," as one physician termed it, seemed to take place in almost every individual, although the age of occurrence might differ.[16] Not every person suffered from the extreme symptoms of madness, for many would feel only irritable or uncomfortable. But to some extent, all could expect to undergo a noticeable transition in character. According to the medical literature of the nineteenth century, many personality traits were determined by sex. Men were thought to be naturally just,

noble, virile, and brave; women were considered nurturant, moral, domestic, and passive.[17] In old age, however, these qualities no longer seemed appropriate. With the climacteric stage of life, a woman became unable to conceive; a man could no longer be portrayed as strong or vital. The basic male and female traits, in fact, seemed to merge in the old until they became almost indistinguishable. After the climacteric, I. L. Nascher explained, "the growth force is now mainly exerted toward the approximation of the sexes and in old age they approach a neutral type."[18] Both elderly men and women were seen as dependent, passive, and weak; their greatest concerns were (or should be) moral and religious. The affairs of the world were best forgotten. The senescent were advised to prepare themselves for their heavenly home.[19]

The climacteric period of life, therefore, marked the division between maturity and senescence. Those in this phase were neither old nor young; their bodies—as well as their status in society—were in a period of transition. Like the passage between adolescence and adulthood, the stage that separated adulthood from old age could be filled with danger.[20] The volatile nature of the body produced physical and mental instability in the climacteric sufferer. This phase, however, lasted only as long as the visible, age-related disease persisted. Once the change had occurred, the old irreversibly separated from their younger selves. It was understandable, then, that physicians considered the illness to be more severe in men than in women. The female could slowly adjust to her new stage of life, while her domestic duties remained the same.[21] For the male, though, the advent of the climacteric implied a radical break with his own past. After describing man at the peak of his strength, Dr. Charles Caldwell lamented: "And I regret to say, I have passed through the last stage of life in which it is not painful to accompany him—because it is the last in which he is comfortable to himself, useful to others or an ornament to his race."[22] In earlier segments of the life cycle, the individual had grown and developed; now he began his "downhill decline."[23]

Thus, physicians cautioned all aging persons to take note of the important divide they had crossed. To the nineteenth-century practitioner, the climacteric was more than an inevitable disease; it marked a point at which most individuals had to accept an entirely new manner of living. "It is the duty then," wrote Dr. Bernard Van Oven:

> of all persons who have attained the climacteric age, carefully to avoid excesses and undue exertions, to watch at all times for the insidious approach of disorders; never to reject any slight ailment, but regard them as forerunners of more serious derangements, seek to repair the most trifling irregularities of function and give rest at once to any organ of the body which shows debility or fatigue.[24]

Above all, physicians warned the elderly that their normal physiological condition had now become one of disease.[25] Although the individual might appear to be in perfect health, old age alone signified disability. With each passing year, the internal organs progressively decayed. Activities that had once been effortlessly accomplished could cause serious infirmities: Overwork might bring on mental exhaustion; physical labor could lead to cardiac arrest or apoplexy. From this perspective, every elderly individual, regardless of the present state of his or her health, became a potential patient. All post climacteric individuals were advised to accept unquestioningly the role of invalid and to place themselves "under the immediate and constant care of the physician."[26] Once in authority, the concerned family doctor could then determine the steps necessary to maintain the fragile existence of the elderly. "Every person," advised Dr. H. C. Wood, "when he advances in years, should go over his whole method of life and personal habits with some wise counselor and should adapt his mode of living to the peculiarities of his particular case."[27]

In a sense, the nineteenth-century studies of pathology had legitimated this role for the physician. By defining physiological old age as a pathological process, they had placed every aspect of senescence in a medical perspective. Choices of diet, clothes, activity, and even occupation became valid professional questions. The earliest gerontological specialists, therefore, devoted much of their writings to the prescription of proper regimens. In general, these programs did not differ practically from the admonitions proffered by the advocates of longevity. In both popular health manuals and scholarly journals, medical authorities instructed the elderly to avoid red meat, be temperate in food and drink, and participate only in those activities that exercised the mind and body without causing exhaustion or worry. Unlike the longevity spokesmen, however, most early gerontologists did not promise that their prescriptions would lead to an extended life. As the body decayed, there was little hope—or desire—for a century-long existence. Additional years would only bring greater organic disability.[28] A correct regimen, therefore, was simply seen as a means of making the body less susceptible to the numerous senile illnesses. Progressive decay could not ultimately be diverted.

Once a senile disease appeared, though, the physician had little beyond palliation to recommend. As the nineteenth-century medical findings broadened the legitimate sphere of the physician, they also deterred him from experimenting with therapeutics.[29] According to prominent pathologists, almost all of the peculiarly senile illnesses were potentially fatal. The organic difficulties that increased with age made the hope of curative treatment illusory. Rather than minister to specific senile diseases, a few individuals attempted to eliminate old age altogether. Through scientific experiments, they searched for the magic elixir that would bring eternal youth. But professional responses to their suggestions only emphasized how patently implausible they seemed. In the 1870s, for example, C. E. Brown-Sequard believed that he could restore the sexual power of the old through a solution derived from ground-up animal testicles. The scientific community generally greeted his experiments with ridicule.[30] In 1903, when Elie Metchnikoff presented his prescription for continuing middle age, he met a similar response. According to Metchnikoff's formula, the scientist was to inject a horse with finely minced particles of human organs such as brains, liver, heart, or kidneys; after a few weeks, he was to drain off the serum.[31] Other physicians suggested the simpler idea of injecting young blood into the old. In terms of curing diseases, however, there were far fewer recommendations. Most American physicians resorted to an assortment of traditional remedies: Opium was prescribed and withdrawn; purgatives, emetics, and diuretics were all endorsed by some and refuted by many.[32] Most senile ailments seemed to remain impervious to treatment.

Any disease, therefore, once it appeared in its senile state, was almost certain to cause the physician innumerable and often insolvable problems. It was futile, he knew, to attempt to return the anatomy of the elderly to its preclimacteric state. Instead, most medical authorities merely reclassified the symptoms of the old in terms of age-related disease entities. Even illnesses that seemed common to all age groups, such as pneumonia, bronchitis, or jaundice, were given special designations to reflect the debilitated condition of the patient. Bronchitis, for example, became "senile bronchitis," its nature and course altered by the pathological vascular tissue and mucous membrane characteristic of the elderly. Physicians believed that such "normally" diseased aspects of the aged organism sharply limited the potential efficacy of therapeutics. In the case of senile pneumonia, for example, George E. Day concluded that three-fifths of all patients would die. Their constantly congested lungs and habitual bronchorrhea gave the physician little hope of ever curing the illness.[33] Well into the twentieth century, practitioners readily agreed with this assessment. In 1907, for example, Dr. Clarence Bartlett declared that "the results from the treatment of old people with pneumonia are so poor that it is difficult to speak with any positiveness as to the efficient measures for their cure."[34]

Senile diseases, therefore, were fundamentally different from illnesses common to other age groups. After midcentury, medical authorities advised practitioners that many diseases cured themselves; the best treatment was often to allow nature to heal the patient. In the old, however, this was hardly the case. The natural course for most senile diseases was either increasing disability or the death of the patient.[35] . . . Senility, once merely "the state of being old," had been transformed into a pathological condition that robbed the individual of both intellect and understanding.[36] The normal state of being old, it seemed, was that of debilitating illness.[37]

Few late-nineteenth-century physicians would disagree with this assessment. Senility, more than any single ailment, came to represent the extreme and inevitable incapacity of senescence. Unlike climacteric disease, however, senile dementia was not the creation of modern physicians. Even in biblical days, the loss of reason in the old had been a well-noted affliction. Medical authorities, however, had generally assumed that this was an abnormal state for the elderly rather than their usual condition. Benjamin Rush, for example, was convinced that most aged individuals would retain full use of their mental powers until they reached the grave. In 1797, in a study of a group of octogenarians, he found that although some elderly individuals had faulty memories of the recent past, their intellectual, moral, and religious powers were completely unimpaired. He did not consider the mere loss of memory a harbinger of more serious problems. For Rush, even a decayed body did not dictate the inevitable loss of one's mental faculties. The spirit and intellect were sure to outlive the material side of one's nature.[38]

With the nineteenth-century medical findings about old age, however, the ability of the senescent to retain their reason came under serious question. As proven by postmortem studies, the anatomical transformations of the organism affected both mind and body. In old age, the brain underwent numerous pathological alterations. Whether physicians believed that dementia was caused by brain lesions, starvation of tissue, dying brain cells, arteriosclerosis, softening of the brain, or even a loss of molecular vitality, most authorities agreed upon the inevitability of the process.[39] In the early nineteenth century, a few physicians, such as Isaac Ray and James Cowles Prichard, attempted to distinguish between normal senile decay and abnormal dementia.[40] The first, they believed, was unavoidable and progressive; the latter, an incurable ailment. "Were it not so," declared Ray in 1838, "every old man would labor under a certain degree of dementia."[41] This was a conclusion he was not prepared to entertain. But Ray, as well as other early expert psychologists, struggled to differentiate between the two diseases. "It may be difficult," he conceded, "to satisfy ourselves whether or not [decay] is accompanied by [derangement], but for any practical purpose it may seldom be necessary."[42] Regardless of whether the disease was called decay or dementia, afflicted individuals slowly lost their reason. First, the memory failed, followed in turn by the powers of perception, recognition, and intellect. There was little the physician could do to deter this process. His only role was to make the patient comfortable as the old man or woman sank into a state of complete mental incompetence.

By the late nineteenth century, few physicians would attempt to distinguish between decay and dementia. "No sharp line can be drawn between ordinary senile dotage and senile dementia," wrote Dr. W. H. B. Stoddard in 1909. "The normal mental deterioration incident upon old age is itself early senile dementia."[43] Senile insanity, like other age-related diseases, had a normal physiological basis. The natural result of gradual decay, it was considered the eventual, inescapable state for all elderly individuals. . . .

Aging was a general, progressive decline; as the body decayed, so did the mind. The concept of mental immortality—endorsed by physicians as late as the early nineteenth century—found few adherents by the end of the century.[44] Vital and intellectual principles were hardly divisible. The brain, like any other organ composed of living cells, underwent physiological decay as it aged. Postmortem studies confirmed this belief. Compared to the brain of the young, clinicians found that the senile organ weighed less, had a thinner cortex, and was subject to lesions and softening.[45] Given such pathological alterations, there seemed little question that as the individual entered the "senile" state, he would suffer from a constantly decreasing mental capability.

On the basis of these data, more than a few physicians began to challenge the traditional image of the old as repositories of great wisdom. The anatomy and physiology of the aged appeared to limit their intellectual achievement. With each passing year, the brain of the old became less sensitive to stimulation and less able to process complicated information. By the time the individual reached senescence, the intellect was all but shattered. Thus, the apparent wisdom of the old was nothing more than the lingering traces of past talents. . . .

In addition, physicians believed that the aging of the mind prevented the elderly from adapting to new circumstances. The molecules of the senile brain had become fixed into well-established arrangements. The organ no longer possessed the plasticity necessary to formulate new patterns. The aged mind, therefore, was incapable of assimilating concepts that were unorthodox or unknown. The physiology of the old, wrote Charles Mercier, confirms that "old and accurate observation that 'you cannot teach an old dog new tricks.'"[46] Business, social affairs, and even family life made little impression upon the aged brain. The old lived in the past; each day, they became less conscious of the world around them.

Intellectual achievement, however, was not the only aspect of mind affected by senility. Nineteenth-century physicians repeatedly asserted that the progressive decay of the brain noticeably altered the personality. The antisocial characteristics that first appeared during the climacteric period now assumed permanent form. The old became perverse instead of reasonable. No longer interested in other events or people, they grew increasingly involved in their own petty concerns. "A change in temper is likewise noticed," continued one late nineteenth-century physician. "Self-control is lost and depression is apt to alternate with irritability. The aged become petulant, selfish, and indifferent to the usual interests of life and to their family."[47] Most practitioners assumed that the old had little real control over these traits. In senescence, their personalities no longer seemed the result of individual backgrounds, tastes, or ideas. Instead, they became the direct reflection of the organisms' pathological conditions. Unchecked by any higher faculty, emotions alone came to dictate the senescent personality.

These uncontrolled passions could easily lead the old into unfortunate, if not dangerous, circumstances. Once senility overtook the aged, they tended to act on any whim. Children were suddenly denied their rightful inheritance, foolish marriages were made, and unwise business deals were transacted.[48] In such a state of mind, the aged individual could become a serious threat to his or her own safety. The suicide rate, according to Dr. Colin A. Scott, revealed "that this crime becomes more frequent at and after the grand climacteric."[49] The case of Margaret Wall, a patient at the Philadelphia Orthopaedic Hospital, was typical. At sixty-five, after her husband died, she became extremely melancholy. As her depression increased and her sense of present-day realities diminished, she made repeated attempts to throw herself down the stairs. Only the constant vigilance of her family prevented her from committing suicide.[50] . . .

The most widely discussed problem created by senility, though, was not intellectual corruption but moral perversion. Most late-nineteenth-century physicians believed that by the time of senescence, the individual had lost both the ability and the inclination for sexual relations. This was nature's way of preserving the body's essential seminal fluids. Through its inability to engage in sexual activity, the organism was saved from "the most exhausting expenditure of nervous and vital energy."[51] With senility, however, the desire for sexual activity often returned, although without the corresponding capability. As a result, the elderly turned into "opulent satyres" or "grotesque monsters" whose abnormal and uncontrollable cravings led them to commit numerous sexual perversions. The senile old man, explained Dr. Allan McLane Hamilton, becomes "amatory, obscene, and fond of telling of the adventures of his youth and living again its gallant frivolities. His leer is lascivious and he goes about with unbuttoned clothes and is lost to all shame."[53] Slovenliness, exhibitionism, and even child molesting could arise out of this pathological mental condition.

Not all the old, of course, would suffer from these extreme symptoms of senility. Yet physicians warned practitioners to be alert to all signs of early dementia. Even in instances where the aged person seemed healthy and active, the brain could be undergoing progressive and irreversible decay. This was especially important when legal matters were involved. Called upon when a will was contested, the physician assumed the role of expert; he had to affirm or deny the mental competence of the elderly testator. In such cases, the practitioner found that he often lacked a clear set of practical guidelines. As we have seen, late-nineteenth-century physicians classified senile dementia as an inevitable part of physiological decay; no distinct line separated the forgetful old person from the insane. The final will of the aged, absent-minded individual, therefore, could easily be contested—especially if the money was donated to a church or charity rather than kin. Religious zeal could be interpreted as senile fanaticism; refusal to acknowledge an heir might be explained as pathological willfulness. The degree of decay then became an issue of legal importance. Did extreme age cause the loss of reason and intellect as well as memory? Did the deterioration of brain cells prevent the individual from knowing the extent and condition of the property?[54]

These were questions, physicians asserted, that could be answered only by the cautious family doctor. Specially trained and familiar with the patient, he alone possessed the knowledge necessary to analyze the subject properly.[55] Even the most concerned judge lacked the wealth of information available to the practitioner. Although he might be able to ascertain if the individual understood the state of his or her business affairs, he was not capable of comprehending the patient's total mental state. "We should bear in mind," Dr. J. Nichols advised, "that in this advanced period though there may be apparent soundness in the operations of the mind, when movement is only in one direction, yet the harmonious play of all its faculties may be greatly disturbed or entirely destroyed."[56] Only the physician could be aware of the individual's usual habits, actions, and beliefs. The slightest change in these areas could be a sign that decay was progressing. In determining the extent of impairment, I. L. Nascher advised, "it is necessary to compare all the faculties with the faculties as they were, and not with the faculties of another at the same age."[57] This could be done only by a person who had watched the elderly individual grow old and could question his daily behavior. Did he act his age? Did he attempt youthful activity unbecoming to his years? Did he have sexual desires inappropriate to the elderly?

For the aged to qualify as mentally competent, doctors implied, they had to act old. Any digression from the standards of senescence was surely a sign of mental regression. "In the young man," T. S. Clouston wrote in 1884, "there is an organic craving for action, which not being gratified there results organic discomfort; in the old man there is an organic craving for rest and not to gratify that causes organic uneasiness."[58]

By the nature of his age and his pathological internal state, the old man was expected to want to retire from active life, to leave his work to junior associates, his family matters to heirs. . . . The old man and woman became, first and foremost, patients in need of constant medical attention. This was, doctors asserted, their physiological destiny. The organic alterations that constituted old age subverted all other possible roles. In terms of caring for the elderly, the physician then assumed the part of expert; every aspect of the senescent's routine was subject to his approval. Yet the same physiological and anatomical changes that had determined that the elderly act the part of needy invalids also stereotyped them as the most unpleasant and incurable patients. The personality characteristics of old age meant that these individuals would be difficult to control and rarely grateful for treatment. In hospitals, they merely filled necessary beds; in mental institutions, they disrupted routines without improving their own condition. . . .

This attitude, voiced by many physicians, certainly limited the growth of geriatrics.[59] In the late nineteenth century, while ambitious young physicians specialized in such fields as surgery, pediatrics, or gynecology, the diseases of the old continued to receive little attention. Therapeutically, there was little hope of implementing curative measures; clinical studies had definitely proven that old

age itself was a disease. Even a medically endorsed total regimen seemed to produce few results. "For a person in the seventies," Dr. James Faugeres Bishop wrote in 1904:

> It is not worth while to make any great sacrifice in the way of money and associations to go in search of health, because the probabilities are that the disturbance of the routine to which he has been accustomed through many years will do more harm than any climate will do him good.[60]

This attitude, however, did not deter the physician from prescribing for the elderly. Autopsies on the old had proven that the senescent could not be treated like all others. They required age-related treatment for their peculiar discomforts. The exterior appearance of the elderly only further supported the need for special regimens. After the climacteric had passed, the individual lacked the necessary vital energy to participate physically or mentally in daily activities. The body had become particularly susceptible to varied and often fatal diseases. The person's only hope was to withdraw from society and submit to the physician's custodial care. Thus, concerned doctors began to categorize the last segment of the life cycle as a period of disability and disease. The classification of the superannuated no longer rested on visible infirmities alone. According to the anatomical view of disease, the internal degeneration found in the elderly body meant that the entire stage was pathological. Those who had become senile had indeed begun to suffer from a progressive and incurable illness.

. . . Simply put, all persons who had grown old were likely to exhibit signs of decay. Thus, in medical and sociological terms, at least, old age was a time when separation from society was both necessary and desirable. Only under the care of experts could the elderly continue to live a peaceful—if no longer productive—existence. In large part, of course, this expanding notion of dependent superannuation was a response to broad economic and demographic changes. In the late nineteenth century, an increasing proportion of the old were indeed being separated from society, not only by the prescriptions of professionals but by their inability to retain control over family, wealth, and possessions. . . . In the late nineteenth century, the almshouse, hospital, mental institution, and old age home all reflected contemporary ideas and realities about growing old.

Discussion Questions

1. Describe the principal assumptions that physicians in the past have made about the physical and mental condition of the elderly.

2. What beliefs about mental decline and sexuality in old age proposed by nineteenth-century physicians persist in present-day thinking about the mental condition, judgment, and behavior of the elderly?

3. How have the medical theories described in this selection contributed to age-segregated programs, such as senior citizen centers, retirement villages, and nursing homes, that separate older people from younger age groups? Have these theories encouraged older people to withdraw from the labor force?

4. Based on your understanding of geriatric medical care today, explain how these older beliefs about later life influence current care of chronic diseases among the elderly.

Notes

1. J. Nichols, "Old Age," *The Rise, Minutes and Proceedings of the New Jersey Medical Society, 1766–1859* (1850), p. 519.

2. Harry Campbell, "Correspondence—The Cause of Senile Decay," *The Lancet*, 2 (August, 1905), p. 403; Henry Holland, *Medical Notes and Reflections* (Philadelphia: Haswell, Barrington and Haswell, 1839), p. 188.

3. James Copland, "Age—'Of the Conditions of a Function Characterising the Advance of Age,'" in *A Dictionary of Practical Medicine*, vol. 1, ed., Charles A. Lee (New York: Harper & Brothers, 1859), pp. 53–4. Holland linked the deposits and alterations of the blood to a loss of vital energy (p. 169).

4. Colin A. Scott, "Old Age and Death," *The American Journal of Psychology*, 8, no. 1 (October, 1896), p. 67; Bernard Van Oven, *On the Decline of Life in Health and Disease* (London: John Churchill & Sons, 1853), p. 53.

5. Ann Douglas, "Heaven our Home: Consolation Literature in the Northern United States, 1830–1880," *American Quarterly*, 26, no. 5 (December, 1974), pp. 496–515; David E. Stannard, *The Puritan Way of Death* (New York: Oxford University Press, 1977), pp. 53, 57, 65, 188–9.

6. George E. Day, *A Practical Treatise on the Domestic Management and Most Important Diseases of Advanced Life* (London: T. and W. Boone, 1849), p. 129.

7. Come Ferran, "Medicine of Senility and the Validity of Prolongation of Senility by Dosimetric Alkaloidotherapy," trans. E. M. Epstein, *The Alkaloidal Clinic*, 9, no. 1 (January, 1903), pp. 18–19.

8. Maclachlan, *A Practical Treatise on the Diseases and Infirmities of Advanced Life* (London: John Churchill & Sons, 1863), p. iv.

9. Richard Harrison Shryock, *Medicine and Society in America 1660–1860* (Ithaca, N.Y., and London: Cornell University Press, 1975), p. 96.

10. John Mason Good, *The Study of Medicine* (New York: Harper & Brother, 1835), p. 15.

11. Professor O'Connor, for example, chastised the clinicians for their failure to recognize climacteric disease because of their reliance on post-mortem findings. "It is," he wrote, "perhaps too much the custom to disregard the consideration of diseases not founded on pathological changes." O'Connor, "On Climacteric Changes," *The Dublin Journal of Medical Science*, 60, no. 42 (July, 1875), p. 78.

12. T. S. Clouston, *Clinical Lectures on Mental Disease* (Philadelphia: Henry C. Lea's Sons, 1884), p. 388.

13. See, for example, Day, *A Practical Treatise*, p. 66; C. M. Durrant, "On the Commencing Climacteric Period in the Male," *The British Medical Journal*, 2 (September, 1865), pp. 233–5; Good, *The Study of Medicine*, p.24; Sir R. Douglas Powell, "Advanced Life and Its Diseases," *The Hospital*, 4, no. 102 (February, 1909), p. 507; J. Madison Taylor, "The Conservation of Energy in Those Advancing Years," *The Popular Science Monthly*, 64 (March, 1904), p. 414; Van Oven, *On the Decline of Life*, pp.104–13; Wells, "The Medical Examiner," p. 133. Physicians believed that, in old age, both men and women were limited by their physiology. For a discussion of medical attitudes toward women, see Carroll Smith-Rosenberg, "Puberty to Menopause: The Cycle of Femininity in Nineteenth-Century America," in Clio's *Consciousness Raised*,

eds. Mary S. Hartmann and Lois Banner (New York: Harper & Row, 1974), pp. 23–7.

14. See, for example, Clouston, *Clinical Lectures*, pp. 388–92; Durrant, "Commencing Climacteric Period," p. 223; Kennedy, "Observations," p. 252; W. Bevan Lewis, "Insanity at the Puerperal, Climacteric and Lactational Periods," *Wood's Medical and Surgical Monographs*, 6 (1890), p. 331; Scott, "Old Age and Death," p. 119.

15. Lewis, "Insanity," p. 341.

16. Durrant, "Commencing Climacteric Period," p. 233.

17. Charles E. Rosenberg, "Sexuality, Class, and Role in Nineteenth-Century America," *American Quarterly*, 25, no. 2 (May, 1973), pp. 131–54; Carroll Smith Rosenberg and Charles E. Rosenberg, "The Female Animal: Medical and Biological Views of Women and Her Role in Nineteenth-Century America," *Journal of American History*, 60, no. 2 (September, 1973), p. 334.

18. Nascher, *Geriatrics: The Diseases of Old Age and their Treatment* (Philadelphia: P. Blakiston's Son & Co., 1914), pp. 6, 16. Charles Mercier believed that in old age man began to "take the feminine view in matters of justice that it would be cruel to punish the offender." Mercier, *Sanity and Insanity* (New York: Scribner & Welford, 1890), p. 309. See also Clouston, *Clinical Lectures*, p. 388; Maclachlan, *A Practical Treatise*, p. 5; Van Oven, *On the Decline of Life*, p. 41.

19. Henry Belfrage, *Discourses on the Duties and Consolations of the Aged* (London: Oliver & Bay, 1827); Joseph Lathrop, *The Infirmities and Comforts of Old Age: A Sermon to Aged People* (Springfield, Ill., Henry Brewer, 1805); John Reid, *The Philosophy of Death: General Medical and Statistical Treatise on the Nature and Cause of Human Mortality* (London: S. Highley, 1841). See also Thomas R. Cole, "Past Meridian: Aging and the Northern Middle Class" (unpublished Ph.D. diss., University of Rochester, 1980), pp. 100–2.

20. The concept of transitional stages was first developed by Arnold Van Gennep in 1909. He wrote:

> The life of an individual in any society is a series of passages from one age to another and from one occupation to another. Whenever there are fine distinctions among age or occupation groups, progression from one group to the next is accompanied by special acts, like those which make up apprenticeship in our trades.

The Rites of Passage, trans., Monika B. Vizedom and Gabrielle L. Caffee (Chicago: University of Chicago Press, 1960), pp. 2–3; see also Mary Douglas, *Purity and Danger* (New York: Praeger Publishers, 1970), pp. 115–18. Recently, historians have focused upon the importance of these transitional periods, especially in terms of adolescence. See Joseph Kett, *Rites of Passage: Adolescence in America 1790 to the Present* (New York: Basic Books, Inc., Publishers, 1977).

21. In addressing an audience of "ladies," Samuel Sheldon Fitch emphasized the important role women could play after menopause. "Although after the cessation of the months," he wrote:

> she cannot again give existence to another, yet she can enjoy the highest charms of society and social intercourse. She can guide the young and everywhere enliven and adorn, and instruct society, by the fervor of her affections to her family, the brilliance of her wit, the polish and charm of her accomplishments, and the generous diffusion of her knowledge and experience, resulting from the stores of her reading and the extent of her observations.

Six Lectures (New York: H. Carlisle, 1847), p. 199. In the mid-nineteenth century, a woman who attained the climacteric period of life was likely to have growing children in the home. Thus, her role as a mother and her domestic duties would continue undisturbed. See Robert V. Wells, "Demographic Change and the Life Cycle," in *The Family in History*, eds., Theodore K. Rabb and Robert I. Rotberg (New York: Harper & Row, 1971), pp. 85–94.

22. Charles Caldwell, *Thoughts on the Effects of Age on the Human Constitution* (Louisville, Ky.: John C. Noble, 1846), p. 14.

23. John Foster, "Old Age," *The Medical Press and Circular*, 27 (February, 1884), p. 203; see also Durrant, "Commencing Climacteric Period," p. 233.

24. Van Oven, *On the Decline of Life*, pp. 110–11.

25. "The weight of evidence," wrote W. H. Curtis, "seems to establish the fact that old age is never physiological, but always pathological, at least its visible and appreciable evidences are pathological ones." Curtis, "Disease in the Aged," *Illinois Medical Journal*, 10, no. 4 (October, 1906), p. 401; see also, as examples, Frederick N. Brown, "Some Observations upon Old Age and Its Consequences," *The Providence Medical Journal*, 10, no. 1 (January, 1909), p. 91; W. C. Bunce, "Some of the Influences that Determine Age," *The Ohio State Medical Journal*, no. 1, (April, 1906), p.

467; Goodno, "Senility, with especial reference to the Changes Developing in the Circulatory Organs, their exciting Causes, and Symptoms," Transactions of the Thirty-Third Session of the Homeopathic Medical Society of the State of Pennsylvania, 33rd issue (1897), p. 244; William Kinnear, "Postponing Old Age," *The Medical Age*, 17, no. 2 (January, 1899), p. 49; E. N. Leake, "At What Period of Life Does Old Age Begin?" *The Medical Examiner*, 6, no. 10 (October, 1896), p. 191; S. Newton Leo, "A Consideration of the Senile State and its Treatment," *New York Medical Journal*, 84, no. 25 (October, 1894), p. 757; Charles G. Stockton, "The Delay of Old Age and the Alleviation of Senility," *Buffalo Medical Journal*, 61, no. 1 (August, 1905), p. 3; Taylor, "Conservation of Energy," p. 407; William Gilman Thompson, *Practical Dietetics* (New York and London: D. Appleton & Co., 1906), p. 312.

26. Day, *A Practical Treatise*, p. 46.

27. H. C. Wood, "The Hygiene of Old Age," *The Therapeutic Gazette*, 2, no. 5 (May, 1886), p. 304.

28. Kinnear, "Postponing Old Age," p. 48.

29. Nascher wrote that "the old man is a poor subject for experimental therapy." He noted, in fact, that ten persons had died from Brown-Sequard's extract. "Treatment of Disease in Senility," *The Medical Council*, 15, no. 8 (August, 1910), p. 274.

30. Peter N. Stearns, *Old Age in European Society: The Case of France* (New York: Holmes & Meier, Publishers, Inc., 1976), p. 98.

31. Metchnikoff did admit two problems in this plan: (1) the removal of organs from dead bodies within twenty-four hours, and (2) deciding the correct dose. Elie Metchnikoff, *The Nature of Man*, (New York: G.P. Putnam's Sons, 1903), p. 246; Stearns, "Old Age in European Society", p. 98; Cole, "Past Meridian," 275–84.

32. Physicians rarely agreed on their prescriptions; therapeutics endorsed by some were often rejected by others. Sir Anthony Carlisle, *An Essay on the Disorders of Old Age and the Means of Prolonging Human Life* (Philadelphia: Edward Earle, 1819), p. 51, Maclachlan, *A Practical Treatise*, p. 42, and Canstatt, "Review of 'On the Diseases of Old Age and their Care,'" p. 111, favor bloodletting, whereas Day, *A Practical Treatise*, pp. 54–5, and Van Oven, *On the Decline of Life*, p. 165, oppose it. In the case of alkalis, Carlisle, *An Essay*, p. 48, J.M. Charcot and Alfred Loomis, *Clinical Lectures on the Diseases of Old Age*, (New York and William Wood and Co., 1881),

p. 160, and Ferran, "Medicine of Senility," p. 1192, favor them, whereas Day, *A Practical Treatise*, p. 57, opposes them. In the case of narcotics, Charcot, *Clinical Lectures*, p. 75, and Henry F. Walker, "Our Counsel to Patients, especially in the Later Part of Life," *Medical Record*, 53, no. 13 (March, 1898), p. 456, suggest them, whereas Day, *A Practical Treatise*, p. 59, disagrees. In the case of purgatives, Maclachlan, *A Practical Treatise*, p. 45, recommends them, whereas Day opposes them. In the case of diuretics, Maclachlan, p. 50, favors them, whereas Canstatt disagrees (cited by Maclachlan, p. 50). Within the same work, in fact, a physician often contradicted his own prescriptions. See, for example, Day on opiates, pp. 59, 129; on metals, pp. 57, 216–17.

33. Day, *A Practical Treatise*, p. 78; see also Charcot and Loomis, *Clinical Lectures*, pp. 194–5.

34. Clarence Bartlett, "Clinical Lectures on Diseases of Old Age," *The Hahnemannian Monthly*, 41 (February, 1906), p. 115.

35. According to I. L. Nascher, "In maturity nature cures; in senility, nature kills. In maturity, the physician tries to aid nature; in senility, he tries to thwart nature and retard the natural senile process which ends in death." "The Treatment of Diseases in Senility" p. 988; Day, *A Practical Treatise*, pp. 52–3.

36. In 1828, Noah Webster included "senility" in his dictionary, although the word did not appear in medical dictionaries. Webster noted that the term was "not much used." By the late nineteenth century, it had become a standard term in medical—and popular—terminology. W. Andrew Achenbaum, *Old Age in The New Land* (Baltimore: Johns Hopkins University Press, 1978), p. 31.

37. *Oxford English Dictionary*, (Oxford. Clarendon Press, 1961), p. 454.

38. Benjamin Rush, *Medical Inquiries and Observations* (Philadelphia: Thomas Dobson, 1797), pp. 308–10.

39. On brain lesions: Clouston, *Clinical Lectures*, p. 408; B. Furneaux Jordan, "Pathological and Clinical Notes with Especial Reference to Disease in the Aged," *The Birmingham Medical Review*, 32 (July, 1892), p. 7.

On starvation of tissue, Julius Althaus, "Old Age and Rejuvenescence," *The Lancet*, 1 (January, 1899), p. 150; Maclachlan, *A Practical Treatise*, p. 21.

On dying brain cells: Althaus, "Old Age and Rejuvenescence," p. 150; W. M. Gibson, "Some Considerations of Senescence," *New York State Journal of Medicine*, 9, no. 9 (September, 1909), p. 382; I. N. Love, "The Needs and Rights of Old Age," *Journal of the American Medical Association*, 29, no. 21 (November, 1897), p. 1038; W. H. B. Stoddart, *Mind and Its Disorders* (Philadelphia: P. Blakiston's Sons & Co. 1909), p. 340.

On arteriosclerosis: Louis Faugeres Bishop, "The Relation of Old Age to Disease, with Illustrative Cases," *The American Journal of Nursing*, 9, no. 9 (June, 1904), p. 677; E. C. Spitza, *Insanity: Its Classification, Diagnosis and Treatment* (New York: Bermingham & Co., 1883), p. 174; F. H. Stephenson, "Senility, Senile Dementia and their Medico-Legal Aspects," *Buffalo Medical Journal*, 40, no. 8 (March, 1901), p. 448.

On softening of the brain: Clouston, *Clinical Lectures*, p. 406; Stoddart, *Mind and Its Disorders*, p. 341.

On loss of the molecules' vitality: Henry Maudsley, *Responsibility in Mental Disease* (New York: D. Appleton & Co., 1874), pp. 259–60; Mercier, *Sanity and Insanity*, pp. 305-6.

40. Isaac Ray, *A Treatise on the Medical Jurisprudence of Insanity* (1838), ed., Winfred Overholse (Cambridge, Mass: Belknap Press, 1962), pp. 205–10; James Cowles Prichard, *Treatise on Insanity and Other Disorders affecting the Mind* (Philadelphia: Haswell, Barrington and Haswell, 1837),pp. 29–30.

41. Ray, *A Treatise*, p. 205.

42. Ibid.

43. Stoddart, *Mind and Its Disorders*, p. 340.

44. Canstatt termed this the "soul-life" "Review of 'On the Diseases of Old Age and their Care,' " p. 103; Caldwell, *Effects of Age*, p. 6; Henry Holland, *Medical Notes and Reflections* (Philadelphia: Haswell, Barrington and Haswell, 1839), p. 106.

45. Charles Segwick Minot, "On Certain Phenomena of Growing Old," *Proceedings of the American Association for the Advancement of Science*, 39 (August, 1890), p. 387; J. Montgomery Mosher, "Old Age," *Yale Medical Journal*, 15, no. 2 (October, 1908), pp. 49–59; Stoddart, *Mind and Its Disorders*, p. 341.

46. Mercier, *Sanity and Insanity*, p. 305.

47. Althaus, "Old Age and Rejuvenescence," pp. 150–1.

48. Maudsley, *Responsibility in Mental Disease*, p. 261; Mercier, *Sanity and Insanity*, pp. 307–8; Mosher, "Old Age," p. 55; Nascher, *Geriatrics*, p. 38; Spitza, *Insanity*, pp. 172–3.

49. Scott, "Old Age and Death," p. 119.

50. Case of Margaret Wall, December 24, 1908, Case Histories, 2:85, Philadelphia Orthopaedic Hospital Casebook located at the College of Physicians of Philadelphia.

51. H. Kellogg, *Plain Facts for Old and Young* (Burlington, Iowa: J. F. Seyner, 1877; reprint ed. New York: Arno Press, 1974), p. 385; see also Van Oven, *On the Decline of Life*, pp. 99–100.

52. Kellogg, *Plain Facts*, pp. 385, 388. Many physicians believed that the senile individual was unable to control his acts, despite the fact that he knew them to be improper. William N. Williams, who entered Philadelphia Orthopaedic Hospital in 1908, was a case in point. At age sixty-seven, he was discharged from work and, according to his case history, "was mentally disturbed as a result." His senile dementia took the form of sexual perversions. "He tampers with little girls and boys. Has been arrested for this; he was let go the next day. Says he knows this is wrong." Case of William N. Williams, June 18, 1908, Case Histories, Philadelphia Orthopaedic Hospital, vol. 2, pp. 67–8. Casebook kept at the College of Physicians of Philadelphia.

53. Allan McLane Hamilton, *A Manual of Medical Jurisprudence* (New York: Bermingham & Co., 1883), pp. 27–8.

54. Ibid., pp. 79–80; Francis Wharton, *A Monograph on Mental Unsoundness* (Philadelphia: Kay and Brother, 1855), p. 16.

55. Ray, *A Treatise*, pp. 211–13; Stephenson, "Senility, Senile Dementia," pp. 560–1.

56. Nichols, "Old Age," p. 522.

57. Nascher, *Geriatrics*, p. 489.

58. Clouston, *Clinical Lectures*, p. 395.

59. Many other physicians expressed similar opinions about the difficulties of treating the aged as patients. See, for example, Bishop, "Relation of Old Age to Disease," p. 676; Brown, "Some Observations," p. 90; Curtis, "Disease in the Aged," pp. 401–6; Clement Dukes, "The Restlessness of Old Age and Its Treatment," *The British Medical Journal*, 2 (December, 1899); p. 1542; J. H. Emerson, "A Group of Aged Patients," *Medical News*, 72, no. 7 (February, 1898), p. 204.

60. Bishop, "Relation of Old Age to Disease," p. 679.

Chapter 5
The Sexless Years or Sex Rediscovered

Benjamin Schlesinger

The preceding selection discussed the medicalization of old age and the belief that aging itself is a disease. A part of the medicalization of old age included the view that older people are incapable of sexual relations but prey to moral perversion. Current social expectations about sexuality in later life echo this nineteenth-century belief that sexuality ceases at a certain age such as 60 or 65 and certainly does not occur among octogenarians or nonagenarians! In the following selection, Benjamin Schlesinger examines myths about sexuality in later life, their relationship to the lack of social value accorded to the elderly, and impediments to sexual activity imposed both by cultural values and by rules in specific settings such as long-term care facilities. Because little attention has been given to sexuality in later life, health professionals have often ignored the sexual needs and behavior of the elderly. Based on what you discover as you read this selection and as you recall previous ones, think about the most effective intervention strategies to bridge the gap between current attitudes toward old age and appropriate recognition of older people's needs and desires, including sexuality. What sorts of training would you design and for whom? What kinds of interventions would you design for older people themselves?

Introduction

The subject of sex is no longer the mystery it used to be, but there exists a persistent belief that sex is not for the old. Old people have come to believe this themselves and often feel that their sexual lives are over, or that they are sexless after 50, 60, or whatever magical number they care to name. Birthday cards tend to prolong this myth by endless jokes about the loss of sexuality as one gets older (Weininger and Menkin, 1978).

Young people have always had difficulty imagining their parents as sexual beings. Even people in their 50s often have great difficulty imagining their own parents being sexual. You're too old for that, they often wisecrack. Our society appears to hold the notion that sexuality stops, severely declines, and/or is not as exciting as it used to be after a person reaches retirement. This attitude produces bad jokes—do old people do it or don't they?—and stems from a potpourri of societal myths and biases (Gordon and Snyder, 1989).

The sexual needs of the elderly are generally misunderstood, stereotyped, and/or ignored. Younger and healthier people tend to believe that sexual desire and activity normally cease with old age. Those elderly individuals who do show an interest in sexuality are regarded as moral perverts or liars. Thus, an honest look at what society expects of the older person is unsettling, because society expects grandparental, nonsexual, nonphysical beings sitting contentedly in rocking chairs while reviewing the past. Reality, however, reveals that this is only an illusion. Older people have physical, social, emotional and sexual needs just as do the rest of the population (Wasow and Loeb, 1977).

People often think of sexual intercourse as the only form of sexual activity. It is often forgotten that touching, holding, genital play, oral sex, and other intimate expressions all constitute human sexuality. Perhaps some older persons place less emphasis on erection, lubrication, or orgasm in favor of other sexual expressions. Does that make them less sexual?

In one instance, a cardiologist was discussing some impending heart surgery with his patient, a 78-year-old woman. He asked her how often she and her 80-year-old husband made love, and she replied, "Oh, we make love every day." The doctor was astonished! "Do you mean you and your husband have sex every day?" he asked. "I think you misunderstand," she answered. "We have sex about once a week, but we make love every day."

The Stereotypes

Since our current societal expectation is that sexual desire declines with age, any older person exhibiting sexual interest, let alone actual behavior, is labeled as aberrant. "Dirty old man" and "old fool" are two labels representing society's dislike for sexual behavior among the elderly usually applied to men. It is even harder for society to accept older women having an interest in sex. Elderly women are usually the focus of labels which describe declining physical appearance as opposed to sexual behavior, for example, "old hag" or "old biddy." For both genders, maintaining an interest in sex is considered evidence of a desire to remain young.

Though women are under less pressure to perform sexually, they remain under constant pressure to remain forever young and sexually attractive; those who do not are often dismissed as undesirable sex partners.

These attitudes have come from a number of sources. The Victorian ethic of being productive as an integral part of the equation of worth has made us see old people as generally valueless. Then, our own fears of growing old lead to stereotyping to create distance between "us" and "them." Furthermore, general misinformation about sexuality leads to ignorance, disguised by silence (Gochros, Gochros, and Fischer, 1986).

In our society romantic love is equated to intense physical love. Its only appropriate sexual expression is characterized by passionate love-making and the achievement of sexual union through simultaneous orgasm. Neither older people nor younger ones can consistently measure up to these expectations, and thus the belief is fostered that "real" sexual pleasure is only for a privileged few.

Despite the substantial portion of older people constituting 12 percent of our population in Canada, little is heard about the sexual needs of this age group.

Every medical study conducted during recent years indicates, however, that there is no physiological reason why older men and women in reasonably good health should not have an active and satisfying sex life. Our culture continues to foster the belief that by the time one is in his or her sixties, sex is neither necessary nor possible; or if it does occur, it is somehow not quite normal, and certainly not nice.

The task today is to break through myths, taboos and misconceptions to give recognition to the reality, the beauty, the problems and the pains of sex in the later years so that we can exercise our legitimate rights as sexual beings and help our senior citizens to do the same (Schlesinger, 1983).

Myths About Sexuality and Aging

Myths regarding sexuality and the elderly have been categorized in a number of different ways. There are five myths: (a) elderly people do not have sexual desires; (b) elderly people are not able to make love, even if they wanted to; (c) elderly people are too fragile and might hurt themselves if they attempt to engage in sexual relationships; (d) elderly people are physically unattractive and therefore sexually undesirable (particularly true for elderly women); and (e) the notion of older people engaging in sex is shameful and perverse. The myths are perpetuated: when society believes that sex is only for procreative purposes; by the fear of imagining parents' engaging in sex; and by the fear of growing old and the loss of one's own sexual abilities.

Hotvedt (1983: 14) summarizes the myths as follows:

In the absence of knowledge, we call upon our folklore about sexuality in the later years. Three repeated themes in these myths stand out:

1. In the later years, we are not sexually desirable.

2. In the later years, we are not sexually desirous.

3. In the later life, we are not sexually capable.

Active Sex Life and Aging

Masters and Johnson (1966) consider their findings in this area to be their single most important piece of research. They have set out two fundamental constants for active enjoyable sex in the later years.

1. The individual must be in a reasonably good state of general health.

2. He or she must have an interested and interesting partner.

Sexually, the male and female can function effectively into their 80s, if they can understand that certain physiological changes will occur and if they don't let these changes frighten them. Once they allow themselves to think they will lose their sexual effectiveness, then, for all practical purposes they will, indeed, lose it, but only because they have become victims of the myth, not because their bodies will have lost the capacity to perform. Masters and Johnson coined the phrase "If you don't use it you lose it."

Elderly Men and Sexual Intercourse

A healthy man should be able to have intercourse at any age, though many do not. Why? The main reason is fear—fear of impotency and the ensuing self-devaluation. The origin of this fear is found in older men's proneness to feelings of depression and unworthiness induced by their altered life circumstances; these feelings have a definite negative effect on male potency. A lack of self-confidence, caused in part by the absence of fairly regular sex habits, is also blamed for impotency (Long, 1976).

Ignorance, in many cases, compounds fear. For example, men who do not realize that more time is required to achieve an erection may become panicky and refrain from further attempts at intercourse. It is also not widely known that an older male may have an orgasm without ejaculating; knowledge and acceptance of this fact would ease the minds of couples who have had this experience. Lack of knowledge perpetuates the current myth that men who engaged in a high level of sexual activity most of their lives can expect to be "burned out" at a rather early age. This was proven false. The nature and interest in sexuality remains fairly constant during the life cycle.

Elderly Women and Sexuality

Women, of course, as the sexual partners, are also greatly affected by the doubts and fallacies prevalent among men. In addition, a pervasive belief of our present generation of older women is that sex is somehow "dirty" and not to be enjoyed or needed. This belief is often Biblically founded, and, though somewhat dependent on individual background, is traditional in Western culture. Researchers have observed that many women lose their desire for sex after menopause, when they are no longer fertile, because sex is linked in their minds with the Biblical injunction to "be fruitful and multiply." The negative feelings, loss of self-worth, and a nagging fear of immorality, would seem to be mutually reinforcing.

Women with broader, more liberal backgrounds, have a different set of psychological factors influencing their sexual relationships. A very important one is derived from their past experiencing of orgasm. Females who had a regular, active sex life and achieved orgasm 99 percent of the time, continued to anticipate and desire this satisfaction (Long, 1976; Visano-Neugebauer, 1995).

The Sexual Changes

Sexual changes are not as dramatic as was once assumed and do not necessarily have an effect on an individual's desire for sexual activity or potential for sexual satisfaction. Nor do they imply the onset of impotence. Also, these changes may affect some people more than others. They may occur at different ages in different individuals (Gordon and Snyder, 1989:151).

Men often notice the following changes:

- It may take longer to achieve an erection.
- The erection may be less hard.
- The ability to delay ejaculation increases.
- Release of semen may be less forceful.
- A second erection may be possible only after a longer period of time.

Some changes occur in women as well:

- Thinning of the vaginal walls can cause irritation during intercourse.

- Less vaginal lubrication can make intercourse uncomfortable.
- A longer time may be required to become excited.
- Orgasm may be shorter or less intense than previously.

Sexuality and Institutional Life

Only a small fraction of Canadians over the age of 65 reside in institutions for the elderly. . . . Research which employs findings derived from relatively independent elders living in the community is not easily transferred to those residing in institutions (Dionne, 1985). Studies about the aged which have been made outside of long-term care facilities cannot be indicative of life in such institutions. For the most part, problems of sexual expression experienced by the aged population in general are greatly amplified for nursing home residents (Schlesinger, 1983).

The essential factors which differentiate institutional and noninstitutional life in terms of the elderly are dependency and control. For the most part, the nursing home resident has much less control over his own life than elderly citizens living in the community. This institutional control extends from the regulation of times and types of meals to the physical layout and furnishing of buildings.

Regardless of the philosophy exuded by institutions in terms of sex and the elderly, restrictions in sexual activity are in many cases influenced by the physical environment of most long-term care facilities. Privacy is a major problem in the institution. In Canada many nursing homes segregate men from women, separating husbands and wives. Single rooms are infrequent in older nursing homes and door locks are generally forbidden. Open spaces designed for large gatherings and easier care are prevalent with private niches being the exception. Ward care remains popular wherein sliding curtains between beds represent the maximum available form of privacy. For reasons related to safety, nursing home personnel have access to all areas; as a result, privacy becomes impossible. Interruptions are guaranteed. Despite a number of studies which indicate that many institutionalized elderly are interested in sex and most nursing home personnel are generally accepting of sexuality among the aged, some authors suggest that there is likely a difference between staff attitudes and actions (Kassel, 1983). In many cases, elderly institutionalized persons become the victims of staff value judgements on morality, religious values and sexuality (Kassel, 1983). In this way natural feelings of sexuality are suppressed, resulting in feelings of guilt and anxiety.

The issue of sex in institutions for the elderly is also compounded by the attitudes of many family members of residents and patients. Children are generally unable to handle thoughts of their parents' sexuality. Having dismissed this disturbing topic from their minds when they reached adulthood, they are unwilling to reactivate the anxieties the subject kindles in them. Frequently they even discourage an enlightened administrator from making any kind of sexual release available to the elderly. In some homes where a room was set aside for privacy, families complained that males might attack their mothers, that the home was experimenting with their parents or that such a room was physically dangerous since it was not immediately supervised (McKinley and Drew, 1977).

For many elderly residents of long-term care facilities, sexual frustration becomes outwardly manifested in the form of masturbation, fantasizing and the demand from staff for back rubs, enemas and other physical contact which represent an attempt to replace or supplement the severely limited physical contact available in such institutions. In many cases these alternate forms of gratification also result in feelings of guilt and shame. Steffl (1978) lists a number of special considerations which can serve to alleviate some of the sexual and emotional needs of institutionalized elderly.

1. We must be aware of the isolation and sensory deprivation.

2. We need more touch for social reasons: hugging, kissing, hand-holding, massage.

3. Build sexuality into (rather than separate) spiritual and emotional well-being.

4. Remember that all meaningful sexual relationships may not be heterosexual. Can we be helpful instead of punishing?

5. Accept and allow masturbation instead of punishing. (Look at the consequences of censure and punishment.)

6. Provide touching and feeling things to handle, fondle, and hold.

7. Live pets provide great sensory stimulation.

8. Provide music: romantic, sentimental, sensuous and erotic.

9. Encourage opportunities for sexes to meet, mingle and spend time together, but do not structure the time or place too rigidly.

Professionals in Institutions

Professionals working with the aged, be they medical personnel, social workers, aides, or whatever, need a better understanding of human sexuality in order to be able to effectively bring about positive changes in institutional policy regarding the sexuality of nursing-home residents. Myths need to be replaced with facts, with professionals feeling more comfortable with their own sexuality. They need to view sexuality in the aged as a good thing rather than something to be eliminated. Indeed, sex counselling services both inside and outside nursing homes should be equipped to provide information that can alleviate some of the normal concerns of the elderly regarding their own sexual functioning.

If some of the elderly have to live in nursing homes, we must be responsible for structuring an environment which doesn't add to the special problems of the aging process. At present, most homes for the aged assume that the elderly are sexless: there are no provisions for privacy, men and women are segregated, conjugal visits are seldom provided for, and nursing-home staff become anxious when confronted with any expression of sexuality by the residents. Their being aged and dying is not sufficient reason to deny to them what joys of affection and sensuality are possible (Wasow and Loeb, 1977).

Interventions by Health Professionals

Positive interventions by health professionals should be based on acceptance of sexual activity in the aging client. Sexuality should be viewed as a birth to death phenomenon. Just as health care providers assist the elderly to walk, eat, exercise and have regular bowel movements, so too should they assist them to be sexual human beings. For the institutionalized elderly, the following strategies are suggested (Osis, 1985: 7):

1. Create an atmosphere that encourages the discussion of sexual feelings.

2. Use group discussions to explore staff's attitudes.

3. Educate staff and residents with factual information.

4. Include sexual data in assessments.

5. Discuss body image changes.

6. Discuss the loss of a partner.

7. Accept masturbation.

8. Provide privacy and time alone for couples.

9. Personalize each individual with jewellery, clothing and after shave lotion.

10. Monitor the effects of drugs and use medications judiciously.

11. Choose behavioral management for behavioral problems whenever possible.

Homosexuality and Aging

Older homosexual adults are perhaps the most neglected and misunderstood group of individuals over 65. Very little sexuality research is available regarding their unique experiences and challenges. About 10 percent of men and women over 65 are homosexual. These individuals, representing older adults from the present cohort, have already endured considerable discrimination and ostracism during a cultural era marked by very negative views about homosexuality and lesbianism. As older adults in homosexual relationships, their potential difficulties are intensified. When one partner becomes disabled, older homosexual couples are faced with complicated and discriminatory practices regarding guardianship and power of attorney. While privacy for heterosexually married couples is too seldom provided in the nursing home, private space for lesbian or gay couples is strictly forbidden. Finally, nursing home staff, reacting to their own fears and discomfort, may be reluctant to deal closely with the homosexual resident; quality of nursing care may be affected as a consequence (Malatesta, 1989).

Selected Facts About Sexuality and Aging

Some of the following sources report varied facts and results of studies related to sexuality and aging.

- People 65 and older are often having as much sex, and in some cases more than people aged 18 to 26 (*The Janus Report on Sexual Behavior*, 1993).
- Elderly people in Sweden who are sexually active have more vitality and better memories than celibate counterparts (*Toronto Star*, Oct 11, 1986).
- A study by Dr. J. A. Silcox, of the University of Western Ontario, examined 800 professional men over 65. The findings revealed that 75 percent had sexual intercourse regularly, and clergymen were the most sexually active (*Toronto Star*, May 6, 1975).
- Most older gays and lesbians prefer to associate with peers of a similar age and have active sex lives with age-appropriate partners (Berger, 1982).
- Many diseases associated with aging may directly affect sexual performance through physical changes or indirectly affect it by negative effects of drug therapy aimed at the primary problem (Osis, 1985).
- About half of both men and women over 65 say their interest in sex is less than when they were young. Women are more interested in "sitting next to someone and talking" and "saying or hearing verbal endearments" than men (Johnson, 1988).

- Four-tenths of the women and half of the men in their 60s masturbate. Two-thirds of the women are sexually active; half or more have sex at least once a week (Brecher, 1984).
- In old age, ignorance of facts surrounding sex is the greatest single deterrent to the active enjoyment of sexuality (Masters and Johnson, 1966).
- While some women report a clear decrease in sexual desire, many women actually feel an increase in erotic appetite during the menopausal years (Hite, 1976).

Research on Aging and Sexuality

Many investigators are either uninterested in the sexuality of older people or are uncomfortable with the idea that old people are sexual. More often than not, the elderly have been excluded from their focus of investigation. Additionally, many older people themselves, or their relatives, seem to be uncomfortable with sex research. It had been seen in one study that even when elderly people volunteered to participate in sex research studies, their relatives often became upset and insisted they withdraw.

Objective and valid information regarding sexual experience is difficult to obtain for other reasons too. Most sex research, but not all, is based on interviews or questionnaires. The honesty or correctness of the answers is unknown. Some elderly male respondents have been known to deny their disinterest or inability in sexual intercourse and have reported feats of virility instead. Others may be reluctant to disclose their thoughts and behaviors. Although this is not sufficient to negate interview methods, it is important to warrant cross-validation by interviews with partners, when possible. In other words, a serious problem of much of the research is its unknown or uncertain validity, as well as its uncertain generalizability (Botwinick, 1985).

Conclusions and Reflections

The maintenance of a satisfying intimate relationship is closely associated with mental health and vitality throughout the life span.

Because many elderly people have lost their partners, sexual outlets are denied to them. Men find replacing intimate partners easier to do than women since the number of elderly women exceeds that of elderly men. In addition, elderly women are denied the cultural prerogative of men to socialize with younger members of the opposite sex.

It's essential for everyone, parents, children and older persons themselves, to accept the proposition that human beings remain sexual throughout their adult lives. Even after age 75, when we notice significant decreases in sexual activity, intimacy and sexual involvement are desired. Closeness to another human being becomes an important link to life.

Positive Aspects of Sexuality and Aging

Butler and Lewis (1973) suggest a number of functional and positive results of sexuality in later years including:

1. The opportunity for expression of passion, affection, admiration, loyalty, and other positive emotions.

2. An affirmation of one's body and its functions—reassurance that our bodies are still capable of working well and providing pleasure.

3. A way of maintaining a strong sense of self-identity, enhancing self-esteem, and feeling valued as a person.

4. A means of self-assertion—an outlet for expressing oneself when other outlets for doing so have been lost.

5. Protection from anxiety as "the intimacy and the closeness of sexual union bring security and significance to people's lives, particularly when the outside world threatens them with hazards and losses."

6. Defiance of stereotypes of aging.

7. The pleasure of being touched and caressed.

8. A sense of romance.

9. An affirmation of a life that has been worthwhile because of the quality of intimate relationships that have been developed.

10. An avenue for continued sensual growth and experience.

One of the most humanitarian services professionals in the health, social work and religious fields can provide is to help families and institutions realize their great opportunity and privilege to reclaim the older person's right to be a sexual human being.

As we approach the twenty-first century, we believe that sexuality has been rediscovered by our senior citizens. Botwinick (1985: 92) pointed this out when he stated:

> The sexual revolution is not only a revolution of the young, but of many elderly people as well.

The last word is left to a senior in her eighties (Reti, 1995: 215).

> Even though our bodies are older, we may move a bit slower, and our bodies don't function as efficiently as they did when we were young, even during lovemaking, not everything has changed. The longing to belong with somebody, to love somebody, to have somebody, and to feel the touch of somebody near us remain equally young, fresh and intact as always. The need for love and intimacy does not change as we get older. Even when our physical capacity for sex wanes slightly, we still have overwhelming feelings of desire, passion and love. As a person in her eighties, I remind everyone of the importance of feeling—with your heart, body and mind. My feelings won't disappear when I turn ninety as they didn't evaporate when I turned eighty or seventy or sixty.

Discussion Questions

1. What are some common myths about sexuality in later life and how do these myths affect men? Do they affect women in the same way?

2. The author proposes interventions that would enable older adults to express their sexuality in long-term care settings. What barriers to sexual expression exist in these settings, and how might they be overcome?

3. What impediments to sexual expression exist for older gay and lesbian adults, both in the community and in long-term care settings?

References

Berger, R. M. (1982). *Gay and Gray*. Urbana, IL: University of Illinois Press.

Botwinick, J. (1995). *Aging and Behavior*. New York: Springer Publishing Co.

Brecher, E. M. (1984). *Love, Sex and Aging*. New York: Little, Brown & Co.

Butler, R. and Lewis (1973). *Aging and Mental Health, Positive Psychosocial Approach*. St. Louis: C.V. Mosby.

Dionne, R. G. (1985). Sexuality and the Aged. Unpublished paper, Toronto: Faculty of Social Work, University of Toronto.

Gochros, H. L., Gochros, J. S. and Fischer, J. (Eds.) (1986). *Helping the Sexually Oppressed*. Englewood Cliffs, NJ: Prentice Hall.

Gordon., S. and Snyder, C. W. (1989). *Personal Issues in Human Sexuality*. Boston: Allyn & Beacon.

Hite, S. (1976). *The Hite Report*. New York: Macmillan.

Hotvedt, M. (1983). The Cross-Cultural and Historical Context. In R. B. Weg (Ed.) *Sexuality in the Later Years* (pp. 13–39). New York: Academic Press.

Janus, S. and Janus, C. (1993). *The Janus Report on Sexual Behavior*. New York: Harper.

Johnson, B. (1988). Still Sexy After All These Years. *Modern Maturity*, February-March, II.

Kassel, V. (1983). *Long-term Care Institutions*. New York: Academic Press, 1983.

Long, I. (1976). Human Sexuality and Aging. *Social Casework*, 57 (4), 237–244.

Malatesta, V. J. (1989). Sexuality and the Older Adult: An Overview with Guidelines for the Health Care Professional. *Journal of Women & Aging*, 1 (4), 93–118.

Masters, W. H. and Johnson, V. E. (1966). *Human Sexual Response*. Boston: Little, Brown.

McKinley, H. and Drew, B. (1977). The Nursing Home: Death of Sexual Expression. *Health and Social Work*, 2, 180–187.

Osis, M. (1985). Sexuality an International Perspective. *Gerontion*, No. 6, 6–8.

Reti, L. (1995). Golden Age and Love: An Insider's Report. In R. Neugebauer-Visano (Ed.) *Seniors and Sexuality: Experiencing Intimacy in Later Life* (pp. 215–216). Toronto: Canadian Scholars' Press.

Schlesinger, B. (1983). Institutional Life: The Canadian Experience. In R. B. Weg (Ed.) *Sexuality in the Later Years* (pp. 259–270). New York: Academic Press.

Steffl, B. M. (1978). *Sexuality and Aging: Implications for Nurses and Other Helping Professionals*. Los Angeles: The University of Southern California Press.

Toronto Star. Sweden's Seniors and Sexual Behaviour, Oct. 11, 1986.

Toronto Star. Seniors, Sexuality and Professional Backgrounds, May 6, 1995.

Visano-Neugebauer (Ed.) (1995). *Seniors and Sexuality,: Experiencing Intimacy in Later Life*. Toronto: Canadian Scholars' Press.

Wasow, M. and Loeb, M. B. (1977). The Aged. In H. L. Gochros and J. S. Gochros (Eds.) *The Sexually Oppressed* (pp. 54–70). New York: Association Press.

Weininger, B. and Menkin, E. L. (1978). *Aging Is a Lifelong Affair*. Los Angeles: The Guild of Tutors Press.

Chapter 6
The Age Boom

Jack Rosenthal

The transformation of old age into a new period of life emerges as a theme in the next selection. According to population estimates, of all the people who ever lived to age 60 or older in the world's recorded history, two-thirds are alive today. Although the size of the world's older population has been gradually increasing for centuries, what is new is the rapid rate of its growth. By 1996, those aged 60 or older numbered 550 million, and by 2025 they are expected to account for 1.2 billion people. As a result of declines in the number of births, the older population in most developed nations is growing faster than the population as a whole. This historical shift from populations with many young and few old people is often described as a "demographic transition." The term describes a gradual process in which a society moves from high birth and death rates to one of low rates. This transition has occurred as a result of several factors: public health measures that reduce disease and improve living conditions, reduction in infectious diseases, better nutrition, and medical advances. The dramatic growth both of proportions and numbers of people who can expect to live longer and healthier lives than most of their parents, grandparents, or great-grandparents, raises questions about appropriate roles in old age.

Just when is one "old" and what does "being old" mean today? In the United States, public policies have traditionally designated people age 65 as officially "old" and thus entitled to certain benefits such as Medicare and Social Security. As more and more people live longer, new lifestyles and challenges to the stereotypes about later life or old age have developed among this segment of the population. As you read the following selection, make a list of the major changes that have occurred for millions of older adults, for their children, and for

American society as a whole. Think about what features of life do and do not change in old age.

When my father died at 67, leaving my mother alone in Portland, Ore., I thought almost automatically that she should come home with me to New York. Considering her heavy Lithuanian accent and how she shrank from dealing with authority, I thought she'd surely need help getting along. "Are you kidding?" she exclaimed. Managing her affairs became her work and her pride, and it soon occurred to me that this was the first time that she, traditional wife, had ever experienced autonomy. Every few days she would make her rounds to the bank, the doctor, the class in calligraphy. Then, in her personal brand of English, she would make her telephone rounds. She would complain that waiting for her pension check was "like sitting on pins and noodles" or entreat her granddaughter to stop spending money "like a drunken driver." Proudly, stubbornly, she managed on her own for 18 years. And even then, at 83, frustrated by strokes and angry at the very thought of a nursing home, she refused to eat. In days, she made herself die.

Reflecting on those last days, I realize that the striking thing was not her death but those 18 years of later life. For almost all that time, she had the health and the modest income to live on her own terms. She could travel if she chose, or send birthday checks to family members, or buy yet another pair of shoes. A woman who had been swept by the waves of two world wars from continent to continent to continent—who had experienced some of this century's worst aspects—came to typify one of its best. I began to understand finally what people around America are coming to understand: the transformation of old age. We are discovering the emergence of a new stage of life.

The transformation begins with longer life. Increased longevity is one of the striking developments of the century; it has grown more in the last 100 years than in the prior 5,000, since the Bronze Age. But it's easy to misconstrue. What's new is not the number of years people live; it's the number of people who live them. Science hasn't lengthened life, says Dr.

Robert Butler, a pioneering authority on aging. It has enabled many more people to reach very old age. And at this moment in history, to say "many more people" is an understatement. The baby boom generation is about to turn into an age boom.

Still, there's an even larger story rumbling here, and longevity and boomers tell only part of it. The enduring anguish of many elders lays continuing claim on our conscience. But as my mother's last 13 years attest, older adults are not only living longer; generally speaking they're living better—in reasonably good health and with enough money to escape the anxiety and poverty long associated with aging.

Shakespeare perceived seven ages of man—mewling infant, whining schoolboy, sighing lover, quarrelsome soldier, bearded justice, spectacled wheezer and finally second childhood, "sans teeth, sans eyes, sans taste, sans everything." . . .

Longer Life

In 1900, life expectancy at birth in America was 49. Today, it is 76, and people who have reached 55 can expect to live into their 80's. Improved nutrition and modern medical miracles sound like obvious explanations. But a noted demographer, Samuel Preston of the University of Pennsylvania, has just published a paper in which he contends that, at least until mid-century, the principal reason was neither. It was what he calls the "germ theory of disease" that generated personal health reforms like washing hands, protecting food from flies, isolating sick children, boiling bottles and milk and ventilating rooms. Since 1950, he argues likewise, the continuing longevity gains derive less from Big Medicine than from changes in personal behavior, like stopping smoking.

The rapid increase in longevity is now about to be magnified. The baby boom generation born between 1946 and 1964 has always bulged out—population peristalsis—like a pig in a python. Twice as many Americans were born in 1955 as in 1935. Between now and the year 2030, the proportion of people over 65 will almost double. In short, more old people. And there's a parallel fact now starting to reverberate around the world: fewer young people. An aging population inescapably results when younger couples bear fewer children—which is what they are doing almost everywhere.

The fertility news is particularly striking in developed countries. To maintain a stable population size, the necessary replacement rate is 2.1 children per couple. The United States figure is barely 2.0, and it has been below the replacement rate for 30 years. The figure in China is 1.8. Couples in Japan are typically having 1.5 children, in Germany 1.3 and in Italy and Spain, 1.2.

To some people, these are alarming portents of national decline and call for pronatalist policies. That smacks of coarse chauvinism. The challenge is not to dilute the number of older people by promoting more births. It is to improve the quality of life at all ages, and a good place to start is to conquer misconceptions about later life.

Better Health

"This," Gloria Steinem once said famously, "is what 40 looks like." And this, many older adults now say, is what 60, 70 and even 80 look like. Health and vitality are constantly improving, as a result of more exercise, better medicine and much better prevention. I can't imagine my late father in a sweatsuit, let alone on a Stairmaster, but when I look into the mirrored halls of a health-club gym on upper Broadway I see, among the intent young women in black leotards, white-haired men who are every bit as earnest, climbing, climbing, climbing. . . .

That people are living healthier lives is evident from the work of Kenneth G. Manton and his colleagues at Duke's Center for Demographic Studies. The National Long-Term Care Survey they started in 1982 shows a steady decline in disability, a 15 percent drop in 12 years. Some of this progress derives from advances in medicine. For instance, estrogen supplements substantially relieve bone weakness in older women—and now seem effective also against other diseases. But much of the progress may also derive from advances in perception.

When Clare Friedman, the mother of a New York lawyer, observed her 80th birthday, she said to her son, "You know, Steve, I'm not middle-aged anymore." It's no joke. Manton recalls survey research in which people over 50 are asked when old age begins. Typically, they, too, say "80." Traditionally, spirited older adults have been urged to act their age. But what age is that in this era of 80-year-old marathoners and 90-year-old ice skaters? As Manton says, "We no longer need to accept loss of physical function as an inevitable consequence of aging." To act younger is, in a very real sense, to be younger.

Stirring evidence of that comes from a 1994 research project in which high-resistance strength training was given to 100 frail nursing-home residents in Boston, median age 87 and some as old as 98. Dr. Maria Fiatarone of Tufts University and her fellow researchers found that after 10 weeks of leg-extension exercises, participants typically doubled the strength of the quadriceps, the major thigh muscle. For many, that meant they could walk, or walk without shuffling; the implications for reduced falls are obvious. Consider what this single change—enabling many, for instance, to go to the bathroom alone—means to the quality and dignity of their lives.

Just as old does not necessarily mean feeble, older does not necessarily mean sicker. Harry Moody, executive director of Hunter College's Brookdale Center on Aging, makes a telling distinction between the "wellderly" and the "illderly." Yes, one in every three people over 65 needs some kind of hospital care in any given year. But only one in 20 needs nursing-home care at any given time. That is, 95 percent of people over 65 continue to live in the community.

Greater Security

The very words "poor" and "old" glide easily together, just as "poverty" and "age" have kept sad company through history. But, suddenly that's changing. In the mid-1960s, when Medicare began, the poverty rate among elders was 29 percent, nearly three times the rate of the rest of the population. Now it is 11 percent, if anything a little below the rate for everyone else. That still leaves five million old people struggling below the poverty line, many of them women. And not many of the other 30 million elders are free of anxiety or free to indulge themselves in luxury. Yet most are, literally, socially secure, able to taste pleasures like travel and education that they may have denied themselves during decades of work. Indeed, many find this to be the time of their lives.

Elderhostel offers a striking illustration. This program, begun in 1975, combines inexpensive travel with courses in an array of subjects and cultures. It started as a summer program with 220 participants at six New Hampshire colleges. Last year, it enrolled 323,000 participants at sites in every state and in 70 foreign countries. Older Americans already exercise formidable electoral force, given how many of them vote. With the age boom bearing down, that influence is growing. As a result, minutemen like the investment banker Peter G. Peterson are sounding alarms about the impending explosion in Social Security and Medicare costs. Others regard such alarms as merely alarmist; either way a result is a spirited public debate. . . .

Politicians respect the electoral power of the senior vote; why is the economic power of older adults not understood? Television networks and advertisers remain oddly blind to this market, says Vicki Thomas of Thomas & Partners, a Westport, Conn., firm specializing in the "mature market." One reason is probably the youth of copywriters and media buyers. Another is advertisers' desire to identify with imagery that is young, hip, cool. Yet she cites a stream of survey data showing that householders 45 and over buy half of all new cars and trucks, that those 55 and over buy almost a third of the total and that people over 50 take 163 million trips a year and a third of all overseas packaged tours.

How much silver there is in this "silver market" . . . is also evident from *Modern Maturity* magazine, published by the American Association of Retired Persons. Its bimonthly circulation is more than 20 million; a full-page ad costs $244,000.

All this spending by older adults may not please everyone. Andrew Hacker, the Queens College political scientist, observes that the longer the parents live, the less they're likely to leave to the children—and the longer the wait. He reports spotting a bumper sticker to that effect, on a passing Winnebago: "I'm Spending My Kids' Inheritance!" Even so, the net effect of generational income transfers remains highly favorable to the next generation. For one thing, every dollar the public spends to support older adults is a dollar that their children won't be called on to spend. For another, older adults sooner or later engage in some pretty sizable income transfers of their own. As Hacker observes, the baby boomers' children may have to wait for their legacies, but their ultimate inheritances will constitute the largest income transfer to any generation ever.

Longer years, better health, comparative security: this new stage of life emerges more clearly every day. What's less clear is how older adults will spend it. The other stages of life are bounded by expectations and institutions. We start life in the institution called family. That's soon augmented for 15 or 20 years by school, tightly organized by age, subject and social webs. Then follows the still-more-structured world of work, for 40 or 50 years. And then —fanfare!—what? What institutions then give shape and meaning to everyday life?

Some people are satisfied, as my mother was, by managing their finances, by tending to family relationships and by prayer, worship and hobbies. Others, more restless, will invent new institutions, just as they did in Cleveland in the 1950s with Golden Age Clubs, or in the 1970s with Elderhostel. For the moment, institutions that figure most heavily for older adults are precisely those that govern the other stages of life—family, school and work.

Family. The focus on family often arises out of necessity. In a world of divorce and working parents, grandparents are raising 3.4 million children; six million families depend on grandparents for primary child care. And that's only one of the intensified relationships arising among the generations. Children have many more years to relate to their parents as adults, as equals, as friends. . . .

School. Increasingly, many elders go back to school, to get the education they've always longed for, or to learn new skills—or for the sheer joy of learning. Nearly half a million people over 50 have gone back to school at the college level, giving a senior cast to junior colleges; adults over age 40 now account for about 15 percent of all college students. The 92d Street Y in New York has sponsored activities for seniors since 1874. Suddenly, it finds, many "New Age seniors" want to do more than play cards or float in the pool. They are signing up by the score for classes on, for instance, Greece and Rome. At a senior center in Westport, Conn., older adults, far from being averse to technology, flock to computer classes and find satisfaction in manning their finances and traversing the Internet.

Work. American attitudes toward retirement have never been simple. The justifications include a humane belief that retirees have earned their rest; or a bottom-line argument that employers need cheaper workers; or a theoretical contention that a healthy economy needs to make room for younger workers. In any case, scholars find a notable trend toward early retirement, arguably in response to pension and Social Security incentives. Two out of three men on Social Security retire before age 65. One explanation is that they are likely to have spent their lives on a boring assembly line or in debilitating service jobs. Others, typically from more fulfilling professional work, retire gradually, continuing to work part time or to find engagement in serious volunteer effort. In Florida, many schools, hospitals and local governments have come to depend on elders who volunteer their skills and time.

Family, School, Work, and Institutions yet to Come. These are the framework for the evolving new stage of later life. But even if happy and healthy, it only precedes and does not replace the last of Shakespeare's age of mankind. One need not be 80 or 90 to understand that there comes a time to be tired, or sick, or caught up by the deeply rooted desire to reflect on the meaning of one's life. For many people, there comes a moment when the proud desire for independence turns into frank, mutual acknowledgment of dependence. As the Boston University sociologist Alan Wolfe wrote in The New Republic in 1995, "We owe [our elders] the courage to acknowledge their dependence on us. Only then will we be able, when we are like them, to ask for help."

That time will come, as it always has, for each of us—as children and then as parents. But it will come later. The new challenge is to explore the broad terrain of longer, fuller life with intelligence and respect. One such explorer, a woman named Florida Scott-Maxwell, reported her findings in "The Measure of My Days," a diary she began in her 80's. "Age puzzles me," she wrote, expressing sentiments that my mother personified. "I thought it was a quiet time. My 70's were interesting and fairly serene, but my 80's are passionate. I grow more intense as I age. To my surprise I burst out with hot conviction. . . . I must calm down."

Discussion Questions

1. What are the major population changes that are occurring in developed nations such as the United States?

2. What changes in health may be due to "advances in perception" as well as to declines in disability?

3. What beliefs about the older population does the bumper sticker statement "I'm spending my kids' inheritance" convey? Is this belief justified by the evidence presented in this article?

4. What are the major social institutions in which older adults are involved and how do they differ from those in which younger people engage? Are any new social institutions needed in later life?

5. How do you see yourself at 80?

Reprinted from: Jack Rosenthal, "The Age Boom." In *New York Times Magazine*, March 9. Copyright © 1997 by the *New York Times*. Reprinted by permission.

Chapter 7
The Process of Successful Aging

*Margret M. Baltes and
Laura L. Carstensen*

*Previous readings in this section examine
views of later life from various historical and
cultural perspectives. A common thread in
these articles has been the cultural constraints
placed upon older people and possible ways to
negotiate old age given these pressures. How
our parents, and eventually how we, will spend
the last one-third of life remains in flux. What
can we do to ensure "successful aging?" What
are the hallmarks of successful aging? The
quest for successful aging is perhaps as old as
time itself, ranging from the search for a fountain of youth to "acting younger." Yet there is
no simple answer, for older people are the most
diverse segment of the population. Is successful aging good health? Economic security?
Friendships and close social ties with others?
Enjoyment of retirement? Rejection of retirement and continuing work or beginning a second career? Volunteering? Or is it feeling satisfied with one's current and past life?*

*In the following selection, Margret Baltes
and Laura Carstensen examine the history of
theoretical attempts to define and describe
"successful aging." Rejecting the "one size fits
all" concept of successful aging, they call attention to the importance of individual and
personal definitions of successful old age. As
you read their process-oriented approach, consider its application to particular individuals
and to social groups. What individual and
group differences in "successful aging" would
you anticipate might exist among very frail elders? Among men and women? Among members of different minority groups? What social
class differences, if any, would you expect to
find?*

Introduction

Since its inception, the primary focus of gerontological research has been in decline and
loss associated with advanced age (Riley
et al. 1994). We neither deny nor minimize
the importance of research on age-related decline. The plight of old age is very real, embracing losses in physical, cognitive and social domains. It is not surprising that anticipation of ageing is characterized by anxiety
and fear both on the part of the individual (*e.g.*
fear of loss) and on the part of societies (*e.g.*
fears of increased costs and burdens). The
plight of ageing, however, is only one side of
the coin. The other side involves growth, vitality, striving and contentment.

Discussion of successful ageing inevitably
raises concern within and outside the academy. In fact, Cole (1983) contends that positive portrayals of ageing are potentially as
pernicious as negative ones in that they deny
the reality of ageing. Cole (1983) and Rosenmayr (1989), for example, believe that unless
this 'enlightened' view of ageing is extended
to include the existential challenges of physical and social decline in old age, it may very
well have baneful effects. Cole writes: 'The
currently fashionable positive mythology of
old age shows no more tolerance or respect
for the intractable vicissitudes of ageing than
the old negative mythology' (1983: 39).

Such concerns are not without merit.
However, even though morbidity and mortality rates do increase with age (Brody *et al.*
1987; Manton and Soldo 1985), we have
reached the point in Western societies where
the reduction in infant mortality and the com-
pression of morbidity (Fries 1990) allow the
majority of people to live out their lives in
relatively good physical health (Manton *et al.*
1993). Recently, several prominent biological
researchers and physicians have argued that
successful and positive ageing must not be
omitted from our conceptions of old age to do
justice to its multifaceted nature and vast heterogeneity (Bortz 1989; Fries 1990; Rowe
and Kahn 1987). In addition, most older people are satisfied with their lives, even more so
than their younger counterparts (Herzog and
Rodgers 1981).

Nevertheless, we agree with critics that the focus on theoretically normative psychological *outcomes*—rooted primarily in middle-class values and, prototypically, in white, male standards—has seriously limited our understanding of successful ageing. The use of normative outcomes pays only minimal attention to the heterogeneity among and within ageing people (Maddox 1987; Thomae 1981), fails to acknowledge the social construction of old age (Dannefer 1987), and ignores the potential for multiple outcomes (Schaie 1983) and diverse standards of success (Boesch 1954). A person living under objectively poor conditions may strive towards self-actualization, another living in an objectively good situation may experience ageing as a tremendous burden. A single individual may be physically ill but psychologically strong, feel despair about family but contentment about work, and experience great dissatisfaction but a profound sense of meaning in life. Furthermore, what is considered successful according to functional norms might not meet with ideal norms, nor square with statistical norms. Definitions of the meaning of success have changed over historical time and will continue to vary along with changes in societal, cultural, and biological norms. Definition of outcomes, therefore, needs to be multidimensional and multilevel and needs to consider both gains and losses.

Furthermore, the research question needs to be broadened from a primary focus on outcomes; that is, from: '*What* is successful ageing?' to include '*How* do people age successfully?' or 'What are the processes that allow for mastery of goals in old age?' We suggest that understanding the *processes* that people use to reach their goals under increasing limitations in resources, be they social, psychological or biological, will lead to additional insights and progress in the field. In this paper we argue that the metamodel of selective optimisation with compensation (Baltes and Baltes 1990) offers a suitable framework within which to pose such questions. The proposed model defines success as the attainment of goals which can differ widely among people and can be measured against diverse standards and norms. The three processes identified in the model—namely, selection, compensation and optimisation—in concert, provide a way to conceptualize the strategies older people use to age well even in the face of loss. We cannot predict what any given individual's successful ageing will look like until we know the domains of functioning and goals that that individual considers important, personally meaningful and in which he or she feels competent.

To provide a context for our argument, we begin by tracing the history of theoretical attempts to define and describe success and successful ageing. Next, we examine empirical findings for the most commonly used criteria of successful ageing. Last, we introduce the process model of selective optimisation with compensation (Baltes 1987; Baltes and Baltes 1990), a metamodel of successful ageing that incorporates a life-span view, builds on empirical evidence about gains *and* losses in old age, permits specification of any desired goal and/or norm to define success depending on the theoretical perspective embraced, and specifies three processes that facilitate striving toward goals in the face of losses.

Defining Success and Successful Ageing

Definitions of success have varied throughout history, implying greater or lesser involvement of luck and/or effort and more or less in the way of evaluative connotations, *e.g.* a fortunate outcome versus any outcome (Edwards 1967; Simpson and Weiner 1989). In modern usage, success typically refers to favourable attainments deriving from one's own behaviour and actions. Very often it is measured by economic accomplishments. Because of such materialistic usages, success is considered by some to be a poor choice for describing positive outcomes in old age. Cole (1984), for example, views the current emphasis on successful ageing as the capitalist takeover of ageing.

Success, however, is not explicitly limited to utilitarian outcomes. Success can refer to the attainment of personal goals of all types, ranging from the maintenance of physical functioning and good health to generativity, ego-integrity, self-actualization and social connectedness (see Baltes and Silverberg 1994; Bellah *et al.* 1986).

Some critics argue that successful ageing is an oxymoron; successful ageing means not ageing at all. History, as well as our modern youth-and-achievement-oriented culture, is replete with tales of the 'Jungbrunnen' or 'fountain of youth' and consumer products that aim to help people maintain a youthful appearance, increase productivity, and optimize physical health. However, a conceptualization of successful ageing founded on denial is ultimately an untenable position. Looking back and seeking to cultivate the still glorious middle years will inevitably lead to despair and eventual defeat (Erikson 1959; Butler 1974).

Unlike earlier developmental stages in which goals and success are defined as the acquisition of survival skills, successful ageing is intricately interwoven with a sense of meaning and purpose in life and thus invokes existential paradigms or ideals (Cole 1984; Cole and Gadow 1986; Rosenmayr 1983 *a, b*; 1985). Rentsch (1992) observes that ageing is the radicalization of the human condition. Ageing is described as a dialectic between self-actualization and self-alienation.

Although influenced heavily by the cultural context of the historical era, a deep ambivalence about ageing can be traced from ancient to modern times. With the advent of industrial capitalism, human value became equated with productivity and, at the same time, retirement was institutionalized as a symbol of non-productivity. Ironically, this more negative view of old people and ageing was facilitated by scientific attention to ageing. By focussing almost exclusively on problems of elderly people—their isolation, dependence, role-loss and illness—researchers reinforced a very negative portrayal of ageing. The view of ageing as a time of decline was further reinforced by well intentioned advocates and politicians who, in order to win support for the infirm elderly, portrayed them as sick and needy. The implementation of the Older Americans Act (OAA) and similar policies in the U.S. and other countries functioned as a double-edged sword by providing

protection but also endangering individual autonomy and integrity (Estes and Binney 1989; Guillemard 1992).

The last two decades have witnessed several important changes in the views of old age held by the scientific community. Findings in biological, social and psychological spheres have pointed to unused and latent potentials of elderly adults. Examples are found in the domain of cognitive ageing, where it has been shown that elders can improve their cognitive output after improved learning and performance conditions (P. B. Baltes and Lindenberger 1988; Schaie 1990); in the domain of social behavior, where dependent self-care behavior can be reversed to independent functioning when given prompts, time and rewards (Baltes 1995; for review *see* Mosher-Ashley 1986/87); and in the domain of physical functioning, where it has been shown that a great number of physical declines can be postponed and temporarily reversed through proper exercise and diet (Baltes and Reichert 1992; Stones and Kozma 1985; Whitbourne 1985). A wealth of empirical findings from both the social and biological sciences have accrued confirming that latent potentials can be activated to compensate for possible losses in old age.

Thus, there appears to be considerable fluidity in old age. Nevertheless, gerontological theories have either focussed on decline or growth. None that we know of have considered gains and losses and their potential interactions conjointly. Many early theories of successful ageing posited highly idealized human states as the adaptive outcomes of old age. Jung (1931), for example, postulated expansion beyond gender constraints towards full humanity and wisdom as criteria for successful ageing. Erikson's stage model (1984; Erikson *et al.* 1986) posited that psychological peace and ego integrity were the criteria for success in old age. Other theorists conceptualized the acceptance of decline as the adaptive task of old age (*i.e.* Bühler 1933). The now classic disengagement theory (Cumming and Henry 1961) characterized success as acceptance of and reconciliation with the loss of power endemic in old age, whereas activity theory (Havighurst and Albrecht 1953; Maddox 1965) posited that the maintenance of activity, replacement of lost roles with new ones and continued psychological involvement in society and interpersonal relationships represented the formula for successful ageing.

More recently, Ryff (1982; 1989 *a, b*) proposed an integrative model of successful ageing based on developmental, clinical, and mental health perspectives arguing that multiple aspects of life must be considered when assessing successful ageing. Her model includes six dimensions, all referring to positive functioning: self-acceptance, positive relations with others, autonomy, environmental mastery, purpose in life, and personal growth.

In summary, over the past 50 years, a number of theories have been proposed to describe successful ageing. The centerpiece of most of these conceptualizations has been the elaboration of focal success outcomes, ranging from disengagement to longevity. No one theory, criterion or even pattern of criteria has been widely accepted as a cogent prescription or explanation for success in old age. Part of this might be due to the empirical findings on successful ageing to which we now turn.

Empirical Findings for Successful Ageing Criteria

Physical health, functional autonomy, and longevity have served as indicators of successful ageing to biological scientists. Physical health is unquestionably tied to psychological well-being at any age (Bowling and Brown 1991; Krause 1990; Rodin 1986) and psychological variables, like perceived social support and life style, appear to influence morbidity and mortality (Blazer 1982; House *et al.* 1988; Vaillant 1990).

However, good physical health cannot be a prerequisite in psychological theories of successful ageing because, as Wong points out, 'even the fittest [eventually] succumb to disabling illness' (1918: 518). In addition, the person who has lived the longest, most likely will also have experienced the most losses, be they loss of friends, loss of own health, etc. The person who strives for autonomy may, at the same time, lose social contacts and expe-

rience isolation. Thus, the criteria of functional autonomy and longevity do not necessarily lead to psychological well-being.

Successful ageing, when studied empirically by psychologists, is most commonly operationalized as *life satisfaction*, high morale or the subjective appraisal of well-being. Researchers have used life satisfaction as an index of success in the retirement transition (Parnes 1981), recovery after widowhood (Wortman and Silver 1990) and a number of other life events. The voluminous literature about the direct and indirect effects of social structural variables on satisfaction (George 1990) reveals that statistically significant differences in satisfaction among groups of people do exist. Income, population density, marital status, years of formal education, and other variables do predict life satisfaction but account for very little of the variance in life satisfaction.

Moreover, the vast majority of people report that they are satisfied with their lives regardless of objective indicators (Brim 1988, 1992; Diener 1984; George 1981; Larson 1978; Lawton 1983, 1984; Schwarz and Strack 1989). One possible explanation is that life satisfaction comprises different dimensions in the old versus the young (Ryff 1989 *b*). Another explanation for preserved life satisfaction in spite of age-related loss is, however, that elderly people adapt to negative changes by using coping strategies such as downward social comparison (Wills 1991).

Relatively recently, a number of researchers from diverse fields, *i.e.* psychology (Dittmann-Kohli 1990; Reker *et al.* 1987; Wong 1989), literature (Weiland 1989; Woodword and Schwartz 1986) and history (Cole 1984), have shifted their attention to *personal meaning* in life as an index of successful ageing. Wong (1989) following Jung (1931) and Erikson and colleagues (1986) argue that finding personal meaning in life is the major developmental task of old age. Personal meaning has been conceptualized as the interpretation of life (Antonovsky 1979), the central focus on values (Cole and Gadow 1986), the cognitive construal of consistency between goals and actions (Rosenmayr 1985), the acceptance of immutable circumstances and integrative reminiscence (Wong 1989, 1991;

Wong and Watt 1991), self-discovery (Tournier 1972), future-orientedness and optimism (Schonfield 1973), and as religiosity and spirituality (Cole 1984).

Summary

We agree with Cole (1984) and Rosenmayr (1985) that a rethinking of successful ageing is necessary in order to avoid a class bias or utopian dream. We disagree, however, that a positive view of the potential of ageing necessarily includes a *prescription* for the outcome, or places sole responsibility for successful ageing on the individual.

We argue that most gerontological theories do not take into account individual or cultural variation in goals and usually apply ideal and/or statistical norms from within one culture, rarely functional or individual norms. But no one criterion has been found acceptable. Indeed, even ranking the array of success criteria is difficult. Can an old person in excellent physical health but deteriorated mental health be considered a successful ager? Should people who live only to 70, but maintain a highly optimistic view of ageing be considered unsuccessful agers? A multi-criteria approach is preferred to a monocriterion approach (Ryff 1989 a; 1991). However, unless we accept all criteria as equally important—which would render the numbers of successful ageing people extremely small—we are left with the problem of ranking the most important criteria.

A solution to this problem seems to be a flexible definition of success outcomes. Success can be defined by different authorities (*e.g.* individual, peer group, society, scientific theory), by different criteria of assessment (*e.g.* subjective vs. objective) and by different norms (*e.g.* functional, statistical, ideal norm).[1] On the most general level, successful ageing implies that people reach personal goals; these might coincide with ideal or statistical norms but may also concur with idiosyncratic goals. Table 7.1 provides an overview and examples of different standards of success.

Allowing variation in goals and norms and identifying the prototypical processes that facilitate successful ageing will potentially lead to increasing precision and strength of our theories of successful ageing and the construction of environmental conditions and life styles conducive to optimal ageing. In short, success needs to be redefined such that it is not just associated with normative and ideal goals or outcomes. Success does not and should not be measured against one standard. Any definition of success based exclusively on theoretically normative outcomes and goals will, by its very nature, lack generalisability and longevity. When the question becomes: *How* is success achieved?, we may find that the processes people use to cope with life and ageing are more universal and less dependent on cultural vicissitudes.

The Metamodel of Selective Optimisation With Compensation

With this said, a useful model of successful ageing must account for the dynamics between gains and losses; that is, on the one hand, for a reduction in reserves and an increasing number of specific losses and challenges in the biological, social, and psychological spheres; and, on the other hand, for potential growth and plasticity in old age. Such a metamodel should be able to harbor a great diversity of outcomes/goals, accommodate different success criteria, and emphasize how elderly people obtain personal goals—that is, age successfully—in the face of simultaneous losses.

Table 7.1

Different Norms in Different Domains With Different Goals

| Norm | Domains/Goals | | |
	Physical Health	Social Integration	Psychological Well-being
Statistical	no major disease	marriage	no pathology
Ideal	complete health	intimacy	happiness
Functional	hearing	communication	independence

In life-span psychology (P. B. Baltes 1987, 1991; P. B. Baltes *et al.* 1980), the major criterion for successful development is the efficacious functioning of the individual in an identified system (biological, social, psychological), domain (sports, leisure, job, family) or task (self-actualisation, cognitive performance, social integration). To augment and enrich one's own reserve capacities and resources, particularly throughout early and middle life, is of the utmost importance since these will also assist successful mastery of developmental tasks in late life. While adherence to the notion of efficacious functioning does not preclude the prescription of developmental goals or outcomes as ideal in successful ageing, it does not bank on them and above all, it allows the operation of diverse norms to evaluate attainment of individually desired goals. Such a model implicitly and explicitly allows for greater variability in successful ageing, with the base being heterogeneity and plasticity, two major findings known about ageing (Baltes and Baltes, 1990).

In this sense, the metamodel of selective optimisation with compensation (SOC) (P. B. Baltes and Baltes 1990; Baltes 1987; Baltes and Reichert 1982) defines success as goal attainment and successful ageing as minimization of losses and maximization of gains. Using the notion of mastery and adaptation allows diverse specifications of the goals and its evaluation criteria depending on the specific theory tested.

The metamodel specifies three processes: selection, compensation, and optimisation. If implemented together, use of the processes enables people to master their goals despite, or perhaps even because of, losses and increasing vulnerabilities. The three processes embrace a great multitude of psychological mechanisms and strategies. For instance, optimisation of one's health may mean for one person to exercise more frequently, for another to diet, and for a third person to reduce stress. According to the model, the same processes are at work even when goals vary over individuals, time or context. Furthermore, the criteria of goal attainment can vary by type of assessment (objective vs. subjective), by the authority (individual, group, family, culture) judging success, and by norms (statistical, ideal, functional).

A real life example might best illustrate the three processes and their interaction. An old marathon runner can maintain the goal of winning by competing within his own age group and running fewer and 'easier' courses (instances of selection); varying footwear and extending warm-up periods (compensation) and using a special diet and vitamins to increase fitness (optimisation).

The metamodel, thus, is considered prototypical in its genotype of mastery, but it can accommodate wide interindividual differences in its phenotypic manifestation. What and how many domains people choose and the specific strategies they use in striving towards successful ageing may differ from person to person. The model is a metamodel that attempts to represent scientific knowledge about the nature of development and ageing with the focus on successful adaptation. Although the three processes have theoretical implications for successful development at large (see Marsiske *et al.* 1995), we will focus here on successful ageing.

Definition of the Three Component Processes and Empirical Evidence

Selection

Selection at all levels of behaviour (input, processing, output) is a core element of any theory of behaviour. Selection can be active or passive, internal or external, intentional or automatic. In development including ageing, selection refers to the increasing restriction of life domains as a consequence or in anticipation of changes in personal and environmental resources. In old age, these changes are often losses. Selection can entail the avoidance of one domain altogether or it can mean a restriction in tasks and goals within one or more domains. An elderly person whose spouse is suffering from a terminal illness, for example, may give up the domain of sexuality altogether, or may restrict some goals and involvements in the social network at large, but increase efforts in the domain of leisure activities and family. The adaptive task of the individual is to select high priority domains, tasks, and goals that involve a convergence between environmental demands, individual motivations, skills and biological capacity.

Although selection connotes a reduction in the number of high-efficacy domains, tasks, and goals, it is not necessarily limited to a continuation of previous goals and domains, albeit in smaller numbers. Selection can also involve new or transformed domains and goals. Thus, the person who lost a spouse might continue to invest love and care by carrying on the political activities of the spouse, for instance, and maintaining his or her legacy. Selection always entails the readjustment of individual goals. Selection can be proactive or reactive. It can encompass environmental changes (*e.g.* relocation), active behavior changes (*e.g.* reducing the number of commitments), or passive adjustment (*e.g.* avoiding climbing stairs or allowing somebody to take responsibility). Proactively, through monitoring current functioning, people predict future changes and losses (*e.g.* death of the spouse) and make efforts to search for tasks and domains that can remain intact even after losses. Selection is reactive when unpredictable or sudden changes force persons to make a selection. If a stroke suddenly severely impairs a person, a decision to remain at home might not be viable, but the person can engage in selection processes about which institution, how much and what kind of self-care, what type of rehabilitation, what activities to engage in, what television program to watch, and when to write a letter or make a telephone call.

Empirical Evidence for Selection Processes

Selection is an integral part of any developmental process. Evidence for selection in the form of channelling or canalization can be found in sociology, biology, and psychology. In *sociology*, selection operates via social structures such as social class (Mayer and Carroll 1987), race, gender and ethnicity (Jencks 1992), social mobility (Blau and Duncan 1976) as well as via immutable variables such as sex (Mayer *et al.* 1991) and age (Hagestadt 1990). Dannefer (1987) has called this process sociogenic differentiation. The cumulative effect of selection on a structural level has been described by Merton (1968) as the Matthew effect, referring to the self-maintaining properties of particular social paths.

In *biology*, selection is the term used to explain canalisation. and specialisation during biological development (Waddington 1975). Cotman (1985), for instance, argues that specialisation on the cellular level involves the loss of alternate courses of cell differentiation. Ontogenetic selection based on the potentials of the genome is a well known fact that pressures development in specific directions.

In *psychology*, there is evidence for selection from multiple sources. For Skinner (1966), for instance, selection played a prominent role in the process of shaping. In human development, maturation involves progressive specialization, which involves both gains and losses. Language provides a particularly elegant example of selection. The ability to learn language is far easier early in life than later and the difficulty in second language acquisition increases as a function of language development (Kellerman and Smith 1986).

In *personality psychology*, findings stemming from self-efficacy theory (Bandura 1977, 1982, 1991) suggest that agency beliefs guide the search, creation, and acceptance of goals, expectations, and environments. By monitoring competencies and demands via self-efficacy beliefs, a person selects which goals to set, what demands to cope with, when to expend effort and when to compromise. People with strong self-efficacy beliefs perceive losses as challenge; those with weak ones perceive losses as threats (Bandura and Cervone 1986; Bandura and Wood 1989). The strength of self-efficacy beliefs determines which and how often anticipatory scenarios are constructed and imagined, which means of control are activated, and how quickly an activity or domain is abandoned or compromised (Bandura and Jourden 1991).

Markus and colleagues (Markus and Nurius 1986; Markus and Wurf 1987) have coined the term 'multiple selves', referring to 'actual', 'feared' and 'hoped for' self-schemata that aid and guide the search for new goals. Similarly, the literature on personal control provides yet another body of evidence for selection. Secondary control (Heckhausen and

Schulz 1993, 1995; Rothbaum *et al.* 1982) and accommodative coping (Brandtsädter and Renner 1990) refer essentially to cognitive selection strategies in that they involve the reorganization of goal structures and goal hierarchies so that a fit between personal competence and environmental demands is achieved.

In, *social psychology*, the social cognitive mechanism of social comparison, which serves to motivate or comfort depending on the reference point, also aids in selection. In the face of difficulties and irreversible losses, downward comparison allows people to adjust and maintain a positive evaluation of the self (Taylor 1983; Wood 1989).

The theory of socioemotional selectivity (Carstensen 1991; 1993) considers selection adaptive in the social arena and specifies goal change as the precipitant to selection. The theory contends that emotional goals become increasingly salient with age and that people engage in active efforts to restructure their social worlds such that they maximize emotionally meaningful experiences. In contrast to the most popular traditional views of social ageing which suggest that maintaining earlier levels of social activity is necessary for happiness in old age (Osgood 1989), socioemotional selectivity theory proposes that the judicious reduction of social contact in adulthood (and especially in old age) fosters enhanced emotional satisfaction and is, thus, adaptive. Analysis of longitudinal data shows that emotional closeness with a select few is maintained or increased from young to middle adulthood even though social contact is reduced during the same time period (Carstensen 1992). Even in very old age, a time when social networks are notably reduced, emotionally close relationships appear to be maintained while more peripheral social relationships are discarded (Lang and Carstensen 1994).

The field of *human factors* is another research area demonstrating empirical evidence for selection. In studies of driving behavior, for instance, it is shown that the elderly driver is faced with an array of physical and environmental barriers (for a summary see the Special Report by the Committee for the Study in Improving Mobility and Safety for Older Persons 1988; also Warnes *et al.* 1991). Conditions perceived as especially problematic were speed, traffic congestion, complex and confusing signs, unfamiliar streets and freeway interchanges. Although almost all studies are about the sensori-motoric and cognitive deficiencies of the elderly aggravating driving behavior, there are a few examples for coping strategies. Selections made by elderly people accommodate these deficiencies and environmental barriers. They select not to drive at dusk, dawn or at night or make only short trips in familiar territory; they avoid peak-period driving and reduce risk-taking and aggressive behavior and instead drive more defensively.

Compensation

Compensation, the second component factor facilitating mastery of loss in reserves in old age, becomes operative when there are person- or environment-associated changes in means-ends resources; *i.e.* specific behavioural capacities or skills are lost or reduced below the level required for adequate functioning. Compensation can also become necessary as the result of selection. The organism might have to compensate in domains that are not selected for further enhancement and thus are given less attention and energy. An example is the delegation of activities to somebody else. Compensation, which can be automatic or planned, refers to the use of alternate means to reach the same goal, *i.e.* accomplish the same outcome in a specific domain; that is, previous means-end strategies are reassessed. If a goal within a domain that includes a large number of activities and means is well elaborated, the person will not experience much trouble in counterbalancing or compensating for a specific behavioral deficiency. If the deficiency is large in scope or if the domains and goals are defined by one or very few activities, compensatory efforts will be more difficult. If, for instance, a master musician defines her expertise only as a soloist, it will be difficult for her to compensate for incurring an impairment, such as hearing loss or arthritis that cuts short her career as a soloist. If, however, she defines her domain of expertise by a number of additional activities aside from playing as a soloist, she may compensate for the impairment by becoming a music teacher, a music critic, or a composer.

Compensation can involve existing behaviours or the acquisition of new skills or construction of new means not yet in one's repertoire. Compensation, thus, differs from selection in that the goal is maintained, but new means are enlisted to compensate for a behavioural deficiency in order to maintain or optimize prior functioning. The element of compensation involves aspects of both the mind and technology. Psychological compensatory efforts include, for example, the use of new mnemonic strategies or external memory aids when internal memory mechanics or strategies prove insufficient. The use of a hearing aid is an example of compensation by means of technology. The world of the handicapped is full of technical means that compensate for impairments and make a more or less independent and successful life possible. An avid reader of literature who becomes blind might learn Braille in order to continue reading or might divert to listening to 'books on tape'. Not only technical means, but human means are often needed to compensate. The assistance of a hand or arm when walking, a hired worker who cooks the meals, or a companion who does the writing may provide the compensatory means that enable elderly people to pursue their lives as fully as possible.

Empirical Evidence for Compensation

Compensation is a multifaceted term that has found its way into biology as well as psychology (Backman and Dixon 1992). In both fields, compensation is possible because of neural or behavioural plasticity, available to the organism when equilibrium is disturbed. In *biology*, compensatory efforts follow brain injury and sensory handicaps. In the case of neural plasticity, compensatory efforts are seen as the source for recovery (Bach-y-Rita 1990).

In the area of *psychopathology*, the vulnerability model of schizophrenia argues for self-healing attempts as compensatory efforts on the part of vulnerable persons to stabilize their psychic equilibrium. Böker *et al.* (1984) demonstrated that persons at high risk for schizophrenia show relatively more attempts than people who are at lower risk to compensate due to heightened vulnerability.

In *cognitive psychology*, the pragmatics of intelligence are considered to have compensatory power to alleviate deficits in the mechanics of intelligence (P. Baltes 1991; Berg and Sternberg 1985; Salthouse 1984).

In *personality psychology*, findings from self-efficacy theory suggest that by delegating control to others, proxy control serves a compensatory function (Bandura 1982). In contrast to selection, proxy control allows the elderly person to maintain earlier goals through the assistance of others. Paradoxically, delegating control to others can be a powerful mechanism for optimizing domains that might otherwise decline. Baltes and her colleagues demonstrated, for example, that dependency can secure and optimize social contact (for reviews see Baltes 1995; Baltes and Wahl 1991).

Socioemotional selectivity theory posits that social selection of long term friends and loved ones (as opposed to acquaintances or hired aids) helps to compensate for losses in areas such as sensory function or memory impairment (Carstensen 1993). In the case of hearing loss, for example, a familiar social partner is more likely to speak clearly or speak into the 'good ear' than someone unfamiliar with special losses. Gould and colleagues (1991) showed positive effects of social collaboration in an oral recall task, clearly a process that benefits most from exchanges with familiar others.

Human factors research is replete with empirical findings suggesting compensation (for a summary see Committee for the Study in Improving Mobility and Safety for Older Persons 1988; also Warnes *et al.* 1991). Here too, driving behaviour in the elderly may serve as an illustration. Elderly drivers compensate, for instance, decreased reaction time by driving more slowly and by using interchanges with lights instead of stop signs only; they compensate for loss in peripheral vision by turning their head when changing lanes. Driving can be facilitated by improvements in transportation technology that would tailor more to the elderly driver, such as improvement in readability of signs, changes in traffic distribution, in certain vehicle design features; in short, by compensatory means introduced by the environment not by the elderly person.

In sum, whether the losses are sensory, cognitive or interpersonal, compensation occurs when a certain behavior (or neural process) is evoked which narrows the gap between actual competence level and environmental demands.

Optimisation

Optimisation, the third component factor of SOC, refers to the enrichment and augmentation of reserves or resources and, thus, the enhancement of functioning and adaptive fitness in selected life domains. Optimisation may occur in existing domains (*e.g.* generativity) or involve investment in new domains and goals consonant with developmental tasks of old age, such as acceptance of one's own mortality. How much selection and compensation must be invested in order to secure maintenance and stimulate optimisation is an empirical question. Recent literature in gerontology suggests that many elderly people, in principle, have the necessary resources and reserves to optimize functions but face restrictive or overprotective environments that inhibit optimisation (Baltes and Wahl 1991). There is no doubt that the process of optimisation will be contingent to a large extent on stimulating and enhancing environmental conditions. Thus, society plays a central role in providing environments that facilitate optimisation. In fact, the success of relatively simple interventions (noted below) suggest that elderly adults often live in a world of under demand rather than over demand. Optimisation is dependent upon available possibilities and opportunities, unless older people actively and individually forge new terrain and frontiers (Rosenmayr 1983 *a, b*).

Empirical Evidence for Optimisation

The psychological literature is replete with evidence for optimisation processes. Improving performance in selected domains is of great interest in education, sport psychology, and cognitive expertise (see Ericsson *et al.* 1993, for review).

Within *gerontology* itself, there is ample evidence for optimisation from intervention studies. This literature evinces plasticity and growth possibilities into very old age. When environmental conditions encourage practice, training and exercise and when attention and motivation are stimulated, declines—long considered to be intractable—can be reversed and improved. This has been demonstrated clearly in the domains of cognition, social behaviour and biology.

A diverse array of intervention studies demonstrates that old people can profit from 'optimizing' environments. Physical exercise improves biological functioning such as pulmonary and cardiovascular functions (for a review see Bortz 1989; Whitbourne 1985); cognitive intervention can increase memory performance (P. B. Baltes and Lindenberger 1988) and can even help to ameliorate the impact of dementia on daily living (Wiedl *et al.* 1987); behavioral interventions can reverse chronic dependent behaviours and increase autonomy (Baltes 1995).

On a macro-level, studies of control-enhancing interventions (Langer and Rodin 1976; Rodin and Langer 1977) have become classics. Despite criticisms concerning the underlying change agents (Munson 1989), these studies have demonstrated substantial improvement in activity level, health, and life satisfaction following relatively minor institutional modifications. Baltes and her colleagues (1994) demonstrated an increase in independent behaviours (autonomy) of institutionalized elderly people following an intervention aimed at changing the institutional context from one that overprotects to one that enhances autonomy and independence. By implementing a training program for caregivers directed at creating greater sensitivity concerning the need for balance between dependency and autonomy (*see also* Parmelee and Lawton 1990), caregivers of elderly adults relinquished their inadvertent tendency to foster dependency and shifted support toward reinforcing independent behavior. Results confirm the malleability of social environmental conditions responsible for dependency in elderly people.

In addition to micro- and macro-level intervention studies, indirect evidence for optimisation in late life can be found in empirical tests of socioemotional selectivity theory. Not only are older couples happier than younger couples (which could be explained by selective attrition), studies of emotion regulation in intimate relationships in old age suggest that, compared to middle-aged couples, older couples display more efforts to quell emotional conflict, *i.e.* express more affection to their partner while voicing concerns (Carstensen *et al.* 1995) and report greater enjoyment from discussions about children, grandchildren, dreams, vacations and doing things together and less conflict surrounding money, religion, recreation and children (Levenson *et al.* 1993)

Summary and Conclusions

The aim of this paper is to advocate a process-oriented approach to successful ageing. We argue that the search for normative success outcomes in old age, whether longevity, ego-integrity or life satisfaction, will ultimately hold limited benefits due to the vast heterogeneity inherent in human ageing. Theoretically derived ideals of what old age and old people should be like have been debated and challenged over the years. Multi-criterial approaches have been offered, yet the focal thrust of this work remains on measuring success or the lack thereof according to normative standards.

We feel that a process-oriented approach has three advantages. First, by accepting personal goals as success outcomes, whatever they may be, a process-oriented approach avoids the problem of imposing universal values and standards. It both acknowledges the heterogeneity of ageing people and avoids the inevitable lack of precision inherent in applying global constructs across diverse groups of people.

Second, a process-oriented approach directs attention to the strategies people use to master specific personal goals. This type of approach accentuates the functional properties of behaviours and strategies. Even behaviours that initially may appear maladaptive, such as limiting social contact, are revealed as adaptive once their function is examined. Consider also a request for assistance walking to the music room. When made by an individual whose primary goal is to continue playing the piano, such a request may be considered compensatory and adaptive. Yet if the individual's goal is to maintain muscular strength, the same behavioral profile may be viewed as maladaptive. In short, in a process-oriented approach classification of goals and strategies rather than outcomes alone becomes the focus.

Third, the process-oriented approach we advocate considers the interplay of gains and losses inherent in old age. Rather than deny the inevitable losses that all old people experience in advanced age, the selective optimisation with compensation model implies that old age holds the potential to be a time when the accumulated knowledge and expertise of a life-time is invested in the realization of a distilled set of highly meaningful domains and goals. In this view, even losses may lead to gains in some highly valued areas of life.

Clearly, more research is needed before the merits of a process-oriented approach will be known. Initial findings from the Berlin Ageing Study (*see* Ageing and Society 1993: 13) are highly encouraging. Evidence for the three processes are found, for instance, in the domain of everyday competence (Baltes and Horgas in press; Baltes *et al.* in press; Marsiske *et al.* 1994) and in the area of self and personality (Staudinger *et al.* in press). Although there is ample evidence of each individual component process of the model, there has been virtually no research on the manner in which the components work together. Whether there is a hierarchy among the three component processes remains an empirical question, for example. It may be that compensation is always attempted first, and only when it fails do selections occur.

We suspect that all three components are activated more easily and readily when there is a rich array of resources available from which to draw. When resources become depleted, an increasingly fine-tuned and subtle interplay among the three components is necessary. We contend, however, that even very frail people can select, compensate and optimize to maximize goal attainment. Given overwhelming evidence that increased loss is associated with ageing, we also suspect that selection and compensation are necessary precursors to optimisation. The time and energy invested in optimizing one domain, task or goal will necessarily influence one's involvements in other domains. The longitudinal extension of the Berlin Ageing Study promises some answers to these questions.

The model of selective optimisation with compensation also suggests new approaches to research. Experimental manipulation of losses could be simulated to study whether, when, and how selective, compensatory and optimizing processes are implemented and to provide precision and strength to predictions about the interplay among processes and goals across people. On a descriptive level, study participants could be selected for similarity in goals in order to analyse the processes used to reach these goals and assess success.

In conclusion, the model proposed in this paper represents a qualitative departure from the traditional social science approach to successful ageing, moving away from a focus on prescribed outcomes and ideal or statistical norms to an analysis in which the primary focus is on the processes people use to obtain desired goals. Skinner (1983), in an account of his own ageing, gave eloquent advice on intellectual management to preserve and continue high productivity in light of failing reserves. It was clear from his writings that the intellectual domain was of high priority and that his life was designed around maximizing function in this selected domain as opposed to others. We argue that this type of selective optimisation with compensation may be the most important tool for successful ageing.

Discussion Questions

1. Why do Baltes and Carstensen suggest that "successful aging means not aging at all" is a flawed argument? Do you agree or disagree with their discussion? Why?

2. Baltes and Carstensen argue that successful aging should be assessed as the mastery of goals resulting from three processes—selection, compensation, and optimization. Define each of these terms and their interplay with one another.

3. Research with older adults indicates that there is "plasticity" in cognitive functioning, such as learning capacity during job training, especially if older adults' use of learning strategies is enhanced in the training situation. Knowing this fact, how would you develop a training program that best achieves Baltes' idea of "selective optimization with compensation"?

4. How may the same concept of selective optimization with compensation be applied to planning one's second or third career in later life?

Note

1. *Statistical norm* means the level of performance, the level of goal attainment that is reached, on average, by a group of people. *Ideal norm* means the highest goal or possible level of achievement towards that goal, as defined by scientific theory, ideology or social values. *Functional norm* means the level of achievement necessary for effective functioning in whatever domain.

Acknowledgements

The writing of this paper was supported by a research fellowship from the Volkswagen Foundation which allowed the first author a year's stay at Stanford University and by a NIA grant RO1-AGO8816 to the second author. Work on this manuscript was completed in part, while the second author was a Visiting Fellow at the Max Planck Institute for Human Development and Education, Berlin, Germany. We are very grateful to Paul Baltes, Barbara Fredrickson, Frieder Lang, Richard Schulz, and Clemens Tesch-Römer for critical comments on earlier drafts of the paper and to Susan Turk for her patient and careful assistance in researching the literature. . . .

References

Antonovsky, A. 1979, *Health, Stress, and Coping*. Jossey-Bass, San Francisco, CA.

Bach-y-Rita, P. 1990. Brain plasticity as a basis for recovery of function in humans. *Neuropsychologia*, 28, 547–554.

Backman, L. and Dixon, R. A. 1992. Psychological compensation: A theoretical framework. *Psychological Bulletin*, 112, 259–283.

Baltes, M. M. 1987. Erfolgreiches Altern als Ausdruck von Verhaltenskompetenz und Umweltqualität (Successful Ageing as a Product of Behavioral Competence and Environmental Quality). In C. Niemitz (ed) *Der Mensch im Zusammenspiel von Anlage und Umwelt* (Men as product of heredity and environment). Suhrkamp, Frankfurt, 353–376.

Baltes, M. M. 1995. Dependency in old age: gains and losses. *Current Directions in Psychological Science*, 4, 14–19.

Baltes, M. M. and Horgas, A. in press. Long-term care institutions and the maintenance of competence. In Schaie, K. W. and Willis, S. L. (eds), *Societal mechanisms for maintaining competence in old age*. Springer, New York.

Baltes, M. M., Lang, F. and Wilms, H. U. in press. Kompetenzerhaltung als Ergebnis einer selektiven Optimierung mit Kompensation. In Kruse, A. (ed) *Jahrbuch der medizinischen Psychologie: Pychosoziale Gerontologie*. Hogrefe, Göttingen.

Baltes, M. M., Neumann, E. M. and Zank, S. 1994. Maintenance and rehabilitation of independence in old age: an intervention program for staff. *Psychology and Aging*, 9, 179–188.

Baltes, M. M. and Reichert, M. 1992. Successful aging: the product of biological factors, environmental quality, and behavioral competence. In Ebrahim, S. (ed) *Health Care for Older Women*. Oxford University Press, Oxford, 236–256.

Baltes, M. M. and Silverberg, S. B. 1994. The dynamics between dependency and autonomy across the life-span. In Featherman, D., Lerner, R. and Perlmutter, M. (eds) *Life-span Development and Behavior*. Erlbaum, Hillsdale, NJ, 12, 41–90.

Baltes, M. M. and Wahl, H. W. 1991. The behavior system of dependency in the elderly: interaction with the social environment. In Ory, M., Abeles, R. P. and Lipman, P. D. (eds) *Aging, Health and Behavior*. Sage, Beverly Hills, 83–106.

Baltes, P. B. 1987. Theoretical propositions of life-span developmental psychology: on the dynamics between growth and decline. *Developmental Psychology*, 23, 611–626.

Baltes, P. B. 1991. The many faces of human aging: toward a psychological culture of old age. *Psychological Medicine*, 21, 837–854.

Baltes, P. B. and Baltes, M. M. 1990. Psychological perspectives on successful aging: The model of selective optimization with compensation. In Baltes, P. B., Baltes, M. M. (eds) *Successful Aging: Perspectives from the Behavioral Sciences*. Cambridge University Press, New York, 1–34.

Baltes, P. B. and Lindenberger, U. 1988. On the range of cognitive plasticity in old age as a function of experience: 15 years of intervention research. *Behavior Therapy*, 19, 283–300.

Baltes, P. B., Reese, H. W. and Lipsitt, L. P. 1980. Life-span developmental psychology. *Annual Review of Psychology*, 31, 65–110.

Bandura, A. 1977. Self-efficacy: toward a unifying theory of behavioral change. *Psychological Review*, 84, 191–215.

Bandura A. 1982. Self-efficacy mechanisms in human agency. *American Psychologist*, 37, 122–147.

Bandura A. 1991. Self-regulation of motivation through anticipatory and self-reactive mechanisms. In Dienstbier, R. A. (ed) *Nebraska Symposium on Motivation, 1990*. University of Nebraska Press, Lincoln, NE, 38, 69–164.

Bandura A. and Cervone, D. 1986. Differential engagement of self-reactive influences in cognitive motivation. *Organizational Behavior and Human Decision Processes*, 38, 92–113.

Bandura, A. and Jourden, F. J. 1991. Self-regulatory mechanisms governing social comparison effects on complex decision making. *Journal of Personality and Social Psychology*, 60, 941–951.

Bandura, A. and Wood, R. 1989. Effect of perceived controllability and performance standards on self-regulation of complex decision making. *Journal of personality and Social Psychology*, 56, 805–815.

Bellah, R. N., Madison, R., Sullivan, W. K., *et al.* 1986. (eds) *Habits of the Heart. Individualism and Commitment in American Life?* University of California Press, Berkeley.

Berg, C. A. and Sternberg, R. J. 1985. A triarchic theory of intellectual development during adulthood. *Developmental Review*, 5, 334–370.

Blau, P. M. and Duncan, O. D. 1976. *The American Occupational Structure*. Wiley, New York.

Blazer, D. 1982. Social support and mortality in an elderly community population. *American Journal of Epidemiology*, 115, 684–694.

Böker, W., Brenner, H. D., Gerstner, G., Keller, F., Miffler, J. and Spichtig, L. 1984. Self-healing strategies among schizophrenics: attempts at compensation for basic disorders. *Acta Psychiatrica Scandinavia*, 69, 373-378.

Boesch, E. 1954. Öber die klinische Methode in der psychologischen Persönlichkeits forschung. *Zeitschrift für diagnostische Psychologie*, 2, 275–292.

Bortz, W. M. 1989. Redefining human aging. *Journal of the American Geriatrics Society*, 37, 1092–1096.

Bowling, A. and Browne, P. D. 1991. Social networks, health, and emotional well-being among the oldest old in London. *Journal of Gerontology*, 46, 20–32.

Brandtstädter, J. and Renner, G. 1990. Tenacious goal pursuit and flexible goal adjustment: explication and age-related analysis of assimilative and accommodative strategies of coping. *Psychology and Aging*, 5, 58–67.

Brim, O. G. 1988. Losing and winning: the nature of ambition in everyday life. *Psychology Today*, 9, 48–52.

Brim, O. G. 1992. *Ambition*. Basic Books, New York.

Brody, J. A., Brock, D. B. and Williams, T. F. 1987. Trends in the health of the elderly population. *Annual Review of Public Health*, 8, 211–234.

Bühler, Ch. 1933. *Der menschliche Lebenslauf als psychologisches Problem* (The Human Life Course as Psychological Problem). Hirzel, Leipzig.

Butler, R. N. (1974). Successful aging and the role of the life review. *Journal of the American Geriatrics Society*, 22, 529–535.

Carstensen, L. L. 1991. Socioemotional selectivity theory: social activity in life-span context. *Annual Review of Gerontology and Geriatrics*, 11, 195–217.

Carstensen, L. L. 1992. Social and emotional patterns in adulthood: support for socioemotional selectivity theory. *Psychology and Aging*, 7, 331–338.

Carstensen, L. L. 1993. Motivation for social contact across the life span. A theory of socioemotional selectivity. In Jacobs, J. (ed) *Nebraska Symposium on Motivation: Developmental Perspectives on Motivation*. University of Nebraska Press, Lincoln, 40, 209–254.

Carstensen, L. L., Gottman, J. M. and Levenson, R. W. 1995. Emotional behavior in long-term marriage. *Psychology and Aging*, 10, 140–149.

Cole, T. R. 1983. The 'enlightened' view of aging: Victorian morality in a new key. *Hastings Center Report*, 13, 34–40.

Cole, T. R. 1984. Aging, meaning, and well-being: musings of a cultural historian. *International Journal of Aging and Human Development*, 19, 329–336.

Cole, T. R. and Gadow, S. D. (eds) 1986. *What Does It Mean to Grow Old?* Duke University Press, Durham.

Committee for the Study on Improving Mobility and Safety for Older Persons 1988. (eds) *Transportation in an aging society: Improving mobility and safety for older persons*, Special Report 218, 1 and 2. National Research Council, Washington, D.C.

Cotman, C. W. (ed) 1985. *Synaptic Plasticity*. Guilford Press, New York.

Cumming, E. and Henry, W. E. 1961. *Growing Old: The Process of Disengagement*. Basic Books, New York.

Dannefer, D. 1987. Aging as intra-cohort differentiation: accentuation, the Matthew effect, and the life course. *Sociological Forum*, 2, 211–236.

Diener, E. 1984. Subjective well-being. *Psychological Bulletin*, 95, 542–575.

Dittmann-Kohli, F. 1990. The construction of meaning in old age: possibilities and constraints. *Ageing and Society*, 10, 279–294.

Edwards, P. 1967. Life, meaning and value of. In Edwards, P. (ed) *The Encyclopedia of Philosophy*. MacMillan, New York, 4, 467–476.

Erikson, E. H. 1959. The problem of ego identity. *Psychological Issues*, 1, 101–164.

Erikson, E. H. 1984. Reflection on the last stage—and the first. *Psychoanalytic Study of the Child*, 39, 155–165.

Erikson, E. H., Erikson, J. and Kivnick, H. 1986. *Vital Involvement in Old Age*. Norton, New York.

Ericsson, K. A., Krampe, R. Th. and Tesch-Römer, C. 1993. The role of deliberate practice in the acquisition of expert performance. *Psychological Review*, 100, 363–406.

Estes, C. L. and Binney, E. A. 1989. The biomedicalization of aging. *The Gerontologist*, 29, 587–596.

Fries, J. F. 1990. Medical perspectives upon successful aging. In Baltes, P. B. and Baltes, M. M. (eds) *Successful Aging. Perspectives from the Behavioral Sciences*. Cambridge University Press, New York, 35–49.

George, L. K. 1981. Subjective well-being: conceptual and methodological issues. *Annual Review of Gerontology and Geriatrics*, 2, 345–382.

George, L. K. 1990. Social structure, social processes, and social-psychological states. In Binstock, R. H. and George, L. K. (eds) *Handbook of Aging and the Social Sciences*. Academic Press, New York, 186–204.

Gould, O. N., Trevithick, L. and Dixon, R. A. 1991. Adult age differences in elaborations produced during prose recall. *Psychology and Aging*, 6, 93–99.

Guillemard, A. M. 1992. Europäische Perspektiven der Alternspolitik (European perspectives of politics in aging). In Baltes, P. B. and Mittelstraß, J. (eds) *Zukunft des Alterns und geseltschaftliche Entwicklung* (Future of Aging and Societal Development). De Gruyter, Berlin, 614–639.

Hagestad, G. O. 1990. Social perspectives on the life course. In Binstock, R. and George, L. (eds) *Handbook of Aging and the Social Sci-*

ences. Academic Press, New York, 3rd ed., 151–168.

Havighurst, R. J. and Albrecht, R. 1953. *Older People*. Longmans, New York.

Heckhausen, J. and Schulz, R. 1993. Optimization by selection and compensation: balancing primary and secondary control in life span development. *International Journal of Behavioral Development*, 16, 287–303.

Heckhausen, J. and Schulz, R. 1995. A life-span theory of control. *Psychological Review*, 102, 284–304.

Herzog, A. R. and Rodgers, W. L. 1981. Age and satisfaction. Data from several large surveys. *Research on Aging*, 3, 142–165.

House, J. S., Landis, K. R. and Umberson, D. 1988. Social relationships and health. *Science*, 241, 540–545.

Jencks, C. 1992. *Rethinking Social Policy: Race, Poverty and the Underclass*. Harvard University Press, Cambridge, MA.

Jung, C. G. 1931. Die Lebenswende (Life's turning point). In Jung, C. G. *Seelenprobleme der Gegenwart* (Psychological Problems of Today). Rascher, Zürich, 248–274.

Kellerman, E. and Smith, M. S. 1986. *Crosslinguistic Influence in Second Language Acquisition*. Pergamon Press, Oxford, England.

Krause, N. F. 1990. Perceived health problems, formal/informal support, and life satisfaction among older adults. *Journal of Gerontology: Social Sciences*, 45, 193–205.

Lang, F. R. and Carstensen L. L. 1994. Close emotional relationships in late life: further support for proactive aging in the social domain. *Psychology and Aging*, 9, 315–324.

Langer, E. J. and Rodin, J. 1976. The effects of choice and enhanced personal responsibility for the aged: a field experiment in an institutional setting. *Journal of Personality and Social Psychology*, 34, 191–198.

Larson, R. 1978. Thirty years of research on the subjective well-being of older Americans. *Journal of Gerontology*, 33, 109–125.

Lawton, M. P. 1983. The varieties of well-being. *Experimental Aging Research*, 9, 65–72.

Lawton, M. P. 1984. The variables of well-being. In Malatesta, C. Z. and Izard, C. E. (eds) *Emotion in Adult Development*. Sage, Beverly Hills, CA, 67–84.

Levenson, R. W., Carstensen, L. L. and Gottman, J. M. 1993. Long-term marriage: age, gender and satisfaction. *Psychology and Aging*, 8, 301–313.

Maddox, G. L. 1965. Fact and artifact: evidence bearing on disengagement theory from the Duke Geriatrics Project. *Human Development*, 8, 117–130.

Maddox, G. L. 1987. Aging differently. *The Gerontologist*, 27, 557–564.

Manton, K. G., Corder, L. S. and Stallard, E. 1993. Estimates of change in chronic disability and institutional incidence and prevalence rates in the U.S. elderly population from the 1982, 1984, and 1989 National Long Term Care Survey. *Journal of Gerontology: Social Sciences*, 48, 153–166.

Manton, K. G. and Soldo, B. J. 1985. Dynamics of health changes in the oldest-old: new perspectives and evidence. *Milbank Memorial Fund Quarterly*, 63, 206–285.

Markus, H. and Nurius, P. 1986. Possible selves. *American Psychologist*, 41, 954–969.

Markus, H. and Wurf, E. 1987. The dynamic of self-concept. A social psychological perspective. *Annual Review of Psychology*, 38, 299–337.

Marsiske, M. M., Lang, F. R. and Baltes, M. M. 1994. Beyond routine: competence and social support in the daily lives of older adults. *Paper presented at the 13th Biennial Meeting of the International Society for the Study of Behavioral Development*, Amsterdam, Netherlands, June/July 1994.

Marsiske, M. M., Lang, F. R., Baltes, P. B. and Baltes, M. M. 1995. Selective optimization with compensation: life-span perspectives on successful development. In Dixon, R. A. and Bäckman, L. (eds) *Compensation for Psychological Defects and Declines: Managing Losses and Promoting Gains*. Erlbaum, Hillsdale, NJ, 35–79.

Mayer, K. U., Allmendinger, J. and Huinink, J. 1991. *Vom Regen in die Traufe: Frauen zwischen Beruf und Familie* (Out of the Frying-pan into the Fire: Women between Job and Family). Campus, Frankfurt.

Mayer, K. U. and Carroll, G. R. 1987. Jobs and classes: structural constraints on career mobility. *European Sociological Review*, 3, 14–38.

Merton, R. K. 1968. The Matthew effect in science: the reward and communication system of science. *Science*, 199, 55–63.

Mosher-Ashley, P. M. 1986–1987. Procedural and methodological parameters in behavioral-gerontological research: a review. *International Journal of Aging and Human Development*, 24, 189–229.

Munson, P.A. 1989. Control and dependency in residential care settings for the elderly: perspectives on intervention. In Fry, P. S. (ed) *Psychological Perspectives of Helplessness and Control in the Elderly*. Elsevier, Amsterdam, 187–215.

Osgood, N.J. 1989. Theory and research in social gerontology. In Osgood, N.J. and Sontz, H. A. (eds) *The Science and Practice of Gerontology*. Greenwood Press, New York, 55–87.

Parmelee, P. A. and Lawton, M. P. 1990. The design of special environments for the aged. In Birren, J. E. and Schaie, K. W. (eds) *Handbook of the Psychology of Aging*. Academic Press, New York, 464–488.

Parnes, H. (ed) 1981. *Work and Retirement: A Longitudinal Study of Men*. MIT Press, Cambridge, MA.

Reker, G. T., Peacock, E. J. and Wong, P. T. P. 1987. Meaning and purpose in life and well-being: a life-span perspective. *Journal of Gerontology*, 42, 44–49.

Rentsch, Th. 1992. Philosophische Anthropologie und Ethik der späten Lebenszeit (Philosophical anthropology and ethics of late life). In Baltes, P. B. and Mittelstraß, J. (eds) *Zukunft des Alterns und gesellschaftliche Entwicklung* (Future of Aging and the Development of Society). de Gruyter, Berlin, 283–304.

Riley, M. W., Kahn, R. L. and Foner, A. (eds). 1994. *Age and Structural Lag*. Wiley, New York.

Rodin, J. 1986. Health, control, and aging. In Baltes, M. M. and Baltes, P. B. (eds) *The Psychology of Control and Aging*. Lawrence Erlbaum Associates, Hillsdale, NJ, 139–165.

Rodin, J. and Langer, E. 1977. Long-term effects of a control-relevant intervention with the institutionalized aged. *Journal of Personality and Social Psychology*, 35, 897–902.

Rosenmayr, L. 1983 *a. Das Alter—ein Stück bewußt gelebten Lebens* (Old age—A Time of Conscious Living). Severin & Siedler, Berlin.

Rosenmayr, L. 1983 *b. Die späte Freiheit* (The Late Freedom). Severin & Siedler, Berlin.

Rosenmayr, L. 1985. Changing values and positions of aging in Western culture. In Birren, J. E. and Schaie, K. W. (eds) *Handbook of the Psychology of Aging*. Van Nostrand Reinhold, New York, 190–215.

Rosenmayr, L. 1989. Wandlungen der gesellschaftlichen Sicht und Bewertung des Alters (Changes in society's perspective toward and evaluation of aging). In Baltes, M. M., Kohli, M. and Sames, K. (eds) Erfolgreiches Altern: Bedingungen und Variationen (Successful aging: Conditions and variations). Huber, Bern, 96–101.

Rothbaum, F., Weisz, J. R. and Snyder, S. S. 1982. Changing the world and changing the self: a two-process model of perceived control. *Journal of Personality and Social Psychology*, 42, 5–37.

Rowe, J. W. and Kahn, R. L. 1987. Human aging: usual and successful. *Science*, 237, 143–149.

Ryff, C. D. 1982. Successful aging: a developmental approach. *The Gerontologist*, 22, 209–214.

Ryff, C. D. 1989*a*. Beyond Ponce de Leon and life satisfaction: new directions in quest of successful aging. *International Journal of Behavioral Development*, 12, 35–55.

Ryff, C. D. 1989*b*. In the eye of the beholder: views of psychological well-being among middle-aged and older adults. *Psychology and Aging*, 4, 195–210.

Ryff, C. D. 1991. Possible selves in adulthood and old age: a tale of shifting horizons. *Psychology and Aging*, 6, 286–295.

Salthouse, T. A. 1984. Effects of age and skill in typing. *Journal of Experimental Psychology: General*, 113, 345–371.

Schaie, K. W. (ed) 1983. *Longitudinal Studies of Adult Psychological Development*. The Guilford Press, New York.

Schaie, K. W. 1990. The optimization of cognitive functioning in old age: predictions based on cohort-sequential and longitudinal data. In Baltes, P. B. and Baltes, M. M. (eds) *Successful Aging. Perspectives from the Behavioral Sciences*. Cambridge University Press, New York, 94–117.

Schonfield, D. 1973. Future commitments and successful aging. 1: the random sample. *Journal of Gerontology*, 28, 189–196.

Schwarz, N. and Strack, F. 1989. Evaluating one's life: a judgment model of subjective well-being. In Strack, F., Argyle, M. and Schwarz, N. (eds) *The Social Psychology of Well-being*. Pergamon, London.

Simpson, J. and Weiner, E. (eds) 1989. *The Oxford English Dictionary* (2nd ed, XVII). Clarendon, Oxford, 92–93.

Skinner, B. F. 1983. Intellectual self-management in old age. *American Psychologist*, 38, 239–244.

Skinner, B. F. 1966. The phylogeny and ontogeny of behavior. *Science*, 153, 1205–1213.

Staudinger, U., Freund, A., Linden, A. and Maas, I. in press. Selects, Persönlichkeit und Lebensgestaltung: Psychologische Widerstandsfähigkeit und Vulnerabilität. In Mayer, K. U. and Baltes, P. B. (eds) *Die Berliner Altersstudie*. Akademie Verlag, Berlin.

Stones, M. J. and Kozma, A. 1985. Physical performance. In Charness, N. (ed) *Aging and Human Performance*. John Wiley and Sons, New York, 261–291.

Taylor, S. E. 1983. Adjustment to threatening events: a theory of cognitive adaptation. *American Psychologist*, 38, 1161–1173.

Thomae, H. 1981. The Bonn Longitudinal Study of Aging (BOLSA): an approach to differential gerontology. In Baert, A. E. (eds) *Prospective Longitudinal Research*. Oxford University Press, Oxford, 165–197.

Tournier, P. 1972. *Learning to Grow Old*. SCM Press, London.

Vaillant, G. E. 1990. Avoiding negative life outcomes: evidence from a forty-five year study. In Baltes, P. B. and Baltes, M. M. (eds) *Successful Aging. Perspectives From the Behavioral Sciences*. Cambridge University Press, New York, 332–358.

Waddington, C. H. 1975. *The Evolution of an Evolutionist*. Edinburgh, Edinburgh University Press, Scotland.

Warnes, A., Rough, B. and Sixsmith, J. 1991. *Elderly Drivers and New Technology*. Project Report 6, Commission of the European Communities.

Weiland, S. 1989. Aging according to biography. *The Gerontologist*, 29, 191–194.

Whitbourne, S. 1985. *The Aging Body*. Springer, New York.

Wiedl, K., Schöttke, H. and Gediga, G. 1987. Reserven geistiger Leistungsfähigkeit bei geriatrischen Psychiatriepatienten und Altenheimbewohnern (Reserves of mental functioning in old psychiatric patients and nursing home residents). *Zeitschrift für klinische Psychologie*, 16, 29–42.

Wills, T. A. 1991. Similarity and self-esteem in downward comparison. In Suls, J. and Wills, T. A. (eds) *Social Comparison. Contemporary Theory and Research*. Lawrence Erlbaum, Hillsdale, NJ.

Wong, P. T. P. 1989. Personal meaning and successful aging. *Canadian Psychology*, 30, 516–525.

Wong, P. T. P. 1991. Existential versus causal attributions: the social perceiver as philosopher. In Zelen, S. (ed) *Extensions of Attribution Theory*. Springer, New York.

Wong, T. P. and Watt, L. M. 1991. What types of reminiscence are associated with successful aging? *Psychology and Aging*, 6, 272–279.

Wood, J. V. 1989. Theory and research concerning social comparisons of personal attributes. *Psychological Bulletin*, 106, 231–248.

Woodward, K. and Schwartz, M. M. (eds) 1986. *Memory and Desire: Aging—Literature—Psychoanalysis*. Indiana University Press, Bloomington.

Wortman, C. and Silver, C. R. 1990. Successful mastery of bereavement and widowhood: a life-course perspective. In Baltes, P. B. and Baltes, M. M. (eds) *Successful aging. Perspectives from the Behavioral Sciences*. Cambridge University Press, New York, 225–264.

Section II

Social Contexts of Aging

This section looks at the social contexts of aging and the ways in which old age is shaped by race, ethnicity, social class, and gender. It explores dimensions of identity to look at the ways in which older people construct their lives through autobiographical narratives and recollections of the past. Research reports, narratives, biography, and autobiography tell a collective story about how we construct our self-concept, individuality, and actions in old age. Gender, race, ethnicity, and social class interlock to frame their stories. The historical period in which people have lived also places them in prescribed social roles, banning or enhancing opportunities and life chances. How they integrate these many variables into their present lives gives a window into their doubts, fears, and survival skills. These selections reveal people seeking answers to fundamental questions of meaning, value, and purpose of their lives in old age.

How do we construct gender and how much variability is there in the ways in which men and women describe themselves as masculine or feminine? In the first selection, using a sample of primarily white, middle-class, and maritally stable high school graduates and their parents, Margaret Huyck, Pninah Zucker, and Cheryl Angellaccio examine developmental shifts in gender identity. Their choice to focus on a restricted cultural group was not an idle one, for it permitted control of other variables that influence how we define ourselves as masculine or feminine.

Their findings show that, even within a culturally homogeneous sample, men and women construct their gender identities in varied ways.

In the second selection, Barbara Formaniak Turner and Priyanthi Silva expand upon the theme of female gender identity among a broader sample of women ranging from youth to old age. They ask the questions: To what extent do self-definitions of what it means to be female vary? How do these delineations vary by birth cohort? Self-definition of one's "femininity" not only reflects past socialization but shapes the ways in which females behave throughout the life course. We see what differences occur not only within but also between birth cohorts as well as noting how both birth cohort and individual personalities intertwine to construct gender identities.

Based on their gender socialization, historical experiences, and personal biographies, men and women have different life courses. Life histories provide a rich tool to understand the life course in perspective and to understand the ways in which living in a specific historical period interacts with opportunity structures and personal characteristics. Marilyn Nouri and Marilyn Helterline in their selection integrate the life histories of working-class whites in the Northeast to show the "story lines" used to make ongoing meaning of "ordinary" lives. Life histories are particularly rich sources of information, for the stories people tell go beyond mere reporting of events. Rather than a photograph of the past, life histories are paintings in process, constantly being created and re-created to give meaning to the present. The elders interviewed by Nouri and Helterline portray themselves as individuals who have survived many vicissitudes. Yet they are surprisingly unaware of the traditional gendered scripts in their stories. Motifs of life as a struggle, life as shared, God, and the American success dream emerge but are distinctly "masculine" or "feminine" interpretations of lived history. Despite gender, the odds these people faced and overcame and their abilities to conserve vitality in the face of declining capacities give them firm bases for self-esteem and competency. Their narratives show how they steered through the many challenges they faced to gain some sense of control, whether through personal agency or belief in the inevitability of their fate.

The voice of disjunction and change becomes clear in the selection by Lydia Minatoya, who recounts her mother's life experiences. This narrative details Mrs. Minatoya's traditional socialization as a young Japanese woman, her pain at the loss of a mother who breached social norms, and her strong filial obligation to her father whether in Japan or the United States. At the time of this narrative, Minatoya, her husband, and her children were one of the very few Japanese-American families living in a medium-size Northeastern city, where they encountered both subtle and blatant discrimination. For example, although he was a well-educated research chemist until his retirement, her husband was paid by his company at the same level as his research assistant; the family was insulted by white neighbors when they finally succeeded in buying a house; and a daughter was denied entry into "gifted classes" until all possibly eligible white students had been selected. Clearly neither education nor achievement insulated them against residual prejudice against the Japanese. Mrs. Minatoya's life history also emphasizes what C. W. Mills (1959) has termed "private troubles" interlocked with "public issues." When World War II broke out, she and her father were among the thousands of Japanese Americans placed in concentration camps by the American government as potential "enemy aliens." Although she was American-born, she shared the same ethnicity as the Japanese enemy. Like other Japanese Americans, their property and belongings were confiscated without compensation until much later. It was not until 1988 that Congress approved legislation officially apologizing for the detention and offering a tax-free payment of $20,000 to surviving detainees. Mrs. Minatoya's reluctance to dwell upon such adverse events as these in her life illustrates survival in the face of hardships. What she does not say highlights the Japanese cultural themes of dignity and family pride in which she was socialized. Nonetheless, we feel her groping for resolution.

In contrast to reticence about detrimental life experiences, the oldest-old African Americans in the selection by Colleen Johnson derive a sense of well-being from comparing their present lives with their pasts. Like Minatoya, they survived racism and discrimination. While their histories in no way detract from the realities of discrimination and blocked opportunity, these elders derive pleasure from their many social supports embedded in black culture. Their entrenchment in a supportive social network extending beyond their families belies the negative portrayal often given to being poor, old, and black in America. Their narratives show that not all old-old are overwhelmed by illness and disability. The stance of oldest-old African Americans as survivors despite poverty and discrimination coupled with the ability to turn negatives into positives give resolution to their lives.

That having a sense of "belonging," to both an ethnic or racial community and to a place, is highlighted in the selections by William J. McAuley and Joan Weibel-Orlando. The all-black towns discussed by McAuley afford an emotional sanctuary against racial discrimination and oppression for elderly blacks in Oklahoma. The towns also accorded these elders opportunities for responsibility and advancement difficult to achieve in predominantly white communities. Small rural communities where all residents are likely to know one another at least by sight are characterized by *gemeinschaft,* or relationships built upon kinship, family, and personal ties. As in other communities throughout the world, some newcomers in town have been less welcome than others, and residents continue to resist the in-migration of whites, who may "take over." Social boundaries do exist based on length of residence, social class, and so forth. Nevertheless, the richly-textured rural life produces opportunities for people to feel good about themselves and to deal with the cultural contradictions imposed by a world demarcated by segregation. The durability of tightly knit all-black rural communities attests to the continuing human desire to maintain physical spaces in which life goes on according to predictable cultural and structural arrangements.

Themes of resistance to structural constraints, survival, and continuity of gender, ethnic, and racial identity characterize the preceding selections. Weibel-Orlando introduces the theme of reclamation of heritage through the return of a Sioux woman, Emma Walking Eagle, from Los Angeles to her reservation. Economic and cultural incentives plus a desire to be close to "Mother Earth" furnish powerful inducements for Native Americans to return to their reservation in later life. Because of the traditional respect accorded to elders as resources and preservers of tribal tradition, many older Native Americans also hope to enact these ancestral roles or to create new roles based on skills they developed when living elsewhere. Unlike the Biblical prodigal son, whose return home was greeted with joy by his family, however, Emma Walking Eagle found that after an initial "honeymoon" period, life was more difficult than she had expected. Regarded by others on the reservation as an "outsider" who had not "paid community dues," she found that the desired, high-status roles she was qualified to fill were not open to her. To reincorporate herself in the Sioux community, she established new roles, displaying both her expertise found when living away from the reservation and her tribal and ethnic identity. Like Johnson and McAuley, Weibel-Orlando emphasizes a constructive view of ethnicity, that is, people create and recreate their ethnic identities based on life experience and circumstances.

Aged immigrants face still a different challenge: to adapt to a new culture while carrying their expectations and values from the old. Even among elders who have lived most of their adult lives in the United States and who have internalized American norms and values, vestiges of their former culture remain. The short story selection by Chang depicts an elderly Chinese-American woman who has lived in America for many years and whose husband has returned to his native China to spend the remainder of his life. She did not accompany him, for, as her husband said, she would be regarded as "foreign" in China; she is "too American." Now old, frail, and alone, she feels both Chinese and American. As she deals with her physical frailty, she values her autonomy and resists advice to enter a nursing home. Contemplating both her past and a new future with a long-lost love, she finds peace within herself and with the limitations imposed by poor health and time itself. Her decisions illuminate the blending of her biculturalism and her commitment to survival.

The final reading in this section presents the perspectives of two African-American centenarians, "Bessie" and "Sadie" Delany, both living together in a middle-class suburb of New York City. The daughters of a father born into slavery and a free-born mother of mixed race, the Delany sisters are the oldest known surviving members of a distinguished southern African-American family. Valuing their independence and autonomy, neither sister ever married. Unlike well-off white women of their cohort who were expected to marry and become dependent upon their husbands, African-American women such as the Delanys were expected to be economically self-sufficient. For African-American women, as K. F. Slevin and C. R. Wingrove have observed,

> Racial hierarchy generated conditions that hindered black Americans while providing automatic privilege for whites. Consequently, black Americans needed more education. . . . Education was both a survival tool in an inhospitable world and a strategy of resistance to those who would deny African Americans the advantages that the educated enjoy. Even

though education might not pave the road to the American dream as many whites would experience it, its absence virtually ensured a life of manual labor for blacks. For black American women, lack of education would mean working in two kitchens—a white woman's as well as their own. (1998, p. 66)

The older of the two sisters, Sadie, who received a master's in education from Columbia University, was the first African American in New York City to teach home economics at the high-school level. Bessie, who earned a doctorate in dental surgery from Columbia University, was the second African-American woman licensed to practice in New York. Both pursued careers until their retirement in the 1950s. Despite their privileged social position, the Delany sisters were never immune to racial and gender discrimination. They grew up in a society bounded by both racial segregation and gender stratification and combated racism and sexism throughout their careers. Living independently in their own home at ages 100 and 102,[1] the narratives by the Delany sisters discredit three undifferentiated images of old age: the old-old as ineffectual, sick, and helpless; women of their race and birth cohort as unable to achieve in a white male world; and all African-American elders as poor, uneducated inhabitants of blighted ghettos.

As you read the following selections, consider the many ways in which these people have aged and the roles that they have played. Also think about how membership in racial or ethnic, gender, and social class groups has shaped their life course.

Note

1. Both Bessie and Sadie Delany died in the 1990s.

References

Mills, C. W. 1959. *The Sociological Imagination.* Greenwich, CT: Greenwood Press.

Slevin, K. F., and Wingrove, C. R. 1998. *From Stumbling Blocks to Stepping Stones.* New York: New York University Press.

Chapter 8
Gender Across Generations

Margaret Hellie Huyck
Pninah Zucker and
Cheryl Angellaccio

*U*nlike the biological designation of sex, gen-der identity is far more complex. Although we frequently use the terms masculine and femi-nine, their meanings vary from society to soci-ety and from one historical period to another. Even within a society, numerous gender iden-tities can coexist among people of the same biological sex, and they can be both negotiated and used to achieve particular social, eco-nomic, and political goals.

How is gender identity constructed? In the following selection, Margaret Huyck, Pninah Zucker, and Cheryl Angellaccio examine how gender behaviors are shaped by the interaction of biological sex, psychological factors, and cultural beliefs. They focus on the degree of variability in the ways adults define them-selves as "masculine" or "feminine" and review types of gender identity among two cohorts of adults—young adults and their parents. As you read the following selection, notice the many styles of "masculine" versus "feminine" self-concept. Think about the extent to which dif-ferences between young adults and their par-ents reflect developmental differences associ-ated with stage in the life course. Consider how age and sex intersect to create a particular self-definition and whether older people tend to be-come more "gender transcendent" or "gender sensitive." Ask yourself whether larger social changes or the desire to develop autonomy from one's parents seems to be more important in developing a particular gender style.

*A*re men and women really from different emotional planets? What makes you feel more masculine? Less masculine? Do you think these feelings will change as you grow older? How easy will it be for you to become your "own kind of woman," unlike your mother and grandmother?

These questions have intrigued scholars and ordinary people for centuries. This selec-tion will explore them by drawing primarily on research with one subgroup in the United States: young adults and their parents living in Parkville, a midwestern community; they are of European American heritage and were selected to represent some of the most stable families in the country.

Over the last two decades social scientists have refined the ways of thinking about males and females, especially in adulthood (Huyck 1989). Today they distinguish sex from gen-der. Sex includes the biological differentia-tion, genetically coded, which leads to repro-ductive specialization, prototypic body con-figurations, and—perhaps—differential vul-nerabilities in health. It is not very clear whether genetic sex also codes for differential cognitive and emotional response patterns (Plomin 1990). The advances in genetic re-search have provided a better understanding that most genetic information codes for sus-ceptibility or likely range of functioning. Ex-perience, including the biochemical environ-ment within the womb after conception, and all that happens after birth interact with ge-netic potential to shape actual (phenotypic) behavior. Gender refers to all the social and psychological consequences of sexual differ-entiation.

There is a great deal of continuing debate about how to conceptualize gender (Turner 1994). Much of the debate refers back to the classic nature-nurture question: is gender part of biological destiny or a social construc-tion? Many now believe that this is the wrong question. Rather, behaviors are shaped by the interacting influences of body, mind, and cul-ture. The body is the bedrock; psychic pro-cesses and cultural constraints must operate within the parameters set by sex-linked ge-netic differentiation, which includes repro-ductive specialization and all that this im-plies. From conception on, however, develop-ment proceeds from the interaction of genetic predispositions, individual responses to experiences, and sociocultural influences.

Cognitive theories about gender explain how the general thinking processes operate to use sex as one of the earliest categorizing variables; once persons are sorted into a category of male or female, all other processing about characteristics is done within existing frameworks of understanding about that category (Cross and Markus 1993). These basic cognitive processes lead persons not only to stereotype on the basis of minimal cues but to act in ways that evoke the expected behaviors (Geis 1993). Although cognitive schemas do change, as a result of repeated instances of poor fit between expectations and reality, change is difficult because new experiences are selectively perceived and interpreted from the perspective of the initial frameworks. The early cognitive frameworks, or schemas, begin to be established in the second year, as part of the acquisition of language and categorizing competencies. The cognitive models do not postulate any inherent content of the schemas beyond stating that schemas reflect experiences as interpreted by the person. Interpretations are influenced by one's temperament and early learning.

Many of the experiences available to the child and adult are shaped by culture. Culture includes all the shared beliefs about what is "natural," "desirable," and permissible for males and females; the social structures developed to implement those beliefs; and the various symbols used to convey the beliefs. Some of these beliefs have been shared by many cultures, such as that women are best suited to care for young infants and that men should be responsible for active warfare. The cultural beliefs may change over time. For example, Michael Kimmel, in his cultural history of manhood in America (1996), described the rise of a "self-made man" as the masculine ideal from 1776 to 1865 and the loss of a clear, shared standard of masculinity in recent decades. There has been substantial debate about the proper place of women in American society, and many social roles have opened for women. In addition, the norms for expressing emotion within marriage, for example, have also changed. In the early part of the twentieth century women were advised to preserve marriage by putting their husband first and avoiding all displays, or even feelings of anger; by the 1970s the advice had shifted toward the importance of wives expecting self-fulfillment and expressing anger openly as one route to power within the marriage (Cancian and Gordon 1988).

These three forces interact to shape one's sense of personal gender identity. As soon as we recognize we are female or male, we begin the process of constructing a sense of what that means to us. The content of the schemas, in terms of the linking of feelings, beliefs, and actions, reflect experiences. The earliest experiences that form the basic sense of love, power, and relatedness, as well as characteristics of woman (mom) and man (dad) are often submerged into subconscious awareness. Often such perceptions are "irrational" and do not fit with more adult conceptions. They linger, however, to influence our automatic responses to events and persons. Because of the split between the ways of knowing rooted in childhood and people's more sophisticated, considered beliefs, many people feel that they continue to hold conceptions of gender that are contradictory and often confusing. To the extent that this is an accurate description, it makes the study of adult conceptions of gender very challenging. When confronted with a questionnaire to fill out in private which asks us what we are like, we may respond in terms of how we wish we were; in a more extended personal discussion, we may admit the ways in which we do not meet our own images of how we wish we were. The authors designed their research to explore the various ways in which adults think about themselves as women or men. They were particularly interested in three related issues: variability in gender identity, possible cohort effects on gender identity, and developmental contributions to gender identity.

Variability in Gender Identity

The first issue in gender is, How much variability is there in the ways that adults define themselves as masculine or feminine? Much of the research has assumed that people think of themselves as masculine or feminine, in rather global ways, and most of the scales designed to measure gender identity are global masculinity-femininity scales. During the 1970s and 1980s, especially, other paradigms emerged (Sedney 1989). People could be gender-typed, or high on the "congruent" characteristics and low on qualities of the "other" gender, or they could be androgynous, or unisex—combining "masculine" and "feminine" characteristics equally. People could be "transcendent"—believing that sex had limited consequences and characteristics and behaviors should not be linked to gender either by oneself or by others. People could even experience "crossover" (Gutmann 1975), whereby they show strong evidence of characteristics associated with the other sex, for example, men come to experience themselves as "feminine" rather than "masculine."

The authors believe that these conceptualizations oversimplify the diverse ways in which women and men describe themselves as gendered and underestimate the extent to which feeling "appropriately gendered" is important to persons themselves and to all who interact with them. They decided to explore the varieties of femininity and masculinity used by adults to think about themselves and others, and to explore how adults dealt with personal qualities they could not fit into their own conceptualization of gender.

Cohort Effects

The second major issue has to do with understanding how sociocultural changes modify such interpretations. It seemed plausible to expect that the efforts of the women's movement to redefine gender would have some impact. It is generally assumed that people develop their basic understandings of what it means to be female or male during their adolescent and young-adult years, when interest in figuring out how to be an adult is strong, and the pressures to conform to social gender expectations arc substantial. People who are socialized into different models of what is "appropriate" ought to show different versions of gender identity. If this model is correct, one would expect to find differences between young adults and middle-aged adults. Generational differences could be in-

terpreted as "cohort effects," where differences reflect differential socialization, particularly if the differences appear in groups that otherwise share similar (never identical) life experiences.

Developmental Influences on Gender

The third issue in gender development is whether conceptualizations of gender undergo transformations because of normal developmental transitions over the life course. Many researchers have reported that, across a variety of cultures, older men seem to be less "masculine" and older women less "feminine" than younger adults (Gutmann 1987/[1994]). David Gutmann has made the most provocative hypothesis about these observations; he proposes that transitions in parental responsibility transform gender-related qualities. In his parental imperative model, younger males and females are socialized into stances that are appropriate to their usual roles as fatherprotector and mothernurturer; the psychological stances required to provide either physical security (fathers) or emotional security (mothers) to the dependent child are accepted by parents as a necessary sacrifice for the well-being of the child. Gutmann argues that good parents routinely repress aspects of themselves that are incompatible with providing security. Fathers, especially, repress their own desires to be dependent and their sense of vulnerability; often they also repress a good deal of sensitivity. Mothers usually repress their own desires to be in charge of their own lives and identify instead with the progress of the child and—in order to preserve the family unit—the father. As children grow up and become more independent, however, most parents at midlife begin to reclaim repressed aspects of the self (Gutmann 1975). Gutmann described a "normal androgyny of later life" in which each gender becomes more like the other and may even become "unisex." In this developmental model, midlife fathers are expected to be less resolutely masculine than their sons, and midlife mothers are expected to be more assertive and comfortable with self-direction than are their young-adult daughters. The predictions from a developmental model are quite different from those derived from a cohort-effects model.

Method: Sample and Data—Parkville

Exploring these issues is not easy. The authors decided to explore developmental shifts in gender identity within a restricted cultural group, preferably one that was similar to the relatively traditional cultures used by Gutmann to develop his hypothesis. The parental imperative model applies specifically to heterosexual couples engaged in long-term parenting relationships, in cultures that validate the social and psychological sacrifices made by both genders in order to parent effectively. Such couples were included in the Parkville sample.

The Parkville sample was recruited from graduates from the public high school in Parkville, an established community outside a major metropolis in the Midwest. Parkville began as an independent village with strong settlement from Western European immigrants. Until the past two decades, the community was almost entirely white, and the sample are all white. Among the parent generation, half of the sample are Catholic; most of the rest are Protestant. They are broadly middle class. The sample was selected to represent the most geographically and maritally stable families; the parents of the high school graduate selected randomly had to be still alive and married to each other, and the young-adult child had to be living within two hours' driving distance of the parental home.

Data collection included three phases. An initial interview was used to gather demographic data and assess appropriateness for inclusion. Those who were selected were asked to complete a packet of self-report questionnaires, including standardized measures for gender and mental health. Following this, personal interviews were conducted; one explored the relationship between parent and young adult and the other explored the individual's life structure. The final sample included members from approximately 140 families; the number available for specific analyses varies. Most of the data were collected in the early 1980s. . . .

Results

The results of the study may be distributed among three questions.

1. How Do Individuals Describe Themselves in Gender Terms?

Our primary assessment of gender styles utilized responses to interview questions about personal definitions of gender. Respondents were asked about the characteristics they associated with masculinity and femininity; how they thought men and women differ psychologically; whether they thought of themselves as feminine (if female) or masculine (if male) and how that self-perception influenced the things they did or did not do; and whether there were any ways in which they were not so feminine (if female) or masculine (if male). Two ratings of the interview materials were obtained. First, discrete, gender-relevant self-attributions were identified by listing every one of the different ways (91 in all) in which respondents described their gender. Second, more global styles were drawn from previous research and a general familiarity with the interviews from this sample. Because the results of the second measure were confirmed by the self-attributions, the findings reported here are in terms of the gender styles. P. Zucker (1988) developed an initial set of styles for 134 middle-aged mothers and 105 middle-aged fathers; C. Angellaccio (1990) found that with minor modifications, the styles could also describe the 66 young-adult sons and 67 young-adult daughters.

Men were classified as experiencing a specific masculine style on the basis of their descriptions of how they were masculine, and women were classified on the basis of their descriptions of how they were feminine. This measure differs from most other measures of gender in using the individual's own conceptual scheme, rather than forcing them to agree or disagree with a preconceived set of "masculine" or "feminine" attributes.

Men's experience of masculinity and women's femininity may be classified as *gender-congruent styles*. In addition, we were interested in exploring how men and women experience aspects of themselves that they associate with the other gender. These experiences may be classified as *gender-expanded* and *gender-compromised styles*.

Gender Styles Described by Men. Men's gender styles fall into three categories: gender-congruent, gender-expanded, and gender-compromised.

Gender-congruent styles. There are three styles that express gender congruence.

- **Macho:** A man presents himself as tough, physically strong, and virile. He tends to deny weaknesses within himself and often emphasizes his bodybuilding and physical-fitness activities. He may project whatever weakness he experiences within himself onto women. He perceives himself as dominating his wife and children (or girlfriend) and reports that they depend on him and look up to him as a source of strength, while he himself is independent. He makes it a point to state he is heterosexual, and he views women as objects of his sexual attraction and desire. His "masculinity" revolves around his inner aggression, which he finds difficult to channel into productive avenues. Instead, he accepts his aggression in its "raw" form and is even proud of it. He may drink, be loud, swear, and get involved in physical fights. He is likely to describe taking physical risks as part of his masculinity.

The macho style draws on the Dystonic Dependency man described by D. Gutmann, J. Grunes and B. Griffin (1982), who opposes his inner striving for nurturance, projects his "femininity" onto a "weak" wife, and adopts a counter-dependant stance. This style also draws on findings of studies that reported that physical attributes, behavioral characteristics, and sexual attitudes were salient to people's experience of gender (Myers and Gonda 1982; Smith and Midlarsky 1985).

- **Leader:** Style of a man who describes his gender identity in terms of the competitive work world. He is confident and assertive and finds it easy to take charge and to lead others. He is not afraid to voice his opinions and stands up for what he believes in and for justice in general. He is not afraid of challenges

and risks, and tasks requiring much effort do not scare him. On the contrary, he likes hard, challenging work. His masculinity seems to revolve around his determination to preserve the social order and thus to protect society in general.

In the leader style, aggressiveness is used to yield success in the man's occupation. This style corresponds to the popular view of masculinity, which equates it with activity, instrumentality, dominance, achievement, independence, assertivity, and aggressivity (Gutmann 1975; Kimmel 1996).

- **Family man:** Style of a man (first termed Husband/Father) who defines himself as masculine because he has proven to be a responsible provider and protector of his wife and children. He respects his wife and children and believes it is his duty to look after them. He views himself as a source of strength for his family, so that they can come to him for support and guidance. He does so, however, not because he is strong and they are weak and therefore to be dominated, but out of his sense of duty to and responsibility for them. Some of the unmarried young-adult men displayed similar conceptualizations when they talked about protecting their (real or anticipated) girlfriends. This man takes pride in channeling aggressive potential into a protective role. The key to this style is the definition of masculinity in a positive interpersonal relationship.

The family man style was proposed since theory and studies have found that family roles are a critical component for men's experience in midlife (Barnett and Baruch 1987; Farrell and Rosenberg 1981; Levinson et al. 1978; Veroff, Douvan, and Kulka 1981).

Gender-expanded styles. There are three styles that reflect expanded gender or androgeny.

- **Activity androgyny:** Style of a man who acknowledges his own potentials for emotion and nurturance within himself in a guarded form by assuming tasks and roles that he associates with women's domain (sharing household chores, cleaning house, cooking, gardening). He is more sensually diffuse and may indicate that he enjoys art, music, and theater, which he mentions when queried about ways in which he is "not so masculine." He may point out that he enjoys women's company (but not primarily as sexual partners); he likes talking to women and enjoys listening to what they have to say. Younger men in the sample were often more apologetic that they still thought of certain tasks in gender-linked terms (e.g., laundry, cooking); but if they indicated that these activities remain gendered, they were coded as showing activity androgyny if they did those activities. If they indicated they had grown up regarding such activities (cooking, laundry, yard work, car maintenance) as gender-neutral signs of independence and self-sufficiency, they were not coded as androgynous even if they mentioned that they had come to realize, as adults, that many people considered these activities sex-typed.

- *Inner androgyny:* Style of a man who is more in touch with his own expanded definition of gender. He comfortably accepts his feminine qualities as part of his human potential rather than as something foreign to him. He acknowledges his emotionality and admits to feeling pain and being hurt on occasions. He also expresses his emotions; he may report he cries at sad movies or when he is slighted. Furthermore, he perceives himself as sensitive to the feelings and needs of others, as a good listener, as tender, and as friendly.

- *Denial of incongruence:* Style of a man who, in response to the question of how he is not masculine, denies any androgynous, feminine qualities and does not consider his masculinity diminished or compromised in any way.

Gender-compromised styles. There are two styles that reflect diminished or compromised gender.

- *Diminished stereotypical masculinity:* Style of a man who presents himself as

either being less "masculine" than he used to be or as not being what he regards as stereotypically "masculine." The qualities that he had and lost, or never had, are seen as typically "masculine" and not feminine; thus, this style is not usefully regarded as a form of gender expansion (or androgyny). He may feel that he is not as physically strong anymore or does not chase women anymore or get involved in physical fights. He may also feel that his authority has diminished together with his leadership position. Younger men in the sample were more apt to emphasize how they are not "stereotypic" men; their point of reference seemed to be an image of man rather than their own prior youth.

- *Facade:* Style of a man who relinquishes his masculine stance, indicating that it has been a strain or a facade all along. (The middle-aged men in the sample indicated that they acted masculine in the past either because it was the social role that was expected of them or because they felt obliged to do so for the benefit of their children.) Acting "masculine" was a role that he played and resented because he did not feel that deep inside he was "masculine" or that he wanted the "masculine" role. At midlife, he accepts his dependency on his wife and would like her to take care of him just as she took care of their children. The younger men in the sample posed this issue in more ideological terms, claiming that sex had no relevance for behavior, that they were unwilling to acknowledge any ways in which their behaviors and choices were influenced by sex, and that they would not be willing to accept traditional male roles such as providing any kinds of security for women and children. That is, they did not identify with any of the "positive" aspects of either masculinity or femininity but backed away from the issue.

Gender Styles Described by Women.
Women's gender styles fall into the same three categories as those of men: gender-con-

gruent, gender-compromised, and gender-expanded.

Gender-congruent styles. There are three gender-congruent styles for women.

- **Femme:** Style of a woman who is concerned with the image she projects in public. She feels that her feminine qualities are reflected in how she dresses and wears her hair and in her feminine manners. She feels feminine when she speaks softly, watches her language, and adheres to etiquette. She appreciates male chivalry, likes male attentions, and wants to be treated like a lady. She reports that she sees herself as dependent on her husband or boyfriend, observes the traditional division of labor at home, and may consider herself to be mechanically incompetent. At times, even though she is capable of more and does not think she is dependent, she chooses to pretend and assume the role of a docile and dependent wife or girlfriend. She may also be quite angry with women who are not like her, possibly because of what that may imply about her own potential.

This style draws on research findings in which femininity was associated with appearance and clothes, attention to manners, and undesirable passivity (Myers and Gonda 1982; Smith and Midlarsky 1985).

- **Nurturer:** Style of a woman who's femininity is not specifically centered on her family. She describes herself as nurturant and affectionate toward people in general. She feels she is feminine because she is in touch with her emotions and is not afraid to express them. People in general, and relationships in particular, are important to her, and she does much to foster them. She feels she is sensitive and responsive to the needs and feelings of others. She considers herself a good friend and a good listener. She is a woman who cares for others.

This style draws on views that associate femininity with affiliation, affectivity, and nurturance (Gutmann 1975; Smith and Mid-

larsky 1985). Thus, in varying degrees, it reflects the femininity scales on the various gender instruments.

- **Family woman:** Style of a woman (first termed Wife/Mother for the middle-aged generation) who defines her femininity in relation to (real or potential) boyfriends, lovers, fiancé, husbands, or children. This woman's femininity revolves around her family. She considers herself as responsible for the emotional welfare of her husband or boyfriend and family and at times lets their needs come before hers. She defines herself as feminine by nurturing them emotionally, being sensitive to their needs and feelings, listening to them, and responding to them. It is important to her to give them a feeling of a home, so she cleans the house, decorates it, does the laundry, and cooks for her family; doing so makes her feel more feminine, and not doing so makes her feel less feminine.

This style draws from theoretical views associating women's role with the emotional well-being of their children (Gutmann 1975), as well as research findings that tie femininity to motherhood and being a homemaker (Smith and Midlarsky 1985).

Gender-expanded styles. Three styles express an expanded sense of gender for women.

- **Activity androgyny:** Style of a woman who accepts her strengths and capacity for autonomy in a limited way, by doing what she herself views as "masculine" things. Her strengths and capacities are mostly expressed as physical strength and mechanical capacity. Thus, she may describe herself as "not so feminine" because she considers herself physically strong, as having a strong body, and as liking or being involved in physical work and activities; consequently, she may not observe the traditional division of labor in the house and may do "hard" chores. She may paint the house, clean the yard, shovel snow, and put up storm windows; and she herself defines these as "masculine" activities. Her physical competence may make her feel competent in general and potentially independent. While many of the middle-aged women in the sample resented having to do such tasks in the past, many felt positive about the present and future benefits of their competence.

- ***Inner androgyny:*** Style of a woman who acknowledges the dynamic, assertive, and independent aspects of herself as part of her human potential, even though she implies or openly acknowledges that these are "masculine" qualities. She views herself as an assertive, outspoken person who is not afraid to voice her opinions. She considers herself to be a capable, achievement-oriented woman who gets the job done, and she may easily assume leadership in groups, being the "take charge" person that she regards herself to be.

- ***Denial of incongruence.*** Style of a woman who denies that there are any ways in which she is not feminine, either because she recognizes qualities in herself that she regards as "masculine" or because she is not as feminine as her internalized social stereotypes of acceptable femininity.

Gender-compromised styles. There are two styles that express women's sense of compromised gender.

- ***Diminished stereotypical femininity:*** Style of a woman who views herself as less "feminine" than she used to be (if middle-aged, or even young adult), or in comparison to what she considers to be reasonable feminine stereotypes (including physical attributes, behaviors, and traits). Thus, the qualities that she may mention are not typically associated with masculinity. Rather, she may *feel* less or not attractive in general, and not attractive to men in particular. She may consider herself less or not invested in her house and family or in her appearance.

- ***Facade:*** Style of a woman who is very uncomfortable with vulnerability or with accommodating to the needs of others. (The middle-aged mothers in the sample indicated that as long as they actively mothered children they managed to deny their assertiveness and needs for autonomy; as they become independent, they no longer found it necessary to deny their true nature.) Such a woman is relieved finally to be true to herself—to be competitive and even aggressive. The younger women in the sample focused more on the irrelevance of gender for behavior and contended that they were unwilling (and unable) to act as if sex or social expectations had any bearing on their behavior. Some of them also indicated that they were quite willing and able to "fake it" and "pass" for being appropriately feminine if it served their purpose, but they were very clear about the split between the pretense (facade) and the "real me."

Variability. The distribution of responses for each of the measures of gender style is shown in Table 8.1. The numbers in each group do not necessarily add up to 100 percent because each person could be classified into several concurrent gender-congruent styles and several gender-expanded or gender-compromised styles.

Among the Parkville men, the most common masculine style was that of family man, men who said they were masculine because they accepted responsibility for the welfare of their wife (or girlfriend) and children; 41.5

Table 8.1

Gender Styles of Men and Women		
	Men **171**	**Women** **201**
Gender-congruent styles		
Macho/femme	28.6%	49.8%
Leader/nurturer	26.3	30.3
Family man/Family woman	41.5	21.9
Denial of incongruence	33.9	27.4
Gender-expanded styles		
Activity androgyny	8.2%	20.4%
Inner androgyny	30.4	26.9
Gender-compromised styles		
Diminished stereotypical masculinity/femininity	25.7%	29.9%
Facade	8.8%	8.8%

percent described themselves in this way. In comparison, only 21.9 percent of the women defined themselves as feminine because of their family care. Half (49.8 percent) of the women described their femininity in terms of appearance and demeanor, the femme. Nearly a third of men and women said there was no way they were not masculine or feminine. However, nearly a third described some way in which they recognized qualities of the "other" gender in themselves, usually in terms of emotional responses (inner androgeny). Men were most apt to describe what they regarded as "feminine" sensitivities to sensuality, criticism, or art; women most often spoke of anger or self-will. Few men (8.2 percent) described themselves as "not so masculine" because they engaged in activities they considered unmasculine; the men either avoided doing things they defined as feminine, or they redefined necessary tasks as gender neutral or even masculine. An example of redefinition are the young men who said they had regarded housework as feminine (and to be avoided) until they began living alone; they then defined it as an aspect of masculine independence and autonomy.

2. Is There a Generation Gap in Gender?

The second question asked in the study concerned possible cohort effects. Are there differences in the ways young adults and midlife adults define their gender identity? Table 8.2 summarizes the responses of the four major groups (age by sex). This analysis suggests that some of the expected cohort effects were evident: young women, especially, were more likely to describe themselves as nonfeminine in some way, as "nonstereotypic," and were less likely to describe themselves as feminine because they nurtured and cared for family or boyfriend. These are the kinds of changes predicted by a model of social change.

3. Are There Developmental Changes in Gender?

In order to explore the possibility that development of the kinds identified by Gutmann shape experiences of gender, the study carried out analyses for each generation. Young adults were compared with their own same-sex parent to see if those who had moved into adult responsibilities of marriage and parenting were more similar to their parents. Midlife parents were compared on moving into the "empty nest" phase of life. Results for the midlife parents have been reported elsewhere (Huyck and Gutmann 1992; Gutmann and Huyck 1994; Huyck 1994); patterns for the young adults are included here.

Table 8.2

Gender Styles by Sex and Generation:
Percentage Endorsing Various Styles, as Coded From Interviews

	Middle Aged		Young Adult	
	Men	**Women**	**Men**	**Women**
	105	**134**	**66**	**67**
Gender-congruent styles				
Macho/femme	27.6%	52.2%	30.3%	44.8%
Leader/nurturer	25.7	29.9	27.3	31.3
Family man/Family woman	46.7	23.1	33.3	19.4
Denial of incongruence	35.2	32.8	34.8	16.4
Gender-expanded styles				
Activity androgyny	17.1%	26.1%	9.1%	9.0%
Inner androgyny	29.5	28.4	31.8	23.9
Gender-compromised styles				
Diminished stereotypical masculinity/femininity	19.1%	14.9%	36.4%	59.7%
Facade	4.8	3.7	15.2	16.4

Each young-adult child was compared with his or her own same-sex parent on the ways in which gender style was expressed. We used this strategy as our best approximation of controlling for the sociocultural milieu, while being able to measure several indices of development. The sample for these analyses included only pairs where gender-style ratings were available for both generations; we had 66 father-son and 67 mother-daughter pairs.

Scale of Masculinity and Femininity

In addition to the gender styles described above, the authors included in the study a standardized self-report questionnaire scale of masculinity and femininity (M and F)(Berzins, Welling, and Wetter 1978). We used three measures of the young-adult child's age: chronological age (21 to 25 and 26 to 31); marital status (single vs. married); and parental status (no children vs. one or more children). Table 8.3a and 8.3b summarize the results in terms of whether the parent-child dyadic pairs were similar (signified by =) or different. In Table 8.3a, a D indicates that the young adult daughters were more

likely to score high (on M or F) or describe themselves in that gender style compared with their own mothers. In Table 8.3b, an S indicates that the young-adult son was more likely to have a high score (in terms of the M and F scale) or describe himself in terms of a particular style; an F indicates that the father was more likely to describe himself in a particular style.

Daughters and Their Mothers. What is striking is the pattern of = signs in four of the six columns, indicating that the daughters were not different from their own mothers on the measures. Dissimilarity from the mother was evident only in the younger women, primarily when the daughter was unmarried. The young-adult women (under 25) showed what we might expect from a social change or cohort model: they reported higher scores on the masculinity scale, and they were more likely to describe themselves as not very feminine or just "passing" when it seemed necessary or useful. However, a cohort model is challenged because the more mature young women do not differ from their own mothers on any of the gender measures.

Table 8.3a

Development of Gender Congruence:
Young-Adult Daughter and Midlife Mother Similarity by Daughter Age

| | **Younger** | | | | **Older** | |
Age Measure	**21–25**	**Single**	**No children**	**26–31**	**Married**	**Parent**
N Dyads	25	27	38	33	31	20
PRF-masculinity	D	D	D	=	=	=
PRF-femininity	=	=	=	=	=	=
Gender-congruent styles						
Femme	=	D	=	=	=	=
Nurturer	D	D	=	=	=	=
Family woman	d	=	=	=	=	=
Denial of Incongruence	=	d	=	=	=	=
Gender-expanded styles						
Activity androgyny	=	d	=	=	=	=
Inner androgyny	=	d	=	=	=	=
Gender-compromised styles						
Diminished stereotypical masculinity/femininity	d	D	=	=	=	=
Facade	d	D	=	=	=	=

NOTE: Single = not married, not a parent; No children = married, no children; Married = no children; Parent = married, children; Younger = 21–25/Older = 26–31; S,D,F = Son, daughter, or father more likely to have high score or style at p < .05; s,d = son or daughter more likely to have high score or style at p < .10

Sons and Their Fathers. When we examine the pattern for the father-son dyads, several differences are evident. As expected from much other research, the young-adult men generally scored higher on the masculinity scale than did their own fathers; however, it is notable that this was not true for the sons who had become fathers themselves. Some of the younger sons seemed to be differentiating themselves from their own fathers by psychologically distancing themselves from gender issues generally. This finding is most evident in the relatively small group of young-adult men (15 percent) who report a facade style. On the one hand, these young men seemed to be saying that the responsibilities of masculinity were too much for them; their interviews made it clear that they did not feel capable of assuming what they regarded as the burdens of being a good provider and protector, and many of them had fathers whom they regarded as abusive. Masculine "strength" was seen as more brutalizing and intrusive than supportive, and they did not seem to have alternative, more positive images of masculinity. On the other hand, the young-adult men who had married were very similar to their own fathers. Interestingly, the more masculine (higher M score) middle-aged fathers were more likely to have sons who married in their 20s, indicating another family influence on these patterns of movement into adulthood.

Discussion

This research has described ways in which a relatively homogeneous sample of adult men and women described themselves in terms of their gender. It is perhaps notable that the families were selected for participation in the study because they represented marital and geographic stability. Virtually all the women easily described ways in which they felt feminine, and most men described ways in which they felt masculine; the conceptions, however, varied. In addition, many described varied ways in which their own characteristics were not congruent with their own conceptions of their gender. The implication is that adult men and women develop complex and individualized schemas in which they experience themselves as acceptably feminine or masculine in ways congruent with their sex. The women seem to rely substantially on controlling their appearance and demeanor; having "secured" their femininity, as it were, they are comfortable with

Table 8.3b

Development of Gender Congruence:
Young-Adult Son and Midlife Father Similarity by Son Age

Age index	Younger			Older		
	21–25	Single	No children	26–31	Married	Parent
N Dyads	22	33	38	34	21	14
PRF-masculinity	=	s	S	S	S	=
PRF-femininity	=	=	=	=	=	=
Gender-congruent styles						
Femme	=	s	=	S	=	=
Nurturer	=	=	=	=	=	=
Family	F	=	=	=	=	=
Denial of Incongruence	=	=	=	s	=	=
Gender-expanded styles						
Activity androgyny	=	=	=	=	=	=
Inner androgyny	=	=	=	F	=	=
Gender-compromised styles						
Diminished stereotypical masculinity/femininity	s	s	s	s	=	=
Facade	s	s	s	s	=	=

actions and stances that they regard as more "masculine." Behaving in such masculine ways, however, does not make them feel unfeminine as long as they have a secure sense of gender-congruent style. Similarly, even when men lose muscular strength (which nearly all the men associated with masculinity) or occupational power, they anchor their sense of masculinity in their willingness to be there for their families, to provide as best they can, to keep concerns to themselves that might worry their wife or children, and to serve as "head" of family to the best of their ability. As long as he can feel he has done this reasonably well, he can feel secure in his gender-congruent identity. From that stance, he can "expand" into other arenas without feeling "unmanned."

What About Gender Expansion vs. 'Androgyny'?

Except for the minority of young adults in this sample who were having obvious difficulty in coming to terms with their basic gender, and who almost refused to admit that being male or female has any social or psychological consequence, the men and women in Parkville were clear about the ways in which they experience themselves primarily in terms of gender-congruent styles. Their first experience of self had to do with how they dealt with their own maleness or femaleness. The persons represented here had developed varied ways of recognizing themselves as "masculine" or "feminine," but the underlying theme was how much and how comfortably they could feel and behave in ways that they believed were congruent with their sex. The primacy of these gender-congruent styles makes good sense in terms of theories that posit that organizing perceptions by sex remains a powerful principle throughout life.

Congruent gender forms the basis for adding (or rejecting) any interests or behaviors associated with the "other" gender. For example, recognizing a desire or propensity to confront criticism by direct challenge is typically experienced as gender congruent by males because it declares a very core aspect of masculinity. Women who recognize the "same" propensity in themselves generally feel ambivalent about it and may control the desire in order to remain gender congruent, or they may act on the desire in order to demonstrate they are not limited by their gender. In any event, such actions are not neutral. Similarly, individuals are not regarded as sexless "persons" by others. The "same" behavior will be evaluated, and responded to, by others in terms of the sex and presumed gender of the actor.

The degree to which behaviors and evaluations of them are linked to gender varies, among persons and probably by historical period and culture. On the basis of previous analyses of the Parkville data, Huyck (1989) suggested that the older middle-aged men are relatively "gender sensitive" and the older, upper-middle-class women are relatively "gender transcendent." However, the basic template for personal awareness and social interactions remains gendered.

Huyck (1994) has argued that it is unrealistic and unreasonable to think in terms of "androgyny," "unisex," or "gender-free" realities. These terms could be dropped from our conceptual vocabulary.

What Have We Learned in Parkville About Gender Development?

According to the Parkville study, gender remains an important dimension of self-identity and appraisals of others, even though adults are challenging some of the "traditional" expectations, even in this "traditional" community. Sixty percent of the young-adult women said they did not conform to stereotypic expectations. This finding supports a cohort, or social-change model of socialization into gender, that is, that our birth cohort or social change influences the way we think about our gender. However, the comparisons of younger and more mature daughters with their own mothers suggests a different story. While the youngest women (21 to 25 and unmarried) were quite different from their own mothers in feeling more "masculine" and less identified with nurture, the young women who were over 25, or married, or mothers, were not different from their own mothers. Although it is possible that even the small difference in age represents a "cohort," a developmental explanation seems more reasonable.

The pattern of similarity to one's own mother, the authors believe (on the basis of familiarity with the interviews and personal experiences), reflects three processes. First, and probably most fundamental, is the daughter's movement into the social-psychological role of wife and partner, where she has linked her life structure to that of a chosen man. Most of these young women also hope, and intend, to become mothers. The patterns of behavior that seem to have worked for their parents in realizing these desires are evoked when the women themselves assume the responsibilities as a wife and mother. In addition, most young women seem to focus on developing autonomy from the mother during their adolescent and younger adult years; if they have done so adequately, they can become like their mother without feeling absorbed or merged. Many of the older young-adult women described this transition in relation to their mother, indicating how they deliberately felt they had to be, or act, differently from their mother in order to gain a sense of their own identity; but having done so, they could see the merits of their mother's position and recognize their own similarity to their mother without feeling threatened. (See Frank, Avery, and Laman 1988, for a discussion of autonomy and relatedness between young adults and their parents in this sample.)

The second process in the pattern reflects the mother's own developmental changes. As has been well documented in other research, many women become more self-confident and assertive in midlife; among the midlife mothers in Parkville, this greater assertiveness was largely evident when they described their marriage relationship as their grown children were leaving home (Huyck 1994).

The third process involves the ways in which both generations are socializing each other, and both are being influenced by larger social changes. The middle-aged mothers in the study described ways in which they had modified their assumptions about what was necessary or even desirable for feminine behavior, on the basis of discussions with daughters and daughters-in-law and by observing how these younger women managed their lives. It is also important to point out that some mothers in the study were watching their daughters and were intensely uncomfortable with what they regard as "unfeminine" behavior, because they feared it would threaten the stability of the marriage or jeopardize the emotional security of their grandchildren. Both generations talked about their awareness of the women's movement; exhortations from the media were filtered through the family culture, which probably helps account for the high mother-daughter congruence.

One third of the young men in the study described themselves as not meeting stereotypic standards of masculinity, and some of them felt clearly uncomfortable seeing themselves as masculine. Overall, the young-adult sons described themselves as more "masculine" than their fathers did; the sons who had become fathers themselves were like their own fathers.

The data do not offer much support for the theory that one's cohort affects one's development. Rather, young adults seem to show ways of differentiating themselves from their own same-sex parents, but this differentiation virtually disappears when young persons marry. While there is clear variability in the ways in which the men and women in Parkville experienced their own gender identity, their own children seemed to follow whatever "family style" had been established. These patterns support the socio-evolutionary model, which assumes that behaviors that are adaptive for family functioning are preserved and activated at the developmentally appropriate points in the life course. The results are also congruent with psychodynamic theories, which postulate that identification with the same-sex parent is a mark of mature, adaptive behavior; and with social-learning theories, which describe the mechanisms through which behaviors might be acquired once the emotional identification specified by dynamic theory has been accomplished.

This conclusion suggests that some of the apparent generational differences that have been reported, particularly in studies utilizing college students, may be linked to developmental issues rather than social change. Overall, the results suggest that both younger sons and daughters differentiate from their own same-sex parent partly by redefining aspects of gender. These kinds of differentiation might suggest a "generation gap" or strong evidence of social change. However, the fact that the "gap" within family-dyads is no longer evident as the young person moves into adult family roles (of marriage and parenthood) strongly supports the developmental explanation of gender style.

What Are the Implications for Theory, Practice, and Further Research?

The ratings based on interviews about gender make it clear that adults develop varied ways of defining themselves as appropriately masculine or feminine. While acknowledging media stereotypes, they are not necessarily coerced by them. This is a positive sign, since it means that social science can help persons identify the diverse ways in which they can be, and are, gender congruent. From this base of security, it seems easier to acknowledge aspects of the self that are not congruent with personal or stereotypic gender and to take pleasure in those expansions.

Gender is more problematic for men than for women. Women, particularly midlife women, seem to be better able to incorporate what they feel are masculine characteristics without feeling compromised in their femininity. The young men who do not feel masculine are less likely to move into the adult roles of marriage and fatherhood. The consequences of psychological passivity for midlife men depends on the wife's response (Gutmann and Huyck 1994); if she is accepting, his passivity is not problematic, but if he feels she demeans it, he is likely to feel very stressed. Clinicians and marriage counselors must remember that a husband's complaints of a domineering wife may reflect his own internalized sensitivities much more than significant change in his wife's behavior. Such sensitivities are likely to reflect his own early developmental problems in separating from his mother.

What Further Research Is Needed?

Researchers need to develop reliable, validated, easy-to-administer measures that are sensitive to the ways that gender-congruent, gender-expanded, and gender-compromised styles are developed, maintained, and modified. The coding scheme developed for the Parkville sample must be tested for applicability with other samples. Barbara Turner and her colleagues are testing the scheme with a more diverse group of adults in the Boston area; while most fit within the Parkville system, some do not (Turner 1994). Since the conceptual framework assumes diversity in self-definitions of gender, this is not surprising. The patterns identified here should be explored in groups that differ from the Parkville sample in terms of age, marital and family history, sexual orientation, ethnicity, and other characteristics that may well influence gender development over the life course.

While this study has attempted to compare cohort and developmental theories of gender change, the research design used can lead only to suggested results. Longitudinal, preferably cross-sequential, cross-cultural research is needed. Although the authors do not believe that gender will ever become irrelevant in terms of personal or social identity, the scope, content, and consequences will continue to shift. We have developed a conceptual model of gender congruence, gender expansion, and gender compromise that should clarify further research.

Discussion Questions

1. Describe the "gender-congruent," "gender-expanded," and "gender-compromised" styles for men and for women. Do you agree with the authors' designations of these styles?

2. What developmental changes in gender styles occurred when young adults moved into marriage (and parenthood)?

3. Discuss the evidence presented to support whether birth cohort or societal change is more important for gender socialization.

4. What results do you think would be found if this study were repeated with a middle-class African American sample of young adults and their parents? With a Latino sample?

5. Among the various gender styles presented, which comes the closest to your own self-identity?

Acknowledgments

The intergenerational research project "Aging Parents, Young Adult Children and Mental Health" was funded by a U.S. Public Health Services grant from the Center on Aging, National Institute of Mental Health, Grant Number ROI Mi-i36264, to the Illinois Institute of Technology from 1982 to 1986, M. Huyck and S. Frank, Co-Principal Investigators. We especially appreciate the guidance of Dr. Nancy Miller and Dr. Barry Lebowitz from NIMH for their guidance in establishing the project. We would like to thank all the respondents who participated and shared their lives with us; Susan Frank for her contributions in establishing the data set; Amy Shapiro for her work as project coordinator; and the students who have helped collect the data and prepare it for analysis. Interviewers included Scott Andrews, Jeffrey Angevine, Larry Antoz, Mike Bloomquist, Yael Buchsbaum, Cathy Butler Avery, Lidia Cardone, Paul Carney, Rita Decker, Helen Dredze, Jim Duchon, Susan Frank, Gall Grossman, Dee Heinrich, Jeri Hosick, Margaret Huyck, Mark Laman, Hunter Leggitt, Bill Pace, Timothy Pedigo, Kate Philben, Martha Scott, and Mary Jane Thiel. Special work on the data reported in this paper was carried out by Christine deGrange and Percy Wang, while they were undergraduate students at IIT.

References

Angellaccio, C. 1990. "Gender Identity of Young Adults." Masters Thesis, Illinois Institute of Technology.

Barnett, R., and Baruch, G. 1987. "Determinants of Father's Participation in Family Work." *Journal of Marriage and the Family* 49 (1): 29–40.

Berzins, J., Welling, M., and Wetter, R. 1978. "A New Measure of Psychological Androgyny Based on the Personality Research Form." *Journal of Consulting and Clinical Psychology*, 46(1): 126–138.

Cancian, F. M., and Gordon, S. L. 1988. "Changing Emotion Norms in Marriage: Love and Anger in U.S. Women's Magazines Since 1900." *Gender & Society*, 2(3): 308–342.

Cross, S. E., and Markus, H. R. 1993. "Gender in Thought, Belief and Action: A Cognitive Approach." In A. Beall & R. J. Sternberg, eds., *The Psychology of Gender*, pp. 55–98. New York: Guilford.

Farrell, M. P., & Rosenberg, S. 1981. *Men at Midlife*. Dover, MA: Auburn House.

Frank, S. F., Avery, C. B., and Laman, M. 1988. "Young Adults' Perceptions of Their Relationships With Their Parents: Individual Differences in Connectedness, Competence, and Emotional Autonomy." *Developmental Psychology*, 24(5): 729–737.

Geis, F. L. 1993. "Self-fulfilling Prophecies: A Social-Psychological View of Gender." In A. Beall & R. J. Sternberg, eds., *The Psychology of Gender*, pp. 9–54. New York: Guilford.

Gutmann, D. L. 1975. "Parenthood: A Key to the Comparative Study of the Life Cycle?" In N. Datan and R. Levine, eds., *Life-Span Developmental Psychology: Normative Life Crises*. New York: Academic Press.

——. [1987] 1994. *Reclaimed Powers: Toward a New Psychology of Men and Women in Later Life*. Evanston: Northwestern University Press.

Gutmann, D., Grunes, J., and Griffin, B. 1982. "Developmental Contributions to the Late-Onset Disorders." In O. Brim and P. Baltes, eds., *Life-span Development and Behavior* (vol. 4). San Diego, CA: Academic Press.

Gutmann, D. L., and Huyck, M. H. 1994. "Development and Pathology in Postparental Men: A Community Study." In E. Thompson Jr., ed., *Older Men's Lives*, pp. 65–84. Thousand Oaks, CA: Sage.

Huyck, M. H. [1989] 1991. "Midlife Parental Imperatives." In R. Kalish, ed., *Midlife Loss: Coping Strategies*, pp. 115–148. Reprinted in B. Hess and E. Markson, eds., *Growing Old in America* (4th ed), as "Parents and Children: The 'Postparental Imperatives,'" pp. 415–426. New Brunswick, NJ: Transaction.

——. 1989b. "Models of Midlife." In R. Kalish, ed., *Midlife Loss: Coping Strategies*, pp. 10–34. Newbury Park, CA: Sage.

——. 1990. "Gender Differences in Aging." In J. Birren & K. W. Schaie, eds., *Handbook of the Psychology of Aging* (3rd ed), pp. 124–134. New York: Academic Press.

——. 1991. "Gender-linked Self-attributions and Mental Health Among Middle-aged Parents." *Journal of Aging Studies*, 5(l): 111–123.

——. 1994. "The Relevance of Psychodynamic Theories for Understanding Gender Among Older Women." In B. Turner and L. Troll, eds., *Women Growing Older: Theoretical Directions in the Psychology of Aging*, pp. 202–238. Newbury Park, CA: Sage.

Huyck, M. H., & Gutmann, D. L. 1992. "Thirty-something Years of Marriage: Understanding Husbands and Wives in Enduring Relationships." *Family Perspective*, 26(2): 249–265.

Kimmel, M. 1996. *Manhood in America: A Cultural History*. New York: Free Press.

Levinson, D. J., Darrow, C. N., Klein, E. B., Levinstein, M. H., and McKee, B. 1978. *The Seasons of a Man's Life*. New York: Knopf.

Myers, A. M., and Gonda, G., 1982. "Utility of the Masculinity-Femininity Construction and Comparison of Traditional and Androgyny Approaches." *Journal of Personality and Social Psychology*, 43(3): 514–522.

Plomin, R. 1990. *Nature and Nurture: An Introduction to Human Behavioral Genetics*. Belmont, CA: Brooks/Cole.

Schaie, K. W., Campbell, R. T., Meredith, W., and Rawlings, S. C. (eds.) 1992. *Issues in Aging Research*. New York: Springer.

Sedney, M. A. 1989. "Conceptual and Methodological Sources of Controversies About Androgyny." In R. K. Unger, ed., *Representations: Social Constructions of Gender*, pp. 126–144. Amityville, NY: Baywood.

Smith, P. A., and Midlarsky, E. 1985. "Empirically Derived Conceptions of Femaleness and Maleness: A Current View." *Sex Roles*, 12(3/4): 313–328.

Turner, B. F. 1994. "Introduction." In B. F. Turner and L. Troll, eds., *Women Growing Older: Theoretical Directions in the Psychology of Aging*, pp. 1–34. Newbury Park, CA: Sage.

Veroff, J., Douvan, E., and Kulka, C. 1981. *The Inner American*. New York: Basic Books.

Zucker, P. 1988. "A Typology of Gender Styles Applicable to the Second Half of Life." Ph.D. dissertation, Illinois Institute of Technology.

M. H. Huyck, P. Zucker, and C. Angellaccio, "Gender Across Generations: Styles of Gender Identity Among Young Adult Children and Their Midlife Parents." Printed by permission of the authors.

Chapter 9

Definitions of Femininity: Youth to Old Age

Barbara Formaniak Turner
and Priyanthi Silva

The preceding selection identified a series of gender styles among middle-class, white young adults and their middle-aged parents. To what extent are these styles characteristic of women more diverse in age, race, social class, and marital and parental status? The following selection explores these questions. As gerontologists, Barbara Turner and Priyanthi Silva were particularly interested in analyzing age differences in the dimensions of gender identity: do dimensions of gender identity differ among women of different ages? They use a statistical technique called factor analysis to identify the various ways in which women describe femininity. Factor analysis is a way of reducing large amounts of data into categories into which responses are placed based on their similarity. It enables the researcher to discover and identify the specific dimensions, called factors, behind many measures.

Think about the various gender styles the authors identified in the following selection and their implications for gender stratification. Note any differences in results from those found by Huyck, Zucker, and Angellaccio. Given the diversity in styles, how meaningful is gender stereotyping? Also keep in mind that their study was cross-sectional; that is, for practical reasons, they were unable to follow the same sample longitudinally over a long period to determine whether birth cohort or social changes, such as the women's movement, were more important in their consideration of age differences in gender styles. Longitudinal studies, although useful in determining the ef-

fects of one's cohort as distinct from the effects of social change, are nevertheless expensive and require a long time for completion.

This selection describes how American women between the ages of 20 and 94 personally define what it is to be feminine, and how they experience their own gender identity. Gender is the social-psychological dimension of one's biological, or chromosomal, sex status. By gender identity is meant "how one defines oneself as a woman [or man], and in what ways one feels feminine or masculine" (Huyck 1994, p. 203). Because a person's gender and gender identity both strongly influence, and are created in, that person's interactions with others, gender identity is an important aspect of overall identity and sense of self.

Until the 1980s, psychologists who studied gender identity usually assumed that people defined their masculinity and femininity in terms of stereotypically feminine and masculine personality traits. Most research used objective paper-and-pencil measures of personality traits to assess a person's masculinity and femininity. Researchers in the 1970s often used such trait tests to classify people into four mutually exclusive gender "types"—high masculine, high feminine, androgynous (high on both masculine and feminine traits), and undifferentiated (low on both) (Turner 1994). Since then, however, psychologists have come to think that masculinity and femininity consist of several dimensions in addition to personality traits, such as physical characteristics, interests, role behaviors, occupational roles and status levels, recreational activities, and more (Deaux and Lewis 1984; Orlofsky 1981; Turner 1994). Given the multidimensionality of gender identity, it is unlikely that a simple typology of four mutually exclusive gender types could accurately describe the ways in which people feel gendered.

In planning this study, the authors assumed, therefore, that women experience themselves as gendered in very complex ways and also that women vary tremendously in these subjective experiences. None of the available standardized paper-and-pencil scales were likely to capture the two types of diversity we expected. For this reason we chose to do in-depth interviews, applying M. H. Huyck's multidimensional set of subjectively experienced gender-identity styles to women's lengthy responses about their gender. This set of gender styles was first developed by P. Zucker in 1988 and revised by Huyck, Zucker, and C. Angellaccio in 1994.

Four of these styles, named femme, nurturer, family woman, and denial of androgyny, were classified as gender-congruent (self-defined as feminine). Two styles, inner androgyny and activity androgyny, were classified as gender-expanded (self-defined as both feminine and masculine). The remaining two styles, diminished stereotypical femininity and facade, appeared gender-compromised (the respondent did not live up to her own standard of femininity or experienced femininity as a phony "act").

Huyck studied an unusually homogeneous and "conventional" group of women. Her 136 middle-aged mothers (aged 43 to 68 years) all were non-Latino White, middle class, and stably married to the fathers of the 76 young-adult daughters (aged 21 to 30 years) in the study. The mothers, whose family sizes averaged 4.4 children, all lived in the suburb of Parkville when interviewed in the early 1980s. Some of the daughters were single, others were married; a very few were divorced. Some were themselves mothers. The authors wondered whether Huyck's gender styles would apply to a sample of women much more diverse in age, race, social class, and marital and parental status. We expected that her styles would apply to such a sample, but that new styles might also appear.

For each woman in Huyck's Parkville study, each of the eight gender styles was coded as either present or absent in the interview material. Women might be coded as expressing one or more gender styles. In fact, among the middle-aged Parkville mothers there were 25 different combinations of styles (Huyck 1994). Even in this homogeneous sample, there was great diversity in the ways that women experienced their gender identity. We expected many more different gender styles in a more heterogeneous sample of women. Most important, we assumed that such complex combinations of gender styles

reflected a smaller set of underlying patterns of subjectively experienced gender identity. Our major purpose in this selection is to delineate these underlying patterns or dimensions of gender identity and to describe the background characteristics of women who scored high or low on each dimension. As gerontologists, we are especially interested in exploring age differences in dimensions of gender identity. Do aspects of gender identity change as a result of aging or of the formative experiences of adulthood such as parenthood and employment? In a cross-sectional study, of course, age differences may indicate cohort differences associated with social change rather than age change.

Sample

The volunteer sample in the authors' study comprised 249 Boston metro area (BMA) women aged 20 to 94 years, with an average age of 43. The sample included 87 percent non-Latina Whites and 10 percent Blacks. (Given the very small numbers of Latina and Asian women, the 4 percent other ethnicity were excluded for these analyses). Sixty percent had a bachelor's degree or more, 19 percent had some college, and 20 percent had completed high school or less. Forty-one percent had high-status (professional or managerial) occupations, 18 percent administrative positions, 30 percent pink-collar (clerical and sales) or blue-collar occupations, and 13 percent were homemakers or full-time students. In addition, some were retired. Forty-two percent were married, 18 percent divorced, 6 percent widowed, and 25 percent never married. The nine percent who cohabited were never married or, occasionally, divorced. Fifty-nine percent of the sample were mothers; of the mothers, only 17 percent had more than two children while 69 percent had children still at home.

The BMA sample was more diverse than the Parkville sample in age, race, marital status, parental status, and social class. The Parkville sample was representative of the American population in the percentage who are Black and fairly representative in the percentage of mothers who are in the labor force for pay. BMA women, however, had more education and more often had professional or managerial occupations than American women in general.

Procedure and Measures

The data, collected in individual interviews between 1989 and 1992, included demographic information, seven open-ended questions tapping gender identity, and two measures of psychological well-being—standard scales of self-esteem (Rosenberg 1965) and mastery or personal control (Pearlin and Schooler 1978). Each gender-identity style was coded as present or absent, following Huyck's coding manual, from the following questions:

What characteristics do you associate with masculinity?

What characteristics do you associate with femininity?

In what ways do you think men and women differ psychologically?

Do you think of yourself as feminine?

In what ways?

In what way does being feminine affect the things you do—or the things you don't do?

In what ways do you think you are not so feminine?

How do you account for that?

How do you feel about it?

In accordance with Huyck's manual, gender-identity styles were coded mainly from the last two questions (do you think of yourself as feminine? in what ways do you think you are not so feminine?). All eight of Huyck's gender styles for Parkville women were readily coded from the BMA women's responses. As we expected, two new gender-identity styles also appeared in our sample. Analysis of the scores by three different coders demonstrated that the gender styles were reliably coded from our qualitative data. The 10 gender-identity styles are named and briefly described in Table 9.1, which also shows the percent of BMA Study women scored with each style.

Because each gender style was coded as present or absent, women might be coded as simultaneously expressing several styles. In fact, 69 different combinations of gender styles characterized the 249 BMA study women. We assumed that the 69 different combinations reflected a much smaller set of ways of experiencing gender. To reduce the number of combinations of styles and ascertain whether they revealed underlying patterns of subjectively experienced gender identity, we performed a factor analysis with varimax rotation on the 10 gender styles. Statistical tests indicated that six factors were appropriate.

The factor analysis is a statistical method that shows which gender styles really go together in women's experiencing of how they feel gendered. In our study, we found that six different factors, or *dimensions*, described the ways that women defined their gender identity. Each woman received a score, ranging from high to low, on *each* factor. Each factor represented a different dimension of gender identity, and each factor was statistically independent of every other factor. This meant that if a woman scored high on the first gender-identity factor, it told you nothing whatever about how she scored on any other gender factor: She could score high, medium, or low on other factors. In other words, a set of gender-identity factors, or gender-identity dimensions, is very different from a set of mutually exclusive gender "types."

Factor scores were calculated for each woman on each factor using all 10 gender styles. The six independent dimensions (factors) are named and described below, using the distinctive patterning of gender styles that appeared on each factor. How gender styles differ is most easily understood by thinking of each style along a continuum ranging from high to low. The simplest way of summarizing the nature of the six dimensions is to look at the high and low ends of each gender factor. Quotes from the women with the highest and lowest scores on each gender dimension are used to clarify gender identity styles and the meaning of high (and low) factor scores. Note that many of the styles are polar opposites.

Table 9.1

Descriptions of the Ten Gender Identity Styles for Women and the BMA Sample Percentage Coded With Each Style (N=249)

Gender Identity Style	Percentage(%)	Description
Gender-congruent Styles		
Femme	57%	The femme defines her femininity (F) in terms of appearance and clothes, attention to manners, flirting and passivity.
Nurturer	41	The nurturer defines her F in terms of interpersonal attachments and sensitivity to people in general (outside the family circle).
Family woman	35	The family woman feels F because she cares for and about her children, husband, fiance, etc.
Denial of androgyny	15	This woman feels that she does not have any masculine (M) qualities.
Gender-expanded Styles		
Activity androgyny	27	This woman performs and accepts activities she defines as traditionally male
Inner androgyny	47	This woman has and accepts traits she defines as traditionally M.
Autonomous responsibility[a]	04	This woman feels she is F and distinguishes M and F activities, but performs them without self-attributing M or F because these tasks must be done to maintain independence and competence.
I am woman[a]	02	This woman identifies not as F but as a woman or female and expresses security in this identity, rejecting "negative" aspects of F.
Gender-compromised Styles		
Diminished stereotypical femininity	18	This woman feels that she is, in some way, either not as feminine as she should be, or less feminine than she used to be.
Facade	04	This woman views aspects of F as phony role-playing and not the "real me," though she may play the role when doing so is strategic.

[a]These 2 styles were developed by Silva and Turner as they emerged in the BMA Study. The other 8 styles are adapted from Huyck, Zucker, & Angellaccio (1994), "Gender Styles Rated From Interviews."

Factor 1: Consistently Inner Androgynous (CIA).

At the high end of the CIA dimension, women expand on feeling basically feminine by acknowledging and accepting masculine personality traits (0.60 on inner androgyny) and might also acknowledge and accept performing masculine activities (0.36 on activity androgyny). Consistent with perceiving that they have characteristics they define as masculine, they do *not* regard themselves as exclusively feminine (-0.91 on denial of androgyny or denial of incongruence). Statements

coded for inner androgyny included: "I'm pretty good at being independent and trying to get what I want. . . . It is being able to have courage to stand up for oneself." Another woman said, "I am sure of myself, know what I want." A third woman said, "I tend to be one of the persevering types . . . go out to work, don't call in sick, anything you have to do you can tough it out." These women are very comfortable with their self-defined masculine traits. Activity-androgyny statements included, "I am independent and like to be able to do things for myself, even fix things around the house."

At the low end of this dimension, women think there is "nothing that isn't feminine about me" (denial of androgyny or denial of incongruence) and, consistent with this perception, do not think they have any masculine personality traits or activities.

Factor 2: Activity-Androgynous Family Women (AAFW)

At the high end of the AAFW factor or dimension, women felt feminine because they nurtured their families (0.75 on family woman) notably, they tended *not* to mention nurturance to people outside their family circle (-0.37 on nurturer). They also acknowledged and accepted performing activities they regard as masculine (0.68 on activity androgyny). In one woman's words, "I take care of the house, clean, cook, do laundry, take care of the baby . . . I certainly fit the housewife model" (family woman). But at the same time she "does not mind doing work outside—yard work, lots of digging holes—and getting dirty" (activity androgyny). Another said she had been "the head of the household. I can't go to school because I have to see my children go to school." And "I can move things like a bed. I must be strong." A third commented, "I give nurturance to kids and husband and I hesitate to put my own needs and desires first." And "I like masculine things, carpentry, hammer and nail and finishing furniture." These women's families "came first." They "did what had to be done" and felt very satisfied with their experiences.

Women at the low end of this dimension tended to nurture people beyond their family but not within it; they were also unlikely to engage in activities they defined as masculine.

Factor 3: Femme-Rejecting–Nurturer (FRN)

Women at the high end of the FRN dimension did *not* define their femininity in terms of appearance and clothes, attention to manners, flirting, or undesirable passivity (-0.91 on femme). Indeed they often explicitly criticized elements of this gender style, which they viewed as undesirable. Rather, they felt

feminine because they cared about people in general (non-kin), (0.42 on nurturer) and also might express security in being women or females, rather than feeling feminine as such (0.25 on I am woman). Rejection of what was perceived as undesirable elements of traditional femininity (femme) appears in the statement, "I have never been 'prissy.' I abhor lace, ruffles, excessive make-up. The whole image of being physical, sexual presentation is atrocious." Another said, "I refuse to look feminine and act feminine and that's one of my feminine things [ways in which she is feminine]." "I think I am *feminine* and the other is societal/patriarchal definition of femininity." These women are concerned about other people. One said she is "concerned for other people and want[s] to help people" (nurturer). Another woman commented, "I gave much higher priority to nurturing and relationships."

Conversely, those at the low end of the FRN dimension *did* feel feminine in appearance and manners (femme): "In my dress I am feminine. I'm feminine in the way I express myself. I am not rough, tough, and nasty." Another said, "I dress like a lady. I walk like a lady. I look like a lady. I act like a lady. I pluck my eyebrows, shave my armpits and legs." The women with the very lowest FRN scores combined the femme and the autonomous-responsibility styles. As one of them said, "I don't think being feminine affects anything you do or do not do. If you are capable of doing something, you are going to do it. I will change a flat tire when the tire is flat rather than waiting for some man to come back and change it" (autonomous responsibility). Finally, women at the low end of this dimension were unlikely to define their femininity in terms of nurturing people in general (non-kin).

Factor 4: Non-role-playing–Nurturer (NRPN)

Like the women at the high end of the FRN dimension, women at the high end of the NRPN dimension felt feminine because they nurtured people outside their family circles (0.50 on nurturer). On the NRPN dimension, however, the nurturer style combines with *not* viewing aspects of femininity as a phony role one plays to gain strategic benefits (-0.91 on facade). Women high on the NRPN dimension also might acknowledge masculine traits (0.28 on inner androgyny). It is important to note that nurturing others in this particular combination of gender styles is statistically independent of the pattern of nurturing others while rejecting femme elements on the FRN dimension. That is, differences in the patterning of gender styles that accompany the nurturer style lend a different flavor to how nurturing others is expressed or experienced.

Women high on the NRPN dimension viewed themselves as "warm, sensitive, and caring . . . I like to take care of people" (nurturer). Another said, "I'm compassionate, spiritual, sensitive to other people." A third commented, "I see it connected to my relationships with other people . . . that real desire for intimate friends, and keeping those friendships up."

At the low end of the NRPN dimension, women feigned or play-acted "femininity" when necessary or useful, though they did not experience it as the "real me;" and they were unlikely to espouse the nurturer style. As one woman said, "I have a sort of soft interior and a hard exterior. When I am relaxed and comfortable, my exterior lets down . . . [but at other times] I act" (facade). Another woman remarked, "What I look like is not a concern, i.e. make-up. Frilly isn't me [but] I pretend."

Factor 5: Independent Woman (IW)

Women high on the IW dimension combined an identification with womanhood or femaleness (0.78 on I am woman), with performing activities they acknowledged as traditionally masculine while avoiding self-descriptions as masculine because these activities must be done nowadays to be independent (0.63 on autonomous responsibility). They tended *not* to mention feeling feminine in terms of nurturing their families (-0.28 on family woman). One woman coded for I am woman remarked, "I think of myself as female. My identity revolves around being a woman . . . if *you* thought feminine meant passive or weak then I don't think I'd be feminine. But I do not buy the original definition." According to another, "Maybe feminine is not the right word—maybe femaleness." These women felt very confident and secure in their "femaleness." A woman coded for autonomous responsibility said, "I don't think of myself as able to do something or not able to do something because I am female. I think in terms of: I am a person." These women acknowledged differences between male and female characteristics but viewed themselves as feminine even though, as one remarked, she did "work that is viewed as traditionally male tasks" (a virtually all-male occupational specialty). They reported feeling competent and independent.

At the low end of the IW dimension women espoused neither the I am woman nor the autonomous-responsibility styles. They might, however, direct nurturance toward their families (family woman) and also might attribute masculine traits to themselves (inner androgyny).

Factor 6: Insecurely Feminine Woman (IFW)

The high end of the IFW dimension is overwhelmingly defined by feeling deficient in meeting one's own internalized standard of appropriate femininity (0.96 on diminished stereotypical femininity). These women felt less feminine than they thought they should be or used to be, in combination with a tendency *not* to acknowledge having masculine personality traits (-0.38 on inner androgyny). Otherwise, insecurely feminine women resembled the rest of the BMA sample in the ways they experienced being gendered (i.e., in choosing or not choosing other gender styles). One woman said, "In my dress I wish I was more feminine but I do not think I ever will be. And I am loud. Maybe I should be more retiring in my demeanor. I feel like I've missed something. I feel dissatisfied. I feel uncomfortable. I feel lacking female-wise. I feel inadequate. On a girl level I feel like I should wear high heels and I don't" (diminished stereotypical femininity). A second woman remarked, "Sometimes I feel like being more 'girly' or feminine. I guess I'm remorseful that I'm missing that side of me. It would have been good to be pampered and take care of myself, my appearance." Another woman said, "I do not take care of myself as much as I should."

Most (75 percent) of the women who felt that they fell short of their own personal standard of appropriate femininity mentioned either one or two types of shortcomings. Most common, albeit just barely, was dissatisfaction with either personal appearance (clothing, grooming, accessories) or physical appearance (too overweight, too large, too old-looking, not pretty enough). These insecurities centered in the femme style of self-presentation. Very nearly as many criticized unladylike behaviors (such as using profanity when alone, or walking down the stairs "like an elephant") and body language ("I do sit with my legs open with a skirt on"), or felt they had too much of a masculine trait that even in men was rather undesirable (such as cynicism, "a tough affect," being "loud and obnoxious," or "when I forget I'm a woman and become domineering"). Unladylike behaviors and body language again reflect femme insecurities. Critiques of too masculine traits deal with the inner androgyny style. These comments suggest discomfort with social displays of masculine traits generally viewed as off-putting even in men (and even more so in women). None of these women criticized themselves for displaying socially desirable masculine traits. Only a few felt they fell short in traditionally "feminine" relatedness to others (nurturer). One such woman commented, "I am not so feminine regarding intimacy in my personal relationships. I don't share or express my feelings as I should or would like to;" another said she had "problems with intimacy and physical sex." A very few felt inadequate in not achieving marriage or, especially, motherhood: "I get sneered at a lot. I feel like a failure because I don't have children"; another woman said, "My infertility . . . I always associated being a woman with having a child and I don't know if that's going to happen." The last comments may reflect some combination of the family woman and femme styles.

These self-doubts indicate women's sensitivity to the sheerly visual components of feminine self-presentation. Their comments emphasize attractiveness and, less often, genteel behavior. Also noteworthy is their sensitivity to negative social feedback about displaying socially undesirable masculine traits.

At the low end of the IFW dimension, women did *not* describe themselves as falling short of their own standard of femininity. Some also acknowledged and accepted having personality traits they defined as masculine.

Correlates of the Gender-Identity Dimensions

What contextual characteristics are related to high scores on each gender-identity factor? To find out, we used a type of statistical technique, regression analyses, to relate scores on each factor to the variables of age (20 to 92), marital status (married, divorced, widowed, never married, cohabiting), motherhood (is not a mother, is a mother), race or ethnicity (non-Latina White, Black), level of education (four or more years of higher education versus some college or less education), and occupational prestige (professional and managerial occupations versus all other occupations). We discarded the variable of paid-employment status (full-time, part-time, not employed) since it showed no relationship to any of the six gender-identity dimensions. The phasing out of parental responsibilities as their children become independent adults is a central determinant of change in gender identity in David Gutmann's (1987) socio-evolutionary theory of transformations in gender identity in midlife (Huyck 1994, 1996). Because two-fifths of the BMA women had no children at all, however, the number with independent-adult children was too small to permit an assessment of the socio-evolutionary hypothesis.

Higher scores on the consistently inner-androgynous dimension were most strongly associated with being younger and with being unmarried (that is, with not being currently married), each time controlling for the other background variables. In addition, women with four or more years of higher education tended to have higher scores on the CIA dimension than those with less education. These findings suggest the possibility of a general societal shift in which later-born cohorts more often incorporate "masculine" personality traits in their gender identity than earlier-born cohorts do. Interestingly, currently married women had *lower* CIA dimension scores than women in all other marital statuses combined. The association of higher CIA scores with four or more years of college suggests the gender-expanding effects of several years of higher education.

Whether or not they were mothers overwhelmingly determined women's scores on the activity-androgynous family-woman dimension. Mothers had higher AAFW dimension scores than nonmothers, controlling for age, marital status, and the other background variables. Many mothers also were wives, but it was the experiences of motherhood that related to high scores on this dimension. In addition, women in managerial and professional occupations tended to have *lower* AAFW dimension scores than women in lower-prestige occupations. To be sure, mothers in high-prestige jobs were slightly less likely to define themselves in AAFW terms. But the majority of women will, in the future, continue to hold the lower-prestige jobs that are associated with higher AAFW dimension scores. These considerations suggest that motherhood in coming decades will go on being associated with being an activity-androgynous family-woman.

Women's scores on the femme-rejecting–nurturer dimension related to race, being a widow, having professional and managerial jobs, and cohabiting, independent of age and the other background variables. Black women and widows had lower FRN scores— they were more likely to feel feminine in femme terms and less likely to define it as nurturing people outside the family than did non-Latina Whites or women in other marital statuses. High femme-rejecting–nurturer dimension scores, on the other hand, were somewhat more likely among women in professional and managerial jobs and among cohabitors. Notably, feeling feminine in terms of appearance and manners, a style espoused by a majority (57 percent) of BMA women, characterized women of all ages and cohorts about equally. In this sample there was no evidence that recent cohorts are shifting to some less "traditional" way of feeling feminine or are more critical generally of "socially undesirable" elements of the femme style.

Mothers and women with four or more years of higher education had higher scores on the nonrole-playing–nurturer dimension, independent of age and the other background variables. In contrast, cohabitors tended to have lower NRPN scores than women in other marital statuses.

Compared to women in other marital statuses, divorced women tended to have higher scores on both the independent-woman dimension and the insecurely-feminine-woman dimension, independent of age and the other background variables. No other background variable was associated with either gender identity dimension. In a cross-sectional design, unfortunately, we cannot specify the causal direction of the relationship between divorce and the two independent gender dimensions. Are highly independent women and women who feel inadequately feminine more predisposed toward divorce, or does divorce lead women to feel inadequately feminine or to redefine themselves as independent women?

Finally, we correlated each of the six gender-identity dimensions with two standard measures of respondents' psychological well-being—self-esteem (Rosenberg 1965) and mastery, or personal control (Pearlin and Schooler 1978). Mastery, or personal control, is people's feeling that what happens to them in life is under their control rather than out of their control. Psychologists long have assumed that masculinity, femininity, and gender are characteristics of individuals related to their psychological well-being (Turner 1994). Past research using standardized paper-and-pencil tests of personality traits usually found that masculine traits predicted better psychological well-being in both women and men (Turner and Turner 1994). The six gender-identity dimensions in our study, however, include many more facets of gender than personality traits. How would these complex multidimensional factors relate to psychological well-being?

Five of the gender-identity dimensions showed *no* relationship to either global self-esteem or mastery scores. Women with high scores on the insecurely-feminine-woman dimension, however, had both lower self-esteem and lower feelings of mastery than women with lower scores on that dimension. Two conclusions strike us as equally important. First, five different patterns of experiencing one's gender were about equally related to psychological well-being (using first-level correlations). Second, this was true only for women who did *not* feel that they fell short of their own standard of appropriate femininity. Women who felt in some way inadequately feminine also had lower global self-esteem and lower mastery. One interpretation is that feeling inadequately feminine diminishes a woman's overall self-esteem and feelings of mastery. Alternatively, feeling inadequately feminine may be a specific instance of a general tendency toward self-criticism (lower psychological well-being).

Conclusions

First, like Huyck (1996) we conclude that the large number of different combinations of gender styles that emerged in our qualitative interviews reveal the tremendous diversity and complexity of the ways that women experience their gender. Indeed, in our more heterogeneous sample two new gender styles and more than twice as many separate combinations of styles appeared. Huyck's analyses of Parkville study data usually have focused on each separate gender style. The specific contribution of the BMA study is to delineate the smaller number of meaningful patterns that summarize how women subjectively experience their gender. Six such patterns appeared among BMA women. Most of all, our findings emphasize the importance of studying the gender styles of women diverse in marital status and race or ethnicity.

Second, it is no surprise that some combinations of gender styles go together in women's thinking about gender more than other combinations. What is surprising is the combinations that did not often appear. If gender identity reflects personality predispositions such as nurturance, for example, then more nurturant women would often describe themselves as both nurturers and family women. Instead, the dimension descriptions show clearly that women usually chose nurturer (41 percent) *or* family woman (35 percent) but infrequently chose both together. Based on the "androgyny" research of the 1970s and 1980s (Bem 1974; Deaux 1984), more masculine or androgynous women often should have experienced both inner androgyny (47 percent) and activity androgyny (27 percent). Instead the two styles generally were independent of each other, though they did tend to be combined on the consistently-inner-androgynous dimension. We think that simple conceptions of personality predispositions toward gender styles will not shed much light on these dimensions. The family-woman and activity-androgyny styles often do go together, probably driven by the parental imperative (Gutmann 1987) or, more simply, the interactional requirements of the mother and single-mother roles. Divorced mothers explained that they had to "be both mother and father" to their children. Married mothers, even a few professional women, usually spoke of performing other types of masculine activities at home.

Third, several gender styles, especially nurturer and inner androgyny, combined with quite different gender styles on separate independent gender dimensions. As noted for the femme-rejecting–nurturer and nonrole-playing–nurturer styles, the same style has a different meaning in different combinations and is associated with quite different background characteristics.

Fourth, we were impressed by the independence of the gender-identity dimensions and psychological well-being (with the important exception of the insecurely-feminine-woman dimension). Contrary to expectation, women at the high end of the consistently-inner-androgynous dimension did not have higher well-being. The facade style, like the diminished-stereotypical-femininity style, was classified as gender compromised (Huyck 1994). But women who described themselves as faking femininity in social situations (those low on the nonrole-playing–nurturer dimension) were not lower in well-being than women who did not choose the facade style. Social pretense may have its uses. Finally, we classified the I-am-woman and autonomous-responsibility styles, the two new styles, as gender expanded. They could, however, be viewed as gender compromised, "backing away from" conventional definitions of feminine and masculine. These styles, which appeared together on the independent-woman dimension and tended to characterize divorced women, may reflect strain and discomfort in gender identity. If so, one might expect women high on the IW dimension to have lower global self-esteem; but they do not. We conclude that the two new styles appear to represent gender expansion more than gender strain.

Finally, we were especially interested in exploring age differences in dimensions of gender identity. To do so, we related respondents' age to their scores on each gender dimension while controlling for several other background variables. In our cross-sectional study, any age differences in gender identity might reflect all age change attributable to developmental family experiences or to maturation. Alternatively, age differences might reflect cohort shifts or some combination of cohort shifts and age change. Age differences in gender identity appeared only on the consistently-inner-androgynous dimension; later-born cohorts of urban women were less likely than earlier-born cohorts to see themselves as nothing but feminine and more likely to incorporate personality traits they defined as masculine. This most likely suggests a general societal shift among women born in recent decades toward accepting personality androgyny. But age differences made no independent contribution to any other gender-identity dimension in the BMA sample, not even to activity-androgynous family-woman. Except for the consistently-inner-androgynous dimension, high or low scores on each gender-identity dimension are related to the social interactions structured by marital statuses, parenthood, socioeconomic status markers, and race or ethnicity.

Discussion Questions

1. Describe the "gender-congruent" styles identified.

2. What is meant by "gender-expanded" styles? Do they differ from those for females as described by Huyck and her associates?

3. What evidence is presented to suggest that gender style is or is not associated with age?

4. What are the advantages and limitations of cross-sectional studies as compared to longitudinal studies?

References

Bern, S. L. 1974. "The Measurement of Psychological Androgyny." *Journal of Consulting and Clinical Psychology* 42: 155–162.

Deaux, K. 1984. "From Individual Differences to Social Categories: Analysis of a Decade's Research on Gender." *American Psychologist* 39: 105–116.

Deaux, K., and Lewis, L. L. 1984. "Structure of Gender Stereotypes: Interrelationships Among Components and Gender Label." *Journal of Personality and Social Psychology* 46: 991–1004.

Gutmann, D. L. 1987. *Reclaimed Powers: Toward a New Psychology of Men and Women in Later Life*. New York: Basic Books.

Huyck, M. H. 1994. "The Relevance of Psychodynamic Theories for Understanding Gender Among Older Women." In B. F. Turner and L. E. Troll, eds., *Women Growing Older: Psychological Perspectives*, pp. 202–238. Thousand Oaks, CA: Sage Publications.

——. 1996. "Continuities and Discontinuities in Gender Identity." In V. L. Bengtson, ed., *Adulthood and Aging: Research on Continuities and Discontinuities*, pp. 98–121. New York: Springer.

Huyck, M. H., Zucker, P., and Angellaccio, C. 1994. "Gender Styles Rated From Interviews." Unpublished document.

Orlofsky, J. L. 1981. "Relationship Between Sex Role Attitudes and Personality Traits and the Sex Role Behavior Scale-1: A New Measure of Masculine and Feminine Role Behaviors and Interests." *Journal of Personality and Social Psychology* 40: 927–940.

Pearlin, L. I., and Schooler, C. 1978. "The Structure of Coping." *Journal of Health and Social Behavior* 19: 2–21.

Rosenberg, M. 1965. *Society and the Adolescent Self-image*. Princeton, NJ: Princeton University Press.

Turner, B. F. 1994. "Introduction." In B. F. Turner and L. E. Troll, eds., *Women Growing Older: Psychological Perspectives*, pp. 1–34. Thousand Oaks, CA: Sage Publications.

Turner, B. F., and Turner, C. B. 1994. "Social Cognition and Gender Stereotypes for Women Varying in Age and Race." In B. F. Turner and L. E. Troll, eds., *Women Growing Older: Psychological Perspectives*, pp. 94–139. Thousand Oaks, CA: Sage Publications.

Zucker, P. 1989. "A Typology of Gender Styles Applicable to the Second Half of Life." (Ph.D. Dissertation, Illinois Institute of Technology.) *Dissertation Abstracts International*, 49.

B. F. Turner and P. Silva, "Definitions of Femininity: Dimensions of Gender Identity From Youth to Old Age." Printed by permission of the authors.

Chapter 10

Narrative Accrual and the Life Course

Marilyn Nouri and
Marilyn Helterline

The preceding two selections dealt with dimensions of gender identity across the life course and provided insights about how gender identity is constructed. The following selection expands upon the theme of dimensions of identity to look at the ways in which older people construct their lives through autobiographical narratives and recollections of the past. Autobiographies and biographies of the rich, famous, or infamous are perennial bestsellers. Reading about their lives offers both a window into distinctly different ways of life and an opportunity to go beyond one's immediate experience. Telling a story about one's life is not confined to the rich and famous, however, for everyone has a story to tell about his or her life. People are constantly involved in constructing narratives about themselves, others, and the world around them in order to give meaning to their histories. These tales are vital to the ways in which we view ourselves throughout the life course, providing the links between continuity and change.

As Marilyn Nouri and Marilyn Helterline point out, life history provides a particularly rich opportunity to give not only factual reports about life events but also meaning to these incidents. Consider the themes of the life history interviews of the older people in the following selection. Pay attention to the values that emerge in their narrations of the American success dream, of life as a struggle, and other themes, and how these older people constructed the "plot" of their life stories. Also note the gender differences in the types of story lines

they tell, and think about the ways in which these differences may or may not relate to the previous selections by Huyck, Zucker, and Angellaccio and by Turner and Silva on gender identity in the life course.

. . . This research will explore the stories we construct about the way we live by "reading" the narratives of elders. The self in the narrative is a *standpoint* from which to view the flow of events and make them meaningful (Spencer 1993). Narrative accrual (Bruner 1991) is necessary for a life's story but is not determined by a single event nor by a single story. How are persons' narratives accrued to make a life story that "centers around a Self acting more or less purposefully in a social world" (Bruner 1991:18)? As persons fictionalize their experiences, age is one of the cultural constructs of meaning that is involved. Age is an ascribed status that moves persons into and out of other status positions as it also moves generations into and out of historical time (Riley and Foner 1972). The interaction of historical time and age in life is likely to have an effect on the story in terms of plot development. Reminiscence is thought by many to be important in the later years. The essence of reminiscence is remembering, but certainly fictionalization is involved as older persons reminisce in an effort to connect the events together into a meaningful whole. Not only is one remembering, but one is also continuing to construct character and tell a moral story. The common adage, "Life is something that happens while we make other plans," speaks to the emergent qualities associated with living a life. Older people are not just ending their stories, they are producing new chapters as well.

The Life History Approach

The population for the research is the cohort of persons born before 1920 who live in a community of upstate New York made up of substantial rural areas and several villages including one small city. Quotas were set to guide sample selection so that the sample is made up of approximately an equal number of men and women and college graduates and non-college-graduates. The sample was selected using "snow-balling" by interviewing one person and then having that person recommend one or two others who might be willing to be interviewed. Life history interviewing requires "a foot in the door" to gain cooperation. The approach does produce biases, but this is not as serious as it might be since the goal is to understand narratives from the point of view of the persons who have produced them rather than to derive estimates of population parameters. The benefit is a low refusal rate. We interviewed thirty persons. The median age of the women interviewed was 79 years and for the men it was 79.5 years. They ranged in age from sixty-nine to ninety-seven years of age. While half of the women were widowed, only 35 percent of the men were. All were White; however, their religious backgrounds were quite diverse and included Jews, Catholics, Unitarians, Baptists, Methodists, and a Quaker. One person lived in a nursing home, one lived with a married daughter, and the rest lived with their spouse or alone. They mostly had lived middle- or working-class lives, and though several were worried at present about their future economic well-being, none were living in poverty, either because their families were supporting them or because they had enough financial support on their own. Most were retired. In order to protect the privacy of the individuals, pseudonyms are used and the descriptions included in this article alter details of lives to disguise identities without altering essential character.

The schedule of in-depth questions and probes used provided a life history interview focused first on memories from childhood and explored work, family, and organizational involvement throughout adulthood. The elders were encouraged to freely talk about their experiences, and probes were used to further explore the topics that the seniors talked about. The second half of the interview asked more specific questions about events in historical time, major problems the person was currently facing and had faced in life, and how that person coped with them. Other questions explored what the person was doing at present and what he or she saw in the future. Typically, the subject was interviewed twice for a total of two to five hours. The interviews were conducted as informal conversations to encourage the telling of stories, but with the interviewee doing most of the talking. We ensured our subjects that whatever they told us would be interesting and important because we wanted to hear about their lives. All of the participants were interviewed in their own homes where they would be most comfortable. We found that once the interviews were started, most were able to quite easily talk about themselves and tell at least some of the stories of their lives. The transcriptions of the interviews were read to identify all narrative-talk. Initial reading of the transcripts made it possible to separate answers into levels of fictionalization, for purposes of analysis. Responses that presented "facts" were treated as first-level abstractions, but not narratives. The facts of life are the ordinary events that do not require fictionalization to make meaning about them; rather, they are what is taken for granted without a need for further explanation. When the respondent moved to the next level, he or she was no loner reporting but interpreting, giving meaning, "building a life's story in history." The subjects were giving narrative accounts and they were accruing the separate narrative accounts into a life's narrative. As Bruner writes, "Even our own homely accounts of happenings in our own lives are eventually converted into more or less coherent autobiographies centered around a Self acting more or less purposefully in a social world" (Bruner 1991:18). The methodology of the long interview encourages narrative talk. These narratives provided the material for analysis. One of the major concerns of our interviewees was that their lives were very ordinary; we found them to be much more than that.

The Story Lines

The seniors talked about many experiences during their interviews. However, as the focus in the analysis was on how persons' lived experiences are accrued to make a life story, specific narratives were less important than how the narratives were woven together into a life's story line. As "the American dream of success" has been identified, culturally, as the dominant story line in our society, the approach to examining the stories was to look for that story line and then to see if and how stories might differ. After all, the culture provides the "community's stored narrative resources and its equally precious tool kit of interpretive techniques" (Bruner 1990:68). Four other narrative forms, in addition to the American dream narrative, were used by the interviewees to relate how the will and the cosmos were engaged with each other in determining the fate of the main character in the story, the self. The other forms were life as a struggle, life as simple, God determines, and life as shared. To understand the process of accrual, it is most informative to focus on one person from each narrative form.

Achieving the American Dream of Success

The dominant myth of American society is how each of us, if we work hard enough and well enough, will be able to overcome adversity to achieve success. That story line was developed in the narratives of seven of the subjects, when they related how through their own will they were able to determine their own fate in relation to the cosmos. Tom Jeneary, an administrator, illustrates this heroic view of his own life course. Tom explains how his family background contributed to the building of his character:

Marilyn N.: When you think of your parents' divorce when you were young, do you remember how it was for you then?

Tom: Yea, I guess. I felt different. This was during the depression years, in the early 30s and because my father had left, our economic situation was not good. I always had the feeling that we were less privileged than my classmates and to this day I often say to myself or sometimes to Veta [his wife], wonder what my life might of been if my father had been around? Kinda forced all four of us to take the strong stand in support of our mother. She didn't work outside the home. . . . It was tough going and I lacked a lot of the conveniences. Never owned a bicycle in my life. Other kids had. However, my mother was a strong supporter of school activities and all of us were very active in school. Music, athletics, dramatic activities. We had a strong family life and still are very strong. . . .

Marilyn N.: So your mother didn't work. Did your father continue to support you then after he left?

Tom: To a very, very limited extent. That's the reason it was tough going for us. We actually had to seek public assistance, social services, welfare. We got no choice and that's kind of a stigma to carry and I always felt different in that regard from my colleagues, but it didn't affect actually their respect me because I did everything that they did in school. For example, was president of my high school class, the last two years in high school, and held other offices and that sort of thing. I don't think it was because of sympathy.

Service through leadership roles can be seen to be accrued as important throughout Tom's life:

Marilyn N.: Some people choose to kind of withdraw from voluntary activities at the same time as they retire . . . and others continue. Why did you decide to continue?

Tom: I guess because I enjoy leadership roles, and while I'm not particularly a leader in everything I belong to, I like the association with other people who are volunteers. I guess basically it's an ingrain and I've even said an inherited trait of doing service for others. Rotary Club motto is service above self. He who serves the best profits most. In my ancestry, great-great grandfather served in the War of 1812 and was quite an outstanding person and I have read something that he wrote indicating that he believed firmly in doing service to other people. Anybody who is Christian, I guess involved in church work. . . . But I do enjoy it.

Tom, in concluding his response to a question about how old he feels, does a "final interpretation" of the earlier accrual:

I guess I'd say I'm at the position of life that I'm prepared to die knowing that I've reached three score years and ten. Feel that I, in my lifetime, I've been a producing member of society.

Good leadership skills and service enabled Tom to see himself as an honorable character in his own story line. It made him "special." He used those same leadership skills in his chosen profession, an administrator. Overcoming the challenges of his childhood enhanced that image as well as provided an explanation for the way he controlled his own fate.

Tom's character fits the ideological "American dream of success" model. All of those who described the relationship between the will and the cosmos in that way also saw the obstacle they had to overcome as character-building rather than as an obstruction. For example, Edith Hayes, a teacher, experienced homelessness at the same time, she said, as most adolescents go through the stage of fighting for freedom. For her, overcoming that difficulty was a start on the rest of her life. It might seem that all the elders might have constructed their stories to match the American dream of success, but that was not the case. Diversity in narrative accrual was found. The story of the "American Dream" is not the fictionalization for everyone. Some describe other kinds of intentionalities; others construct stories that generate a valued self at the end of the story when the hero role does not fit as a way of making sense of a life.

Life as a Struggle

This story line (used by nine of the subjects) depicts life as a continuing struggle. The self is seen less as a heroic figure; rather, life is hard and one does what one has to do throughout one's life and the outcome is that "you win some and you lose some." The contrast with the first type of accrual rests with the recognition that the adversities of life continue and no constant pattern is found for meeting them. There are two variations within this category, and which one is used depends on whether one finally wins or loses. Hans Henrickson is an example of the first type. He managed businesses in Midwestern farming communities most of his life and was concerned with making a good deal. In describing changing jobs, he remarked:

> I went back up to Michigan and then came back that fall and I told my Dad, I said, "You know if you hear of any jobs you think I can get, I am willing to leave that job in Michigan." . . . by that time I was

married and had a boy and I had a paying proposition in town.

Hans saw himself finally paid off for some free labor he had done for his brother early in his life when he recently inherited some land from that same brother. He continues to be involved with land he owns and wants to make the best deal he can in passing it on to his children. Cunning is a valued characteristic. As he describes his work, he talks of his ability to solve problems and make money, but the description of self lacks the moral overtone that is associated with the heroic figure. Hans was offered the job of managing an elevator that was facing financial difficulty:

> I said, "I know I can go to the bank." The banker told me I got no limit to what I can borrow, but, I said, "I don't want to. I am going to borrow it from you and from you." These two friends. "I want three thousand from you and I want five thousand from you. You fellows have got that money laying, not even using it. You are not getting a cent and I will give you five percent interest." And five percent interest in 1943 and 1945 was pretty high interest for idle money. And I said, "I will pay you at the end of the year each year. Pay the interest out so the notes will stay the same. How long we going to need them is going to depend on what luck we have."

Hans goes on to describe the ups and downs of the struggling business and how through his own cunning, he was able to find solutions.

With deals, luck is an important element, and Hans certainly recognized the significance of getting a good break, as was mentioned above. His approach to his personal life also recognized the significance of luck. His wife, later in their life together, was dying of cancer. He described how they decided to go to their daughter's wedding in England, in spite of her health:

> Why I put it this way, "Alright, we will go to England." Our daughter married an Englishman and we wanted to be there. If your time is up, not the best doctor in the world can save you . . . and I said, "If your time isn't up, you are going to come back feeling just as good as you left, maybe better." That is exactly what happened. 'We

was there three weeks and she was feeling much better.

Hans uses his present bank account and the land he has to pass on to his children as evidence of having finally won: "It was hard work, we worked hard. But it paid out." Being on the receiving end of life's rewards is a way that final outcomes can lead to winning. The fate-problem is resolved for one is finally coming out on top. Again, the narratives have been accrued into a general story with the statement that "it paid out."

Losing at life is a different story. John Dalton got a deferment from military service during World War II, because he was trained as a biologist. He felt he ought to make use of his training as a biologist since it allowed him to avoid serving, but he saw life as full of problems that made that goal an elusive one. Neither good luck nor winning played much of a part in John's story, and his plight was portrayed differently. When John was younger, he felt that he could go out and conquer the world. "As you grow older, you realize that it's not that easy." He was unable to establish himself in a career as a biologist:

Marilyn H.: When you were eighteen, what did you think your future would be?

John D.: I was working very hard in college and I thought when I finished, it would be easy, but it hasn't been.

Marilyn H.: Can you explain how it has been different?

John D.: In science we were taught to be honest, never to fudge results or steal another person's findings, but it wasn't like that. Everyone was out for themselves and people would stab you in the back.

When John was asked to describe the biggest problem he faced in his life and how he handled it, he replied:

Of course, my whole life. Gee, I don't know. Life is full of problems. Graduation from college, finding a job, gaining employment, I can't really answer that much more than that.

Rather than describe a flawed or failed character, the story line of life as a struggle pro-

duces a fate that is the result of a difficult cosmos that could not be overcome.

Life Is Simple

The third theme used to accomplish narrative accrual appears in the stories of two men. In both cases, there was little talk about the relationship between the self and the world and the self was described more as a benefactor of the good life rather than a creator of it. Life is more a matter of fact than of story. These were the shortest of the interviews as the movement from the concrete and phenomenal to the narrative form was less elaborate. Ernest France, a lawyer, had dedicated his life to his career. His father had been a lawyer, he had always wanted to be a lawyer, he did that kind of work when he served in World War II, and he is still lawyering part time for senior citizens. Excerpts from his story illustrate:

Marilyn H.: Can you tell me anything about living in Albany and being a new lawyer?

Ernest: Very pleasant firm. Was one of the happiest years I ever spent, first year out of law school.

Marilyn H.: Why was it happy?

Ernest: Just a wonderful place to work, wonderful bunch of fellows, nice town to live in. Just everything sort of came together.

Later in the interview, Ernest describes another time in his life:

Marilyn H.: When you came back and set up practice, what was it like getting started?

Ernest: With my father here, and my name was known, that may of been one of the main reasons I came back, easy to get started.

It is likely that he may have had many narratives about lawyering, but if he did, he did not volunteer them. Now, the present and future are problematic for him because he is no longer really working as a lawyer and life is empty. His wife, who had made his family life comfortable and easy, died several years ago, and this has created an even bigger void in his life. He has created no narrative to make sense of this period of his life any more than in the earlier years, at least in any way that enhanced self-esteem or life's quality. Life is still simple, but in the present it is sad.

God Determines

In this type of story line (used by five of the subjects), religion is important, for it provides direction for how to handle the cosmos. In this narrative, persons are more than simply religious; they see God as determining their relationship to the world. Trust in God is an important idea. Ellen Taylor, a beautiful woman of eighty-seven, describes her own life very clearly as a true believer. She is amazed that she is still alive and explains it this way:

> Marilyn N.: Do you view these last years that you've been living now as a particular time in your life that has meaning?

> Ellen: Well, if my life was going to mean anything, it's got to be God-driven. . . . You have to follow. But, that's the meaning. He needs me for something, so he lets me live.

> Marilyn N.: Do you have any clues as to whether God has any particular meaning for your life at this stage?

> Ellen: Yes, I can see many, many instances. I know God has directed. I just know it. . . . And he's with us always, you know. I think that's how come I can get through these things. And I don't know why I've been selected to do it.

Most interviewers gave significance to religion in their lives, but the people in this group included religion specifically in discussions of the relationship between the will and the cosmos. God's will provides the intentions of life.

Life as Shared

Several of the women (seven of the subjects) had a shared story line. They could not separate their story lines from those of other family members, most often their husband's, but sometimes their children's, or the society at large. To illustrate the different ways that life is shared, excerpts from three different women's stories are used. Edna Brown's narrative was found among the stories about her husband and her children and her relationships with them:

> Marilyn H.: Your marriage seems to have been happy—

> Edna: Oh, wonderful. I think I was one of the happiest women around, because Martin worked real hard eight hours. Came home. I always had a good dinner, of course, for everybody. And then he would go up to his room . . . and paint all the time. I think he did hundreds of paintings; they are all over the world.

Later in the interview, Edna describes her dedication to her husband:

> Marilyn H.: What did you do after your children were grown and left home?

> Edna: I kept house for Martin. Took good care of his health in every way that I could and I still did to the last drop in the bucket. He was here [the nursing home] for two years, and I came to see him. We gave our home up and I came and lived in Hillside Apartments. And I came up every day and I was in his room from 11:00 to 3:00, every day. I was in his room every day for that length of time. I collapsed; I had a heart attack.

One of Veta Gunnery's many stories in her narrative illustrates the blending of a mother's life with the life of the children:

> Marilyn N.: How did you deal with it while he [her son] was over there [Vietnam]? That must've been—

> Veta: I'll tell you how I dealt with it. He went in September. One day I went over to have my teeth cleaned at Dr. B's office. . . . The hygienist, she was chatting all the time . . . and she said, he's going to have to do something about this, answering the phone and cleaning teeth at the same time. . . . So I said well if he decides, I might be interested. . . . The best thing ever happened to me. . . . It became quite a job. . . . While I was in that office I didn't think too much about it. It was always on my mind. How did we deal with it? I'd say it was rough. But thank God I had that job.

When one's own story is strongly connected to another's, the talk about character and fate changes. The character and/or fate of another person or persons becomes important to one's own.

One woman described her character and fate in relation to the cosmos, in general. Earlier in her life she had been involved in causes; more recently she is trying to develop a more passive and spiritual relationship with the world. Her philosophy of life earlier had included a belief in the ultimate triumph of goodness. A pacifist most of her life, Margaret continues to hold those same values but sees herself moving toward a more Buddhist philosophy:

> My philosophy has changed in terms of trying to eliminate things I no longer believe that I learned at such an early age in Church and Sunday school, that they are very hard to eliminate, and now things that I want to believe, that are more of a Buddhist cast, don't fit into that early training and I am hung up between the two. I don't think that I have a mind to formulate in either terms a viable philosophy. I think I am like the conscientious objector who was questioned by the authorities as to what he believed and he said, "I can't tell what I believe until I see what I do."

Later in the interview Margaret is asked to describe herself:

> Marilyn H.: When you think of yourself in the past and in the present and in the future and who you think you are, how would you describe yourself? That part of you that is sort of continuous throughout your life?

> Margaret: Oh this is a big subject. I might be, think of myself as my parent's child or as my husband's wife, but can I think of myself as just somebody independent? If I think of myself standing out in the wet woods listening to some bird that is kind of an exercise in shedding any identity, trying to identify with Pan, as it were. I think I have always been trying to get away from having a personal self. This is a very knotty subject.

Margaret is trying to blend character and fate into one, but it is the fate of the "Great Self," rather than her self and her fate.

Fate-talk requires narrative accrual, as life's many stories are pulled together to pro-vide a narrative in the present. Many of the elders used all the types of fate-talk at one time or another, but in each case there was one that was dominant. Heroes might be just as religious as were subjects who thought that "God determines," but for them, God's part in the narrative about the relationship between the self and the cosmos was a different one. Those who told heroic stories developed a continuous theme of character in their story line; for others, character was a less important theme. The weaving of character and fate into the stories allows persons to make sense of social reality and their place in it. In will and cosmos talk, people produce reasons both for what they do and for the outcomes that result.

Lived Experience and the Story Lines

There is no way to know how persons come to choose one narrative form over another to make sense of their relationship to the cosmos, but it is reasonable to consider some factors that might be related to that choice. Both the content and the form of the stories are influenced by the lived experiences of everyday life and the culture of the historical time in which they occur. An examination of the story lines of the elders reveals two contributing factors, in particular. One is gender and the other is the basic oppositions in the cosmos that persons confront. Gender emerged as a result of discovering how differently the men and women were distributed among the five types of narrative accrual.

Table 10.1

Type of Story Line by Gender (n = 30)		
Type of Story Line	**Male**	**Female**
American Dream of Success	4	3
Life is simple	2	0
Life as a struggle	7	2
God determines	1	4
The shared story	0	7
Total	14	16

Gender

One way of thinking about gender is that it is socially constructed as people live their lives. Table 10.1 presents the distribution of type of story line by gender. As can be seen, there are significant differences between men and women in the form their story lines take. Two of the three women who described their life course in terms of the American dream were single, which suggests that it was not common for married women to see themselves that way. Edith Hayes, the educator, supports that interpretation by something she said about her career and the fact that she had never married (her fiancé had been killed in World War II):

Marilyn N.: You did say, early on, that you did think that women who were married didn't do as good a job teaching because they were divided.

Edith: I think that's true, I really do, and I think I would have done the same thing. I think I would have had a hard time accepting one or the other, and I don't know if I would have made a success at marriage. I'm a pretty hard-hearted person to change their mind. I'm willing to accept a change if I feel it is justified. . . . I stand firm sometimes, and I suspect I might have done that if I'd been married. I think that's my makeup. I might have ended up with a divorce or something. Either that, or I would have had so many kids I wouldn't have known whether I was coming or going. And I wouldn't have had to think about it. You can't tell.

Edith commented that if she had married and left teaching, she probably would have turned into one of those "club women who run everything in town."

Something else happened in the interviews to lend credibility to the interpretation that a story line is constructing gender. Men, when being interviewed, often failed to mention marriage and the birth of children as they were telling their life histories until considerably past the time it would have occurred; alternately, women would go into detail about both the courtship and the marriage and never leave out the birth of children. For most of the men, family brought pleasure and activity to their lives; for women, it was more often central to their story line. Even the one married woman who saw herself as accomplishing the American dream saw herself doing that in partnership with her husband. Her husband also saw himself as achieving the American dream but did not relate it as a partnership with his wife.

The one man who saw his life as determined by God had originally thought of becoming a priest. Later in life, his son was seriously ill and he and his wife prayed to "a saint within our religion, St. Jude, who is attributed to take on hopeless cases," and they still pray because they are so thankful that a miracle happened and their son improved. Other men were religious, but they saw religion either from a social and/or service point of view, rather than that God determines fate.

The story lines of most of the women (eleven out of sixteen) would indicate that they did not particularly see their fate to be in their own hands. It was not so much that they saw themselves as dependent on God or their husbands, and, in fact, independence was valued; it was that their stories were so intertwined with the stories of significant others in their lives that they were unable to make a strong singular connection between their own will and the cosmos as experienced. We specifically asked the elders what the fact that they were a woman or man meant to them at this time in their life. This was not an easy question for them to answer. We struggled to ask it in several different ways and still most replied that they hadn't thought much about it or that it is just the way it is or that they wouldn't want to be what they were not. Except for the two single women with careers, there was very little acknowledgment of any of the issues addressed by the women's movement of the 1960s generation.

Gender has a substantial impact on the story lines, but it seems invisible to the men and women. Men construct male identities as individual heroes or as individuals struggling with the cosmos. Only when one tells of a less traditional identity, it would seem, does it become an intentionally authored part of the story. These men and women were raised with a generation that saw gender as a biological reality; hence, it was not an issue to be narrated but a "fact of life."

The significance of gender in how the fate-problem was addressed shows how lived experience enables and restrains us and how what happens and how we narrate it are intertwined in complex ways. It is likely that the three other significant sociological variables of age, social class, and race/ethnicity would also be differentially constructed in addressing the cosmos. Our sample, because it was small, was intentionally homogeneous on those characteristics.

Oppositions

The basic tension between the cosmos and the will provides the frame for the story line in providing a plot. Social interactions provide the locations for that tension to be experienced. The fate-problem would suggest that we have to narratively construct solutions that enable us to face "demons that would diminish us." Oppositions that lead to struggle provide the substance for the story line. In so doing, we develop the "character" of our selves as well as the "characters" of others and descriptions of events in which the "characters" develop. These oppositions can be thought of as the "troubles" or "plight" that provide the plot and are essential to being able to tell a story at all. Our theoretical focus on the relationship between the will and the cosmos led us to find oppositions in the stories. Each type of story line has its own form of opposition, a point that is exemplified in the excerpts that follow.

Veta Wright, an immigrant who saw herself and her husband as a success in making a go at farming, described their efforts:

> We started to improve on the house. Thank God, we were very pleased. I managed the money. That credit belongs to me. My husband was a very hard working young man.

The great odds they faced were all those imagined and real problems that threaten anyone who buys a farm on borrowed money, and from Veta's point of view, they each did their part to insure that success.

For those whose story portrayed life as a continuing struggle, the oppositions were many and they kept changing over the life course. No constant character was described, either. The following narratives given by four of the men in this group about their philosophy of life illustrate:

> Manfred: I don't think too much. I don't get too uptight that is all, about things that are wrong in the world. I try to live to as nearly, nearly to the best that I know, which I don't always do, but—things will be all right.

> Harold: Way it is now, you take one day at a time. You can't plan ahead. Every time you plan ahead, something comes up and that knocks it in the head.

> Bob: Well, in some aspects of my life, I have tried to preplan it. . . . Think about it to see if I couldn't improve it, you know, in some manner. It was never to a high degree. . . . There was never too much of a necessity for that, you know, outside of [military] service.

> John D.: Right now, the last several years, basic philosophy of life, I don't know, go with the flow, I guess. . . . You come to realize that these problems come up and it's part of life and you just have to accept them and do the best you can.

For life as shared, the threats to being able to prevail are many, for not only does one have to face the oppositions of one's own life, but those of others as well. Rose Edwards, who had a rewarding career of her own, might have fit the hero model except for the challenges of her family life. Her husband was an alcoholic, one son was rebellious during his adolescence, and a daughter had a learning disability that required Rose to spend hours tutoring her most evenings:

> Marilyn N.: Most people have a basic philosophy about life. Do you?

> Rose: My family has always been considered above, not detrimental, caring for others. Everyone is equal as a human being. Feeling that way. Going out of your way to be kind and to help other people.

Rose's commitment to her family took much of her time, energy, and compassion. The problems of her family were ones that she could not ignore or fix. Relationships, then, are the basis of a shared story, but oppositions are still involved. Successful resolution of problems brings considerable pleasure and/or pride to the life as a shared story and to the characters within it. Rose described during the interview a letter she had received from her "learning-disabled" daughter who is now a successful career woman. In that letter, her daughter includes a paper she had written in which she tells how much Rose's help had made a difference in her life. To Rose, that letter meant everything. Life as shared was the story line only of women. They narratively developed a sense of self-worth out of a shared life, something that men did not do.

When God determines what happens, interestingly, not much is learned about the other or the self. Ellen, who sees her life as driven by God, describes her influence on others:

> Well, it's like I tell so many that come in here, God is love. And it begins with that. . . . Take someone who hasn't ever thought about it and do a little thinking about it. They come in here. You can influence folks. My grandchildren, figure them first and worry about their life. I don't mean, what they're going to put into it, but what's coming to them. And so I try. I had two grandsons in here together the other day and I had the opportunity. Now God would've punished me if I hadn't taken care of it. . . . And I could see they were absorbing it. . . . But I don't go out of the house, but I seem to be an influence nevertheless. And I thank God it's an influence for good rather than anything else.

And Carrie, a devout Catholic who saw religion as providing a set of rules to live by, describes her own philosophy:

> Just what I said. Do unto others as you'd have others do unto you. There is good in everybody. Some people brings out the worse, not the good. And be tempered in all things.

Carrie expressed strong opinions about what was morally right and morally wrong in the world, and those opinions came from her Catholic faith:

> The moral issue today to me is a grave one. Young people today are like the dogs and cats on the street. They go out and mate up and think nothing of it, live together, isn't right.

Common among those who saw religion as determining were ideas of good and bad, right and wrong. They try to be good, and they describe others as good people. Most issues are discussed from a moral perspective. For Tony, one of the things that makes him the saddest is that his children, now in adulthood, have not chosen to regularly practice their faith. The opposition such persons face is all that is evil or wrong in the world, and the failure to follow God's will.

The last group to consider are those for whom life is simple. It is hard to find any oppositions in their stories about their life course; perhaps that is what made their lives "read" as simple. Undoubtedly, the lawyer could have detailed the oppositions that are a routine part of the profession of law. He did not, and the interview was not oriented to encourage such explorations. For him, his family life had brought him pleasure but was not particularly defining. Now, as a widower, that part of his life seemed to be over as well. His children, though still in touch, were not described as important.

For the American hero, the defeat of the demon builds character, the character that enables the person to go on to success. For those who see life as a struggle, the demon comes in many colors and the self is constantly and differently challenged. For those with a shared story line, the demons are not only one's own, but those of others that are important to them. The demons for those who saw their lives as determined by God's will were what is evil and bad in the world. And for those for whom life seemed simple, there were few challenges to be met; rather, life just was.

Gender and oppositions show how important context is to addressing the fate-problem. They reinforce the claim fundamental to the sociological enterprise, that social interaction and culture matter in the fictionalization of events into stories.

Continuity, Change, and Narrative Accrual

Continuity and change have always been important themes in exploring the life course.

There has been considerable debate in the aging literature about whether lives are dominated by continuity or change. Narrative accrual connects the various stories of a person's life into a whole, so it also addresses continuity and change, but as an element in a life's story. Narrative treatment of the interaction between the will and the cosmos is concerned with continuity and change because life's challenges invite it. One's fate is seldom determined by a single event, instead, narratives accrue by connecting into a life's story. The risks and troubles of life are seldom resolved once and for all. How did the subjects include continuity and change in their narratives as they addressed the fate problem?

Three sources of change dominated the stories. Those were historical events, personal events, and the inability to handle the hassles of day-to-day living. There is no doubt that many changes have occurred in the world in which these seniors have lived. When the stock market crashed in 1929, the youngest person in the sample was eight years old and the oldest was thirty-six years of age, and their median age was eighteen. Much has changed since that time. But how is historical time involved in persons' stories about their own lives? The elders were specifically asked about historical events and how they might have made a difference, so there was opportunity for such talk to occur. When events mattered (became part of life's narratives rather than narratives about society), it was because lives were personally affected. Edith Hayes became homeless during college due to the Depression's effects, and two other women changed their plans about going to college for the same reason. Edith's misfortune became fortunate, as she describes it:

> Edith: My family home was disbanded. My mother went to work at Homer Folks [a TB Sanitarium], my father took a job working as a builder on Griffith Air Base, and it was at this time I really became a second daughter in this family here in Shelby. . . . And so, the Jensen family were just my family, and I loved them dearly. And this is the Jensen homestead, which I inherited. And, I have small inheritances from the relatives out on the fringe areas,

so that really proved that I was a member of this family. . . . That was the beginning of a long-term relationship. Yes, it was. When my family got back to where they could reestablish a home, I would go and spend some time with them, but I felt that this was my home. . . . It didn't make me not have as much love for my family, I still did, I think it was, you just have a heart that can expand, that's the way I look at it.

Alberta, who didn't get to go to college because her father had a setback, financially, describes the impact on her fate rather passively:

> Marilyn H.: Were you disappointed you couldn't go to college since you had been planning on it?
>
> Alberta: I didn't brood over it because I understood the circumstances and so I went to work and then I went to work at two or three different places then I went to work for the telephone company. I worked there thirty-six years.

Later in the interview Alberta brings up college again:

> Alberta: To tell you the truth, I never, I just took things as they came each day. I never wished that I had done something else. I wanted to go to college. I had taken college courses in high school, but I didn't dwell on it, to the extent that it made me unhappy. I knew that I couldn't go, so as things came along, I took them up. I wasn't despondent over it at all.

The effects of World War II, when narratively included in peoples' life histories, were almost without exception positive, and over half had such an experience. None of the sample had seen combat. It was a time, instead, of adventure, pride, opportunity for service to the country, and the building of self-esteem. Harold Lodge, one of the two men who had almost no stories to tell, told his longest story about an experience while in the military. Wives described the feeling of independence that came with following their husbands across the country. The exception was Edith whose fiancé was killed during the war. After that, for her, work became more important than any relationship. For a few, the

1960s were a challenging time because their children were coming of age. Veta, whose story line was shared, agonized over the plight of her sons who were in Vietnam. She thought that it was enough that her husband had served in World War II; did her sons have to serve in Vietnam as well?

Historical events had the capacity of transforming persons' lives, as in the case of the women who did not go to college because of the depression or the one whose fiancé was killed in World War II. Alternately, events in history also provided excitement, drama, and, consequently, stories that enhanced character. They also provided the stories that justified worldviews. They were the extraordinary events of life that provided exciting substance for narration.

Personal events likely to produce change but not directly connected to historical events involved a wide range of situations. Adulthood is sometimes described as being based on love and work, and such personal events of enough significance to be mentioned were mostly in one of those two areas. It is in personal events that talk of coping strategies emerges (Nouri and Helterline, 1993). Without doubt, the most serious personal event was the death of a family member, most often a spouse, child, or a parent. Women explored the significance of the death of loved ones much more than men did. The most tragic case is illustrated by Ellen who lost two of her children, each when they were two years of age:

> Ellen: . . . when my first baby died, their father said we'd better go back to Brookside to live, where you have your mother and father, too. So we did that. Now that was the greatest help right there. And when Mary died, that didn't seem possible. That God needed both of them. And that was so hard, too, and always when I say something about Mary, why I see Jimmie there on the bed crying for me. No, let's not talk of that.

At another point in the interview, Ellen, when asked about the effect of losing children at such an early age, asserts, simply, but with certainty, "I guess it made me what I am today." The most important consequence of personal difficulties was their effect on the fate-problem. Central to successful coping was the maintenance or enhancement of the self. In the face of difficulties, the self is threatened; ability to cope provides a narrative that affirms the self. Continuity and change are both foundational to narrative accrual.

As the interviewed seniors looked ahead to their own futures, a definition of old age emerged in their narratives and again points to the intersection of continuity and change in persons' life stories. Routine problems, successfully resolved, were an affirmation of self as a competent person. The inability to handle those routine problems was a marker for the beginning of old age. When asked if they felt older some days than others, usually our subjects would describe poor health as something that makes them feel old. But as they talked about their problems, it was also clear that worry about or inability in facing the hassles of day-to-day living was a part of it as well. Being old tends to be associated with not being able to "get through the day."

There were several new fictionalizations used by the elders to maintain a sense of vitality in spite of declining capacities. One was to compare themselves to others of a similar age, not to younger persons. Bob Edwards got up out of his chair and demonstrated how one man he knows walks in a very bent-over manner; compared to him, Bob sees himself as quite vital. A second method was to pursue less. If prevailing in life is the pursuit and accomplishment of a series of expectations, then one way to continue to prevail is to reduce expectations. Sometimes associated with this was an explanation of how the world had changed in such a way that life just isn't the same as it used to be, an account that justifies reduced expectations. A third method is to be amazed at how long one has lived and to define any remaining quality of life as a bonus. At some chronological age, persons are impressed with simply being alive, and that is enough in and of itself. What age that is, we do not have enough information to pinpoint, but it appears to be in the nineties. And, last, many of our subjects had no difficulty in enhancing their sense of self by talking about their children and grandchildren. Most of the subjects who had children saw them on a regular basis and the children and grandchildren were very important to them. Those whose children lived elsewhere waited for phone calls and letters and liked visits and visiting. Pictures adorned the buffets and walls of the homes of our subjects and were often shared with us. The more they talked, the more it was clear that while they may not have too many accomplishments to brag about at this stage in their life, they certainly liked to describe the successes and accomplishments of their children and grandchildren. The strategies used to put off old age were used by both genders equally. It may be that in the final confrontation of the limits of the body, the resources that can be called upon are not as gender specific, are new, and require new narratives.

Summary

Dignity in the later years is dependent on being able to prevail, to have some sense that one is coping. When self-efficacy runs out, old age sets in. Descriptions of intentionality with values dominate talk about continuity and change, and they are used to make sense of the events of life. Intentional action is based on choices, especially in problematic situations, and as such, involves valuing to make the good choice. The "American dream of success" story line only fits a minority of the subjects interviewed in this research. Three other types of narrative accrual also enabled persons mostly to prevail in their own life stories. Life as a struggle, life as shared, and God determines as story lines also were ways of "encountering and temporarily surmounting the projected demons that would diminish us" (Ochberg 1994:143). Clearly self-efficacy is too much of a value in people's lives to develop a story line that diminishes its significance or takes it out altogether. The mastery and self-esteem that make up self-efficacy are threatened at the end of life. New coping strategies are developed to enable the maintenance of self and hold off the "demons of old age."

Gender emerged as an important dimension in narrative. Women often accrue the narratives of their lives differently than men. Gender was not an explicit topic for most of our subjects even if gender was an important outcome in their stories. With the changes in how women and men are now constructing the life course, it is likely that the narratives themselves, and the process narrative accrual as well, are more intentionally gendered. How the resulting story line has been affected by this consciousness of gender is the more interesting question. Analysis of the stories of the next generation of elders will help to answer that question. The significance of gender in the narratives suggests that other differences would also be important. Race or ethnicity, social class, and rural/urban contrasts would likely be involved in both the process of narrative accrual and the content of the narratives.

Finding that gender and oppositions were so important to the narratives supports the claim that in fictionalizing our stories we do so within the cultural webs of meaning in which we live and that we are both enabled and constrained by the resources available to us. Narrative analysis explores the variety of means available to fashion a life. Debates about whether the life course can be seen as continuous or changing seem to miss the point when one considers narrative structures. Narrative accrual, necessary to making sense of all the events of persons' lives, also needs both continuity and change to make the "good story." . . . Whether people develop, continue, or change, they do continue to construct meaning that negotiates the cultural themes and the oppositions they face in a way that maintains their sense of self and the world in which they live.

Discussion Questions

1. Describe the four major types of narrative accrual used by the older people in this selection and how they hold off the "demons of old age" to give meaning to their current lives.

2. What are the gender differences in the narratives of older men and women? On the basis of your readings thus far, would you expect members of the baby boom generation to show the same gender-linked patterns? Why or why not?

3. The narrators in this study were all White, middle-class or working-class people in

rural areas, villages, and small cities. How might you expect the narrative themes to differ from these among urban, economically disadvantaged African-American elders, urban, poor Puerto-Ricans, middle-class Japanese Americans, or recent elder immigrants from Southeast Asia?

Authors' Note

Funds for the research that provided the background for this article were received from the Walter B. Ford Foundation. The authors wish to thank all of the persons who willingly shared their time and their life histories with us. We also wish to thank two anonymous readers for their very helpful comments on an earlier draft of the article.

References

Bruner, Jerome. 1990. *Acts of Meaning*. Cambridge, MA: Harvard University Press.

——. 1991. "The Narrative Construction of Reality." *Critical Inquiry* 18:1–21.

Nouri, Marilyn, and Marilyn Helterline. 1993. "Coping Strategies, Gender and Aging." Paper presented at the Eastern Sociological Association, March, Boston, MA.

Ochberg, Richard. 1994. "Life Stories and Storied Lives." Pp. 113–44 in *Exploring Identity and Gender: The Narrative Study of Lives*, edited by Amia Lieblich and Ruthellen Josselson. Thousand Oaks, CA: Sage.

Riley, M. W., and Foner, Anne. 1972. *Aging and Society*. Vol. 3, *A Sociology of Age Stratification*. New York: Russell Sage.

Spencer, Martin. 1993. "The Idea of Fate: Literature, History, Character, and the Modernization of Consciousness." Paper presented at the Eastern Sociological Association Meetings, March, Boston, MA.

Chapter 11

My Mother's Music

Lydia Minatoya

The previous selection on narrative accrued throughout the life course emphasized the importance of telling life stories as a way of integrating one's past in order to give meaning to the present. The following selection, recounted by an American-born Japanese-American daughter who grew up with her parents in upstate New York, details her mother's childhood in Japan and her early life in the United States, and her mother's marriage, arranged while she was interned as a potential saboteur during World War II. The history of Japanese immigrants, like Mrs. Minatoya's, is marked by discrimination. Although the first Japanese to settle in the continental United States arrived in 1869, Japanese and those of Japanese descent were refused citizenship twice by the U.S. government (once in 1870, a second time in 1911). In 1924, Congress passed an Immigration Act stating that no alien ineligible for citizenship should be admitted to the United States, thus stopping all legal immigration from Japan. (The American-born children of Japanese immigrants were, however, citizens.) When the United States entered World War II after Pearl Harbor was bombed by Japan in 1941, feelings against people of Japanese origin escalated. In early 1942, President Roosevelt signed an executive order giving the War Department authority to exclude anyone who might be potentially disloyal, whether American born or not, from the western United States. This order not only effectively banned all Japanese-born and American-born Japanese from the states in which the majority lived but also began the evacuation of about 110,000 people of Japanese descent to 10 detention camps located in remote inland areas.

Notice how the author's mother, Mrs. Minatoya (called Okaa-chan, which means "sweet honorable mother" in Japanese) describes her girlhood, the gender socialization she received as a child, and her relationship to her parents. See if you can detect patterns of family loyalty and the ways in which that loyalty led to her marriage. Think about the ways in which her forced relocation during World War II affected her subsequent life. Pay attention to the themes in her life history and what she includes and does not include to give meaning to her life.

"I believe that the Japanese word for wife literally means honorable person remaining within," says my mother. "During the nineteen twenties, when I was a child in Japan, my seventeen-year-old cousin married into a wealthy family. Before her marriage, I would watch as she tripped gracefully through the village on her way to flower arrangement class. Kimono faintly rustling. Head bent in modesty. She was the most beautiful woman I had ever seen. After her marriage, she disappeared within her husband's house. She was not seen walking through the village again. Instead, she would send the clear, plucked notes of her okoto—her honorable Japanese harp—to scale the high courtyard wall. I used to pause to listen. In late spring, showers of petals from swollen cherry blossoms within her courtyard would rain onto the pavement. I would breathe the fragrant air and imagine her kneeling at her okoto, alone in a serene shadowy room. It seemed so romantic, I could hardly bear it." My mother laughs and shakes her head at her childhood excess. After a moment she speaks. "Courtyard walls, built to keep typhoons out, also marked the boundaries of a well-bred wife. Because of this, in other ways, the Japanese always have taught their daughters to soar."

"And you?"

"When I was eleven years old, my father gave me okoto."

During the 1950s, in our four-room flat on the south side of Albany, New York, my mother would play her okoto. Sometimes on Sunday afternoons when the jubilant gospel singing had faded from the AME Zion Church across the alley, my mother would kneel over a long body of gleaming wood, like a physician intent on reviving a beautiful patient, and pinch eerie evocative chords from the trembling strings of her okoto.

"Misa-chan, Yuri-chan," she would call to my sister and me, "would you like to try?"

"*Hai*, Okaa-chan"—yes sweet honorable mother—we would murmur, as if stirred from a trance.

"I was a motherless child," says Okaa-chan, when I have grown to adolescence. "My father gave me okoto to teach me to cherish my womanhood."

"Your womanhood?"

My mother plucks a chord in demonstration. "The notes are delicate yet there is resonance. Listen. You will learn about timelessness and strength. Listen. You will understand how, despite sorrow, heart and spirit can fly."

An American daughter, I cannot understand the teachings of my mother's okoto. Instead, I listen to the music of her words.

A formal, family photograph is the only memento my mother has of her mother. In 1919, an immigrant family poses in a Los Angeles studio and waits for a moment to be captured that will document success and confidence in America; a moment that can be sent to anxious relatives in Japan. A chubby infant, pop-eyed with curiosity, my mother sits squirming on her father's lap. My forty-five-year-old grandfather levels a patrician stare into the camera. By his side, wearing matching sailor suits, his sons aged three and five stand self-conscious with pride and excitement. My grandmother stands behind her husband's chair. In her early twenties, she owns a subdued prettiness and an even gaze.

My seven-year-old aunt is not in the picture. She has been sent to Japan to be raised as a proper ojo-san—the fine daughter of a distinguished family. Within the next year, her mother, brothers, and baby sister will join her. Five years later, my grandmother will be banished from the family. The circumstances of her banishment will remain a family secret for over forty years.

"Your grandmother loved to read," says Okaa-chan. The year is 1969. Okaa-chan and I sit in the kitchen, drinking tea at a table my father has made by attaching legs to a salvaged piece of Formica. It is after midnight; the house lies sleeping. "She was a romantic, an adventurer. In Japan, she caused scandal when she bought a set of encyclopedia."

"A scandal?"

"You must understand these were country people. A young wife wasting her time on reading, spending her money on frivolous facts, people must have thought, What nonsense! My honorable older brothers recall that each day she would read to us from the encyclopedia. She would tell us about science and foreign countries. I think she liked to dream about possibilities." Okaa-chan tilts her head and looks into the distance. "I was too young to remember this but it is a nice memory, neh Yuri-chan?"

"But why was she sent away? Why did your father divorce her?" Direct, assertive, American, I break into my mother's reflection and pull her back to the story I want to hear.

"*Saa neh*," Okaa-chan wonders. "Ojii-chan—your honorable grandfather—lived in America maybe ten to fifteen years before he went back to Japan and married. Our family is descended from samurai. We thought of ourselves as aristocracy; and Ojii-chan needed a wife from another samurai family."

"And the divorce?" I persist.

"Perhaps my father was naive about people."

"What do you mean?"

"When he brought my mother to Los Angeles, Ojii-chan owned a pool hall. It was very popular with young Filipino workers. It was against the law for them to bring family to America. They were lonely and restless; and pool halls helped to kill times. My mother worked by Ojii-chan's side, and being young and pretty she was good for business. When work was done, Father would leave us alone. My mother had read all the European, great romantic novels. She was much younger than Ojii-chan. She was lonely, and she fell in love with a young Filipino who could read and speak Japanese. He courted her by bringing books."

"She had a love affair!"

"They were very sincere." Okaa-chan is quick to correct any impression that her mother had been a libertine. "The man wanted my father to divorce my mother so she could remarry. Ojii-chan started moving us from house to house, trying to hide Mother, but her lover keeps locating us."

"Why didn't she just take you children and run away with him?"

"You must understand, my mother was from a good family. She would not consider taking her children from a respectable family into a disgraceful situation. She would not think of taking her husband's children from him. Romance is a private peril. Others should not suffer." Okaa-chan pours herself some more green tea. Its aroma is faintly acrid. "Perhaps Ojii-chan finally thought, This is embarrassing nuisance. He sent us all back to Mother's parents in Japan."

"But why did Ojii-chan wait five years to divorce your mother?"

Okaa-chan sighs. "That was a cruel mistake, *neh*? Ojii-chan was a highly honorable man but often he did not understand how his action would affect others. If he had divorced my mother when he first found out, in America, then she could have married her lover." Okaa-chan is silent again. Perhaps she is saddened to recall a flaw in the only parent she clearly can remember. "Ojii-chan divorced as an afterthought. He may have wondered; Why am I supporting this woman? Why is her family raising my children? He broke a promise to my mother's parents."

"A promise?"

"When Ojii-chan sent my mother back to her parents, they begged him not to divorce her. It was a small village. If Ojii-chan and Mother divorced, her parents would have no choice but to send their daughter from their house."

"And so, when they divorced . . . "

"My mother's ancestral home was adjacent to Ojii-chan's ancestral home. There had been warm feelings and intermarriages between the homes for centuries. With the divorce, relations had to be severed."

Okaa-chan is silent for a long time.

"After the divorce, my mother's parents would come to edge of Ojii-chan's ancestral home," she finally says. "My grandmother would be carrying a plate of sweets and she would call to her grandchildren. They only wanted to see us, to give us some candies. We would long to run to them but we knew it was

forbidden. Instead, we would turn and run into the house to hide."

I stand and move to the sink and stove, heating more water, helplessly wanting to give Okaa-chan a cup of tea to compensate for losing her grandmother's sweets.

"Did you know beforehand? Did you know the divorce was coming?"

"Oh, no, I was maybe five years old, little more than toddler. But looking back, there are certain memories."

Okaa-chan is quiet as she moves back within her memories. "One day, Mother took us to a photographer's studio for a formal portrait. I was excited and I turned to call my mother's attention to something. She was wiping away tears with her kimono sleeve. I never before had seen her cry and thought, Why in the middle of such a grand adventure?" Okaa-chan pauses. "I suppose that happened just before Ojii-chan had us sent from her house."

There is a longer pause.

"How I wish I could have a copy of that picture," she says.

In the quiet, I notice that the sky is lightening outside the kitchen window; birds are beginning to stir. Finally, Okaa-chan resumes her story.

"My clearest memory is this. I am sleeping beneath billowing mosquito netting with my sister and brothers. Suddenly I am awakened. It is a summer night and the rice paper screens are open. In the courtyard are the sounds of crickets and the glows of fireflies. My mother is standing, holding two candles inside white paper lanterns. They make pretty shadows. I am still sleepy as Mother leads us across the courtyard. Our wooden geta scrape along the footpath. It is damp and cool with dew. Mother holds one lantern. Eldest brother holds the other. As we get to Ojii-chan's ancestral home, Mother embraces us. Ojii-chan's sister stands waiting. '*Itte!*' Mother commands. Go!"

The second hand sweeps noiselessly around the kitchen clock. From somewhere in the darkened house, my sister coughs and turns in her bed. After a long time, Okaa-chan speaks. "I never saw my mother again."

When my mother is fifty-one, she takes me to the Japanese village where she spent fourteen years of her girlhood.

"I want to tell you about my regret," Okaa-chan says suddenly as we recline on the cool straw mats. In this house where Okaa-chan spent her childhood, the late afternoon air feels sultry and unpredictable. A typhoon has been forecast.

"After I graduated from the Charlotte School of Costume Design in Los Angeles"— my mother always uses the full title of her alma mater; as if the formal labor of carefully pronouncing all those multiple syllables affords her more time to savor her pride— "your Ojii-chan wanted to return to Japan. I accompanied him and became a fashion designer at a large department store. One day I received a letter, from Manchuria, addressed to me through the store. It was from my mother."

"What did you do?"

"I was only twenty years old. It is such a young age. My mother was little older than twenty when she was sent away." Okaa-chan sighs. "I excitedly showed my mother's letter to my father. May I write back? I begged him. I knew nothing of the anger that can be between husband and wife."

"Did Ojii-chan scold you?"

"No. He took my mother's letter from me. He told me not to write back. We never spoke of the letter again." Okaa-chan pauses. "My greatest regret, Yuri-chan, is that I obeyed. I did not write to my poor mother. I do not have her letter. She never wrote to me again."

In the restless, August afternoon, Okaa-chan strokes my hair. I am moved and discomforted by her confession. I am twenty years old.

"Tell us how you and Daddy met!" my sister and I would beg Okaa-chan when we were children. The idea of our parents courting seemed both romantic and silly, and we would become giddy and giggly at the telling.

"During the war, your daddy's daddy and my family were in the same relocation camp—Heart Mountain, Wyoming," Okaa-chan invariably would begin. "Your daddy was in Chicago, at the University of Illinois and your daddy's daddy was very worried about him."

"Why?"

"Because he was thirty-three years old, unmarried, and far from family." Okaa-chan would smile in recollection. "Your daddy's daddy was the sweetest man. Since I am here in camp, Daddy's daddy thought, I will make most of it. I will find my son a good bride."

"You were the good bride!" I would giggle from behind my hands.

"But first there were other steps," Misa would interrupt. Being older and more orderly, Misa's job was to make certain that the whole story was told in the correct sequence.

"Yes," Okaa-chan would oblige us. "Daddy's daddy decided that his son should marry a Kibei Japanese born in America and raised in Japan. As you know, your daddy has a temper and sometimes can be stubborn."

Misa and I would chortle knowingly.

"Daddy's daddy thought, If Katsuji marries a Nisei—a Japanese born and raised in America—or a non-Japanese, there will be too much commotion in the household. So Daddy's daddy began to ask all his friends."

"Do you know of any nice Kibei girl for my boy, Katsuji, to marry?" Misa and I would chorus. We knew this part by heart.

"Daddy's daddy was a widower in his late sixties. He was separated from all seven of his sons. The bride search made his life in camp more meaningful."

"Tell us about the haiku man."

"Well, Ojii-chan liked to write. He belonged to a haiku poetry group. One of Ojii-chan's haiku poetry friends knew Daddy's daddy. When the haiku friend heard Daddy's daddy ask—"

"Do you know of any nice Kibei girl for my boy, Katsuji, to marry?"

"The haiku friend said, 'Oh, Yes. I know the finest Kibei girl. She is an ojo-san—a proper daughter from a fine household—and she even comes from same prefecture in Japan.'"

"And you were that finest Kibei girl!" I triumphantly would shout, overeager for the happy culmination of the story.

"Tell us about Daddy's visit," Misa would urge, savoring the tale.

"When war ended, your daddy came to Heart Mountain to visit his daddy. He planned to stay two weeks. The first week of the visit was agony for Daddy's daddy. He wanted your daddy to agree to meet the Kibei girl, but all your daddy did was eat ravenously and sleep late! Finally, about six days before he was to return to Chicago, your daddy accompanied the haiku man to our barracks and was introduced to my father and me."

"Daddy broke a date for you," Misa reminds Okaa-chan.

"Well, not really, that would have been rude," Okaa-chan explains. "The next evening, your daddy had agreed to play bridge with a young Nisei woman. She had been married to a Hakujin—a white man—but he had divorced her in the midst of wartime hysteria. She was very nice girl."

"But not the girl for Daddy!" Misa and I would gloat at Okaa-chan's victories over shortening time and a nice Nisei woman.

"Instead of playing bridge, your daddy again came to our barracks. This time, the haiku friend did not accompany him. By the end of the week, when Daddy went back to Chicago, our marriage had been arranged. Just before he left, there was an engagement party." Okaa-chan laughs affectionately, "Your daddy and I were still strangers: shy and dazed. The most happiest person at party was your daddy's sweet daddy!"

In the fall of 1945, Okaa-chan and Daddy's Sweet Daddy took a train to Chicago, where my parents were to be married. In formal recognition of the new familial network, Ojii-chan accompanied them to the train station. There in the desert, amidst the howling, whipping winds, Okaa-chan's father stood on the train platform. He held his hat in his right hand; his arms hung straight at his sides. He stood bowing deeply from the waist, long after the other well-wishers had drifted from the platform. He stood bowing, until the train carrying his child and her new father had vanished into the horizon.

In romance, my father's timing was lucky. Until only a few months before she met him, Okaa-chan had been spoken for.

Her engagement had begun on an early autumn morning in 1940. She and Ojii-chan were boarding an ocean liner docked in the busy international harbor of Yokohama. They were returning to Los Angeles after a sojourn of two years in Japan.

Sunlight sliced the crisp sea air. Ships sounded. Everywhere was the commotion of loading. My mother wore high heels and a slim, pinch-waisted suit she had designed herself. My grandfather was regal in pinstripes.

Also boarding was a sophisticated woman in her late twenties, sailing off with her second husband. She and my grandfather began to converse. It seems that, distantly, their great family houses were linked. The woman's brother—a college educated, handsome young baseball idol in the glittering city of Tokyo—was there to bid his sister adieu. He pushed back the brim of his new fedora—the better to see my twenty-year-old Okaa-chan—and immediately fell in love.

And so, in time, a marriage was arranged. Between a bilingual fashion designer, from the city of motion pictures, and a Japanese baseball star. Truly, it was to be a marriage of the twentieth century, of a shining new age at its height. But then came the war and everything changed and wedding plans fell into dust.

When my sister and I were children, we viewed Okaa-chan's wartime Relocation simply as the provident event that enabled her to meet our father. As we grew older, Misa and I began to ask Okaa-chan about the war years themselves.

"Like every American of that era," Okaa-chan says, "I will never forget December seventh, nineteen forty-one. Ojii-chan, my eldest brother, and I were visiting an auntie in San Pedro, California. Ojii-chan had just returned from visiting Japan. It had been the last Kobe-San Francisco sailing, before war. We were laughing and talking when the telephone rang."

Okaa-chan pauses, searching for a way to describe that moment. "Sometimes you catch, out of the corner of your eye, a view of someone's posture suddenly change, just a little," she says, "something so small, and you know that everything has gone terribly wrong."

"Who was it on the telephone?" Misa and I ask.

"Someone from Japanese American community perhaps. My auntie said nothing. She carefully put the receiver back on the telephone, turned like a sleepwalker to the radio, and switched it on. When she faced us, the sight of Auntie's anguished face and the sound of the news came at the same moment."

"Then what happened? What did you do?"

"San Pedro is a harbor." Okaa-chan recalls, "There was immediate panic about Japanese American fishermen. The federal government issued an order blockading all roads leading out of the city. No Japanese were allowed to leave the city and anyone doing anything suspicious was to be arrested and detained indefinitely. Auntie got word from friends that government agents were going from house to house, arresting the leaders of Japanese culture clubs."

"Weren't you terribly frightened?"

"I was paralyzed with fear. Ojii-chan was Issei—born in Japan and not allowed to become American citizen. He had just come from Japan; he was considered a community elder. He was an old man, in his seventies. I was afraid if he was arrested, we never would see him again."

"What did you do?"

"I did nothing. I was too frightened. Oniisan—my honorable older brother—decided that we had to return to Los Angeles. Onii-san wrote to the Los Angeles county clerk's office. He asked for notarized copies of his and my birth certificates. They would be proof of our American citizenship. He selected a time when the military police were likely to be too busy with traffic to search each car. He made our father lie down in the back of car and completely covered him with clothes. It had been one week since that horrible moment when Auntie had turned on the radio. That moment had never ended; it had only grown worse. When we approached the military police station, my brother calmly handed over our identifications paper. The guard looked at us closely; he leaned through the window and stared at the pile of clothes. I wondered if the clothes were moving. I waited for the guard to stiffen, for him to aim his rifle, for him to drag Father from the hiding place. He stepped back and waved us through."

I am a psychologist. People often ask me, "How did wartime Relocation affect Japanese Americans?" Relocation was a wall that my mother's music could not scale.

When asked about her feelings and thoughts during her three years in Relocation Camp, Okaa-chan has little to say. Her memory, usually so rich with character and mood and nuance, becomes oddly unyielding.

"How long did you have to get ready, what did you take?" My sister and I try to encourage her with questions.

"Oh," Okaa-chan stops and thinks. She shakes her head impatiently, as if trying to shake a dormant memory into wakefulness. "Let's see, maybe two weeks? We could bring what we could carry. Everything else had to be sold or given away." Okaa-chan trails off and looks at us with worry. She is disappointed by her memory and afraid that we will be disappointed with her. When Okaa-chan speaks of her years in Relocation Camp, her voice is hesitant. Often it fades: confused and apologetic. Her recollections are strangely lifeless. In this way, the Wyoming desert, with its cruel extremes, with its aching cold and killing heat, still holds my mother against her will.

Discussion Questions

1. Describe the dilemmas and tensions Mrs. Minatoya faced in the relationships with her mother and father. How are these related to her gender socialization as a Kibei?

2. Outline the events leading to Mrs. Minatoya's internment in a detention camp during World War II. In what ways was this event unexpected?

3. The narrator says: "Relocation was a wall my mother's music could not scale." Explain this statement, given what you know about life history thus far from preceeding selections.

4. Compare the pattern of Okaa-chan's courtship with what you know of your mother's courtship. What cultural differences do you find and how did gender socialization influence their respective betrothals?

Reprinted from: Lydia Minatoya, *Talking to High Monks in the Snow*. Copyright © 1992 by Lydia Minatoya. Reprinted with permission of HarperCollins Publishers, Inc.

Chapter 12
Adaptation of Oldest Old Black Americans

Colleen L. Johnson

Aging, although a universal process, varies widely among individuals, and so do sources of satisfaction in later life. Older people interpret their life experiences in many different ways that relate not only to their individual characteristics but also to their social class, race, and ethnicity. Studies of older minorities often inadvertently stress the disadvantages their members have faced, such as racial or ethnic discrimination, poverty, and limited life chances, and ignore the positive aspects of ethnicity, race, and membership in a minority group. In the following selection, Colleen Johnson details the ways in which a group of oldest old black Americans[1] derive a sense of well-being by comparing their present lives to their pasts. Strong social supports from various sources, values in black culture emphasizing old age as a natural process, and satisfaction over having survived a lifetime of discrimination and economic disadvantage enhance life satisfaction among very old black Americans. As you read, note the types of available social supports that have been helpful in dealing with poverty and discrimination. Appraise the beliefs, norms, and values in black culture that have a positive effect on well-being. Think about the relevance of feeling that one has "beaten the odds" as it relates to well-being and personal satisfaction in later life.

This exploration of adaptation of 122 Black Americans 85 years and older has puzzling findings. Despite harsh conditions and many adversities throughout their long lives (Jackson 1988), most blacks in advanced old age express more contentment with their lives than do their white age peers (Johnson 1994). In fact, their contentment prevails even though they are more likely to view their health as poor and to complain about inadequate economic resources. Questions arise as to the strategies blacks have devised to adapt not only to the predictable difficulties of advanced old age, but also to possible belated effects of difficulties experienced over the life course. Is it because blacks derive more contentment from their religious beliefs, their church activities, their families and friends? Or is it because black culture provides greater pride with the special status of a survivor despite great odds, what we refer to as the aura of survivorship? Or does it come from changing their aspirations, expectations, and reference points used as a basis for assessing the quality of their lives?

In the following, I will address these questions through illustrations of three types of effects that may be contributing to the subjective well-being of oldest old blacks. First, very old blacks benefit from extensive social resources, if not from their family, then from the black church and community. Second, cultural effects are found in the black community that offers values, beliefs, and a coherent set of meanings that integrate their life history with their present situation in order to make sense out of their special status as survivors. Third, by changing their reference points from which to evaluate their current quality of life, they draw upon their own life history, usually a life plagued by many hardships, to compare with their greatly improved current life. . . .

Our initial aim was to select respondents from public voting records in San Francisco and Oakland, California, and then to use snowballing techniques where respondents secured from the voting records referred us to their age peers. These voting records include date of birth and current addresses that facilitate locating respondents. Since blacks 85 years and older comprise a very small proportion of the local population, we encountered some difficulty in locating sufficient numbers from voting records, so it was necessary to also secure names from various community associations. In total, 34 percent came from voting records, 32 percent were randomly selected from a clinic serving older blacks, and 34 percent were secured through snowball techniques or referrals from community associations. Letters were sent to individuals, 85 years and older, followed by telephone calls to schedule an interview. Of those contacted who were judged competent enough to be interviewed, 24 percent refused. Competency to participate in an interview was established by asking potential respondents to confirm their age, date of interview, address, and telephone number. . . .

Interviews lasting two to three hours were held in the respondents' homes and conducted either in one or two sittings. A focused interview technique was used, one that combined both open-ended and structured questioning and standard instruments to measure health, functioning, and mood. Verbatim notes were taken by hand and later transcribed. Where measures were warranted, relevant open-ended portions of each interview were coded by two members of the research staff, with an intercoder reliability of 81 percent. Structured questions included demographic information and economic status and expectations for their economic status. Selected life histories were analyzed that reflected the patterns of adaptation described in the following. . . .

Table 12.1 describes the sample and compares demographic variables by gender. Like the general sample of the very old who still live in the community, a large majority are women (79 percent), few (15 percent) are married, and a large proportion are living alone (60 percent). Men, however, differed significantly from women with more being married and living with others. Few respondents (22 percent) in this cohort of blacks had twelve years or more of education, and few (16 percent) held skilled or white collar positions. Only one-third describe their economic status as good, although as many as 71 percent said it was better than they had anticipated. Table 12.1 also includes the proportion who experienced the early loss of a parent. Thirty-eight percent of the sample had lost one or both parents by the age of sixteen with 19 percent having lost a mother, 10 percent a father, and 9 percent losing both parents. In family structure during childhood, as many as 53 percent did not grow up in a family with both parents present for all or a major part of their childhood.

Determinants of Adaptation

Social Integration

Blacks have long been noted for their flexible family values that have assisted them in dealing with the stressors stemming from poverty and discrimination (Stack 1974). Most respondents define their family to in-

Table 12.1

Sample Characteristics by Gender			
	Male (n=26) 21%	Female (n=96) 79%	Total (n=122)
Mean Age	88.5	88.2	88.3
Marital Status			
Married	38%	8%	15%
Not Married	62	92	85*
Household			
Alone	35%	67%	60%
With Others	65	33	40*
Parent Status			
Childless	35%	48%	45%
Living Children	65	52	55
Education			
12 Years or More	15%	24%	22%
7 to 11 Years	27	41	38
6 or Fewer Years	58	35	40
Occupation			
White Collar/Above	15%	16%	16%
Skilled Blue Collar	27	17	19
Semi/Unskilled	58	67	65
Perceived Economic Status			
Good	38%	31%	32%
Fair	50	60	58
Poor	12	9	10
Expectations			
Better	88%	66%	71%
Same	4	19	15
Worse	8	15	14
Loss of Parent			
No	58%	64%	62%
Yes	42	36	38
Had Nuclear Family			
No	62%	51%	53%
Yes	38	49	47

*$p < .05$.

clude, not only children and members of their immediate families, but also distant relatives and fictive kin. As to their current family resources, very few, 15 percent, are married, but 36 percent live with a family member. While only 13 percent have a child functioning as a caregiver, two-thirds receive some instrumental support from at least one child. When children are present, grandchildren and great grandchildren are also usually a source of sociability and support.

Potential vulnerabilities are particularly apparent among the 45 percent who are childless. The fact that 30 percent of the sample have no contact or rare contacts with relatives reflects the high percentage of childless. In t-tests to explore the effects of this dearth of family relationships, we found that those with no relationships do not differ significantly from those with some family in mood, in involvement with friends and associations, and in their satisfaction with their families. (Not reported in tabular form.) The presence of fictive kin, however, was significantly more common among those with few or no family contacts. Those with little family involvement are significantly more likely to create kin out of nonkin relationships. This pattern is important, for it suggests that mechanisms are present that can expand helping networks even when family members are not present.

The following illustrations of family life range from those with many descendants to those who have no ongoing family relationships. Mrs. M. is fairly typical of those with large families. She has eight surviving children, 29 grandchildren and "So many great grandchildren I can't count that high." For her 89th birthday party, five generations were present and the attendees filled every seat in her church. She lives with her daughter, but most of her children are in the area and drop in frequently or at least speak by telephone. Mrs. M is very much in control of her family life and in fact her children refer to as "the queen mother." Each morning she calls her children and tells them what to do. Even with these frequent social contacts, Mrs. M. still finds time to be active in her church, which has been a source of numerous friendships. She reports that she is never depressed. "I let bygones be bygones. I don't look at the ugly

things in life. I have my family to look after me and I look to the Lord to handle everything else."

Even large families with considerable social disorganization usually meet the needs of the oldest generation by a variety of means. Mr. B at 90 years of age has some needs for help, because of his own infirmities and because his wife of 66 years is bedfast and unable to care for herself. They are able to stay in their large house only because of the efforts of numerous people. His wife had two sons when they married, but both of them died some years ago of alcohol-related diseases. He and his wife raised the four children of one son whom he considers as his own grandchildren. One granddaughter functions as caregiver with the county paying her to come daily in the hours between her shifts as a school bus driver. Her daughter, their great granddaughter lives with them along with her baby daughter, and she also helps out. Another great granddaughter lives nearby and stops in frequently. Another grandson lives "out back" in a small cottage. He is an alcoholic who comes and goes, but causes Mr. B. no problems. Finally a friend is also paid to come weekly to clean their house. Shortly after our first contact, his wife died. Although he said he was lonely, his life was full of activities with family members who continued their supports. "I have people around most of the time with lots of friends from church coming too. People want me to come and live with them, even my niece in Louisiana, but I'm too old to move." When asked about his mood, he reported, "I've had a beautiful life even when I'm sick. I am pretty hard to upset. I've been through so many trials and tribulations for so long, I don't pay no more attention to problems and trouble."

Where such extensive families are unavailable, informal community resources become substitutes. For example, some respondents create fictive kin out of fellow church members, long-term friends, or even more casual relationships. Mrs. C. at age 87 lost her only son five years previously, a child raised by her mother because of her own alcoholism. Consequently, she was never very close to her son. Because of difficulty walking, she is unable to get out, so she spends most of her days in her one-room apartment in senior housing. A choreworker comes three mornings a week, and her neighbors and friends from her church take care of her other needs. During the interview, her "niece" came and kissed her, calling her "Auntie." This niece is really not a niece, but a young roommate of a "relative," whose actual relationship is unclear.

Her "grandson" takes her shopping, but he is not the son of her son. She also reports, "My church sisters and brothers see to me all the time. That woman you saw downstairs is a church relative. I call her 'daughter' and she calls me 'mama.' She brings me my food." When asked about the last time she cried, she responded, "The other day I got to thinking how good people are to me, even those I see out on the street. They talk to me so kind and help me out." In her life review, she said, "The best time in my life was when I started to change. I was feeling it was time to give up drinking. Ever since then, the Lord has looked over me and I am by his side. There's nothing left to worry about now."

Even when kinlike relationships are not formalized, members of the community tend to replace the family as helpers. Such helpers can come from a variety of sources. For example, one woman living alone benefitted from renting out her garage to a young man who knocks on her door each morning to see that she is all right. He shops for her on his way home from work. If she needs anything else, a neighbor across the street will also shop for her even though she does not even know this neighbor's name. The landlord leaves his car in her driveway at night to increase her security.

The Cultural System and the Aura of Survivorship

The black culture contains relevant beliefs, norms, and values that designate expectations and shape standards of evaluation about their lives. Three value orientations were observed that are likely to have positive effects on well-being. First, in agreement with reports in the literature, blacks in general tend to value the aged and old age (Taylor 1982; Register 1981). Aging is not usually viewed as a problem, but rather it is accepted as a natural process or, if life is prolonged, as a gift from God. These black respondents are generally contented with their lives and proud of having reached advanced old age. When problems arise, they are not likely to dwell upon them, instead appreciating the mere fact that they are still alive to deal with them. With such beliefs, the effects of any disadvantages are minimized. In fact, in response to a question, "What is the most difficult problem you have to deal with?", one-third of the respondents reported no problems, while another 37 percent only complained about physical problems. "Nothin' wrong. I don't let things bother me." "I don't have anything hard to handle any more." "I just forget my problems—push them out of my mind." Even physical complaints are minimized. "Only problem is when my knee is hurtin'." When asked, "What's it like to live so long," a large majority gave positive responses. "It's wonderful." "I'm thankful—I'm still around and have my mind."

Second, the widespread belief in the benevolence of a supernatural power has important implications in how very old blacks deal with potential stressors in their old age. Religiosity is high with 65 percent attending church regularly. Frequent church attendance not only benefits them in terms of coping with stress and in receiving social supports, their religious ideology offers a coherent system of meaning that explains and sometimes rationalizes the effects of the many adversities experienced throughout their lives. Their supernatural being is viewed not only as responsible for their having lived so long, but also for their safety and contentment in late late life. "The Lord let me live so long. He take care of me and give me health." "I don't be fretting over things that are not my concern. I live in the Lord and I do good to others." "I'll stay around until the Lord calls me."

One 88-year-old woman can remember little about her past. In fact, in her eyes, her life began in 1957 when she found the Lord. "My life is good. I don't have no complaints about my past life . . . no regrets. I can take a little pain and sickness now, because God give me a lot of thing[s] most don't get. It means a lot when God can use you in a lot of things. The older I get the closer I get to the Lord—more deeper in him every day. It makes me satisfied with whatever comes."

Third, these beliefs are particularly relevant to adaptation in advanced old age, because they establish guidelines on the appropriate level of control they should exercise over their lives. A complete trust in the supernatural relieves them of personal responsibility for their past and present problems. Such beliefs have important implications. If individuals accept their situation and put their lives "in the hands of the Lord," past failures and present inadequacies become less significant in the grand scheme. It is likely that aspirations change, and acceptance of dependency becomes more common, a situation that can have positive effects.

Mr. D at 87 years offers a particularly clear example of how, upon finding the Lord, his life changed dramatically even to the point that his perceived status in society improved dramatically. This 87 year-old man reported that he had reformed after being a gambling man and a lady-chaser. He concluded, "I'm glad of being this old and not being hungry, shoeless, and bedless. I don't have to go out in the cold rain to work any more. My life is in God's hands. He blessed me and he helped civilize me. I wish I had started civilized. When God came to me, I don't have to take no back seat. I'd been driven like a mule, turned away, and shamed. Now He will make a way for me to heaven in the front seat."

Changing Reference Points Over the Life Course

A content analysis of these discussions indicates that the reference points used to compare oneself with others are also redefined when reviewing their lives. These very old blacks rarely venture out into the white world, so whites are not mentioned as a standard of evaluation and as a basis for their expectations. Since most of their age peers are dead, they can no longer act as reference points from which to make comparisons with one's own status. As the following will suggest, one's past life becomes their reference point to evaluate life in advanced old age. A widespread theme was, "Life was hard but I survived." In making such life course contrasts, individuals are likely to find their current status considerably improved over their past situations, so their aspirations and expectations are being met. Such findings are consistent with the model offered by Brown and Harris's developmental studies (1978). Earlier adverse events seem to leave an impact on one's present life only if they also must deal with current provoking agents.

A large majority of these respondents grew up in the rural South as children or grandchildren of slaves. Most defined a good childhood as always having food on the table or never going to bed hungry. They were proud of parents who provided well for them and who instilled the value of hard work and respect. Their childhood early in this century was commonly affected by three occurrences: the early death of one or both parents; extreme poverty; and difficult early work experiences. Some had to work in the fields at an early age or take care of younger siblings while a child themselves.

Others worked for white people for very little money. "At 13, I had to walk two miles every day to work, and the white lady only gave me $2.50 a week." "I was orphaned at seven and raised by my sister. When she died I was 16. I didn't want to move in with a mean uncle, so I got married." "Mother died when I was fourteen. I had five brothers and sisters with the youngest only seven months old. That's when I became the lady of the house." "Daddy died and Mama had to work on the plantation. I stayed home and took care of nine brothers and sisters." "My parents separated and my father wouldn't let Mama have us. She left Louisiana, remarried, and had seven more children. She came and got me but then he took me back. I was glad when he died, so I could go back to my mama."

Mrs. A. aptly illustrates the influence of earlier problematic experiences as contrasted to a contented life in advanced old age. An 86-year-old widow, she lives in a middle-class black suburb. She was born in Washington D.C. Despite the deaths of most of her loved ones in her childhood, she was able to improve her life considerably. "Mother died when she was 30. I took care of her youngest five children. My grandmother and father died three months after my mother. I was trapped—almost like being in slavery. I raised my mama's children, then my sister's children after she died. I took over where others had started and never had no opportunity to have children of my own. I got caught in a trap. Then at 21, the man I was supposed to marry didn't show at the altar. That was a blessing in disguise though. It made me escape my trap and come to California. Everything worked out for me here. I had a good husband, even though I never had children."

Those who were barely surviving economically suffered greatly during the Depression. When World War II broke out and news of defense industry jobs in California reached the South, the more adventuresome moved West. Most reported good wages, at least until the end of the war. By then, however, they were firmly lodged in the growing black community and unwilling to return to the rural South. Two cases illustrate a number of themes in the interviews—the early loss of a parent, a life time of hard work, and for men particularly, a period of "running around." Strong religious beliefs provide a coherent system of meanings through which they can come to terms with the past and appreciate their present rewards.

Mr. B., age 87, illustrates how a combination of events and decisions over a life time eventually led to a relatively comfortable and contented life in advanced old age. He was born in rural Texas. His father died three months before he was born and his mother died when he was three years old. "I was the only one. My grandmother raised me but really her teenage daughter, my auntie, raised me. I was on my knees at my mother's death bed, promising her that I would obey my grandmother, that I'd be living in the hands of the Lord and he'd take care of me. She was right. I've looked death in the face many times since then, and the Lord protected me."

When asked about his childhood, he reported, "I was a big boy and wanted to get off the farm that my granddad had that I was raised on. I finally did get off the farm and found a job in a foundry. It folded during the Depression. First one thing and then another. My wife took in washing and we washed and ironed clothes all night. We made it." (later) "The truth is as a young man, like most, I run

around. But when I likely died of pneumonia, I decided, no more running around. I told my wife that I admit I wasn't the husband to suit her, that I was running around, but no more. I wasn't raised to run around with a wife and children at home. My grandmother knew the Scriptures—She would say 'Have only one God and one baptism, only one wife and one set of children.' She had thirteen children all by the same man. I said one day, I not gonna chase women no more. The Lord blessed me since I straightened up."

Mr. B. came to San Francisco in 1943 and worked in the shipyards for two years. When he accumulated money, he sent for his wife and children. When his defense job ended, he drove a streetcar. "We always had a close family. All my life has been good. I was born with a roof over my head. As soon as I was old enough, I went to work. I always had a job. I never laid hungry and none of my children have either. We always led a Christian life. The future beyond the grave is all taken care of—nothing to worry about. If there's a heaven, I'll be there, for I live by the Bible. Nothing is difficult. I just keep living."

Mrs. C. also has had a difficult life but at age 85 she is very contented with her life. Shortly before our first contact, she had had her leg amputated because of diabetes. She got around her one-room apartment in a wheel chair and never went out. Her two children live 100 miles away, where her daughter takes care of Mrs. C.'s invalid son. Even in the absence of her children, her life is not isolated, for friends, prayer groups, and play children (fictive kin) are constantly dropping in. She reports that her health was good. "I only have diabetes and a bad leg." She did not view the amputation as a problem.

She never knew who her father was, and her mother died when she was born. She was raised by her grandmother whom she referred to as her mother. "I came up poor, very poor. I'd come home to a dinner of syrup and bread. Thank God we had that. My mother cut cane all week and went to white folks on Saturday to do a little laundry. That bought us a piece of meat for Sunday. At seventeen I had my first child. I stayed with their father for five years but never married him. He started playing around with women, so I left."

She later moved to New Orleans to give her children a better education. There she worked as a seafood cook at a well known cafeteria. When her daughter came to California, she followed her. When recounting her past, she said, "I have had no disappointments. My whole life has been good. I'm thankful to the Lord that I've lived. I take life as he wishes. He always makes a way for me. Nothin' is hard for me. I's a happy old lady, because I've come through it all. I lost one baby to cancer and lost a second baby in me. Then last year I lost my leg because of my sugar problems. The Lord brought me through all these trials. I've got a good mind, food on my table, a home on this earth, and a home when I leave it."

Conclusions

Models and theories on adaptation or successful aging do not generally focus upon minority elderly, yet there is considerable evidence that their status in old age is widely variant from the dominant group. Thus this inquiry is exploratory and has to evolve a conceptual framework to organize our data on adaptation of very old Black Americans that hopefully is culturally specific. I have explored those factors that are related to a high level of subjective well-being late in their lives. Most respondents had very difficult lives punctuated by poverty and racism, and late in their lives, they complain of poor health and economic problems. However, their mood is significantly better than their white age peers. Because they do not seem to have been affected by numerous negative events, they must have effective means to cope with their problems. I have indicated three social and cultural effects evident in their current life that can account for their impressive adaptation.

First, a large majority are well integrated into supportive social networks and community institutions. Where the family has scant resources, they flexibly create kinlike relationships sometimes formalized into fictive kin. When they are without extensive relationships, the black church offers a supportive family-like setting as well as a belief system that takes into account their life-long hardships. As they discuss their lives, respondents also restructure the meanings about their past, a technique that results in a strong sense of achievement about their long-term survivorship.

Second, inherent in black culture are values and beliefs that extol old age and create an aura of survivorship that enhances well-being. Also the ideology stemming from their religious beliefs explains and interprets their survival and serves to integrate past experiences with the current life. Part of these beliefs center on the view that the supernatural is responsible not only for their survival but also their contentment in late late life. As a result, these beliefs relieve them of responsibility for potential problems.

Third, I suggest that as they age, very old blacks tend to change their reference points previously used that compared their own status with whites and other blacks. Instead most have turned to their past life as a basis for evaluating their current life. A cultural restructuring of the past tends to occur where previous problems and tragedies are put into the context of their special status as survivors. Having suffered racism, deprivation, and numerous losses as well as prejudice and discrimination, the mere fact of being one of the few in their age group to survive takes on added meanings. Consequently, they are mostly contented and secure in having reached advanced old age. Because of the almost impossible odds facing them over their lives, their status is subjectively viewed as considerably improved over their past. While such a positive view of survivorship is also evident among oldest old whites (Johnson and Barer 1993), such an aura of survivorship among whites had not been achieved with the marked disadvantages their black age peers had experienced.

These conclusions are consistent with the developmental model used in England to explore interactions between the earlier loss of a mother and depression in adulthood. The effect of this loss is apparent in this long-term research, but only if the respondents face current stressors and socioeconomic problems. With the very old blacks studied here, the potential vulnerabilities arising from life course events may then be ameliorated by social and cultural aspects of the black community as well as the aura of survivorship.

Discussion Questions

1. What are the major forces cited in the Black Americans' social support system?

2. What values in black culture contribute to a sense of well-being in old age? Given other ethnic or racial groups with which you are familiar, to what extent are these values present or absent?

3. If comparing one's past to present circumstances promotes positive adaptation to later life among disadvantaged Black Americans, what differences, if any, would you expect to find among Black Americans of more privileged socioeconomic backgrounds? What differences would you expect to find among whites from disadvantaged backgrounds?

Acknowledgements

This article is based upon research funded by the National Institute on Aging 1 R37 AG06559. The author wishes to thank Barbara Barer for her comments on an earlier version of this article.

References

Bradburn, N. M. 1969. *The Structure of Well-Being*. Chicago: University of Chicago.

Brown, G. W. and T. Harris. 1978. *The Social Origins of Depression*. London: Tavistock Publications.

Campbell, A., P. E. Converse, and W. L. Rodgers. 1976. *The Quality of Life: Perceptions, Evaluations, and Satisfactions*. New York: Russell Sage Foundation.

Dowd, J. and V. Bengtson. 1978. "Aging in Minority Populations: An Examination of the Double Jeopardy Hypothesis." *Journal of Gerontology* 33: 427–436.

Ellison, C. G. 1990. "Family Ties, Friendship, and Well-being among Black Americans." *Journal of Marriage and the Family* 52: 298–310.

Ford, A., M. Haug, P. Jones, A. Roy, and S. Folman. 1990. "Race-Related Differences among Elderly Urban Residents: A Cohort Study, 1975–1984." *Journal of Gerontology: Social Sciences* 45: S163-SI70.

Genevay, B. 1992. "Creating Families: Old People Alone." *Generations* 17: 61–64.

George, L. 1988. "Social Participation in Later Life: Black and White Differences." Pp. 99–128 in *The Black Elderly: Research on Physical and Psychosocial Health*, edited by J. S. Jackson. New York: Springer.

Gibson R. and J. Jackson, 1992. "The Black Oldest Old: Health, Functioning and Informal Support." Pp. 321–340 in *The Oldest Old*, edited by R. M. Suzman, D. P. Willis, and K. G. Manton. New York: Oxford University Press.

Jackson, J. S. 1988. "Social Determinants of the Health of Aging Black Populations in the United States." Pp. 69–98 in *The Black American Elderly: Research on Physical and Psychosocial Health*, edited by J. S. Jackson. New York: Springer.

——. 1989. "Race, Ethnicity, and Psychological Theory and Research." Guest Editorial. *Journal of Gerontology* 44: PI-P3.

Johnson, C. L. 1994. "Differential Expectations and Realities: Race, Socioeconomic Status, and Health of the Oldest Old." *International Journal of Aging and Human Development. Special Issue. Social and Cultural Diversity of the Oldest Old* 38: 41–50.

Johnson, C. L. and B. M. Barer. 1990. "Families and Social Networks among Older Inner-City Blacks." *The Gerontologist* 30: 726–733.

——. 1993. "Coping and a Sense of Control." *Journal of Aging Studies* 7: 67–80.

——. 1994. "Childlessness and Kinship Organization: Comparisons of Very Old Black and White Oldest." *Journal of Cross-Cultural Gerontology* 10.

Krause, N. 1995. "Race Differences in Life Satisfaction among Aged African Americans." *Journal of Gerontology* 48: S235-S244.

Krause, N. and T. Van Tran. 1989. "Stress and Religious Involvement among Older Blacks." *Journal of Gerontology: Social Sciences* 44: S4–S14.

Ortega, S. T., R. D. Crutchfield, and W. A. Russing. 1983. "Race Differences in Elderly Personal Well-being: Friendship, Family, and Church." *Research on Aging* 5: 101–118.

Perry, C. M. and C. L. Johnson. 1994. "Families and Social Networks among African American Oldest Old." *International Journal of Aging and Human Development* 38: 41–50.

Register, J. C. 1981. "Aging and Race: A Black-White Comparative Analysis." *The Gerontologist* 21: 438–443.

Rodin, J. 1986. "Aging and Health: Effects of a Sense of Control." *Science* 233: 1271-1276.

Spitze, G. and S. Miner. 1992. "Gender Differences in Adult Child Contact among Black Elderly Parents." *The Gerontologist* 32: 213–218.

Stack, C. 1974. *All Our Kin: Strategies for Survival in a Black Community*. New York: Harper and Row.

Taeuber, C. M. and I. Rosenwaike. 1992. "A Demographic Portrait of the America's Oldest Old." Pp. 17–49 in *The Oldest Old*, edited by R. M. Suzman, D. P. Willis and K. G. Manton. New York: Oxford University Press.

Taylor, S. P. 1982. "Mental Health and Successful Coping among Aged Black Women." Pp. 95–102 in *Minority Aging. Sociological and Social Psychological Issues*, edited by R.C. Manuel. Westport, CT: Greenwood Press.

Taylor, R. J. 1985. "Receipt of Support from Family among Black Americans: Demographic and Familial Differences." *Journal of Marriage and the Family* 48: 67–77.

Taylor, R. J. and L. M. Chatters. 1986. "Church-Based Informal Support among Elderly Blacks." *The Gerontologist* 26: 637–642.

Chapter 13
History, Race, and Attachment to Place

William J. McAuley

The previous selection emphasized the strengths oldest-old African Americans derive from social supports, the values associated with black culture, and survival in the face of adversity. This selection by William McAuley expands this theme and investigates attachment to place as a positive factor in successful aging. Few of us stop to think about how much a specific geographic locale affects our lives and personalities. For members of minority groups who have faced a lifetime of discrimination and limited opportunities for upward mobility, a racially or ethnically homogeneous community can provide a special haven in a hostile world. McAuley points out that attachment to a specific community or town results not only in familiarity and comfort with one's surroundings but also reinforces social ties and accords a sense of selfhood. As you read this selection, listen to the voices of the older residents of the all-black towns in Oklahoma and think about the sense of freedom that membership in these communities gave to their inhabitants. Pay attention to the perceptions of attack by whites who wanted to enter these towns and the pride felt by older residents in withstanding threats to their way of life. Think also about the significance of social class, racial, ethnic, or religious similarity in constructing the meaning of one's personal old age.

This article draws upon data from a research project aimed at comprehending the lived experiences of older residents of the all-Black towns of Oklahoma. The term "all-Black town" is commonly used by town residents to refer to the incorporated municipalities in rural Oklahoma that were established by African Americans. The general thesis of this article is that the issues of history and race, especially the African American history of Oklahoma, are important integrating themes for understanding social and autobiographical insideness and the levels of place attachment that are expressed in the life narratives of the elders in these towns. I use the term "race" in this article not as a biological term, but to denote social constructs that are reflected in social institutions as well as in group and individual actions (Gregory & Sanjeck, 1994).

The all-Black towns of Oklahoma are small rural African American communities scattered throughout the eastern half of the state. Most Oklahomans, White or African American, find it difficult to name more than 2 or 3 of the 12 towns that remain out of the approximately 30 that once existed. By focusing on these special rural communities, we may uncover themes that expand our understanding of place attachment, especially within racially homogeneous minority settings.

Background

Place attachment is a concept that geographers and demographers have used to describe the strong social-psychological attraction to a specific location among long-term residents. Through his work in a rural Appalachian community in West Virginia. Graham Rowles (1980, 1983a) enhanced our understanding of the dimensions of place attachment in old age. According to Rowles, place attachment can be expressed in three categories of geographical insideness. These dimensions include the following: (a) physical *insideness*—based upon familiarity with surroundings, (b) social *insideness*—the social integration of the elders into the community, and (c) autobiographical *insideness*—or the lifelong accumulation of experiences in the community. The more "inside" one is with regard to these dimensions, the deeper the level of identification with a place and the greater the sense of belongingness to it (Relf, 1976). This article focuses specifically upon autobiographical and social insideness and the roles of history and race in the development of these forms of attachment. Though an equally compelling argument might be made for the relevance of physical insideness to the place attachment of older residents of the all-Black towns, space does not permit a full explication of this argument.

Autobiographical and social insideness may be particularly powerful aspects of place attachment in old age. With regard to autobiographical insideness, aging in place promotes the temporal layering of actual experiences and fictional elements that converge to establish one's personal identification with a place (Rowles, 1983b). The development and reinforcement of social ties can also bond the older person to the community by creating a high degree of social insideness that establishes a sociogeographic "refuge" for coping with the transitions that occur in old age.

Because racism and racial segregation are powerful and pervasive in their impact on minority group consciousness (Brazziel, 1973), research on place attachment in minority communities may be counterproductive unless investigators directly examine the nature of racism and its consequences for attachment to specific locations. Among older minority group members, the autobiographical and social insideness associated with a community may be influenced by a lifetime of discrimination, limited life chances, and minority group identification (Broman, Neighbors, & Jackson, 1988; Smith & Thornton, 1993). The social context in which minority groups are reared, including their collective deprivation, influences the level of minority group consciousness (Smith & Thorton, 1993).

Discrimination, segregation, limited life chances, and minority group consciousness act in concert to create socially and historically relevant cultural regions. The boundaries of these cultural regions may be congruent with or different than geographic or political boundaries, but they nevertheless establish insiders and outsiders and distinguish "us" from "them" (deMause, 1982; Stein & Hill, 1993). These cultural regions should be particularly salient with regard to the place attachment of older long-term residents when (a) they have maintained their cultural homogeneity for an extended period, and (b) their histories are imbued with elements of racial identification, racial discrimination, and racial pride.

About the All-Black Towns of Oklahoma

A majority of the all-Black towns of Oklahoma could be easily overlooked—it is quite literally difficult, with a good map, to know for sure whether you have successfully located certain of them. They tend to be very unlike the image many urban residents may hold of a "town." Many of their streets are unpaved. It would be an indulgence to call the roads gravel, because in many cases it has been years since any gravel has been applied. Even the main access roads to certain of the towns are unpaved. . . .

The census data indicate that certain of the towns have relatively large White populations and many young adults, although this is not what one sees when one visits them. Boley is a good case in point. A few years ago, Boley annexed a nearby correctional facility that houses many young adults and Whites who, due to their incarceration, have no involvement with the town. Langston is the home of Langston University, a historically Black state university whose student body remains predominately African American. Therefore, much of the town's young adult population consists of students at the university. The permanent population in Langston has a higher percentage of African American elders than is suggested by the census.

The town residents are defined by the census as rural-nonfarm. They tend to have low incomes, and the quality of the housing stock is generally very poor. The median age of homes in certain towns is over 40 years, although some towns do have at least a few modern, well-constructed homes. Some homes are without indoor plumbing and many do not have access to natural gas. Some of the towns have sewage and/or water systems, although not all residences are connected.

There are few businesses in any of the towns today. Some have a convenience store. A few have a cafe. One has a liquor store, and one has a blues club. In many cases, the schools that once served the children in the towns are abandoned; some have burned down. With the exception of Boley, which still has public schools, the children now attend consolidated schools elsewhere. A number of the towns continue to make use of the old school buildings as town halls or community centers. Some of the towns have managed to garner sufficient state and district grant funds to build new community centers or to remodel older buildings for this purpose. Churches are frequently the most prominent buildings in town.

In spite of their small size, the communities are incorporated and have mayors and town councils. The governmental structures tend to be simple, but they are sources of great pride. Town services, such as water and sewage, are managed by volunteers in many cases. Some towns have small police departments. A few also have fire departments (usually volunteer), whereas others depend on services from nearby communities.

Method

A variety of approaches were combined to gather information about the lived experiences of elders in the all-Black towns of Oklahoma. I visited each of Oklahoma's all-Black towns at least once and most many times. Some of the visits were for the purpose of observing and recording the characteristics of the towns, whereas others were made to conduct interviews. During and after each visit I wrote field notes that have been incorporated into the analysis. When traveling to towns in which I had previously interviewed, I also made informal return visits to past respondents. These return calls, although primarily social in nature, sometimes resulted in new information.

Research by Rowles (1988) has shown that qualitative interviews can be a rich source of information about the meaning of residence to elders in a particular area. Active interviewing, with its emphasis on both the process of meaning making and collaboration between the interviewer and the respondent, is a valuable method for guiding the participants through the identification and discussion of salient topics encompassing an issue (Gubrium, 1993; Holstein & Gubrium, 1995). This interview approach was used with nine

older residents in three of the all-Black towns. The respondents were selected by means of a combination of purposive and opportunity approaches. I approached some after spotting them in their yards or in other locations on my travels to the towns. I was introduced to some respondents by community leaders, and others were recommended to me because of their age and their long tenure in the town. The four men and five women range in age from 61 to 91. Two are married, and five are widowed. All of the individuals have lived for an extended time in their town. With the exception of one respondent who arrived in her town in early adulthood through marriage to a resident, all were born in or very near the towns. Some of the individuals have spent time away from the towns for education or work or to serve in the armed forces. Two left school before completing high school. Seven completed high school, and two of these completed some college.

I used a semistructured interview guide. Because a major focus of the project was to understand the health situations of the residents, the guide focused on the health status, health perceptions, health practices, and health care utilization of residents. Additional questions were designed to elicit descriptions of the history of the towns, the personal life narratives of the respondents, and their general views about life. The interviews required from approximately 80 minutes to 5 hours to complete. Most interviews were carried out over at least two sessions.

In addition to these individual interviews, I conducted a group interview with seven female residents of one of the towns, all within the age range for the investigation (60 and over) and all members of the town's informal Retired Senior Volunteer Program group. I also interviewed a group of three male residents of one town: a former mayor and two town council members. Two of these people were over 60 years of age.

For those towns that have post offices, I made a point of regularly stopping by on my visits to the towns. The post offices are, in many cases, the towns' centers of activity. More than once, I met people at the post office whom I already interviewed or who might become respondents. The postmasters are familiar with all of the adult residents and know a great deal about their circumstances and activities. Although I did not ask postmasters to share their insider's knowledge with me, they sometimes volunteered useful information.

I completed face-to-face interviews with the current mayors of three towns. One of the mayors accompanied me around town to introduce me to some of the older residents. In another town, a former mayor drove through town with me and identified the homes where elders reside. This type of support was common, and it helped a great deal gaining acceptance. All of the individuals whom I asked to serve as respondents/informants agreed to do so.

I also interviewed two African Americans who, although not residents of the all-Black towns, have made the study of the history of African Americans in Oklahoma their mission. Ms. Eddie Faye Gates, a resident of Tulsa, has spearheaded a number of historical displays and oral history projects in northeastern Oklahoma. Mr. Napoleon Davis, of Muskogee, has single-handedly built an impressive Creek Freedmen Memorial. As a descendant of Creek freedmen, he has spent decades gathering and archiving information about his ancestors.

I also regularly attended the bimonthly meetings of Oklahoma Council of Black Mayors. This group consists of the mayors of the original all-Black towns, as well as the African American mayors of other Oklahoma communities. I used these meetings as a forum to explain my research and to work with the mayors on projects beneficial to their towns. The Council endorsed my work and gave me a regular place on the agenda of each meeting. The Council meetings were an extraordinarily rich source of information and of contacts.

One valuable way of "locating" a place in social research is to consider its historical context. Because the all-Black towns have rich histories, which include issues of race pride and racial discrimination, there is value in bringing the social-historical context of the towns to light in the analysis. Therefore, another critical element of my work has

been a review of historical documents pertinent to Oklahoma's African American history, including *The WPA Oklahoma Slave Narratives* (Baker & Baker, 1996), photographs from the photographic archives of the Oklahoma Historical Society, and the literature on the history of the all-Black towns of Oklahoma.

All told, I completed several hundred hours of field work and interviews and have reviewed a large quantity of primary and secondary historical information. This article draws upon all of these resources. The analysis has consisted of multiple phases of listening to audio recordings and reading transcripts, field notes and other written materials, along with note-taking regarding emerging themes. Each new review phase consisted of (a) discovery of new themes; (b) searches for passages that confirm, refute, or refine the themes; and (c) refinement of themes. In the findings section, respondents' names are pseudonyms and towns are referred to by number to protect confidentiality.

Historical Context: The Development of the All-Black Towns

The history of the all-Black towns is more than an interesting backdrop to their current circumstances. The distinctive social-history of these communities establishes the context that substantially defines their current character and condition. Also, through their narratives, the older residents link the social history of the towns with their lived experiences as they attach meaning to the communities. Although the history of each town is unique and is relevant to the issues under investigation, space limitations permit only a brief general overview.

Early Establishment

The all-Black towns of Oklahoma were organized during the period from just after the Civil War into the early 1900s. Most of the approximately 30 original all-Black towns were established in the section of Oklahoma that was designated as Indian Territory (Carney, 1991) prior to statehood. In many cases, individuals who developed the towns did so on land that had been previously assigned by the federal government to African American freedmen of one of the Five Civilized Tribes at the conclusion of the Civil War (Knight, 1975). Many freedmen of these tribes received land allotments due to the revised treaties that the Five Civilized Tribes were forced to sign after the Civil War (Teall, 1971; Tolson, 1972).

African American freedmen of Indians rarely settled in the towns (Crockett, 1979). Instead, the towns grew through the continued in-migration of southern freedmen or their descendants. Some town promoters distributed circulars throughout the South to attract settlers (Carney, 1991). The documents advertising the availability of land in the towns appealed to African Americans on several levels, including economic opportunities related to the opening of the West, the chance to live with members of their own group and be in charge of their own destiny, the prospect of personal and family safety, and freedom from White domination (Bogle, 1994; Carney, 1991). A recruitment bulletin for the town of Langston exemplifies these themes.

> To better our sad conditions, we must act at once; if not we will let our best and only chance for independence pass. . . . Our city is incorporated. Not a single white person lives in our town. . . . What will you be if you stay in the South? Slaves liable to be killed at any time, and never treated right; but if you come to Oklahoma you have equal chances with the white man, free and independent. Why do southern whites always run down Oklahoma and try to keep the negroes from coming here? Because they want to keep them there and live off their labor. White people are coming here every day. . . . Langston City and its addition promises to be one of the great cities of Oklahoma. A negro city for the exclusive use of and benefit of our own race. (Tolson, 1952, pp. 66–70)

The towns grew rapidly during the period from 1880 through Oklahoma's statehood in 1907 (Carney, 1991). As African American farmers from the South settled in the nearby countryside, the communities became agricultural commercial centers with a large array of businesses (Tolson, 1952). In 1912, the Boley Commercial Club claimed that Boley was the largest and wealthiest exclusively African American city in the world (Jackson, 1968). The towns attracted professionals from southern states in large numbers prior to statehood due to the possibility of establishing an all African American state (Crockett, 1979). Oklahoma's potential for entering the Union as an African American state was quite real toward the end of the nineteenth Century. There were sufficient numbers of African Americans in Oklahoma to encourage E. P. McCabe, developer of the all-Black town of Langston (Carney, 1991; Franklin, 1982), to meet with President Harrison in Washington in 1890 to seek Harrison's approval for the establishment of an African American state in the Oklahoma Territory (Tolson, 1966). The President was generally in favor of the idea, providing [that] a majority of the residents in the region were African American at the point of a petition for statehood. Ultimately, African American migration to Oklahoma was not sufficient to establish a majority African American population.

Racial Identity and African American Pride

There is evidence of strong African American racial pride and concern for racial fulfillment within the all-Black towns. These communities were settled less as racial ghettoes than as enclaves where racial fulfillment and self-realization could be sought without interference from Whites and Indians (Bittle & Geis, 1957). After visiting Boley in the early 1900s, Booker T. Washington wrote:

> Boley . . . represents a dawning of race consciousness, a wholesome desire to do something to make the race respected: something which shall demonstrate the right of the negro, not merely as an individual but as a race, to have a worthy and permanent place in the civilization that the American people are creating. (Washington, 1908, p. 31)

Mozell Hill, a sociologist, has described the "Great Black March Westward" as a classical social movement based upon a powerful positive race ideology. He saw the organization of the all-Black towns of Oklahoma as the culmination of the institutionalization phase of this social movement—a phase in which African American group ideology was permanently established by the towns' residents.

> This racial ideology is giving permanence to the development and stability of the society. Under these conditions, it has become apparent that the movement has become established, it has become institutionalized. (Hill, 1946a, p. 264)

In the mid 1940s, Hill compared the attitudes of the youth in an Oklahoma all-Black town with African American young people in a more biracial community in another state. He found that the youth in the all-Black town were far more likely to view positively such characteristics as dark woolly hair, dark skin, a flat nose, and thick lips—evidence of African American pride and positive race ideology (Hill, 1946b). The cohort that Hill interviewed is now within the age group targeted for the current research.

In line with Hill's findings, Crockett contended that within the all-Black towns the residents asserted a robust sense of racial pride and experienced genuine freedom from White oppression.

> In home, church, and school, black-town youth were taught self-respect, and the glorification of past racial accomplishments. . . . To the sensitive, the black town offered a social paradise with freedom to walk the streets without encumbering the thousand subtle reminders of membership in a subordinate class. Also one need not fear that a look or gesture might be misinterpreted and bring down the physical wrath of whites. Each day the community blanketed the individual with a sense of well-being, and some who were born and grew up there became addicted to the environment. (Crockett, 1979, p. 185)

Racial/Ethnic Animosity

Initially, Whites, who were also settling the region at this time, were unconcerned about the development of the all-Black towns. As a matter of fact, the concentration of African Americans in specific locations may have been encouraged, because it limited the interchange between Whites and African Americans (Hill, 1946a). White intimidation began to be more open and destructive after the turn of the century, due in part to the

possibility of African American statehood (Bogle, 1994). White Oklahoma farmers began to organize "Anti-Negro Farmer's Associations" to encourage farming by Whites and to discourage and harass African American farmers (Elahi, 1968). In the early twentieth century, lynchings and house burnings by "Whitecappers" and the Ku Klux Klan were quite common in Oklahoma (Tolson, 1972). Whites began forcing African American residents out of many mixed-race towns (Franklin, 1982).

One very clear marker of the extent of White animosity toward African Americans in Oklahoma was the Tulsa race riot of 1921, one of America's worst urban racial conflicts. It started when an African American man was accused of attacking a White girl. The man was arrested and jailed. White and African American mobs formed at the jail, and a shot was fired. The fight soon moved to the African American district, where shooting continued during that evening and into the next day. Ultimately, approximately 9 Whites and 68 African Americans were killed. Thirty city blocks that had previously housed 15,000 African Americans, were torched (Smallwood & Phillips, 1993; Tolson, 1972).

As a result of these occurrences, the all-Black towns increasingly became places in which African Americans sought safety from White oppression. Some of the towns (i.e., Redbird and Tullahassee) showed population increases following the Tulsa race riot of 1921 (Knight, 1975).

As the towns developed and grew, there was also some animosity between two groups of African Americans that resided in rural eastern Oklahoma: the former slaves of Indians and the former slaves of southern White slaveowners and their descendants. For example, there is historical documentation of freedmen of Indians "shooting up" the town of Boley in the early years (Crockett, 1979). An explanation is in order regarding some of the terms used in this article. With apologies for the sexist connotations of the terms, but in keeping with the preferences of most African Americans whose ancestors came to Oklahoma with the Five Civilized Tribes on the Trail of Tears well before the Civil War, I refer to them as "freedmen of Indians" or

"Indian freedmen." For purposes of consistency, former slaves of Southern White slave holders are called "southern freedmen." Although these two groups of African Americans arrived in the Territory from the South, they came during different periods and under very different circumstances.

Perhaps one reason for the initial disagreement between freedmen from the South and Indian freedmen was the fact that southern freedmen lobbied the government heavily for the right to land allotments in the Territory, based upon a misreading of the 1866 treaties between the Federal government and the Creeks and Seminoles (Tolson, 1972). If the southern freedmen had won this right, it would have been to the detriment of Indian freedmen. In addition, many of the Indian freedmen, who had little experience in land management or real estate transactions, lost the land they received as a result of the 1889 bill requiring allotment of the remaining Indian reservations in the Territory (Teall, 1971). In some cases, the land was lost through exchanges with southern freedmen.

Older Residents' Narratives

Narrative Descriptions of Town Histories

Most of the older residents of the all-Black towns can recount in considerable detail the early and recent history of their town and their family's role in its founding and development. Autobiographical and social insideness emerged as important themes in their descriptions of the town's histories, and racial oppression and racial pride are frequent components of their narratives. Ms. Hanford is the oldest living resident of Town 1. Her story of her father's migration out of Texas to Town 1 includes references to the desire for freedom from the racial and economic oppression associated with tenant farming. Her father "slipped off" (Segment 1.2–1.3) because he owed for share cropping and saw that he could never buy his way out of debt in Texas.

1.1 He didn't get quite along so good with all the White folks what he had to work with in Texas.

1.2 So he had some people what had come from Texas up here and said it was a nice place, and everything.

1.3 So he slipped off and came over *here*. . . .

1.4 [You said he slipped away. What do you mean by that?]

1.5 Well, the folks didn't know he was *leavin'*!

1.6 See. . . . \\at that time they'll still kinda hold onto ya in one way or the other.

1.7 If you owed them, you couldn't leave the community. They had that goin' down there.

1.8 And so he had to get outa there at night. And, that's what he did.

It should be noted that all narrative segments have been edited for continuity. I have attempted to maintain the basic pronunciation within the text. A modified version of Labov's (1972) text annotations have been used: ( ) explanations or replacements provided by the author, [ ] Questions or comments of the interviewer during the interview . . . narrative text omitted, \ hesitation (more marks indicate longer hesitations), and passages spoken with greater volume.

Expressions of opportunities for race fulfillment and freedom were also expressed in the respondents' stories about the town histories. In her narrative history of Town 2, Ms. Murton describes the land runs as extraordinary opportunities for African Americans to seek racial equality.

2.1 Well, it all began . . . with my grandfather . . . He was \ a minister.

2.2 And . . . in the South, as we all know, conditions were not very good, and people were leaving.

2.3 So, . . . during the time they were leaving, was, oh, back in the '80's when . . .

2.4 the first real opportunity, equal opportunity . . . came along,

2.5 which was the Oklahoma Land Rush.

An important element of Mr. Bartle's narrative history of Town 3 is that it was controlled by African Americans. In describing the history of the town, he mentions several businesses; then he shows that White access was limited by describing the number permitted "inside."

3.1 They . . . operated ever'thang here. . . . the Negroes did.

3.2 So later on \\ they . . . let two . . . Whites come in,

3.3 and one put in a feed store, and the other one put in a hardware.

Themes of the Towns as Refuges from Racial Oppression

Many of the older residents of the all-Black towns still leave their doors unlocked. More than once, when visiting a town post office I have found a car left by a patron with the engine running and the door open. There are many robust themes in the narratives of the towns as refuges, places of safety. Several residents mentioned the lack of "drive-by shooting," "gangs," and "drugs"—qualities that might be viewed as positive characteristics of many rural communities. However, many narratives also addressed the importance of the towns as refuges from race discrimination and oppression. Mr. Jennings describes the need to isolate oneself in urban areas. In the larger context of his narrative, the concept of "hiding" is related to both avoiding general crime and to avoiding problems with Whites.

4.1 Really, when you in, in Oklahoma City or anywhere else . . .

4.2 You hide from one element and you induce another element.

4.3 So, you not, \ you not really hid. . . . Right here, I feel pretty free.

Mr. Jennings summarizes his viewpoint by offering a multifaceted perspective on Town 1 as a refuge. Passage 5.1–5.2, with its emphasis on freedom of action, is reminiscent of Crockett's description of the towns in earlier times.

5.1 So, that's the reason I like to live in (Town 1). Because, not the high hustle and bustle. The high crime rate.

5.2 The freedom of activity. The freedom to get up in the mornin' \\\ and go.

Ms. Murton offers another version of how Town 2 has served as a refuge from White oppression in both her youth and her adulthood. She describes how, when she was young, her father would take her into a nearby town in the wagon. He would go into the general store, and have her stay in the wagon. White children would gather around the wagon and taunt her.

6.1 Hey, little piccaninny! Hey, little piccaninny!

In a later conversation with Ms. Murton, she elaborates on the theme of racial harassment in later years.

7.1 I was comin' from Oklahoma City. . . . I had to change buses in, ah, (nearby town).

7.2 Well, I don't know if you know anything about (town).

7.3 But (town) used to have the signs there about, you know, "Don't let the sun go down on you in (town)."

7.4 They didn't want to see a Black *face* there after dark. . . .

7.5 Well, I was standing on the sidewalk waiting for the bus.

7.6 And a lady came by, and she had a little girl. And of course, the child, in passing by me ,. . . stepped off . . . the sidewalk.

7.7 Well, the lady . . . pulled her and . . . tell her "No!"

7.8 She scolded her, "You never get off the *sidewalk* for a \\." And I just looked at her.

7.9 The bus couldn't come fast enough for me.

Ms. Merton was always happy to return to Town 2, where she was not subjected to this type of racial abuse. Her narrative description of the town today conjures potent images of its continuing value as refuge. Segment 8.1–8.5 also offers a glimpse into her notion of "insideness" and "outsideness."

8.1 Well, we have peace. . . . I tell the people that I don't think that they realize just what we have.

8.2 Like you don't have to answer to a lot, you know, on the outside. It's like bein' your own boss.

8.3 My mind goes back to Grandfather . . . in establishin' a place \\\ which was \\\ like a haven of \\\ rest.

8.4 Place to be away from a lot of things.

Another refuge-related theme has to do with opportunities to practice race pride and the freedom to reside with one's minority group—suggestive of Hill's description of the towns as the culmination of a social movement based on racial ideology. Mr. Bartle succinctly expresses this theme in the following passage.

9.1 I ain't nothin' much, but I'm a race pride person.

9.2 [Tell me what you mean by that.]

9.3 I believe be with your race \\\. That's what I mean by it.

9.4 I don't mean to dislike you. But I just want to stay with my own race.

Insideness, Outsideness, and Boundary Violations

I also identified numerous passages in which the elders describe various forms of assault on the towns. These narrative elements strengthen the evidence that the towns serve as refuges from racial oppression. According to Mr. Hastings, Whites have long sought to do away with Town 3 because it is an all-Black town.

10.1 (White) people been tryin' to kill (Town 3) off for the last 40 years.

10.2 [Why do you think that is?]

10.3 Black people.

There are also many examples in the narratives of various physical encroachments, especially by Whites, that have served to heighten the elders' awareness of the towns' boundaries and of what it means to be "inside" and "outside." Mr. Bartle speaks of Whites burning down Town 3's school building.

11.1 I remember when they had this big school up there in (Town 3). And when they went to

11.2 integratin' they tried to break it up . . . and couldn't break it up. . . .

11.3 And they set that school afire and burnt it down.

11.4 [Who did that?]

11.5 The White people. \\ set it afire and burned it down.

Mr. Bartle describes another incident many years ago that shows how a nearby White community violated Town 3's boundaries by seizing the train station late one evening.

12.1 The train station was straight down the hill there. And it was operated by Negroes.

12.2 And you know, we went to bed one night, and that station was down there and the next mornin' we woke up and it was right down here (points to nearby White community).

12.3 [Is that right?]

12.4 They loaded that thing on a track and pulled it down there with a train, an' set it up there.

12.5 Yeah they . . . thought once they was just gonna take . . . over.

Ms. Murton also introduces an incident showing that town residents and town property are vulnerable to racial attack. Her sister, who lives out of town, maintains a mobile home in Town 2 that has been broken into several times. She speaks of a recent episode.

13.1 They came in through the kitchen window.

13.2 And they . . . takes this black paint, \\ and they just put it all over the walls \\\ KKK. \\\

13.3 Went all over the mirrors, all over the walls, on the table.

For Mr. Jennings, the issues of "insideness" and "outsideness" of Town I took on considerable importance in his youth. He tells how he had to deal with descendants of Indian freedmen and with Whites when he journeyed to an nearby town.

14.1 If I wadn't fightin' my way to town, then I was outa' town.

14.2 Fightin' my way to town with the colored boys, and fightin' my way outa town with the White boys.

Narrative statements about White encroachment, as well as mistreatment by Whites outside the towns, appear to demonstrate the elders' sense of individual and group vulnerability. The result is a strengthened social and autobiographical insideness, resulting in greater place attachment.

Descendants of Slaves of Indians as Outsiders

Intertwined with the issue of insideness versus outside in Passage 14.1–14.2 are perceived group differences between African American descendants of Indian freedmen and African American descendants of southern freedmen. The colored boys Mr. Jennings describes fighting with were descendants of Indian freedmen. In general, the descendants of Indian freedmen continue, as in the early days, to reside in settlements outside the all-Black towns, although I interviewed two who resided within the boundaries of the communities. The older town residents can name communities where descendants of Indian freedmen once lived, or where they live today, and these communities are clearly geographically and socially separate from the all-Black towns.

In a variety of ways, the descendants of Indian freedmen and descendants of southern freedmen are identified as separate African American groups by residents of the all-Black towns. For example, a number of terms, in addition to "Indian freedmen," are used by descendants of both Indian and southern freedmen to refer to this group, and thus establish their otherness: "Indian Territory Blacks" (often abbreviated to "ITs"), "natives," "Indian raised," and "African Americans of Indian descent". Conversely, the descendants of southern freedmen are also called "state raised" or sometimes "people of migration" by the town elders of both groups. Two elements of the language used by the elders, the diverse taxonomy for referencing Indian freedmen and southern freedmen and the facility with which they use this referential terminology, suggest that the two groups have held separate identifications for a long

period. The fact that the elders rarely speak of individuals as descendants of one or the other group, but instead refer to them as members of a contemporary group (e.g., "he is an IT", or "she is state raised") indicates that there is a currency to the issue of group membership.

Ms. Hanford makes it clear that the majority of descendants of Indian freedmen live separately and were not responsible for the development of Town 1.

15.1 They settled about three miles south and east of here.

15.2 That's where they are put.

15.3 When these people (southern freedmen) came from the *states*, this was woods, and like that.

15.4 So they bought . . . little lots. . . .

15.5 And that's why the *town* was created, because of *them*.

Mr. Hastings discusses the descendants of slaves of Indians as living apart from Town 3.

16.1 Here's what we called them "natives." They were Negroes that came here with Indians, see.

16.2 And there were quite a few of 'em down at (nearby town). . . .

16.3 Let me tell you. You fought one and you'd have to fight the whole crew.

16.4 Cause they'd jump on you and they'd eat you up!

16.5 Boy, down in (town) and (town) . . . when you go down there brother, you'd better go on your best behavior, cause . . . they had them 30–30's 'n they'd run you out of *town*!

Ms. Hanford explains the reasons for the rancor between the two groups in terms of the feeling of superiority on the part of the descendants of Indian freedmen, due to their land holdings.

17.1 Naturally, they (southern freedmen) just came and didn't have nothin' but themselves.

17.2 But these Indian raised people or what not, they inherited 40 acres of land.

17.3 Well, that made them feel that they were superior than the people that didn't have anything . . .

17.4 And that kinda grew up in people my age. They had it *real* bad that they were *superior* to the people that came from the states.

17.5 Like I'm tellin' you. They didn't want to have nothin' to do with one another. It was terrible!

Mr. Jennings claims heritage from both groups—a fact that made it somewhat difficult for him to be accepted back into Town 1 after living elsewhere, even though some of his ancestors were among the original town settlers and community leaders. He offers a version of what led to the animosity (what he calls "Black on Black") that incorporates issues of land allocation, education, intelligence, and jealousy.

18.1 It is a matter of have and have nots.

18.2 It's the same thing that has, has gone on in the world from the beginnin' of time.

18.3 The strong take away from the weak, and the smart take it away from the strong . . .

18.4 So, the ITs or people of \\ African Americans of Indian descent . . . had the land. People of migration, Blacks that was migrated from Mississippi, Georgia, Alabama, and Arkansas, did not have that right.

18.5 So there had to be a turnover \ some kinda way. The land had to be usurped. . . .

18.6 I would say (southern freedmen were) intellectually at a level a little higher than African Americans of Indian descent. . . .

18.7 All of this was caused by jealousy and undereducated people, because the ITs had no schoolin'.

All of the older all-Black town residents introduced thus far express very strong positive place attachment in their narratives. Their regard for their towns is high, and they frequently describe the towns with terms denoting deep affection. Ms. Murton's description of Town 2 as a "haven of rest" (Segment 8.1–8.4) is indicative of its deep meaning to her. According to Ms. Hanford,

19.1 (Town 1) is my heart.

Ms. Nash, another older resident, expresses similar views.

20.1 I just *looove* here! \\ I've been away workin' but I come back.

20.2 You know, this is home. . . . (Town 2) is my home.

In their narratives, place attachment is frequently related to social-historical circumstances that give meaning to the elders' residence within the towns. The towns have been locations where the elders could experience race pride and freedom from much of the racial oppression that occurs on the outside, thereby enhancing their social and autobiographical insideness. Social-historical events have also established the towns as places in which Whites and White society are viewed as being on the outside. Negative experiences with Whites outside the towns and negative incursions of Whites into the communities have enhanced the meaning of the towns as racial refuges, thereby amplifying the social and autobiographical insideness of the elders.

Social-historical events have also led to the identification of one group of African Americans, Indian freedmen, as outsiders. Thus, the meaning the residents attach to their towns is partly related to the process of identifying themselves as autobiographical and social insiders and partly related to identifying Whites and some other African Americans as social and autobiographical outsiders.

Narratives of Marginal Residents

It is beneficial, when examining issues of place attachment and integration, to seek the views of more marginal individuals in the community. I interviewed two such individuals who, like the other seven respondents, were long-term residents of their communities. Mr. Lincoln considers himself a marginal resident of Town 1. His pronouncements of community marginality are in consonance with his circumstance. He is a descendant of Indian freedmen in an all-Black town, which consists chiefly of descendants of southern freedmen, and his home, a mobile home, is just barely within the town limits on a perimeter street. He often speaks of leaving town, although he is deterred by the fact that his ancestors are buried nearby.

21.1 My holy grounds is in the field of a White man.

21.2 A White man got hold of that property *soooome* kinda way, and he got a fence around it.

21.3 And my holy grounds have been desecrated.

Mr. Lincoln is very proud of his heritage. He calls himself an "African American of Native American descent" or, sometimes, an "aboriginal." Like many of the other respondents, Mr. Lincoln evokes racial themes in his description of the town's history. However, his narrative is offered from the vantage point of someone whose ancestral group was manipulated by others, both White and African American.

22.1 The people that incorporated (Town 1) were trained by slave masters somewhere else . . .

22.2 Slave masters that *realized* beforehand what was gonna happen . . . trained people to come out here and to marry into our families.

22.3 So that when we died, half of our property would go automatically to them.\\\

22.4 We lost it.

Another marginal person, Ms. Bradford, also a descendant of Indian freedmen, came to Town 1 because of marriage. Like Mr. Lincoln, she lives just within Town 1's perimeter. Ms. Bradford, who has a daughter living very nearby, has tended to maintain her distance from other residents, even though she has lived in Town 1 for many decades. She attends church outside of town, a behavior that further establishes her marginality. Although her narrative does not associate her treatment by other residents directly with her heritage, she feels that she has not been dealt with properly by town residents.

24.1 There's too many people didn't treat me right.

24.2 The things they done, I didn't appreciate it. So, that's the way it is.

Ms. Bradford expresses her sense of personal marginality when asked about how important living in Town 1 is to her.

25.1 Well, I'd miss it and call it home. But the truth is, I don't care that much about it.

Thus, the expressed marginality of these two elders is related in part to the social-historical circumstances that establish their social and autobiographical status as neither insider nor outsider. On the one hand, their long-term residence in the town (their physical insideness), along with Ms. Bradford's having family nearby and Mr. Lincoln's attachment to his family's burial grounds, bonds them to their town. On the other hand, their membership in a group that most other older residents view as outsiders diminishes their autobiographical and social insideness as expressed in their narrative descriptions of place attachment.

Discussion

The social-history of the all-Black towns and the personal histories of the older residents, as expressed through their life narratives, provide a fresh perspective on the place attachment of elderly rural minority residents. The findings serve to extend Rowles' conceptualization of social and autobiographical insideness and place attachment by showing that (a) place attachment is not a constant, even among long-term residents; (b) social-historical factors can play an important role in the level of place attachment; (c) race can be a salient aspect of place attachment among older minority group members; (d) experiences outside the community, such as racial segregation and discrimination, can influence the level of social and autobiographical bonding to the community; and (e) subgroup identity within minority groups can be associated with variations in community place attachment. To most of the older residents, whose place attachment is strong, the positive and negative aspects of racial history, including their narrative histories of the towns and of their personal experiences, give meaning to their lives in the towns. Their narratives establish horizons of meaning (Holstein & Gubrium, 1995) between their social insideness, their autobiographical insideness, and their place attachment. As Hill (1946b) noted, there is, for many older residents, a well-defined group ideology that influences their attachment to the town. By focusing on history and race as they relate to the autobiographical and social insideness voiced in their narratives, we gain a deeper, more multifarious view of the development of place attachment. It should be noted that although social and autobiographical insideness are distinct concepts, I did not address them separately in this article, because they tightly intertwined in the elders' narratives.

An important finding of this research is that historically based minority subgroup identity is fundamental to our understanding of the marginality of some of the older residents of the towns. Many of the elders I interviewed drew distinctions between two African American groups—descendants of freedmen of Indians and descendants of freedmen of White southern slave holders. Many of them described bitterness between the two groups. In most cases these differences are presented as being most salient in earlier times. However, some elders offer stories of continuing divisions, and there is relatively little social interchange between the groups today. Competing versions of how the land in the towns was obtained play a role in the social distance between the two groups and also in the level of place attachment among older town residents.

This research has focused chiefly on how place attachment in an older rural minority population can be influenced by history and race. However, the findings also add to the increasing body of research suggesting that older rural populations, even within such apparently "homogeneous" groups as rural nonfarm African American populations, are anything but homogeneous. It has been written that "the search for a simple definition of rural in the context of growing old is probably a quest for an unattainable holy grail" (Rowles, 1988, p. 121). Support for this statement is the finding that in Oklahoma there are socially and spatially meaningful differences among African American rural nonfarm residents living in relatively close proximity to one another. The differences that emerge in the narratives are rooted in social-historical occurrences that predate the Civil War period, yet they appear to bear upon older respondents' current descriptions, social interchange, and place attachment.

It should be noted that the factors attracting individuals to a particular location may change over the life course. I did not specifically ask the elders what led them to remain in the towns during their young adulthood or at other points in their lives; nor did I ask what led them to return when jobs or military commitments took them away. I also did not seek out elders who have left the towns to determine how they differed from those who have remained. It would be most informative to compare versions of social-historical, racial, and minority subgroup expression in the life narratives of movers and stayers. These are valuable avenues for further research. . . .

Discussion Questions

1. In what ways is the meaning that older residents attach to their towns related to the process of identifying themselves as "autobiographical and social insiders?"

2. Discuss the evidence presented for historically based minority subgroup identity in the communities studied and the relationship of subgroup identity to marginality.

3. Assume that, for some reason, such as a massive natural disaster, all residents of the rural all-Black towns described were forced to relocate to different areas. What would you anticipate the results would be on the lives of those relocated?

4. Thinking about the community in which you have spent most of your life, how important is attachment to place to you? What social class, cultural, ethnic, racial, or religious aspects of this community have given you a sense of place? To what extent have your feelings of personal identity been influenced by this particular community?

Acknowledgments

This article is a revised version of a paper presented at the 1996 Gerontological Society of America Annual Meeting in Washington, D.C. Partial support for this research was provided by the Presbyterian Health Foundation of Oklahoma. I appreciate the contributions made by Jo Anna Grant, Marcia Safewright, Loretta Pecchioni, Linda Womack, and Rebecca Courreges to this investigation.

References

Baker, T. L., & Baker, J. P. (1996). *The WPA Oklahoma Slave Narratives*. Norman: University of Oklahoma Press.

Bittle, W. E., & Geis, G. L. (1957). "Racial Self-fulfillment and the Rise of an All-Negro Community in Oklahoma." *Phylon*, 18, 147–260.

Bogle, L. (1994). "On Our Way to the Promised Land: Black Migration From Arkansas to Oklahoma, 1889–1893." *The Chronicles of Oklahoma*, LXIII, 160–177.

Brazziel, W. E (1973). "White Research in Black Communities: When Solutions Become a Part of the Problem." *Journal of Social Issues*, 29, 41–44.

Broman, C. L., Neighbors, H. W., & Jackson, J. S. (1988). "Racial Group Identification Among Black Adults." *Social Forces*, 67, 146–158.

Carney, G. O. (1991). "Historic Resources of Oklahoma's All-Black Towns." *The Chronicles of Oklahoma*, 69, 116–133.

Crockett, N. L. (1979). *The Black Towns*. Lawrence: Regents Press of Kansas.

deMause, L. (1982). *Foundations of Psychohistory*. New York: Creative Roots.

Elahi, L. 1. (1968). *A History of Boley, Oklahoma, to 1915*. Unpublished master's thesis, University of Chicago, Chicago, IL.

Franklin, J. L. (1982). *Journey Toward Hope: A History of Blacks in Oklahoma*. Norman: University of Oklahoma Press.

Gregory, S., & Sanjek, R. (Eds.). (1994). *Race*. New Brunswick, NJ: Rutgers University Press.

Gubrium, J. F. (1993). *Speaking of Life: Horizons of Meaning for Nursing Home Residents*. New York: Aldine de Gruyter.

Harel, Z., McKinney, E., & Williams, M. (1987). "Aging, Ethnicity, and Services." In D. Gelfand & C. Baressi (Eds.), *Ethnic Dimensions of Aging* (pp. 196–2 10). New York, NY: Springer.

Hill, M. C. (1946a). "The All-Negro Communities of Oklahoma: The Natural History of a Social Movement." *The Journal of Negro History*, 31, 254–268.

Hill, M. C. (1946b). *The All-Negro Society in Oklahoma*. Unpublished doctoral dissertation, University of Chicago, Chicago, IL.

Holstein, J. A., & Gubrium, J. F. (1995). *The Active Interview*. Thousand Oaks, CA: Sage.

Jackson, L. R, Jr. (1968, November 29). "Shaped by a Dream: A Town Called Boley." *Life*, 65, 72–74.

Knight, T. (1975). *Black Towns in Oklahoma: Their Development and Survival*. Unpublished doctoral dissertation, Oklahoma State University, Stillwater, OK.

Labov. W. (1972). *Language in the Inner City: Studies in the Black English Vernacular*. Philadelphia: University of Pennsylvania Press.

Relf, E. (1976). *Place and Placeness*. London: Pion.

Rowles, G. D. (1980). "Growing Old 'Inside': Aging and Attachment to Place in an Appalachian Community." In N. Datan & N. Lohmann (Eds.), *Transitions of Aging* (pp. 153–170). New York: Academic Press.

Rowles, G. D. (1983a). "Between Worlds: A Relocation Dilemma for the Appalachian Elderly." *International Journal of Aging and Human Development*, 17, 304–314.

Rowles, G. D. (1983b). "Place and Personal Identity in Old Age: Observations from Appalachia." *Journal of Environmental Psychology*, 3, 299–313.

Rowles, G. D. (1988). "What's Rural About Rural Aging? An Appalachian perspective." *Journal of Rural Studies*, 4, 115–124.

Smallwood, J. M., & Phillips, C. A. (1993). "Black Oklahomans and the Question of 'Oklahomaness': The People Who Weren't Invited to Share the Dream." In H. F. Stein & R. F. Hill (Eds.), *The Culture of Oklahoma* (pp. 48–67). Norman: University of Oklahoma Press.

Smith, R. J., & Thornton, M. C. (1993). "Identity and Consciousness: Group Solidarity." In J. S. Jackson (Ed.), *Aging in Black America* (pp. 203–216). Newbury Park, CA: Sage.

Stein, H. F., & Hill, R. F. (1993). Introduction. In H. F. Stein & R. F. Hill (Eds.), *The Culture of Oklahoma* (pp. xv–xxvii). Norman: University of Oklahoma Press.

Teall, K. M. (1971). "Black History in Oklahoma: A Resource Book." Oklahoma City: Oklahoma City Public Schools.

Tolson, A. L. (1952). *A History of Langston, Oklahoma, 1890–1950*. Unpublished master's thesis, Oklahoma Agricultural and Mechanical College, Stillwater, Oklahoma.

Tolson, A. L. (1966). *The Negro in Oklahoma Territory, 1889–1907. A Study in Racial Discrimination*. Unpublished doctoral dissertation, University of Oklahoma, Norman, OK.

Tolson, A. L. (1972). *The Black Oklahomans: A History, 1541–1972*. New Orleans, LA: Edwards Printing.

Washington, B. T. (1908). "Boley, a Negro Town in the West." *Outlook,* 88 (January), 28–31.

Chapter 14
You Can Go Home Again

Joan Weibel-Orlando

The previous selection emphasized the importance of lifelong identification with a community. Attachment to a specific community results not only in familiarity and comfort with one's surroundings but can reinforce social ties and give a sense of selfhood. Ethnic identity may be reinforced and used to promote satisfaction with one's own current life. Ethnic membership may be mobilized to provide resources that enable individuals to make meaning of their lives in the face of poverty and discrimination. In this selection, Joan Weibel-Orlando presents an analysis of a life history of an elderly American Indian woman whose identification with her community is illustrated by her return to her reservation after living in a large city for more than two decades. The author focuses on how Emma Walking Eagle used her ethnic identity and ethnically based coping strategies to return.

Representing a small but rapidly increasing population, older American Indians face particular problems often overlooked by the larger society. Poverty is widespread, and many older American Indians suffer disproportionately from acute and chronic diseases. Nearly half of older American Indians live in just four states: Arizona, California, New Mexico, and Oklahoma. Although the majority live on or near reservations, the number living in urban areas is increasing. In later life, many American Indians in cities may, like Walking Eagle, return home to the reservation where they grew up. It is important to keep in mind, however, that "American Indian" is an imposed classification, symbolizing a legal relationship between victorious Whites and diverse conquered societies. Rather than as "American Indian" or "Native American," members of this broad ethnic group identify themselves by tribe, such as Cherokee, Sioux, or Navajo. Despite the variations among American Indian tribes, anthropological reports of Indian life have emphasized the veneration generally accorded to elders in societies largely dependent upon oral tradition.

As you read this selection, think about the role of federal policy in Indian relocation to urban areas and to the roles that both economic expediency and spiritual connectedness play in the decision to move back to the reservation. Notice the ways the woman separated from her urban Los Angeles social club and the process of her reentry to the reservation community. Think about the problems she faced in adapting to ethnic community life; the roles she accepted, challenged, and created; and whether she became an "autobiographical and social insider."

. . . Indian elderly are viewed by some as disenfranchised members of their communities (Block 1979) constituting a double and even triple jeopardy (Jeffries 1972). It has been a common view that lack of social cohesion and well-being among contemporary Indian elderly results from younger Indians adopting the dominant society's values and mores and, in the process, losing much of their own cultural ethos. As a result, elderly Indians are no longer considered the most important members of their society. Often neglected, they live out lonely lives of poverty and depression (National Indian Council on Aging 1978).

While some authors devote themselves to documenting the deplorable physical and psychological conditions of life among contemporary Indian elderly (Benedict 1971; Doherty 1971), others suggest that negative findings regarding the aged Indian may be somewhat overstated and possibly inaccurate. Hockschild, (1973), for example, insists that previous studies are "age centric" and ignore the elderly's view of themselves and their viable roles in society. Still others (Schweitzer 1983, Amoss 1983) wax eloquent about a golden age of Indian familism and maximal social integration. Then the aging Indian was not simply regarded as old, but as an "elder"; a person of substance and value, inviolate dignity, and worthy of great respect. Councils of elders were the active loci of tribal decision making and commanded highest prominence in governmental and political affairs. It was through the elders that the culture lore was transmitted across generations. Lacking a written tradition, the entire history, language, art, and value system of a people were passed on to younger generations by the elderly through their oral traditions (National Indian Council on Aging 1978).

In many traditional tribal societies, the elderly are still a needed and highly respected people. Their wisdom and experience (the products of having lived a long time) are of value to the rest of the community. Elderly Indians can and do make valuable contributions to their communities. They are included in tribal councils; many function as spiritual leaders of their communities (Amoss 1981, Schweitzer 1983). Some participate in foster grandparent programs in both urban and rural reservation areas (Weibel-Orlando in press). Identification of these and other culturally viable roles or old age careers and their contribution to successful aging are other foci of this article.

With these suppositions in mind, this article presents a processual analysis of a life history of a Sioux woman who returned to her reservation in South Dakota after spending twenty-six years in Los Angeles. . . .

Emma Walking Eagle[1] is one of twelve Sioux who returned to their South Dakota reservation homelands. Emma and I have known each other since 1978. We first met when she applied for a community outreach position on a research project I was initiating in the Los Angeles Indian community. At that time she was highly involved in all three dimensions of ethnic experience. She took great personal pride in her Sioux heritage, traveling back each summer to visit friends and family on the reservation. The majority of her circle of close friends in Los Angeles was other Indians. And she sat on advisory boards of several Los Angeles-based, Indian-run social service agencies, social clubs, and political action groups. In the next three years before she went back home we saw each other regularly at various Los Angeles Indian social and organizational gatherings.

When she announced her decision to return to her reservation I immediately enlisted her as a field research representative as I was about to initiate a comparative study of rural and urban Indian drinking patterns and had hoped to conduct a survey among the South Dakota-based Sioux. It seemed a stroke of extraordinarily good luck, a positive omen, that a competent and trusted indigenous co-worker was about to relocate to an area in which I was planning to conduct research the following summer.

Our co-worker relationship provided the rationale for my monthly telephone calls to her when, in May, 1981, Mrs. Walking Eagle returned to her childhood reservation home in South Dakota. While the research on which this article is based had not begun when she moved back to the reservation, the notes taken during each telephone conversation provided a running narrative of the process by which she reentered her community of origin. We worked together in South Dakota during the summers of 1981, 1984 and 1985.

In the summer of 1984, using the structured ethnographic interview protocol Myerhoff, Simic and I (1982) designed to elicit comparable life history data across our three ethnic-American groups to direct our conversation, Emma and I set about recording her life history. In the summer of 1985 a research assistant and I returned to South Dakota to videotape Emma both in conversation with me and as she went about her daily and ceremonial activities. In the interim periods we continued to correspond and to have lengthy telephone conversations on a regular basis. In all, we recorded 24 hours of her life history recollections and videotaped five hours of her interactions with her family and ethnic community members.

During and subsequent to the field research periods these data were analyzed for their theoretical import, particularly their ability to depict ethnically-inflected processes and patterns of behavior. Processual analysis involves the identification of a set of actions over time which eventuate in either change or continuity of a particular state or circumstance. Of particular interest were actions which influenced individual shifts or continuities in cognitive, informal social, formal activity and/or locational states vis-à-vis the person's ethnic community.

It is important to note that the life history presented here is a "success story." Most, but not all, of the twenty-eight American Indians who returned to their ancestral homes and with whom I worked and have been in touch with since 1981 have been as successful in their use of ethnicity as a resource. Emma Walking Eagle exemplifies that majority of the returnees who have successfully reincorporated into ethnic community membership and who view their ethnicity as a positive force and a major social-organizational principle of their lives. Her positive reincorporation into ethnic community life (attainment of satisfying community roles, acknowledgment of her rights to membership by her community, a sense of belonging and contentment with her present life situation), however, is not shared by every Indian who "goes home." The reasons why some people reincorporate more successfully than others is not the focus here but of future analysis. Rather, identification of the positive contributions ethnic group membership make to well-being in old age and the strategies by which an ethnic elder successfully negotiated her reincorporation into her ethnic community are illustrated by the life history analysis that follows.

Of the possible "success stories" which could have been chosen to examine and refine our original model of ethnic career trajectories . . . I chose Emma's for the following reasons: (1) we enjoy a long term collegial relationship that allowed for easy and continual communication; (2) her articulateness, insightful introspection, and understanding of my research goals led to analytical discussions and the eventual refinement of the early and hypothetical model, . . . (3) her cultural, informal social network and formal ethnic community involvement trajectories over her lifetime are representative of those of the other Indians in this study who successfully have "gone home again."

Findings

Life History as a Processual Document of Intensity of Ethnic Involvement

Emma Walking Eagle spent a self-defined idyllic early childhood living with her mother and maternal grandparents on their farm on a Sioux reservation in South Dakota. She was nine years old before she experienced her first long-term contact with the non-Indian world. At that time and though she spoke only Lakota, she was ordered to attend the Catholic Indian Boarding School some distance from her home. She was allowed visits to her grandparental home only at Christmas and during the summer break. She remained in Indian boarding schools until she was 18 at which time she left to marry her first husband, another "full-blood" Sioux.

Her early and complete immersion in the culture of her ethnic group is consistent with our conceptualization of the inversely parabolic nature of ethnic involvements over the life span. For the first nine years of her life her cognitive, informal, and formal social experiences were purely Lakota.

As a young adult Emma worked as a nurse's aide in one of the non-Indian Nebraska farming towns which border her reservation. She was within a day's easy drive of her ancestral home until her mother died. Only then, when in her late-thirties, divorced, and with two adolescent and one infant sons in tow, Emma boarded a bus headed for Los-Angeles.

. . . The exigencies of having to support herself and her three children pulled her into a more heterogeneous social matrix in early adulthood. During the work week her contacts were, for the most part, non-Indian. However, strong psychological ties to family and land pulled her back to the family with regularity and prohibited her from realizing her personal wish to move to California as so many of her ethnic and age cohorts were doing until her daughterly commitments to an ill mother and elderly grandparents had been fulfilled. Structurally and interactionally, her involvement in ethnic community activities was becoming attenuated. Psychologically, however, ethnically inflected tenets of filial respect and familial responsibility remained high and governed her behavior well into mid-life.

In the twenty-six years Emma lived in Los Angeles she remarried, bore a fourth child (her only daughter), became a grandmother many times over, and worked for twenty years in hospitals, in the aircraft industry, and for the Long Beach School District. Her and her third husband's incomes provided the capital to buy a pleasant house in a largely Anglo suburb of Long Beach. Although the majority of her informal network of friends was other Sioux who had migrated to Los Angeles, she also established friendships with non-Indian co-workers, relationships that have survived her return to reservation life. Until her daughter became interested in pow-wow dancing (Emma was in her mid-fifties at the time) her involvement in formal Indian events in Los Angeles was minimal. She did, however, return for two weeks every summer to the reservation to visit friends and kin and, as she puts it, "to reinforce my Indian spirituality so that I could go another year in that thing [Los Angeles]" (In interview, 1985).

Her life trajectory continued to parallel our refined model of differential ethnic involvements over the life span. . . . In mid-life her informal and formal ethnic networks became increasingly attenuated. The cultural (cognitive, psychological and spiritual) dimension of ethnicity, however, was sustained providing an essentially internalized ethnic experience. Only in late mid-life did she become actively involved in Los Angeles Indian social and political affairs. Her teen-age daughter's interest in participating in the public ethnic displays at Indian dance events called powwows and Emma's early retirement provided the rationale and time to effect a reentry into the formal and public spheres of Los Angeles Indian community life.

By the time I met Emma in 1978 she was deeply committed to several Indian-run social programs and was considered by many of her urban Indian ethnic cohorts as a person who exemplified honored Indian elderhood. In 1981 her husband took an early retirement. It was this major career disruption that prompted their return migration to Emma's homeland.

Emma's reinvolvement in formal Indian activities in Los Angeles in middle age completes the parallel fit of her life trajectory with our inversely parabolic model of ethnic involvement through the life course. While she had, throughout her life, been proud of her Lakota Sioux heritage, her expressions of it had been essentially private most of her adult life. It was only upon approaching old age

that she effected public displays of her ethnicity. These pursuits continued to escalate culminating with the decision to "go back home" or to completely reimmerse herself in ethnic community life in old age.

Important to the "going home" process is the fact that she had maintained ties to her ethnic group of origin throughout her sojourn in the city. Though public ethnic involvements were eclipsed in mid-life, the private and psychological, and informal and social dimensions of her ethnic identity were sustained through yearly pilgrimages to the homeland, a regimen of private spiritual rituals and the maintenance of social ties to kin, tribesmen and other Indians both at home and in Los Angeles.

Toward a Processual Model of Ethnic Group Reincorporation: Separation From the Non-ethnic Social Milieu

Continuity of ethnic identity and expression was integral to the successful life-career shift Emma made when, in 1981, she decided to "go home again." How that reentry was accomplished provides a second theoretical model-community reincorporation as ethnically-inflected social process.

On the second Saturday of April 1981, Emma attended the powwow hosted by the Los Angeles-based Indian social club of which she had been an active member for some years. She came in full Northern Plains dance regalia with several grandchildren in tow. She asked and was afforded the privilege of having a special dance held in honor of her grandchildren. The dance had the dual function of recognizing her grandchildren as members of the Los Angeles community and underscoring the community's collective responsibility to "watch over" those Indian children in their grandmother's absence.

Rather than hold a yard sale to redistribute her unneeded material accumulations of 26 years, Emma elected to sponsor a second, particularly Indian, ritual—the give-away.[2] Following the powwow honoring dance she distributed hundreds of personal items she would or could not take with her to South Dakota as gifts to the assembled crowd. Friends, kin, and complete strangers received a token of Emma's *largesse* during an hour-long secular ritual. The give-away symbolized her appreciation of the support she had received over the years from the Los Angeles Indian community and her expectation that those reciprocal ties would remain operational even in her absence.

Re-entry

Emma had been back on the reservation approximately two weeks when I called in mid-May, 1981. She and her husband had been staying at her sister's home, just 3 miles from their proposed home site.

We haven't stopped for a minute. Everybody I went to school with and remember me from when I lived with my Grandpa and Grandma . . . come round at all hours to welcome me back. It's like old home week over here. (In interview May, 1981)

Emma was infused with the flush of early acceptance as evidenced by the general, if *pro forma*, signs of her welcome by her neighbors. Obviously pleased and proud of the interest shown by her old friends and kin in her return, she, at that time, had little thought about negotiating status and roles for herself in the community as anything other than as a returned co-ethnic.

Settling In: Routinization of a Personal Schedule

In June, 1981 Emma had been back on the reservation for approximately six (6) weeks. She was busy with plans for building a new house on land she had inherited from her mother and purchased from "land-poor" neighbors. She and her husband had already planted a garden and anticipated freezing a year's supply of fruits and vegetables in the Fall. Her daily activities had become routinized. They included a drive into the hamlet for the mail, a stop at the laundromat and general store, and a free lunch which the Tribal Chapter House provided daily to all reservation elderly. At that point her daily routine, except for conferences with her building subcontractors, paralleled that of any of her co-ethnic neighbors. She was, in effect, settling in.

Post-Reentry Depression: Learning the Parameters of Her Welcome and Place in the Community

A month later when I called, Emma was in an atypically dark mood. She missed her children and grandchildren dreadfully and continually lobbied them to come visit and/or live with her. Her children, however, had their own ties to friends and activities in Los Angeles and resisted her suggestions to relocate. Her entreaties to send one or two of the grandchildren to live with her also fell on deaf ears. Even her intonations of traditional Lakota child care practices ("Lakota grandmothers always took at least the first grandchild to raise because they were more mature and could teach them the Lakota ways more correctly" in interview July, 1985) carried no psychological weight with her urban-bred children—much to her displeasure and frustration.

Accustomed to a busy social life in Los Angeles, and having grown bored with the narrow sameness of the daily routine of reservation life, Emma had applied for employment as a teaching assistant in the local Bureau of Indian Affairs school. She was warned, however, that "locals," as well as young people with children to support, would probably get hired before she would.

Emma was experiencing the limits to which she could immediately effect reimmersion in ethnic community life. In a society in which steady, paid employment is a scarcity, informal hiring rules prevail. "Locals", people who had "paid their community dues", so to speak, could claim social prerogatives not available to "outsiders" or "newcomers", no matter how qualified or motivated to do good. Emma simply had not been back long enough to be considered a "local."

The Search for a Culturally Viable Role

By the time I arrived at her home in August, 1981 Emma had been attending the monthly Tribal Chapter House meetings in her district for a couple of months. She was toying with the idea of running for Tribal Council membership. She, however, sensed that one or two of the older people in the community resented her outspokenness and "city ways." References had been made to her long absence from and only recent return to the reservation when she had voiced her opinions at chapter house meetings. People eager to discredit her public suggestions for change and/or action suggested that though the changes Emma suggested might work in the city, "That's not the way we do things back here" (in conversation August, 1981).

Apparently neither age, nor competence warrants respect nor guarantees ascriptive status in contemporary Sioux society. Desired, high status public roles she felt qualified to fill seemed closed to her at the time because of their honorific and culture-specific application criteria. In that first summer of our work together Emma was having difficulty dealing with her marginality in the community in which she wished total immersion and had expected an unquestioned membership. Community reincorporation (acceptance) was proving to be a more lengthy process than she had anticipated.

Community Versus Self-created Roles for the Returnee

When I talked with Emma in September, 1981 she complained about a role her neighbors had fashioned for her which she found untenable. They had come to think of her as a source of ready credit. Her neighbors' ambivalence about her presence in their midst was expressed in both grudging references to her "having made good in the city," "being loaded" "spending money like water" and the ease with which they approached her for loans.

> They do it in the Sioux way. Nobody would just ask me for money. Instead, they come over with a star quilt, or some beadwork, or a gun and ask me to hold it for them until their checks come in. Usually they need it to get into town, or the clinic, or for food, so I give it to them if I have it in the house. But if they're drunk . . . or if I know they are heavy drinkers I don't unless they look desperate. I make sure they know that it is for food or gas and if I see them drunk I won't ever loan them money again. I want to help out. I don't want people to think I've forgotten how to be a Sioux. But, golly, it's getting to be expensive. I don't know how much longer I can keep it up! (In interview Sept., 1981)

The concepts of community responsibility for its members (sharing, generosity, and generalized reciprocity) are ingrained in the character profile of the ideal Sioux (Driver 1975, Erikson 1963, Grobsmith 1981). Family and community members are, from earliest childhood, enmeshed in a complex weave of social, emotional and financial obligations. One obvious resource Emma brought to the community in which unemployment can run as high as 75 percent was an apparent supply of ready cash. She would have "not acted like a Sioux" if she had refused to share her cash reserve with those less fortunate members of her community.

The criteria by which Emma limited the loans are both idiosyncratic and culturally appropriate. While she very occasionally takes a drink, she holds strong views about the alcohol abuse which devastates large numbers of her community peers. Her views echo those of the several church organizations, social service agencies and family members of the afflicted on the reservation. Her unwillingness to support alcohol abuse would be understood and supported by large numbers of people in her community, many of whom are members of the service agencies and political associations to which she had hoped to gain membership. Her response to this imposed role had been culturally correct. Emma was proving to her neighbors and herself that she, indeed, did know "how to act like a Sioux."

Rites of Incorporation: Public Displays of Ethnic Group Membership

Emma's lack of success in her initial attempts to attain certain highly visible statuses in the community was due, in part, to her impatience. At the time of her abortive attempt to find gainful employment on the reservation she had not been formally reincorporated, through ritual, into her community. Recognizing that birthright, age, and competency were not enough to insure her a desired role in community life, Emma began, through public tribal ritual, to demonstrate the viability of her ethnic group membership.

She decided to hold another give-away. She was busy planning the gift list in October, 1981, even though the ritual would not be held until the next Spring. The overt purpose of the give-away and the occasion on which it would take place was the dedication of a tombstone she had purchased for her mother's unmarked grave. Everyone in the community would be invited to participate. It would take her six months to make or purchase the gifts she would give to everyone who attended that memorial give-away. While she did not consciously state it, the give-away would express, in a public and culturally viable way, her knowledge of Sioux ceremonial traditions and acknowledgment of and adherence to the continuing strength of the mother/daughter dyad in Sioux family structure.

Establishing Viable Community Statuses and Roles

One year later when I called to check on her data collection activities, Emma was in the brightest spirits since her return. She had recently been elected to represent her community's Senior Citizens Center at the regional senior citizens social services governing board meetings. This is a status and role particularly suited to a woman who had been actively involved in similar Indian community activities in Los Angeles. Both she and her neighbors had found a way to maximize her urban-honed skills, i.e., political leadership, fiscal acuity, and, most especially, Indian advocacy when interfacing with social service officials from the non-Indian sector of our society.

The happiest development for her, however, was the opportunity she had been given by her tribe to assume a traditionally viable older woman's role. Two Sioux children who were distant blood relations of Emma had been made wards of the tribe. Emma had offered to be their temporary foster parent. In September, 1982 she had had those children in her home for two months. She spent the better part of our telephone conversation happily indexing for me all the things she was doing for the children. "It feels so good to have kids around the house. I feel useful again" (In interview September 1982).

Informal adoption of orphans or children from impoverished or disrupted homes is another well-established Sioux tradition (Driver 1975, Grobsmith 1981, Schweitzer 1983).

Grandmother caretakers freed the younger tribal women from constant surveillance of their children and allowed them to take on the essential tasks of food gathering, skin preparation, and clothing manufacture. For Emma, foster child care served both emotional and social needs. Not only was the caretaking role fulfilling for her but she also realized that the status, foster grandparent, demonstrated her willingness to take on work traditional to older Sioux woman and much needed by the community in general.

In November, 1982 she had applied and received formal authorization by the tribal social services agency to serve as a foster grandparent. Since that time she has had at least one, and as many as four grandchildren (both foster and biological) in her home at one time. At this writing two biological grandchildren are living with her and have been since 1984.

Assessment and Acceptance

Approximately eighteen months after her return to reservation life Emma and I had another in our series of marathon telephone conversations. During the course of the dialogue she reminisced about her early days back home. She remembered the initial flush of good feelings, the subsequent loneliness as a result of the separation from her children and grandchildren, and the longer-than-expected wait for formal, public recognition by the community of her incorporation into community affairs. But, by Christmas time, 1982, she felt that she and her husband were fully acclimated to reservation life.

> We had two big gardens this year. We make our own bread and pies. We can or freeze our own fruits and vegetables. We collect wild fruit and berries to make jelly with. We're living like pioneers. It's just like the good old days when I was young and living with my grandparents. (In interview December, 1982)

The level of contentment with which Emma purred her summation and assessment of the events which had shaped the last eighteen months of her life cannot be adequately portrayed here. It seemed apparent to this Sioux grandmother that the circle of her life was being completed in ethnically appropriate ways and that that process constituted a personal success.

> I always knew I'd come back to South Dakota. My roots are here, my family, my ancestors, and friends. Even after all those years in L.A., I knew I'd go back. That's where the Sioux spirits are . . . That's where I want to be when I die. . . . (In interview July, 1985)

Discussion

"Going home" is processual, can take on the elements of and be validated by ritual, and appears to be composed of sequential components or phases. An initial period of heady anticipation, reapproachment, and a steady whirl of positively-toned social engagements and superficial gestures of welcome and acceptance mark the reentry period. This stage is followed by a more sober and instrumental settling-in period in which the essentials of "nest building" and establishment of assistance networks and life support systems are established. Once the pragmatics of reentry are accomplished, the returnee is faced with the more subtle and complex task of establishing membership viability in the chosen homeland. This period may be prefaced by a period of estrangement or rootlessness, due, in part, to lack of immediate access to the roles by which community membership is demonstrated and to which the returnee both aspires and qualifies.

The development of viable status relationships mutually acceptable to the ethnic community and the reentering individual, and the performance of roles consistent with the community view of appropriate status enactment is the next phase of reentry into ethnic community life. This process is buttressed by regular and ritualistic displays of ethnic group membership and cultural competence. Successful reincorporation is realized when an individual assumes achieved or ascribed statuses and roles both acceptable to the community and satisfying to self. Full immersion in ethnic community life through role attainment creates a new steady-state or community/member equilibrium that appears to have both personal and sociopsychological value for the reincorporating individual.

For Mrs. Walking Eagle the process, "going home", included exploration of viable statuses and roles available to her in an ethnic community from which she had been separated geographically, but not cognitively, for over a quarter of a century. After a year and a half of experimentation, Emma had resolved the dissonance and disjuncture in her life that separation from her urban Indian community had caused through attainment of two ethnically-inflected, age-appropriate statuses. Election to office in an ethnic service organization was peer validation of her community membership. Grandparental caretaking is not only a recognized Sioux tradition, but also, a role uniquely suited to an older woman who has raised four children of her own as well as various sets of biological grandchildren. These statuses and roles provide the mechanisms by which a Sioux woman could not only "go home" but also, in old age, feel "useful again."

Conclusions

Rosenthal (1986) provides three models of ethnicity as: culture, inequality, and traditional ways of thinking and behaving. Here ethnicity has been shown to be a resource, available to all who have attained, either through ascription or achievement, the validating markers of ethnic group membership. Ethnicity's uses, however, can result in both positive or negative consequences, be acknowledged or abandoned, manipulated to one's advantage, or perceived as placing one, inexorably in "double jeopardy."

In answer to Rosenthal's question. "Does ethnicity make a difference?", I offer that it does if the individual member of an ethnic group wishes it to do so. Rosenthal argues, "It is vital that behavior be kept conceptually and analytically distinct from culture" and that cultural "meanings guide but do not determine behavior" (1986: 20).

The life history data presented here strongly support the notion that culture (ethnicity) does influence behavior and that the tenets of an ethnic group can be invoked by individuals to enhance individual prestige, create new careers and provide for a sense of well-being in old age or by the ethnic group to restrain and sanction individual behavior. The power of ethnicity to shape behavior lies in the individual's acceptance of the ethnic group's right to sanction behavior, level of interest in ethnic group incorporation, and cultural acuity. However, the availability and use of cultural knowledge are never uniformly acquired or executed. Rather, optimum resource management depends, in great measure, on life career trajectories and the felt need on the part of an individual for inclusion in the social arena that ethnic group membership provides.

Finally, Rosenthal asserts that "ethnicity and aging research has suffered from a lack of conceptual clarity". Analysis of retrospective life history accounts and longitudinal observation of old age ethnic community careers have shown ethnicity to be a multidimensional phenomenon, experienced at a personal, psychological, cognitive (cultural) level throughout life's course. Intensity of membership in informal social networks of kin and ethnic group cohorts and involvement in formal ethnic institutions and activities, however, can vary dramatically across time depending on the individual's life career trajectory. An eclipsing of ethnic involvement during periods of the life span on one or more of the dimensions, however, does not mean total and irretrievable loss of ethnic culture or identity. Rather, our longitudinal observation and processual analysis of life history data provide the methodology for identifying, expanding and clarifying ethnic dimensions, determining the relative persistence of ethnic influences on the individual across the life span and demonstrating the flexibility with which individuals can and do access ethnic resources in providing a measure of self worth and well-being in old age. . . .

Discussion Questions

1. Describe at least two motives for older American Indians to return to the reservation.

2. Outline the problems Emma Walking Eagle experienced in defining a culturally viable role for herself when she returned to her home community. To what extent did these problems reflect structural factors in the Sioux community as distinct from issues individual to her?

3. What Sioux traditions or rituals enabled Walking Eagle to become a respected elder in the community?

4. Explain how "going home" enabled her to "age successfully."

Notes

1. The name, Emma Walking Eagle, although stylistically Sioux, is fictitious. I have used this pseudonym and purposely not identified her reservation community to protect the anonymity of the person who graciously shared her life, home, and life history with me.

2. A give-away is a traditional Sioux ceremony in which political, familial, and assistance relationships are publicly acknowledged and sustained through redistribution of highly valued goods.

References

Amoss, P. T. 1981 Cultural Centrality and Prestige for the Elderly: The Coast Salish Case. In *Dimensions: Aging, Culture, and Health*. C. Fry, ed. Pp.47–63. Brooklyn: J. R. Bergin.

Amoss, P. T. and S. Harrell, Eds. 1983 *Other Ways of Growing Old*. Stanford, CA: Stanford University Press.

Benedict, R. A. 1971 *A Profile of Indian Aged*. Occasional Papers in Gerontology 10: 51–55.

Block, M. R. 1979 Exiled Americans: The Plight of Indian Aged in the United States. In *Ethnicity and Aging: Theory, Research and Policy*. D. E. Gelfand and A. J. Kutzik, Eds, Pp. 184–192. New York: Springer Publishers.

Doherty, R. P. 1971 Growing Old in Indian Country. In *Employment Prospects of Aged Blacks, Chicanos, and Indians*. Washington, D.C.: National Council on Aging.

Driver, J. 1975 *Indians of North America*. Chicago: The University of Chicago Press.

Erikson, E. 1963. *Childhood and Society*. New York: W. W. Norton and Company, Inc.

Grobsmith, E. S. 1981 *Lakota of the Rosebud: A Contemporary Ethnography*. New York: Holt, Rinehart and Winston.

Hockschild, A. R. 1973 *The Unexpected Community*. Los Angeles. Prentice Hall.

Jeffries, W. R. 1972 Our Aged Indians. In Triple Jeopardy: Myth or Reality? Washington D.C.: National Council on Aging.

Myerhoff, B., A. Simic and J. Weibel-Orlando 1982 Ethnicity, Continuity and Successful Aging. An unpublished grant proposal submitted to the National Institute on Aging, Washington, D.C.

National Indian Council on Aging 1978 The Continuum of Life: Health Concerns of the Indian Elderly. Final report on the Second National Indian Conference on Aging. Billings, Montana: National Indian Council on Aging.

Rosenthal, C. J. 1986 Family Supports in Later Life: Does Ethnicity Make a Difference? *The Gerontologist* 26:19–24.

Schweitzer, M. M. 1983 The Elders: Cultural Dimensions of Aging in Two American Indian Communities. In *Growing Old in Different Societies*, J. Sokolovsky, (Ed.), Pp. 168–178. Belmont, CA. Wadsworth Publishing Co.

Weibel-Orlando, J. C. (in press) Grandparenting Styles: American Indian Perspectives, In *Old Age in Culture's Context: World-wide Perspectives*. Jay Sokolovsky, ed. Boston: Bergin and Garvey.

Chapter 15
Falling Free

Diana Chang

During the nineteenth century, many Chinese men came to the United States to build the transcontinental railroads. Prohibited by immigration laws to bring wives with them or to send for brides, those remaining in the United States formed an almost exclusively male community. After World War II, however, restrictive immigration laws were repealed, and many Chinese men and women, a high proportion of whom were well-educated professionals, emigrated to the United States where they adopted the norms and values of the majority culture and stayed on to grow old. The rate of Chinese-White marriages among the children of older Chinese immigrants has been high. Within the past few decades, however, some Chinese-Americans have returned to their country of origin to contribute their skills and knowledge and to rekindle old kinship ties.

The following selection by Diana Chang is a short story describing the experience of an elderly Chinese woman, Kiki Kuo, as she considers her life and identity as a Chinese and as a successful American costume designer for Broadway plays. Now frail, she searches for reaffirmation of both her Chinese and American identities and her relationships with those people whom she has loved and loves. Pay attention to the interweaving of her bicultural identity, and the role that this played in her decision not to return to China with her husband. Think about how, despite her declining health, she strives to remain vital and independent. Notice the importance of time in her narrative and the freedom and constraints time places on her independence, affection for her grandson, and reaffirmation of love and romance.

Let it go, let it go. This is peace. I am what I am now, one with this house I spend my hours in—its lines which travel past corners my only distances. My worn chair reflected in the window is ghosted before my time. Such whiteness I face from wall to wall. White is the color of mourning where Ying has gone, the awesome color which is absence, is purity, is outward-boundness, a flight of the pale body into pitch blackness.

Our son-in-law looks tribal or like a gypsy with green eyes shaded by thick straight lashes. He's part Welsh, part Portuguese. Ying, my husband, said, "I'm of two minds regarding miscegenation. You think it's a simple matter? I'm a liberal, however, a liberal," he repeated, his foot tapping.

"Mimi," I said, "is of one mind." She wanted that gypsy-like assistant professor, and he desired her, our fine-boned daughter.

I'm almost color blind now. At any rate, green and blue I find hard to distinguish in the evening. The world in shrinking imploded into our grandchild's face and body. I can't take my eyes off him. I lean too close, I'm sure, absorbing his features, their mixed aspects, raceless or twice bred, as they slip into combinations surprising and new.

Let it go. I'm of my years airing themselves in my breath. I should not have written Timothy. I passed commonsense over to him to employ—which he'll do. He shall. He won't get in touch with me.

How long is it that I've been the sensible one? If we count it from when we met—decades, only decades. By writing Timothy, Ying's colleague, I handed over commonsense. All I want is aloneness now, the choreography of meals, the pruning of plants, a walk to the corner, the easement of lying in bed, my form stretched out before me to look down at, as though I've already left it behind.

I *will* Timothy not to call. Anyway, I won't let him leave Boston.

All of us are Chinese some of the time, I say. But I'm not certain what I mean. Other times, I'm a Calvinist, familiar with dimity and yokes. My favorite summer dress is Danish, my gold ring Greek, my face cream French, my daydreams I can't place. For someone so unsure of who I am, from time to time I have such definite statements to make. My thoughts are reckless, braver than Ying's. Yet, for decades, I ignored Timothy, ignored even the thoughts I refused to think. *That* is Chinese.

The phone rings. It has a cutting edge. I look at it. One. Two. Three. I once had a cat who stared at phones when they rang. Now I stare, too. Four. It stops, leaving the house emptier. Fragrances have leaned against me. There's so much speech in silent things.

For a long time, I was young. Spaces happen now which I can't fill. I'm often away from myself. The past tense can bury me like a landslide. The past tense is the most populated country of the countries I've lived in. Friends have gone. Mimi, our daughter, has died. There was no one for Ying to stay in the States for, except me.

He writes twice a month. He sounds more and more Chinese. It's life which will divorce me. It'll leave me behind, receding.

Timothy.

It's too late. His name's just a reflex. I no longer secrete longing. I'm beached; and the moon's a dead pebble. My dry hands seek my dry cheek. My clocks move but return to the same hour twice a day, on time. I'm noticing in new, dry-eyed ways. As for my age, I'll never catch up with Ying's, which puts me ahead like daylight saving. I'm months and months younger, enough months to count as years, and I always rubbed it in. "You're getting on!" I declared thirty years ago. "It's too bad!"

Ying said in St. Croix, "Compared to these people you look like an eleven-year-old."

I was forty-seven and he fifty-three then and, made self-conscious, I tugged at my bikini. "It's all that butter and sides of beef and hard liquor they stow away," I said. "And have stowed away since Druid times. They can't help it, you know."

They. Americans were they. German tourists, Swedish ones. But so were Chinese. "Look," Ying said, "they have to catch up with technology." He was worrying over mainland China. "They're of nowhere."

"From nowhere," I corrected him.

"With all its ills," he went on, "they can't bypass industrialization. Mao will learn the hard way, mark my words."

Ying's part of that "they" now. I'm now from nowhere, no longer part of a "we." Interesting. I'm only I, I am. I still am, however. So far and meanwhile. Till I leave even me.

Timothy's last name is Ayres. Scottish. I'll explain to him I was having one of my lapses when I wrote that letter.

I try not to think of China because its fate hurts so. The other side of everywhere, of everyone, living and unlived, forced to try to catch up with—to keep pace with—imperfections of driven, self-searching barbarians.

I have to save my eyes. But what for? I don't watch television anymore and don't miss it. My desk, my sofa, the refrigerator, the radio are islands in a sea of floor. I take beads on distances before embarking toward the letters, cushions, eggs, music—the other soul in this house.

Impossible lamp. I turned you off at four this morning. Full of yourself, you snap back on! There's a break in the shrubbery which is lined up with an aisle between a neighbor's trees. Through it, dawn rises like water filling a bathtub.

I'm to soak myself because of the insistence in my thigh and back. Perhaps camel's humps are trying to grow out of me, repositories of memory which won't lie down, go away. My hands seek out past days to knead, to work out their ache.

When I was in the hospital, I heard him say, "No heroic measures." I believe Dr. Walsh was talking to my grandson. "At her age, you understand." And then the two lads at the foot of my bed traveled away on platforms until I could no longer hear them.

When Dr. Walsh reappeared suddenly, I scrabbled at the sheets, swung my legs, moved toward him. It was as though my skirts were tied at the bottom.

"Mrs. Kuo! You do my heart good," he declared, plunging toward me.

"Nothing's wrong with mine," I said. "I'm strong. Don't think I'm on my last legs."

He carried me, put me back to bed as though, as though I were the child. Determination returned to me. Like the lamp, I snapped back on. And you see, I'm here at home again, the two of me—the me and the you. It comes of talking to oneself; however, which one of us would stop me? We laugh together. You tell me who's to stop us. I've never been freer. I think anything I like, do as I please. I'm as single as I was at nine, a sweet age. My mind is clear and could shine.

I stare at the telephone. One; two; three? Yes, four; five. It rings on, disappoints me. Bitter, yet I am also relieved.

Probably my neighbor, a strong woman, across the street and half a block down. She's short of cash, so helps out with storm windows, mowing, raking.

I'm looking at albums she took down from the attic for me, my nose a couple of inches from faces. "See," I say to you, "that was when Timothy arrived in a convertible, his scarf looped around his neck." Timothy, our guest, was Ying's colleague, both of them involved with Venus scrutinized from Yerkes Observatory, tracking gases and speeding light. They dealt with infinity, seemed to wonder at nothing. My physicist husband, Ying, was sure of me, while Timothy, married often, waited.

If only I knew I could stay in touch with myself forever.

The camera is a gun shooting down moments. I take in small people, tiny views I don't remember from where: outside Athens, on a French canal? Is that lake Swiss or in Hangchow, the honeymoon city, the sheen of one sky continuing into the next?

I expel exasperation. I will not have it. Buds, nodes, appear on my knuckles, rosaries to tell. You and I laugh. It's the beads have things to tell, not I. My neck feels yoked by an influence I'm to serve. Mimi, our daughter, was swayed by a rare disease of the blood when she was thirty-three, four months and seven days. Winston, our grandson, Ying and I brought up mostly, though his gypsy-like father would claim otherwise.

Simply because it rings, must I answer it? It yelps, so willful. You see, you're withdrawing, I point out to myself. But this is peace! I'm what I am now. My ledges, plants, cant of roof upraised. I'll leave through the skylight, God sucking me upward through his straw. I rather like that thought, I must say, vain, as usual. He'll vacuum me up, aspirate me. For once, I'll be his aspiration, momentarily in the light and years of galaxies. Ying could never get used to my most natural thoughts. After fifty-five years here, he had to go all the way to China to get away from me. That's my next-to-final thought about him. There's always more to think, have no fear. The life of radioactivity is forever. The life of death is everlasting. I've been married over fifty years, years made contingent by Ying's need to go home.

I'm sorry I wrote that letter. I simply won't answer the phone for a week. I'm content, after all.

He stepped out of the convertible, rather tall; I remember being nonplussed, as though his height put me in a quandary. Sitting, Timothy folded into another man. As he approached us, Ying standing next to me, the scarf around his neck slipped out of its loop. He picked it up and, as Ying introduced us, Timothy flung it over my head like a skipping rope, flicking one end through the other. The fringe, though almost weightless, prickled. We smiled at one another slowly, as if remembering, though we'd never met before.

"It's yours," Timothy talking, I recognized, to fill stopped time I knew we both heard, "It suits you. Besides, Ying, I forgot to bring a present. You know me. So this is your pearl of the Orient."

"For Pete's sake, come in," Ying answered, taking Tim's arm. Ying was American that day. "You're full of baloney, come what may." Sometimes he sounded like a Rotarian, but a xerox of one, though he didn't know it then or now.

"Leave May out of it," Tim retorted, referring to his wife who was suing him for the first of what turned out to be their two divorces. That day we were only writing our stories or reading one another's, while now our lives have become knowledge of endings. I feel I know nothing; yet I also know volumes to be remaindered. One comes to the end of mysteries generating themselves; to the end of wanting. It's a thought. Yes. I'll leave off everything except this containment, this management of myself in my home.

I wound it around my neck twice so it wouldn't slip off. Its silk is the color of moonlight on a pond, a blond presence, the color of sheen.

Friends call; visit; take me for rides. Miriam across the street goes marketing with me. There're plenty of people left. More than enough.

I'm the center. I stand in the middle which, according to the Chinese, is the fifth direction. Ying who often sounded like a Rotarian when it suited him here, is now Peking man, imagine. I'm the center, a Chinese direction. He needn't think I'm so American yet!

In a section of plate glass the length of a building, I saw a woman hurrying along. Her knees raised themselves to climb but the sidewalk was level. Her stepping was hurried, stiff, floating. I gasped; she, too. "That's you!" I said to me. I—who used to move like a dress hung on a hanger loose in the wind.

The woman's hair was as silver as anyone's here. That's why I didn't grasp who she was. So, finally, she resembled the rest, weathered silver like any Caucasian. Hers was a new gait, a new identity. At the corner, she and I put hands out for support on rear fenders of cars. "You're me," I said to her. "You're me," she said back. What I saw mirrored before me was also everything behind me.

Polarity, space, time. Ying and I reflected on such matters. "You, of course, in your way," he never neglected to add, which in the long run never did match his.

"You must remember you have lapses," Dr. Walsh said in his grown-up manner. "You mustn't go out any more without a companion. And I forbid you to drive."

The mind is punishing the body, denying it in exactly the way I would. The mind simply absents itself, rehearsing for the eviction of evictions. And the tenement lets in the sky even below the stairs. I sometimes feel like mesh dissolving into light. I almost died in the crash, which was my fault.

So busy; busy; so busy. In this house, I put out my palms to stroke the flanks of time. At last I have time. It lies at my feet like rugs; hangs in mid-air unsupported. By staring down time, I still it. I need no one—finally!

So busy, busy, busy! I was interviewed; won awards for my designs. I turned out costumes for *Kismets*, *Kings and I's*, and Rattigans, too. Ying Y. Kuo, the young physicist,

was backstage when a relative of his was in *The King and I*. He picked me up off the floor when a bolt hit me out of the blue. It was heavy metallic fabric and knocked the breath out of me, so I didn't notice that he fell in love on the spot. "I was the one hit," he told me, laughing abruptly, astonished.

"Really?"

"Definitely."

He saw and he loved. "I was the one hit," he said many times, astonished.

"You felt hit?" I asked.

"Definitely."

Timothy said, "Admit to it. Just admit to it and I'll leave you alone."

I never admitted to it. I never said to him, "I saw and loved." Timothy admitted to it all, over the years, during which he married two or three or however many times. He signed notes slipped into my hand at parties, at a lunch or two: "Perpetually, comma, perpetually, Tim."

I said to him, "Sure. You'll always be perpetually Timothy Ayres."

"You're a coward," he said.

"I'm married. I've a daughter. I love Ying Y. Kuo, who happens to be my husband."

"All three are true," he answered. "But something more is also true."

"You're just another star-gazer," I told him. Ludicrous. Transcendent. Intrepid; wild with themselves, with grace. Shamelessness a part of their genius.

The Chinese are matter-of-fact. Didactic. Categorical. Yes. There are ways to be; and they know those ways. They do. These Westerners. What keeps them together, I wonder? So selfish, so soulful. I'm a canal with locks. Timothy the open sea, his stole of silk streaming on the wind of the cosmos. Women threw him out of their beds; he abandoned ship and struck out alone, not once, not twice. I stayed happy with Ying, together we weathered Mimi's illness and death. I saw that that was the meaning of marriage. Any Chinese would agree. I even agree with myself.

For decades I longed. It was like a disease of the blood, which took Mimi away. Heart and womb, the one over the other, waited. I laughed at myself. At Palo Alto, Ying was promoted over him. It was a sign from outer space.

Timothy left Palo Alto. We lost track of him for three years. He sent cards with no return address from Paris, Buenos Aires, Baltimore. A book came out. For a season he was famous in celestial circles. I took that as a sign, too. He belonged now to his success. Thank my lucky stars.

This house is in a state of sleep. The porch snores softly. I wake into its dream daily.

The phone rings four, five, six times. I'm disappointed when it doesn't ring; disappointed when it rings too often. On the first ring, I jumped to turn off the alarm. But you're awake. It's not the clock. I'm awake like a cat or a dog, unknowing. Is that armchair wondering where Ying's gone? "China, China!" I cry out. "He's gone to a different condition, you fool," I tell the head rest. "Make no mistake. The Chinese *can* go home again." But it's given me a turn, I can tell you.

Winston, his Eurasian brow furrowed, his exasperation unconcealed, said, "I thought Chinese women were cooperative." My grandson didn't use the words, "docile," "passive." He knows better than that. "Why the hell can't you see you should be in a home? With people. You'll be taken care of. Don't you want to be safe, happy? Grandpa had no business splitting—at his age. At yours. And he was always grinding the Chinese ax of propriety. How would this look! How would that look! As though anyone's wasting a glance. You want to know what it is? It's unseemly— his favorite word. A disgrace. Abandoning you. I'm getting you into a home, I don't care what."

I banged my fist on his arm. "I like it here. This *is* my home. As he said, what would I be doing in Peking. I don't blame Gramps one bit."

"Gramps," Winston repeated. "This bi-cultural, sitting on the cusp, oh, so Westernized, mixed up family! And it isn't Peking. It's Beijing, and if we don't practice, we'll never catch onto this new spelling. Tell me straight—is it Chinese to abandon your wife when she's as old as the century?"

"Here they abandon earlier. You're the one bringing up this ethnic stuff. You true blue Chinese-American Eurasian. I used to think

I belonged nowhere. But not so. I belong everywhere, anywhere, even on Maple Lane in Westchester. And I'm only seventy-nine. Try to get my age straight."

He guffawed in the agony of a twenty-seven-year-old and stopped himself in time from slapping my back. He could have broken me in two, which may be my natural condition, come to think of it.

"Winston," I said to him, "I stopped thinking in Chinese when I was just about your age. Chinese is another syndrome. But what would you know about it." I leaned too close, intrigued with his features.

"Suppose you fall and can't get to the phone."

"I'm not saying you're wrong. But Gramps is right, too. He's being Chinese. You know how they are about family. Hopeless cases."

"You're something else," Winston said. His body movements are like James Dean's or Alan Ladd's, but though his hair is brown he has Shantung[1] bones. I remember the day he arrived in America—purplish-red and kicking out of Mimi at Doctor's Hospital, the mayor oblivious a couple of blocks away of still another Oriental who'd slipped over a border. I laugh. How Chinese of me to claim him as Chinese when he's half Caucasian.

I'm at the border. This grayness may not be dusk, but a dawning. Remember that, I order myself, the thought already gone.

Mimi died on an operating table twenty years ago. How old would she be now? While I remained her horizon, she would have been becoming my past ages. My son-in-law remarried so he's no longer my son-in-law. So he, too, left. Or am I confused? No, Lewis moved back to Indianapolis. Winston, some sort of junior curator, is with a museum in Los Angeles. He makes appearances and vanishes as though I rub whatever makes genies come and go.

He wants me in an old-age home. Without a daughter how can I know my age? Since Mimi died, I've felt ageless. Periodically, Winston gives up on me. I annoy young people more and more.

The phone. I count: one, two, three, four and so forth. It's beautiful to be alone here on the sofa. I shall not answer the phone all day; I will not. This is enough. Once a week my neighbor takes me marketing. She describes new ways of making jello. I marvel at her kindness. We have supper out, my treat, and feel girlish about it. Friends take me to the movies once, twice a month, and I sit down front. What more do I want? The window sills are strands, the bush outside the kitchen is all I need of parks, and as for flowers, my thickened knuckles smart with feverish buds. I put my hand before my face, press against time's haunch. Time has volume here.

Before departing, Ying said, "I'm thinking of you alone here. Though the financial arrangements are secure, more than secure. Winston's a man now, too, and will look out for you."

"From California," I didn't put in, for there are telephones in this country. It's not the Australian outback, unconscious next to insomniac cities.

I said instead, "I want you to stay, but . . ." I reassured him, "you must go. I do understand."

"I am Chinese," he said.

"No need to say," I said in Chinese, as if losing my bearings.

He said, "A man must die in his native land."

"You talk," I declared, "as if winding up a speech at a banquet." My remark was of the sort which always derailed his trend of thought. Not that my comment was so American, but that his rock bottom mode is Chinese, and he feels defined by the use of maxims.

I continued, "Die! All this talk about dying! You're only eighty-two." We didn't smile. That was three years ago when the detente was well-established, and his brother who had been imprisoned in a windowless closet under the stairs of a school building by seventeen-year-old Red Guards, asked him to visit. And to stay. By letter, he'd instructed them to ask him, I didn't let on I knew. His letter had said, "It will be easier on my wife, if you and Erjieh demand that I return. Suddenly, I'm overwhelmingly homesick, a sign, perhaps, that my time is short."

"You won't be able to adjust," he said to me. "You're too advanced in years, even if you *are* appropriately younger than I, and too used to comforts, luxuries. Where do you suppose you can get sauna treatments? Is your arthritis getting any better? How can I ask you to make such sacrifices at your age? I can't be so unreasonable, can I?"

Enough. Enough. In one breath, he asked so many questions.

He had another one. "They'll find you so foreign, don't you agree?"

I've taught myself to need no one. Long since, long since. The moon's no longer pulling at my blood. Long since.

"My native land," he said. "Fatherland." Words, phrases turned in the manner of a cadenza, the mind braking the way an ice skater does after a flourish, making himself into an exclamation point. "It's a proper goal, a fitting conclusion to my life, my career. I can bring something to China, too, as a physicist emeritus, above politics, beyond self-interest."

I remembered myself, a girl, riding through China, provinces slipping through the loop of the train.

Timothy's convertible waited outside. We proceeded indoors to our living room. Or was that when we had our first apartment in even earlier days? A tree grew through our second-floor deck. Was my hair long then, heavy as liquid coal, glinting maroon in the sunlight, or was it cropped short again? The first time its bob made me the talk of Shanghai, when I was fourteen, and here, too, a little later. My father, a magistrate educated in France, was weak in my hands, so I was told by those who found me spoiled, oh spoiled rotten. But I wasn't ruined then. It's now that I am, that things could be described as spoiled. Timothy was spoiled, too, leading directly to his being single today after three wives. Two did die of natural causes, it's perfectly true, one of them May—just before their third time together. He's irresistible, to hear everyone tell it, though I've never been fooled. I'm not Chinese for nothing. But he is also intelligent and far-sighted, focused on the horizon when most of us don't look past sills.

The four of us were at the Princeton Club. Ying was greeting someone half a room away.

Timothy was looking at him, while he said to me, "Have you ever heard me? Answer me!"

I told him, "I'm all ears, all ears, but no heart." I felt nothing at all for him, for his second wife coming down the hall from fixing her hair. Tall and single-minded about being his wife, she was perfect for him, as Ying'd been the one to observe.

Through his teeth, Timothy repeated, "Remember how I feel."

I did; I do. I remember how we felt.

"Leave me alone!" I cried. Like a mirage in the Gobi desert in August, his wife shimmered toward us . . . a trick of my eyes, I suppose.

"I never will," he said, angrier at himself than at me.

"You want to wreck my life. I hate you."

"Never."

As a last resort, I said, "I am *Chinese*."

"And cruel," he retorted, the patient one.

But he was cruel, too, his presence a hardship.

"You're so foreign!" I exclaimed, in disgust or in despair?

Oh, the phone. I count. I turn away, go to the front door, open it. It's rained. The lawn is Ireland, the flagstones like ancient Chinese mirrors before glass came into being. Freshness rushes into the house like a young athlete, wholesome, muscular. Knocked back, I lean against the door. The athlete reaches the bedroom, bounds up the stairs I no longer use. I then step back with extraneous motions and close out the glare, the universal air. What was I doing just now? Mail falls out of my hand. That's it, I'd picked up the mail left on the doormat, a special concession of the postwoman to save me a trip down the driveway in bad weather. I bend in stages, pick up all of it a second time and, hand on hip, straighten up inch by inch to go to the desk.

No letters from anyone I know this time. Most are away. Migratory. I've lived out a century of refugees, and tourists. I, too, am waiting for exit papers. I laugh at myself laughing. In the hospital they gave me quarts of someone's blood, lymph and elixirs of values not my own. Perhaps her name is Jane Smith. The tree I crashed into should have shared my semi-private room, hooked up to

plant foods. Poor traumatized being, it doesn't climb aboard planes, leave and write me love's rationalizations. I'm sorry I hurt you, tree. Thank you for stopping me half dead in my tracks. I might have crashed into anti-matter instead.

"These Americans," Ying has said. "Those Chinese." I, too, have uttered these and those words. We would have been rendered speechless otherwise. Ying said, "Timothy doesn't marry for good. We Chinese are taught to love once, deeply and faithfully."

"Divorce isn't easy for anyone, including them," I put in. "That he remarries the same girl makes him nice, don't you think?"

"You always generalize from too little."

He was right and for all his star-gazing was more down to earth.

"We marry as much for the sake of the institution as for ourselves," I said, surprising myself. "We serve the institution. They marry for the sake of one another and of themselves."

"Another aspect of individualism again."

"Why don't you say what you think?"

"Selfishness," he said. "Shamelessness, too. They don't care what anyone thinks."

"I'm so glad you'll never divorce me," I said.

"I have no reason to."

He was right. I gave him no reason to go home. And we're not divorced. It's Timothy who ended up with no one. Serves him right. It's Timothy who's alone.

And I.

We Chinese are rational. It's good to know, to bank on.

At the supermarket yesterday, I said to Miriam, "These people look familiar."

She misunderstood. "Uhn-uh . . . your eyes," she said. "Hold onto me."

Americans look familiar now. After all, I did go to college here. My name was Kiki Lee before it became Kiki Kuo. Kiki Kuo. People calling me have sounded like crickets all these years, all because my father studied at the Sorbonne, and thought Kiki sounded Chinese. After Ying dies, will he still be Chinese? I feel neither Chinese nor not Chinese. I feel incredulous, living here on Maple Lane.

It's Timothy Ayres who's making me carry on like this. You see, if you marry your own kind you don't have to engage in so much realizing.

I have some tea. I neaten up the counters. It's ten-thirty. I take off my silk crepe robe, designed for a production of the *Mikado*. I dress well all of the time now, no longer saving things for better occasions. I throw the robe to a chair. It slips off, but I leave it. The sleeve is snagged in several places by the chair's unrepaired arm. I will never wear out my clothes accumulated over the years. I keep three diamond rings on my left hand at all times, and wear seven bracelets and five fine gold chains. Other things are in the safe deposit for Winston's future wife. I will love her sight unseen. I love her already, whoever she may be.

The phone. One, two, three; yes, of course, four, and so on. I suppose I'll have to call my neighbor so she doesn't worry. I don't need anyone! I wash my neck and arms gingerly as if water were scarce. I don't take off the bracelets and necklaces. I put on my lacy nightgown, plait my hair, perfume my shoulders. It's a bit macabre, I agree.

I ease myself into bed, pull the comforter up to my chin. Ah. It's good to lie down. I feel capable, lying down, the way young people feel standing and ready to go.

In sleep I am ready to go. It's only a longer lapse in my day. I don't sleep so much as I swoon, aware of time passing and refusing to pass, of time hanging like curtains of snow. White is the color of mourning in China. In the dark I stare down time, as though I could win against it. I fall asleep, I suppose. I dream of a white face at the whitening window.

The ring jangles through me. I am fully awake. Two. Three rings. Then silence. Only three rings! My eyes widen. I am robbed clean of any thoughts to think. I begin to count slowly, as I told Timothy I would . . . and fifty-five, and fifty-six, and fifty-seven and fifty-eight and fifty-nine. Sixty. The phone begins to ring again. I am breathing with my lips parted. My mouth is dry, but my mind is a fair day on a plateau.

My letter had said, precisely, "If you are still there for me, phone me from Boston. I'm not what I used to be, so ring three times. Then hang up and, a minute later, ring again. That way I'll have time to get to the phone."

Lying on my side, I reach out. My thin braid is caught under my back. I jerk at it. I pick up the receiver.

"What an hour to call," I declare. "You're so inconsiderate!"

In such a rush, he doesn't hear me, he says what he has to say, "I've been in the hospital—nothing serious. Just got your letter last night." He sounds as if he's been running. "How are you?"

Leaning on an elbow, I take in his voice.

"I wanted to wake you up," he says, and hears himself. A pause. "Finally."

I laugh, throw back my head and lie flat listening.

"I'm not in great shape," he says. "I hope you're good and rickety, too."

"Worse than that."

He sighs. "Wasted."

"You threw yourself away on too many women."

"Wasted *years*." Voices don't change any. He sounds the way he did at the beginning.

"I've been playing dead," I say. Where do the words come from? I didn't know I'd been playing dead. "I thought it'd be easier. Isn't that turned around though?"

"Did you worry I wouldn't call?"

"No, not at all." I remember he said I was cruel. "Yes," I say.

And so we continue. What was once so hard is now so easy. We're beyond differences, situations, exempt at our age from most things, even regret. And he's agreeing to everything. That he rent an apartment nearby for now. That we take each day as it comes, staring down time together.

Fragments of conversations we've had, the scarf the color of moonlight, postcards from Brussels and Baltimore, I possess in this montage, time not a corridor but a meadow surrounding a center, a maypole rippling with ribbons. I can blossom; I can attract bees.

I'm a woman in a lacy gown, making my own way. I shall put up my silver hair for an old man to take down.

"I'm well past longing," I say into the phone, stretching an arm above my head.

I've summoned him, haven't I, to the task of our prevailing?

Note

1. Northern province in China.

Discussion Questions:

1. Discuss Kiki's statement, "I feel neither Chinese nor non-Chinese."

2. What physical health problems does Kiki confront? How does she deal with them?

3. Describe the relationship between Ying and Kiki. Was he more or less Americanized than she and how did this affect their relationship?

4. Do you agree or disagree with Kiki's grandson, Winston, when he advises her to go into an old-age home? Does his advice ignore or confirm her own sense of self and hopes for the future?

5. Does Kiki's decision to reunite with her long-lost love, Timothy, surprise you? Why or why not?

Chapter 16
Having Our Say

Sarah Delany and
A. Elizabeth Delany
with Amy Hill Hearth

The narrator in the preceding selection had plans for a new life despite physical frailty. She is not an oddity, for the average life expectancy of the population increased dramatically in the twentieth century, and the majority of elders have ambitions for their future lives. The number of people living to be age 100 or older is also expanding rapidly in the United States. What is it like to live to be that old or even older? Are centenarians generally happy and healthy, or are they more often miserable, physically and mentally disabled, and dependent on other people? As with so much about later life, the answer is variable and influenced by the health and life satisfaction of the centenarians themselves. This selection, narrated by Sarah (Sadie) and Elizabeth (Bessie) Delany, two African-American sisters ages 100 and 102, presents their perspectives on their past and current lives. The daughters of a father born into slavery and a free, mixed-race mother, the Delany sisters are the oldest known surviving members of one of the most eminent families in North Carolina and Harlem. Despite their own professional and personal accomplishments, neither sister was sheltered from the effects of racism and discrimination.

Their recollections and accounts of their daily lives and personal relationships shatter stereotypes of what it means to be old and African American. The sisters' relationship with each other has also helped them maintain optimism and a sense both of continuity and futurity that contradicts the idea that the elderly look to their past for self-identity and comfort. As you follow their story, pay attention to their past and present activities and coping skills. Notice their self-esteem and humor enhanced by the passage of time. Think about how their membership in a privileged social class has interlocked with gender and racial discrimination to shape their lives and opinions.

Sadie

. . . Bessie and I have been together since time began, or so it seems. Bessie is my little sister, only she's not so little.

She is 101 years old, and I am 103.

People always say they'd like to live to be one hundred, but no one really expects to, except Bessie. She always said she planned to be as old as Moses. And when Bessie says she's going to do something, she does it. Now, I think Moses lived to 120. So I told Bessie that if she lives to 120, then I'll just have to live to 122 so I can take care of her.

Neither one of us ever married and we've lived together most all of our lives, and probably know each other better than any two human beings on this Earth. After so long, we are in some ways like one person. She is my right arm. If she were to die first, I'm not sure if I would want to go on living because the reason I am living is to keep *her* living.

Bessie and I still keep house by ourselves. We still do our shopping and banking. We were in helping professions—Bessie was a dentist and I was a high school teacher—so we're not rich, but we get by. Papa always taught us that with every dollar you earn, the first ten cents goes to the Lord, the second goes in the bank for hard times, and the rest is yours, but you better spend it wisely. Well, it's a good thing we listened because we're living on that hard-time money now, and not doing too badly.

We've buried so many people we've loved; that is the hard part of living this long. Most everyone we know has turned to dust. Well, there must be some reason we're still here. That's why we agreed to do this book; it gives us a sense of purpose. If it helps just one person, then it's worth doing. That's what Mama used to say.

Bessie and I have lived in New York for the last seventy-five years, but Raleigh will always be home. Raleigh is where Mama and Papa met, as students at Saint Augustine's School, which was a school for Negroes.

Mama and Papa got married in the campus chapel back in 1886 and raised all ten of us children right there at good old "Saint Aug's." Papa became vice principal and Mama was the matron, which meant she ran things day-to-day at the school.

I don't remember my mother ever calling my father by his first name, Henry. He was always "Mr. Delany" or "Your Pa." Now, I do recall that my father would call my mother "Miss Nan" in private moments, but he usually called her Mrs. Delany in front of everyone, including us children. Now, you might think this seems a bit formal. But the reason they did this is that colored people were always called by their first names in that era. It was a way of treating them with less dignity. What Mama and Papa were doing was blocking that. Most people never learned their first names.

In 1918 Papa became the first elected Negro bishop of the Episcopal Church, U.S.A. That's a long way for a man who was born a slave on a Georgia plantation. But if you had known Papa, you wouldn't be surprised. He was always improving himself, and he and Mama brought us up to reach high.

Papa was a smart, good-looking Negro man. Actually, his skin was a reddish-brown, on account of his mother being part Indian. Mama, who was from Virginia, was an issue-free Negro.[1] Mama looked white but she never did try to "pass." She was proud to be a colored woman!

People would look at us Delany children and wonder where in the world this bunch came from. We were every different shade from nearly white to brown-sugar. I was one of the lighter children, and Bessie was browner. As children, we were aware we were colored but we never gave it a second thought. Papa was dark and Mama was light and so what? It's just the way it was.

I came into this world at 7:30 in the evening on the nineteenth day of September, 1889. It was a long day of hard labor for Mama. Poor, dear Papa! There wasn't a thing he could do for Mama but worry and pray.

Everyone was nervous, because I was Mama's second baby, and the doctor had to be brought in after my older brother, Lemuel, was born two years earlier. This time, Mama wanted her sister, Eliza, by her side. That's why I was born at Lynch's Station, Virginia, where Eliza lived. Mama just got on that old train and headed up there when she was about ready to drop me.

Eliza's presence was calming, and the doctor was not needed. As a matter of fact, after the midwife left, Mama sat up in bed and declared she was hungry! Eliza was just tickled to death at Mama's appetite and cooked up the biggest plate of fried apples and hot biscuits Mama ever saw. Mama said she ate every bite. They named me Sarah Louise, but I have always been called Sadie.

Mama got her confidence back with my birth, and went on to have eight more healthy babies. Next in line was Annie Elizabeth, born two years after me and known as Bessie. I don't remember life without Bessie.

"Queen Bess," as Papa used to call her, was born on the third of September, 1891. Like all my younger brothers and sisters, she was born in Raleigh. She arrived at 9:30 in the morning, after keeping poor Mama up all night pacing those pine floorboards, which creaked loud enough to wake the dead. Bessie was so alert at birth that Mama said she had a funny feeling that child would have a mind of her own.

Bessie was what we used to call a "feeling" child; she was sensitive and emotional. She was quick to anger, and very out-spoken. Now, I was a "mama's child" and followed my Mama around like a shadow. I always did what I was told. I was calm and agreeable. The way I see it, there's room in the world for both me and Bessie. We kind of balance each other out.

Bessie

People learned not to mess with me from day one. When I was small, a neighborhood girl started taunting me: "Bessie Delany, you scrawny thing. You've got the skinniest legs and the longest neck I ever did see." Now, this girl was a bully, and I had seen her technique before: She would say nasty things to other girls, and they'd burst into tears and run crying to their mama. She was a lot bigger than me, but I didn't care. I said, "Oh, why don't you shut up. You ain't so pretty yourself!" And she never bothered me again.

Papa used to say, "You catch more flies with molasses than vinegar." He believed you could get further in life by being nice to people. Well, this is easy for Sadie to swallow. Sadie is molasses without even trying! She can sweet-talk the world, or play dumb, or whatever it takes to get by without a fuss. But even as a tiny little child, I wasn't afraid of anything. I'd meet the Devil before day and look him in the eye, no matter what the price. If Sadie is molasses, then I am vinegar! Sadie is sugar, and I'm the spice.

You know, Sadie doesn't approve of me sometimes. She frowns at me in her big-sister-sort-of-way and says it's a wonder I wasn't lynched. Well, it's true I almost was. But I'm still here, yes, sir!

What worries me is that I know Sadie's going to get into Heaven, but I'm not so sure about me. I'm working on it, but it sure is hard to change. I've been trying to change for one hundred years without success, that's not so good, is it? I'm afraid when I meet St. Peter at the Gate, he'll say, "Lord, child, you were *mean*!"

I have trouble with the idea of forgiving and forgetting. You see, I can forgive, but I can't seem to forget. And I'm not sure the Lord would approve of that at all. I remember things that happened long, long ago that still make me madder than a hornet. I wish they didn't. Most of the things that make me mad happened to me because I am colored. As a woman dentist, I faced sexual harassment—that's what they call it today—but to me, racism was always a bigger problem.

Most of the people I'm still mad at are long dead. If I say something mean about them, Sadie will say, "Now Bessie, of the dead say nothing Evil." And I try to be good.

Sometimes I am angry at all white people, until I stop and think of the nice white people I have known in my life. OK, OK, there have been a few. I admit it. And my mother is part white, and I can't hate my own flesh and blood! There are good white people out there. Sometimes, they are hard to find, but they're out there, just look for them.

But the rebby boys tend to stand out, make themselves known. Rebby is what we used to call racist white men. I guess it's short for rebel. I'll tell you, the way those rebby types treat colored folks—well, it just makes me sick. If I had a pet buzzard I'd treat him better than the way some white folks have treated me! There isn't a Negro this side of Glory who doesn't know exactly what I mean.

Why, the rebby boys start early in life learning to hate. I remember encountering some who weren't more than ten or twelve years old. They were cutting through the fields at Saint Aug's one day, and I had strayed a few yards from where I was supposed to be. I was about six years old. My little petticoat had slipped down a bit, and they made some nasty remarks about this little colored girl and her underpants. I'm not even sure I understood what they were saying, but I got their meaning.

The rebby boys don't give colored folks credit for a thing, not a single thing. Why, I think we've done pretty well, considering we were dragged over here in chains, from Africa! Why, colored folks *built* this country, and that is the truth. We were the laborers, honey! And even after we were freed, we were the backbone of this country—the maids, cooks, undertakers, barbers, porters, and so on.

Those rebby types! What do they think, anyway? When we get to the Spirit World, do they think colored people are going to be waiting on their tables, pouring their tea? I think some of them are in for a big surprise. They're going to be pouring tea for *me*.

Now, Sadie doesn't get all agitated like this. She just shrugs it off. It's been a little harder for me, partly because I'm darker than she is, and the darker you are, honey, the harder it is. But it's also been harder on me because I have a different personality than Sadie. She is a true Christian woman! I wish I were more like her but I'm afraid I am a naughty little darkey! Ha ha! I know it's not fashionable to use some of the words from my heyday, but that's who I am! And who is going to stop me? Nobody, that's who! Ain't nobody going to censor *me*, no, sir! I'm a hundred-and-one years old and at my age, honey, I can say what I want!

Now, don't go thinking that I'm *all* mean. I am not so angry that I cannot laugh at myself! One thing most Negroes learn early is how to laugh at their situation.

If you asked me the secret to longevity, I would tell you that you have to work at taking care of your health. But a lot of it's attitude. I'm alive out of sheer determination, honey! Sometimes I think it's my meanness that keeps me going. . . .

Sadie

One thing I've noticed since I got this old is that I have started to dream in color. I'll remember that someone was wearing a red dress or a pink sweater, something like that. I also dream more than I used to, and when I wake up I feel tired. I'll say to Bessie, "I sure am tired this morning. I was teaching all night in my dreams!"

Bessie was always the big dreamer. She was always talking about what she dreamed the night before. She has this same dream over and over again, about a party she went to on Cotton Street in Raleigh, way back when. Nothing special happens; she just keeps dreaming she's there. In our dreams, we are always young.

Truth is, we both forget we're old. This happens all the time. I'll reach for something real quick, just like a young person. And realize my reflexes are not what they once were. It surprises me, but I can't complain. I still do what I want, pretty much.

These days, I am usually the first one awake in the morning. I wake up at six-thirty. And the first thing I do when I open my eyes is smile, and then I say, "Thank you, Lord, for another day!"

If I don't hear Bessie get up, I'll go into her room and wake her. Sometimes I have to knock on her headboard. And she opens her eyes and says, "Oh, Lord, another day?!" I don't think Bessie would get up at all sometimes, if it weren't for me. She stays up late in her room and listens to these talk-radio shows, and she doesn't get enough sleep.

In the mornings, Monday through Friday, we do our yoga exercises. I started doing yoga exercises with Mama about forty years ago. Mama was starting to shrink up and get bent down, and I started exercising with her to straighten her up again. Only I didn't

know at that time that what we were actually doing was "yoga." We just thought we were exercising.

I kept doing my yoga exercises, even after Mama died. Well, when Bessie turned eighty she decided that I looked better than her. So she decided she would start doing yoga, too. So we've been doing our exercises together ever since. We follow a yoga exercise program on the TV. Sometimes, Bessie cheats. I'll be doing an exercise and look over at her, and she's just lying there! She's a naughty old gal.

Exercise is very important. A lot of older people don't exercise at all. Another thing that is terribly important is diet. I keep up with the latest news about nutrition. About thirty years ago, Bessie and I started eating much more healthy foods. We don't eat that fatty Southern food very often. When we do, we feel like we can't move!

We eat as many as seven different vegetables a day. Plus lots of fresh fruits. And we take vitamin supplements: Vitamin A, B complex, C, D, E, and minerals, too, like zinc. And Bessie takes tyrosine when she's a little blue.

Every morning, after we do our yoga, we each take a clove of garlic, chop it up, and swallow it whole. If you swallow it all at once, there is no odor. We also take a teaspoon of cod liver oil. Bessie thinks it's disgusting. But one day I said, "Now, dear little sister, if you want to keep up with me, you're going to have to start taking it, every day, and stop complainin'." And she's been good ever since.

As soon as we moved to our house in 1957, we began boiling the tap water we use for our drinking water. Folks keep telling us that it's not necessary, that the City of Mount Vernon purifies the water. But it's a habit and at our age, child, we're not about to change our routine.

These days, I do most of the cooking, and Bessie does the serving. We eat our big meal of the day at noon. In the evening, we usually have a milk shake for dinner, and then we go upstairs and watch "MacNeil Lehrer" on the TV.

After that, we say our prayers. We say prayers in the morning and before we go to bed. It takes a long time to pray for everyone, because it's a very big family—we have fifteen nieces and nephews still living, plus all their children and grandchildren. We pray for each one, living and dead. The ones that Bessie doesn't approve of get extra prayers. Bessie can be very critical and she holds things against people forever. I always have to say to her, "Everybody has to be themselves, Bessie. Live and let live."

Bessie can be very kind, though she usually saves her kind side for children and animals. She has a little dog who belonged to someone in the neighborhood who didn't want him anymore. He's part Chihuahua and I don't know what else, and he has some nasty habits, but Bessie loves him. She never eats a meal without saving the best piece for her little dog.

I'll tell you a story: Not long ago the Episcopal bishop of New York had a dinner to honor me and Bessie. A couple of days beforehand, Bessie announced that she was going to bring a doggie bag to the dinner. I said, "Whaaaat? Why, Bess, people will think you're a peculiar old woman." And she said, "So what, maybe I am a peculiar old woman. I hear they're having prime rib, and I would die of guilt if I had prime rib and didn't save any for my little dog."

Sure enough, when they served the dinner, Bessie took a bag out of her pocketbook and started to cut off the nicest part of the meat. And the bishop, who was sitting right there, asked her what she was doing. Next thing I knew, the bishop was cutting off a piece of *his* prime rib and wrapping it in a napkin for Bessie's little dog, and everybody else started doing the same thing, because the bishop did.

When we got home, Bessie was so excited she was almost giddy. She kept saying, "I've got enough prime rib to feed my little dog for a week!" I said, "Well, I certainly hope he enjoys the bishop's dinner."

Before Bessie got her little dog, we had a stray cat we named Mr. Delany, since we don't have a man in the house. He had been run over by a car, and had crawled up on our doorstep. So we brought the kitty in the house, rubbed salve into his cuts, and splinted him up. We fed him by hand and fussed over him, day and night, for two weeks. And you know what? He was just fine. But one day, he ran off. Bessie's still grieving

for that old cat. She says, "I know he must be dead, or he would have come back."

If only I could get Bessie to be as sweet to people as she is to her animals. Bessie can be a little bit nasty sometimes, you know. She thinks it's her God-given duty to tell people the truth. I say to her, "Bessie, don't you realize people don't want to hear the truth?"

One time, there was a woman in our neighborhood who was furious at her granddaughter for moving in with a boyfriend. This woman was running around the neighborhood complaining to anyone who would listen. I was sort of sympathetic but Bessie said to her, "You shouldn't be running all around bad-mouthing your own kin." Of course, Bessie was right. But that poor lady was embarrassed and has avoided us ever since.

Another time, a priest was over here visiting us and I noticed he'd put on a little weight. I thought to myself, Uh-oh, I bet she says something to him. Well, when he was leaving, Bessie said, "Now, Father, it seems to me you are getting fat. You've got to lose some weight!" He laughed and said, yes, he knew he needed to go on a diet. When he left I said to Bessie, "What did you have to go and say that for?" And she said, "I care about people's health, and sometimes people need somebody to give it to 'em straight."

Bessie does not mince words, and when she has a strong opinion—especially when it involves me—she's not shy! Not long ago, one of our nieces died, and somebody was over here describing the place where she died. It was called a hospice, and it sounded awfully nice. I said, "Well, maybe when my time comes, y'all should take me to a hospice." But Bessie got real mad. She said, "You ain't dying in no hospice. You ain't dying nowhere but upstairs in yo' bed!"

Over the years, we've buried a lot of people. Even the generation younger than us is starting to die off. I don't know why I'm still here and they're not, but I don't fret over it. It's in God's hands.

You know, when you are this old, you don't know if you're going to wake up in the morning. But I don't worry about dying, and neither does Bessie. We are at peace. You do kind of wonder, when's it going to happen? That's why you learn to love each and every day, child.

Truth is, I've gotten so old I'm starting to get a little *bold*. Not long ago, some young men started hanging out in front of our house. They were part of a gang from the Bronx, and they just thought our dead-end street here was a good spot to play basketball and do drugs and I don't know what-all.

Well, Bessie said to me, "I'll go out there and get rid of them." And I said, "No, Bess. For once, I'm going to handle it. You stay in the house."

I went out the backdoor and around to the sidewalk where they were hanging out. And I said, "You boys better get out of here." They were kind of surprised. And then one of them said, "You can't make us leave. This is a public street."

And I said, "Yes, it's a public street, but it's not a *park*, so get moving."

And this fella said to me: "Just how do you think you're going to make us go?"

I pointed to my house. I said, "My sister is inside and she has her hand on the phone to call the police." Of course, this was a little white lie because we don't have a phone, but they didn't know that.

So the leader of this group laughed at me and he said, "You think the police are gonna come when some old *nigger woman* calls them?"

I said, "Yes, they will come. Because I own this property here, and I own this house, and I pay my taxes. They *will* come, and they will boot you on out of here."

Well, they grumbled and complained, and finally they left. They came back about a week later, and our neighbor ran them off. And they never did come back.

Bessie was kind of surprised that I took those boys on like that. To tell you the truth, so was I.

Bessie

I was mighty proud of Sadie for taking on those no-good fellas and running them on out of there. It just goes to show she can be tough when she puts her mind to it. I said to her, "Sadie, our Grandpa Miliam surely would have been proud."

I was just thinking about Mr. Miliam this morning. There was a cute little squirrel in my yard, and I said, "Oh, you better be glad Mr. Miliam and his gun ain't around. Cause he'd shoot you and fry you up for his breakfast."

You know how when you come up on a squirrel, it'll run around to the other side of the tree? Well, Mr. Miliam would send one of us grandchildren to chase the squirrel back around to his side, and he would shoot it dead while the child stayed hid behind the tree. But don't worry. Mr. Miliam was an excellent shot, and nobody ever got hurt.

I wonder what Mr. Miliam would think of his granddaughters living this long. Why, I suppose he'd get a kick out of it. I know he'd have lived longer if Grandma hadn't died and it broke his heart. Sometimes, you need a reason to keep living.

Tell you the truth, I wouldn't be here without sister Sadie. We are companions. But I'll tell you something else: Sadie has taken on this business of getting old like it's a big *project*. She has it all figured out, about diet and exercise. Sometimes, I just don't want to do it, but she is my big sister and I really don't want to disappoint her. Funny thing about Sadie is she rarely gets—what's the word?—depressed. She is an easygoing type of gal.

Now, honey, I get the blues sometimes. It's a shock to me, to be this old. Sometimes, when I realize I am 101 years old, it lilts me right between the eyes. I say, "Oh Lord, how did this happen?" Turning one hundred was the worst birthday of my life. I wouldn't wish it on my worst enemy. Turning 101 was not so bad. Once you're past that century mark, it's just not as shocking.

There's a few things I have had to give up. I gave up driving a while back. I guess I was in my late eighties. That was terrible. Another thing I gave up on was cutting back my trees so we have a view of the New York City skyline to the south. Until I was ninety-eight years old, I would climb up on the ladder and saw those tree branches off so we had a view. I could do it perfectly well; why pay somebody to do it? Then Sadie talked some sense into me, and I gave up doing it.

Some days I feel as old as Moses and other days I feel like a young girl. I tell you what: I have only a little bit of arthritis in my pinky finger, and my eyes aren't bad, so I know I could still be practicing dentistry. Yes, I am sure I could still do it.

But it's hard being old, because you can't always do everything you want, exactly as *you* want it done. When you get as old as we are, you have to struggle to hang onto your freedom, your independence. We have a lot of family and friends keeping an eye on us, but we try not to be dependent on any one person. We try to pay people, even relatives, for whatever they buy for us, and for gasoline for their car, things like that, so that we do not feel beholden to them.

Longevity runs in the family. I'm sure that's part of why we're still here. As a matter of fact, until recently there were still five of us, of the original ten children. Then, Hubert went to Glory on December 28, 1990, and Hap, a few weeks later, in February 1991. That leaves me, Sadie, and Laura, our baby sister who moved to California with her husband.

Now, when Hubert died, that really hurt. He was just shy of ninety years old. It never made a bit of difference to me that Hubert became an assistant United States attorney, a judge, and all that. He was still my little brother.

Same way with Hap. You know what? Even when he was ninety-five years old, Sadie and I still spoiled him. When he didn't like what they were cooking for dinner at his house, he would get up and leave the table and come over here and we'd fix him what he liked to eat.

Good ol' Hap knew he was going to Glory and he was content. He said, "I've had a good life. I've done everything I wanted to do, I think I've done right by people." We Delanys can usually say that, when our time comes.

You know what I've been thinking lately? All those people who were mean to me in my life—all those *rebby boys*—they have turned to dust, and this old gal is still here, along with sister Sadie.

We've outlived those old rebby boys! That's one way to beat them! That's justice!

They're turning in their graves, while Sadie and me are getting the last word, in this book. And honey, I surely do love getting the last word. I'm having my say, giving my opinion. Lord, ain't it good to be an *American*.

Truth is, I never thought I'd see the day when people would be interested in hearing what two old Negro women have to say. Life still surprises me. So maybe the last laugh's on *me*. I'll tell you a little secret: I'm starting to get optimistic. I'm thinking: *Maybe I'll get into Heaven after all*. Why, I've helped a lot of folks—even some white folks! I surely do have some redeeming qualities that must count for something. So I just might do it: I just might get into Heaven. I may have to hang on to Sadie's heels, but I'll get there.

Discussion Questions

1. What roles do past and current social supports play in the Delaney sisters' current lives?

2. What effects do memories of past relationships have on their present lives?

3. How do the sisters' lifelong coping strategies enable them to deal effectively with their day-to-day lives now?

4. Despite having faced racial discrimination throughout their lives, the Delany sisters are relatively advantaged socioeconomically. What differences in their current lives would you expect had their education and opportunities been more limited earlier in their lives? What differences do you think their life courses might have taken had they been White and relatively advantaged socioeconomically?

Note

1. An issue-free Negro was a person who had some black ancestry but whose mother was a free person, not a slave.

Section III

Work, Retirement, and Income Security

Work is an integral part of most people's lives and one aspect of their identity. Like work, retirement is a social status, implying transition out of one formally recognized status, that of employed worker, into the ambiguous status of, retiree. "Retirement" encompasses several meanings: leaving paid employment; a new paid or unpaid career; and a stage within the life course. Unlike aging, an intrinsic characteristic of living beings, retirement is very much a social creation of industrialized society and does not exist in many less industrialized nations. Starting in the nineteenth century, creation of public and private pension plans enabled people to retire. Ending paid employment was induced or rewarded by pension payments, in part reflecting employers' beliefs that workers age 65 no longer were able to work efficiently or effectively. More recent research has shown, however, that age is not a significant factor for performance in many jobs (Waldman and Avolio 1986). Although mental and physical capacities such as speed, strength, visual acuity, and reaction time decline with age, these changes are small and may be balanced by greater experience and skill (Welford 1993).

A second, perhaps more significant, factor stimulating the creation of retirement incentives has been an ample supply of younger workers, who are often willing to work for less money. In 1935, when Social Security was enacted in the United States, the nation was in the depths of the Great Depression.

Providing public pensions encouraged older workers to leave the labor force to make room for younger workers. Social Security also reduced the likelihood that older workers would be financial burdens on their families. Older workers were no longer needed except as a reserve labor force.

Retirement thus has at least two functions. It both rewards the worker for a lifetime of labor and provides a tool for corporations and a society to manipulate the supply of workers. This section explores work and retirement further by examining participation in the labor force, retirement patterns, and income security in later life.

Ironically, as life expectancy has increased, age at retirement has decreased in the United States. Participation in the labor force decreases sharply for both men and women from about age 55. Two-thirds of men and half the women age 55 to 64 are either employed or seeking work, but relatively few of either gender are still working at ages 75 or over. According to the Bureau of Labor Statistics projections, in 2005 about 23 percent of all men age 65 to 74 and 8 percent of those 75 and over will be in the labor force. Comparable figures for women are 16 percent and 4 percent (Fullerton 1995). The labor force will also be more ethnically and racially diverse with Latinos, Asians, African Americans, and women representing a larger proportion than ever before (Sterns, Sterns, and Hollis 1996). But age discrimination continues, reducing both incomes and life

183

chances of millions of Americans. According to one report, one in seven people age 55 and over who were not working were willing to work but unable to find a suitable job (Commonwealth Fund 1993).

It is difficult to predict the future: whether older workers will be encouraged to continue in their current jobs, retrain for new jobs, seek part-time employment, or retire. Recent public policies, such as laws prohibiting mandatory retirement, can encourage the continued working life of older people. Recent Social Security changes that will raise the full-benefit age to 67 by 2022 may also reverse trends toward early retirement. The baby boom generation of workers is growing older and will be followed by a shortage of "baby bust" generation workers. To date, however, no consensus exists among either employers or employees about what older workers want, can, and should do. Employers agonize about the future cost of pensions; tax payers and politicians brood about the costs and solvency of Social Security; and employees worry about future postretirement benefits.

What can we learn from the work and retirement experiences of women, nonwhites, and the less affluent that will shed light on the relationships of power and privilege across the life course? Using retirement as an example, the selection by Toni Calasanti emphasizes the importance of diversity if we are to understand the lives of *all* old people. Basing retirement policies only on middle-class white male workers gives an unrealistic view of what retirement is like for others. Focus on the voices of elders with less authority, such as women, African Americans, and other traditionally powerless groups gives a more complete view of social reality than centering on the more influential and socially privileged. The experiences of African American working-class males are not those of working-class white males. Nor are their experiences those of African American working-class females, female members of the "black bourgeoisie," or white middle-class males. With the growth of a global economy, we must be attentive to international differences in the meanings of work and retirement if we are to have a more complete picture of old age.

During the past two decades in the United States, corporate downsizing, increased use of part-time and contract employees, automation, and less job security have created a climate where older workers are at high risk of losing their jobs to younger workers. According to a Harris survey, only one in eight of the 400 companies surveyed felt a need to respond to the aging of the labor force, and only one in three offered older workers opportunities to transfer to jobs with less responsibility (Administration on Aging 1999). In their selection, William Crown and Charles Longino turn their attention to labor-force trends in the United States and their consequences for future policy on the aging. Noting that the decision to retire reflects decisions at three levels—public policy, employment policy, and personal decisions made by employees and their families—they point out the interplay of these levels with population aging, technological change, and organizational decisions. Concern over the future of the Social Security retirement trust fund, coupled with an anticipated decline in the number of younger workers, should make older workers more attractive to employers. Yet employers continue to provide incentives that encourage older workers to retire, with the result that workers with adequate incomes may be more willing to accept lower incomes than to forego the leisure time that retirement promises. Public policies limited to Social Security modifications provide insufficient incentives to retain workers in the labor force, for policy makers, employers, and individual workers have distinct, often opposite, values, motivations, and goals.

The effects of workplace technology on the availability of jobs and on the need to update skills throughout the life course influence current and future employment and retirement policies. Lisa Hollis-Sawyer expands upon this theme in her selection, suggesting that greater attention be paid to the Age Discrimination and Employment Act and the Americans with Disabilities Act. Both pieces of legislation forbid overt discrimination on the basis of age or disability and urge employers to make "reasonable accommodations" to meet the special needs of older or disabled workers. When their jobs are finished or are overdemanding, older or disabled employees face a dilemma; they must either leave their current jobs or update their work skills if they are to avoid being fired or retired (Farr, Tesluk, and Klein 1998; Sterns and Camp 1998; Tepas, Duchon, and Gersten 1993). Rather than offer older workers incentives to retire, employers and human resource managers should ensure that the provisions of these laws are met. By modifying testing procedures and making work modifications designed to increase job tenure and job productivity, older workers' knowledge, skills, and abilities can be matched to the changing job demands of the twenty-first century.

Some workers, however, are trapped in jobs with no opportunity to learn new skills or to use what they know. This situation clearly will affect their income and opportunities in retirement. The ironic poem by Pedro Pietri describes the soul-deadening jobs held by many Puerto Rican Americans in New York City. Hindered by ethnicity or race, class, and sometimes gender, these people never realized the American Dream. Their jobs have been figuratively and literally dead ends where the last stop is the Long Island cemetery.

Although paid employment is part of many people's lives, rites of passage, or rituals, surrounding passage from the status of worker to retiree are few in American society. Joel Savishinsky in his selection discusses the absence of appropriate rites of passage that mark retirement. Using interviews with both men and women from various work backgrounds and social classes, he reports that retirees' feelings about impersonal, employer-sponsored, formal retirement ceremonies are generally negative. These "official" rituals are far less significant than informal rites, such as parties. Informal celebrations give the retiree chances to focus on personally meaningful people, personal interests, and dreams—choices markedly absent from "official" retirement observances. Informal retirement flings also enable people to voice their fantasies and discontents about their jobs. Travel, too, may be an informal rite of passage from worker to the retiree; a transition between an old and new stage of life.

The income situation of the elderly has drastically improved in the past few decades, and the extent of their poverty is less than that among the rest of the population. Nonetheless, a closer look shows pronounced economic disparities: women, African Americans, Hispanics, persons living alone, the very old, and elders living in rural areas are disproportionately poor. Ill-paid work affects retirement options for both men and women. Women are usually at a disadvantage. They are more likely to be concentrated in poorly paid job categories such as service industries and retail work. Shorter work histories and lower earnings affect their Social Security benefits and private pension coverage. Most obviously, women tend to have lower lifetime earnings than do men, owing to lower wages, less continuous participation in the work force, and fewer and shorter career ladders. Not only are Social Security benefits linked to wages but private pensions are least likely to be available in those occupations where women are disproportionately represented (Dressel, Minkler, and Yen 1997). Women workers are typically in jobs that do not provide private pensions and that do not pay enough for substantial IRA investments. Furthermore, for many women, retirement does not reduce the time spent in homemaking and may even increase it. Interestingly, compared to men, older women are more likely to have health problems but still outlive their husbands.

American elderly women living alone are especially vulnerable to poverty compared to women in other industrialized nations; such American women have a poverty rate five times higher than Canadian older women alone and more than 40 times higher than their counterparts in the United Kingdom and France (Burkhauser and Smeeding 1994). Moreover, while the economic position of elderly women in other nations has improved over the last decade or so, the relative position of American women has not. That a larger proportion of old women in the United States have lower incomes than in other nations reflects differences in pensions and means-tested programs—specifically, in other nations the greater availability of universal pensions, policies to divide pension credits equally between spouses, and means-tested supplemental benefit levels. Nor is the financial situation for elderly American women expected to improve in the next 30 years. According to one projection, by the year 2020, two out of five elderly women will be living on incomes of less than $9,500 in today's dollars and primarily dependent on Social Security and Supplemental Security Income.

Emphasizing the importance of the concepts of diversity and power relationships as they structure work and retirement across the life course are Studs Terkel's interviews with Jessie de la Cruz and Charles Hayes. Drawing attention to race, ethnicity, and economic disadvantage, Terkel has his respondents describe how their work histories and lives are interwoven with inequalities and with caring about others. The son of an African-American farm laborer, Hayes at age 76 is a former U.S. congressman from Chicago who has devoted much of his life before his congressional appointment to opposing discriminatory labor practices affecting minorities. De la Cruz, widowed and a former agricultural worker, was one of the first women organizers of the Farm Workers' Union. At age 74, she is, as she points out, "definitely not retired from life" and remains a union organizer and activist in the Mexican American community. Their stories highlight structural barriers they themselves have faced and that still remain, affecting the life chances of minority young people for education, employment, and economic security.

How do disadvantaged women fare in retirement? Katherine Allen and Victoria Chin-Sang address ways in which the context and meaning of older, working-class African-American women's past work histories structure their retirement life courses very differently from those of middle-class whites. Paid labor has long been a part of African-American women's lives. Hampered both by race and social class, they were forced to work. Although postretirement leisure in general has attracted scholarly and popular attention, relatively little is known about how poor, elderly African-American women spend their time. Retired from paid employment, they are free to enjoy leisure, an unaccustomed luxury enabling them to spend their time as they choose. Yet for these women, work is never done. The women described by Allen and Chin-Sang incorporate service to others as part of their leisure, despite one or more chronic health problems. For them retirement is not just liberation from toil; it is an opportunity to express an ethic of caring for others, an aspect of less affluent women's life that is not confined to women of color.

Kathleen McInnis-Dittrich in her selection discusses the plight of poor, rural, white Appalachian elderly men and women who have lived in poverty all their lives. In old age, their plight is worse. They have fewer connections to the labor force and throughout their lives have been handicapped by substandard housing, inadequate diets, and meager health care. Social classes of "haves" and "have nots," all of whom would be considered poor in another social context, further divide residents of Appalachia, creating fear and distrust of political and social institutions. Geographically isolated and fiercely independent, they rely on informal bartering and extended family support systems rather than public entitlements. Current social policies have failed to be sensitive to their unique situation. Both short-term and long-term solutions are needed. Short-term solutions can alleviate the needs of those who are old now, but long-term solutions are required if the cycle of poverty is to be broken for younger cohorts.

Early retirement, continued participation in the labor force, or late retirement are outcomes of the interactions among individual biographies, positions in social hierarchies, and structural factors in a specific sociocultural and historical context. Retirement is increasingly accepted as a predictable part of the life course in the United States. Individual, social, and political attitudes remain ambiguous and sometimes contradictory. Abolition of mandatory retirement discourages withdrawal from the labor force and also would reduce the Social Security and pension burden foreseen by some analysts. But age discrimination in employment continues. High levels of financial and social insecurity among both employed and unemployed older people persist, especially among women and people of color. The majority of elders remain members of a cheap reserve labor force.

As you read through the selections in this section, realize that American employment policies as well as budgetary priorities are characterized by conflicting social ideologies that color both social policies and personal beliefs about the value of work. Ours is a society based upon the work ethic—that work is valued as an end in itself. What is "owed" the elderly? The cultural construction of old age for both men and women in postindustrial society encourages elders to internalize their own limitations and to settle for less than their actual capacities (Philipson 1982) and shades attitudes about benefits and entitlements for work and retirement in later life. Americans are forming new social constructions of work and retirement in later life, but the development period is long and painful. How older Americans will fare in our economy and society in the future is allied to the social ideologies and economic decisions you and others will choose.

References

Administration on Aging, U.S. Dept. of Health and Human Services. 1999. *Age Discrimination: A Pervasive and Damaging Influence.* Washington, DC: U.S. Administration on Aging Fact Sheet (Internet www.aoa.dhhs.gov/factsheets/ageism.hml).

Burkhauser, R. V., and Smeeding, T. M. 1994. *Social Security Reform: A Budget Neutral Approach to Reducing Older Women's Disproportionate Risk of Poverty.* Policy Brief no. 2/1994.

Syracuse, NY: Syracuse University, Maxwell School of Citizenship and Public Affairs/Center for Policy Research.

Commonwealth Fund. 1993. *The Untapped Resource.* New York: Commonwealth Fund.

Dressel, P., Minkler, M., and Yen, I. 1997. "Gender, Race, Class, and Aging: Advances and Opportunities." *International Journal of Health Services* 27(4): 579–600.

Farr, J. L., Tesluk, P. E., and Klein, S. R. 1998. "Organizational Structure of the Workplace and the Older Worker." In K. W. Schaie, and C. Schooler, eds., *Impact of Work on Older Adults.* Societal Impact on Aging Series, pp. 143–206. New York: Springer.

Fullerton, H. N., Jr. 1995. "The 2005 Labor Force: Growing, but Slowly." *Monthly Labor Review* 118(11): 29–44.

Philipson, C. 1982. *Capitalism and the Construction of Old Age.* London: Macmillan.

Sterns, H. L., and Camp, C. J. 1998. "Applied Gerontology." *Applied Psychology: An International Review* 47(2): 175–198.

Sterns, A. A., Sterns, H. L., and Hollis, L. A. 1996. "The Productivity and Functional Limitations of Older Adult Workers." In W. H. Crowne, ed. *Handbook on Employment and the Elderly,* pp. 276–303. Westport, CT: Greenwood Press.

Tepas, D. I., Duchon, J. C., and Gersten, A. H. 1993. "Shiftwork and the Older Worker." *Experimental Aging Research,* 19(4): 295–320.

Waldman, D. A., and Avolio, B. J. 1986. "A Meta-Analysis of Age Differences in Job Performance." *Journal of Applied Psychology* 71(1): 33–38.

Welford, A. T. 1993. "Work Capacity Across the Adult Years." In R. Kastenbaum, ed. *Encyclopedia of Adult Development.* Phoenix, AZ: Oryx Press.

Chapter 17

Incorporating Diversity

Toni M. Calasanti [1]

One of the most important long-term effects of the social movements of the 1960s has been the entry of large numbers of minority men, working-class youth, and women of all races and ethnicities into higher education, and ultimately, academic research, who brought with them sets of experience, feeling, and belief very different from those of existing elites. These new viewpoints have challenged the dominant conceptual models of the social sciences, which until recently reflected the world as seen by whites, men, and the privileged. Hence, there is a new emphasis on "diversity," on taking into account the hierarchies of class, race or ethnicity, and gender. Can we learn something from the life histories of women, non-whites, and the less affluent that illuminates the relationships of power and privilege in the society as a whole?

In the following selection, Toni Calasanti shows how incorporating diversity into models of aging involves more than just including data on subpopulations (the "mix and stir" approach). Using retirement research as her example, she details how this broader brush produces a more complex and fluid picture of social reality, in which various strata engage in reciprocal interchanges. For example, remaining in the labor force involves very different costs and benefits for men and women and for people at different income levels. Some women can continue in the labor force because other, poorer, women care for their homes; some men are able to enjoy comfortable pensions because other men are in jobs that do not provide retirement benefits.

In addition to diversity within a society, we must also be aware of diversity among nations, especially in this era of a global economy.

Most other Western societies have social-welfare systems more supportive of women and the poor than does the United States. But as these nations, especially those of Eastern Europe, come under international economic pressure to reduce social spending, it is the elderly and women who will suffer most. As you read this selection, think about the concept of diversity and the distinction between diversity and heterogeneity. Consider why membership in one or another ethnic or racial group in relationship to the broader society matters in understanding later life. Notice how the experience of retirement is shaped by gender, class, race, and ethnicity. Pay attention to the different meanings these characteristics have for retirement in different societies.

In the last several years, "productive aging" has become a rallying cry for many gerontologists. However, "while almost everyone . . . seems to have heard and talked about productive aging and may have formed some opinions about it, does anyone really know what it means?" An affirmative answer still does not imply any *shared* understanding, as productive aging "frequently means many different things to as many different people" (Robinson, 1994; p. 33).

So too has been the fate of "diversity." Alternately upheld and vilified, it has often served as a banner to be adopted or rejected more on the basis of expedience or politics than shared understanding. While it will neither be a panacea for all social ills nor result in reverse discrimination, incorporating diversity into theory and research is, I believe, critical for enhancing the quality of life of *all* old people.

My present goal, then, is to consider, first, what it *means* to do research which incorporates diversity, and the importance of doing so. Next, I will discuss some ways diversity has been and could be incorporated into aging research. Here, I will focus on the power relations most commonly explored in the literature to date—predominantly racial/ethnic, gender, and class relations. I will begin by comparing diverse groups within the United States, and then move to discussion of the international-comparative level and old people's experiences across diverse welfare states. I will argue that gathering information on other countries uncovers structural and ideological processes which influence diverse aging and retirement experiences in the United States. Finally, I will discuss some of the implications that including diversity suggest for theorizing about aging.

Many theoretical perspectives speak to diversity. I will draw from feminist theories and research, particularly socialist-feminism, an approach I have treated more thoroughly elsewhere (Calasanti & Zajicek, 1993). While many of the ideas I present below are not unique to this perspective, areas of divergence may well exist. Throughout my discussion, I will be referring to similarities and differences among and within different populations, as it is through such comparison that both the existence and the social construction of diversity are revealed. And, for clarity and simplicity's sake, prior to my discussion of the international-comparative level, I will focus on the United States. Finally, while my comments apply to the field of aging in general, my examples will mainly draw from, and relate to, the work/retirement relationship.

The Meaning and Importance of Incorporating Diversity

Understanding the importance of incorporating diversity into aging research requires disentangling the word "diversity" from its various uses. For myriad, often political reasons, it has been widely adopted in sometimes atheoretical or contradictory manners. As a result, "diversity" is often devoid of *theoretical* meaning. This lack of conceptual clarity adversely affects knowledge and practice, as studies are rendered incomparable, or debates rage based upon miscommunication. Certainly, this has been true of other concepts. Gender, for example, has been—and continues to be—used to refer, variously, to essential sex differences, or women, or power relations. The differences among these meanings are enormous yet rarely made explicit.

Diversity or Heterogeneity?

Much confusion could be alleviated if we clearly distinguished between diversity and heterogeneity. Because both indicate differences among the old, there is a tendency to use these terms interchangeably. However, while they often focus on the same phenomena, diversity and heterogeneity represent different lenses and actually connote disparate sources of variations.

For example, gerontologists caution against generalizing to all those aged 65 and over as this population typically represents a 40-year age range: a potentially heterogenous group. Similarly, attempts to counteract ageism or ageist stereotypes often point to the heterogeneity of the old. In this context, when we warn that group stereotypes cannot be assumed to fit some or even most individuals, or that individuals "age" at different rates, we are talking about heterogeneity, not diversity. Heterogeneity, then, refers to individual-level variation.

By contrast, diversity, discussed more thoroughly below, refers to examining *groups* in relation to interlocking structural positions within a society. No doubt, some of the confusion surrounding these concepts is due to their interrelatedness. Certainly, heterogeneity among individuals may result from their diverse social locations. Further, awareness of individual differences—heterogeneity—within a particular racial/ethnic group could point to other structural sources of differences, such as gender relations. Obviously, we need to consider both heterogeneity and diversity, while not conflating the two. Recognition of the distinction between the two is emerging, as exemplified in recent attempts to examine both in relation to families and aging (Bengtson, Rosenthal, & Burton, 1990).

Content or Approach?

For many gerontologists the term "diversity" has until recently been equated with "gender," although among still other researchers, diversity has been taken to refer only to race/ethnicity. Empirical and theoretical challenges provided by women of color (such as Hooks, 1981; Thornton-Dill, 1983, among others), have led to the recognition of multiple bases of social privilege and inequality (Collins, 1990), including race/ethnicity, class, and, recently, sexual orientation. However, what is involved in recognizing diversity on these and other grounds is often still unclear.

A pervasive view is that incorporating diversity entails focusing on the situation, special problems, or experiences of some "special group." That is, diversity is taken to be synonymous with the *content* of a study. Indeed, a common justification for choosing research questions related to diverse groups has been allusion to their relative neglect in previous research. While descriptions of neglected groups are vital to knowledge formation, this does not address some critical, basic questions. Why has this group been neglected? And why does this matter? Why be concerned about, for example, racial/ethnic groups or relations in the first place? At issue is not merely "does race matter," but rather why membership in one racial/ethnic group rather than another matters. The answer cannot simply refer to socioeconomic correlates, or any others, for that matter; statistical relationships are only that and nothing more. Both African Americans and Mexican Americans have relatively high risks of poverty in retirement; if the importance of race/ethnicity is its relation to socioeconomic states, then why investigate these two groups separately? And why not just examine socioeconomic status?

Certainly, research that is sensitive to diversity involves comparison. However, examining similarities and differences across and within groups is only the method. Incorporating diversity involves more than content, or comparison. It provides a theoretical framework that is built upon the experiences of a particular group or groups as they are situated in the web of interlocking power relations. It therefore also involves theorizing about underlying relations. What I am suggesting, then, is a subtle but critical distinction in how we examine and interpret differences in our theories and research. Merely positing that the experiences of a racial/ethnic group are "different" places them in the category of "other"—a special "deviant" case—with the dominant group serving as the often unacknowledged "norm." By contrast, addressing *why* groups diverge places the dominant group in relation to oppressed racial/ethnic groups, and all in relation to one

another. For instance, *all* are seen to "have race"—"white" is also a "color"—and the experiences of one is understood only as it relates to the experiences of others.

For example, looking only at whites' experiences provides an incomplete view of retirement. Examining African Americans' experiences of retirement by seeing if they "match" those of whites tells us if and when they are "not white" but does not tell us what they are. Incorporating diversity, then, first requires that we investigate various racial/ethnic groups from their standpoint, privileging their knowledge (Andersen, 1995). When, how, and why oppressed groups differ is invisible when viewed through a privileged lens. Interpreting African American men's experiences from a typically white, middle-class, men's view of a work/retirement dichotomy or a "career" would not reveal that many working-class, African American men self-identify as disabled (Gibson, 1987). The second step, using the knowledge of racial/ethnic groups derived in this manner to compare to whites, exposes the racial/ethnic dynamics which shape aging experiences, including previously invisible aspects of the privileged group's experiences. For instance, it would reveal that whites' ability to identify as either retired or still in the labor force rests squarely upon the often unintentioned but structured domination of those racial/ethnic groups who have occupied secondary jobs, worked in the informal economy, provided cheap reproductive labor, and so on. Thus, critical aspects of the retirement matrix in *general* would be missed if we did not consider the racial/ethnic relations revealed when we include the experiences of oppressed groups.

Further, attending to African Americans' voices better illuminates racial/ethnic relations than listening to whites'. The oppressed are far more aware of the lives and views of the privileged, as social institutions express these, and of the processes through which dominance is maintained than vice-versa. The "outsider" is more able to see that which the "insider" takes for granted (Andersen, 1993, Collins, 1986).

Incorporating diversity, then, ultimately means broadening our knowledge of *all* groups (Andersen, 1993); uncovering and exploring the power relations constitutive of social reality stems from examining the similar and different experiences of a variety of groups. This comparative process is rendered even more complex by the dynamism and simultaneity of various power relations. That is, individuals experience their race/ethnicity, gender, class, and sexual orientation at the same time. For example, my experience as a woman in United States society is simultaneously an experience of being a white woman of a particular class and sexual orientation. I do not experience my gender first, with my race "added" to this. Thus, the effect of interlocking power relations on lives is most aptly described by allusion to a matrix (Collins, 1990). Privilege on one dimension is not "cancelled" or negated by oppression on another, nor are oppressions additive, resulting in "double" or multiple jeopardy (Markides, Liang, & Jackson, 1990).

The importance of incorporating diversity, then, rests on the realization that social reality, including our knowledge of it, is relational. Oppression only exists to the extent that privilege does, and vice-versa; beginning with the experiences of the oppressed is necessary for understanding those who are privileged, as well. It is not only the case that what it *means* to be a woman or a man is constructed in relation to one another, but embedded within these dynamic meanings are the inequalities that define the privilege of one as directly related to the oppression of the other. As social scientists who seek to understand social reality as it pertains to aging, then, we first recognize diverse experiences and meanings; unpack, or deconstruct, them to discover the social relations embedded within; and construct our theories and interventions accordingly. Our subsequent concepts are inclusive; they pertain to the whole picture, not just part. Incorporating diversity, then, is synonymous with being inclusive, and I use these phrases interchangeably.

Finally, using the term "oppressed" or its variants does not connote victimization or weakness. Instead, as noted above, it indicates a *social relationship*—to those who are privileged, i.e., possess unearned advantage by virtue of their social location (McIntosh, 1993). Thus, privilege also is not synonymous with intentionality.

Below, I provide selective examples from the area of retirement to help clarify the link between exploring diverse experiences and gaining a more complete knowledge of aging. In this discussion I assume that the work/retirement relation provides a context for understanding the retirement process for at least two reasons. First, the intersection of paid and unpaid labor over the life course shapes subjective and objective aspects of retirement. Second, the State and social policies influence such things as the timing of retirement, reentry, sources of retirement income, and retirement activities. Each of these may vary across diverse groups.

Diversity Within the United States and Knowledge Construction

Often, when we examine the influence of social structures and ideologies on aging experiences, we look to aging policy. In relation to retirement, for instance, an appropriate focus has been on retirement income policies and programs, such as the initial Social Security legislation and subsequent amendments, mandatory retirement laws, and regulations concerning age discrimination in employment. To a lesser extent, gerontologists have also considered workplace legislation and policies which, while not directed specifically at older workers, have an obvious impact. These might include mandates concerning types and amounts of benefits employers must provide; laws concerning part-time, temporary, and other forms of employment that are not full-time, year-round; and policies which influence labor supply in general.

Incorporating diversity broadens this focus considerably by making us aware that while such policies create barriers and opportunities for older workers and retirees, both the form and extent of their impact can vary considerably across diverse groups. Further, to understand these disparate effects often requires examining the influence of these and other policies over the life course. This latter point is not novel or unique to exploring diversity. However, sensitivity to oppressed groups shifts our focus to policies that we might otherwise ignore in relation to retirement as they do not seem to relate to the experiences of white, middle-class men (such as child-care provision or welfare legislation related to families). Equally important, it also makes us aware that, in fact, such policies do influence the work and retirement experiences of white, middle-class men. Child-care policies that restrict or enhance women's labor force participation influence men in myriad ways, facilitating or constraining their possibilities, in both the workplace and the home. Similarly, welfare legislation that limits or opens opportunities to engage in paid labor or to types of jobs is shaped by, and in turn shapes, race, class, or gender relations by challenging or maintaining workplace or familial practices.

Disparate retirement experiences point to processes through which gender, class, and racial/ethnic relations can affect objective and subjective aspects. To illustrate, I provide just a few examples of similar and different retirement experiences as these emerge among groups variously situated with the matrix of power relations. I begin by examining retirement in relation to some aspects of labor market experiences, broadening my focus to include domestic labor when I discuss more subjective dimensions. I then discuss some explanations of diverse retirement experiences that examine power relations and the State.

Diverse Retirement Experiences

Examining "objective" aspects of diverse retirement experiences exposes the gender, class, and racial/ethnic relations embedded therein. Beginning with gender relations, labor market inequality, such as the low wages that typically accompany "women's jobs," is reflected in the financial aspects of women's retirement. As of December 1994, retired men received an average monthly Social Security benefit of $785.24; same-status women garnered only $601.26 (Social Security Administration, 1995). Further, women's dependence on men, embedded in the Social Security Act (Rodeheaver, 1987), persists. The reproduction of gender relations in the family—and heterosexual norms—are apparent

in the observation that the combined benefits of dual earners still fall below those of male single-earner families of the same annual income (Burkhauser & Smeeding, 1994). Finally, women are far less likely to receive pensions than men (Quadagno & Harrington Meyer, 1990).

Considering the intersection of gender and race/ethnicity is even more revealing. In 1993, white men averaged $772.50 in monthly Social Security benefits compared to $588.60 for white women (Social Security Administration, 1994). Black men, who averaged $627.30 a month, were in a financial position similar to many white women; low wages received in secondary market occupations depress retirement incomes (Gibson, 1987; Social Security Administration, 1994). Exploring this similarity can expose particular interactions of racial/ethnic, class, and gender relations. A still different configuration of privilege/oppression is indicated by women's common and divergent retirement experiences. For example, white women have lower poverty rates than African American women due, in part, to their historical ability to exploit women of color (Glenn, 1992). In fact, African American women's average monthly Social Security benefits, $508.50 (Social Security Administration, 1994), are substantially less than white women's, despite their longer employment histories (Belgrave, 1988). In addition, both African Americans and Hispanics of either gender are less likely to receive pension benefits than white women (Gibson & Burns, 1991).

At a macro level, the recent bouts of recession and unemployment in the United States have influenced retirement decisions and resources of all. Old displaced workers remained unemployed longer than their younger counterparts and also received lower median weekly earnings when reemployed than they received in their prior job (Herz, 1990; Love & Torrence, 1989; Rodeheaver, 1990). Diversity existed among displaced workers, however. People of color experienced higher unemployment rates than whites; men of both races were more likely to be rehired than women; white women fared better than their African American counterparts (Amott &

Matthaei, 1991; Gibson & Burns, 1991; Kletzer, 1991; Zsembik & Singer, 1990).

While undoubtedly critical to retirees' lives, objective indicators, such as pension levels, do not tell us *how* they affect experiences. The "subjective" aspect of retirement involves retirees' construction of their lives: the descriptions, the interpretations, the *meanings* they attach to their experiences. In the wake of such phenomena as labor force reentry, researchers have become increasingly concerned with what constitutes retirement (Ekerdt & DeViney, 1990). Interestingly, the general approach seems to be to derive "objective" indicators that approximate some type of "fit" between such things as hours worked, part-time employment, temporary employment and the like, and a taken-for-granted notion of retirement.

Considering the ways diverse groups construct their retirement is critical in this regard. Gibson (1987, 1991) has already demonstrated that working-class black men do not identify themselves as retired as readily as their white counterparts. The "markers" white men use to form their "retired" identity are not as available. The life-long labor force instability that working-class, African American men experience blurs the work/retirement dichotomy. It also reduces the likelihood and amount of Social Security and pension receipt, two other "indicators" of retirement. Mexican American men and women share a similar propensity in this regard, no doubt partly due to their similar labor force experiences. At the same time, Mexican American men and women differ from one another, with men more likely to call themselves retired if they receive retirement income, while women tend to identify themselves in relation to their activities (Zsembik & Singer, 1990).

These divergent identities raise a number of related issues. First, they challenge the utility of trying to measure "retirement" along the "usual" dimensions. Second, they point to the exclusivity of the concept itself, as it assumes white, middle-class men's experiences: a stable work history, one that has a clear beginning and end, and is followed by retirement income. Overall, then, these discrepant identities question the notion of retirement itself. If, for example, researchers find a statistically significant "fit," what then would retirement *mean*?

My own research (Calasanti, 1993) suggests that white men and women both view retirement as "freedom from labor." Yet, what it *means* to equate retirement with freedom diverged, again revealing the matrix of power relations embedded within. To illustrate: Walter typified many of the men I interviewed. A white, working-class retiree, Walter described how much he enjoyed his opportunities to engage in new activities in the home. He learned to paint pictures by watching television shows; he began to produce his own wine. He especially liked to experiment with cooking when the mood struck him.

White, working-class retired women's expressions of freedom were similar to Walter's in that they conveyed a feeling of happiness with their expanded choices. At the same time, significant differences emerged. For instance, both Annie and Lois noted that they no longer felt that they had to do laundry on a particular day. Still others said that being retired meant they no longer had to stay up late at night to finish housework. As Lorraine put it, before she retired, her life was "rush, rush, rush;" in retirement, she could, "take my time . . . I don't have to rush" (Calasanti, 1993; p. 144).

In terms of their activities, these retirees were all engaged in domestic labor. But for Walter, his work was a matter of choice: while he might now define himself as a cook, he could choose to cook or not, without any obligation. In contrast, women's experiences of freedom were interpreted in terms of their double burden: experiencing less stress as, having lost one job, they had more time for the other. "Choice" for these retirees meant being free to select a different day to do domestic tasks (Calasanti, 1993).

In these examples, white, working-class men and women experienced retirement in similar and different ways. Similar expressions of freedom could well reflect their common class position; exploring disparities in what freedom meant to each uncovered the gender relations which define women as workers in the domestic realm. What is critical is not only that such disparities exist but understanding *why* they exist. One source of explanation is presented below.

Diversity: Theorizing Retirement Experiences at the State Level

Numerous social scientists have identified structural and ideological mechanisms through which the contemporary United States welfare state incorporates, reproduces, and reshapes power relations. A long tradition of political economic and Marxist investigations has concentrated on uncovering class relations, lately becoming more attuned to the contradictory nature of structural and cultural factors, historical context, and human agency (Quadagno & Fobes, 1995). Gerontologists too have found the lens of political economy to yield fruitful insights into the relationships among the State, classes, and aging (Estes, 1979; Myles, 1984). More recently, feminists and others have looked at the interactions between the welfare state and gender or racial/ethnic relations as well as the intersections of these power relations and class (for example, Orloff, 1993; Quadagno, 1994; Quadagno & Fobes, 1995). Although gerontologists have only recently discussed the need to examine aging within the context of a gendered and racialized State (Estes, 1991), promising analyses have begun to emerge, directing attention to the effects of *in*action—steps *not* taken—as well as State actions (Harrington Meyer, 1994).

Differences in men's and women's retirement experiences can be traced to androcentric and capitalist notions of work and production, as well as traditional ideas about the private sphere embedded in Social Security (Calasanti, 1993). Because production was defined as that which white, middle-class men do—paid work—reproductive labor was not the basis for calculating Social Security (Quadagno & Harrington Meyer, 1990; Scott, 1991). A similar androcentric bias, unchallenged by the State, helps explain why women are less likely to receive pensions: pension rules "naturally" reflect men's work and family lives, thereby penalizing women for reproductive labor (Quadagno, 1988). Yet, men's freedom to engage in paid labor generally depends upon women's reproductive ac-

tivities (Smith, 1987). Further, when the concept of productivity is expanded to include unpaid labor, research shows that women spend more time than men in productive activities throughout their lives (Calasanti & Bonanno, 1992; Herzog et al., 1989). As a consequence of the restricted meaning of production, however, women receive lower Social Security benefits.

Similarly, racial/ethnic and class relations were codified in the initial Social Security legislation which excluded occupations most often found among the poor and working classes and people of color. For example, farm and domestic service work, low-waged areas in which large numbers of racial/ethnic women found employment, were not covered until the 1950 and 1954 revisions to the Social Security Act (Amott & Matthaei, 1991; Scott, 1991). Further, as noted above, Social Security benefits assume the stable work histories most characteristic of white, middle-class men.

These disparities, based on industrial and occupational segregation and low earnings, have been further reinforced by State actions. The Job Corps, for instance, an anti-poverty program of the 1960s, ostensibly challenged power relations while simultaneously incorporating structural and ideological processes that reproduced the intersections of particular gender, class, and racial/ethnic inequities. Young African American men's job training provides some basis for challenging traditional labor market discrimination, but their female counterparts were taught skills that kept them firmly ensconced in paid and unpaid forms of domestic labor (Quadagno & Fobes, 1995).

Interestingly, when the intersections of gender and race/ethnicity are examined, the gender difference in productivity holds across whites and African Americans. Women in both groups engage in more productive labor, although the overall configuration of factors leading to such activity varies across racial/ethnic groups. Significantly, white men have the greatest number of enabling resources, yet they engage in less productive activity than black men or women of either racial/ethnic group (Danigelis & McIntosh, 1993). But because of the power relations embedded within Social Security, benefits actually reflect the reverse of these productivity levels.

Divergent retirement experiences reveal class dynamics and their complex and contradictory relation to the State. For instance, some point to the continued labor of retirees as an important indicator of "productive aging" (Robinson, 1994). However, retirees' experiences of this labor suggest that it is not necessarily the boon—either to them or society—that is typically portrayed. The reasons retirees give for employment, as well as the amount and type of "choice" they have in this regard, reflect the divergent social positions they occupy within the matrix of power relations. At the same time, these choices and activities are filtered through contradictory power relations at the State level (Calasanti & Bonanno, 1992). For example, the class dynamics involved in reentry into paid labor are evident in the types of jobs the old obtain. The well-publicized professional positions comprise the experiences of some, but the relatively low average hourly wages of "working retirees" testify to the job experience of the majority (Iams, 1987). Gender and racial/ethnic relations further intersect with class, as women have greater difficulty finding employment; gendered occupational segregation is reproduced; and white and African American working-class men and Chicano men and women appear to be most likely to reenter (Boaz, 1987; Gibson, 1987, 1991; Iams, 1987; Zsembik & Singer, 1990).

Contradictory power relations at the State level are implicated in the formal and informal labor experiences of retirees in numerous ways; here I elucidate just a few. The gendered, racialized, and class-based nature of Social Security benefits helps explain why working-class and particular racial/ethnic retirees are more likely to reenter paid labor. Their greater need for employment also underlies the differences in retirees' job experiences. Less obviously, class interests are evident in State actions that enable accumulation by facilitating the provision of low-waged labor, an experience in which ageism intersects with gender, class, and racial/ethnic relations. Legislation concerning part-time work, wages, and benefits make cheap labor a possibility; particular groups of old, defined by their marginalized social locations, are likely to be involved in its actualization. Further, the provision of *minimal* financial protection through Social Security and Supplemental Security Income makes minimum- or low-waged employment more viable, especially in combination with means testing. At the same time, "cheap labor" is a relative term; if legislation allows employers to side-step certain benefits, they could pay wages well above the minimum and still realize lower labor costs. This helps explain the ability of more privileged groups of retirees to engage in "consulting" or other higher-paid jobs that give them "extra money" they can use to maintain status (Calasanti & Bonanno, 1992). From this perspective, the State might be depicted as subsidizing low-waged labor and reproducing oppressive relations. Similarly, the extent of the informal economy, who participates, and what services and products are provided are greatly affected by the State and the power relations therein.

As I hope my examples have shown, analyzing diverse aging experiences within the United States reveals critical, previously hidden dimensions of social reality. Uncovering still other aspects rests on our ability to go beyond our taken-for-granted notions of the State itself. This challenge is facilitated by examining diverse experiences at the international level.

Diversity and Knowledge: International-Level Comparisons

What it means to incorporate diversity at the international level does not change so much as it becomes broader, involving additional analyses. It builds upon the widely acknowledged value of crosscultural research (Keith, 1990; Streib & Binstock, 1990), bringing a particular theoretical dimension to this comparative approach: a sensitivity to power relations both within and across countries. This implies two different units of analysis: diverse experiences within nations, my focus here, and states as they exist in a global context.

Diversity and the State: International Comparisons

To uncover further connections between the State, power relations, and experiences of aging in the United States, it is important to examine variations across unique political economies. Parallel to my earlier discussion, the United States cannot serve as the implicit "norm" against which other nations are compared. What is at stake is not only the problem of "judging" diverse structures and processes, but missing them altogether. Numerous studies of Middle Eastern society, for example, have typically portrayed women as having little power. However, because these investigations use Western, patriarchal notions of power and political activities and structures, researchers had missed the informal and familial-based forms of power wielded by women in these societies (Coles, 1990).

Further, fruitful international comparisons are contingent upon sensitivity to power relations *within* a country *prior* to cross-national comparisons. These relations themselves needn't be the research focus, but analysis should include them. For example, Zelkovitz (1990) examines different class relations, among other factors, to understand why and how Swedish aging policy avoids the "conservative bias" of other Western welfare states, such as the United States. His initial attention to the Swedish welfare system, without reference to others, allows him to uncover its "transformative" nature. Through comparison with the United States, he then demonstrates the vital importance of strong working-class representation in generating this policy posture.

Similarly, Coles' (1990) work has broadened the concept of power and its sources by uncovering the informal channels through which aging Hausa women in Nigeria exercise power. Further, she demonstrates that men's and women's power exist in relation to one another. Finally, she indicates the intersection of class and gender, noting that while wealth may increase a woman's power, it is not the only basis for it.

Considering diversity challenges us to (re)examine our assumptions concerning what actually *constitutes* a welfare state, and how this relates to actual and potential aging experiences of different groups. For example, in the Czech Republic, the move *toward* a capitalist welfare state means less social spending: a *retraction* of government support. An economic adviser to the Czech parliament spoke to the difficulties such policy changes entail for the government, as the Czech people were "used to a generous society." She further noted that the "old in particular say they don't like capitalism so well" (Procházková, 1994). For them, a welfare state is a "conservative" structure that is increasingly denying them their due as citizens of that country.

Essentially, exploring the power relations embedded in diverse aging experiences in other countries and comparing these to the United States renders at least two critical and related insights. First, it uncovers otherwise hidden processes of the present welfare state: aspects that are taken for granted or seen as intractable, including the ways in which systems of inequality are structured into its present workings. Importantly, this also opens up a wider range of alternatives to the status quo. Second, international variations in the expression of power relations forcibly remind us of their socially *constructed* nature at all levels of society, including the State. This also gives us the tools to unpack discourses supporting inequality, including those supportive of cuts in social spending for the old in general or particular groups of old.

Below, I offer my own and others' observations to demonstrate how international comparisons—examining diversity within and then across nations—offer critical insights into the dynamics through which power relations can influence retirement experiences.

Diversity and International Comparisons: Retirement in Central Eastern Europe

Exploring the impact of German reunification on the former East German women's pensions demonstrates the effects of different patriarchal forms on gendered retirement experiences. In the former East Germany, the extant political economy made the worker identity central. This identity remained male-defined despite the large numbers of women in the paid labor force. To simultaneously address labor shortages and a declining birth rate, contradictory policies developed to encourage women to combine work and motherhood. However, the work-related maternity "benefits" served to define and reinforce domestic labor as women's alone, thereby increasing their double burden. Further, the "special" treatment women received based on their domestic obligations also provided legitimation for workplace inequality (Ferree, 1993). In essence, within the work-centered society, women were penalized for their family status, and their workplace-defined pensions were relatively meager, given their predominantly low earnings. But they were also relatively uniform: the range was minimal. With unification and consequent changes that occurred under West German law, this range has increased dramatically. The greater disparities among former East German women are based on marital status: the patriarchal (and heterosexist) basis of West German law rewards women for marriage through higher pensions (Allmendinger, 1994).

These different pension experiences graphically illustrate varying intersections of patriarchy and political economies. Still other intersections of class and gender relations might well be revealed in comparing recent changes in Germany with another Western, advanced capitalist country. For instance, the assumption has been that State fiscal crises within such countries have led to welfare "retrenchment." Yet, partly in response to workers' pressure, Germany recently *expanded* provisions for care of the old, a task most often the purview of women.

The welfare expansion in Germany certainly challenges the "truism" that welfare state fiscal crises in general, and in the United States in particular, are largely a result of expenditures for "too many old." Further, numerous scholars have questioned this link, pointing to nations with demographic profiles similar to the United States but greater social spending for the old *and* strong economies (Butler, 1989). Examining some of the Central Eastern European countries pushes this challenge even further, standing the assumed connection between provision for an

aging population and economic crisis on its head.

Both the Czech Republic and Poland, among others, face enormous economic problems in providing pensions and other social programs for the old (Laczko, 1994). Yet, these countries are younger than Western nations (Velkoff & Kinsella, 1993). Of more importance than age in the Polish and Czech cases are the large numbers of pensioners, spurred by the increase in early retirement (Laczko, 1994). While the United States is experiencing a similar trend, the reasons for this phenomenon, as well as its gendered nature, show significant cross-national divergence.

Throughout Central Eastern Europe, the age for full pension eligibility is significantly lower than in the United States. The one exception is Poland, here men must wait until age 65. But prior to 1989, the Polish communist government encouraged early retirement to maintain full employment levels and depress wages. As an inducement, retirees faced no earnings tests; further, years of continued work were factored into future pension levels (Laczko, 1994). Additionally, gender relations in the domestic realm and pronatalist policies resulted in women's ability to collect full pensions at age 60, five years sooner than men, in "recognition" of their reproductive labor. Similar gender relations in the Czech Republic, where men can retire at 60, allow women who are childless to retire at age 57; one year is subtracted for each child born, up to four children. In these countries, then, the "burden of the old" on the welfare state is not as much a demographic phenomenon as a situation constructed by the State for political economic reasons (Calasanti & Zajicek, 1994). The fiscal problems faced by these countries arise from the intersections of the contradictions within their gendered political economies and ageism: the gendered "use" of old workers and retirees to maintain some aspects of the political economic system is negated by others. Similar conclusions based on divergent contexts have been made in relation to advanced capitalist nations of the West (Estes, 1979; Myles, 1984).

Comparing the similar and different bases for these assertions by exploring cross-national diversity both broadens our conception of political economy and sensitizes us to historical *context*, thereby maintaining a dynamic nature to our explanations. Importantly, it also enables us to deconstruct the rhetoric surrounding such issues as "the burden of the old" within a society. This is critical as such discourses define reality in such a way that possible "solutions" to "problems" are also delimited.

While cross-national comparisons enable some level of generalization, sensitivity to diversity prohibits formulations of "templates" that can be placed upon particular "types" of countries to "explain" aging experiences. Inability to derive such templates is, perhaps, disheartening to some. However, the dynamism and existence of variation points as well to the malleability of structure and ideology: to human agency and the always-present possibility of change.

Discussion: Incorporating Diversity and Theorizing About Retirement and Aging

As the previous examples illustrate, incorporating diversity reveals—or reinforces—several critical, related points about social aspects of retirement and aging that have a bearing on how we theorize these phenomena. First, they indicate the importance of *context*. The same observation—such as the extent to which women engage in paid labor—can simultaneously tell us similar and very different things about gender relations. For instance, Central Eastern European women who "return to the home" may well be oppressed. However, understanding the historical context renders a somewhat different reading of their return to domesticity: an act of resistance against the oppression of being "forced" to work for pay—it was the State's decision to "grant equality" to women by employing them, and not the result of a grass roots movement—and carry a double burden.

This relates to the second critical point—the importance of *agency*. Welfare states, ideologies, or other institutionalized forms of power relations are *not* deterministic; peo-

ple's actions can and do dramatically alter the roots and outcomes of these relations (Quadagno & Fobes, 1995). Indeed, this underlies the wide variation in experiences across groups and societies at any given point in time. The interaction between patriarchal ideology and structure in the Czech Republic was such that virtually the same "human capital" reasons were given to account for the similar gender gap in wages there as are given in the United States: women workers possess the wrong kinds or levels of skill, and their family obligations result in lower productivity. Yet, this explanation was given to justify the *low* pay of medical doctors—an occupation in which Czech women constitute the majority—and secretaries (Procházková, 1994).

The third point that examining diversity reveals is the *dialectical* nature of structures and ideologies. That is, they are *dynamic* and *contradictory* processes which significantly influence life-long experiences and retirement. Polish women's domestic return is an act of resistance and liberation; it is simultaneously oppressive, induced by capitalist and patriarchal ideologies and structures. It reinforces their economic dependence on men, and further limits their future options, especially in retirement (Calasanti & Zajicek, 1994). Similarly, poverty among the old in Central Eastern Europe is on the rise and will increasingly be a "woman's problem." Women in these countries receive lower pensions based on their lower wages and the contradictions within State pension policies. In the Czech Republic, the early retirement "reward" that women's reproduction earns carries a simultaneous penalty. Men retiring at age 60 can receive a maximum of 67 percent of their previous earnings. Women retiring at 57 can only receive 64 percent of their (already relatively lower) earnings. Their further "reward" for childbearing, the ability to retire one year sooner for each child, reduces this percentage: 63 percent for 1 child, 60 percent for 2, and so on.

Fourth, considering diversity is geared toward uncovering dimensions of social reality otherwise obscured by power relations; it is not a form of "victimology." That is, incorporating diversity is neither an effort to place groups on some sort of grid to decipher "who is most oppressed" nor does it seek to portray different groups as passive victims. If reality *is* dialectical, then situations and human actions have both oppressive and liberatory potential. Thus, if we are truly sensitive to diverse experiences, we will not only uncover forms of resistance but we will also, again, be compelled to foreground context. Context helps explain when and how one aspect might be more prevalent. For example, the oppressive situation for old Czech women also contains elements of potential strength. Given the child-care crisis, one of the few areas of informal labor open to these old women—care of grandchildren—represents a potential avenue for maintaining their status in the family not open to men.

Fifth, incorporating diversity implicitly calls us to consider the *historical* context. How and why the social reality of aging comes to be constituted in a particular way is contingent upon the confluence of the dynamics of various power relations at a specific point in time. Further, as the examples from Central Eastern Europe make clear, comparisons of similarities and differences in diverse aging experiences *over time* are an integral part of understanding the present constitution of power relations.

Finally, taking the standpoint of diverse groups as the starting point of our theorizing, as the notion of inclusion requires, returns *fluidity* to structures and focuses us on processes. That is, coming face to face with the contextual, dynamic, and social constructed aspects of the social world "de-reifies" the State and other social institutions. Social reality neither consists of deterministic structures nor is it the result of random processes. Rather, it is constituted by simultaneously dynamic and patterned processes that reconstitute and are shaped by permeable structures. Essentially, then, incorporating diversity restores the agentic element often missing from theorizing, without denying or losing sight of structure. Losing the rigidity that more static notions of social reality assume means that we cannot derive immutable "truths" about the social aspects of aging or retirement. Instead, our research redirects our attention to uncovering processes that both maintain inequality and are avenues for change.

Conclusion

Incorporating diversity compels us to begin with different aging experiences, using these as the basis for scrutinizing power relations at all levels as these influence the life course. It thus has the potential to provide gerontologists the theoretical tools that Marshall (1995) asserts are necessary for understanding present and future aging experiences.

Incorporating diversity refers to more than the content of a study. It is an approach to social reality that applies to and benefits *all* theorizing and research, including studies dealing with only one group—even if that group is composed of white, middle-class, heterosexual men in the United States. The critical difference between research that does and does not incorporate diversity is not necessarily which group(s) is investigated, but rather how. Being sensitive to diversity involves an awareness of lived experience as embedded in power *relations*: relations that are constituted by *both* oppressed and privileged groups. Because privileged groups have long served as the "norm," researchers often forget that their experiences are shaped by the same power dynamics as those who have been oppressed.

Being inclusive does not mandate that all research focus on differences and similarities across groups or simultaneously examine all power relations. It does, however, require acknowledging the unique configuration of a group within the matrix of power relations, being sensitive to the importance of these cross-cutting relations, and not making undue generalizations. The experiences of black working-class men, for example, cannot serve as a "proxy" for black working-class women, nor can the latter serve as a proxy for "black women of the bourgeoisie" (Giddings, 1984). At the same time, we can and should compare similar research across groups; indeed, this is an aspect of theory-building. But we need to bear other critical social relations in mind or risk losing critical parts of the picture as well as hampering theory-building by others.

In understanding diverse experiences within our own welfare state, I have stressed the importance of international comparison for understanding diversity as it enables us to situate experiences within variable state structures. The next step would be to examine diverse experiences within the context of global power relations. To the extent that the United States is able to exploit developing countries in particular ways, for example, different groups of elderly United States citizens will have both the access and ability to consume certain products. Further, with economic globalization has come the weakening of nation-states; increasingly social relations are analyzed within the context of "transnational" states (Araghi, 1995; Bonanno, 1994). Moving to the global level enabled Diamond (1992) to indicate the transnational political economic processes that influence both the race/ethnicity and gender of certified nursing assistants in long-term care institutions in the United States (Diamond, 1992).

The ideas I have presented concerning diversity are not themselves new, and many of the issues I have discussed are quite familiar to some. However, as we become increasingly specialized—between "theorists" and "practitioners," between "sub-areas" within aging, between levels of analyses—theoretical developments in one area are often not communicated to others, nor are linkages across areas as well developed as they could be. My goal, then, has been to facilitate this dialogue by discussing what diversity means, why it is vital to our efforts to understand and intervene in aging experiences, and how we might therefore incorporate this into our work.

Discussion Questions

1. How does Calasanti define "diversity" and "heterogeneity"?

2. Explain the statement "The 'outsider' is more able to see that which the 'insider' takes for granted."

3. Why might an elderly Polish woman office cleaner prefer the old communist regime rather than the new capitalist system?

4. What are the major effects of social class on the timing and meaning of retirement?

5. Can cross-national and historical comparisons enable us to disentangle such issues as the view that American "greedy geezers" are costing younger taxpayers money? If so, how?

Note

1. My sincere thanks go to my colleagues, Anna Zajicek, who commented on an earlier draft, and Rachel Parker-Gwin, with whom I discussed my thoughts. I am also grateful to Andrea Wilson and especially Barbara Townley for their help in manuscript preparation. Finally, I would like to acknowledge the support of Jill Grigsby, Jon Hendricks, Stephen J. Cutler, and Annamarie.

References

Allmendinger, J, (1994). "Discussant Comments, Symposium on Women's Retirement in Industrialized Countries." Meetings of the International Sociological Association, Bielefeld, July.

Amott, T. L., & Matthaei, J. A. (1991). *Race, Gender, and Work: A Multi-cultural Economic History of Women in the United States*. Boston, MA: South End Press.

Andersen, M. L. (1993). *Thinking About Women*, 3rd ed. New York: Macmillan.

Andersen, M. L. (1995). "From the Editor." *Gender & Society*, 9, 269–271.

Araghi, F. (1995). "Global Depeasantization, 1945–1990." *The Sociological Quarterly*, 36, 337–368.

Belgrave, L. L. (1988). "The Effects of Race Differences in Work History, Work Attitudes, Economic Resources, and Health on Women's Retirement." *Research on Aging*, 10, 383–398.

Bengtson, V., Rosenthal, C., & Burton, L. (1990). "Families and Aging: Diversity and Heterogeneity." In R. H. Binstock & L. K. George (Eds.), *Handbook of Aging and the Social Sciences* (pp. 263–287). San Diego: Academic Press.

Boaz, R. F. (1987). "Work as a Response to Low and Decreasing Real Income During Retirement." *Research on Aging*, 9, 428–440.

Bonanno, A. (Ed.). (1994). *From Columbus to ConAgra: The Globalization of Agriculture and Food.* Lawrence: University of Kansas Press.

Burkhauser, R. V., & Smeeding, T. M. (1994). *Social Security Reform: A Budget Neutral Approach to Reducing Older Women's Disproportionate Risk of Poverty.* Policy Brief No. 2., Syracuse University: Center for Policy Research.

Butler, R. N. (1989). "Dispelling Ageism: The Cross-cutting Intervention." *Annals of the American Academy of Political and Social Science*, S03, 138–147.

Calasanti, T. M. (1993). "Bringing in Diversity: Toward an Inclusive Theory of Retirement." *Journal of Aging Studies*, 7, 133–150.

Calasanti, T. M., & Bonanno, A. (1992). "Working 'Over-time': Economic Restructuring and Retirement of a Class." *The Sociological Quarterly*, 33, 135–152.

Calasanti, T. M., & Zajicek, A. M. (1993). "A Socialist-feminist Approach to Aging: Embracing Diversity." *Journal of Aging Studies*, 7, 117–131.

Calasanti, T. M., & Zajicek, A. M. (1994). "Economic Restructuring in Poland and Retirement Experiences". Paper presented at the meetings of the International Sociological Association, Bielefeld, July.

Coles, C. (1990). "The Older Woman in Hausa Society: Power and Authority in Urban Nigeria." In J. Sokolovsky (Ed.), *The Cultural Context of Aging* (pp. 57–81). New York: Bergin S. Garvey.

Collins, P. H. (1986). "Learning from the Outsider Within: The Sociological Significance of Black Feminist Thought." *Social Problems*, 33, S14–S31.

Collins, P. H., (1990). *Black Feminist Thought: Knowledge, Consciousness, and the Politics of Empowerment.* Boston: Unwin Hyman.

Danigelis, N. L., & McIntosh, B. R. (1993). "Resources and the Productive Activity of Elders: Race and Gender as Contexts." *Journal of Gerontology: Social Sciences*, 48, S192–S203.

Diamond, T. (1992). *Making Gray Gold: Narratives of Nursing Home Care.* Chicago: University of Chicago Press.

Ekerdt, D. J., & DeViney, S. (1990). "On Defining Persons as Retired." *Journal of Aging Studies*, 4, 211–229.

Estes, C. (1979). *The Aging Enterprise.* San Francisco, CA: Jossey-Bass.

Estes, C. L. (1991). "The New Political Economy of Aging: Introduction and Critique." In M. Minkler & C. L. Estes (Eds.), *Critical Perspectives on Aging: The Political and Moral Economy of Growing Old* (pp. 19–36). New York: Baywood.

Ferree, M. M. (1993). "The Rise and Fall of Mommy Politics: Feminism and Unification of (East) Germany." *Feminist Studies*, 19, 89–115.

Gibson, R. C. (1987). "Reconceptualizing Retirement for Black Americans." *The Gerontologist*, 27, 691–698.

Gibson, R. C. (1991). "The Subjective Retirement of Black Americans." *Journal of Gerontology: Social Sciences*, 46, S204–S209.

Gibson, R. C., & Burns, C. J. (1991). "The Health, Labor Force, and Retirement Experiences of Aging Minorities." *Generations*, 15, 31–35.

Giddings, P. (1984). *When and Where I Enter: The Impact of Black Women on Race and Sex in America.* New York: Bantam Books.

Glenn, E. N. (1992). "From Servitude to Service Work: Historical Continuities in the Racial Division of Paid Reproductive Labor." *Signs: Journal of Women and Culture in Society*, 18, 1–43.

Harrington Meyer, M. (1994). "Gender, Race, and the Distribution of Social Assistance: Medicaid Use among the Frail Elderly." *Gender & Society*, 8, 8–28.

Herz, D. E. (1990). "Worker Displacement in a Period of Rapid Job Expansion: 1983–87." *Monthly Labor Review*, 133, 21–33.

Herzog, A. R., Kahn, R. L., Morgan, J. N., Jackson, J. S., & Antonucci, T. C. (1989). "Age Differences in Productive Activities." *Journal of Gerontology: Social Sciences*, 44, S129–S138.

Hooks, Bell. (1981). *Ain't I a woman: Black Women and Feminism.* Boston: South End Press.

Iams, H. M. (1987). "Jobs of Persons Working After Receiving Retired-worker Benefits." *Social Security Bulletin*, 50, 4–19.

Keith, J. (1990). "Age in Social and Cultural Context. Anthropological Perspectives." In R. H. Binstock & L. K. George (Eds.), *Handbook of Aging and the Social Sciences* (pp. 91–111). San Diego: Academic Press.

Kletzer, L. G. (1991). "Job Displacement, 1979–86: How Blacks Fared Relative to Whites." *Monthly Labor Review*, 114, 17–25.

Laczko, F. (1994). *Older People in Eastern and Central Europe: The Price of Transition to a Market Economy.* London: HelpAge International.

Love, D. O., & Torrence, W. D. (1989). "The Impact of Worker Age on Unemployment and Earnings After Plant Closings." *Journal of Gerontology: Social Sciences*, 44, S190–S195.

Markides, K., Liang, J., & Jackson, J. S. (1990). "Race, Ethnicity, and Aging: Conceptual and

Methodological Issues." In R. H. Binstock & L. K. George (Eds.), *Handbook of Aging and the Social Sciences* (pp. 112–129). San Diego: Academic Press.

Marshall, V. W. (1995). "The Next Half-century of Aging Research—and Thoughts for the Past." *Journal of Gerontology: Social Sciences*, 50B, S131–Sl33.

McIntosh, P. (1993). "White Privilege and Male Privilege: A Personal Account of Coming to See Correspondences Through Work in Women's Studies." In M. L. Andersen & P. H. Collins (Eds.), *Race, Class, and Gender*, 2nd ed. (pp. 76–87). Belmont, CA: Wadsworth.

Myles, J. (1984). *The Political Economy of Public Pensions*. Boston: Little, Brown, and Company.

Orloff, A. (1993). "Gender and the Social Rights of Citizenship: The Comparative Analysis of State Policies and Gender Relations." *American Sociological Review*, 58, 303–328.

Procházková, E. (1994). Special Counselor in Economic Policy, Parliament of the Czech Republic. Personal conversation, Prague, July.

Quadagno, J. S. (1988). "Women's Access to Pensions and the Structure of Eligibility Rules: Systems of Production and Reproduction." *The Sociological Quarterly*, 29, 541–558.

Quadagno, J. (1994). *The Color of Welfare: How Racism Undermined the War on Poverty*. New York: Oxford University Press.

Quadagno, J. S., & Fobes, C. (1995). "The Welfare State and the Cultural Reproduction of Gender: Making Good Girls and Boys in the Jobs Corps." *Social Problems*, 42, 171–190.

Quadagno, J. S., & Harrington Meyer, M. (1990). "Gender and Public Policy." *Generations*, 14, 64–66.

Robinson, B. (1994). "In Search of Productive Aging: A Little Something for Everyone." *Ageing International*, 21, 33–36.

Rodeheaver, D. (1987). "When Old Age Became a Social Problem, Women Were Left Behind." *The Gerontologist*, 27, 741–746.

Rodeheaver, D. (1990). "Labor Market Progeria." *Generations*, 14, 53–58.

Scott, C. G. (1991). "Aged SSI Recipients: Income, Work History, and Social Security Benefits." *Social Security Bulletin*, 54, 2–11.

Smith, D. (1987). *The Everyday World as Problematic: A Feminist Sociology*. Boston: Northeastern University Press.

Social Security Administration. (1994). *Annual Statistical Supplement, 1994*. Washington, DC: U.S. Government Printing Office.

Social Security Administration. (1995). *Social Security Bulletin*, 58(l).

Streib, G. F., & Binstock, R. H. (1990). "Aging and the Social Sciences: Changes in the Field." In R. H. Binstock & L. K. George (Eds.), *Handbook of Aging and the Social Sciences* (pp. 1–16). San Diego: Academic Press.

Thornton-Dill, B. (1983). "Race, Class, and Gender: Prospects for an All-inclusive Sisterhood." *Feminist Studies*, 9, 131–150.

Velkoff, V. A., & Kinsella, K. (1993). *Aging in Eastern Europe and the Former Soviet Union*. Washington, DC: U.S. Government Printing Office.

Zelkovitz, B. M. (1990). "Transforming the Middle Way: A Political Economy of Aging Policy in Sweden." In J. Sokolovsky (Ed.), *The Cultural Context of Aging* (pp.163–180). New York: Bergin S. Garvey.

Zsembik, B. A., & Singer, A. (1990). "The Problem of Defining Retirement Among Minorities: The Mexican Americans." *The Gerontologist*, 30, 749–757.

Chapter 18
Labor Force Trends and Aging Policy

William H. Crown and Charles F. Longino, Jr.

Is there some neat formula that would allow us to predict the likelihood of a person's retirement? Employers and legislators have considered policies that in theory would encourage or discourage a worker from leaving the workforce. Yet, short of mandatory retirement, which was effectively reduced by the 1978 Amendments to the Age Discrimination in Employment Act, such manipulations are only partially effective. This is so because of the sheer number of factors that enter into the equation—primarily one's own health and that of family members, financial situation (a function of lifetime employment history), and the influence of significant others—but each of these has also been profoundly affected by race, ethnicity, sex, education, marital status, and place of residence. And we have not even mentioned qualitative factors such as work satisfaction and alternative sources of well-being.

William Crown and Charles Longino examine several of these factors as they relate to three levels of policy making: by government, by employers, and interpersonal. They note the push-and-pull of demographic forces intersecting with policy. For example, firms have an interest in cutting costs through downsizing or early-retirement incentives for older, less productive workers, yet one of the proposals to shore up the Social Security system has been to raise the age of eligibility. The employer benefit pushes you out; Social Security policy pulls you back. But not everyone enjoys a private pension or retirement benefits; these are available primarily to upper-level employees, disproportionately male and White. Most women and minority men in the labor force have no such additional financial resources, depending almost exclusively on their Social Security benefits. As you read the following selection, think about the possible results of changing the age of eligibility. Will the result then be a two-tiered system in which the well-off can choose their time of retirement, while the majority of those who labor in relatively unrewarding jobs are forced to remain at work?

How workers make decisions about when to retire is enormously complex. They are influenced by retirement incentives and disincentives in Social Security and private pension plans, by their own health status, by the retirement decisions of their spouses, the level of their earnings, the meaningfulness and intrinsic satisfaction they derive from their work and many other factors. Employers and public policy makers who attempt to alter the timing of retirement decisions invariably are able to influence only a portion of the total set of factors that enter into the retirement decision. Nonetheless, the incentives and disincentives of Social Security and pension income are a large lever and must be examined in creative ways.

One only has to glance at the age structure of the U.S. population to understand why there is a growing interest in the connection between labor force trends and future aging policy. It has to do with the Social Security Retirement Trust Fund and the concern that the imminent retirement of the baby boom generation will put a difficult if not impossible burden on the system. Policymakers, therefore, have an obvious interest in mechanisms that encourage older workers to stay in the labor force.

Several demographic trends currently under way could cause older workers to become more attractive to employers over the next several decades. Of these, population aging is the most frequently cited as leading to a future growth in demand for older workers. In fact, several studies in the 1980s pointed to increased demand for older workers because of an anticipated decline in the number of young, new labor force entrants.

However, this simple equation assumes that population is the only dynamic factor affecting employment. In reality, change is also operating in the technological and organizational dimensions, and all three stand in an interdependent relationship to one another in the workplace.

Technological change is as obvious to an untrained observer as is the aging of the population, and it has had a significant impact on labor force trends. The wave of information technology that has washed over the workplace during the past decade was only the most recent technological change to affect the workforce. For more than a century, the response of employers to increased labor costs has been the replacement of workers by more efficient ways of getting work done. Machines have played a large part in this process.

The aging labor force may be at odds with the increased training needed for taking advantage of technological innovations. In the face of rapid technological change at work, older workers may find their skills increasingly obsolete, thereby decreasing their value to employers.

Most employers are concerned about the higher costs and lower productivity of older workers relative to younger workers. The evidence to date indicates that, indeed, older workers are more expensive than younger workers, and there is no strong evidence that older workers are also more productive, Consequently, it is not surprising that most employers remain more concerned with structuring incentives for older workers to retire than with encouraging them to remain in the labor force.

Early retirement incentive programs (ERIPS) developed in the late 1970s and early 1980s have become a popular way for employers to reduce their personnel costs without exposing themselves to charges of age discrimination. The return of sluggish economic growth during the late 1980s and early 1990s, along with continued computerization of work, stimulated labor force reductions in many industries. Downsizing was accomplished largely by ERIPS, which worked in concert with private pensions to augment income and perhaps health benefits of retir-

ees to the point where they could begin receiving Social Security benefits and Medicare.

Interest in increasing labor force participation by workers of retirement age has been keener among public policy analysts than among employers. The 1983 Social Security amendments contained several provisions designed to encourage later retirement. Smaller than anticipated effects of these amendments, however, may stem from the health and economic status of early retirees.

Individuals with health limitations may have little flexibility in the timing of retirement. As a result, the increased actuarial penalties for early retirement will have the effect of lowering their retirement incomes. Many older workers with adequate incomes may not delay their retirement even though the policy disincentives for early retirement have the effect of lowering their incomes somewhat. For these workers the economic disincentives are outweighed by the desire to consume more leisure time.

On the other hand, raising the normal retirement age may have a comparatively large effect on encouraging the increased labor force participation of low-income older workers, many of whom may be compelled to continue working until they reach the new (higher) normal retirement age in order to obtain a more adequate retirement income. These considerations, of course, raise serious equity issues.

Public policy focusing on Social Security alone may not be sufficient to reverse early retirement trends. A combination of Social Security and private pension incentives may be especially important in inducing delayed retirement. The age at which pension wealth can be drawn by employees, for example, at least by those who cannot claim a health disability, can be raised through public policy embodied in government regulations. In addition, public policy that increases the cost of early retirement incentives for employers, whatever the mechanism employed, would serve to reinforce the retirement disincentives of the Social Security amendments for workers.

Public policy focusing only on Social Security amendments may not be enough to fulfill the goal of keeping older workers in the labor force until age 65 or later. Coordinating policy at the public, the employer and the individual levels, however, is a little like trying to herd cats. Each has its own set of goals, values and motivators.

Discussion Questions

1. Which factors would have greatest impact on your decision to retire and why?

2. How can employers encourage workers to stay or go?

3. Discuss the implications of current demographic trends for older workers.

4. In what ways would retirement decisions vary by sex and race?

5. What workplace conditions would have the strongest effect on the decision to retire?

Reprinted from: William H. Crown and Charles F. Longino, Jr., "The Implications for Future Aging Policy." In *Critical Issues in Aging*, 1, Fall 1997, pp. 16–17. Copyright © 1997 by The American Society on Aging, San Francisco, CA. Reprinted by permission.

Chapter 19

Reasonable Accommodation in the Workplace

Lisa A. Hollis-Sawyer

Although there are many supporters of capitalism who would claim that it is unfair to ask employers in the private sector to make special adaptations to retain older or disabled workers, in 1967 the United States Congress, recognizing the political power of older Americans, enacted the Age Discrimination in Employment Act. The mid-1960s, unlike the past three decades, was a period of legislative activism on behalf of the elderly in general, including liberalization of Social Security benefits and the establishment of Medicare. It was not until 1990 that a similar effort was mounted on behalf of disabled people of any age, leading to the passage of the Americans with Disabilities Act. As their titles indicate, both pieces of legislation prohibit overt discrimination on the basis of age or disability and urge employers to make "reasonable accommodations" to meet the special needs of older or handicapped workers.

In the following selection, Lisa Hollis-Sawyer details the many accommodations that employers and human resource managers can use to ensure fairness in testing, as well as modifications in the work environment that would enhance productivity. Such suggestions assume that employers are willing to make these changes, some of which could place them at a competitive disadvantage by increasing production costs. Given the very tight labor market at the present, employers may well be able to afford the expense; a trained and loyal employee would be far less costly than a new hire at competitive wages. But what if the economy drifts into recession and unemployment rates rise, or if younger and cheaper workers flood the labor market? Think about how deep the

nation's commitment to its older and disabled workers is. Consider who judges what is fair and by what criteria. How would you run your factory? Appraise these questions and how you would answer them as you read this selection.

How can employers and human resource managers maximize the fit between the needs and abilities of a graying work force and the job needs and requirements in an increasingly technological work environment? Focusing on this issue, the following analysis examines the role of two employment-related pieces of legislation: the Age Discrimination and Employment Act (ADEA) and the Americans with Disabilities Act (ADA). Through this analysis, it is possible to delineate employers' and human resource managers' dilemmas regarding career work life extension policies in the workplace and to suggest "test-fair" procedures for job testing of older workers.

Organizations are becoming increasingly aware of the need to pay attention to heterogeneity and diversity and their impact on human resource management practices. An often overlooked heterogeneous group is the rapidly growing proportion of older workers in the labor force. To safeguard the participation of older adults in the workforce, the Age Discrimination in Employment Act of 1967 prohibits discrimination in selection and other personnel decisions on the basis of an individual's age (Snyder and Barrett, 1988). To avoid age discrimination, organizations should utilize selection devices and procedures that accurately assess job-related performance capabilities in order to identify qualified workers regardless of age (Arvey and Mussio, 1973; Sterns and Alexander, 1987). To ensure fair assessment procedures, employers should review tests and selection devices to ensure that they are appropriate to administer to older adults.

Although the differential validity of tests for minority and non-minority candidates has been frequently studied (see, for example, Hunter, Schmidt, and Hunter, 1979), only more recently have researchers begun to examine potential problems of validity in testing older adults (Sterns and Barrett, 1992). While research-based overviews of testing issues relevant to older adults have begun (Lindley, 1989; Hertzog and Schear, 1989), accurate testing of older adults remains an issue for employers and managers.

Many testing factors interact with age and affect performance. Performance on many tests may be multidimensional; that is, tests tap more than one ability. Consider, for example, a typical test of mathematical ability, reasoning or knowledge. Many mathematics or quantitative tests also involve a reading component and tend to be highly speeded, requiring test takers to complete a large number of problems in a limited time. Administration factors also affect performance: for example, whether calculators can be used. These two examples are just part of a series of considerations that potentially affect the test performance of older adults.

In this article, I review relevant age changes and discuss how these characteristics interact with test factors. In discussing age related changes, it is useful to distinguish three types: developmental changes, cohort effects, and non-normative changes.

Developmental Changes

Test performance often involves multiple cognitive process components, as when mathematics tests also require related abilities such as reading, short-term and long-term memory. The degree to which reading or memory is important will vary, as will the job relatedness of reading and memory. However, if the major concern is with testing mathematics knowledge, the effects of additional factors should be controlled in some way.

Why the measurement of additional, non-job-related abilities should be of concern becomes more apparent when one considers possible age-related declines in test taking performance which could represent a decrease in the ability that the test was designed to measure or predict (Hertzog and Schear, 1989). Furthermore, each component or dimension has an associated weight to predict the test score. If the test component(s) related to age declines are given more weight in test score prediction, older adults will probably perform worse on the test.

A related question is whether the test component(s) receiving more weight are job-related. If a test component associated with greater age related decline is also less related to job relevant abilities, age bias is present in the testing. Older workers who have a deficit in one component ability, such as decreased ability to access long-term memory, during the testing process could ameliorate the effect of this ability decline on the job by using a compensatory strategy, such as a notebook or computer to store numbers or formula

Speed

Another factor entering into mathematics testing is speed, although speed in performing quantitative operations is not always related to the requirements of a specific job. In general, older adults experience a relative slowing in reaction time that can be partially offset by experience (Cerella, 1990; Salthouse, 1985). Thus a major concern when testing older adults is the possible effect of speed on testing, including both the speed at which the test is presented and at which responses are required. Apparent age declines in test performance can be decreased if speed is controlled statistically. Unless related to job-specific variables, tests should be designed to allow sufficient time both in processing test items and in responding thereto (Hertzog and Schear, 1989; Lindley, 1989).

Vision

Age-related vision declines can impair the test performance of older adults. High levels of visual acuity are often required on tests involving rapid scanning of material or that use relatively small print in test materials. Accordingly, attention should be paid to test layouts, including font size and placement and space of response grids. Vision is also affected by age-related reductions in the ability of the eye to adapt to changes in lighting and to glare, as well as reduced ability to discriminate brightness and color.

Other Environmental Factors

It is possible that older adults become more fatigued during long testing sessions and more susceptible to environmental conditions, such as extreme heat and air quality, than do younger test takers. Thus additional environmental factors to be considered in the design or selection of administration sites include having shorter testing sessions rather than a few long ones and reducing distracting, irrelevant information, including extraneous noise (Hertzog and Schear, 1989; Lindley, 1989).

Cohort Effects

Cohort effects reflect historical and cultural differences rather than aging effects. For example, we might expect a group of 40 year olds to outperform a group of 20 year olds on a mathematics test requiring the use of a slide rule. If we were developing an intelligence test similar to the WAIS information subtest,[1] we would expect 20 year olds to outperform on questions about members of the Rock and Roll Hall of Fame. It is thus important to design the contents of a test to avoid creating an advantage or disadvantage for specific age cohorts. However, not all job-related cohort effects can or need be minimized. For example, if a specific job requires that typing be done on a word processor, it would be illogical to require all applicants to take a typing test on a manual typewriter in order not to hamper older applicants!

Non-normative Changes

Non-normative aging effects, such as a physical disability due to a work-related accident, can affect performance. Although few older individuals are disabled, their incidence of disability due to accidents is higher than that of younger workers (Sterns and Barrett, 1992). In addition, some older job applicants and employees may have a non-work related disability, such as arthritis, mild hearing loss, and so on, that would not impair their performance on specific jobs.

In selecting workers, regardless of age, the question that arises in personnel selection is whether a candidate's disability would have a potentially negative effect on his or her performance on a selection test, even though that same person could perform the "essential functions" of the job with or without "reasonable accommodation." Although not specifically focusing on older workers, the passage of the Americans with Disabilities Act of 1990 (ADA) ensures fair selection practices and employment opportunities for adults, regardless of age, who wish to participate in the workforce. The ADA thus specifically prohibits discrimination against "qualified" disabled applicants, including older workers.

Conclusion

A diverse workforce will include older workers as applicants, trainees, and entry level workers and not just long-term experienced employees. Since the Age Discrimination and Employment Act prohibits discrimination in the workplace against any individual on the basis of age, organizations and assessment professionals should be aware of ways to reduce the possibility of age bias in the selection processes and subsequent personnel decisions (Sterns and Alexander, 1987). Practitioners in the field of personnel assessment need to ensure that selection tests are designed and implemented to identify the abilities or strategies that are essential to the job for which testing is being conducted. A selection test (or tests) and the testing process must be job relevant, valid, and reliable, able to distinguish the most qualified candidate(s) for a position without regard to age-related but job-irrelevant test performance factors.

In designing age-sensitive tests and testing environments, the following suggestions are offered:

1. Tests should be reliable and valid, measuring job-related knowledge, skills, abilities, or behaviors.

2. Careful attention should be paid to the test contents, ensuring that only job-related abilities are being measured.

3. Test information should avoid cohort or generational effects unless the knowledge is specific to the job requirements.

4. Testing sessions should be designed to allow sufficient time to process and respond to items.

5. Attention should be paid to the layout of the test including such issues as font size, placement and size of response grids, and quality of copying.

6. Attention should be paid to the testing site environment to reduce extraneous

factors that can reduce test performance, such as poor lighting, inadequate temperature control, and faulty noise control.

7. Adequate rest breaks should be provided; that is, batteries should be designed so that there are several shorter testing sessions rather than one long one.

8. Policies should be developed to provide "reasonable accommodations" for people with disabilities.

Discussion Questions

1. As the twenty-first century opens, what might be some new job-related knowledge or skill issues for workers across the life course?

2. What age by race and age by gender interaction issues affect efforts by employers and human resource managers to help qualified older workers stay active?

3. Describe how one's cohort can affect testing results.

4. More than ever before, the population is living longer. How will future workplace design be affected if the average (mean) age of the workforce continues to increase?

Note

1. The WAIS is a commonly used measure of intelligence in adults and comprises many subtests.

References

Arvey, R. D., & Mussio, S. J. (1973). "Test Discrimination, Job Performance, and Age." *Industrial Gerontology*, 16, 22–29.

Cerella, J. (1990). "Aging and Information-processing Rate." In J. E. Birren and K. W. Schaie (Eds.), *Handbook of the Psychology of Aging*, 201–221. New York: Springer.

Hertzog, C., & Schear, J. M. (1989). "Psychometric Considerations in Testing the Older Person." In T. Hunt and C. J. Lindley (Eds.), *Testing Older Adults* (pp. 24–50). Austin, TX: Pro-ed.

Hunter, J. E., Schmidt, F. L., & Hunter, R. (1979). "Differential Validity of Employment Tests by Race: A Comprehensive Review and Analysis." *Psychological Bulletin*, 86(4), 721–735.

Lindley, C. J. (1989). "Assessment of Older Persons in the Workplace." In T. Hunt and C. J. Lindley (Eds.), *Testing Older Adults*, 232–257. Austin, TX Pro-ed.

Rhodes, S. R. (1983). "Age-related Differences in Work Attitudes and Behavior: A Review and Conceptual Analysis." *Psychological Bulletin*, 93(2), 328–367.

Salthouse, T. A. (1984). "Effects of Age and Skill in Typing." *Journal of Experimental Psychology: General*, 113(3), 345–371.

Salthouse, T. A. (1985). *A Theory of Cognitive Aging*. Amsterdam: North-Holland Publishing.

Snyder, C. J., & Barrett, G.V. (1988). "The Age Discrimination in Employment Act: A Review of Court Decisions." *Experimental Aging Research*, 14(l), 3–55.

Sterns, H. L., & Alexander, R. A. (1987). "Industrial Gerontology." In G. L. Maddox (Ed.), *The Encyclopedia of Aging*. New York: Springer.

Sterns, H. L., & Barrett, G. V. (1992). *Work (paid employment) and Aging*. Paper presented at National Institute of Aging Workshop entitled "Applied Gerontology Research: Setting a Future Agenda," August 12–13, Bethesda, MD.

Sterns, A. A., Sterns, H. L., & Hollis, L. A. (1996). "The Productivity and Functional Limitations of Older Adult Workers." In Crown, W. H. (Ed.), *Handbook on Employment and the Elderly* (pp. 276–303). Westport, CT: Greenwood Press.

Lisa A. Hollis-Sawyer, "Reasonable Accommodation in the Workplace: Implication of the ADEA and ADA for Older Workers." Printed by permission of the author.

Chapter 20
Puerto Rican Obituary

Pedro Pietri

Although Puerto Ricans have been U.S. citizens since 1917, it was not until the 1950s that large numbers began to arrive on the U.S. mainland as a result of the collapse of the sugar industry on their native island. The majority have settled in Northeastern states, especially New York, New Jersey, and Connecticut. Characterized by a mixture of Spanish, Indian, and African ancestry, they have been subjected to racial and ethnic barriers to upward mobility. The majority have been employed in low-skill, low-paying service jobs that provide little or no springboards into more rewarding and better-paying occupations.

The following selection by poet Pedro Pietri characterizes the life of Puerto Rican workers in New York City. He identifies heavily with the marginalized underclass workers whom he describes. As you read his ironic verses, pay attention to his message of broken social promises and the unfilled American dream for these people. Notice the occupational roles and the ethnic slurs. Consider how the Long Island cemetery is both a metaphor for their lives in America as well as a final end to their existence.

They worked
They were always on time
They were never late
They never spoke back
when they were insulted
They worked
They never took days off
that were not on the calendar
They never went on strike
without permission
They worked
ten days a week
and were only paid for five

They worked
They worked
They worked
and they died
They died broke
They died owing
They died never knowing
what the front entrance
of the first national city bank looks like

Juan
Miguel
Milagros
Olga
Manuel
All died yesterday today
and will die again tomorrow
passing their bill collectors
on to the next of kin
All died
waiting for the garden of eden
to open up again
under a new management
All died
dreaming about America
waking them up in the middle of the night
screaming: Mira Mira
your name is on the winning lottery ticket
for one hundred thousand dollars
All died
hating the grocery stores
that sold them make-believe steak
and bullet-proof rice and beans
All died waiting dreaming and hating. . . .

Juan
died waiting for his number to hit
Miguel
died waiting for the welfare check
to come and go and come again
Milagros
died waiting for her ten children
to grow up and work
so she could quit working
Olga
died waiting for a five dollar raise
Manuel
died waiting for his supervisor to drop dead
so he could get a promotion

Is a long ride
from Spanish Harlem

to long island cemetery
where they were buried
First the train
and then the bus
and the cold cuts for lunch
and the flowers
that will be stolen
when visiting hours are over
Is very expensive
Is very expensive
But they understand
Their parents understood
Is a long non-profit ride
from Spanish Harlem
to long island cemetery. . . .

Juan
died dreaming about a new car
Miguel
died dreaming about new anti-poverty
    programs
Milagros
died dreaming about a trip to Puerto Rico
Olga
died dreaming about real jewelry
Manuel
died dreaming about the irish sweep-
    stakes. . . .

Juan
Miguel
Milagros
Olga
Manuel
All died yesterday today
and will die again tomorrow
Hating fighting and stealing
broken windows from each other
Practicing a religion without a roof
The old testament
The new testament
according to the gospel
of the internal revenue
the judge and jury and executioner
protector and eternal bill collector. . . .

They are dead
They are dead
and will not return from the dead
until they stop neglecting
the art of their dialogue
for broken english lessons

to impress the mister goldsteins
who keep them employed
as lavaplatos porters messenger boys
factory workers maids stock clerks
shipping clerks assistant mailroom
assistant, assistant assistant
to the assistant's assistant
assistant lavaplatos and automatic
artificial smiling doormen
for the lowest wages of the ages
and rages when you demand a raise
because is against the company policy
to promote SPICS SPICS SPICS

Juan
died hating Miguel because Miguel's
used car was in better running condition
than his used car
Miguel
died hating Milagros because Milagros
had a color television set
and he could not afford one yet
Milagros
died hating Olga because Olga
made five dollars more on the same job
Olga
died hating Manuel because Manuel
had hit the numbers more times
than she had hit the numbers
Manuel
died hating all of them
Juan
Miguel
Milagros
and Olga
because they all spoke broken english
more fluently than he did

And now they are together
in the main lobby of the void
Addicted to silence
Off limits to the wind
Confined to worm supremacy
in long island cemetery
This is the groovy hereafter
the protestant collection box
was talking so loud and proud about

Here lies Juan
Here lies Miguel
Here lies Milagros
Here lies Olga

Here lies Manuel
who died yesterday today
and will die again tomorrow
Always broke
Always owing
Never knowing
that they are beautiful people
Never knowing
the geography of their complexion. . . .

Discussion Questions

1. What impact has ethnic and racial discrimination had on the occupational opportunities of the people described in the poem?

2. How has their relationship with one another been affected by blocked mobility?

3. What effect has being a member of an oppressed minority had upon their sense of self-esteem?

4. How would you try to convince Pietri that the American Dream is real?

Reprinted from: Pedro Pietri, "Puerto Rican Obituary." In H. Augenbaum and Margarite Fernandes Olmos (eds.), *The Latino Reader.* Copyright © 1973 by Monthly Review Press. Reprinted by permission of Monthly Review Foundation.

Chapter 21

The Unbearable Lightness of Retirement

Joel Savishinsky

One of the key concepts in anthropology is that of the rite of passage, a communal ritual that marks a person's transition from one important social status to another: birth, coming of age, marriage, parenthood, and death. At these moments, the community comes together not only to assist the individual through the transition but to convey the message that the group as a whole has a stake in a successful outcome. In simple societies, where the kinship group and age peers are primary sources of support, these rituals assume major importance in demarcating stages in the life course. In modern complex societies, there are many comparable ceremonies: baptism, confirmation or Bar Mitzvah, weddings, and funerals, involving a relatively small segment of the community.

But what of retirement—the passage out of paid labor into "what?" In the following selection, Joel Savishinsky notes that this transition in American society is almost devoid of compelling or even standard rituals. Possibly, because few earlier societies had a comparable status passage, there is little tradition upon which to draw. Or perhaps the "lightness" of such recognition reflects the ambiguous connotation of "nonwork" in a society founded on the work ethic. Conversely, the do-it-yourself nature of retirement ritual could ease the transition for those who are leaving paid employment but not other forms of work. As you read the following selection, think about whether the lack of strong, communal gestures of support through ritual places another burden upon the retiree, who must then navigate the passage as best she or he can, through informal parties, travel, and even leaps of fantasy.

Culture has often been thought of in terms of tradition, but modern culture is more often noted for its inventions. The novelties of our time include not just the obvious and dramatic new technologies—the gene-splicers, CAT scanners, word processors, and spaceships of recent decades—but also new social forms. Feminism, single parenthood, nursing homes, rap music, psychobabble, and deconstructionism are just a few of these innovations. But, one of the most important developments has been in the life course itself where our century has seen the invention of retirement as a new stage of life with its own name, organizations, magazines, an economic and legal infrastructure, and full-blown planned communities.

Traditionally, when anthropologists have studied tradition, they have focused a lot on ritual, and many of the rituals they have addressed are rites of passage. These ceremonies help individuals move from one stage of life to the next by transforming their identities and by investing both the passage and the person with deep cultural meaning.[1] Societies that fail to provide timely and appropriate retirement rites may lay themselves open to intergenerational tensions and discontent among their elders (Foner 1984; Nadel 1952). In the culture of modernity, the potential dilemmas have been exacerbated: Rituals have been played down, and to act ritualistically is to risk being put down rather than socially elevated. Later life, in particular, is characterized by a dearth of expectations and ceremonies in industrial societies (Hazan 1994; Myerhoff 1984), and these deficits occur during a developmental period of great social discontinuity when rites of passage could potentially be the most helpful to individuals and the social order (Fortes 1984; Keith and Kertzer 1984). For most retiring employees, Maddox (1968) once observed, "this significant transition appears to be unceremonious, perhaps intentionally so, as though retirement were an event which one does not wish to mark especially" (p. 357). More recently, Manheimer (1994) has noted that retirement is still "a rite of passage we haven't figured out how to celebrate" (p. 44).

One of the most attentive students of retirement, Robert Atchley (1976, 1991), has observed that we do not know much about retirement ceremonies, how commonly they are held, or what part they play in this important transition. A similar point has been made by Linda George (1980), who comments that the "symbolism and subjective meaning of retirement as an event is a rich and largely unexamined area of study" (p. 56). Atchley notes that, unlike rituals such as weddings and graduations, retirement ceremonies are not standardized in our culture. Some rites are personal and informal events, others highly organized and elaborate; some honor one person, others feature a group of individuals; some are sponsored by employers, others by friends; some bestow meaningful gifts whereas others fail to; and although the atmosphere of such events is usually positive, the speeches and rhetoric focus on the past rather than on the transition that lies ahead (Atchley 1976, 1991).

Given the lack of careful attention to retirement rites, the absence of ceremonial standardization, and the uncertain significance of such rituals, several important issues remain to be addressed. What happens, ceremonially, when people enter the new life stage of retirement? Who organizes these events, and how are they arranged and put together? And what are the sources of meaning and support that retirees find, or hope to find, in these ritual experiences?

These are three of several questions I have been asking in a longitudinal study of retirement as a life passage in a rural American community. With the collaboration of my students and a developmental psychologist, I have been following a group of 26 people as they approach retirement and experience its first 3 years. Recruited through a combination of letters and notices to local employers and unions, and by a process of snowball sampling, study participants are equally divided by gender but represent a diversity of work backgrounds and personal circumstances. They include people who have been teachers, doctors, and professors, a lawyer, a secretary, a postman, a designer, an accountant, a human service worker, a biologist, a librarian, a musician, and a salesman. They are variously married, single, or divorced individuals, some of whom have children and grandchildren, and others who have neither. Their states of health vary, as do their financial situations. Their ages at the time of retirement ranged from 54 to 77, and about half have elderly parents or in-laws still alive. The methods involved in this project have emphasized formal and informal interviews, life-history analysis, and participant observation. The latter has included attendance at people's retirement rituals and parties, and the sharing of such mundane events as hanging out together at local coffee shops, shopping malls, and the weekly farmers' market (see the appendix). My concern in this article is with the way these people have experienced the public marking of their retirement with rituals, and with how these events reflect their social support systems, and the models they have developed of what this new state of life will be like for them.

Formal Rituals

Retirement marks the end of work but not of responsibility, and one of those responsibilities is to mark retirement itself with ritual. Employers usually feel obligated to host farewell ceremonies, and prospective retirees feel compelled to attend them. The formal nature of these events tends to follow a fairly standard formula: advance announcements of the party's time and place; brief speeches by supervisors or senior personnel; the bestowal of a gift and a commemorative certificate or plaque; and the serving of food or a meal, accompanied by a toast. Although the course and content of such rites are fairly predictable, the expectations of workers, and the best laid plans of mice, men, and management are not always congruent. Nor are the results necessarily fulfilling.

At the age of 61, Martin Karler had been anticipating his retirement for months, and knew that it would only take one day in April to finish off the work of 37 years. For over 3 decades he had been employed in the production department of an appliance manufacturer. Rising slowly in its ranks, he wound up his career in charge of advertising and media. Martin was content with what he called his last promotion's "comfortable responsibility," and in the preceding 5 years had especially enjoyed the novelty of being a kind of model and mentor to younger workers just starting out in the division.

Martin saw himself as a very practical man. And—other than attending his children's college graduations and weddings—he was no lover of ritual. But with the end of work about to begin, he privately hoped that its public celebration would make the passage to retirement easier for him. He wanted some validation for what he had accomplished in the past and an acknowledgement of the brave new world he was about to enter. But the ceremony held to mark his last day of work was a disappointment. Like most retirees in the study, Martin found the formal ritual at his workplace to be "very nice" but also pallid and predictable. His boss said a few words, a plaque and a present were given, a toast was made, and people quickly turned to the buffet. Martin and other study participants have been witness to nearly identical ceremonies held for older coworkers, and what they had once seen was now what they themselves got. The climax to years of work was anticlimactic. There were, of course, minor variations in the content of speeches, the words on the card, and the value of the check or gift. In most cases, a few anecdotes were told by colleagues, and the retiree's history of work and contributions was recounted; but only the most general remarks were made about the person's family ties or future plans. The rhetoric and the proceedings followed a fairly standard formula, and in Martin's words, "even the laughter came on cue and sounded canned."

People retiring from some of the area's larger employers—a university in several cases, a financial corporation in others— were faced with another dimension, the fact of numbers. In these instances, the work year fell into well-defined periods, and there were clear junctures in time when groups of people, approaching retirement, were expected to leave and mark that event together. In such situations, retirees were forced to share an already weakened spotlight with others whom they either barely knew or who—in at least two cases—they actively disliked. These experiences underscored how distinct a social experience the retirement rite could be from a seemingly similar ceremony such as graduation, which often marked a person's entry into the world of work. Though adolescence and early old age parallel one another as times of transition, powerlessness, and identity confusion (Keith and Kertzer 1984), their rituals can differ in significant ways. Unlike a high school or college graduation, there was no collective or class identity at the end of work to bind retiring celebrants together. Employees generally began and lived their work lives as individuals, not as a cohort; and yet at the end of their careers, they were lumped into a collectivity of ceremonial convenience.

Even some of the people who felt negatively about the formal rites nevertheless felt compelled to attend them. In some instances, they did not want to disappoint those who desired to acknowledge their departure. In other cases, the compulsion was their own. Whether hollow or not, the rite was still an important form of closure these retirees preferred not to forego. In one case, that of Nate Rumsfeld, a public service employee was offered a window of time during which to take an early retirement. Encouraged by younger coworkers anxious to move up, pressured by his supervisors, and left to fend for himself by his union, Nate took the window at age 57 but did so with strong feelings of ambivalence and uncertainty. Although several others also made the same decision Nate did, none of these men or women was offered a party, and no one thought of organizing even the most minimal of departure rites for them. Although Nate felt he would not have especially enjoyed such an event, he nevertheless resented its absence. It was one more insult in a hurried, unsatisfying, and alienating process.

In a second case, that of Stefan Nokalsky, a man who chose to leave work in his mid-50s was told by his employer of 20 years that this step could not technically be called a retirement. The personnel director insisted on the phrase "voluntary separation from employment." To call it a retirement, Stefan's superiors explained apologetically, would require the company to begin his pension and other benefits. Yet in Stefan's own mind, though he was not asking for early benefits, this was his retirement, and the withholding of that title felt like a betrayal. Feeling a hostage to language and bureaucracy, he worked hard to get his employer to at least include him in the end-of-the-year's retirement party because this event, when it happened, did finally allow him to lay personal and public claim to a status that those he called the "language police" had barred him from.

Another factor that made official rites of retirement so unfulfilling for many was that the organizers of these ceremonies—the bosses, supervisors, and administrators—only knew the retiree in a one-dimensional way, that is, as an employee or coworker. Because this was the only part of the person's identity they could speak to, they could not address all the other dimensions of the retiree's life that would be affected by this transition, such as family ties and friendships, personal dreams and life goals, and health status and finances. Only the people who knew the retiree in a more rounded, multifaceted way could relate to these other aspects of who they were. This was one reason why the informal rites that intimates organized for retirees were usually more meaningful.

Informal Rites

One of these invented rituals reveals the structure and significance of such events. In the case of Alice Armani, retirement came at the end of 15 years of administrative work for a small, nonprofit human service agency—a very demanding, low-paying, yet high-profile position. This organization had only had two previous directors—neither of whom had retired after leaving—and so there was no institutional culture to frame a ceremonial tradition. When Alice decided to retire at the age of 67, her decision was prompted by a combination of burnout, a growing sense of her own age, and a feeling of diminished capacity and trust in her own memory and attentiveness. She was proud of what she had accomplished in her work but haunted by doubts of her own efficacy.

The retirement event created by Alice's staff, her board of directors, and the agency's volunteers included a dish-to-pass supper, the presence of Alice's adult children, a dance band featuring several of her colleagues, a song composed in her honor, and several speeches—brief but rich in detail—recounting episodes from Alice's career and highlighting the qualities of her character. There was also a memory book in which most of the six dozen people present wrote at some length about their feelings for Alice. Finally, there was a gift of a hand-carved easel, reflecting people's awareness of Alice's intention to focus her energy on her great passion, painting, once retirement began. The gift's presentation, which Alice's grown children participated in, focused specifically on the kind of painting Alice loved, and some of the actual landscapes she dreamed of visiting. Those who spoke obviously knew Alice's heart as well as her art. What also made the entire event so meaningful to Alice was not just the individual attention and the personal tone it embraced, but—as she put it—"The knowledge that my work had not been in vain, that I wasn't as incompetent as I feared I had become." The main reward, then, even more valuable than the easel, was the gift of reassurance and self-worth.

The very steps by which such informal rites were planned unveiled another of their important attributes, namely, the significance of process and selection. We found, for example, that preparing the guest list for a private celebration was itself a significant process in that it gave retirees a chance to sort through the people in their life and decide who constituted their real support system and circle of significant others. Ursula Chalfin, a biologist, reflecting on her recent party and the steps she had participated in to plan it, compared the experience of making the guest list to cleaning out her office and lab: The two processes had enabled Ursula—aged 63—to figure out what and who was memorable and meaningful in her history, not just in a material, but also in an emotional way. She remarked that it "put things together by helping me put some things, and some dreams and people, away."

These informal or intimate rites revealed one other important dimension of retirement, namely, fantasy. In the safe and supportive company of friends, families, and colleagues, the more inventive and imaginative retirees articulated their vision of what they would have wanted their ideal departure to be like. At their party, sparked by the presence of confidants and a seasoning of alcohol, they spoke and joked about who they would have told off, for example, and in what words, or to what degree of drama and fanfare. Listening to them was like listening to people's fantasies of how they would have wanted to leave a bad relationship; it had all the theatricality, flair, and well-considered words that we come up with only in our dreams or on the morning after. A 63-year-old professor, Felix Davis, spoke at his party of wanting to hold his retirement rite on the main quad of his campus; in his fantasy he saw himself dressed in golfing clothes and awaiting a vintage Sopwith camel that would fly low over the college, land on the quad, and taxi up to where he stood, surrounded by campus dignitaries. In Felix's dream he then saw himself mount the wing of the plane, hurl piles of bureaucratic forms and invective on the unprecedentedly silent college president, emit one huge fart, and roar off into the sunset. To be able to describe such dreams, mouth the words, and—in a few cases—even act them out before an appreciative group, lent a cathartic quality to the retirement event. Like court jesters, clowns, and other marginal figures licensed to express outrage and ridicule, ritualized fantasy also allowed these elders to use humor and their liminal status as platforms for social commentary and criticism (cf. Myerhoff 1984; Turner 1969). As Turner (1969) has emphasized, being marginalized does not necessarily disempower people. It is often from the margins that individuals can see, and voice, what those in the center of things may miss or choose to suppress. For retirees, ritual here was the opportunity for the repressed to find its voice, for intimates to become an audience, and for kin and colleagues to stand witness to an adulthood's accumulation of love and hate.

Travel

In listening to people talk about retirement, and in following their lives during its first 2 years, we discovered an unexpected and unceremonious way that many of them had for dealing with this transition. Their method was travel. For quite a number of women and men, a major trip in the immediate postretirement period was not just a special reward that they gave themselves, it also served a number of significant social, emotional, and symbolic functions. Travel itself, beyond its inherent pleasures of leisure and excitement, allowed them to separate from work, home, hometown, the daily round of life, and the common flow of social ties. They found that when people persistently (and sometimes irritatingly) asked, "What are you going to do in your retirement?" they could simply answer, "I'm going to take a trip"; this would often satisfy others and shut them up. But, travel was more than merely a quick and convenient retort. New retirees used the time away not only to relax but to reflect on themselves and the past, put its immediacy behind them, and give thought to what they wanted from their future and their own life.

Teri Rogers, for instance, after her retirement at the age of 57 from teaching high school, took a long, leisurely, cross-country trip by train with her husband, visiting many of the national parks that she had dreamed about for years. The experience not only fulfilled a long-held ambition of Teri's but built on the growing sensitivity to environmental issues that she had developed while serving on her local civic association's executive board. By the time Teri returned home, she had decided to put her trip, her retirement, and her consciousness to work by devoting her energy to her town's fledgling efforts to develop a land preservation trust.

Teri's experience bears out the remarks of novelist and travel writer Lawrence Durrel (1957), who has observed that

Journeys . . . flower spontaneously out of the demands of our natures—and the best of them not only lead us outwards in space, but inwards as well. Travel can be one of the most rewarding forms of introspection. (p. 1)

Several other participants said, as did Teri, that when they came back from their trip, their new identity as a retiree was "more real." They acknowledged that, except for the absence of work, the things around them were the same, yet they had changed. It was, in effect, easier to go away and come back as a different person than it would have been, in Teri's words, "to simply change in place."

These experiences add a special dimension of meaning to the role of travel in the period after people exit from the work force. Atchley (1991) has noted that one of the paths that some individuals follow after retiring is to actively pursue the activities they had not been able to engage in before. Among men and women who start out adopting this euphoric honeymoon approach, extended travel is a common feature for those with adequate income. Our study suggests that, for the persons on such a path, the pursuit of this particular form of pleasure is also a transformative process. Travel thus constituted a de facto rite of passage in the classic sense of that term; that is, the initial postretirement trip served as a mediator between statuses, and qualified as a transitional or liminal period between a person's separation from and subsequent reincorporation into the society at large. As Turner (1969) has so persuasively argued, the liminal phase of rituals needs to be more fully acknowledged and more carefully studied because it constitutes the period during which personal identity is actually reconstituted. This theme is congruent with the ritual emphasis on separation in retirement's broader meaning (Atchley 1976, p. 54). Thus, although many cultures have rites of passage (such as pilgrimages and the vision quest) that involve travel, here—for retirees—travel itself is ritualized, and helped them pass from an old to a new stage of life.

Summary and Conclusions

Modern times have presented Western peoples with many forms of novelty in the domain of lifestyle as well as technology. These include important questions and new reflections on the idea that one's job is a central source of personal and social meaning (De Grazia [1962] 1994). Just as the Indus-

trial Revolution and the 19th century gave birth to the weekend and modern forms of leisure (Rybczynski 1991), they have also restructured the life cycle of contemporary workers by creating the very concept of retirement (cf. Graebner 1980; Haber and Gratton 1993; Hannah 1986).

Studying how people cope with the transition to retirement is neither trivial nor esoteric: This passage is the gateway to a period of time that could amount to a third of their lives. The main findings of this study indicate, however, that the rituals held to mark people's entry into retirement take a number of different forms, and offer varying degrees of fulfillment. The key points may be summarized as follows.

1. For most participants in this study, the formal and public recognition of retirement was marred by the pale content of the official rituals meant to dramatize it. These ceremonies were formulaic, predictable, and cliched; they were officiated over by individuals who did not know the retirees in a rounded way, and they sometimes lumped together a group of honorees who wanted to be acknowledged as individuals. These were the cases in which ritual did become "mere ritual." Because most of our subjects were in decent financial circumstances, what they were faced with then was not the culture of poverty but rather the poverty of their culture.

2. The private and informal ceremonies created for retirees were more fulfilling for a number of reasons. These included the content and tone of the rhetoric; the informed and sympathetic presence of people who knew the retirees, along with their histories and their dreams; the thoughtful process of selecting gifts and the reflective experience of formulating a guest list; and the opportunities provided for retirees to engage in fantasy, physical separation, and freedom of expression. The latter features of ceremonies opened the doors for catharsis and personal transformation.

All of these rewarding attributes suggest that the ritual entry into retirement is heavy with meaning and full of potential for people. Unfortunately, the language of the participants' culture and the rhetoric of formal ritual continue to convey the subtle and airy nature of this new phase of life, its aura of nothingness (Atchley 1976). People retire from work, which is an activity. They retire to bed or Florida, which are simply places. But there are still no prepositions or figures of speech to indicate what retirement is, for older individuals do not retire to a purpose, activity, or function. What they do in the place they retire to is ill-defined and largely up to them. Going through retirement strips people of a long-held identity and bestows nothing concrete to replace it (Hazan 1994). Personal uncertainty is compounded by the fact that retirement's impact can also vary with social class, gender, education, and work history, and so it is not "a single experience with a predictable consequence" (Maddox 1968, p. 364). Lacking a consensual model of retirement, most persons in this study tended to invent or seize on a metaphor that felt suitable to them: It was a "vacation" to those who anticipated its freedom; it was a "sentence" to those who could not escape its confinement; it was like "adolescence" to those who saw it, with either fear or hope, as a kind of "starting all over again." Like being, itself, whether retirees consciously followed the weighty philosophy of Sartre (1956) or floated along passively with the characters of Milan Kundera (1985), it was this undefined nature, this cultural lightness of retirement that made it so personally heavy to bear.[2]

Anthropologists and historians have shown how people, faced with the unexpected circumstances of modernity, commonly create new forms of behavior to pattern their unprecedented lives. The historian Eric Hobsbawm (1983), in fact, has pointed out how a good deal of what now passes for tradition is really of recent invention, created especially in the years since the start of the Industrial Revolution. And in Barbara Myerhoff's (1978) now classic study of elderly East European Jews in California, she observed how people created definitional ceremonies, that is, their own rites of passage, when their combination of New- and Old-World cultures failed to provide them with meaningful rituals. Private rites were here elaborated to compensate for the lack of effective public ones (Myerhoff 1984).

Our study has also shown that there are several positive ways in which the ritual handling of retirement can be made to work for people, just as it suggests that students of this life stage should give more careful regard to the details of its celebration. Indeed, it is the close observation and thick description found in other recent ethnographies of aging—such as Sankar's (1991) work on dying, and Gubrium's (1993) book on meaning—that demonstrate the power of qualitative gerontology for illuminating and critiquing the texture of older people's lives. In that spirit, and based on what retirees themselves have found in their own experiences, we would suggest that colleagues and kin pay more attention to the following five areas in planning people's retirement ceremonies.

Informal rites. The rites that people invent for their friends and family are a rich source of cultural creativity. They do, say, and provide more than the standardized rituals that have grown up in the American work place. Such private, intimate, and informal ceremonies should be encouraged, studied, learned from, and adapted to individual circumstances, and not be overshadowed by the pro forma events that usually occur at people's place of employment. As Martin's experience suggests, the transition to retirement is too important to be left to employers and managers, and—as Nate and Stefan's cases demonstrate—they are too critical to be allowed to suffer from the benign neglect of significant others.

The gift. The gift a retiree gets should have some direct relationship to his or her history and hopes. All-purpose presents, such as money or gift certificates, should be avoided: Retirement is a meaningful transition, and its meaning should be reflected and expressed in what is given. A gift that is connected to an activity that the retiree is looking forward to, such as Alice's easel, makes the ritual more personal, more future oriented, and thus more fulfilling.

The guest list. Although the gift for an informal event may be a surprise, the guest list should not be. Rather, it should be prepared with care, and the retiree should have a primary role in drawing it up. Family and friends who work on this process with the retiree should encourage her or him to talk about the reasons for including or excluding people. For some individuals, such as Ursula, this process becomes a valuable experience in sorting through one's social ties and work history. Some people find it helpful to begin with a very large list of potential guests—lots of colleagues, coworkers, family, and friends—and then winnow out those who are not meaningful, and identify those who are.

Travel. Travel turns out to be a potent, transformative experience for certain retirees, and its functional equivalent to a rite of passage should be recognized and reconsidered. Those planning their own retirement and those who help others plan for theirs might want to consider the efficacy of travel in this light, and think of ways to enhance its potential. Journeys should occur within a reasonable time (approximately 6 months) of actual retirement, and involve—as Teri's experience shows—a destination or itinerary that has some special meaning for the retiree.

Fantasy. Finally, retirement is a transition that brings out both memories and dreams and so it bears a strong link to the unconscious world of fantasy. The ritual celebration of this life passage offers a rich opportunity to express and act out those fantasies, and people should be given—or, as Felix did, they should give themselves—a chance to enjoy this possibility. If the American dream is one that has been built around the world of work, perhaps it is time for people to dream new worlds, and avenge themselves on old ones, when this time of transition is at hand.

Appendix

Sample and Methods

Study participants were recruited by means of letters and notices sent to major employers and unions in a rural county in upstate New York. Personnel departments also helped us to identify people who were likely to retire within a specific 12-month period. In addition, an article about the study in the area's major newspaper brought the project to people's attention. Once a core of

participants was identified, individuals in this group told us of other women and men whom they thought would probably retire within the next 6 to 8 months. Such snowball sampling yielded a cohort of 26 people.

Methods employed in the study have included formal and informal interviews, life-history analysis, and participant observation. Initial structured interviews with all participants were held prior to their formal retirement: These occurred, on average, about 4 months before people retired. To date, two additional rounds of interviews have been held: The second round took place between 6 and 12 months after retirement, and the third round between 18 and 24 months of retirement. Formal and informal interviews, and casual conversations with retirees and family members, have also yielded a considerable body of life-history material. The specific topics we have collected data on include people's educational, work, and medical histories; their financial status; their family background and living situations; their expectations of, and reflections on, retirement; their mode of planning for retirement; their perceptions of individuals whom they feel constituted good and bad models of retirement for them; their views of how retirement has affected key relationships and activities; their involvement in travel, volunteer and paid work; and their views of the meaning of life.

Discussion Questions

1. What would you construct as an ideal retirement rite of passage?

2. Would this ritual be different for men and women?

3. Are there advantages to a "light" rite?

4. How does the exchange of gifts reinforce social ties?

5. Why would you expect rites of passage to differ in a modern society compared to a less industrially developed society?

Notes

1. Important studies of rites of passage by early and more recent scholars include the works of Bateson ([1936] 1958), Gluckman (1962),

Herdt (1981), Myerhoff (1978), Turner (1969), and van Gennep ([1909] 1960).

2. A caveat about retirement, issued many years ago by Maddox (1968, p. 363), continues to retain its relevance:

> Failure to conceptualize reaction to retirement as a variable (rather than as a social event with a single meaning) related to the particular configuration of experiences which constitute an individual's biography has been a crucial flaw in many studies of retirement.

One effort to address that flaw is Prentis' (1992) book that contains 40 brief case histories of individual women and men dealing with various phases of the retirement experience. Another approach is represented by ethnographies of communities of retired people, a number of which have appeared since the early 1970s, including Hochschild (1973), Jacobs (1974), Johnson (1971), Keith (1977), Myerhoff (1978), and Vesperi (1986).

Author's Note

An earlier version of this article was presented at the 93rd Annual Meeting of the American Anthropological Association, Atlanta, Georgia, November 30, 1994 to December 4,1994. The research reported on here is being supported by a grant to the Gerontology Institute at Ithaca College. I would like to acknowledge the help provided by the Institute, the cooperation of the study's participants, and the assistance of my students and my collaborator, Janet Kalinowski, of Ithaca College's Department of Psychology. To protect people's privacy, the names used in the text are pseudonyms, and some biographical details have been altered. For reprints, write to Anthropology Department, Ithaca College, Ithaca, NY 14850-7274.

References

Atchley, R. 1976. *The Sociology of Retirement*. Cambridge, MA: Schenkman.

——. 1991. *Social Forces and Aging: An Introduction to Social Gerontology*, 6th ed. Belmont, CA: Wadsworth.

Bateson, G. [1936] 1958. *Naven*, 2nd ed. Stanford, CA: Stanford University Press.

De Grazia, S. [1962] 1994. *Of Time, Work and Leisure*. New York: Random House.

Durrell, L. 1957. *Bitter Lemons*. New York: E. P. Dutton.

Foner, N. 1984. *Ages in Conflict. A Cross-Cultural Perspective on Inequality Between Old and Young*. New York: Columbia University Press.

Fortes, M. 1984. "Age, Generation, and Social Structure." Pp. 99–122 in *Age and Anthropological Theory*, edited by D. Kertzer and J. Keith. Ithaca, NY: Cornell University Press.

George, L. 1980. *Role Transitions in Later Life*. Monterey, CA: Brooks/Cole.

Gluckman, M., ed. 1962. *Essays on the Ritual of Social Relations*. Manchester: Manchester University Press.

Graebner, W. 1980. *A History of Retirement: The Meaning and Function of an American Institution*. New Haven, CT: Yale University Press.

Gubrium, J. 1993. *Speaking of Life: Horizons of Meaning for Nursing Home Residents*. Chicago: Aldine de Gruyter.

Haber, C. and B. Gratton. 1993. *Old Age and the Search for Security: An American Social History*. Bloomington: Indiana University Press.

Hannah, L. 1986. *Inventive Retirement: The Development of Occupational Pensions in Britain*. Cambridge: Cambridge University Press.

Hazan, H. 1994. *Old Age: Constructions and Deconstructions*. Cambridge: Cambridge University Press.

Herdt, G. 1981. *Guardians of the Flutes: Idioms of Masculinity*. New York: Columbia University Press.

Hobsbawm, E. 1983. "Introduction: Inventing Traditions." Pp. 1–14 in *The Invention of Tradition*, edited by E. Hobsbawm and T. Ranger. Cambridge: Cambridge University Press.

Hochschild, A. 1973. *The Unexpected Community*. Englewood Cliffs, NJ: Prentice-Hall.

Jacobs, J. 1974. *Fun City: An Ethnographic Study of a Retirement Community*. New York: Holt, Rinehart & Winston.

Johnson, S. 1971. *Idle Haven: Community Building Among the Working Class Retired*. Berkeley: University of California Press.

Keith, J. 1977. *Old People, New Lives: Community Creation in a Retirement Residence*. Chicago: University of Chicago Press.

Keith, J. and Kertzer, D., eds. 1984. "Introduction." Pp. 19–61 in *Age and Anthropological Theory*. Ithaca: Cornell University Press.

Kundera, M. 1985. *The Unbearable Lightness of Being*. Translated by M. H. Heim. New York: Harper & Row.

Maddox, G. L. 1968. "Retirement as a Social Event in the United States." Pp. 357–65 in *Middle Age and Aging*, edited by B. Neugarten. Chicago: University of Chicago Press.

Manheimer, R. J. 1994. "The Changing Meaning of Retirement." *Creative Retirement* 1:44–9.

Myerhoff, B. 1978. *Number Our Days*. New York. Simon & Schuster.

———. 1984. "Rites and Signs of Ripening: The Intertwining of Ritual, Time, and Growing Older." Pp. 305–30 in *Age and Anthropological Theory*, edited by D. Kertzer and J. Keith. Ithaca, NY: Cornell University Press.

Nadel, S. F. 1952. "Witchcraft in Four African Societies." *American Anthropologist* 54:18–29.

Prentis, R. S. 1992. *Passages of Retirement: Personal Histories of Struggle and Success*. Westport, CT: Greenwood Press.

Rybczynski, W. 1991. *Waiting for the Weekend*. New York: Viking.

Sankar, A. 1991. *Dying at Home: A Family Guide for Caregiving*. Baltimore, MD: Johns Hopkins University Press.

Sartre, J. 1956. *Being and Nothingness: An Essay on Phenomenological Ontology*. Translated by H. Barnes. New York: Philosophical Library.

Turner, V. 1969. *The Ritual Process: Structure and Anti-structure*. Chicago: Aldine.

van Gennep, A. [1909] 1960. *The Rites of Passage*. Translated by M. Vizedom and G. Caffee. Chicago: University of Chicago Press.

Vesperi, M. 1985. *City of Green Benches: Growing Old in a New Downtown*. Ithaca, NY: Cornell University Press.

Chapter 22
Charles Hayes, 76, and Jessie de la Cruz, 74

Studs Terkel

Studs Terkel has made a career of interviewing the forgotten workers of America, not the movers and shakers but members of the faceless masses who see that the buses run on time, that food is in the supermarket, that your trash is picked up. This labor force has always been disproportionately composed of the most recent ethnic or racial or religious migrants to our shores, in addition to indigenous minorities. Terkel has also had a lifelong interest in the union movement, with its history of extraordinary bravery in the early decades of this century, through its peak of power in the 1950s and 1960s, and its recent slow decline.

In this selection, two veterans of the union struggle speak to Terkel of their seven decades of experience as farm workers, labor organizers, and now retirees still actively engaged on behalf of the relatively deprived. Charles Hayes owed his first break with poverty to the New Deal programs of the 1930s, which provided a job and job training for unemployed and underprivileged youth of all races. From there, he moved into labor organizing and ended his career as a member of Congress from the Chicago area.

Jessie de la Cruz, in contrast, grew up in California, where her family followed the crops as migrant laborers, with little expectation of breaking out of the cycle of poverty— that is, until Cesar Chavez began to organize the largely Chicano farm workers. Chavez promised more than steady wages and decent working conditions; he pledged to restore dignity to an oppressed minority. Jessie de la Cruz became one of Chavez's first women organizers and has never left the movement. Its causes

remain her crusades even in retirement, as she fills a number of volunteer positions in organizations providing legal assistance to migrant workers, who continue, even today, to labor for minimal wages in unsanitary and unsafe conditions.

Charles Hayes, 76
Chicago, Illinois

"I*n 1983, when Harold Washington became mayor of Chicago, I took over his seat in Congress and remained there until January 3, 1993.*" *He had previously been an official of the United Packinghouse Workers of America (UPWA-CIO).*

***

I was the second oldest of twelve kids in the family. I was born down in Cairo, Illinois, between the Ohio and the Mississippi Rivers. The Mason-Dixon line, they said, was below that, but you couldn't tell the difference. [*Chuckles.*]

My father was a farm laborer. I started work with him at nine years old. We chopped cotton, baled hay, harvested corn. I made seventy-five cents a day. My father got paid $1.25 a day, for ten hours. A hard life, but it was challenging to me. I was determined to go to school. I graduated from grade school, all black. Me and a neighbor boy caught the freight train every day. We lived near the tracks where they switched trains. We'd hop on that train when they spliced them together, and ride to the north end of Cairo, where the train went across the Ohio. Whenever a train goes on a bridge, it slows down almost to a stop. We would leap off and roll all the way down the hill. A ten-mile trip. That's the way I got to school. [*Chuckles.*] We finally got a ride with my cousin, who was our English teacher. My mother would pay her with milk or butter.

We had algebra, geometry, English, and what they called manual training. I learned a little bit how to make furniture. I didn't think I'd be able to attend my graduation, we were so poor. Didn't even have money to pay for my robe. Didn't have a suit. My father said, "You'll just have to get your diploma on the fly," My mother was determined and, God bless her soul, she borrowed money from a relative to pay four and a half dollars for a graduation suit and some shoes. [*Chuckles*.] I'll never forget it. Thirty-five of us in the class of 1935.

It was right in the throes of the depression. I remember they used to give us flour. I'd walk seven miles to pick up a twenty-four-pound sack. And every now and then, you'd get some canned beef. It was tough, but we did everything we could to survive. That's why I get mad when I see no real commitment by Congress to create jobs for people who want to work. I should know this, because I was part of that Congress.

In the Roosevelt days, there was the WPA (Works Progress Administration) the Civilian Conservation Corps (CCC). Right after I graduated from high school, I went into the CCC camps. We set out trees on the banks of the Mississippi to stop erosion of the soil—not too far from Galesburg. It was an all-black camp, patterned after the armed services. The officers were white. I got $30 a month and sent $25 home. Of the $5 I kept, I still had some money left at the end of the month.

I wanted to go to college in the worst way. I had aspirations to become a doctor. It was just impossible, being black with no money. After I came out of the CCC camp. I had a job for a few months helping rebuild the tracks of the Missouri & Pacific after a devastating flood.

The first long-time job I had was with a hardwood manufacturer in Cairo. Their headquarters was in Memphis, so they really knew how to practice racism. I started out stacking lumber with older black men. Then I was moved inside the factory.

I'll never forget the time I stepped playfully on some hardwood floor that I thought was no good. The superintendent, walking through the plant, hollered, "Come here, boy!" I came over. "Don't you know you're not supposed to step on that flooring?" I said, "But I thought it was a throw-out." He said, "Let me tell you one thing and don't you ever forget it. You don't get paid to think here. I do." I never forgot it. I just said, "Uh huh."

I always had a degree of independence. I used to read quite a bit. I had read something about a union that seemed to have some jurisdiction over this kind of work. At the time it was called the Federation of Carpenters and Joiners. I wrote a letter to their headquarters in Indianapolis. I got a response. They sent an international rep and he met with me. I went to some of the older black guys who were miserably mistreated. I said, "We need some protection. You can't deal with these bosses on a one-to-one basis, because they'll fire you one at a time. But if we get together and stick together, they can't fire all of us." They agreed. I was making $7.50 a week. So about five of us sent $2.50 a piece to apply for a union charter and we got it.

Wasn't the carpenters' union lily-white?

Yeah, yeah. [*Chuckles*.] The guy they sent in was pretty decent, so we were able to form an all-black local, Local 1424. The whites at the plant had the better jobs, grading the flooring and running the saw mills. They refused to join. Of course, the company refused to recognize us, so we went on a six-week strike, all black. It worked. They recognized us, and I was elected president of the local. I was still pretty much of a kid. That was my beginning in the labor movement.

After the strike, some of the white guys saw that they weren't being treated right either. So they joined our union. This was at a time when the trades were segregated. We elected one white guy secretary-treasurer and put another on the committee with me. He and I had to negotiate our first contract in Memphis, the company's headquarters. We got on the train at Cairo, and I never saw him until we reached Memphis. We were in different cars. I was the first black guy who ever sat across the table in that company's office. There was just no way they could get around me. I was president of the Cairo local. [*Chuckles*.]

I still wanted to go back to school. I had an uncle who worked in the Chicago stockyards. He said, "Why don't you come up here? I'll find you a job in the yards and you can go to school." So my wife and I came to Chicago.

He got me a job as laborer for Wilson. We were getting seventy-five cents an hour, much more than we got in Cairo. I was working at night in the pork-boning department, hauling meat to the wagon and cleaning up. They had women boning the pork shoulders for sausage and lunch meat.

This was in 1942 and they were just organizing in the stockyards. Armour had already recognized the union, but Wilson was one of the most vicious anti-union outfits. They had a company union. Though I was a new guy with hardly any seniority, I had organizing experience. So I joined with the pro-union people immediately.

We went through two NLRB (National Labor Relations Board) elections and two strikes. One lasted two weeks in 1946, and there was a bigger one in 1948. Along with three other guys, I was fired for union activity. We were reinstated by the NLRB. In 1949, I was made full-time international field representative. I traveled to Kansas City, Omaha, wherever there were challenges.

The union became my life, but I still wanted to go to school, at least, learn a trade. I applied at Coyne Electrical College. I'll never forget what they told me: "We have no facilities for colored." So it was all union work from then on. I stayed all the way through, including two mergers. I had to resign my post when I entered Congress in 1983. I'm told I was the first elected union official ever to become a congressman. I served nine years and six months.

Our union was far in advance of many others in breaking down unfair practices. Male laborers were getting seventy-two cents an hour. Women, doing the same work, were getting sixty-two cents. We broke that down. White women worked in the cleaner departments, meat processing. Black women were stationed on the killing floors. We changed all that.

We realized that changing the working conditions was only part of our job. We had to do something about the conditions where the workers lived, in the community. That's why I had become so active in the civil rights movement. That's why Martin Luther King came to Chicago. Talking about crime doesn't add up to anything, unless we get at basic causes.

The closing of the stockyards in Chicago was devastating. Swift moved to Rochelle,

Illinois. Wilson moved to Monmouth. They said they had to move closer to their sources of supply. The Chicago plants were getting old and outmoded. I remember, back in the '70s, when twenty thousand workers had a mass rally to save their jobs. But it was no use.

Some were able to take what was then early retirement. Some women who had worked in the yards actually put their birth dates back in order to be eligible for social security. [*Chuckles*.] They were that desperate. They'd come to me: "Look, I'm really older than I've been saying I was. You've got to help me prove it." I wrote many a letter to the social security department in Baltimore trying to straighten out ages. [*Chuckles*.] We did very well. We had a strong union.

What happened to that strength? Aside from corporate greed, the labor leadership got more interested in themselves than in those they were supposed to represent. Some of the leaders have greater allegiance to the Democratic Party than they do to their members.

I learned a lot during my tenure in Congress. Traveling around the world, comparing educational systems, it became obvious to me that, in contrast to European countries, especially Scandinavia, we're a Third World nation in that respect. We're always crying we don't have the money for education, but your mind boggles at the billions squandered on Star Wars.[1]

I think there's very little care as to whether or not poor kids get an education, especially African Americans. So we move toward privatization of the public school system, and you don't hear the trade union movement saying too much about it—as though there were no connection between schooling and jobs and crime.

I can see what's happening in my own community. I really feel things are going to get worse before they get better. The value of human life means nothing to some young people. My wife—she's gone to glory now—had bars put on our windows and installed an alarm system. I've made sure they're preserved. [*Chuckles*.] I don't like to go out at night. When I was in Congress, I had a guy from the sheriff's office with me all the time. He had a gun. Now I don't have that kind of security. If I go anywhere at night, I take somebody with me, even if it's my grandkid.

People—that is, whites—think crime is inherent to black life. I know better. I was born and bred in black areas. It's spread everywhere. Everybody who is out of a job is not lazy. Most would rather have a job than be on public assistance. The reality is that technology has eliminated a lot of jobs. But we're still fooling ourselves that things are getting better. We're still using the band-aid approach. It's not going to work.

I remember when the federal government stepped in—Roosevelt times. My daddy worked on the WPA when I was in the CCC camp. He worked on shoring up river banks and levees. He worked on highways. Today, our infrastructure is falling apart. Every major city needs rebuilding. Millions of young people would be glad to work, yet our government is not making a move in this direction.

Without work, kids are just loitering around, standing on the corner. There are so many panhandlers that I try to avoid going down the street. Yet the only talk we hear is for more prisons, sterner sentences, and more police. How long will it take us to discover that that won't cut it? You don't get at cancer with just a surgeon's knife. You get at the cause or it just spreads on and on and on.

I would really have liked to have spent two more years in Congress, but my big regret was not getting to go to college. Yet. [*Chuckles.*] One thing I know: I've had more experience at being a black than I have had at anything else. I've got seniority there. [*Laughs.*]

Jessie de la Cruz, 74
Fresno, California

When I first visited her in Fresno, she lived with her husband in a one-family dwelling. A small well-kept garden was out front. "I always looked at those flowers in other people's gardens and said, 'If I could only have my own hose and garden.' We couldn't as migrant workers. Now, as you walk onto my porch, everything you see is green. [Laughs.] I have a garden now."

Her husband died four years ago. She lives by herself in a mobile home, though her children are in constant touch with her. "It's a

double trailer, with two baths, two bedrooms, dining room. Everything is compact. Real nice. A porch and a small garden out front, where I can plant anything I want. Beautiful."

***

I'm definitely not retired from life. Right now, there's a big fight going on in Fresno. We wanted to name a street in honor of Cesar Chavez, who did so much for all the people. The city council voted four to three against. At first they voted for it. There were complaints from some people, who were always against Cesar and the union. So they called another meeting and one councilman changed his vote from yes to no. Now the city is divided.

The growers are the ones who gathered the signatures of the business people on Ventura Boulevard. Some have just recently arrived, Arabs, who don't even know what's happening. The others are the ones who've always fought us. We have 100 percent support from the black people of West Fresno, though it was the black councilman who changed his vote. He was pressured, of course. Oh, we're going to keep on fighting. We want that street named after Cesar Chavez, to remember him by.

My health is fine, thank God. I guess keeping busy does it. Last year, I went back and worked for the union full time for about ten months. The first month I was down in Delano, cooking for seventeen volunteers. Then I was sent to Coachella Valley, about a hundred miles north of the Mexican border.

We'd get up about 2:30 in the morning, shower, and be in the office at about 3:15. We were dispatched out to different fields, telling the workers about their rights. It's the desert, about 117 degrees out in the sun. They were working without any shade, no fresh drinking water, no rest rooms, no nothing. Some of the women were pregnant, kneeling in the hot sand picking grapes. They just had a little jug by their side.

We told them there's a federal law that protects these workers and they should stand up and enforce it. We told them the wages they were getting were very low. We convinced them to walk out of the fields. They did, and they got the rest rooms. They got a table with an umbrella overhead, where they stood and packed. They got fresh drinking water. We had thousands of people out there, marching. Last summer, I get a shot of adrenaline when I'm out there, being involved in things. I have to be where the action is.

About five years ago, I suffered a mild stroke that paralyzed an optical nerve. I was seeing double for a time. I had to wear a patch on one eye one day, and a patch on the other eye the next day. But I got over that. They told me I could have surgery or wait and it might go away by itself. So I waited and am fine.

I've been as active as ever. I was president of the California Rural Legal Assistance Migrant Association, referring farm workers to lawyers who wouldn't cheat them. I'm still with the State Bar of California Access for Justice, getting funds for low-income people who can't afford a lawyer. Mostly, I talk to people, tell them about the laws and what they have to do for themselves. Whatever it is, if there's a need, I'll go.

I get up in the morning, have a cup of coffee, a piece of toast, and I'm ready to go. I haven't got a car, haven't the money for it. Somebody drops by, I get a ride or walk downtown. See what's going on, talk to friends, and whatever needs to be done, I'll do.

I live on social security, which is not very much. After paying my rent and utilities, there's about one hundred dollars left over, which I have to stretch for a whole month before I get another check.

I keep getting all these calls because they heard we didn't get the street named for Cesar. People from all walks of life are calling, not just farm workers. We'll keep on fighting, I tell them. There are some meetings coming up.

It's getting worse for the farm workers with this Republican government we have. A lot of them are hiding because they're not legally here. That's what the labor contractor wants. He hides them because he can exploit them by paying them lower wages and having them live in old barns or chicken coops.

And the pesticides. That's another thing. I've seen children that were born without spines. That's why we're boycotting grapes—the pesticides. Many of the children have died. Especially in these rural communities and these little towns around here.

More and more people are becoming aware of these pesticides. They wouldn't listen to us before, but the experts have been out there, exposing the harm. Some are being banned. Whenever I talk to anybody, I tell them about the grapes and the vineyards and the pesticides being sprayed by the tons every year. I study these things and read everything I get my hands on.

There's new leaders out there, new people from the community. Especially the Chicanos. They see how we've been rejected, wherever we go, whatever we try to do. Just the other night at the city council meeting, when somebody stood up before the microphone to talk and he couldn't speak good English, he had a translator. They always ask somebody to help them out. The whites behind us whispered, "Why don't those stupid Mexicans go back to Mexico where they belong." But we're Americans!

This anti-Mexican feeling is strong, especially here in Fresno County, where the growers try to control everything. They have the money and they figure, well, they're the boss of everything. But we're going to prove them wrong. Oh, they know me, all right. But they hardly come out this way. They go shopping in San Francisco or New York, not Fresno. Most of our business is moving out of here. Big shopping centers are being built up in the northern part, moving out of downtown.

It makes me sad to see everything that's going on, especially among our young people—drugs, jail. I wish they could open their eyes and see what society is doing to them. They put the small dope dealers in jail, sixteen-, seventeen-year-old kids. But the big fish, the ones way up who make millions, the government hardly touches.

It's the young who worry me the most. They're fighting each other, being divided. The Chicano kids are told the blacks are no good, the black kids are told the Chicano kids are no good. But among us older people, we're still together. Cesar Chavez taught us we're all in the same boat. He never saw race, he saw people.

Cesar's passing away was a big blow, but we're going to keep on going. That's one thing he always pointed out. "If anything happens to me, there always has to be somebody else." He said, "I don't want our movement to go the way the civil rights movement vanished when Martin Luther King got killed. We must go on."

We're holding up, yes. About a month ago we had a big march, five thousand people marching all the way down from King's Canyon, Ventura. Our Lady of Guadalupe was up front. Even if I don't go very much to church, I pray here at my house. I know there's a God. Otherwise we wouldn't have any rain, flowers. Look outside this trailer. What do you see? A small garden, flowers, tomato plants, whatever.

My children think the same way I do, they think the same way my husband did: the family should have roots. Remember when I told you about the cooperative we had—six families? Everybody pitched in when the big storm was coming. The day before it hit, everybody—grownups, little kids—covered all our tomato plants with little paper cups, cone-shaped. The wind was blowing so strong those cups were just torn from our hands, flying all over the place. Oh, it was hard, but everybody, without exception, put them back. We covered them gently with dirt. My little nephew, four years old, was out there running and helping. And the next day, after the storm, all the plants were there! Oh, it was so wonderful. I said, "Thank God. There is a God."

A big grower would have said, "Let the storm come. What's the difference? What the heck, we'll replant tomorrow." People like us, we don't have the money, show more respect for the land. We try the best we can to conserve the land and enjoy the trees, the fruits they bear, the flowers. Even though you don't eat the flowers, you still enjoy them. They're colorful, they smell good, they're beautiful. It makes you feel good just to have them around. You have to respect everything. Not just the land, but the animals, the people, everything.

I look at myself in the mirror and I know I'm old. But I don't feel old! Last year, they celebrated my birthday—I was seventy-three—at our union headquarters in La Paz, near Bakersfield. They had a big cake and a gift and

Cesar got up and told them how old I was, and they didn't believe it. I got up and said, "When I was younger, I never said my age. Now I'm proud that I am old."

I married when I was young, and I never thought about how long I was going to live. How long am I going to be on this earth? You just live day by day. You get older and you realize there are many things you can do besides just staying home, besides feeling sorry for yourself. There's always something to do, no matter what age, as long as you can get up and walk and talk. There's always hope. We have a saying: *La esperanza muere al ultimo.* Hope dies last. Hope for whatever you want to do. If you can't do it today, there's always tomorrow or the next year. I'm going to spend Christmas with my doctor son in Sacramento, come back and make some tamales for the rest of the family out here. And then I'll get back in action again at the Fresno city council. That's my way of enjoying life—doing something.

Discussion Questions

1. What were the long-term accomplishments of organized labor in the United States?

2. Describe how each of the narrators is spending his or her "retirement."

3. What do Jessie de la Cruz and Charles Hayes see as the major challenges for U.S. society?

4. What are the possibilities for organizing low-skill, low-wage workers today? In what ways do you think being nonunionized will affect their retirement prospects?

Note

1. Reagan's Strategic Defense Initiative, a program to develop and deploy a multi-billion dollar missile defense system, popularly known as "Star Wars."

Reprinted from: Studs Terkel, *Coming of Age,* pp. 105–109, 120–123. Copyright © 1995 by Studs Terkel. Reprinted by permission of The New Press.

Chapter 23
A Lifetime of Work

Katherine R. Allen and
Victoria Chin-Sang

When is retirement not retirement? When you are a rural, aging African-American woman who has done nothing but work all her life, although not always for pay. Helping with the crops a child, keeping house, raising children, volunteering at church, assisting kin, caring for elders—the transition from unpaid to paid work, typically as agricultural help or in domestic or other service-sector jobs, have never been clear across the life course. Like others in U.S. society, such women in this study perceived leisure in old age as "free time," but unlike so many Americans, who define it as time for themselves, many of these women saw leisure in retirement as opening up more space for continued service to kin, church, and now, the senior center.

In the following selection, Katherine Allen and Victoria Chin-Sang portray self-reliant but hardly self-centered women, who have few memories of enjoyable leisure time in the past. Pay attention to their strength and resilience, honed through a lifetime of marginal employment, poverty, and lack of educational opportunity and medical care, shining through the narratives. Consider how, like poor women of all races, work for them is a never ending reality, not something that can be compartmentalized as it is for so many men.

The importance of leisure as an aspect of the post-retirement years is often assumed (Atchley, 1980; Gordon, Gaitz, & Scott, 1976). However, the topics of older adults and leisure (Mancini, 1984; Roadburg, 1981); older women and leisure (Henderson et al., 1989); and black Americans and leisure (Stamps & Stamps, 1985) have received minimal systematic attention. Further, the examination of aging black women's leisure experiences is almost nonexistent. Descriptive work is needed to address biases about leisure, aging, race, and gender. The selection of a sample of aging black women underscores the importance of understanding the meaning and context of leisure from their point of view (Shaw, 1985a, 1985b), a view that is sensitive to the disadvantage, self-reliance, and diversity that characterize their lives (Dill, 1983, 1988; Dressel, 1988; Higginbotham, 1982; Padgett, 1989).

This paper examines the interrelated contexts of work and leisure, as perceived and experienced by aging black women, from a life course perspective. We argue that work history and minority group status underlie black women's current perceptions of leisure and the ways in which they experience leisure in their later years.

Theoretical Framework

The rationale for this study is based on three assumptions: 1) the exclusion of aging black women from leisure studies has contributed to misrepresentation of their lives as well as distortion of our understandings of leisure experience as people age; 2) in examining the experiences of a neglected group of people, an interactionist definition of leisure as an experience of everyday life is preferred to a focus on leisure as recreation or activity because divergent population groups may differ in their leisure definitions (Shaw, 1985a); 3) a life course approach offers a historical, contextual, and culturally sensitive way to interpret current patterns and personal meanings of a neglected minority group (Dilworth-Anderson & McAdoo, 1988). These assumptions underlie the use of qualitative, in-depth interviews to explore and describe aging minority women's experiences (Padgett, 1989).

Leisure as an Experience of Daily Life

. . . The experiential definition rejects earlier notions of leisure as simply nonwork time or a type of activity (Henderson, 1990). Participants can attach their own meanings to leisure experiences if a definition is not imposed through prior categorization of activities.

Samdahl (1987) further elaborates a symbolic interaction-based experiential definition of leisure. Leisure is a particular definition of the situation whose defining qualities arise from the perceived context as opposed to a psychological state. Leisure is "a distinctive pattern of perceiving and relating to ongoing interaction" (Samdahl, 1987, p. 29). Samdahl found that freedom from role constraint and increased opportunity for self-expression are the key dimensions that distinguish pure leisure (engaging free time) from other experiences such as anomic leisure (empty time), enjoyable work, and obligatory tasks. The definition of leisure as an experience of everyday life (Henderson et al., 1989; Samdahl, 1987; Shaw, 1985a) provides a framework to explore how aging black women distinguish work, leisure, and service.

The Experience of Work and Leisure From a Life Course Perspective

Although leisure is a complex, elusive concept with varied meanings, it has been studied almost exclusively from a white, middle-class male perspective (Shaw, 1985b). A life course approach alerts the researcher to contextual issues of process, time, and historical location that are needed to uncover hidden aspects of the lives of neglected groups (Allen, 1989; Elder, 1981).

The life course perspective focuses on the interface between personal biography and social-historical time (Elder, 1981; Erikson, 1975; Mills, 1959). Individuals share certain regularities with cohort members by virtue of entering the world at the same period in history (Ryder, 1965), yet each life is punctuated in diverse and unique ways by idiosyncratic events and experiences (Runyan, 1984).

. . . A key connection in life course experience is between work and leisure. For women, work includes unpaid caregiving labor as well as paid and underpaid market work. These are distinct, yet interrelated experiences, and the meanings and activities associated with each converge and change over time. For black women over age 65, work has dominated their lives (Padgett, 1989; Smith, 1985). Now retired from paid employment, it is likely that they have more

freedom from the constraint of needing to work for someone else in order to survive. Leisure emerges as a more salient life course context. Yet certain continuities, such as work and service, persist over time and are incorporated, perhaps with new meanings, in daily experience in old age. . . .

. . . The research question addressed in this study is how the context and meaning of past work history can distinguish leisure from work and other non-leisure experiences in their current lives.

Methods

In-depth, qualitative interviews were conducted with 30 African-American women. The sample was selected from a population of older adults, with a high concentration of black women, attending urban senior citizen's nutrition and activity programs in northwest Florida. These programs serve a full range of individuals from diverse racial and ethnic backgrounds and socioeconomic levels. Permission was granted to obtain a sample by 25 nutrition center coordinators, who selected six representative centers. Coordinators of the six centers were contacted by telephone to arrange a date and time to meet with potential respondents. An oral explanation of the study was given to groups of older black women, and questions were answered. The 30 participants met two criteria: they were African American and at least 65 years of age. Invitations were extended based on the woman's willingness to participate and desire to express herself on leisure experiences. A nonprobability sample (Babbie, 1989) was obtained in which respondents were selected based on the researcher's judgment about who would be most informative or representative.

The average age of the 30 women (born between 1896 and 1923) was 75.3. Twenty-one were widows, two were separated, one was divorced, five were married, and one was never married. Nineteen women reported having living children (15 women had one to four children; four women had five to ten children). Ten women did not attend school beyond the sixth grade. Of the remaining 20, six completed high school, and one completed one year of college. All of the women were retired, with the exception of four who worked part time for less than 20 hours a week. Before they retired, they worked as domestic workers, factory workers, beauticians, nurses, and the like. The four part-time workers were employed as domestic workers, a practical nurse, and an elder care assistant. All 30 women lived on fixed incomes, and were active members of Protestant churches. Twenty-three lived independently in their own homes or apartments; seven women lived with a family member. Most women had one or more chronic health problems, including hypertension, arthritis, and diabetes. . . .

Audiotaped, in-depth interviews of 60–90 minutes duration were conducted with the 30 participants over a 4-month period, either in their homes or a private room at the senior center. The interview guide consisted of open-ended statements asking each woman to describe her contemporary leisure experiences and work histories. The interviews began with an explanation of the purpose of the study, and as they progressed, each woman was given the opportunity to ask questions to clarify any concerns about the study. In addition to the collection of demographic and experiential data, the women were asked to look at a 7-day calendar and discuss the activities they participated in during the last week that they would classify as leisure, and those that they would not classify as leisure. Interviews ended when the women felt they had provided as much information about the topics as possible. . . .

Following the method described by Taylor and Bogdan (1984), a qualitative content analysis was used to process and interpret the data from the verbatim transcriptions of the interviews. This method involved three phases: discovering themes and patterns in the data, coding the data, and interpreting the data once it had been synthesized and processed. . . .

The Context and Meanings of Leisure

Women described their past and current experiences of leisure within the context of a lifetime of hard work. The discussion below reveals how past work history and adversity associated with multiple jeopardies of minority group status structured life course experience. The meanings of past and present leisure experiences are seen within this context, where the women's present day leisure activities show a mixture of continuities and discontinuities with their work histories. Their self-reliance from years of adaptability in dealing with oppressive systems reveals a pattern of service to self and mostly other women in their later years. The interrelated contexts of work, leisure, and service can be distinguished by using the proposed interactionist-life course framework.

The women's perceptions of past leisure and work experience are presented in Table 23.1. When asked how their definition and experience of leisure had changed over the years, most women said that they had no leisure in the past. Only 13 women replied that there was some type of enjoyable leisure activity in which they engaged before retirement. What is intriguing about their experiences is that only six women described what Samdahl (1988) referred to as pure leisure (engaging free time). The other seven women who claimed to have had leisure experience in the past defined it in relation to either work or service. Work clearly was the prominent feature of their lives. The context of a lifetime of hard work is described below.

The Context of Leisure: A Lifetime of Hard Work

These 30 women described a lifelong involvement in structured work activities that began in childhood and extended into old age:

> I started to work when I was 9. That's how I bought my school clothes. The lady paid me one dollar a week to walk her baby 2 hours every day after school. I started pressing when I was 12 years old, and I've been a professional presser for 52 years. I'm still doing it off and on when they call me.

Their work histories followed a pattern of mostly unpaid agricultural work in childhood, paid work during adulthood typically in agricultural, domestic, and service industries, and volunteer work or self-employment in old age. The availability of employment for uneducated black women was limited to the work reported here, a commonality of their lives that is well documented in the historical literature (Rodgers-Rose, 1980; Smith, 1985). Only in old age did flexibility in job choice increase. All the women in this study worked in at least two job categories during their lifetime.

Table 23.1

Perceptions of Aging Black Women About Past Leisure and Work Experiences

Perception	Respondent *n* (*N* = 30)
No past leisure time[a]	17
Past leisure, defined as:	
Work[b]	4
Service[c]	3
Leisure[d]	6

Note. The following quotes typify the perceptions of leisure.
[a]"I was always working; I had no leisure time."
[b]"I was content working in my free time."
[c]"I helped people when I had spare time."
[d]"I'd come and go as I pleased."

Childhood Work. Their work careers began during childhood, where they worked in the cotton, tobacco, and vegetable fields along with parents and siblings. Childhood labor was mostly unpaid and was necessary to contribute to self and family care:

> Daddy was a big farmer. He started me working when I was about 10 years old and you talk about work, I worked hard! I was the oldest of 12 children, and my daddy made a plowboy out of me.

Adult Labor. As adults, nine women received wages for field work, including those who worked in the fields as children: "Up until 12 years ago I was still working in the fields picking cotton, tobacco, butterbeans, and peas."

Domestic service was the other occupation open to the women during their early and middle adult years. Eighteen women worked in the homes of white families, doing housework, cooking, laundry, and child care. Paid work had personal meanings beyond the necessity of earning a wage:

> I was 18 or 19 when I started doing domestic work. That's hard work. You have to put all of your whole heart, soul, and mind in it.
>
> I washed and ironed for people from when I was 14 until I was 50. I raised all my children by washing and ironing.

Several women continued to take domestic jobs until retirement:

> I've done domestic work all of my life. I retired 5 years ago. I stopped being a housekeeper and cleaning people's homes. I wasn't ill or nothing. I just reached the age where I thought I should stop working.

Additional service occupations opened to them as they aged. Six women worked in laundries:

> For 10 and a half years, I folded, counted, wrapped, and boxed sheets.
> I worked in laundries all over this city. I worked until my wrists just gave out.

Nine women became employed in food service jobs that had been previously closed to them. The skills that were used in domestic work were transferred to jobs in restaurants and food processing plants. Several reported their expertise in cooking and baking.

Eight women had paid work experience in health care service, doing what they considered was natural for them—caring for others. Nurturing others, their domain, was broadened to include the sick and infirm in the homes of others and in hospitals. They became skilled at caring for others' physical and emotional needs.

Seven women reported a stint at self-employment. They established their own grocery stores, lunchrooms, and hairdressing salons. One woman described her experience with renting a flea market stand:

> I got tired of staying home and I told my husband we had to do something. I thought it would be good for us to be out of the house. You just can't sit around all the time doing nothing. So I thought of having a stand at the flea market. Sometimes we make money, sometimes none, but we have a good time. At least we're not sitting home feeling sorry for ourselves.

When we're out there we forget about our aches and pains.

A Wish for a Job. The importance of work, whether paid or unpaid, was further expressed by six women as "a wish for a job." Their entire life course was organized around work, and work was associated with self and family survival. In discussing their retirement, six women expressed a desire to work now, revealing the importance of work as a defining feature of their lives:

> Work is great, I love it. I've always said, even if I was rich, I would want to be working. I've always loved work because that's all I've ever done. I wish I had a job now.

Each woman's work history was diverse, yet they all shared a focus on the importance of work as a central organizing feature of their existence. For most of their lives, these women were involved in subsistence labor outside their families in order to promote familial survival. Much resourcefulness was needed for them to provide for their families, because their wages and opportunities were so limited.

The Meanings of Leisure for Aging Black Women

Before retirement, the women's experience of leisure was restricted primarily to the context of working. The resourcefulness they developed in dealing with a lifetime of hard work set the stage for their interpretation of leisure after they retired. . . .

The demarcation between the women's definitions of work and leisure . . . disappears, however, when the women's current leisure experiences are examined. . . . They described three experiences: leisure, work, and service. The third category consists of service to others and self-care activities . . . for these women, the current meanings and context of leisure often overlapped with work and service.

Leisure Time as My Time. These women considered leisure time in old age to be free time, whereas working for someone else had dominated the majority of hours in their adult years. They drew strength and became resourceful in taking care of themselves and others by surviving the weight of disadvan-

tage that is black women's history, especially in the context of southern race relations (Dill, 1988; Higginbotham, 1982; Mann, 1989). Their self-reliance and freedom to spend their time as they pleased in old age were important accomplishments that they valued and protected.

The women engaged in a variety of activities, including solitary, passive experiences and physical activities that were active or affiliative. They spent time alone, reading the Bible or newspaper, watching TV, and just sitting and relaxing. They exercised, kept house, gardened, and made crafts.

The church and senior center provided important contexts for their leisure involvement. Voluntary activities allowed them to use skills and talents gained in previous work and caregiving experiences. The reciprocal function and importance of the church and community groups in the lives of black women is well documented, though their organizational complexities are not widely studied. Black women's traditions in community institutions have been among the most underdeveloped topics of social investigation (Gilkes, 1985).

The Church. These women viewed the church as a shelter, a refuge, and a place to be connected to others: "I started volunteering at church, feeding the street people. I started it because I wanted to do something other than sitting here. I had gotten in a rut." They saw themselves as the backbone of the church and expended great energy to maintain the place where they relax, serve, and worship:

> Church is not leisure and not work, it's worship. The Lord gives me a lot of strength to do whatever I do every day. He has given us all these days to do what we want to do, so we should give him his time.

A few women were ambivalent about the church, consistent with Grant's (1982) finding that the church can be a mixed blessing for black women, a fundamental feature of their lives, yet a potential source of exploitation. Overall, however, they expressed the dual meaning of the church as a context for leisure and for service:

Church is a place that I like to go on one account, to hear the preacher preach and study the Bible because I don't know it all. Them ministers can't save me, but if I can get that word and live by it, then maybe I can make it in. I get as much pleasure going down there and cleaning up my church as somebody would get for making a big speech and getting all the applause he wants. I'm just as happy in that church as he is on that podium.

The Senior Center. Whereas church is a place for leisure and service, the senior center was described as a context in which leisure and work were combined, reflecting a continuity in these women's lifelong involvement in work:

I've been a diet aide helper at two nutrition sites for more than 6 years. I help set up trays by putting the cold food on the trays. After everyone eats I help wash the trays, clean the tables, clean the place up, and leave it nice. When I'm not there I miss it very much.

I come to the center once a week. I belong to the Urban League. I'm financial secretary of the homeowner's association and president of the local chapter of the AARP. I feel that I'm going to these meetings and organizations to help other people and more or less to just simply be there.

Finally, many of these women did not have involvement with family members, either through death or neglect, so they created their own community. This strategy of creating fictive kin relationships is an aspect of African American experience examined by Stack (1974): "I spend most of my time in the streets, marketing and at the center. Those people treat me very nice, like I'm their sister or daughter. They found alternative family arrangements in the senior community among other women, with whom they felt an undeniably strong bond:

I like to help people out, do the housework, run errands if I'm able to go and it's not too far. [It] makes me feel good to know I could do some of these things for them. [I] think the Lord will bless me for doing that.

Conclusions

The work histories—unpaid childhood labor; low-paying agricultural and service jobs in adulthood; volunteer work in later life—of women in this study are consistent with the experiences of black women in previous research (Collins, 1989; Dill, 1988; Mann, 1989). The supportive services they created and found for themselves reveal the strength and resilience of older black women who have survived uniquely adverse conditions of poverty, lack of medical services, and lack of opportunities (Jackson, 1972; Padgett, 1989). They put their lifetime of hard work into practice as they aged, and incorporated work and care for others into their leisure experiences by tending to peers in their own communities.

The meaning of leisure for these women was revealed by addressing the life course context of work. . . . Work was the context in which leisure was described, yet, in response to questions about what is leisure and what is not leisure, the women elaborated their own meanings, as well. Consistent with Samdahl's (1987) findings, the women in this study also described leisure as both freedom from the constraint of needing to work in order to survive and a form of self-expression, whether active or passive, solitary or affiliative. What had been missing during their working years was time just to relax or to have the freedom to work with and for others as they chose. Now with free time, these self-reliant strategists incorporated important community institutions—the church and senior center (Gilkes, 1985; Stack, 1974)—into their daily experience of work, leisure, and service.

Several conclusions can be drawn from this study. First, work was a life course continuity that dominated their childhood and adulthood, and was incorporated into both past and present leisure experience. For example, grocery shopping, some aspect of housekeeping, and helping others were listed under each of the three categories of leisure, work, and service in their activities within the past 7 days. . . . The inclusion of caregiving in all three categories suggests the pervasive and hidden meanings of women's caring labor. We concur with Henderson (1990) that the ethic of care is an important context of women's leisure activities.

Second, the meaning of work seemed to change, however, from the necessity of earning a living for self and family survival to becoming an aspect of freedom from the constraint of having to work (Samdahl, 1987). Thus, working was continuous throughout the life course, but the meanings associated with work changed to incorporate new definitions and contexts.

Third, church was defined by the women as either leisure or service, but not as work, suggesting the uniqueness of this experience for many of the women. . . . The unique relationship between black women and the church is a way in which women's lives are differentiated. There is no unilateral way that all women experience leisure.

Finally, the inclusion of service as an inter-related context with leisure and work in these women's lives departs from the traditional white male definition of leisure as a segmented experience of the life course. Unlike definitions of men's leisure experience, which show a clear work/leisure dichotomy (Henderson, 1990), the aging black women in this study were much more like the aging rural white farm women described by Henderson and Rannells (1988). They found that the women's work was time consuming and never ending, valued and enjoyed, and connected to caregiving and community responsibilities. They did not view their lack of free time or leisure as problematic. Rather, these farm women "found meaning and leisure through an integration of work, family, and community experiences" (Henderson and Rannells 1988, p. 41).

Like the women in Henderson and Rannells' (1988) study, these aging black women worked hard all their lives in the service of self and family survival. In their later years, they placed more emphasis on freely choosing their leisure pursuits, but the context in which they expressed their leisure was related to their lifelong involvement in work and in the particular way that black women have provided service for others. The finding that church is neither work nor leisure, but perhaps a unique type of service experience these women share with each other requires

further exploration to see if it is shared with other groups and cohorts of women and men.

Discussion Questions

1. How do poverty and race intersect in the lives of these women?

2. Discuss the role of the church in the African-American community.

3. What are the advantages and drawbacks of the qualitative data-gathering approach used in this study?

4. In what ways would the experience of poor white women be similar or different from that of these women?

References

Allen, K. R. (1989). *Single women/family ties: Life histories of older women.* Newbury Park, CA: Sage.

Atchley, R. (1980). *The social forces in later life* (3rd ed.). Belmont, CA: Wadsworth.

Babbie, E. (1989). *The practice of social research* (5th ed.). Belmont. CA: Wadsworth.

Bengtson, V. L., & Allen, K. R. (in press). Life course theories and methods applied to the family. In P. Boss, W. Doherty, R. LaRossa, W. Schumm, & S. Steinmetz (Eds.), *Sourcebook of family theories and methods: A contextual approach.* New York: Plenum.

Collins, P. H. (1989), The social construction of black feminist thought. *Signs, 14,* 745–773.

Dill, B. T. (1983). Race, class, and gender: Prospects for an all-inclusive sisterhood. *Feminist Studies, 9,* 131–150.

Dill, B. T. (1988). Our mothers' grief: Racial ethnic women and the maintenance of families. *Journal of Family History, 13,* 415–431.

Dilworth-Anderson, P., & McAdoo, H. P. (1988). The study of ethnic minority families: Implications for practitioners and policymakers. *Family Relations, 37,* 265–267.

Dressel, P. (1988). Gender, race, and class: Beyond the feminization of poverty in later life. *The Gerontologist, 28,* 177–180.

Elder, G. H., Jr. (1981). History and the family: The discovery of complexity. *Journal of Marriage and the Family, 43,* 489–519.

Erikson, E. H. (1975). *Life history and the historical moment.* New York: Norton.

Gibson, R. C. (1987). Reconceptualizing retirement for black Americans. *The Gerontologist, 27,* 691–698.

Gilkes, C. T. (1985). "Together and in harness": Women's traditions in the sanctified church. *Signs, 10,* 678–699.

Gordon, C., Gaitz, C. M., & Scott, J. (1976). Leisure and lives: Personal expressivity across the lifespan. In R. H. Binstock & E. Shanas (Eds.), *Handbook of aging and the social sciences* (pp. 310–341). New York: Van Nostrand-Reinhold.

Grant, J. (1982). Black women and the church. In G. T. Hull, P. B. Scott, & B. Smith (Eds.), *But some of us are brave: Black women's studies* (pp. 141–152). Old Westbury, NY: Feminist Press.

Henderson, K. A. (1990). The meaning of leisure for women: An integrative review of the research. *Journal of Leisure Research, 22,* 228–243.

Henderson, K. A., Bialeschki, M. D., Shaw, S. M., & Freysinger, V. J. (1989). *A leisure of one's own: A feminist perspective on women's leisure.* State College, PA: Venture.

Henderson, K. A., & Rannells, J. S. (1988). Farm women and the meaning of work and leisure: An oral history perspective. *Leisure Sciences, 10,* 41–50.

Higginbotham, E. (1982). Two representative issues in contemporary sociological work on black women. In G. T. Hull, P. B. Scott, & B. Smith (Eds.), *But some of us are brave: Black women's studies* (pp. 93–98). Old Westbury, NY: Feminist Press.

Jackson, J. J. (1972). Black women in a racist society. In C. Willie, B. Kramer, & B. Brown (Eds.), *Racism and mental health* (pp. 185–268). Pittsburgh: University of Pittsburgh Press.

Johnson, J. E. (1982). The Afro-American family: A historical overview. In B. A. Bass, G. E. Wyatt, & G. J. Powell (Eds.), *The Afro-American family: Assessment, treatment and research issues* (pp. 3–12). New York: Grune & Stratton.

LaRossa, R. (1988). Renewing our faith in qualitative family research. *Journal of Contemporary Ethnography, 17,* 243–260.

Mancini, J. A. (1984). Leisure lifestyles and family dynamics in old age. In W. H. Quinn & G. A. Hughston (Eds.), *Independent aging: Family and social systems perspectives* (pp. 58–71). Rockville, MD: Aspen.

Mann, S. A. (1989). Slavery, sharecropping, and sexual inequality. *Signs, 14,* 774–798.

Mills, C. W. (1959). *The sociological imagination.* London: Oxford University Press.

Padgett D. (1989). Aging minority women: Issues in research and health policy. In L. Grau (Ed.), *Women in the later years: Health, social, and cultural perspectives* (pp. 213–225). Binghamton, NY: Haworth.

Passuth, P. M., & Bengtson, V. L. (1988). Sociological theories of aging. In J. E. Birren & V. L. Bengtson (Eds.), *Emergent theories of aging* (pp. 333–355). New York: Springer.

Roadburg, A. (1981). Perceptions of work and leisure among the elderly. *The Gerontologist, 21,* 142–145.

Rodgers-Rose, L. R. (1980). The black woman: A historical overview. In L. F. Rodgers-Rose (Ed.), *The black woman* (pp. 15–25). Beverly Hills, CA: Sage.

Runyan, W. M. (1984). *Life histories and psychobiography.* New York: Oxford University Press.

Ryder, N. (1965). The cohort as a concept in the study of social change. *American Sociological Review, 30,* 843–861.

Samdahl, D. M. (1987). A symbolic interactionist model of leisure: Theory and empirical support. *Leisure Sciences, 10,* 27–39.

Shaw, S. M. (1985a). The meaning of leisure in everyday life. *Leisure Sciences, 7,* 1–24.

Shaw, S. M. (1985b). Gender and leisure: Inequality in the distribution of leisure time. *Journal of Leisure Research, 17,* 266–282.

Smith, E. (1985). Black American women and work: A historical review—1619–1920. *Women's Studies International Forum, 8,* 343–349.

Stack, C. B. (1974). *All our kin.* New York: Harper Colophon.

Stamps, S. M., & Stamps, M. B. (1985). Race, class and leisure activities of urban residents. *Journal of Leisure Research, 17,* 40–56.

Stryker, S. (1959). Symbolic interaction as an approach to family research. *Marriage and Family Living, 21,* 111–119.

Taylor, S. J., & Bogdan, R. (1984). *Introduction to qualitative research methods* (2nd ed.). New York: John Wiley.

Wilkinson, D. Y. (1984). Afro-American women and their families. *Marriage and Family Review, 7,* 125–142.

Chapter 24

Too Little, Too Late

Kathleen McInnis-Dittrich

The great majority, two-thirds, of poor people in the United States today are native-born whites. Some live in the inner ring of America's decaying urban centers, but most are rural residents, from the forests of Maine to the sun-baked dirt streets of run-down villages in the Southwest. But when we think "rural white poor," the picture that comes to mind is a white family in the hollows of West Virginia, hauntingly captured by the photography of Gordon Parkes during the Great Depression. There is the gaunt woman, probably only 30 but looking twice that age; the grim-faced, unshaven father; the barefoot, hollow-eyed children, all posed before a decaying wooden shack of a home.

Despite tens of millions of dollars poured into the region called Appalachia during the short-lived War on Poverty of the late 1960s, the prevalence of poverty remains stubbornly unchanged. Few health-care professionals serve the area; schools are chronically underfunded and understaffed. Young adults flee to more urbanized areas where there are jobs, however low-paying. And their parents will "age in place," rarely eligible for Social Security (having had little in the way of covered employment) and dependent on Supplemental Security Income (SSI), which provided a minimal monthly benefit, roughly $440 per month in 1997, to people whose incomes remained below the poverty level even when all sources of income are measured. But even this flimsy thread of a safety net was shredded with passage of legislation in 1997 replacing federal guarantees with block grants to the states and urging the needy to seek employment first. The problem for many in Appalachia, however, is that paying jobs have been scarce since the coal

mines were shut down, and the land is too harsh for crops.

Kathleen McInnis-Dittrich details the unique situation of the Appalachian elderly, their culture of independence and isolation. Think about the problem of providing supportive services across a difficult and sparsely populated terrain. Long-term solutions to Appalachian poverty would involve far greater public expenditures than the current Congress or public mood is willing to expend. As you read, appraise short-term, concrete steps that can be taken to alleviate the pain of this cohort of older rural "folk."

Introduction

The geographical region known as Appalachia is comprised of 399 counties within a 13-state region of the United States, extending from upstate New York to Alabama. With an aggregate overall poverty rate of over 32 percent in the early 1960s, this region became a center of attention for President John F. Kennedy's War on Poverty (Appalachian Regional Commission 1997). The heart wrenching pictures of poor children in dirty, tattered clothes along with their gaunt faced, unemployed parents posing in front of ramshackle mountain cabins brought the United States to a heightened awareness of the faces of intense and chronic poverty. Due in part to the short-lived War on Poverty programs and the few anti-poverty efforts that survived the tumultuous economic cycles of the 1970s and 1980s, current poverty rates in this region have been slashed to 15.2 percent compared to 13.8 percent for the total U.S. (U.S. Bureau of the Census 1997). These aggregate statistics hide the dramatic variations within the Appalachian region where poverty rates in 1996 ranged from a low of 4.0 percent in Gurnnett County, Georgia to a high of 52.1 percent in Owsley County, Kentucky (Appalachian Regional Commission 1997). The most economically distressed areas within Appalachia are rural, heavily concentrated in the states of Kentucky, Mississippi, Tennessee, or West Virginia, and disproportionately elderly (Deavers and Hoppe 1992).

Among the impoverished coal miners and tobacco farmers pictured in the War on Poverty photographs who are now elders, poverty rates soar as high as 70 percent (Rowles and Johansson 1993) while the national elderly poverty rate is 10.5 percent. Although the obstacles that face Appalachian elders are similar to those facing any low income rural elderly, the physical characteristics of the region and the unique traits of the changing Appalachian culture exacerbate both the intensity of the poverty and the difficulties involved in planning and providing services to the elderly population.

The paper will begin with an overview of the causes and consequences of poverty in the Appalachia region emphasizing the complex interaction of social, economic, and structural issues in both the development and maintenance of poverty. Four specific problem areas unique to Appalachian elders are explored in detail using the real life experiences of elders who face these challenges every day. The paper concludes with recommendations for social policy and service adaptations which address the unique situation of Appalachian and other isolated rural elders.

The Life Course Perspective on Poverty in Appalachia

The dynamics of poverty among the elderly in Appalachia are best understood from the "life course" perspective. The life course perspective examines the biopsychosocial realities of elders as a function of shared lifelong experiences with a birth cohort. Many of the elders in Appalachia along with all of their relatives and friends have been poor all of their lives. In other words, many elders share similar health problems, experiences in being married and raising families in the region, relationships with neighbors and friends, and ways of coping with the intensity of emotions that accompany a life of chronic poverty. While being poor in Appalachia is in part due to human capital factors (Schiller 1995) such as limited education, skills, and training, poverty is also the function of historical, structural and social factors that have affected the economic experiences of the entire birth cohort of elders in the region.

Historical Factors

The Appalachia region of the United States was first settled in the late 1700's by Irish, Scottish and German settlers. These early settlers were primarily subsistence farmers and fostered a rural culture that stressed freedom, democratic values and fundamentalist Protestantism (Billing and Walls 1980). While the land was beautiful and rich in natural resources, it was cut off from large scale settlement by rocky, mountainous terrain. This isolation that served the settlers well in terms of being left alone by others created formidable obstacles to building both physical and social connections to a rapidly developing outside world. Historically, the region has been bypassed for economic development because of the difficulty of accessing the region. Highways and railroads are difficult to build and maintain.

The discovery of rich veins of coal in the region and advances in the lumbering industry began to make the region attractive to outside capital starting in 1870 (Billing and Walls 1980; Duncan 1992). The Appalachian region's economy became heavily resource-based meaning that what little industry existed in the region was based on the use and processing of natural resources. Lumbering, mining, small scale farming or manufacturing served as the primary source of employment for men. These jobs rarely gave men an opportunity to qualify for retirement pensions or to accumulate resources for retirement. Industries were owned by entrepreneurs who lived outside the region and when resources were depleted or it became too expensive to implement federally mandated safety standards in the mines and mills, the industries folded, leaving local residents few, if any, employment options (Eller 1986). Thus chronic unemployment has become a way of life for residents of Appalachia. Jobs in the region have always been scarce so it is a common experience for women to marry early, not work outside the home, and raise families. With their economic well-being intimately connected to the economic experiences of their husbands, they suffered the same, if not worse, economic insecurity (Rowles and Johansson 1993).

For elders of both genders, this means that a life time of low income and sporadic or chronic unemployment has translated into few, if any economic resources for later in their lives (McLaughlin and Holden 1993). For those few men (or women who worked outside the home) who qualified for Social Security, benefit levels reflect the modest earnings on which benefit payments are calculated. For those elders relying on Supplemental Security Income (SSI), the federal means-tested income maintenance program for low-income, blind and disabled persons, state supplements in states in the Appalachian region are rarely sufficient to raise their income above the poverty line (Rowles and Johansson 1993). Their historical experience of low-income and subsistence living compounds the extreme of poverty in their old age.

Structural Factors

The economic dichotomy created by the owners of industry, the "haves," and the laborers in the mines and mills, "the have-nots", continues to play itself out in many Appalachian counties today in an "entrenched patronage-driven political system." (Duncan 1992, 11). A small number of farmers who have historically owned either land or industry continue to control a small number of jobs in the region. Lack of economic diversity in many Appalachian communities places severe limitations on the availability of even minimum wage jobs. While the aggregate unemployment rate for the entire Appalachian region in 1995 was 6.0 percent (compared to 5.6 percent for the U.S.), the unemployment rate in rural Appalachian counties is 7.2 percent (Appalachian Regional Commission 1997). This rate climbs to over 9 percent in counties for which coal mining is the sole industry. If a select group of families controls who gets available jobs based on patronage, lifelong poor families will find the traditional ways of leaving poverty through education and employment blocked. Historically, "poor families have been assigned a permanent place at the bottom of the social structure" (Duncan 1992, 131). Even today, social stratification is reflected in the operation of the school system, social services, and public services such as road repair, fire, and police protection.

Social Factors

Elders living in Appalachia are adept at using a complicated system of resources used to mitigate the direct effects of severe poverty. These include the wide use of gardens to supplement food supplies, an informal bartering system for the exchange of services, and reliance on extended family support systems (Rowles and Johansson 1993). Family support may consist of intergenerational transfers of money, food, or personal assistance.

Use of a "social credit" system was and continues to be seen in low-income populations such as Appalachia as well as poor urban areas. By helping a neighbor who has difficulty paying a utility bill or clothing the children, an individual accumulates social credits. When individuals who have helped others in the neighborhood need help in return, they can expect to approach family members and neighbors for assistance based on their own personal pattern of helping. Many elders rely on a complex system of social credits to buffer the effects of severe poverty (Gove, Ortega and Style 1989). The social credit system is a prime example of the social context of poverty in rural Appalachia. Even people with severely restricted incomes may not consider themselves poor when they compare their own situations with others they know. There is a tacit expectation that life involves some degree of hardship and poverty. While that belief may help people survive, elders may be tolerant of deprivation so severe it actually threatens their physical health and well-being (DePoy and Butler 1996).

These historical, structural and social factors constitute the framework in which poverty exists in Appalachia. Looking specifically at elders in the region, four problem areas can be identified within this context of entrenched poverty. These include the effects of lifelong poverty, cultural attitudes about independence, geographical isolation, and enduring rigid social class structure.

The Cumulative Effects of Poverty Over the Life Course

As the history of the region illustrates, many Appalachian elderly have been poor their entire lives. As elders, they have less connection to the labor market than at any time in their lives and are subsequently more likely to remain poor (Adams and Duncan 1992). Living in chronic poverty creates a greater risk for developing a chronic health problem, dying from accidents or disease, living in substandard housing, being witness to or the victim of violence and suffering from physical and intellectual damage resulting from poor nutrition (Deavers and Hoppe 1992; Richardson 1987). These deleterious effects are exacerbated when individuals reach old age. While older adults of all socioeconomic groups are more likely to suffer from heart disease, hypertension, and diabetes, Appalachian elders may begin to experience the disabling effects of these conditions in early middle age. Appalachian elders also experience more frequent illnesses due to social isolation, chronic stress and erratic weather (Deitz, 1991). Lack of access to early medical intervention and/or the inability to pay for such care means that these conditions are less likely to be treated than is the case for other elders.

Ruth, an 83 year old woman living alone in a dilapidated farm house, is a good example of the disastrous effects of lifelong poverty. Ruth raised ten children in a six room house with no plumbing situated two miles off a main road. The family supplemented their subsistence-level income by raising and preserving much of their own food. Ruth often fed her children and husband first. If there was no food left, she simply did not eat for a few days. As she states "we got by somehow." Her husband, a tobacco farmer, died when Ruth was 60 years old and the children were grown. Her adult children remain within the county but are busy with children and grandchildren of their own. Breaking ice to haul water in the winter and trudging to the outhouse were feasible when Ruth was younger, but now she suffers from severe arthritis, hypertension, impaired hearing and gynecological problems. Living in a cold house, performing intense physical labor throughout her lifetime, too many meals of soup beans and cornbread and no routine medical care have taken their toll. Untreated ear infections as a child have damaged her hearing. Ten difficult births supervised by an untrained midwife neighbor have contributed to current life threatening health problems. While Ruth finds her deep religious faith comforting, the chronic discomfort and pain she experiences have contributed to severe depression.

Ruth's health problems are not unique to her rural residence. However, these conditions are exacerbated as a consequence of chronic lifelong poverty. Poor medical care, inadequate diet, and substandard housing although challenging when Ruth was younger are life-threatening issues to her as an elder.

Social Attitudes About Independence

A well-meaning social worker or nurse would see Ruth as an excellent candidate for specialized elderly housing. With access to on-site medical services, nutrition programs, and even the simple matter of better plumbing facilities, the immediate danger to Ruth's health would be dramatically reduced. It is easy to believe that what sounds acceptable and attractive to professional helpers would be equally appealing to an elder in Ruth's situation. However, prevailing social attitudes about independence among Appalachian elders and expectations around who will care for dependent elders indicate otherwise.

Many Appalachian elders who raised their families under the most destitute of conditions without the help of public assistance benefits, food stamps, or housing subsidies (and cared for their own aging parents as well) represent a very sturdy and proud low-income population (Spence 1993). When they had nothing else to offer their children, they had their pride in having "taken care of their own." Even now it is difficult to convince some elders in the region that they are both eligible for and entitled to SSI or special visiting nurse benefits. Elders may cling to the idea that it is the responsibility of their children to care for them and their children's failure to do so reflects poorly upon them as parents.

They are relying on the "social credit system" described earlier in this paper. This complicated picture of social credits and the social buffers which isolate Appalachian elders from some of the most devastating effects of a lifetime of low income is a functional way of counteracting poverty. However, this system is rapidly disappearing in the area. Young people are leaving the area to seek better and more stable employment in urban areas, leaving elders without the assistance that once enabled them to continue to live independently despite severe poverty and isolation (McCulloch and Lynch 1993). The Appalachian region has seen an out-migration of 15 percent of its total population since 1950 although this rate has slowed dramatically since 1990 (Appalachian Regional Commission 1997). Elders who once relied on each other as they raised their own families, now find themselves with limited resources to share and more in need of services than able to share it with others. The buffer zones which mitigated the problems of poverty are rapidly disappearing.

Another factor which reinforces Appalachian elders' perceptions of the importance of remaining independent of outside social institutions is their deep love of and attachment to the land on which their homes are located. Land often represents the only capital low income elders have ever had and the stunning beauty of much of the Appalachian region makes it clear why elders may be hesitant to leave their homes. Ruth's husband's family homesteaded the ten acres on which the house is located. She still sleeps in the bed in which she delivered all of her children and in which her husband died. The idea of leaving the land passed down from generation to generation in her husband's family is too painful for Ruth to even consider. Her husband and all of his extended family from four generations back are buried several hundred yards from the house. The graves are cared for with great devotion, an enduring cultural practice in this region. These factors far outweigh any chance that even with severe medical problems, Ruth will consider leaving her home for what she considers to be the sterile, unfriendly environment of elderly housing.

Geographical Isolation

Ruth's house, like many other Appalachian elders whose homesteads predated the development of a system of local roads, is far away and difficult to access. Harsh mountain winters, torrential spring rains, and the hostile terrain make both road construction and maintenance extremely precarious. Although snowfall is not uncommon in the more mountainous areas of the region, county governments own little snow removal equipment, and it is rarely used to plow out remote roads. Even if supportive services such as visiting nurses, meals-on-wheels, and homemaker services do exist in Appalachian counties, it is difficult to get the service to the elder in need.

Howard is a 76 year old man who lives alone in a cabin located some 20 miles from even the smallest town in the county. He was discovered only recently by an outreach worker from a local Christian philanthropic organization who ventured down Howard's road in a four-wheel drive vehicle quite by accident. The road to his cabin has fallen into disuse and Howard cannot afford to pay for repairs. He has always owned the house and adjoining land where he and his wife raised five children. His wife left him 20 years ago after the children were grown because of his chronic alcoholism and abusive behavior. Howard worked only sporadically throughout his life and relied on Supplemental Security Income (SSI) for his limited income until recently. Howard's needs are limited and the SSI check was sufficient to at least meet his basic needs for food. Recipients of SSI are allowed to keep their homes and still receive benefits which is what happened in Howard's case until he sold a portion of the land to a neighbor and used the money pay off old debts. Someone reported the sale to the Social Security Administration and Howard's SSI checks were stopped. The Social Security Administration considered the money from the land sale to be income which made Howard ineligible for SSI. Hence, Howard gets no monthly income and has lost the medical insurance, Medicaid, which accompanies SSI.

A lifetime of heavy drinking has left Howard with severe cirrhosis of the liver, diabetes, and a paranoid personality, most likely the result of the beginnings of organic brain disease. Some days, he is so weak and sick he cannot get out of bed. He has never learned to monitor his diabetes and continues to drink despite his medical condition. The only place he can receive medical care without health insurance is at a public hospital located 75 miles away. After a bad experience there some years ago, Howard refuses to go. Despite the severity of the situation, Howard can probably survive in his own home with the right support services but how do helping professionals get to him?

Howard's case is a good example of the dilemma that faces providing services to extremely isolated rural elders. Howard owns his house and adjoining land including the road to it therefore is financially responsible for maintaining the road. He cannot afford to do it but is so bound to the land he also will not leave his home. While he is eligible for free support services from a county visiting nurse, despite his lack of medical insurance, they cannot provide the service because he is inaccessible. The values of both nursing and social work professions indicate that people such as Howard cannot be left to die; the professional codes of ethics do not indicate how to overcome the severe isolation which precludes delivering the service.

Despite the high drama, Howard's case is not unique. Thousands of Appalachian elders who continue to live on land which remained in their families for generations, like Ruth, are simply too isolated to take advantage of the limited services that do exist in home care for the elderly. While early settlers in Appalachia may have relished the isolation from others and homesteaded on scenic wooded land, their descendants find themselves elderly, alone, and isolated.

Enduring Social Class Issues

Howard's case is a vivid example of another problem area for Appalachian elders, an enduring social class structure. As was illustrated earlier in this chapter, social classes of the "haves" and "have nots" continue to influence the social and political institutions of the Appalachian area. It is important to emphasize that the "haves" in Appalachia are not wealthy by traditional standards of measuring economic success. More accurately, most are working class. However, in comparison to the destitutely poor, they appear rich. Their power exists not so much in access to personal resources but through control of public monies through political office. County officials wield tremendous power over road repair, building permits, and civil service employment. The decision about who gets a load of gravel on the road to their home or is plowed out first in a snowstorm may seem inconsequential to an outsider but reflects a deeply entrenched system of political patronage.

For many generations, Howard's extended family has been regarded as a "bad turn" family. That is, the family has a history of criminal activity, extreme poverty, illegal trade in moonshine, womanizing, and failure to assume family responsibilities. No doubt some of Howard's behavior in his lifetime has contributed to the family's reputation. While in more urban areas and in other cultural settings, reaching old age has a forgiving effect on what behavior people engaged in prior to old age, Appalachian culture has a long memory. Persons regarded as "have nots" when they were younger remain permanently relegated to a position on the bottom of the economic and social ladder. An elder's position in this social structure is maintained on the basis of enduring social class issues. Howard's position on the bottom of the social ladder explains why someone reported him to the Social Security Administration when he sold a portion of his land to liquidate cash. The mean-spirited behavior on the part of someone else does not justify Howard's failure to report the land sale; the law is very clear on that requirement. Unfortunately it does illustrate that even as a very sick, dying old man, he cannot escape his diminished social status.

The perception that political power over already limited resources in the region favors "the haves" has led to a pervasive distrust in social institutions in general by low income Appalachian elders (Davis 1988; Spence 1993). Elders and their families may fail to even apply for assistance because they have heard stories about either how the poor are treated or the likelihood they will receive benefits if they do apply. Although the stories of poor treatment may be more myth than fact, [and] they act as a powerful deterrent to help-seeking behavior in this population.

Elizabeth, a 60-year-old divorcee whose 98-year-old mother recently died, is a vivid example of the power of these myths. Elizabeth was married briefly in her late teens to an abusive alcoholic husband. Following her divorce, she returned to her widowed mother's home with her two children. She raised an immense garden and took care of all the housekeeping while the family survived on her small welfare check. When her children left home, her welfare stopped but her mother became eligible for Supplementary Security Income due to her age. While her mother's disabilities were severe enough to warrant full time nursing home care, Elizabeth refused to even consider the possibility of placing her mother in the local nursing home. She had heard horror stories of the home's poorest residents being ignored or abused by the staff. Elizabeth and her mother were able to live quite comfortably on her mother's check until her mother's death. For over 25 years, while she cared for her mother, Elizabeth saved the state and federal government hundreds of thousands of dollars that might have been spent on nursing home care. Her intent of course was to provide better care not save the government money, but nonetheless this charitable act placed her own financial well-being in jeopardy. Elizabeth never worked outside the home which would have enabled her to accrue Social Security credits. She had not been married long enough to draw Social Security benefits from her former husband's account. At 60, she was not eligible for SSI based on age. She had no income from any source after her mother's death despite a lifetime of hard work.

Elizabeth was fearful of applying for SSI based on the disabling nature of her severe arthritis because she had heard discouraging stories about how rural mountain people were treated in the disability application process. She heard one had to be severely mentally ill or so crippled one could not walk to qualify for assistance. She also believed no one ever got SSI on the first try, having to submit to a long series of humiliating medical and psychiatric appointments. Elizabeth was willing to forego the application process until she was eligible on the basis of age, five years in this case, to avoid personal degradation.

There is no way of accurately documenting how many people are in situations similar to Elizabeth or have been arbitrarily denied SSI benefits. What is perhaps as significant as her refusal to even apply for assistance based on what she had heard is the public perception that qualification for SSI is in some way a reward or punishment for membership in a particular social class. Elizabeth eventually did apply for and receive SSI benefits through the advocacy efforts of a private philanthropic agency that serves the Appalachian region. The workers at the private agency did find the process grueling and the decision-making process at the Social Security Administration somewhat puzzling. However, the difficulty in securing benefits more likely stems from errors in the application process which occur more frequently in a population with limited literacy.

Implications for Social Welfare Policy and Services

Appalachian elders' experiences in weathering lifelong poverty and extreme geographic isolation combined with the prevailing attitudes about independence and social class have significant implications for social welfare policy and services. While these elders represent an extreme case in terms of poverty and isolation, the policy recommendations suggested by their plight are applicable to the larger population of elders as well.

An overarching theme in addressing the problems of Appalachian elders is reducing the numbers of persons below the poverty line in the region. Initiatives that focus on the development of non-resource-dependent manufacturing activities and the improvement of education must be top priorities. Detailed recommendations for eliminating poverty are beyond the scope of this paper but it is clear that reducing the prevalence of poverty among younger families is the most promising way to avoid low-income related problems later in life.

There are, however, specific policy initiatives that focus on programs of immediate concern to Appalachian elders. The first is the revision of eligibility requirements for SSI. SSI is underutilized in other parts of the country due to both elders' lack of awareness of their own eligibility and the stigmatization attached to the program. In the Appalachian region, elders age-eligible for benefits use the program at much higher rates due to a simple lack of alternative income sources. Appalachian elders actually need the assistance *before* they reach age 65 as was evident in Elizabeth's case described earlier in this paper. With limited lifelong connections to the labor force and little accumulation of financial resources, Appalachian adults need SSI earlier in their lives. Women, in particular, rarely have the option of seeking employment if they are widowed or divorced. Few jobs exist and they bring limited human capital to the labor market. The same argument applies to many middle-aged adults of color, particularly Native and African Americans. If they are not eligible for traditional public assistance benefits (because they no longer raise dependent children) or are not severely disabled, they have no income source. It is unconscionable that a whole segment of the population has no financial safety net.

In 1983, changes in Medicare reimbursement schedules forced the closing of many health care facilities in rural areas throughout the country (McCulloch and Lynch 1993). Low income persons of all ages and racial groups have suffered as a result. Elders, however, have borne the brunt of this change as 80 percent of this population seeks medical care in any given year (U.S. Congress Office of Technology 1990). It is also critical that community health clinics that serve rural areas especially those with high concentrations of elders, receive state and federal subsidies to ensure their continued survival. While younger persons with transportation see an hour's drive to a physician as an inevitable change in health care, elders simply will not obtain medical care if the service is inaccessible to them.

Social and health care systems serving rural areas need to be extraordinarily flexible. Location specific solutions must be allowed under Medicare and Medicaid provisions for physician and mental health services. Some rural locations may be best suited to comprehensive community health centers served by visiting service providers from larger medical facilities. Other geographical areas may benefit from an arrangement where familiar local service providers bring the appropriate service directly to the elder. Public health care services have already instituted a "circuit rider" model for delivery of preventative services to elders in rural areas. That is, nurses make house calls in four wheel drive vehicles for diabetes, blood pressure and medication checks. While these nurses cannot provide the full range of medical care, early intervention efforts can spot treatable medical conditions in the isolated elderly. This circuit rider model can also be applied to social services, mental health counseling, and advocacy services (McInnis-Dittrich 1997). Developing on-going relationships with the isolated can help social workers and other advocates identify and address social problems before they become as severe as Howard's situation illustrated earlier in this paper.

Establishing more flexible and non-traditional models of service delivery suggests the use of social institutions that are more familiar to Appalachian elders such as local churches and schools (DePoy and Butler 1996). Holding something as routine as a flu shot clinic for elders in a local church, rather than a sterile and unfamiliar clinic, promises better participation by the elders. Familiar social institutions serve a second function; to serve as information dissemination (and rumor control) centers. Helping elders to be aware of the variety of services that exist to meet their needs, the application process for these services, and the caveats of each program will both increase utilization when appropriate and reduce error related application problems. Elders are more likely to listen to their ministers talk about these programs than a stranger from the Social Security Administration. As illustrated earlier in this paper, this approach might have soothed Elizabeth's fears about applying for SSI long before her financial situation became so desperate.

Finally, physical and mental health professionals need to become familiar with the culture and customs of rural communities. Although television has brought much information about urban culture to rural areas, the reverse is not true. Only 10 percent of physicians and fewer mental health workers choose to practice in rural areas (U.S. Congress Office of Technology 1990). Those practitioners need to be aware that every rural area has its own cultural character whether it is rural Appalachia or rural North Dakota. Social class structures, informal helping networks, and the rigors of the local terrain will have a definite effect on how and where physical and mental health services are delivered.

Summary

This paper has examined the problems of poor, rural elders in the Appalachian region of the United States. The multifaceted nature of poverty in this region is best understood through a life course perspective that includes special consideration of social and historical factors. The effects of lifelong poverty, cultural attitudes about independence, geographical isolation and a rigid social class structure have been particularly problematic for Appalachian elders. Social welfare policy and service efforts that concentrate on alleviating poverty for the next generation of elders will prove to be the most valuable long-term solution. However, more short-term solutions are needed to meet the immediate needs of the current cohort of elders. Recommendations for health and welfare policy initiatives include revisions in SSI eligibility requirements, subsidized community service clinics, flexible service delivery systems and cultural training for physical and mental health service providers. These suggestions balance the pragmatics of policy and service provisions with a sensitivity to the unique cultural character of rural Appalachia.

Discussion Questions

1. How would you construct a viable social-service system in rural Appalachia?

2. Describe the unique characteristics of Appalachian culture.

3. What is the role of community organizations and the church?

4. Why should we care about people too proud to accept assistance?

5. How do the rural areas in your home state differ from those in Appalachia?

References

Adams, T. K. and G. J. Duncan. 1992. "Long-Term Poverty in Rural Areas." In C. M. Duncan (Ed.) *Rural Poverty in America*, (pp. 63–93). New York: Auburn House.

Appalachian Regional Commission. 1997. *General Economic Indicators: Appalachia and the United States, 1965–present*, Washington, D.C.: Author.

Billing, D. and D. Walls. 1980. "Appalachians." In S. Thernstrom (Ed.) *Harvard Encyclopedia of American Ethnic Groups*, (pp. 125–128). Cambridge, MA: Harvard University.

Butler, S. 1993. "Older Rural Women: Understanding Their Conceptions of Health and Illness." *Topics in Geriatric Rehabilitation* 9(l): 56–68.

Davis, L. F. 1988. "Rural Attitudes About Public Welfare Allocation." *Human Services in the Rural Environment* 12(2): 11–19.

Deavers, K. L. and R. A. Hoppe. 1992. "Overview of the Rural Poor in the 1980s." In C.M. Duncan (Ed.) *Rural Poverty in America*, (pp. 3–20). New York: Auburn Press.

Deitz, S. M. 1991. "Stressors and Coping Mechanisms of Older Rural Women." In A. Bushy (Ed.) *Rural Nursing*, (pp. 267–280). Newbury Park, CA.: Sage.

DePoy, E. and S. S. Butler. 1996. "Health: Elderly Rural Women's Conceptions." *AFFILIA* 11(2):207–220.

Duncan, C. M. 1992. "Persistent Poverty in Appalachia: Scarce Work and Rigid Stratification." In C.M. Duncan (Ed.) *Rural Poverty in America* (pp. 111–133). New York: Auburn Press.

Eller, R. D. 1986. "Appalachia: Still Waiting for Spring." *Seeds*, October: 12–15.

Gove, W., S. Ortega and C. B. Style. 1989. "The Maturational and Role Perspective on Aging and Self Through the Adult Years: An Empirical Evaluation." *American Journal of Sociology* 94: 117–129.

McCulloch, B. J. and M. S. Lynch. 1993. "Barriers to Solutions: Service Delivery and Public Policy in Rural Areas." *Journal of Applied Gerontology* 12(3): 388–403.

McInnis-Dittrich, K. 1997. "An Empowerment-Oriented Mental Health Intervention with Elderly Appalachian Women: The Women's Club." *Women and Aging* 9(1/2):91–106.

McLaughlin, D. K. and K. C. Holden. 1993. "Nonmetropolitan Elderly Women: A Portrait of Economic Vulnerability." *The Journal of Applied Gerontology* 12(3), 320–334.

Richardson, H. 1987. "The Health Plight of Rural Women." *Women and Health* 12, (3/4): 11–54.

Rowles, G. D. and H. K. Johansson. 1993. "Persistent Elderly Poverty in Rural Appalachia." *Journal of Applied Gerontology* 12(3): 349–367.

Schiller, B. 1995. *The Economics of Poverty and Discrimination*. 6th Edition. Englewood Cliffs, N.J.: Prentice Hall.

Spence, S. A. 1993. "Rural Elderly African Americans and Service Delivery: A Study of Health and Social Service Needs and Service Accessibility." *Journal of Gerontological Social Work* 20(3/4): 187–202.

U. S. Bureau of the Census. 1997. *Poverty 1996*, Current Population Surveys, March 1996. Washington, D.C.: Government Printing Office.

U. S. Congress. Office of Technology Assessment. 1990. *Health Care in Rural America* OTA-H434. Washington, D.C.: Government Printing Office.

Kathleen McInnis-Dittrich, "Poor, Rural Elders in Appalachia: Too Little, Too Late." Printed by permission of the author.

Section IV

Family, Social Relationships, and Intergenerational Reciprocity

Social scientists are particularly interested in social networks that provide assistance, emotional support, love, and care in later life. Family and friends are important sources of social support throughout the life course, especially in old age. This section will look at social relationships, including family, friends, and patterns of intergenerational reciprocity and assistance and the ways in which these connections vary by gender, race, ethnicity, and needs and preferences. It will explore the ways in which older people participate in friendship and family networks.

Rooted in Emile Durkheim's social integration theory formulated in *Suicide* [1897] (1966), the concept of a social network has been variously defined as "support accessible to an individual through social ties to other individuals, groups, and the larger community" (p. 109) and as "the experience of being supported by others" (Lin et al. 1979, pp. 114–115). Effective social ties diminish psychological distress, offset the impact of stress, and help maintain physical and psychological well-being in later life (Chappell 1995; Krause 1990; Palinkas, Wingard, and Barrett-Conner 1990).

Despite popular belief, total social isolation—the absence of any social contacts, interaction, and support networks—is rare among the elderly, with only about 4 percent reporting extreme isolation (Kahana 1995). Nor are the majority of elders abandoned by their families to live in nursing homes or other institutions. Only about 5 percent of people over the age of 65 are in institutions, and the majority of elders requiring care because of chronic disease receive assistance from a family member. A look at national data underscores the importance of the availability of an *immediate social network* in providing care. According to National Nursing Home Survey information, more than eight in ten nursing home residents are single, divorced, widowed, or separated; almost one third have no living children. In contrast, only about four in ten of the noninstitutionalized elderly are without a spouse and two in ten have no living children.

Gender plays a significant role in the structure of social networks, with women likely to have larger support systems and to give and receive more assistance throughout the life course than men. Women traditionally not only have been the "kin keepers" but also their lifelong tendency to have significant friendships often intensifies in old age (Wright 1986). In their selection, Hiroko Akiyama, Kathryn Elliott, and Toni Antonucci study four types of same-gender and cross-gender close relationships—spouse, children, siblings, and friends—and shedding new light on the patterns of intimacy in later life. Although both genders tend to have more women in their social networks and receive more support from these women, they are not necessarily psychologically or geographically closer to women than to men. Rather, the type of relationship—spouse, child, sibling, or friend—is more important. Whether male or female, people almost always feel most intimate with their spouses, followed by their sons and daughters, and less connected to siblings and friends. Popular myths to the contrary, family members remain the core of elders' social-support systems, with friends and neighbors in secondary roles.

Throughout human history, family structures have varied widely: from multigenerational, extended patriarchal and authoritarian families, bound by filial piety and subordination of younger people who owed absolute obedience to parents, to the nuclear family, held together by mutual affection, identity, and support and characterized by egalitarianism between husband and wife and between parents and children rather than filial obligation or duty. In the United States today, families differ as well; there is no "American family" but a gamut of formations that vary to meet people's needs at sundry times during their lives or are forced upon them by circumstances. The great majority of elderly, whether couples or single, live in their own households, although 10 percent of men and 18 percent of women are in the household of someone else, usually an adult child. African American and Latino elderly are more likely than whites to be in the household of another, usually an adult child, as are recent immigrants from Asia and the Pacific islands (Woroby and Angel 1990). In part, this pattern reflects ethnic cultural norms but is largely dictated by economic conditions that make separate households untenable.

In American later-life families, the ability of parents to demand automatic respect and obedience from their children and grandchildren has dwindled, for they no longer hold the key to their adult children's power, prestige, and property. Gunhild Hagestad elaborates in her selection on family relationships, pointing out the ways in which mortality patterns, life paths, and family arrangements deviate for men and women in later life. Current portrayals of older families tend to stress illness and disability rather than the increasing vitality of later-life family relationships. Comparing the old-old and the soon-to-be-old, she highlights the ways that social and structural changes present opportunities for new roles for older people and new potentials for their family life in the twenty-first century.

Not only are family roles in later life changing, but family size is altering as well. In 1900, for example, the average American couple had four children; today, the average couple has one or two. What implications do smaller families have for parent-child relationships in later life? Although the experience of growing up as an only child has been studied, little attention has been given to being the elderly parent of an only child and its meaning in later life. Marcene Goodman and Robert Rubinstein in their selection explore this often neglected area, considering the relationship between elderly mothers of one child and their son or daughter. Contrasting qualitative findings from interviews of mothers of one child and mothers of four or more children, they report that mothers of only children are much more likely to be focused on their adult child to the exclusion of other potential sources of gratification. Exaggerating the positive aspects of their child's life served as an "adaptive illusion," providing emotional equilibrium and validating their sense of accomplishment as a parent in old age. It is interesting to speculate whether the dependency on one's child for emotional gratification observed among these mothers is confined to these women's birth cohort when larger families were the norm, or whether future cohorts of women who elect to have only one child will resemble these mothers.

Expectations of support from adult children vary by characteristics such as ethnicity, religion, income, and race. What older white parents expect from their children and what they believe their children expect from them is the subject of the selection by Susan Sherman. Through interviews with 81 people, ranging in age from 41 to 96, she identifies three major patterns: independence, with no expectations for support to or from children; one-way exchange of support from adult children to older parents; and mutuality, where support would be exchanged as needed between generations. Although motifs for anticipated mutual exchanges varied, reciprocity in exchange was the most common expectation regardless of the age of the respondents. From an exchange-theory perspective providing support to a family member is delayed reciprocity for past nurturing, whether by one's parents or other family members. It may also be viewed as a moral duty: "the right thing to do." Her findings emphasize the contemporary trend among recent cohorts of elderly parents to live and be independent from their children and to expect to give or receive assistance only when it is needed.

What about the role of grandparents? Are grandparents like the fictional Grandma and Grandpa Walton in the 1970s television serial, where they played wise family counselors, respected by the entire family? Did such a pattern ever exist in the United States or is Walton Mountain, where the extended family lived harmoniously during the Great Depression of the 1930s, a romantic myth? Evidence suggests that the latter is true, for grandparents in Grandma and Grandpa Walton's birth cohort were not only less likely to survive into old age but were more likely to be distant authority figures than warm, caring nurturers (Cherlin and Furstenberg 1986). Because of increases in life expectancy, most of us can expect to live to be grandparents and perhaps great-grandparents—a dramatic change from the past when few people survived until the birth of their first grandchild. Grandparents today, however, may be almost any age from early 30s to more than 100. Not only do the ages of grandparents vary widely, but the very meaning of grandparenthood differs among different groups, in different societies, and at different points in history. In Kenya, for example, grandmothers traditionally played the role of "cultural experts," advising and instructing their granddaughters on sex, marital behavior, and other aspects of life. This role altered dramatically as Kenya became less culturally and economically isolated, for many grandmothers have little experience of this changing society. Yet close ties remain where grandmothers raise their granddaughters' children and granddaugh-

ters in turn provide assistance to a frail grandmother when needed (Cattell 1998). Norms of reciprocity now exist where assistance flows from the person more able to give it. Intergenerational reciprocity between a granddaughter and grandmother is illustrated in the short story by Helena Maria Viramontes, which illuminates the secret connection between a dying Chicana grandmother and her teen-age granddaughter. The story portrays the strong family loyalty and tenderness, sometimes disguised as roughness, that characterized their relationship and their mutual caring for each other even unto death. This story illustrates the point that just as there is no single American family pattern, there is no "typical grandparent" or "grandchild"; roles vary according to the needs and desires of the family members. Rachel Pruchno and Katrina Johnson expand upon this theme in their selection and discuss the multiplicity of grandparental roles, including those of surrogate parents and caregivers for one or more grandchildren—a pattern very different from Grandma and Grandpa Walton.

Providing care within the family, whether to a grandchild or to an elderly family member, is often stress laden. As Sherman's research indicates, expectations for support from adult children vary by personal experience throughout the life course. Expectations also differ according to characteristics such as race, ethnicity, religion, and social class. Ethnic and racial differences exist in the size of families and household composition, filial expectations, social support, amount of care given, and the degree to which caregivers experience caregiver burden. The selection by Maria Aranda and Bob Knight addresses the functions of ethnicity and culture in the stress and coping process among African American, Anglo, and Latino family caregivers. Noting that the meaning of a specific disease or impairment varies among ethnic or racial groups, they point out that caregivers of older Latinos face special challenges in caring for relatives at risk for specific chronic diseases and with multiple disabilities. Like African Americans, Latinos have been objects of prejudice and discrimination. To assume that Latinos are homogeneous, however, ignores their diversity, for they represent a range of social classes from affluent to middle class to very poor, reflecting their social class, level of acculturation, and life opportunities. Latinos share Spanish as their major common bond; their immigration histories and cultural traditions vary as widely as do their countries of origin and length of time in the United States (Markides and Mindel 1987). Differing levels of acculturation also beget stress, for Latinos who are more acculturated might hold views about appropriate care different from those of their impaired relative. Cultural traditions stressing caregiving and self-sacrifice without outside assistance not only create a heavy burden for family caregivers but actually exacerbate dependence and disability among the relatives for whom they care. It is important to understand the diversity of health beliefs and caregiving patterns if stress and burnout are to be reduced among African American and Latino family caregivers and care recipients.

Approximately two-thirds of all informal caregivers in the United States are women—wives, daughters, and other female relatives or in-laws. Only between 5 and 10 percent of elders receive care exclusively from formal-service providers. Among aging couples, wives are almost twice as likely to be the primary caregiver, reflecting both the greater life expectancy of women and the persistence of traditional gender roles. Men caregivers are likely to provide typically "masculine" services such as home repairs, financial management, and money; women provide hands-on care and socio-emotional support. Frida Kerner Furman has challenged this norm, asking:

> But what, specifically, makes driving, dressing, bathing, and feeding a desperately sick person a gender-specific job? I would say economics and power tied to cultural conventions. . . . A long tradition of devaluing women, and concomitantly, their work of caring. . . . Women are socialized to serve and care for others, . . . this expectation probably emerges far more from women's lower status in society than from a natural predisposition in these directions. (1997, pp. 141–142)

Tish Sommers and Laurie Shields in their selection address the role of women as caregivers to focus on its burdens and frustrations: first for an elderly wife who provides care to her terminally ill husband until she herself becomes ill, then her adult daughter who assumes the caregiver role for both. Their selection illustrates the dilemma of gendered caregiving for a disabled family member. Socialized to be nurturers, women are likely to be trapped between traditional gender roles stressing care and obligation to a spouse and parents and their own hopes for individuation and self-expression.

Anna Quindlen's 1994 novel that was subsequently made into a film, *One True Thing*, depicts a 24-year-old woman urged by her father to return home to care for her dying mother, emphasizes how caregiving within the family is gendered. Rather than taking a leave of absence to care for his wife, her father states: "It seems to me that another woman is what is wanted here" (Quindlen 1994, p. 25). In the selection by Edward Thompson, he challenges the belief that caregiving is a female job as depreciating both men and women. By assuming that caregiving is a gendered task where women are somehow innately more competent as caregivers, the caring and skills that men can bring are belittled and women are locked into stressful "feminine" roles. Both suffer from gender stereotyping, inasmuch as the managerial and detached-concern model of care more characteristic of men is just as valid as the more emotionally involved prototypical pattern for women.

Older people who have provided *lifelong* care to a disabled family member are discussed by Jennifer Hand and Patricia Reid. Directing attention to families who have provided around-the-clock care for their developmentally disabled relatives from childhood to old age, they describe the dilemmas and difficulties these caregivers face. A key issue is that of who will provide the shelter, assistance, and affection the developmentally disabled elder will require when the current caregiver becomes frail or dies. Will they become "hand-me-down people," passed from one relative to another? What plans can be made to ensure a comfortable quality of life outside of an institution?

Changes in life expectancy have meant that more generations are alive today than ever before in human history. As a result, the role of an adult child is also changing; today people can expect to spend more years as adult sons or daughters than as parents of children younger than 18. Increased health and longevity present new possibilities for family, kin, and friendship relationships in later life. Adult children and their elderly parents are involved in more mutual-exchange relationships, where assistance runs up and down between generations, than in family models characterized by filial piety. As future cohorts age, intergenerational links, characterized by affection and caring, are likely to become more compelling because of the increased years of life shared by adult children and their parents.

Yet issues remain. Unless patterns of mortality change, more women can expect to live as widows. If divorced, women are less likely to remarry as the likelihood of remarriage decreases rapidly with age; men, when divorced, are likely to marry a woman younger than themselves. They can also expect to spend at least some time caring for a relative, whether a spouse, child, grandchild, or other relative. There is still much to learn about social relationships among very diverse ethnic, racial, and socioeconomic groups throughout the life course.

What social-support changes will occur among future cohorts of elders as new immigrants become assimilated? What effects will divorce have on the social networks for the elderly of tomorrow? Will stepparents and stepchildren and children raised by one parent but not the other be bound together by norms of reciprocity? What impact will greater female participation in the labor force have upon caregiving? To what extent will male roles change to encompass more "kin keeping" and caregiving? Relationships in future older families, as in older families today, will be shaped by numerous factors, including individual choices; membership in the hierarchies of gender, race or ethnicity, and social class; and sociohistorical events. As you read the following selections, think about the ways in which you hope to participate in family and friendship networks in later life and the social structural arrangements that might promote or impede these aspirations.

References

Cattell, M. G. 1998. "'Nowadays It Isn't Easy to Advise the Young': Grandmothers and Granddaughters Among Abaluyia of Kenya." In J. Dickerson-Putnam and J. K. Brown, *Women Among Women: Anthropological Perspectives on Female Age Hierarchies*, pp. 30–51. Urbana: University of Illinois Press.

Chappell, N. 1995. "Informal Social Supports." In L. A. Bond, S. Cutler, and A. Grams, eds., *Promoting Successful and Productive Aging*, pp. 171–185. Thousand Oaks, CA: Sage.

Cherlin, A. J., and Furstenberg, F. 1986. *The New American Grandparent*. New York: Basic Books.

Durkheim, E. [1897] 1966. *Suicide*. New York: Free Press.

Furman, F. K. 1997. *Facing the Mirror: Older Women and Beauty Shop Culture*. New York: Routledge.

Kahana, B. 1995. "Isolation." In G. L. Maddox, ed., *Encyclopedia of Aging*, 2nd ed., pp. 526–527. New York: Springer.

Krause, N. 1990. "Perceived Health Problems, Formal/Informal Support, and Life Satisfaction Among Older Adults." *Journal of Gerontology: Social Sciences* 45:S193–S205.

Lin, N., Simeone, R. S., Ensel, W. M., and Kuo, W. 1979. "Social Support, Stressful Life Events, and Illness: A Model and an Empirical Test." *Journal of Health and Social Behavior* 20: 108–119.

Markides, K. S., and Mindel, C. H. 1987. *Aging and Ethnicity*. Newbury Park, CA: Sage.

Palinkas, L. A., Wingard, K. L., and Barrett-Conner, E. 1990. "The Biocultural Context of Social Networks and Depression among the Elderly." *Social Science and Medicine* 30: 441–447.

Quindlen, A. 1994. *One True Thing*. New York: Random House.

Woroby, J. L., and Angel R. 1990. "Poverty and Health: Older Minority Women and the Rise of the Female-Headed Household." *Journal of Health and Social Behavior* 31: 370–383.

Wright, P. H. 1986. "Gender Differences in Adults' Same- and Cross-Gender Friendships." In R. G. Adams and R. Bliesner, eds., *Older Adult Friendship: Structure and Process*. Newbury Park, CA: Sage.

Chapter 25

Same-Sex and Cross-Sex Relationships

Hiroko Akiyama
Kathryn Elliott and
Toni C. Antonucci

Throughout our lives, family and friends are important as companions, sources of affection, and support. Unlike family relationships where people are bound by blood relationship or kinship ties, friendships are voluntary. Together, family and friends form our personal social networks, usually marked by feelings of positive regard, commitment, and personal value. The people in one's social network are potential sources of assistance and encouragement and are also important resources for maintenance of physical and emotional health.

Who comprises the social network of older people, and how does it differ by gender? Some researchers have argued that women, because of their greater concern with interpersonal relationships, are more likely than men to have both a larger network and to provide more emotional support to others. Hiroko Akiyama, Kathryn Elliott, and Toni Antonucci, examining four types of close relationships among older men and women, consider the importance of gender and its relationship to the size and composition of social networks. As you read the following selection, notice the structural characteristics, such as size and membership, of same-gender and cross-gender relationships. Consider the roles of psychological and geographic closeness and their association to the gender of network members. Think about the role of "femaleness" in social networks.

In this selection, "sex" denotes both biological characteristics and gender.

An individual's location in the social structure influences the opportunities, resources, demands, and constraints that he or she is likely to encounter in life. Such structural conditions shape the individual's life experiences—including the nature of one's relationships. Sex is indisputably a powerful component of structural milieu that cuts across societies as does social and economic class, race/ethnicity, and age. The goal of this study was to examine how sex affects the nature of relationships between older adults and the people in their immediate social environment, i.e., their personal networks. Specifically, we examined different roles occupied by male and female spouses, children, siblings, and close friends in the personal networks of older men and women. Capitalizing on a unique national probability sample with detailed information on individual network members, we sought to identify sex-specific patterns in their relationships and inquire into their etiology.

It is well documented in the literature that sex differences are significant in structuring personal networks of older adults (see Antonucci, 1990, for a review). Older men and women have personal networks that differ in size, composition, and support exchanges. In general, women are likely to have a larger network with greater diversity and to engage in support exchanges which exceed men's in terms of the variety and amount of support. Married men tend to rely on their wives for all types of support. In contrast to the level of attention which this line of research has given to the sex of older persons, the sex of network members has not received adequate attention. . . .

Prior research on sex of network members can be summarized under three principles: (1) relation hierarchy (2) femaleness; and (3) sex commonality. First, according to the principle of relation hierarchy, the key factor which determines who provides which form of support for older persons is the primacy of the relationship. Thus, the serial order depending on availability is/would be: a spouse, then children, siblings, other relatives, and friends/

neighbors (Cantor, 1979; Cantor & Little, 1985; Chappell, 1992; Shanas, 1979). Sex of older persons or network members makes little difference in the provision of support.

Second, the principle of femaleness theorizes that sex differences in personal relationships are a function of the femaleness of the dyad. The more women included in the dyad, the closer the relationship (Bengtson, Rosenthal, & Burton, 1990; Gold, 1989; Troll, 1994). . . .

Another line of research supports the principle of sex commonality which posits that same-sex dyads are closer than cross-sex dyads. . . . Rossi and Rossi (1990) examined sex symmetry in help exchange between elderly parents and adult children. They found that while daughters were much more likely than sons to provide mothers with personal care/support (i.e., comfort, sick care, and advice), sons and daughters were equally likely to provide fathers with comfort and sick care. Sons were also more likely than daughters to provide advice to fathers. Given women's family specialization in personal care/support, this finding suggests that people do feel especially at ease in same-sex parent-child relationships. . . .

A review of the literature concerning sex differences in close relationships clearly indicates the significant impact of marital status on the personal network of older persons. It is perhaps the strongest factor to influence the structure and nature of the entire personal network (Dykstra. 1993). . . . Given that a spouse is normally identified as the closest network member in all aspects, it is conceivable that the presence or absence of a spouse intricately affects both same-sex and cross-sex relationships of older persons. Furthermore, a marked difference in marital status between men and women in the older population makes it crucial to examine personal networks of the married and the unmarried separately; otherwise, observed differences might actually reflect confounded effects of sex and marital status.

. . . The present study aims at a systematic investigation of same-sex and cross-sex close relationships among different relational characteristics and relation types using a national probability sample of community-dwelling older adults. Specifically, we examine three basic relational characteristics: psychological closeness, geographical proximity, and support exchange in four types of close relationships: spouse, children, siblings, and friends. Sex and marital status of older respondents, sex of network members, types of relationship, and relational characteristics will be systematically examined. The major questions to be addressed are fourfold:

1. Do the size and composition of older men's and women's personal networks differ in terms of same-sex and cross-sex relationships?

2. Are sex differences in same-sex and cross-sex relationships consistent across relational characteristics: psychological closeness, geographical proximity, and support exchange?

3. Are sex differences consistent across relationship types: spouse, children, siblings, and friends?

4. Does marital status differentially affect same-sex and cross-sex relations of older men and women?

First, we will identify and compare the structural characteristics, such as size and composition, of same-sex and cross-sex relationships in men's and women's personal networks. Second, we will compare the reported closeness of men and women. We will examine same-sex and cross-sex relationships on three basic dimensions: affectional, associational, and functional ties. Prior research has often focused on a single dimension of close relationships rather than examining multiple dimensions of the relationship as a whole (see Bengtson, Cutler, Mangen, & Marshall, 1985; Rossi & Rossi, 1990, for exceptions). Many studies that we reviewed focused on the provision of specific instrumental support, while others looked at affective ties. It is not obvious that sex differences in the provision of support are associated with sex differences in psychological closeness. We will consider whether women provide more support than men because they are psychologically closer to their parents, spouses, siblings, and friends. Third, sex differences in close relationships are presumably mediated by the social role occupied. Consistency and variations in sex differences across various types of relationships will identify relation-specific sex differences from those that are common across all types of relationships, which would elucidate the grounds for the sex differences. Finally, we will examine the effect of marital status. Although there is ample evidence confirming differential effects of marital status on the personal network of men and women, still little is known about how the presence or absence of an intimate cross-sex network member (i.e., spouse [or partner]) affects the same-sex and cross-sex relationships with other network members. Answers to these questions will delineate intricate ways in which sex affects close relationships of older persons and facilitates our understanding of the etiology of the sex differences.

Method

Sample

Data are drawn from the national survey *Social Networks in Adult Life*, which was conducted by the University of Michigan, Survey Research Center (Antonucci & Akiyama. 1987b). A two-stage nationwide probability sample of 2,458 households was screened for eligible respondents (individuals 50 years or older). If the household had more than one eligible respondent, one was randomly selected. Trained interviewers administered in-home, face-to-face interviews approximately one hour in length. The response rate was 73 percent. The sample consisted of 718 people (298 men and 420 women) ranging in age from 50 to 95. Four hundred twenty people were married and 268 were unmarried. Among the unmarried, 95 percent were previously married. Health status, labor force status, and other demographic characteristics of the sample showed general agreement with major national data sets, such as the Current Population Survey of the U.S. Bureau of the Census. The sample characteristics are summarized in Table 25.1.

Measures

Network structure was established by presenting a set of three concentric circles with a smaller circle in the center in which the word "you" was written. The respondent was told, "I'm going to ask you to help me draw a diagram which we will refer to as your personal network. This is you in the middle [showing a blank diagram to the respondent]. The inner circle would include only the one person or persons that you feel so close to that it's hard to imagine life without them. People you don't feel quite *that* close to, but who are still very important to you, would go in the middle circle. People whom you haven't already mentioned but who are close enough and important enough in your life that they should also be placed in your network, would go in the outer circle. Circles can be empty, full, or anywhere in between."

Respondents then were asked a series of questions concerning structural and func-

Table 25.1

Sample Characteristics

| | Married | | | | | | Unmarried | | | | | |
| | Men | | | Women | | | Men | | | Women | | |
	Mean	SD	Range	Mean	SD	Range	Mean	SD	Range	Mean	SD	Range
n	233			187			47			221		
Age	64.66	10.27	50–92	64.21	9.00	50–85	66.21	10.22	51–95	68.22	10.13	51–93
Years of education	11.00	3.88	0–17	10.67	3.28	1–17	10.02	4.75	0–17	9.85	3.63	0–17
Income*	20.05	15.06	2.5–60.0	18.79	15.65	2.5–60.0	12.66	10.25	2.5–40.0	8.42	9.93	2.5–60.0
No. of health problems	2.16	2.01	0–10	2.19	1.95	0–11	2.18	1.96	0–9	2.48	1.87	0–8
Employed	50%			25%			43%			29%		

*A figure represents the mean income based upon taking a midpoint of the following 8 categories from which respondents chose: under $5,000; $5,000–9,999; $10,000–14,999; $15,000–19,999; $20,000–24,999; $25,000–34,999; $35,000–49,999; $50,000 and over.

tional characteristics of the first 10 people listed in their network. Structural characteristics analyzed in this study were network size, sex, relationship to the respondent, psychological closeness, geographical proximity, and frequency of contact. Relationship was coded into 11 categories: spouse, son, daughter, brother, sister, grandson, granddaughter, male friend, female friend, other male relative, and other female relative. Psychological closeness was assessed based on the circle in which a network member was placed in the network diagram: inner circle = 3, middle circle = 2, and outer circle = 1. Geographical proximity is a measure of distance between the residence of respondent and a network member that was scored as a dichotomous variable: 1 = living within a one-hour drive and 0 = not living within a one-hour drive. Contact frequency was measured by a 6-point scale: 6 = live together, 5 = being in touch daily, 4 = weekly (or more often), 3 = monthly (or more often), 2 = yearly (or more often), and 1 = not at all.

Network functions were measured as six types of social support given and received by the focal person: they are (1) confiding about things that are important; (2) being reassured when feeling uncertain; (3) being respected; (4) being cared for when ill; (5) talking with someone when upset, nervous, or depressed; and (6) talking with someone about one's health. The respondents were asked to identify each network member from whom they received each type of support as well as each network member to whom they provided each type of support. A transaction of support (provision or receipt) was coded as 1 and no transaction as 0. "Support received" from a specific network member (e.g., a daughter) is the number of different types of support that a respondent received from the daughter. The value ranges from 0 to 6. Zero (0) indicates that the respondent received none of the six types of support from the daughter, whereas (6) indicates he/she received all six types of support from the daughter. "Support provided" to a specific network member was calculated in a similar way. The descriptive statistics of these five relational characteristics are presented in the Results section. However, since "geographical closeness" and

"contact frequency" (.43 to .68) as well as "support received" and "support provided" (.45 to .65) were highly correlated, "contact frequency" and "support provided" are not included in regression analyses.

Results

The 718 older adults (298 men and 420 women) nominated a total of 6,341 network members. Since the detailed information is available on only the first 10 network members nominated by each respondent, our analysis included 5,199 network members. Table 25.2 shows the composition of personal networks of married and unmarried men and women. The numbers in the table are the average number of people in certain relationship categories. For example, the married men included, on the average, 1.22 sons in their personal network.

Table 25.2 reveals notable sex differences in several aspects of network structure. First, there is a sex difference in the size of personal network. Unmarried men's network size (5.72) is significantly smaller than that of married men (7.16), whereas marital status has little effect on the network size of women (7.37 and 7.38). Second, all four groups of older adults (i.e., married and unmarried men and women) reported having more women in their network than men. This trend is most prominent among unmarried women. They reported significantly more daughters, sisters, and female friends than sons, brothers, and male friends in their networks. Third, with respect to friends, however, respondents were more likely to include same-sex friends. Only unmarried men reported about equal numbers of male and female friends in their network.

Table 25.3 presents the mean scores of five relational characteristics (psychological closeness, geographical proximity, contact frequency, support received, and support provided) in same-sex and cross-sex relationships in four relation types (spouse, children, siblings, and friends). Grandchildren and "others" categories are not included due to the lack of sufficient number of cases for the analysis. The table shows a strikingly systematic pattern of differences in virtually all relational characteristics by relationship types rather than by sexes. Older men and women almost always placed their spouses in the inner circle (i.e., psychological closeness = 3) and children (both sons and daughters) mostly in the inner circle. Siblings (both brothers and sisters), however, were mostly placed in the middle circle (i.e., psychological closeness = 2), and friends of both sexes were placed either in the middle or outer circle (i.e., psychological closeness = 1). Similar systematic differences among the relationship types are observed in the rest of the relational characteristics. Such findings indicate that, in general, older persons' close relationships are strongly determined by the relationship type rather than the sex of network members. A comparison between the married and unmarried samples suggests differential effects of marital status on men's and women's networks. Whereas the unmarried women reported closer relationships with their children, siblings, and friends than the married women, the unmarried men are more distant from their children but closer to their siblings and friends, particularly to female friends, compared with their married counterparts. . . .

While we have known for some time that men's networks are often smaller than women's, the findings from this national sample offer valuable specificity about the nature and prevalence of this sex difference. In this sample, men's networks were smaller than women's. It is noteworthy, however, that the network size of married men and women was not very different. On the other hand, the network size of unmarried men and women was significantly different. Unmarried men reported significantly fewer children and grandchildren in their personal networks than married men. Not only did they have fewer children in their networks but, as Table 25.3 indicates, they contact the children less frequently than their married counterparts. These findings appear to support the notion in the literature suggesting that married men's connections with their network members, especially kin relationships, often operate through their wives (Troll, 1994). Obviously, what we can argue from the cross-sectional data is limited. It requires a longitudinal study to assess changes in men's interactions with their network members before and after the change in marital status to pro-

Table 25.2

Who Are in Older Adults' Personal Networks?

	Married						Unmarried					
	Men			Women			Men			Women		
	Mean	SD	Range	Mean	SD	Range	Mean	SD	Range	Mean	SD	Range
Spouse	0.94		0–1	0.93		0–1						
Son	1.22	1.26	0–6	1.15	1.23	0–6	1.04	1.28	0–5	1.07	1.22	0–5
Daughter	1.17	1.11	0–7	1.25	1.06	0–5	1.09	1.25	0–5	1.27*	1.33	0–8
Brother	0.48	0.87	0–5	0.40	0.77	0–5	0.38	0.82	0–3	0.44	0.89	0–4
Sister	0.59	0.96	0–5	0.74**	1.00	0–6	0.62*	1.05	0–5	0.64*	1.05	0–4
Grandson	0.21	0.69	0–4	0.29	0.75	0–4	0.06	0.32	0–2	0.35	0.86	0–4
Granddaughter	0.14	0.52	0–3	0.22	0.68	0–4	0.11	0.37	0–2	0.37	0.86	0–6
Male friend	0.73	1.29	0–6	0.16	0.51	0–3	0.70	1.21	0–6	0.30	0.71	0–4
Female friend	0.27**	0.66	0–3	0.91**	1.34	0–7	0.66	1.26	0–5	1.39**	1.83	0–10
Other males	0.65	0.96	0–4	0.57	0.90	0–4	0.45	0.83	0–4	0.56	0.97	0–4
Other females	0.76	1.04	0–5	1.11	1.35	0–7	0.60	0.92	0–4	0.97	1.10	0–6
All males	3.29	1.91	0–8	3.39	1.66	0–7	2.63	1.79	0–7	2.73	1.80	0–7
All females	3.87**	1.78	0–8	3.99**	2.02	0–9	3.09*	1.99	0–8	4.64**	2.18	0–10
Total	7.16	2.58	0–10	7.38	2.45	2.0–10	5.72	2.79	0–10	7.37	2.71	0–10

Note: Asterisks indicate significant differences in the number of male and female network members in a specific relation (e.g., the average number of male friends vs female friends in the married men's networks is significantly different).
*$p < .05$; **$p < .01$.

Table 25.3

Relationships of Older Adults With Male and Female Network Members

	Married													
	Older Men's Network Members							Older Women's Network Members						
	Wife	Son	Daughter	Brother	Sister	Male Friend	Female Friend	Husband	Son	Daughter	Brother	Sister	Male Friend	Female Friend
n	220	284	273	111	138	170	62	173	215	233	75	139	30	170
Psychological closeness														
Mean	2.97	2.64	2.57	2.09	2.06	1.56	1.55	2.97	2.76	2.73	1.92	2.15	1.83	1.71
SD	0.20	0.54	0.55	0.58	0.59	0.60	0.56	0.17	0.44	0.49	0.56	0.65	0.65	0.65
Geographical proximity														
Mean	1.00	0.67	0.60	0.46	0.51	0.78	0.76	0.99	0.64	0.55	0.49	0.50	0.83	0.79
SD	0	0.49	0.49	0.50	0.50	0.41	0.43	0.08	0.48	0.50	0.50	0.50	0.38	0.41
Contact frequency														
Mean	6.00	3.80	3.76	2.78	2.82	3.69	3.61	5.98	3.82	3.83	2.61	3.20	3.63	3.72
SD	0.07	1.32	1.34	1.02	1.00	1.09	1.00	0.17	1.20	1.22	1.08	1.26	1.07	1.21
Support received														
Mean	4.82	2.57	2.43	1.36	1.66	1.71	1.90	3.85	2.73	3.23	1.35	2.31	2.23	2.59
SD	1.49	1.67	1.68	1.43	1.74	1.66	1.74	1.98	1.54	1.77	1.38	1.91	1.19	1.82
Support provided														
Mean	4.92	3.82	3.58	2.14	2.43	2.11	2.16	4.28	3.55	3.97	2.72	3.20	2.37	3.22
SD	1.60	1.85	1.95	1.89	2.03	1.95	2.12	1.75	1.82	1.79	1.86	2.04	2.17	2.06

continued on the next page

Table 25.3

Continued

| | Older Men's Network Members | | | | | | Older Women's Network Members | | | | | |
	Son	Daughter	Brother	Sister	Male Friend	Female Friend	Son	Daughter	Brother	Sister	Male Friend	Female Friend
n	49	51	27	43	46	43	236	282	120	152	69	325
Psychological closeness												
Mean	2.61	2.51	2.19	2.26	1.72	2.23	2.85	2.87	2.28	2.32	2.00	1.94
SD	0.61	0.61	0.79	0.79	0.72	0.75	0.39	0.37	0.61	0.66	0.82	0.73
Geographical proximity												
Mean	0.51	0.45	0.67	0.65	0.89	0.90	0.67	0.62	0.59	0.53	0.77	0.88
SD	0.51	0.50	0.48	0.48	0.31	0.30	0.47	0.49	0.49	0.50	0.43	0.33
Contact frequency												
Mean	3.43	3.08	3.48	3.74	4.20	4.12	3.92	3.96	3.12	3.41	3.69	3.78
SD	1.46	1.48	1.45	1.29	0.98	1.00	1.40	1.33	1.30	1.25	1.27	1.13
Support received												
Mean	2.98	2.43	2.22	2.91	2.33	3.56	3.17	3.73	1.88	2.18	2.07	2.09
SD	2.07	1.69	1.95	2.07	2.06	1.98	1.71	1.70	1.73	1.85	1.54	1.63
Support provided												
Mean	3.22	3.39	2.44	3.37	2.46	3.37	3.17	3.77	2.13	2.90	2.65	2.69
SD	2.12	2.13	1.80	2.04	2.20	2.23	2.08	1.88	1.82	1.87	1.77	1.99

Unmarried

vide more direct evidence for the role of wives in men's connections with their offspring.

Also consistent with prior reports is that older adults, both men and women, had more female network members than male network members. However, this tendency was not consistently observed. A greater salience of female network members was most pronounced among the unmarried women. Among different relation types, sisters were more likely than brothers to be included in the networks of all four groups of older adults. However, daughters did not always exceed sons. Indeed, the married men reported more sons than daughters in their networks. As to friends, there were more same-sex friends than cross-sex friends reported in the networks, although unmarried men reported almost as many cross-sex friends as same-sex friends.

We were interested in whether older persons not only have more women in their network but also have closer relationships with women. That is, are older persons psychologically and geographically closer to and do they receive more support from female network members than male network members? Although our older respondents overall reported more women than men in their networks, there was little indication that they were psychologically or geographically closer to female network members (i.e., wives, daughters, sisters, and female friends) compared with male network members. One exception was that female friends were more likely to live closer to unmarried older persons than male friends. On the other hand, older persons were more likely to receive support from women than men. In short, our data suggest that although older persons tend to have more women in the network and receive more support from those women, they are not necessarily closer, either psychologically or geographically. to women than men in their networks. Thus, it does not appear that sex differences are consistent across the relational characteristics.

We should reiterate here our finding that, compared to the sex of a network member, the relation type (e.g., spouse, children, siblings, and friends) is more important in determining the structure and function of older people's support networks. It suggests that the norms for adult children in relation to elderly parents are stronger than sex norms in structuring the support network. Therefore, under circumstances where daughters are not available, sons, who occupy the same type of relation in the opposite sex, are more likely to be substituted than those who have a different type of relation in the same sex (e.g., sisters).

Finally, the data reveal notable differences between married and [presently] unmarried older persons in the nature of their same-sex and cross-sex relationships. Although the respondents overall reported more women than men in their network, the data (see Table 25.3) indicate intimate relationships between the married respondents and their same-sex network members. The married respondents reported receiving more support from same-sex children than from cross-sex children and feeling closer to same-sex siblings and friends than cross-sex ones. On the contrary, the unmarried men and women both received more support from female network members, such as daughters and sisters, than sons and brothers.

In this vein, there is a finding which deserves special attention. Married respondents reported that sons in their networks live closer than their daughters do. This finding is somewhat intriguing, because there is a general belief that older persons tend to live close to and have frequent contact with their daughters. There are two possible interpretations for this finding. One is simply that sons tend to live closer to their married parents than daughters. Another possibility is that older people tend to include sons in their personal networks if they live nearby, whereas they include daughters even if they live a greater distance away, because sons are less likely to keep in touch with their parents once they have moved away. Although the data do not provide information which directly supports or refutes either explanation, the first explanation appears more plausible than the second one. If the second explanation were valid, we would expect the married respondents to have more daughters than sons in their network. However, this is not the case. Furthermore, the first explanation is consistent with the recent report based on the 1990 Census data that a significantly larger proportion of single adult men live with their parents than single adult women (U.S. Census Bureau, 1992). This is a relatively new phenomenon. Although the nature of such relationships between adult children and their parents has not been fully investigated, it appears that an increasing number of "resourceless" adult children continue to stay in or move back to their more "resourceful" parents' households. In such relationships, support is more likely to flow from parents to adult children rather than the other way. Why are sons more likely to stay with their parents than daughters? Some speculate that parents have different expectations for their sons and daughters in various aspects of their lives, such as how much freedom they are allowed and how many household chores they should share. Since parents may tend to be more permissive and tolerant of their sons than their daughters, sons might feel more comfortable living with their parents. We found that sons lived closer to their married parents than daughters did. We did not, however, find a similar sex difference for the children of unmarried older persons, who tend to have fewer resources and need more support than their married counterparts. Thus, our finding appears to support the speculative explanation of the sex difference in single adults' living arrangements which was found in the 1990 Census.

Referring back to the three principles—relation hierarchy, femaleness, and sex commonality—which have guided research on sex in close relationships, our data offer strong support for the relation hierarchy principle and limited support to the other two. The findings indicate that relation type (children, siblings, friends, etc.) is the primary factor in determining the structure and function of an older person's support network, and sex is secondary, although both of them are decisive factors. The norms associated with specific relations appear to be more powerful than sex norms. At the same time, however, we found that married older persons tend to maintain close relationships with their same-sex children and siblings, which is consistent with the sex commonality principle, whereas

women play more central roles in the network of unmarried persons, which is consistent with the femaleness principle. More specifically, our data suggest that the femaleness principle operates on the provision of support. Unmarried older persons were more likely to receive support from women rather than from men. However, we failed to find evidence of the femaleness principle in a more strict sense. That is, we did not find the most extensive support transactions in female-female dyads which were followed by female-male dyads and male-male dyads in this order. Furthermore, the data indicate that those unmarried older persons maintained a relatively similar level of psychological and geographical closeness with men and women in their networks. These results highlight the distinctive nature of relationship (or role) of women in the personal network of older persons, that is, it is more likely women who provide support to older persons when these elders require increasing care. Thus, we found support for the femaleness principle as well as the sex commonality principle only in specific relational characteristics in specific segments of the older sample.

These findings lead us to the following conclusion. Sex differences in older persons' close relationships are complex and require our attention not only to the sex of older persons but also to the sex of their network members, relation type (e.g., children, siblings, and friends), and relational characteristics (e.g., psychological closeness, geographical proximity, and support exchange). Our data also suggest that married and unmarried persons have different relationships with their same-sex and cross-sex network members. Thus, men and women serve intricately differential functions in the various types of relation and situational circumstances which evolve around aging individuals.

The results of our analysis have implications for further development of research which inquires into the etiology of sex differences in older persons' close relationships. First, sex differences in older persons' personal networks are multidimensional and complex. They differ in their structure, function, and quality. Research must continue to examine complex relationships among these dimensions. Second, although the structure, function, and quality of the personal networks of older men and women are influenced greatly by their current circumstances, those networks are at the same time a culmination of their personal relationships over the life course. Research from a life-span perspective, which investigates the emergence and development of sex differences over the life course, will be a more direct and powerful avenue to identify their determinants. Finally, another promising approach is an examination of the universality and variations in sex differences among societies which differ in family system, kinship relations, and/or role expectations. Such cross-cultural comparative research will further advance our understanding of the etiology of sex differences in close relationships.

Discussion Questions

1. How does the size of the social networks of men differ from that of women?

2. Describe the typical gender composition of the social networks of men and women.

3. To whom are older men and women likely to be most close: Who makes up the inner circle?

4. What effect does marital status have on elders' social networks, and does this differ for men and women?

5. Explain the statement: "Our data offer strong support for the relationship hierarchy principle and limited support to the other two."

6. How might the growing number of gay or lesbian partnerships affect our understanding of support networks of the elderly?

Acknowledgments

This study was supported in part by the National Institute on Aging, Grant AG-01632. Appreciation is extended to Halimah Hassan for her assistance in data analyses.

Dr. Richard Schulz was Editor of the *Journal of Gerontology: Psychological Sciences* at the time the manuscript was submitted and was responsible for the review process and acceptance of this article.

Address correspondence to Hiroko Akiyama, Institute for Social Research, the University of Michigan, Ann Arbor, MI 48106-1248 (E-mail: akiyama@umich.edu).

References

Antonucci, T. C. (1990). Social supports and social relationships. In R. H. Binstock and L. K. George (Eds.), *Handbook of aging and the social sciences* (3rd ed., pp. 205–226). San Diego, CA: Academic Press.

Antonucci, T. C., & Akiyama, H. (1987a). An examination of sex differences in social support among older men and women. *Sex Roles, 17,* 737–749.

Antonucci, T. C., & Akiyama, H. (1987b). Social networks in adult life and a preliminary examination of the convoy model. *Journal of Gerontology, 42,* 519–527.

Bank. S. P. (1982). *The sibling bond.* New York: Basic Books.

Bengtson, V. L., Cutler, N. E., Mangen. D. J., & Marshall. V. W. (1985). Generations, cohorts, and relations between age groups. In R. H. Binstock & E. Shanas (Eds.), *Handbook of aging and the social sciences* (2nd ed., pp. 304–338). New York: Van Nostrand Reinhold.

Bengtson, V. L., Rosenthal, C., & Burton, L. (1990). Families and aging: Diversity and heterogeneity. In R. H. Binstock & L. K. George (Eds.), *Handbook of aging and the social sciences* (3rd ed., pp. 263–287). San Diego, CA: Academic Press.

Blieszner, R., & Adams, R. G. (1992). *Adult friendship.* Newbury Park, CA: Sage Publications.

Brody, E. M. (1990). *Women in the middle: Their parent care years.* New York: Springer.

Cantor, M. H. (1979). Neighbors and friends: An overlooked resource in the informal support system. *Research on Aging, 1,* 434–463.

Cantor, M. H. (1983). Strain among caregivers: A study of experiences in the United States. *The Gerontologist, 23,* 23–43.

Cantor, M. H., & Little, V. (1985). Aging and social care. In R. H. Binstock & E. Shanas (Eds.), *Handbook of aging and the social sciences* (2nd ed., pp. 745–781). New York: Van Nostrand Reinhold.

Chappell, N. L. (1992). *Social support and aging.* Toronto, Canada: Butterworths.

Chodorow, N. (1978). *The reproduction of mothering: Psychoanalysis and the sociology of gender.* Berkeley: University of California Press.

Chown, S. M. (1981). Friendship in old age. In S. W. Duck and R. Gilmour (Eds.), *Personal relationships, Vol. 2: Developing personal relationships*. London: Academic Press.

Cicirelli, V. G. (1993). Sibling relationships in adulthood. *Marriage and Family Review, 16*, 291–310.

Dykstra, P. A. (1993). The differential availability of relationships and the provision and effectiveness of support to older adults. *Journal of Social and Personal Relationships, 10*, 355–370.

Finley, N. J., Roberts, M. D., & Banahan, B. F. (1988). Motivators and inhibitors of filial obligation toward aging parents. *The Gerontologist, 28*, 73–78.

Gold, D. T. (1989). Sibling relationships in old age: A typology. *International Journal of Aging and Human Development, 28*, 37–51.

Griffith, J. (1985). Social support providers: Who are they? where are they met? and the relationship of network characteristics to psychological distress. *Basic and Applied Social Psychology, 6*, 41–60.

Horowitz, A. (1985). Sons and daughters as caregivers to older parents: Differences in role performance and consequences. *The Gerontologist, 25*, 612–617.

Lopata, H. Z. (1979). *Women as widows*. New York: Elsevier.

O'Bryant, S. L. (1988). Sex-differentiated assistance in older widows' support networks. *Sex Roles, 19*, 91–106.

Rosenthal, C. J. (1985). Kinkeeping in the familial division of labor. *Journal of Marriage and the Family, 47*, 965–974.

Rossi, A. S., & Rossi, P. H. (1990). *Of human bonding: Parent-child relations across the life course*. New York: Aldine de Gruyter.

Shanas, E. (1979). The family as a social support system in old age. *The Gerontologist, 19*, 169–174.

Sheehan, N., & Nuttall, P. (1988). Conflict, emotion, and personal strain among family caregivers. *Family Relations, 37*, 92–98.

Sollie, D. L., & Leslie, L. A. (1994). *Gender, families, and close relationships*. Thousand Oaks, CA: Sage.

Stoller, E. P. (1990). Males as helpers: The role of sons, relatives, and friends. *The Gerontologist, 30*, 228–235.

Suggs, P. K. (1989). Predictors of association among siblings: A black/white comparison. *American Behavioral Scientist, 33*, 70–80.

Suitor, J. J., Pillemer, K., Keeton, S., & Robison, J. (1995). Aged parents and aging children: Determinants of relationship quality. In R. Blieszner & V. Hilkevitch Bedford (Eds.), *Handbook of aging and the family* (pp. 223–242). Westport, CT: Greenwood Press.

Troll, L. E. (1989). Myths of midlife intergenerational relationships. In S. Hunter & M. Sundel (Eds.), *Midlife myths; Issues, findings and practice implications* (pp. 210–232). Beverly Hills, CA: Sage.

Troll, L. E. (1994). Family connectedness of old women. In B. F. Turner & L. E. Troll (Eds.), *Women growing older* (pp. 169–201). Thousand Oaks, CA: Sage Publications.

U.S. Census Bureau (1992). *1990 census of population, volume 2: Social and economic conditions*. Washington, DC: U.S. Government Printing Office.

Wright, P. H. (1989). Gender differences in adults' same- and cross-gender friendships. In R. Adams & R. Blieszner (Eds.), *Older adult friendship: Structure and process* (pp. 197–221). Newbury Park, CA: Sage Publications.

Reprinted from: Hiroko Akiyama, Kathryn Elliott, and Toni Antonucci, "Same-Sex and Cross-Sex Relationships." In *Journals of Gerontology, Series B, Psychological Sciences and Social Sciences*, 51:B, 1996. Reproduced by permission of the publisher, Gerontological Society of America, via Copyright Clearance Center, Inc.

Chapter 26

Able Elderly in the Family Context*

Gunhild O. Hagestad

[handwritten: Researcher Family Life + elders Norway? Chicago Published 1987 Gerontologist]

Among all the topics studied by social scientists, the family tops the list. Today, the majority of older people can expect to live in a family past the childbearing and child-rearing years. This is a twentieth-century phenomenon, however; in the past, due to shorter average life expectancies, few couples survived to live much beyond the last child leaving home. Today, a couple marrying in their early twenties can expect their marriage to last approximately 50 years, unless, of course, it is dissolved by divorce. What is family life like for older couples and for those who have become widowed?

Unlike the traditional family in some cultures such as prerevolutionary China, the modern late-life American family, like that in many industrialized nations, is held together by mutual affection, identity, and support rather than filial obligation or duty. Media portraits often dwell upon lonely elders and neglectful children. Yet the evidence indicates that the opposite is true. Although the majority of older adults prefer to live in their own homes as long as possible and maintain "intimacy at a distance," they maintain close reciprocal ties with their children and other kin. In the following selection, Gunhild Hagestad examines changes in later life among yesterday's and tomorrow's young-old and the potentials that these shifts have for family and careers. For the first time in history, it is likely that most elders will not only spend many years in retirement but also will play roles as grandparents. As you read the following selection, think about the positive aspects of recent demographic changes that increase capacities for family roles in later life. Pay attention to any barriers that may limit these capacities. Notice the different-gendered worlds of men and women in later life and consider the implications of these two worlds for family interaction.

We live in a watershed period characterized by revolutionary demographic changes. It is an era which calls for reexamination of old assumptions, perceptions, and expectations. As Laslett (1977) put it in a discussion of aging in recent history: "Our situation remains irreducibly novel; it calls for invention rather than imitation." Comparing the life experiences of age-cohort groups currently in the population can help illustrate the magnitude of demographic and social changes which have reshaped the social context of lives and relationships. Two groups were chosen: individuals who are currently over the age of 85, and early baby boomers, the first of whom are now turning 40. These two groups represent yesterday's and tomorrow's young-old. Contrasts between them reflect dramatic changes in mortality and life expectancy, fertility patterns, educational attainment, and work careers. These contrasts point to sharply different adult experiences among those who entered old age in the mid-20th Century and those who will be the young-old in the first decades of the 21st Century.

Although sweeping changes associated with the aging of society have opened up new vistas for individual life experiences and the maintenance of family ties, recent literature has been focused on the problematic aspects of recent demographic change. It is time to look at the opportunities presented in an aging population, which is comprised of millions of able, independent elders. In the family realm, recent changes offer increased complexity of family networks, relationships of unprecedented duration, decades of shared experience, and the opportunity to forge new roles. Modern grandparenthood illustrates all of these possibilities.

In mortality patterns, life paths, and family role constellations, recent changes have affected men and women differently. Some emerging contrasts between men and women provide ground for reflection and present challenges to policy-makers as well as researchers.

The Changing Context of Lives: Contrasting Two Cohorts

Society currently has cohorts of people whose experiences of given life phases have been worlds apart. To illustrate how dramatically lives have changed, contrast two age groups: the present oldest old (Suzman & Riley, 1985), those 85 and older, and the first waves of the postwar baby-boom individuals who are now approaching midlife and will constitute the young-old in the early part of the 21st Century.

Many of the current oldest old probably never expected to reach their present age. At the time they were born, general life expectancy was 49. For people who had survived to the age of 20, the average length of remaining life was about 42 years (Torrey, 1982). These elderly remember a past when death was a part of life for all age groups. A majority of them had lost a parent or a sibling by the age of 15 (Uhlenberg, 1980). In their youth, they survived an influenza pandemic which killed millions, young and old. Later, among those who became parents, there was a constant fear of childhood diseases, many of which were potential killers.

Less than a third of these men and women finished high school, and under 10% attained a college degree (Rosenwaike, 1985). Many of them had worked for nearly two decades when Social Security was introduced in 1935. Almost half of the men in this group were still employed in their late 60s (U.S. Bureau of the Census, 1984). Although strong data are lacking on how many of the oldest old have children, it is reasonable to assume that close to 70% of them have at least one living child (Shanas, 1979; U.S. Bureau of the Census, 1984). The average age of these children is about 59 (Torrey, 1985). Among oldest old parents, three-fourths are also grandparents and great-grandparents.

This society currently has approximately two million members who are counted among the oldest old. It is estimated that by the time the first cohorts of baby boomers reach this age bracket, about ten million Americans will be over 85 (Suzman & Riley, 1985; U.S. Bureau of the Census, 1984). The 21st Century's 85-year-olds, with roots in the postwar baby boom, will look back at lives which were strikingly different than those remembered by today's oldest old.

As the first baby boomers approach their 40th birthday, most of them have both parents living. It is estimated that by the time they reach their late 60s, nearly one-third of the women in this group will still have at least one surviving parent (Winsborough, 1980; Wolf, 1983). Some of them have living grandparents. In the world of their childhood, deaths in the nuclear family were rare and unexpected crises and they have come to think of serious illness and death as events which typically occur in life's later decades. During their early years, recent advances in medicine had produced inoculations for most serious childhood diseases, and antibiotics kept common infections from becoming life-threatening. At the time of their birth in the early postwar years, general life expectancy was about 67. By the time they reached 20, they could expect an average of 53 more life years. More than 80% of these baby boomers were graduated from high school; 20% have a college degree. Because of their educational level, members of this group were relatively late in entering the labor force, but they are expected to leave it at an earlier age than was the case for people born early in this century. It is estimated that less than 10% of the men in these cohorts will be in paid employment when they reach their late 60s (U.S. Bureau of the Census, 1984).

Between the baby boomers and the oldest old are today's young-old. These are transitional cohorts, individuals who have some knowledge of a demographic world that has been left behind and who have been characterized as "demographic pioneers" (Shanas, 1980). Having survived to the age of 65, they can expect nearly two more decades of life (U.S. Bureau of the Census, 1984). Constituting about 60% of those classified as old, individuals aged 65–74 overwhelmingly function without limitations on activities due to health problems. Less than 10% of them require institutional care or assistance with daily living (U.S. Senate, 1983).

New Patterns of Aging: Problem or Promise?

Recent changes in mortality, work patterns, and educational levels represent whole new potentials for family life and individual life careers. Yet, mass media, as well as gerontological literature, have taken a surprisingly dim view of the new demographic realities. All too often, the word aging is associated with the word problem. The dominant popular image of old age is one of inevitable decline, senility, and dependency. At the World Congress of Gerontology in New York last summer, a participant could have spent the entire Congress listening to papers on Alzheimer's disease and senile dementia. On the other hand, an attendee looking for sessions on the old as a resource would have had a lot of free time.

In discussions of the family, the recurrent theme in recent gerontological literature has been the burden of parent care. There is growing concern over the strain experienced by families who provide care for impaired elderly members (e.g., Brody, 1984; Cantor, 1983; Ory, 1985). Many of these discussions are focused on women in middle generations, who tend to be the main providers of care. It is frequently argued that today's families face more of a care load than was the case before societal aging. Unfortunately, there are no available historical data to judge the accuracy of such claims, but it is important to keep in mind that before our society had rectangular survival curves, illness and death were experiences which were encountered in all phases of family life. Families have always been caregiving units. The most significant difference between today's families and families of the past is not likely to be in the number of hours spent on the provision of care, but in the focus of care.

In no way is it desirable to forget the problems and heartaches which confront many families in an aging society. But when will the positive outcomes of demographic change be considered? When will it be realized that more financial support goes from old to middle-aged and young family members than flows in the opposite direction along generational lines (Hill et al., 1970, Morgan, 1983)?

When will it be understood that an aging society offers expanding, not constricting, opportunities for family life? When will it be acknowledged that even in advanced old age, millions of people function independently? When will it be recognized that most old people do not represent dependency and a drain on familial and societal resources, but rather that they indeed constitute a vastly underutilized social resource? When will it be grasped and realized that there are rich new possibilities presented by recent demographic and social changes?

In a recent discussion of emergent patterns of longevity, M. Riley and J. Riley (1986) listed four types of new potentials presented by recent demographic change: increased complexity of social networks, increased duration of relationships, prolonged opportunities to accumulate experience, and new chances to complete or change role assignments.

The Rileys pointed out that such potentials are not fully realized in society because currently there is an imbalance between a rapidly growing, vital older population and opportunities available in the social structure. Similar points have been presented by Rosow (1974, 1976) in his discussions of aging in modern society. He argued that society currently offers "tenuous roles" to its older members. These authors are focusing on a macro-social level. On a micro–level of social reality, however, such as in family groups, the four types of potential outlined by the Rileys may be considerably closer to being realized than in society at large.

New Potentials for Family Life

Complex Family Networks

A growing number of families now have four or more generations (Shanas, 1980; Townsend, 1968). Members of multi-generational families interact in a complex set of family roles and relationships. For example, in a four-generation family, there are three tiers of parent-child connections; two sets of grandparent-grandchild relationships, and two generations of people who are both parents and children. Older members of such families typically have steady contact with siblings, children, grandchildren, and great-grandchildren. Most of these ties endure for decades.

Durable Relationships

As was briefly outlined, family relationships now have an unprecedented duration (Hagestad, 1986). Siblings may share eight decades of life, and for most of those years, they will regard each other as age peers. The majority of parents and children will have about half a century of shared lives; many will have 60 to 70 years together. Grandparents and grandchildren will have relationships which last two or more decades. These figures represent rich, varied personal experiences, but also an enormous wealth of shared living and interdependent biographies.

The Accumulation of Experience

In enduring family relationships, individuals build unique webs of experiences, memories, stories. The longer the relationship, the more complex the web. "As two or more persons have a succession of shared experiences, they develop a wider and more firmly rooted common conception of reality—setting them apart from others, who have not been part of the same experience circle" (Turner, 1970). Recent research on marriages which have survived into the retirement years has demonstrated the effects of accumulated shared experiences. The longer a couple has been married, the higher their rates of agreement on personal goals (Atchley & Miller, 1983). In the case of parents and children, the passage of time often leads to the softening of earlier contrasts, to the development of common ground, and to greater tolerance of differences. At a recent social gathering, a woman in her late 60s the mother of four commented on her current phase of life: "I love being my age! It's the first time in my life that all my children liked me!"

Through long-lasting ties in the family, individuals not only build bonds through the accumulation of shared experience, they also help one another deal with a changing historical context. In a society which often erects structural barriers against contact and communication between members of different age-cohort groups, the family provides critical generational bridges. Interwoven lives,

long-standing personal knowledge, and long-term reciprocities can help soften and modify age-related contrasts and chasms which exist in society at large. Older family members help the young build bridges to the past, and the young can help make a rapidly changing culture and technology more understandable. Today's elderly often rely on younger generations to help them deal with complex bureaucracies (Shanas & Sussman, 1977) and, in many modern families, children are tutors for parents and grandparents who find it trying to adjust to the computerization of everyday life. Some years ago, we interviewed a middle-aged woman who gave a vivid illustration of how intergenerational family ties bridge generational contrasts in society at large. She was worried about how long the interview would take, because she had a full program that evening: Her mother and grandmother were going to teach her how to can fruit the old way and her grandson was taking her disco-skating.

Changing Roles

At this time in history, the number of life years has increased, but the proportion of adulthood spent actively involved in two key roles has decreased. As noted previously, the work role is entered later and left earlier than was the case before. It has been estimated that it may now be common to spend one-fourth of adulthood in retirement (Riley, M. & Riley, J. 1986; Torrey, 1982). In the family, the trend towards fewer, closely spaced children means that a decreasing number of years are spent involved in the day-to-day tasks of childrearing and the empty nest phase is a normal, predictable part of modern family life (Glick, 1977). These role changes in a long-lived society may have shaped a new kind of grandparent.

There are several trends worth noting with regards to modern grandparenthood. Although the entry into the grandparent role most likely has always been a transition which typically took place in middle age (Sprey & Matthews, 1982), it is now more clearly sequenced in relation to parenthood than it was earlier (Hagestad & Burton, 1986). Because women finish childbearing fairly early in adulthood, the days of active parenting are likely to be over by the time they become grandmothers. After the emptying of the nest, they may function as what Gutmann (1985) calls "emeritus parents," monitoring and supporting members of the younger generations:

> Precisely because she is now detached from active, hands-on parenting, the older woman can graduate to the next vital parenting level: The management of the extended rather than the nuclear family; and, by extension, of the individual parental couples within the extended family.

Grandparents have been found to be important supports for their children's parenting (Tinsley & Parke, 1984). With nearly half of all grandparents becoming great-grandparents (Shanas, 1980), it may also be found that they become important stabilizing forces for adult grandchildren. Although many young children have grandparents who are actively involved in work roles, the grandparents of young adults are likely to be retirees, and many of them will have experienced widowhood. The few investigations which have explored relationships between young adults and their grandparents (Hagestad & Speicher, 1981; Hoffman, 1979–1980; Robertson, 1976) have found that these grandchildren see grandparents as highly important people in their lives. The emerging picture of today's grandparent, especially in the later phases of grandparent-grandchild relations, is one of a family member who operates without some of the role constraints characteristic of earlier adulthood, who has lived and learned to put things in perspective, whose most important function may just be being there for younger generations (Hagestad, 1985). The comforting presence of grandparents may often be felt despite geographic distance between them and the younger generations.

For members of several younger generations, grandparents serve critical safety-valve functions: They are people who can be counted on in case things go wrong (Troll, 1983). There is growing evidence that in times of crises, grandparents do indeed step in with help and support. A case in point is divorce. Recent research has found that grandparents serve as significant stress-buffers following family disruption (Cherlin & Furstenberg, 1986; Hetherington, et al., 1978). Although it is not known how often divorce leads to three-generational living, or how often grandparents provide substantial financial support to grandchildren following divorce, recent studies have shown that grandparents on the custodial side are significant factors in post-divorce adjustment. Marital breakup often intensifies relationships with maternal kin, but presents a threat to relationships in the paternal line (Furstenberg et al., 1983; Hagestad et al., 1984). Research on divorce has confirmed previous findings regarding the role of men and women in the maintenance of family ties.

The Worlds of Men and Women

It has repeatedly been found that women are the linchpin of family contact and cohesion. They are the kin-keepers, the ministers of the interior, who orchestrate family get-togethers, monitor family relationships, and facilitate intergenerational contact (Rosenthal, 1985). Women in middle generations are most centrally involved in kin-keeping, and the mother-daughter link is pivotal, both in the maintenance of family contact and the flow of support across generations (Daatland, 1983; Kendig & Rowland, 1983). As was mentioned earlier, daughters are more involved in parent care than men are. A recent study of family caregivers (Horowitz, 1985) found that two-thirds of them were adult children, and, among offspring providing care, daughters outnumbered sons 3 to 1. This research also showed that when sons were caregivers, they relied heavily on assistance from their wives. In other words, "caregiving as a primary female role clearly extended to daughters-in-law as well as daughters" (Horowitz, 1985, P. 615). It has been common, especially in the popular press, to suggest that when women are in the labor force, they will spend less time and effort on kin-tending. There is little empirical evidence to support this claim (Cantor, 1983; Horowitz, 1985; Noelker & Poulshock, 1982; Soldo & Myllyluoma, 1983). Indeed, Stoller (1983) recently found that employment significantly reduced caregiving to aging parents among sons, but this was not a statistically significant trend for daughters.

Because of gender differences in life expectancy and age at marriage, the oldest member of a family lineage is likely to be a woman. In society at large, as well as in families, the world of the very old is a world of women. Among today's oldest old, there are only 41 men for every 100 women (Siegel & Tauber, 1986). Even among the young-old, those aged 65 to 74, there are only 75 men per 100 women (U.S. Bureau of the Census, 1984). The steady increase in the number of old people living alone which has been observed over the last two decades (Kobrin, 1976) is mostly accounted for by women, who constitute 80% of elderly primary individuals. There has been public concern over the well-being of the old who live alone, but a current national study found that they are far from isolated (National Center for Health Statistics, 1986). The majority live close to family and have frequent contact with relatives. Of those with children, 72% said that a child could get to their home in a matter of minutes. Only 5% of people living alone reported no contact with family or friends during the two weeks prior to the interview. Most of these isolated individuals were men. The first reports from this study concluded that it may indeed be steady contact with family and friends which makes it possible for older women to live alone and function in everyday living. Although they were somewhat older than people who were living with others, they rated their health more positively, and two-thirds perceived themselves as a lot more active than other people their own age. It appears that although most women in the later phases of old age do not have a horizontal linkage to a spouse, they have strong intergenerational, vertical ties which help them sustain independent living. There are few indications that this will change in the near future. Some things are likely to change, however.

As society enters the 21st Century, generations of women who have high levels of education and high rates of labor force participation will be in the early phases of old age. About half of them will have experienced marital disruption earlier in adulthood and will have spent a number of years on their own. The needs of these older women are going to confront social service agencies and informal networks with a different challenge from that represented by past cohorts, who after decades of traditional marriage and motherhood faced decades of widowhood.

Young-old mothers in the 21st Century may have more shared experiences with their daughters than has been the case for older women at the end of this century. In the future, mothers and daughters will typically look back at involvements in education, work, and family. Many of them will also share some of the life changes associated with aging. A greater fund of shared life experiences may make the female axis even more central as the dominant force in the maintenance of intergenerational cohesion and continuity. In addition, there are recent social trends which may weaken men's intergenerational ties. Divorce has already been mentioned. Often, marital disruption leads to what Preston (1984) called "the disappearance act of the American father." The increase in non-marital fertility is another trend which entails young generations who grow up with little or no contact with a father and paternal kin. Although women's intergenerational ties are more durable, rich, and varied than ever before in history, a growing number of men may now have highly precarious vertical family ties (Eggebeen & Uhlenberg, 1985; Hagestad, 1986). In contrast with recent discussions of how demographic and cultural changes may have created new gaps between the worlds of men and women, there are suggestions that male and female life patterns may show increasing convergence in an aging society. Three trends have been identified as contributing to such convergence: the decreasing life course involvement in work and parenting, the androgyny of later life, and the feminization of the population.

As was discussed in the comparison of yesterday's and tomorrow's young-old, two key role activities now occupy a smaller proportion of the adult years than was the case for previous cohorts: work and day-to-day parenting. Many observers have noted that men's and women's differential investments in these roles create sharp gender differences in early adult experiences, but wane in importance after midlife (Gutmann, 1985; Livson, 1983, Rossi, 1986).

From psychodynamic and biological perspectives, it is also argued that as men and women age, they become more alike (Turner, 1982). Giele (1980) discussed this as part of what she calls "the cross-over pattern." Gutmann (1985), who sees the parent role as the critical factor in early adult gender differentiation, has argued that older men gravitate toward the domestic sphere and an emphasis on affiliation. Aging women, on the other hand, become more aggressive and agentive, assuming a role as administrators of extended family networks.

Rossi (1986) reminded us that the larger the proportion of elderly in the population, the greater the tendency to a female majority in that population. Thus, an aging population is one in which androgenous qualities may be more in evidence, but also one in which may be seen greater salience of female values, such as an emphasis on connectedness and reciprocal caring. Increasingly, for men and women, the strongest thread of continuity across 8 or more decades of life will be found in the fabric of family life.

Summing Up

Although much recent attention has been focused on issues of dependency in an aging society, there is a need to recognize the enormous potentials for family life under the new demographic conditions. Current patterns of longevity create new opportunities for long-lasting, complex relationships and emerging roles for the able elderly. They represent a major family and societal resource. Gutmann (1985) discussed the challenge facing social scientists in today's society. His words could apply to policy-makers as well:

Instead of thinking of the aged as hapless recipients of services over which they can have little control, they can begin to study the ways in which postparental potentials can be transformed—into resources and capacities—not only for the elders, but for us all.

Discussion Questions

1. What assumptions are often made that stress the elderly as an expensive burden rather than an underutilized social resource?

2. Describe the four new potentials for family life.

3. What key roles are changing in later life?

4. Describe "the worlds of men and women."

5. What is meant by "androgyny" and how may it affect family life for both men and women?

Note

* Work on this paper was supported by a Research Career Development Award from the National Institute on Aging, Grant No. 1 K 04 AG 00203.

References

Atchley, R. C., & Miller, S. J. (1983). Types of elderly couples. In T. H. Brubaker (Ed.), *Family relationships in later life*. Beverly Hills, CA: Sage Publications, Inc.

Brody, E. M. (1984). Parent care as normative family stress. *The Gerontologist, 25,* 19–29.

Cantor, M. H. (1983). Strain among caregivers: A study of experience in the United States. *The Gerontologist, 23,* 597–604.

Cherlin, A., & Furstenberg, F. F., Jr. (1986). *The new American grandparent: A place in the family, a life apart*. New York: Basic Books.

Daatland, S. 0. (1983). Use of public services for the aged and the role of the family. *The Gerontologist, 23,* 650–656.

Eggebeen, D., & Uhlenberg, P. (1985). Changes in the organization of men's lives: 1960–1980. *Family Relations, 34,* 251–257.

Furstenberg, F. F., Jr., Peterson, J. L., Nord, C. W., & Zill, N. (1983). The life course of children of divorce: Marital disruption and parental contact. *American Sociological Review, 48,* 656–668.

Giele, J. Z. (1980). Adulthood as transcendence of age and sex. In N. J. Smelser & E. Erikson (Eds.), *Themes of work and love in adulthood*. Cambridge, MA: Harvard University Press.

Glick, P. C. (1977). Updating the family life cycle. *Journal of Marriage and the Family, 39,* 5–13.

Gutmann, D. L. (1985). The parental imperative revisited: Towards a developmental psychology of adulthood and later life. In J. A.

Meacham (Ed.), *Contributions to human development*. Basel: Karger.

Hagestad, G. O. (1985). Continuity and connectedness. In V. L. Bengtson & J. Robertson (Eds.), *Grandparenthood*. Beverly Hills, CA: Sage.

Hagestad, G. O. (1986). The aging society as a context for family life. *Daedalus, 116*, 119–139.

Hagestad, G. O., & Burton, L. (1986). Grandparenthood, life context, and family development. *American Behavioral Scientist, 29*, 471–484.

Hagestad, G. O., & Speicher, J. L. (1981, April). *Grandparents and family influence: Views of three generations*. Paper presented at the Society for Research in Child Development biennial meeting, Boston.

Hagestad, G. O., Smyer, M. A., & Stierman, K. L. (1984). Parent-child relations in adulthood: The impact of divorce in middle age. In R. Cohen, S. Weissman, & B. Cohler (Eds.), *Parenthood: Psychodynamic perspectives*. New York: Guilford Press.

Hetherington, E. M., Cox, M., & Cox, R. (1978). The aftermath of divorce. In J. H. Stevens, Jr. & M. Matthew (Eds.), *Mother-Child, Father-Child relations*. Washington, DC: National Association for the Education of Young Children.

Hill, R., Foote, N., Aldous, J., Carlson, R., & MacDonald, R. (1970). *Family development in three generations*. Cambridge, MA: Schenkman.

Hoffman, E. (1979–1980). Young adults' relations with their grandparents: An exploratory study. *International Journal of Aging and Human Development, 10*, 229–310.

Horowitz, A. (1985). Sons and daughters as caregivers to older parents: differences in role performance and consequences. *The Gerontologist, 25*, 612–617.

Kendig, H. L., & Rowland, D. T. (1983). Family support of the Australian aged: A comparison with the United States. *The Gerontologist, 23*, 643–649.

Kobrin, F. E. (1976). The fall in household size and the rise of the primary individual in the United States. *Demography, 13*, 127–138.

Laslett, P. (1977). *Family life and illicit love in earlier generations*. New York: Cambridge University Press.

Livson, F. B. (1983). Gender identity: A life-span view of sex role development. In R. B. Weg (Ed.), *Sexuality in later years*. New York: Academic Press.

Morgan, J. N. (1983). The redistribution of income by families and institutions in emergency help patterns. In G. J. Duncan & J. N. Morgan (Eds.), *Five thousand American families—patterns of economic progress* (Vol. 10).

Ann Arbor: The University of Michigan, Institute for Social Research.

National Center for Health Statistics, Mary Grace Kovar. (1986, May 9). Aging in the eighties, age 63 years and over and living alone, contacts with family, friends, and neighbors. *Advance Data from Vital and Health Statistics* (No. 116, DHHS Publication No. PHS 86-1250). Hyattsville, MD: Public Health Service.

Noelker, L. S., & Poulshock, S. W. (1982). *The effects on families of caring for impaired elderly in residence* (Final report submitted to the Administration on Aging). Cleveland. OH: The Margaret Blenkner Research Center for Family Studies, The Benjamin Rose Institute.

Ory, M. G. (1985, Fall). The burden of care: A familial perspective. *Generations, 8*, 14–18.

Preston, S. H. (l984). Children and the elderly: Divergent paths for America's dependents. *Demography, 21*, 435–457.

Riley, M. W., & Riley, J. W., Jr. (1986). Longevity and social structure: The potential of the added years. In A. Pifer & L. Bronte (Eds.). *Our aging society: Paradox and promise*. New York: W. W. Norton & Company.

Robertson, J. F. (1976). Significance of grandparents: Perceptions of young adult grandchildren. *The Gerontologist, 16*, 137–140.

Rosenthal. C. J. (1985). Kinkeeping in the familial division of labor. *Journal of Marriage and the Family, 47*, 965–974.

Rosenwaike, I. (1985, Spring). A demographic portrait of the oldest old. *Milbank Memorial Fund Quarterly, 63*, 187–205.

Rossi, A. (1986). Sex and gender in the aging society. In A. Pifer & L. Bronte (Eds.), *Our aging society*. New York: Norton & Co.

Rosow, I. (1974). *Socialization to old age*. Berkeley: University of California Press.

Rosow, I. (1976). Status and role change through the life span. In R. E. Binstock & E. Shanas (Eds.), *Handbook of aging and the social sciences*. New York: Van Nostrand Reinhold Company.

Shanas, E. (1979). Social myth as hypothesis: The case of the family relations of old people. *The Gerontologist, 19*, 3–9.

Shanas, E. (1980). Older people and their families: The new pioneers. *Journal of Marriage and the Family, 42*, 9–15.

Shanas, E., & Sussman, M. B. (Eds.). (1977). *Family, bureaucracy, and the elderly*. Durham, NC: Duke University Press.

Siegel, J. S., & Tauber, C. M. (1986. Winter). Demographic perspectives on the long-lived Society. *Daedalus, 7*, 118.

Soldo, B. J., & Myllyluoma, J. (1983). Caregivers who live with dependent elderly. *The Gerontologist, 23,* 605–611.

Sprey, J., & Matthews, S. H. (1982, November). Contemporary grandparenthood: A systemic transition. *Annals of the American Academy of Political Science, 464,* 91–103.

Stoller, E. P. (1983). Parental caregiving by adult children. *Journal of Marriage and the Family, 45,* 851–858.

Suzman, R., & Riley, M. W. (1985, Spring). Introducing the "oldest old." *Milbank Memorial Fund Quarterly Health and Society, 63,* 177–186.

Tinsley, B. R., & Parke, R. D. (1984). Grandparents as support and socialization agents. In M. Lewis (Ed.), *Beyond the dyad.* New York: Plenum.

Torrey, B. B. (1982). The lengthening of retirement. In M. W. Riley, R. P. Abeles, & M. Teitelbaum (Eds.). *Aging from birth to death, Vol. II. Sociotemporal perspectives.* Boulder, CO: Westview Press.

Torrey, B. B. (1985). Sharing increasing costs on declining income: The visible dilemma of the invisible aged. *Milbank Memorial Fund Quarterly Health and Society, 63,* 377–394.

Townsend, P. (1968). Emergence of the four-generation family in industrial society. In B. L. Neugarten (Ed.), *Middle age and aging.* Chicago: University of Chicago Press.

Troll, L. E. (1983). Grandparents: The family watchdogs. In T. Brubaker (Ed.). *Family relationships in later life.* Beverly Hills, CA: Sage.

Turner, B. F. (1982). Sex-related differences in aging, In B. S. Wolman (Ed.), *Handbook of developmental psychology.* Englewood Cliffs, NJ: Prentice-Hall.

Turner, R. H. (1970). *Family interaction.* New York: John Wiley & Sons, Inc.

Uhlenberg, P. (1980). Death and the family. *Journal of Family History, 5,* 313–320.

U.S. Bureau of the Census, T. Siegel, & M. Davidson. (1984). Demographic and socioeconomic aspects of aging in the United States. *Current Population Reports* (Series P-23, No. 138). Washington, DC: U.S. Bureau of the Census.

U.S. Senate. Select Committee on Aging. (1983). *Aging America: Trends and projections.* Washington, DC.

Winsborough, H. H. (1980). A demographic approach to the life cycle. In K. W. Back (Ed.), *Life course: Integrative theories and exemplary populations.* Boulder, CO: Westview Press.

Wolf, D. A. (1983). *Kinship and the living arrangements of older Americans: Final report submitted to the National Institute of Child Health and Human Development* (Contract No. N01–HD-12183). Washington, DC; Urban Institute.

Chapter 27

Parenting in Later Life

*Marcene Goodman and
Robert L. Rubinstein*

*Are you an only child? If so, it is likely that
your relationship with your parents in later life
will be very different from what it would be if
you were one of several of their adult children.
Although considerable research has been
undertaken on the importance of birth order in
the family and on the experience of growing up
as only child, rare are the studies that experientially examine that dynamic from the elderly
parent's perspective. Even more rare are studies that address qualitative differences in the
parenting experience of elderly mothers of one
child versus mothers of several children. The
following selection by Marcene Goodman and
Robert Rubinstein reports on a study that examines late-life developmental changes
among mothers who had parented only one
child. It introduces the notion that mothering
an only child may have consequences for
women that affect their well-being in late-life.
Their results suggest that having only one
child intensifies a mother's attachment to her
offspring, narrows sources of life satisfactions,
and limits the variety of her activities. As you
read, think about the possible effects that the
birth cohort of the mothers in this study may
have had on their responses. Specifically, these
are women who, for various reasons, had only
one child during a period when most American
women were having two or more. In that sense,
they deviated from the norms of childbearing
for their cohort. If smaller families, with only
one child, were the norm, would you expect to
find the same results reported here? If not,
why?*

Scholarly literature on intergenerational
connectedness has failed to capture the rela-

tional nuances that exist between adult children and their parents, or the substance,
complexity, and history of the life-long dynamic that eventuates in aging-parent-adult-
child relationships. Rarely do we find studies
that experientially examine that dynamic
from the elderly parent's perspective (Blieszner and Mancini 1987; Matthews 1993).
Even more rare are studies that address
qualitative differences in the parenting experience of elderly mothers and elderly fathers.
This article reports on a study that examined,
from a phenomonological perspective, late-
life developmental sequelae of mothers who
had parented only children. It introduces the
notion that mothering an only child may have
consequences for women that singularly impact on their well-being in late life. Our data
suggest that having one child intensifies a
mother's attachment to her offspring, narrows the loci of her life satisfactions, and limits the diversity of her commitment to activities that foster a sense of continuity.

Three themes relating to the fulfillment of
maternal, social, and self-expectations were
uniquely expressed in single-childed mothers. First, from the mother's perspective, the
emotional content and the meaning of the
mother/child relationship appeared to remain unchanged with time. The perceived
centrality and steadfastness of the tie endured, despite the occurrence of new events
in both mother and child's lives, evolving developmental needs of the mother, or the process of the child's own individuation. Second,
a critical issue of adult identity was solved for
these women by having borne a child, often
in problematic or non-normative circumstances (late life pregnancy, multiple miscarriages, other health problems, or a bad marriage). In having a child, they felt they had
managed to legitimize their womanhood, fulfilling what was seen, for that cohort, as the
destiny of women and generative tie to the
future (Erikson 1963).

Lastly, as their single vehicle of self-per-
petuation, most women shared the need to
believe in the perfection, happiness, or success of their child. This was expressed in their
tendency to give unstintingly glowing evaluations of their child's personality, social
skills, and intellect, and to downplay or deny

their failures. Indeed, we found that the emotional lives, identities and future care expectations of single-childed mothers hinged, to a great extent, on what appeared to be inflated images they held of their only child. We feel these inflated images served several adaptive functions for these women. In supplying a "happy ending" to the child's life, the mothers could take comfort in knowing that *their* lives had been of some value, or had "paid off." Further, believing in their child's security helped them to alleviate anxiety over their own. The provision of successful outcomes for their child gave them hope for the future, enabling them to put satisfactory closure on life. We have labeled this apparent construction of reality in the service of well-being "adaptive illusion" and have found evidence of its use in most of the single-childed women we interviewed. In turn, we found that its absence was associated with feelings of hopelessness and despair.

Our goal is to contribute to intergenerational theory by calling attention to one particular parenting dynamic and its ramifications for late life development. We present data derived from in-depth interviews of older mothers of only children, introduce themes that differentiated single-childed mothers from mothers of larger families, and suggest why having an only child uniquely colors the parenting experience of aging mothers. Literature pertaining to the nature and quality of intergenerational relationships, the parenting of only children, and the impact of parenting on late life development are reviewed. We follow with a description of the study, highlights from our data that support our position and illustrate differences between mothers of one and mothers of many, and close with a discussion that argues the relevance of maternal self-representation to well-being in older age.

Background

The Ties That Bind

The most scrutinized family dynamic in gerontological research has been the reciprocal exchange between adult children and their aging parents. A good portion of this research is devoted to the conceptualization of a relationship based on the care of aging parents and the willingness and ability of adult offspring to provide it (For reviews of filial responsibility and expectations see, Cicirelli 1983; Nydegger 1991; Shanas 1979, 1984; Troll 1986). In a reversal of "caregiving" roles a more recent body of literature examines the experience of aging parents who are forced to revisit the economic and emotional burdens of parenting because of the marital or financial problems of adult children.

Both types of intergenerational studies have common features. First, research in this area is almost singularly based on quantitative assessment of well-being measures associated with quality-of-life in older age (for example, morale: Quinn 1983 or Seelbach and Sauer 1977; avowed happiness, Connidis and McMullin 1993; personal satisfaction as a function of filial interaction, Lee and Ellithorpe 1982). Second, studies evaluating the adult parent/child interaction are seldom gender specific in spite of a literature that identifies the mothering experience as socially, emotionally, and physically distinct from that of the father (For cross-disciplinary references see, Chodorow 1978; Cook 1988; Littlewood and Hoekstra 1991; Gerson 1986; Nydegger and Mitteness 1991; Russell and Radojevic 1992). Finally, intergenerational studies seem more concerned with what older parents expect from their adult children rather than what they hope or expect *for* them.

The intergenerational literature seems clear on the issue of what aging parents want *from* their adult children. Overall, findings suggest a shift in the need for "instrumental" care to a desire for "expressive" caring (Hess and Waring 1978). This is evident in the trend of recent cohorts of elderly parents to live and be independent from their children, turning to them only when help is needed (Hagestad 1987; Mancini and Blieszner 1989; Seelbach 1977; Seelbach and Sauer 1977; Shanas 1979). Elderly parents are also anxious to, and do, remain emotionally close to their children in spite of the distances that increasingly divide contemporary families (Blieszner and Mancini 1987; Cicirelli 1983, 1991; Connidis and

McMullin 1993; Roberts et al. 1991; Rossi and Rossi 1991; Troll and Smith 1976).

While mutual affection explains the persistence of adult-child/aging-parent relationship across time, the extent to which filial ties contribute to peace of mind in the lives of older parents varies according to study. Affectional ties with adult children may (Connidis 1989) or may not (Lee and Ellithorpe 1982) be the central source of well-being in older persons, but health unequivocally is (Connidis and McMullin 1993; Quinn 1983). Thus, kin interaction, while it may be critical, appears to be secondary in contributing to the well-being of elderly persons (Lee and Ellithorpe 1982).

Taken together, intergenerational studies paint a picture of parent/filial relationships that is generally positive. Until recently, studies have not addressed the conflictual dimensions in these relationships, nor have they probed for the negatives in parenting adult children. Bengtson and associates were among the first to recognize a disparity between younger and middle-aged cohorts in interpreting the depth and nature of intergenerational cohesiveness (Bengtson and Kuypers 1971; Bengtson et al. 1991). Where older parents need to insure their continuity and support by feeling close to their offspring, children, whose task it is to individuate, may tend to evade and deny this cohesiveness. As a result, young adults and the middle-aged write a relational script commensurate with their own developmental needs. In keeping with this notion of "developmental stake," older parents are also more likely to describe relationships with their children in positive terms, and are less likely than their children to acknowledge the changing nature of those relationships (Hagestad 1987).

A recent, and as yet small body of work purposefully examined conflict between parents and adult children and its impact on parental morale. This avenue of inquiry developed in response to current divorce and economic trends which increasingly propel adult children back to their parent's home in search of financial, familial, and emotional support (Crimmins and Ingegneri 1990; Mancini and Blieszner 1989; Pillemer and

Suitor 1991; Umberson 1989). These studies find that problems in the life of a child are potential causes for distress among the elderly (Pillemer and Suitor 1991), with mothers being more vulnerable to children's misfortunes than fathers (Greenberg and Becker 1988; Suitor and Pillemer 1987; Umberson 1989).

Parenting Only Children

While the impact of being an only child has stimulated some research, the experience of being a parent who rears one has received little attention from developmental psychologists. Thus, psychological and behavioral profiles of single-childed parents are lacking. Parents of only children have been characterized as more anxious about parenting (Schachter 1959), a trait that appears to make them more sensitive to, and "unrealistic" about, their child's behavior (Falbo and Polit 1986). Because the parental concerns center around one, the child "experiences greater quantities of high-quality parent-child interactions" (Falbo and Polit 1986). This singular investment of time and energy sets up expectations for achievement on the part of parents that are believed to promote motivation in the child (Falbo 1984).

Some research suggests that women who are limited biologically (by age, fertility problems, or other reasons) from having more than one, harbor a wish for more children (Polit 1980). Mothers who *plan* to have one, however, are "more positive about their family configuration" (Katz and Boswell 1984). Falbo (1984) speculates that attitudes toward raising a single child are dependent on whether the parents anticipate having more children. As for the textural or longitudinal fabric of the maternal/filial relationship, studies examining the mother/single-child dyad outside of adolescence are rare. One study of single-childed mothers who are themselves single, suggests pathological outcomes for both mother and child when "prolonged symbiosis" interferes with mothers' ability to differentiate the needs of her child from her own (Bogolub 1984). Finally, if older parents have biased estimates of filial loyalty and involvement as developmental stake theory suggests (Bengtson and Kuypers 1971),

the phenomenon may be empirically demonstrated in the wedding of our data and
those of Kivett and Atkinson (1984). Where
we suggest that mothers of one affect closeness through illusion, their data find that parents of only children, in fact, receive less help
and attention from that child.

The Developmental Significance of Parenting an Only Child

Elson (1984), in a psychoanalytic/develop-
mental analysis of parenting, cites the gradual individuation of parent from child as the
prerequisite to social and emotional maturation in both. In her words, "support of the
forming and firming narcissism in the child
is the developmental *task* of parenthood. The
continuing transformation of their own narcissism is the developmental *process* of parenthood" (p. 299). Elson (1984) is suggesting
that a critical component in successful parenting is the ability to empathize with the
child's evolving needs rather than one's own.
She cautions that middle-aged parents who
"need to bind the child . . . to their own ambitions and goals" to seek solutions to their
own problems will regress to more primitive
forms of narcissism. Although not specific to
single-childed parents, Elson's theory is exemplified in the cognitions, behaviors and af-
fectual outcomes of the 20 single-childed
women we interviewed in this study.

Our findings may be explained, in part, by
social ideologies at play during the ripening
or puberty of these women. Because cultural
credibility and self-worth were contingent on
marrying and raising a family, motherhood
offered the best, and for some, the only means
of self-validation, self-expression, and self-
perpetuation. These women, having managed to produce at least *one* child, were
spared the stigma of marginality experienced
by childless women, *and* given a single
chance to live on through the lives of children
and prospective grandchildren (Alexander
et al. 1992). We found that the penchant in
some of these women to deny the negatives
and embellish the positives in their child's life
further validated the sense of achievement
they had in their own. We called this tendency
to mentally adjust for reality "adaptive illusion" because its use appeared to be associ-

ated with emotional equilibrium in the mothers who practiced it, and hopelessness and
despair in mothers who did not. Indeed, we
contend that elderly mothers' illusions of cohesion and centrality in their only child's life
are critical to maintaining their sense of identity into late-life.

Method

The Sample

The forty women discussed in this paper
were sub-samples in a larger study entitled
"Lifestyles and generativity of childless older
women" (N= 160). These subjects comprised
two groups of six that distinguished women
on the basis of their status as mothers or as
childless women. Childless groups included
(1) women who had never married, (2) women
who were widowed, and (3) women who
were currently married (n=90); mothering
groups included (4) those who have borne
and raised a single one child, (5) those who
had borne and raised over three children, and
(6) bereaved mothers who had lost children
they had raised to adulthood (n=70). Women
in mothering groups were either widowed,
divorced, or currently married. Demographic specifics of the single-child and
mother-of-four groups contrasted here are
outlined in Table 27.1.

Most of the twenty women who were mothers of only children considered themselves to
be homemakers whose working careers
(mostly secretarial or clerical) lasted until the
birth of their child. The few exceptions were
women whose skills enabled them to work
from their homes (a music teacher, an interior decorator) or at jobs compatible with domestic schedules (a teacher, a social worker).
In short, the primary profession of most
mothers in this group was mothering. In contrast, only one mother of the four-or-more
group considered herself to be solely a housewife. In addition to mothering large families
(ranging in number from 4 to 10 children),
these women often had careers outside the
home (a nurse, a Board of Education supervisor, a legal secretary). Approximately half
the mothers-of-one had a current annual income of below $10,000 while the income of
the remaining half ranged from $10,000 to

Table 27.1

Demographic Characteristics of Mothers

	Mothers of One Child (n=20)	Mothers of Four or More Children (n=20)
Age Range	64 to 83	61 to 80
Mean Age and SD	74.2, 5.6	70.6, 5.3
Currently Married	3	9
Widowed	16	10
Divorced	1	1
White	20	18
African American	0	2
Protestant	5	4
Catholic	4	13
Jewish	10	3
No Religion	1	0
Range in Years of Education	14 to 18	8 to 16
Modal Years of Education	12	12
Living Alone	17	6
Living with Husband	3	5
Living with Husband and Child(ren)	0	3
Living with Child and Grandchild(ren)	0	6

$30,000. Women with four or more children were better off financially, presumably because more were living with husbands, had held pension producing jobs, or were receiving their late husbands' pensions. Sixteen of these women had incomes ranging from $20,000 to $30,000. Only one woman had an income of below $10,000 while two had incomes in excess of $30,000.

The women of only children gave several reasons for having a single child. Most (12) had erratic histories of fertility and childbirth or medical problems associated with childbearing. These included miscarriages, stillbirths, infant deaths, or problems with menstruation and conception. Five had married late in life which limited their potential for mothering a larger family. Three attributed their single-childed status to bad marriages, two that ended in divorce soon after the birth of their son or daughter. These women never remarried. In all, ten of the women in the single-child group had daughters while the other ten had sons. Only one woman in the group had adopted her child. No women in the four-or-more-children group had exclusively sons or exclusively daughters.

The Procedure

Women in the study responded to ads placed in local newspapers, fliers in senior centers and senior housing, or were recruited through church and synagogue groups or among volunteer workers in charity organizations. A $40 honorarium was paid to all women who were interviewed. Ethnographic in nature, the semi-structured interview was designed to evoke life histories, to estimate the nature and strength of generative ideation and behavior, and to provoke self-assessment in a life-review format. Interviews were conducted in respondents' homes and lasted anywhere from two hours during a single visit to twelve hours spread over multiple visits. Interviews, which were audiotaped, were transcribed and analyzed for thematic content relative to self-image, motherhood, and, aging as the mother of a single child (Luborsky 1993).

Results

Themes That Characterized Mothers of One

Mothers of only children were distinguished by the stringent nature of their relationships with their child and their idealizations of the intellects, career successes, or matrimonial conquests of their sons or daughters. In many cases, mothers appeared to establish terms of endearment that prohibited the individuation of adult children. This, for some mothers, resulted in bitterness and acrimony toward the child who they often perceived as uncaring, ungrateful, and non-supportive in spite of his or her achievements. Filial disappointment for these women seemed to be magically transformed through the self-healing mechanism we described as "adaptive illusion." Thus, the subjective qualities they assigned to their son or daughter served to mask any indications of indifference, neglect, or hostility they perceived on the part of the child. We characterized these women (n=8) as extremely-attached and vicariously dependent on their child for self-affirmation.

Attached and Dependent Mothers

Women in this group voiced regret over having had only one child; the basis of regret was their current loneliness and confusion over their child's need to physically or emotionally distance from them. In various ways and to varying degrees, most felt that their selflessness in raising their child was, if not reciprocated, unappreciated. All were continually child-referenced, in spite of the multidimensionality of the interview. They appeared preoccupied with the lives of their children, often to the exclusion of their husbands or other commitments in life.

Themes apparent in the narratives of these mothers were the need for exclusivity in the hierarchy of their child's affections, the yoke of martyrdom, a reticence to "let go," resentment over what they perceived as interference from their child's spouse in the mother/child relationship, and concerns over potential dependency on the child. Dialogue from the life history narrative of Mrs. Bergen, age 73 and widowed, illustrates several of these themes as she describes the vicissitudes of connectedness between her and her 43 year old daughter Barbara.

Interviewer: Do you have anything you consider to be your 'job in life?'

Mrs. Bergen: Well, when my daughter Barbara was born it was everything for Barbara. Barbara this and Barbara that. It was one child. . . . The main thing when you are a mother is you have to give. . . . I was the mother first . . . I guess I am still the mother first, still doing. . . . It is still Barbara this and Barbara that. . . . That is one of the problems I had. I have been, maybe, too close or too dependent . . . and I know of different ways she tried to break away. . . . When she got divorced, naturally, I saw more of her. Then, I guess maybe I was telling her too much because she resented it, so I hurt. . . . But then when she started going with the person she's engaged to now, of course, I saw less of her and I guess I felt left out. . . . While I was cooking and everything she would come. . . . It was to her benefit . . . I wanted to see her, so if you want to make yourself wanted you have to keep doing. . . . Now I don't work. I have time. My daughter's working, she's busy, there is no time . . . I have the time, she doesn't. . . . If you have a few children you would not give as much of your time and it would be spread out. . . . My trouble is I don't let go.

Reconciling the discrepancy between the need for prominence in her daughter's life and her daughter's distancing, Mrs. Bergen's evaluation of motherhood seemed contradictory. Seemingly more content in the knowledge that she had mothered than in the results of her mothering, her ambivalence is evident when she advises:

If you want children, you know you have to work . . . you have to make sacrifices. But then, that is how you get something. Because after they have grown, it is *wonderful*. They turn out right.

Mrs. Feldman, a 74 year old widow, focused on her 45 year old son's intellectual prowess and her daughter-in-law as obstacle to the ambitions she held for him. Throughout a lifetime of delivering him from insolvency and financing his false starts, Mrs. Feldman continues to revere his "brilliance" and maintain her belief in his lack of control over the negative events that shaped his life.

Interviewer: What were one or two of the saddest times in your life?

Mrs. Feldman: Well, of course it has to do with my son dropping out of college. He had a nervous breakdown. And he lost his scholarship. And I was very pleasantly surprised after that, you know . . . he was given a fellowship, so I thought that was like hope returning. He was offered one to Harvard, which at that time he didn't take and later he was offered one to Trenton State which he took.

Interviewer: You had a lot invested in his academic success?

Mrs. Feldman: Yes. Yes, well because he was always very brilliant, you know . . . I had to do some very difficult planning on a very tight budget. . . . When I moved in here it was a nightmare financially, emotionally, and if I could have divorced myself from my son and not cared, not worried about his problems. Mine are compounded because I thought about him. . . . My son went through a very difficult period. One of the things that showed up was the parking tickets. Hundreds and hundreds of dollars. He'd just park any old place and the tickets came in droves.

Interviewer: He paid them?

Mrs. Feldman: My husband paid them, because, I'll tell you, money didn't mean anything to him [my son]. I'm the one that suffered . . . if I were only thinking of myself I could have squeezed through quite easily . . . they were buying a house, thanks to me through years and years of thrift, saving it up over the years and saying, well, you can have it when you need it . . . my daughter-in-law loved to move, move, and move, and move . . . but [she] was very wasteful . . .

When asked what things she would change about her life if she could, Mrs. Feldman centered her response around her son.

You know, my son had received a large grant from a top school amongst a lot of other grants. The others were much smaller. . . . But it's a field that leads you no place. . . . This wasn't my original plan for him. . . . He's a fine gentleman. First of all he's got a brilliant mind. He's got a compassionate nature and he's very honest.

Mrs. Kempler's need to share in the lives of her daughter's family structured her life. Interviews were dominated by descriptions of her daughter's developmental history, Mrs. Kempler's ministrations to, and sacrifices on behalf of her child, and her determination to remain central in her daughter's life. By her own admission, the need for filial cohesiveness often caused problems between her and her husband, and a fusion of identity between her and her daughter. The following monologue in response to questions about their relationship reveals the all-consuming, uncompromising nature of her mothering, and the fidelity she expected and (from her accounts) got from her daughter in return.

> . . . I could not live, I mean that literally. I could not live if I was angry at my daughter. That's it. . . . Our family, our children come first. We come second. . . . It's her house but I feel like it's my house too. . . . Like I put things in her drawers or I'll go to the closet and straighten [it out]. . . . They're her children but I feel like they're my children. . . . When my Ricky [grandson] was born, I remember this distinctly, I never forgot it . . . it was her first child, you know . . . I told her what to do. I don't domineer her, I really don't . . . we get along good . . . and I said something to her. And she said, 'Mom, he is *my* baby and please don't tell me what to do.' So I said, 'Don't you ever dare to say that to me again, that he is *your* baby. He is my baby too. Your child is like my child. I love him like you love him. I want to see what you want to see in him. Don't you ever say that to me again.' And she never did.

The identities of many mothers in the study were tenuous outside of their mothering role. According to these women, their contentment was dependent upon their child's contentedness, a theme which unfolded in "if she's okay, I'm okay" reasoning.

"She's Okay, I'm Okay" Mothers

Women in this group (n=7) professed independence from their child, tended to deny entitlement to the child's attention, yet gave conflicting messages about their satisfaction with the extent and nature of the current parent/child bond. Failure to meet mothers' expectations for achievement or connectedness were rarely expressed in criticisms of the child. Rather, they were cloaked in justifications on his or her behalf. Here again, adaptive illusion in the form of idealizations helped mothers to overcome the shortcomings of their child, to defend against the child's inattentiveness, or to generally explain away problems.

The following are examples of how two devoutly Catholic women, Mrs. Dougherty, an 82 year old sister of a priest and grandmother of eight, and Mrs. McAndrew, age 75, whose four sisters were nuns, neutralized the significance of their only children's divorces in their own lives.

Interviewer: Who is the most important person in your life right now?

Mrs. Dougherty: My daughter.

Interviewer: What's she like as a person?

Mrs. Dougherty: Outgoing and loving, kind and generous. She has all the attributes. . . . She was a very good student, you know . . . she had very high marks, she was always on the honor roll . . . [but] she had a sad life with her first husband.

Interviewer. It sounds like it had a happy ending though.

Mrs. Dougherty: Yeah. A wonderful fellow that she's marrying . . . I think she's getting a splendid man. . . . She had eight children by this [first] husband who drank. . . . She [finally] got him away from the saloons. Of course, it didn't take. And the fact that she divorced him, he wasn't sending any money. . . . I had to get all these papers because they were trying to get an annulment because she'd be ostracized out of her religion by marrying this fellow.

Mrs. McAndrew also appeared to gloss over her son's two divorces by accentuating the positives in his life.

Interviewer: What's your son like?

Mrs. McAndrew: He's studying to be a psychologist, you know, he's going to school. . . . My son is quiet, he's retiring. . . . He's very, very intelligent. I don't know where he got that. Extremely intelligent . . . outside of his marriages, he's a good son.

Feelings of neglect were never directly expressed by women in this group, but came through in the form of ambivalent statements made throughout the interviews. Some mothers, for instance, spoke of their child's attentiveness in one breath and wistfully wished they had had more children in the next. Statements such as, "I'm very proud of him, and he's a very good man, has always been a very good son, a religious man, a caring man" were routinely followed by, "I have envied my sister-in-law who has two children, two sons. You get more attention, naturally, from two children. You get two cards on your birthday, or two phone calls . . . and, you'd have two visits." Or, "I sort of hang my star on my son," followed by ". . . when I get sick, who is going to be around to take care of me?'.

The words of Mrs. Weiskoff, age 74, gave title to the mindset of women in this category. The question, "What things have recently given you the most pleasure?" stirred memories of a reciprocity with her own mother which Mrs. Weiskoff's daughter refused to allow Mrs. Weiskoff to replicate in their adult relationship.

I've done a lot of things that I've enjoyed . . . I audited some courses at the university . . . I have a subscription to theater and so forth . . . I've been doing all nice things. And just thinking about myself. I might add that as long as everything is all right with my daughter, if she's happy, I'm happy . . . which, incidentally, happens to be the truth, because if she wasn't happy, I couldn't be happy. She said [to me], 'Mother I want you to enjoy for *yourself*. It wouldn't make me happy knowing that your happiness depends on me being happy.' So I said to her, you know, grandmom always used to say, 'If you go, that makes me happy. I am with you.' So every time I go someplace I say, 'Mom, I'm here.' [Now tearful] So anyway, . . . I'm thinking of myself, all right?

Five mothers in this group were, by their own accounts, emotionally, or emotionally and physically detached from their only child. For these women, tenuous or severed relationships [had] resulted in self-deprecation, anger, and despair.

Detached and Depressed Mothers

These women referred to themselves as survivors. Each described a life driven by the need to overcome personal tragedy or historical destiny, where self-preoccupation became the rule rather than the exception. The dialogues of these women were notable in their egocentrism and lack of child-related material.

Women who were detached appeared to view the raising of a child as a ball and chain affair. Detachment was an early and ongoing feature of the mother/child relationship that appeared to result from insufficient bonding rather than unfilled promise. Detached mothers were openly critical of their child during the interview. They admitted to no great maternal commitment and, in some cases, vexation over having found themselves pregnant with their son or daughter. They described the relationship with their child as being peripheral or of secondary importance to their other interests, goals, or problems. Additionally, these women appeared to resent the child's inability to appreciate the nature of their life-struggle. Because of their limited maternal investment, these women made few demands on their children for financial, social, or emotional support, nor did they hold illusions about their children's capacities or successes. We found their lives to be marked by loneliness, isolation, and lack of hope for the future.

Mrs. Lewin, age 77, began her story by admitting, "misfortunes [are] what I had most of my life." As a youngster she and her parents escaped from Eastern Europe and were separated for the next eleven years. Her parents, who had immigrated to Palestine when they fled Germany, did not join her in the United States until after the birth of Mrs. Lewin's daughter and the death of Mrs. Lewin's first husband which followed shortly after the birth of the child. Mrs. Lewin was twice more married and widowed. She described herself during the interview as "floating" through life and several times referred to herself as someone "selfish" with her affections. As she was generally noncommittal about her daughter, we were never permitted to know how the emotional distance between them [had] developed. The following exchange illustrates the nature of their relationship.

Interviewer: Who would you say is the most important person in your life right now?

Mrs. Lewin: My daughter.

Interviewer: What's she like?

Mrs. Lewin: She is a very happy person right now, after she got divorced. And she's extremely active. In my opinion too active because I'm afraid she's one day going to collapse, but I cannot interfere with her life.

Interviewer: Would you say that you are close?

Mrs. Lewin: Not particularly.

Interviewer: Are there any ways in which you share closeness?

Mrs. Lewin: Not any more . . . I hope that she has a happy life and not go through such upheaval like I had. . . . First of all, she doesn't have to leave America. Secondly, she has a good education . . . and nobody can take that away from her.

Detached mothers were reticent to discuss their child outside of the disillusionment and regret that appeared to result from the failed relationship. Mrs. Harold, 73 and widowed, told our interviewer, up front, that she had no wish to discuss her 46 year old son. She touched on the lapse of their relationship, however, in discussing her current state of loneliness and despair.

Interviewer: Have you felt at a disadvantage in the last five years for having had only one child?

Mrs. Harold: With my life at this stage, yes, because my son is not a very close person. He is a selfish individual . . . college students, they go to college and all of a sudden you know nothing and they know it all. . . . I had a friend that I met at a senior citizen hall and this woman would brag about her children, one is a college professor. She died of a broken heart, she saw so little of them . . . what is the use of bragging about them if it doesn't mean anything.

Interviewer: Does your son have a role in your life today?

Mrs. Harold: Unfortunately, my son and I are on opposite sides of the fence. He didn't have the problems of other children or to have to contribute to the welfare of a family, or stop going to school because you had to go to work to help the family.

Interviewer: Who will take care of you if needs be?

Mrs. Harold: I don't have anyone. You can't rely on people, not even children. . . . I feel that I am alone. I really mean it. There isn't anybody. Were I to do it over again, I would have had more than one child.

Interviewer: Do you have any grandchildren?

Mrs. Harold: No. I hope not.

Mrs. Morgan, age 71, married the father of her only son to give legitimacy to the child's birth, and soon after divorced him. Most of the child's younger life was spent in boarding schools while Mrs. Morgan moved around the country changing jobs, and, by her telling, companions. Any attempts at domestic harmony between mother and son always ended in frustration, solidifying the space between them. She and the boy "didn't get along well" and she described their relationship as being like "two people living together, two strangers, really." Her aversion to motherhood and its consequences are revealed below.

I hate the word commitment. . . . It's just like the cat. I couldn't think of having another cat. Twenty years of worrying about that cat. I think the term is 'hostage to fortune,' or something like that. When you bear a child you are eternally responsible for them. . . . Mitchell and I are not your standard mother and son thing. At the time I wasn't a good mother. I wasn't. . . . We were only close in a buddy-buddy kind of way, after he was no longer my responsibility . . . we weren't getting along, he was a teen-ager and I was busy with my own life and working hard and everything, and I must have said something, and he said, 'I didn't ask to be born.' And then [I] say, 'Well, I didn't have to keep you, and I didn't have to have you in the first place. I could have had an abortion.'

About 15 years ago, her son, now age 50, moved without her knowledge, leaving no forwarding address. Eventually he contacted her from San Francisco and he has since permanently relocated in Asia. Although she occasionally hears from him, she hasn't seen him since 1982. Mrs. Morgan says she is plagued by isolation and loneliness and "that awful time before dinner [when there] is that endless night." She states, "When you get older . . . you feel alone, very alone. . . . Things are not going to get any better, I can tell you that. I don't have any hope."

Thematic Differences Between Mothers of One and Mothers of Four or More Children

Mothers of four or more (n=20) either planned to have large families or, in the words of one women, let nature take its course by "doing what comes naturally." In stark contrast to mothers of one, mothers of four or more generally expressed laissez faire attitudes about mixing in grown children's affairs. As a group, they were more multidimensional, husband or family oriented as opposed to child-centered, candid about their children's shortcomings, and forthright about their unmet needs and unfulfilled goals. They were more realistic about their own limitations or responsibility as parents in dissolving the obstacles to success or happiness encountered by their children. A sampling of statements from mothers-of-four-or-more illustrates their general approach to child rearing and their expectations as parents.

. . . . There are a lot of times I might disagree with what my kids are doing with their kids, but I just keep my mouth shut!

. . . . We were all involved in just about everything, Girl Scouts, Boy Scouts, Cub Scouts, [helping to] form the Middletown Library. . . .

. . . . Being a wife was a very big part of my life. That is something I have passed along to my daughters, 'Don't get completely wrapped up in children!'

. . . . They were just ordinary kids. I didn't have a talented child in the bunch. . . . No geniuses. . . . I am disappointed that they have not gone farther in their education. . . .

. . . . There are problems when you're grown, of your own making, and you should be able to solve them yourself.

Mothers-of-four-or-more were more positive about life in spite of children's financial, medical, or marital woes. Troubling as their children's problems might be, mothers of large families seemed sensitive to the changing demands of the parenting role and the reciprocal rhythm of the adult child/parent relationship. As one women humorously quipped, "You have to do an awful lot of tongue biting." Taking on the trials and joys of mothering from a seemingly selfless perspective, mothers of many expressed a belief in the ephemeral or transitory nature of mothering. Two women spoke for most in the group when discussing the principles that guided their late-life parenting.

. . . . I don't feel I have any right to interfere in their lives unless they invite me in . . . my responsibility is to be there should the children need me . . . you know, just to be in the background. To be sort of like an anchor. That is all. Not to be *in* their lives, you know, just to be on the peripheral edges.

. . . . I don't think children are required for happiness. Besides they are not yours to keep anyway. They are only loaned to you. You have the pleasure of bringing them up. You also have all the headaches that go along with it. But, you don't own them.

Mothering, for mothers of large families helped to define the totality of these women's lives, particularly as they aged. For most, the "duties" of mothering connected them to commitments outside their homes. Immersion in volunteer activities on behalf of their children (library or school aides, scouting) kept them involved in community work long after their sons and daughters had grown and left home. These women continued to mentor others' children, sponsor or organize charity drives, and generally operate within a rich cooperative of children, grandchildren, children's friends, and their children. As one woman put it, "I think you're surrounded by life going on." For mothers of many, this con-

nectedness seemed to pay off in the guarantee of future care. Where mothers of only children often expressed concern over their care needs being met, mothers of four or more seemed confident that they could always turn to one of their "kids."

Discussion

Our data suggest that having an only child distinctly shapes a woman's response to mothering and her approach to the developmental issues of aging. We find that long-established patterns of mother/child interaction in single-childed mothers determine, in part, their sense of well-being in later-life. Most mothers of one child had the tendency to gloss over or deny the negatives of their child's lives. They appeared to rely on the kudos and status of motherhood, rather than the activities of mothering for self-fulfillment. They were emotionally invested in ways that precluded individuation from their son or daughter, and worked to create a mental representation of a relationship in keeping with their own needs for, or from the child. Hopelessness and despair were associated with mothers who faced the objective realities of their only child's life without the use of these self-conciliatory measures.

For the following reasons, we interpret the use of illusory reasoning as a buffer against the developmental realities of their own aging. First, their history of problematic fertility, pregnancy, and late-life childbirth uniquely colored their experience as mothers. Having barely managed, in their view, to conform to the social norms of their day, they considered their baby a "miracle child" whose birth spared them from the stigma of childlessness (Alexander et al. 1992). While their child's exclusivity allowed them to perceive their son or daughter as a *gift*, their concentrated nurturing enabled them to perceive the child as *gifted*. Research shows that close affiliation between only children and their parents results in intellectual gains and achievement orientations for their children (Falbo 1984; Falbo and Polit 1986); however, the effect of this investment on mothers is unknown (Katz and Boswell 1984). We contend that elderly mothers' illusions of cohesion and centrality in their only child's life are critical to maintaining their sense of identity into late-life.

Second, the singular investment mothers-of-one made in their children appeared to leave little room for, or interest in, developing other outlets for generativity (Kotre 1984). As with many women in this cohort, mothering was their work in life, resulting in the need to produce a successful product. Because the value of her own life depended on what she made of her child's, mothers of one *controlled* for disappointments by creating whole truths out of the positives and ignoring or relegating the negatives to past chapters in their child's life.

Finally, the illusion that all was financially and emotionally well with the child served to stave off fear of the mother's own increasing dependency needs. In our study, single-childed women were less apt to clearly define a plan for future care. This indication of under-developed contingencies for emotional or physical support is not found in elderly childless women (Rubinstein et al. 1991), nor was it found in the multi-childed women we studied.

If the totality of life is reconciled during its final stages (Generativity versus Stagnation, Integrity versus Despair; Erikson 1963), the compensatory nature of "adaptive illusion" argues for its existence as a normal function of aging. This is particularly true when it comes to basing one's worth on the accomplishments of one's children. We recognize that negative and positive feelings about offspring often go hand-in-hand. We also acknowledge that there is nothing unusual about mothers-of-one simultaneously praising their child and bemoaning his or her exclusivity. Even the most objective of parents have "blind spots" about children's performance, where subjectivity fills the gap between expectation and disappointment. In all likelihood, "adaptive illusion" is used in varying degrees by *all* parents when it comes to mentally adjusting for those disappointments. What is notable here is the *vicarious stake* mothers-of-one appeared to have in their only child's success and the degree to which their own contentment depended on positive outcomes for that child.

Although we have identified this phenomenon in both Jewish and Christian mothers, we acknowledge that mothering styles are in part determined by culture. The differences we observed between mothers of one and mothers of four or more, however, seemed less a function of religion or ethnicity than the psychosocial effect of biological circumstance (See Goodman et al. 1991, for a review of cultural differences in mothering). The intergroup tendencies we identified seemed to transcend children's gender, or mothers' marital or socioeconomic status. Since no African-American mothers-of-one were interviewed, we cannot speak to the issue of race in contributing to these differences.

Given the possibility that the attitudes expressed by our single-childed women are peculiar to our sample, we offer our observations and interpretations as a contribution to theory building in adult parent/child relationships. At the very least, we feel that the meaning of parenting to elderly parents should be studied from a *phenomenological* perspective. The economic realities of raising numerous children and the career bias of contemporary women make it seem likely that the single-child family will be common. Younger cohorts of women who *elect* to have one child may face other issues as they age, but there is need for understanding today's elderly, who, because of circumstances sometimes beyond their control, negotiated a life course as the mother of one.

Discussion Questions

1. Describe the ways in which the beliefs and expectations about their children differ among mothers of only children and mothers of four or more.

2. Explain the function of "adaptive illusion" among mothers of one child.

3. In what ways is adaptive illusion maladaptive?

4. Assume you were designing a support group for elderly parents with only one adult offspring. What elements would you want to include for the group to discuss and why?

References

Alexander, B., R.L. Rubinstein, M. Goodman, and M. Luborsky. 1992. "A Path Not Taken: A Cultural Analysis of Regrets and Childlessness in the Lives of Older Women." *The Gerontologist* 32(5): 618–626.

Bengtson, V.L. and J.A. Kuypers. 1971. "Generational Difference and the Developmental Stake." *Aging and Human Development* 2: 249–260.

Bengtson, V.L., G. Marti, and R.E. Roberts. 1991. "Age-Group Relationships: Generational Equity and Inequity." In *Parent-Child Relations Throughout Life*, edited by K. Pillemer and K. McCartney. Hillsdale, NJ: Lawrence Erlbaum Associates.

Blieszner, R. and J.A. Mancini. 1987. "Enduring Ties: Older Adults' Parental Role and Responsibilities." *Family Relations* 36: 176–180.

Bogolub, E.B. 1984. "Symbiotic Mothers and Infantilized Only Children: A SubType of Single-Parent Family." *Child and Adolescent Social Work Journal* 1(2): 89–101.

Chodorow, N. 1978. *The Reproduction of Mothering*. Berkeley: University of California Press.

Cicirelli, V.G. 1983. "Adult Children and Their Elderly Parents." In *Family Relationships in Later Life*, edited by T.H. Brubaker. Beverly Hills: Sage.

——. 1991. "Attachment Theory in Old Age: Protection of the Attached Figure." In *Parent–Child Relations Throughout Life*, edited by K. Pillemer and K. McCartney. Hillsdale, NJ: Lawrence Erlbaum Associates.

Connidis, I.A. 1989. *Family Ties and Aging*. Toronto: Butterworths.

Connidis, I.A. and J.A. McMullin. 1993. "To Have or Have Not: Parent Status and the Subjective Well–Being of Older Men and Women." *The Gerontologist* 33(5): 630–636.

Cook, J.A. 1988. "Dad's Double Binds: Rethinking Fathers' Bereavement from a Men's Studies Perspective." *Journal of Contemporary Ethnography* 17(3): 285–308.

Crimmins, E.M. and D.G. Ingegneri. 1990. "Interaction and Living Arrangements of Older Parents and Their Children." *Research on Aging* 12(l): 3–35.

Elson, M. 1984. "Parenthood and the Transformations of Narcissism." In *Parenthood: A Dynamic Perspective*, edited by R.S. Cohen, B.J. Cohler, and S.H. Weissman. New York: The Guilford Press.

Erikson, E. 1963. *Childhood and Society*, 2nd edition. New York: Norton.

Falbo, T. 1984. "Only Children: A Review." In *The Single-Child Family*, edited by T. Falbo. New York: The Guilford Press.

Falbo, T. and D.F. Polit. 1986. "Quantitative Review of the Only Child Literature: Research Evidence and Theory Development." *Psychological Bulletin* 100(2): 176–189.

Gerson, M. 1986. "The Prospect of Parenthood for Women and Men." *Psychology of Women Quarterly* 10(l): 49–62.

Goodman, M., R.L. Rubinstein, B. Alexander, and M. Luborsky. 1991. "Cultural Differences in Coping with the Death of an Adult Child." *Journal of Gerontology* 46(6): S321–329.

Greenberg, J.S. and M. Becker. 1988. "Aging Parents as Family Resources." *The Gerontologist* 28(6):786–791.

Hagestad, G.O. 1987. "Parent-Child Relations in Later Life: Trends and Gaps in Past Research." In *Parenting Across the Life Span*, edited by J.B. Lancaster, J. Altmann, A.S. Rossi, and L.R. Sherrod. New York: Aldine De Gruyter.

Hess, B.B. and J.M. Waring. 1978. "Parent and Child in Later Life: Rethinking the Relationship." In *Child Influences on Marital and Family Interaction*, edited by R.M. Lerner and G.B. Spanier. New York: Academic Press.

Katz, P.A. and S.L. Boswell. 1984. "Sex-Role Development and the One-Child Family." In *The Single-Child Family*, edited by T. Falbo. New York: The Guilford Press.

Kivett, V.R. and M.P. Atkinson. 1984. "Filial Expectations, Association, and Helping as a Function of Number of Children among Older Rural-Transition Parents." *Journal of Gerontology* 39(4): 499–503.

Kotre, J. 1984. *Outliving the Self: Generativity and the Interpretation of Lives*. Baltimore: Johns Hopkins University Press.

Lee, G.R. and E. Ellithorpe. 1982. "Intergenerational Exchange and Subjective Well-Being among the Elderly." *Journal of Marriage and the Family* (February): 217–224.

Littlewood, J.L. and J. Hoekstra. 1991. "Gender Differences in Parental Coping Following Their Child's Death." *British Journal of Guidance and Counselling* 19(2): 139–148.

Luborsky, M. 1993. "The Identification and Analysis of Themes and Patterns." In *Qualitative Methods in Aging Research*, edited by J.F. Gubrium and A. Sanker. New York: Sage Publications.

Mancini, J.A. and R. Blieszner. 1989. "Aging Parents and Adult Children: Research Themes in Intergenerational Relations." *Journal of Marriage and the Family* 15: 275–290.

Matthews, S.H. 1993. "The Use of Qualitative Methods in Research on Older Families." *Canadian Journal on Aging* 12(2): 157–165.

Nydegger, C.N. 1991. "The Development of Paternal and Filial Maturity." In *Parent-Child Relations Throughout Life*, edited by K. Pillemer and K. McCartney. Hillsdale, NJ: Lawrence Erlbaum Associates.

Nydegger, C.N. and L.S. Mitteness. 1991. "Fathers and Their Adult Sons and Daughters." *Marriage and Family Review* 16: 249–266.

Pillemer, K. and J.J. Suitor. 1991. "Relationships with Children and Distress in the Elderly." In *Parent-Child Relations Throughout Life*, edited by K. Pillemer and K. McCartney. Hillsdale, NJ: Lawrence Erlbaum Associates.

——. 1991. "Will I Ever Escape My Child's Problems? Effects of Adult Children's Problems on Elderly Parents." *Journal of Marriage and the Family* 53: 585–594.

Polit, D.F. 1980. "The One-Parent/One-Child Family: Social and Psychological Consequences [Final Report]. (Contract No. NO1-HD-82852). Cambridge, MA: American Institute for Research.

Quinn, W.H. 1983. "Personal and Family Adjustment in Later Life." *Journal of Marriage and the Family* (February): 57–73.

Roberts, R.E., L.N. Richards, and V.L. Bengtson. 1991. "Intergenerational Solidarity in Families: Untangling the Ties That Bind." *Marriage and Family Review* 16(1–2): 11–46.

Rossi, A.S. and P.H. Rossi. 1991. "Normative Obligations and Parent-Child Help Exchange Across the Life Course." In *Parent-Child Relations Throughout Life*, edited by K. Pillemer and K. McCartney. Hillsdale, NJ: Lawrence Erlbaum Associates.

Rubinstein, R.L., B. Alexander, M. Goodman, and M. Luborsky. 1991. "Key Relationships of Never Married, Childless Older Women." *Journal of Gerontology* 46: S270-277.

Russell, G. and M. Radojevic. 1992. "The Changing Role of Fathers? Current Understandings and Future Directions for Research and Practice." *Infant Mental Health Journal* 13(4): 296–311.

Schachter, S. 1959. *The Psychology of Affiliation*. Stanford, CA: Stanford University Press.

Seelbach, W.C. 1977. "Gender Differences in Expectations for Filial Responsibility." *The Gerontologist* 17(5): 421–425.

Seelbach, W.C. and W.J. Sauer. 1977. "Filial Responsibility, Expectations, and Morale Among Aged Parents." *The Gerontologist* 17(6): 492–499.

Shanas, E. 1979. "Social Myth as Hypothesis: The Case of the Family Relations of Old People." *The Gerontologist* 19(l): 3–9.

——. 1984. "Old Parents and Middle-Aged Children: The Four- and Five-Generation Family." *Journal of Geriatric Psychiatry* 17(l): 7–19.

Suitor, J.J. and K. Pillemer. 1987. "The Presence of Adult Children: A Source of Stress for Elderly Couples' Marriages?" *Journal of Marriage and the Family* 49: 717–725.

Troll, L.E. 1986. "Parent-Adult Child Relations." In *Family Issues in Current Gerontology*, edited by L.E. Troll. New York: Springer Publishing Company.

Troll, L.E. and J. Smith. 1976. "Attachment Through the Lifespan: Some Questions about Dyadic Bonds among Adults." *Human Development* 19: 156–170.

Umberson, D. 1989. "Relationships with Children: Explaining Parents' Psychological Well-Being." *Journal of Marriage and the Family* 51: 999–1012.

Chapter 28

Intergenerational Reciprocity

Susan R. Sherman

Americans frequently romanticize the past as a golden era in which family ties were stronger and filial obligations to parents more intense. Despite the numerous changes in structural arrangements of family life that have occurred during the past few centuries, ties between parents and children remain throughout the life course, and parents have expectations for their children and their children for their parents. These expectations encompass various behaviors: contact, affection, respect, agreement, and assistance between generations. What parents expect from their adult children and what they believe their children expect from them is the focus of the following selection by Susan Sherman.

It has been well documented that elderly family members receive help from their children in both the instrumental, or task-oriented, and emotional spheres. Yet, as numerous research studies have pointed out, it is a mistake to think that older people are always the recipients of assistance. Sherman first provides a review of previous studies on intergenerational mutual assistance and then focuses on how a sample of white, working-class and lower-middle-class midlife and older adults define what they anticipate as their due for support and assistance from family members. As you read, notice the types of expectations older parents have from their children. Pay attention also to what the respondents feel adult children should expect from their parents. Look for patterns of reciprocity. Think about such patterns in your own family.

A great deal of attention has been devoted over the last couple of decades to the study of intrafamilial assistance, especially assistance flowing upward from middle-aged daughters to older parents. Varieties of upward assistance include financial, emotional, housekeeping, support in activities of daily living (e.g., bathing, dressing), all the way through taking the older parent into the child's home. Less attention has been directed either to assistance flowing downward from the oldest generation to succeeding generations or to motivations for intrafamilial assistance. The present qualitative study addresses the expectations that middle-aged children and older parents have of themselves and of the other, and examines to what extent these expectations are reciprocal. As context for the research the study briefly reviews the literature in historical development of these expectations and the motives and contingencies underlying normative expectations. It focuses in particular on the neglected area of assistance received by adult children from older parents.

History of Intergenerational Expectations

In their analysis of the ethical dimensions of family caregiving, presumably ethics that would be shared by both parties to the exchange, S. Selig, T. Tomlinson, and T. Hickey (1991) point to the early biblical injunction to "honor thy father and thy mother." Much later, in preindustrial times, frail parents living in the child's household were as likely to be giving help (household duties or child care) as to be receiving the benefits of filial responsibility. Selig, Tomlinson, and Hickey also suggest that in earlier times filial responsibilities were not as costly to adult children and were more vital—hence less optional—for the parents. Over historical time, however, norms have shifted from duty to personal choice in adult familial relationships (Stein 1992). Given that there is a choice in intrafamilial assistance, there are a number of reasons why one generation might choose to help the other.

Motives and Contingencies in Intergenerational Assistance

Much research assesses the quantity or frequency of assistance of various sorts, without asking about motives. Why should there be intrafamilial assistance? What is the basis for it? Some authors specifically indicate that such norms are shared by both generations; others focus primarily on adult children's expectations or primarily on expectations held by the parent. Some have studied norms and moral obligations; others have studied the ability to assist; still others have studied active behavior. There has been debate about the role of self-interest in intrafamilial assistance. A. S. Rossi (1993), for example, takes issue with the exchange model of intergenerational relations and suggests rather altruism or irrational love. The motives found in the literature generally fall into the following groups: reciprocity or gratitude for past gifts or sacrifices in child rearing; affection, loving concern, attachment, family cohesion, or emotional bonding; sense of the "right thing to do," altruism, filial piety; quality of care, patient well-being, need; and reverence (Bengtson 1993; Foner 1993; Rossi 1993; Sanborn and Bould 1991; Selig, Tomlinson, and Hickey 1991; Stein 1992; Wallhagen and Strawbridge 1995; Wolfson, Handfield-Jones, Glass, McClaran, and Keyserlingk 1993).

Given that these norms or motives are pervasive in American culture, enacting them is still contingent on a variety of factors: geographic location and ease of visiting; need; income, ability, and competing demands upon caregiving; and past or present intergenerational relationships (Hoyert 1991; Logan and Spitze 1996; Stein 1992; Wallhagen and Strawbridge 1995; Whitbeck, Hoyt, and Huck 1994; Wolfson et al. 1993). Furthermore, a lack of congruence has been noted between endorsing general norms about filial responsibility and wishing to enact the role of recipient oneself. The view of M. I. Wallhagen and W. J. Strawbridge's respondents was: "I helped my parents and I don't ever want my children to be put through what I have been through—or at least I think so now."

Expectations about intergenerational exchange frequently contrast expressive and instrumental support. C. Wolfson et al. found that emotional, physical, and financial aid were endorsed in that hierarchical order. R. R. Hamon and R. Blieszner (1990) found agreement between elderly parent and adult child regarding emotional support but less agreement on instrumental support; parents were less likely than their children to approve of financial assistance from children or of having children change their work schedules in order to assist.

Downward Assistance

Although there is an overwhelming amount of research on assistance given by adult children to their elderly parents, with emphasis typically placed on caregiver burden or stress, the literature pertaining to assistance in the other direction is by contrast sparse and of more recent interest. People take for granted downward assistance from young-adult parents to their young children, but then norms of adult development and the ethic of independence suggest that adult children are no longer to expect assistance from their parents; at some point attention shifts to focus on adult children's upward assistance to elderly parents. Recent attention to downward assistance addresses primarily problematic situations, e.g., unemployment, divorce, or mental illness. This attention needs to be broadened to include ordinary exchanges in families, be they instrumental or expressive.

Regardless of norms of independence, there is abundant empirical evidence that money, care, and support flow across generations in either direction, with money primarily flowing downward (Johnson 1995). Indeed, J. R. Logan and G. D. Spitze (1996) suggest the presence of a norm that parents should be "givers rather than receivers." They found that parents were at least as likely to help adult children with chores as they were to receive such help. More help flows downward until late old age. Most interestingly, consistent with Selig, Tomlinson, and Hickey's report of the preindustrial period, Logan and Spitze found that when co-residence occurred, it was more likely to fulfill the adult child's need than the older parent's. Distance, marital status, gender of parent and adult child, and custodial status of divorced daughters with children have been found to influence assistance from older parents to adult children (Hoyert 1991; Logan and Spitze 1996; Ingersoll-Dayton, Starrels, and Dowler 1996; Rossi 1993).

Having sketched a brief historical description of intergenerational expectations and motivations and contingencies for such exchange, the author made the distinction between endorsement of generalized norms and enacting them oneself. The author also noted the distinction between expressive and instrumental assistance. Particularly motivated by an interest in downward assistance, this study asked a wide variety of persons about intrafamilial expectations.

Method

As part of a larger study of socialization, sanctions, age identity, and role models for aging (Sherman 1994), purposive sampling was used to select respondents living in a variety of living environments (senior housing as well as conventional housing), encompassing a wide age range. Fifty-three women and 28 men were interviewed in their homes, senior centers, nutrition sites, and offices. Ages ranged from 41 to 96. Marital status was equally divided between married and widowed, with 42 percent in each group. Another 5 percent were married but not living with spouse, 6 percent were divorced, and 5 percent were never married. Respondents ranged from blue-collar workers to professionals (past or current occupation). Education was inversely related to age, as in the general population.

Nineteen percent of the sample had at least one child and at least one living parent. Sixty-five percent had children but no longer had living parents. Sixteen percent had neither children nor a living parent. Similar to much research in this area, this study did not attempt to interview related parent-child dyads. That would have limited sample size and would have restricted the sample to those

who were able and willing to have their child or parent respond to the interview.

An open-ended format was used and content analysis was performed on written transcripts of audiotaped interviews. About one-quarter of the interviews were coded by two advanced graduate students, with the remainder coded by the author. The analysis for the present report focuses on responses to questions about intergenerational expectations but considers the interview in its entirety. The major themes reported below emerged inductively from the data, rather than having been predicted beforehand. These findings are presented using the respondents' own words; for context, the age and gender of each respondent are given.

Results

When asked *"Are there certain things an older parent should expect from his/her children?"* about a fifth said no, with others commenting that the parent should be independent. When there *were* expectations, the most common were respect and expressive support. Expectations for instrumental support were rare. Respondents age 70 and over were more likely to mention respect and less likely to mention help, advice, and financial assistance as compared to those persons under 70, perhaps expressing cohort values. The older cohort was also more likely to say there was *nothing* they should expect, or that the parent should be independent.

When asked *"Are there certain things grown children should expect from an older parent?"* again about a fifth said no. The usual responses were respect and love, with a few suggestions for help, advice, and financial assistance.

For middle-generation respondents (about one-fifth of the sample), the questions addressing generational expectations could result in an unacknowledged role shift or dual focus, that is, both from a child's vantage and from a parent's. Of those with a living parent and child, nearly half saw the self as parent, and half (all in their 40s) saw the self as child. Two saw the self as both parent and child.

One can learn more by looking at the two sets of responses together. Six patterns emerged. (Two respondents, both male, could not be coded in any category.) The first two patterns may be characterized as upward expectations only and downward expectations only. The remaining four categories are forms of reciprocity, the focus of this selection. (The dominant theme is reported in those cases where more than one was mentioned.) It will be noted that some respondents spoke more in terms of general societal norms, while others referred more specifically to their own expectations regarding themselves and their families. Still others wove in both perspectives.

Upward Expectations Only

Fifteen respondents (eight men and seven women), ages ranging from 41 to 84, reported expectations of assistance only from the adult child upward to the parent. The thinking was that the children should be independent now. Most of the assistance that was expected was expressive.

A 48-year-old man who had neither living parents nor children spoke in terms both of general norms and his own experiences.

> Enfeebling certainly must be frightening. I'm sure that aged parents would like to have the comfort of having their offspring look out for them. I think there's a good deal of socialized guilt involved with being the child of an aging parent and I think that they expect to be put in the position of having, ultimately, to become the parents of their parents. My mother's disease made me more and more concentrate on the aging process. Her experience was a poignant one for me.

Downward Expectations Only

Six respondents (five men and one woman), all in their 70s, only expected assistance going downward from the aged parent to the adult child. One of these, a 71-year-old man, supported his premise with an interesting contrast of societal discontinuity in norms, but familial continuity.

> Not like the old days. You got to do it yourself. Not look for help from them. They have their own family and life to do. [What do children expect from parents?] What they expected from you all your life, that's

what they expect you to keep doing. As long as you're able to do it.

Another respondent in this category commented that her child has a different lifestyle, "everybody goes in different directions." Yet she has helped her daughter financially.

The four remaining patterns found are forms of *reciprocity*, the major interest in this selection. The first two refer to reciprocity in the *present*, and the last two refer to reciprocity in the *past*.

Reciprocal Independence

This pattern, focusing on the present, can be characterized as "I don't expect anything from my children and they shouldn't expect anything from me either." Fourteen persons (eleven women and three men), ages ranging from 42 to 89, could best be characterized by this response. Normal development across the life span, including both connectedness and separation/individuation, was reflected in C. H. Stein's (1992) five factors of felt obligation. Stein's factors not only included contact/ritual, assistance, and personal sharing, but also self-sufficiency and avoidance of conflict. The responses of several in this study's reciprocal-independence category reflected the motivation for self-sufficiency. These respondents included those with children whose parents were no longer living (the next four examples), as well as those who were in the middle generation, who had children as well as living parents (the fifth and sixth examples).

An 80-year-old woman said, "Some of them don't want their children to be helpful to them because they have their own problems. [What do children expect from parents?] Just to keep well so they won't be a problem. According to a 74-year-old man, "Well it goes both ways. We shouldn't expect anything from them and they shouldn't expect anything from us."

A woman, 73, said,

> Well you should not expect it because you're a parent. You don't have children so that when you are older they will take care of you. That's not the purpose. They will take care of their parents if they are able to do it from some kind of human

kindness. But the parents should not expect it in that sense, because quite often they won't get it anyway. Some people are selfish and some people cannot really help. [What do children expect from parents?] Not any more than the parents should expect from the children.

This response sounds partially like a warning not to have too many expectations because they might not be fulfilled.

A woman, 74, said, "I don't expect anything from the kids. They tell me I'm too independent. I don't ask for anything as long as I can get by. My two girls don't expect anything from me." Some in the reciprocal-independence category, after asserting that parents and children should not *expect* too much, then went on to describe how much their children do for them. One respondent's daughter had asked her to come to her house when the respondent returned from the hospital, and the mother commented, "I know if I needed something and asked them that I'd get it." A 55-year-old woman said, "I don't think you should expect to burden your children with total care, nor should children expect elderly parents to provide for them." A woman of 42 said, "I don't believe that older parents should expect anything from their children. I don't think that was my purpose for becoming a parent, so that in my old age the kids could help me.

By contrast, the next example comes from a 74-year-old woman (never married and parents no longer living) who endorses independence in the sense of permitting each generation its own autonomy.

Let the parent do whatever they're able to do. Don't decide you're going to take over and make their decisions. I've seen younger children, especially if there's the death of one of the parents, they'll say, 'well you come with me,' and it never works. So give them all the latitude you can. [What do children expect from parents?] To keep busy in their own lives and not expect to live their children's lives.

The final example of reciprocal independence reflects the subthemes of both autonomy and self-sufficiency.

According to a 54-year-old woman,

They have the right to lead their own life without the children telling them what to do. Sometimes it flip flops at that age and I think parents should have the right at that point not to take instructions from the children. Grown children should expect an older parent to attempt to do what they can do for themselves. I don't think that the older parent is entitled to sit back and feel that the child owes them a living. The grown child has the right to lead their own life without a lot of advice from the parent unless they are seeking that advice. At some point the tie has to be cut there where the grown child has to lead their own life the way they want to lead it.

Reciprocal Interdependence

In contrast to reciprocal independence (but also referring to the present), the pattern of reciprocal interdependence—by far the largest group—can be characterized as "My children may expect things from me and I may expect things from them." Twenty-eight respondents best fit this category (20 women and 8 men), ages ranging from 43 to 96. These respondents referred primarily to expressive assistance. A typical response would refer to respect and love—"It goes both ways." A smaller number referred to both instrumental and expressive assistance, and only a couple referred solely to instrumental aid. Some in the reciprocal-interdependence pattern do not directly express expectations for interaction but say what they do for each other, even if it is only "keeping in touch."

A man, 71, said, "Grown children should expect the same things as the parents expect [support, keep in touch]. It should be reciprocal." A woman, 69, said, "I expect their respect and I give it, and love which we have for each other. It's a mutual thing." According to a woman, 70, "She could call on me anytime and I can call on them anytime too. Just being there, that's all you should expect from your family. [What do children expect from parents?] Just respect and love and that you're there and you would help them anytime.

Another woman of 70 responded,

I think grown children shouldn't expect too much from their parents. But they should get respect, too, from their parents. You know it can be the other way around where parents think everything should come from the children, but it has to be 50–50. What comes from the child has to come from the parent too.

According to a woman of 53,

I believe family members should be available to each other in all ways. What people should expect from each other within their families and going in both directions, back and forth, children/parents, parents/children, etc., is psychological security. That there is this finite group of people there that you can absolutely depend on, no questions asked. I am not a drain on my kids and my kids are not a drain on me. But I know that I can call on them and they will come, no questions asked, and they know they can call on me and I will go, no questions asked.

This respondent, who has children and a living parent, went on to add an "additional layer of family": "The grandparent should be able to call on the children and grandchildren, and vice versa. Grandchildren, parents, call on the grandparents." This respondent did refer to the past, as will be described more fully below: "You shouldn't be forced to support somebody who has not earned your love and your trust and your respect."

Similar to research reviewed earlier, responses in this study expressed contingencies in intergenerational assistance. The first contingency was the *needs* of the recipient (parent or child). A 71-year-old woman said,

I could call on her most anytime to help me if I needed it. And if it was absolutely necessary I could always go there. If we need each other we should reach out to one another. Not too much. I don't think you should take advantage of the other person. But I think in need you reach out to one another.

A woman of 73 replied,

It depends on the children a lot and of course, it depends on whether your parents are financially independent or whether they need help from you. In a relationship where maybe young people have to work and have children, maybe the parents can help babysit but they're not compelled to do it, but I think it's nice if they're capable of doing it.

The last phrase adds the contingency of the *abilities* of the donor. The next respondent, a 78-year-old woman, also included needs *and* abilities. "It's according to the situation; if there's an older parent who has a lot of money and [the children] are struggling. Although they're married they have a right to expect their parents to help them and to respect their children. It's a two-way street."

After having described a pattern of contemporaneous exchanges between parent and adult child, the study turns to those responses that took a longer view, an exchange across time.

Two-Generational Reciprocity in the Past

V. L. Bengtson suggests that in a period of population aging, a continuing belief in a "cyclical process of being helped and helping throughout life" (1993, p. 22) supports an optimistic prediction of less intergenerational conflict in the next century. Societal norms about intergenerational exchange are negotiated within individual family life-cycle histories; however, research on adult intergenerational relationships typically overlooks earlier intrafamilial relationships and relationship histories (Stein 1992; Whitbeck, Hoyt, and Huck 1994). The next two patterns explicitly refer to reciprocity for past intergenerational exchange.

First, there is an earlier two-generational exchange. There were 11 women in this category, and only 1 man; ages ranged from 41 to 80. N. Foner (1993) refers to this pattern as delayed or lifetime reciprocity: children see elder care as repayment for earlier care they received; elders, likewise, view it as a reward for fulfilling earlier responsibilities. In a community where child bearing is the norm, L. M. Burton (1996) found two-generational exchange between grandparents and grandchildren. Grandchildren expected to be the caregivers for their grandmothers, as it was the grandmother who had raised them. Even where there was a "debt owed," however, respondents saw reciprocating primarily along expressive rather than instrumental dimensions. A woman, 70, said, "A parent who has raised up her children what I would consider in a mannerly, thoughtful way should expect children to keep in touch with the parents." Another woman, 74, said, "You don't get respect from children unless you have earned it. You have to start at a very early age to earn respect you want when you become older. It depends upon the kind of rearing the children had, how they would respond to the parents as the parents got older." Another woman of 74 said, "I think the parent did so much for the child for so many years and I feel in an emergency to help [the parent] out I think they should." This respondent had taken care of three young grandchildren when her daughter (their mother) was divorced. However, perhaps because she had earlier been burdened with a great deal of care for her own parents (with a brother who thought it was her responsibility, not his), she went on to express a preference for a home aide, so the older person could maintain independence.

A woman, 75 responded, "It depends a lot on what kinds of parents you are. But no matter what, there's a certain filial duty that you owe your parents. After all, they did bring you into the world. I don't say you have to love your parents, but let us say respect them as such." She maintained that adult children are also entitled to the same respect. Denying that assistance is obligatory, she, however, had given direct care to her parents and father-in-law.

Regarding the gift of life, H. Berman (1987) claims that we can never repay our parents for this first gift; as it was given voluntarily, it is an irredeemable obligation. A related distinction is made by Selig, Tomlinson, and Hickey: ordinary childrearing is expected (duty); good childrearing (favor) requires repayment. In Rossi's framework, parental affection and access are important not merely to be "paid back," but as *modeling*. This duality is reflected in the following response by a 77-year-old woman:

> They must have been good parents when they were young; they must have treated their children well to be so loved by their children. When I see how well loved they

are by their children, I think, she must have been some mother or father for those kids to still go out of their way to do the things for their person.

Other respondents also spoke of reciprocity for past deeds but put the emphasis on not expecting much if the parent did not provide much. Foner found this in her study of nonindustrial cultures as well: if the oldest generation did not invest in the future by establishing relationships with grandchildren, then they could not expect help when they needed it. Selig, Tomlinson, and Hickey suggest this framework be used in counseling to help the adult child establish limits to parental duties. According to a woman, 43, "Whatever the relationship has been all along is going to continue to be what it's like when the parent is older. So people can't expect something they've never had in a relationship before." A woman of 72 said, "It depends on what they have given them. You can't be anything you'd like to be or say anything and then expect from them what you don't do yourself. You have to be the primary example. You can't expect anything you don't give." and a woman of 41 responded, "To reap the benefits from whatever they gave their children so if they didn't give them much then they can't expect too much and if they really did give them a lot, then they can probably but not necessarily expect attention and caring in return." This last phrase, "probably but not necessarily," spoken by a middle-generation respondent, is also reflected by the following mother, 74, disappointed by a lack of reciprocity: "You raise them, they go away, they have it so good and they forget you."

Three-Generational Reciprocity in the Past

The last pattern of reciprocity involves a three-generational exchange, with assistance flowing either downward or upward. There were three women and one man in this category, with ages ranging from 42 to 72. Processional or transitive caregiving suggests that adults pay back their parents for what they received as a child, not by reciprocating directly to parents, but by giving in turn to their own children (Johnson 1995).

Rossi argues that rather than parents expecting to be "repaid," they expect their children will in turn "invest" in the succeeding generation. Using a three-generational reciprocal time frame, one 72-year-old mother expressed a yearning for downward assistance: her mother hadn't lived long enough to help her out when she had had young children. However, because she missed this, she would help out her children: "If you can be helpful to [adult children] you should be. Cause I never had anybody to be helpful for me cause my mother died when I was born. And so I brought up my children alone. So I feel if they need me I'm going to be there for them."

Another type of three-generational exchange, focusing on upward assistance, can be characterized as "I helped (or didn't help) *my* parents and I expect my children to do the same for me." Each generation in old age will *receive from* the next generation. Foner suggests that this is a conscious setting of an example for one's children. Although most of Wallhagen and Strawbridge's respondents did not want their children to do for them what they'd done for their parents, there were those who did. One respondent, a woman of 50, expressed this upward three-generational reciprocity: "My parents never had to ask me to make sure that their life continued in a decent way. I had to look for those changes that happened to them and I would hope that this would carry through to me and my daughters."

One might speculate whether it is more acceptable to expect care from one's child in old age because of what one gave one's parent than because of what one gave that child. Perhaps positive role modeling is a loftier motivation for exchange than is expecting what one is due from the donor herself. These two emphases fit well into a life-course framework: we reciprocate for our parents' gifts to us by giving to our children as long as we can. When that is no longer possible, we hope that our children will assist us in the same way we assisted our parents.

Conclusion

Eighty-one persons, age 41 to 96, were asked what older parents should expect from their children, and what grown children should expect from an older parent. The sample included a middle-aged group, enabling a study of persons in the process of formulating ideas about intergenerational exchange based on current observations of their parents. A diversity of socioeconomic statuses and living arrangements were represented in the sample.

Intergenerational expectations were more likely to be for expressive than for instrumental assistance, frequently for respect and love. Expectations pertained both to general societal norms and to respondents' own families. A common theme was for independence with availability, a mutual expectation between parent and adult child of "being there if needed." Resentment about filial responsibilities was rare, either from middle-aged respondents currently involved or from older respondents speaking from memory. In contrast to much research on intergenerational assistance, the study noted considerable attention to assistance going from parents downward to adult children.

When studying intergenerational exchanges, it appears that the notion of reciprocity needs to be considered. Reciprocity is frequently seen in general terms. This study, however, found mutual expectations for both independence and interdependence and different time frames for the reciprocal exchanges. Turning to the first of these distinctions, note that the notion of reciprocity has primarily emphasized a mutual exchange of benefits. It is important, however, to acknowledge those who "agree not to exchange." Two groups of respondents reflected such a distinction; the latter pattern was labeled reciprocal independence and the former, the larger group, reciprocal interdependence. Respondents tended to recommend reciprocal independence because of a belief that persons should be self-sufficient and because of a desire for autonomy. Some fitting the reciprocal-interdependence pattern expressed contingencies of needs of the recipients and abilities of the donor. Both of these sets of expectations, independence and interdependence, referred to the present.

It is also important when describing reciprocity to note that some respondents use a longer time frame. Those in the two-generational group in the past expected that adult children would reciprocate to their parents for benefits received from them earlier in life—delayed reciprocity. Finally, there was a complex pattern of reciprocity using a three-generational time frame and focusing in both directions. Adults were expected to reciprocate for benefits received from parents by assisting their children; and children would assist their parents when needed, just as the parents had helped their own parents.

In conclusion, by combining the expectations older parents should have with expectations that grown children should have, the study noted a four-part framework. Four different types of reciprocity were used by middle-aged and older persons to describe their intergenerational expectations for both giving and receiving assistance. These findings should be useful for those working with individual families in counseling situations. For example, in a family where assistance flows primarily from the adult child to the older parent, both parent and child can be helped by pointing out interdependency and mutual exchange in the past as well as in the present. The findings also should be useful for those interested in setting policy for the future. Policy makers need to recognize that when intergenerational exchange is considered, some people are considering current exchange, others focus on past benefits from parent to young child, while still others focus on past benefits to the previous generation. Therefore, it is apparent that a recognition of both present and past reciprocity, as well as reciprocity for both independence and interdependence, has both micro and macro implications.

Discussion Questions

1. Describe the expectation patterns for giving or receiving assistance and how these differ from forms of reciprocity.

2. What distinguishes respondents who advocate reciprocal independence from those championing reciprocal interdependence?

3. Based on what you know or have read thus far, what dominant expectation and reciprocity patterns would you believe you are most likely to find among Asian Americans? African Americans? Latinos?

4. How would you apply the patterns of expectations and reciprocity from this selection to your family or to the lives of people with whom you are well acquainted?

References

Bengtson, V. L. 1993. "Is the 'Contract Across Generations' Changing? Effects of Population Aging on Obligations and Expectations Across Age Groups." Chapter 1 in V. L. Bengtson and W. A. Achenbaum, eds., *The Changing Contract Across Generations*. New York: Aldine DeGruyter.

Berman, H. 1987. "Adult Children and Their Parents: Irredeemable Obligations and Irreplaceable Loss." *Journal of Gerontological Social Work* 10: 21–34.

Burton, L. M. 1996. "Age Norms, the Timing of Family Role Transitions, and Intergenerational Caregiving Among Aging African-American Women." *The Gerontologist* 36: 199–208.

Foner, N. 1993. "When the Contract Fails: Care for the Elderly in Nonindustrial Cultures." Chapter 6 in V. L. Bengtson and W. A. Achenbaum, eds., *The Changing Contract Across Generations*. New York: Aldine DeGruyter.

Hamon, R. R., and Blieszner, R. 1990. "Filial Responsibility Expectations Among Adult Child—Older Parent Pairs." *Journal of Gerontology: Psychological Sciences* 45: 2110–2112.

Hoyert, D. L. 1991. "Financial and Household Exchanges Between Generations." *Research on Aging* 13: 205–225.

Ingersoll-Dayton, B., Starrels, M. E., and Dowler, D. 1996. "Caregiving for Parents and Parents-in-law: Is Gender Important?" *The Gerontologist* 36: 483–491.

Johnson, M. L. 1995. "Interdependency and the Generational Compact." *Ageing and Society* 15: 243–265.

Logan, J. R., and Spitze, G. D. 1996. *Family Ties: Enduring Relations Between Parents and Their Grown Children*. Philadelphia: Temple University Press.

Rossi, A. S. 1993. "Intergenerational Relations: Gender, Norms, and Behavior." Chapter 10 in V. L. Bengtson and W. A. Achenbaum, eds., *The*

Changing Contract Across Generations. New York: Aldine DeGruyter.

Sanborn, B., and Bould, S. 1991. "Intergenerational Caregivers of the Oldest Old." *Marriage and Family Review* 16: 125–142.

Selig, S., Tomlinson, T., and Hickey, T. 1991. "Ethical Dimensions of Intergenerational Reciprocity: Implications for Practice." *The Gerontologist* 31: 624–630.

Sherman, S. R. 1994. "Changes in Age Identity: Self Perceptions in Middle and Late Life." *Journal of Aging Studies* 8: 397–412.

Stein, C. H. 1992. "Ties That Bind: Three Studies of Obligation in Adult Relationships With Family." *Journal of Social and Personal Relationships* 9: 525–547.

Wallhagen, M. I., and Strawbridge, W. J. 1995. "My Parent—Not Myself." *Journal of Aging and Health* 7: 552–572.

Whitbeck, L., Hoyt, D. R., and Huck, S. M. 1994. "Early Family Relationships, Intergenerational Solidarity, and Support Provided to Parents by Their Adult Children." *Journal of Gerontology: Social Sciences* 49: S85–S94.

Wolfson, C., Handfield-Jones, R., Glass, K. C., McClaran, J., and Keyserlingk, E. 1993. "Adult Children's Perceptions of Their Responsibility to Provide Care for Dependent Elderly Parents." *The Gerontologist* 33: 315–323.

Susan R. Sherman, "An Exploration of Intergenerational Reciprocity." Printed by permission of the author.

Chapter 29
The Moths

Writer

Helena Maria Viramontes

Mexican Americans (Chicanos and Chicanas) comprise the single largest subgroup of Latinos in the United States today. Many are descendants of people living in the Southwest prior to its annexation by the United States; others are from families that have lived in the United States for several generations, and some are more recent immigrants. Regardless of their tenure in the United States, the Chicano family has traditionally been characterized by familism, that is, the deep importance and loyalty of family members to one another and reliance on the family in times of need. Also traditional has been the greater authority of older generations over younger ones; elders held important roles both in family decision making and child rearing. Although these traditional patterns are changing as later generations become assimilated into the majority culture, exchanges of aid and services within the family remain higher than among Anglo Whites. In the following short story, Helena Viramontes explores the relationship between a 14-year-old tomboy, always in trouble at home, and her grandmother, Abuelita. Abuelita, who had rescued her granddaughter from numerous "unladylike" scrapes with siblings and others, is terminally ill. As you read the following selection, pay attention to the connection between grandmother and granddaughter and the ways in which the grandmother has expressed her love. Think about the role reversal when Abuelita is ill. Notice the moths, and their appearance twice in the story. What is their symbolism? How do they relate to the affection and loss the granddaughter experiences?

I was fourteen years old when Abuelita requested my help. And it seemed only fair. Abuelita had pulled me through the rages of scarlet fever by placing, removing, and replacing potato slices on my temples; she had seen me through several whippings, an arm broken by a dare jump off Tío Enrique's toolshed, puberty, and my first lie. Really, I told Amá, it was only fair.

Not that I was her favorite granddaughter or anything special. I wasn't even pretty or nice like my older sisters and I just couldn't do the girl things they could do. My hands were too big to handle the fineries of crocheting or embroidery and I always pricked my fingers or knotted my colored threads time and time again while my sisters laughed and called me Bull Hands with their cute waterlike voices. So I began keeping a piece of jagged brick in my sock to bash my sisters or anyone who called me Bull Hands. Once, while we all sat in the bedroom, I hit Teresa on the forehead, right above her eyebrow, and she ran to Amá with her mouth open, her hand over her eye while blood seeped between her fingers. I was used to the whippings by then.

I wasn't respectful either. I even went so far as to doubt the power of Abuelita's slices, the slices she said absorbed my fever. "You're still alive, aren't you?" Abuelita snapped back, her pasty gray eye beaming at me and burning holes in my suspicions. Regretful that I had let secret questions drop out of my mouth, I couldn't look into her eyes. My hands began to fan out, grow like a liar's nose until they hung by my side like low weights. Abuelita made a balm out of dried moth wings and Vicks and rubbed my hands, shaped them back to size, and it was the strangest feeling. Like bones melting. Like sun shining through the darkness of your eyelids. I didn't mind helping Abuelita after that, so Amá would always send me over to her.

In the early afternoon Amá would push her hair back, hand me my sweater and shoes, and tell me to go to Mama Luna's. This was to avoid another fight and another whipping, I knew. I would deliver one last direct shot on Marisela's arm and jump out of our house, the slam of the screen door burying her cries of anger, and I'd gladly go help Abuelita plant her wild lilies or jasmine or heliotrope or cilantro or hierbabuena in red Hills Brothers coffee cans. Abuelita would wait for me at the top step of her porch, holding a hammer and nail and empty coffee cans. And although we hardly spoke, hardly looked at each other as we worked over root transplants, I always felt her gray eye on me. It made me feel, in a strange sort of way, safe and guarded and not alone. Like God was supposed to make you feel.

On Abuelita's porch, I would puncture holes in the bottom of the coffee cans with a nail and a precise hit of a hammer. This completed, my job was to fill them with red clay mud from beneath her rosebushes, packing it softly, then making a perfect hole, four fingers round, to nest a sprouting avocado pit, or the spidery sweet potatoes that Abuelita rooted in mayonnaise jars with toothpicks and daily water, or prickly chayotes that produced vines that twisted and wound all over her porch pillars, crawling to the roof, up and over the roof, and down the other side, making her small brick house look like it was cradled within the vines that grew pear-shaped squashes ready for the pick, ready to be steamed with onions and cheese and butter. The roots would burst out of the rusted coffee cans and search for a place to connect. I would then feed the seedlings with water.

But this was a different kind of help, Amá said, because Abuelita was dying. Looking into her gray eye, then into her brown one, the doctor said it was just a matter of days. And so it seemed only fair that these hands she had melted and formed found use in rubbing her caving body with alcohol and marijuana, rubbing her arms and legs, turning her face to the window so that she could watch the bird of paradise blooming or smell the scent of clove in the air. I toweled her face frequently and held her hand for hours. Her gray wiry hair hung over the mattress. For as long as I could remember, she'd kept her long hair in braids. Her mouth was vacant, and when she slept her eyelids never closed all the way. Up close, you could see her gray eye beaming out the window, staring hard as if to remember everything. I never kissed her. I left the window open when I went to the market.

Across the street from Jay's Market there was a chapel. I never knew its denomination, but I went in just the same to search for candles. There were none, so I sat down on one of the pews. After I cleaned my fingernails, I looked up at the high ceiling. I had forgotten the vastness of these places, the coolness of the marble pillars and the frozen statues with blank eyes. I was alone. I knew why I had never returned.

That was one of Apá's biggest complaints. He would pound his hands on the table, rocking the sugar dish or spilling a cup of coffee, and scream that if I didn't go to mass every Sunday to save my goddamn sinning soul, then I had no reason to go out of the house, period. *Punto final*. He would grab my arm and dig his nails into me to make sure I understood the importance of catechism. Did he make himself clear? Then he strategically directed his anger at Amá for her lousy ways of bringing up daughters, being disrespectful and unbelieving, and my older sisters would pull me aside and tell me if I didn't get to mass right this minute, they were all going to kick the holy shit out of me. Why am I so selfish? Can't you see what it's doing to Amá you idiot? So I would wash my feet and stuff them in my black Easter shoes that shone with Vaseline, grab a missal and veil, and wave goodbye to Amá.

I would walk slowly down Lorena to First to Evergreen, counting the cracks on the cement. On Evergreen I would turn left and walk to Abuelita's. I liked her porch because it was shielded by the vines of the chayotes and I could get a good look at the people and car traffic on Evergreen without them knowing. I would jump up the porch steps, knock on the screen door as I wiped my feet, and call, Abuelita? Mi Abuelita? As I opened the door and stuck my head in, I would catch the gagging scent of toasting chile on the *placa*. When I entered the *sala*, she would greet me from the kitchen, wringing her hands in her apron. I'd sit at the corner of the table to keep from being in her way. The chiles made my eyes water. Am I crying? No, Mama Luna, I'm sure not crying. I don't like going to mass, but my eyes watered anyway, the tears dropping on the tablecloth like candle wax. Abuelita lifted the burnt chiles from the fire and sprinkled water on them until the skins began to separate. Placing them in front of me, she turned to check the *menudo*. I peeled the skins off and put the flimsy, limp-looking green and yellow chiles in the *molcajete* and began to crush and crush and twist and crush the heart out of the tomato, the clove of garlic, the stupid chiles that made me cry, crushed them until they turned into liquid under my bull hand. With a wooden spoon, I scraped hard to destroy the guilt, and my tears were gone. I put the bowl of chile next to a vase filled with freshly cut roses. Abuelita touched my hand and pointed to the bowl of *menudo* that steamed in front of me. I spooned some chile into the *menudo* and rolled a corn tortilla thin with the palms of my hands. As I ate, a fine Sunday breeze entered the kitchen and a rose petal calmly feathered down to the table.

I left the chapel without blessing myself and walked to Jay's. Most of the time Jay didn't have much of anything. The tomatoes were always soft and the cans of Campbell soup had rust spots on them. There was dust on the tops of cereal boxes. I picked up what I needed: rubbing alcohol, five cans of chicken broth, a big bottle of Pine Sol. At first Jay got mad because I thought I had forgotten the money. But it was there all the time, in my back pocket.

When I returned from the market, I heard Amá crying in Abuelita's kitchen. She looked up at me with puffy eyes. I placed the bags of groceries on the table and began putting the cans of soup away. Amá sobbed quietly. I never kissed her. After a while, I patted her on the back for comfort. Finally: "¿Y mi Amá?" she asked in a whisper, then choked again and cried into her apron.

Abuelita fell off the bed twice yesterday, I said, knowing that I shouldn't have said it and wondering why I wanted to say it because it only made Amá cry harder. I guess I became angry and just so tired of the quarrels and beatings and unanswered prayers and my hands just there hanging helplessly by my side. Amá looked at me again, confused, angry, and her eyes were filled with sorrow. I went outside and sat on the porch swing and watched the people pass. I sat there until she left. I dozed off repeating the words to myself like rosary prayers: when do you stop giving when do you start giving when do you . . . and when my hands fell from my lap, I awoke to

catch them. The sun was setting, an orange glow, and I knew Abuelita was hungry.

There comes a time when the sun is defiant. Just about the time when moods change, inevitable seasons of a day, transitions from one color to another, that hour or minute or second when the sun is finally defeated, finally sinks into the realization that it cannot, with all its power to heal or burn, exist forever, there comes an illumination where the sun and earth meet, a final burst of burning red-orange fury reminding us that although endings are inevitable, they are necessary for rebirths, and when that time came, just when I switched on the light in the kitchen to open Abuelita's can of soup, it was probably then that she died.

The room smelled of Pine Sol and vomit, and Abuelita had defecated the remains of her cancerous stomach. She had turned to the window and tried to speak, but her mouth remained open and speechless. I heard you, Abuelita, I said, stroking her cheek, I heard you. I opened the windows of the house and let the soup simmer and overboil on the stove. I turned the stove off and poured the soup down the sink. From the cabinet I got a tin basin, filled it with lukewarm water, and carried it carefully to the room. I went to the linen closet and took out some modest bleached white towels. With the sacredness of a priest preparing his vestments, I unfolded the towels one by one on my shoulders. I removed the sheets and blankets from her bed and peeled off her thick flannel nightgown. I toweled her puzzled face, stretching out the wrinkles, removing the coils of her neck, toweled her shoulders and breasts. Then I changed the water. I returned to towel the creases of her stretch-marked stomach, her sporadic vaginal hairs, and her sagging thighs. I removed the lint from between her toes and noticed a mapped birthmark on the fold of her buttock. The scars on her back, which were as thin as the lifelines on the palms of her hands, made me realize how little I really knew of Abuelita. I covered her with a thin blanket and went into the bathroom. I washed my hands, turned on the tub faucets, and watched the water pour into the tub with vitality and steam. When it was full,

I turned off the water and undressed. Then, I went to get Abuelita.

She was not as heavy as I thought, and when I carried her in my arms, her body fell into a V, and yet my legs were tired, shaky, and I felt as if the distance between the bedroom and bathroom was miles and years away. Amá, where are you?

I stepped into the bathtub, one leg first, then the other. I bent my knees to descend into the water, slowly, so I wouldn't scald her skin. There, there, Abuelita, I said, cradling her, smoothing her as we descended, I heard you. Her hair fell back and spread across the water like eagle's wings. The water in the tub overflowed and poured onto the tile of the floor. Then the moths came. Small, gray ones that came from her soul and out through her mouth fluttering to light, circling the single dull light bulb of the bathroom. Dying is lonely and I wanted to go to where the moths were, stay with her and plant chayotes whose vines would crawl up her fingers and into the clouds; I wanted to rest my head on her chest with her stroking my hair, telling me about the moths that lay within the soul and slowly eat the spirit up; I wanted to return to the waters of the womb with her so that we would never be alone again. I wanted. I wanted my Amá. I removed a few strands of hair from Abuelita's face and held her small light head within the hollow of my neck. The bathroom was filled with moths, and for the first time in a long time I cried, rocking us, crying for her, for me, for Amá, the sobs emerging from the depths of anguish, the misery of feeling half born, sobbing until finally the sobs rippled into circles and circles of sadness and relief. There, there, I said to Abuelita, rocking us gently, there, there.

Discussion Questions

1. In what ways has Abuelita guided and supported her granddaughter?

2. Discuss how the healing power of moths' wings symbolizes the narrator's feeling safe, protected, and not alone during her adolescent struggle with her parents and siblings.

3. In what ways does this short story illustrate intergenerational reciprocity?

4. To what extent is familism a theme in the relationships discussed?

5. Discuss the granddaughter's confrontation and feelings of loss at her grandmother's mortality and the dawning awareness of her own finitude.

Chapter 30

Research on Grandparenting

*Rachel A. Pruchno and
Katrina W. Johnson*

*The traditional American picture of a grand-
parent is a white-haired elder, perhaps
Grandma baking cookies or Grandpa tossing a
ball to his grandchildren. This romanticized
view of grandparents is not borne out by reality
in present-day society, for as Rachel Pruchno
and Katrina Johnson point out, grandparents
are not necessarily old; their ages may range
from 30 to 110. Shaped by the historical, cultural, and social context in which they live,
grandparents' roles are structured by countless
factors, including their relationships with
their children; their children's marriages, divorces, and remarriages; or the ages of their
grandchildren. The emotional meanings and
the actual role responsibilities associated with
the grandparent-grandchild relationships at
various points in their lives are also key. Gender, ethnic, racial, and social-class patterns
also contour the role of grandparent, as do life
events in their children's and grandchildren's
lives. They may provide "parenting" when the
mother or father is unavailable for any reason;
by 1997, seven percent of all families with children under age 18 were maintained by grandparents. In other families, grandparents may
be peripheral to their grandchildren's lives and
seen only on birthdays, holidays, or other family occasions. Or they may be keepers of family
tradition and sources of family history. They
may be confidants and wise advisors. The following selection examines recent studies of
grandparenting and points both to multifaceted roles that may be played by grandparents
and to the gaps in current knowledge about the
nature of grandparenthood. Consider the multiple meanings of being a grandparent in
American society today, ranging from full-
time caregiver of young children to a once-a-
month or less visiting relative or far-away
grandparent living in a distant state. Think
also about the various emotional meanings
that being a grandparent or grandchild may
have.*

Grandparenting is about generations, but
not necessarily about old age. Grandparenting research, therefore, encompasses a wide
spectrum of approaches in which aging is
seen in a life-course perspective. The following is a brief review of current scientific
knowledge about major topics related to
grandparenthood.

Demographics

Today, an unprecedented number of people in American society are grandparents.
Treas and Bengtson (1982) suggest that two
key demographic changes have altered the
nature of grandparenthood in our society: increased life expectancy and new rhythms in
the family life cycle. Changes in mortality and
fertility mean that an estimated three-quarters of adults will live to be grandparents.
Omitting those who do not have children
themselves, 94 percent of older adults are
grandparents (Hooyman and Kiyak, 1988),
and nearly 50 percent are great grandparents
(Roberto and Stroes, 1992). Aldous (1995) la-
ments that presently not enough is known
about the sheer number of grandparents in
the United States or their age, gender, and
social composition. Some data are available,
however. For example, it is known that grandparents are not defined by age—they can be
30 or 110 years old! Most middle-aged people
become grandparents around age 45
(Hagestad, 1985). One recent estimate places
nearly half of grandparents at less than age
60, one-third at less than age 55, and one-fifth
at age 70 or older (Schwartz and Waldrop,
1992). Additionally, because of changed family configurations through divorce or remarriage, that "new" grandchild can be an infant
or a retiree. Longer lives also mean that the
grandparent role has been extended. It is no
longer uncommon for women to be grandmothers for more than four decades
(Hagestad, 1988). Many people who are

grandparents are still busy rearing their own children and participating actively in the work world, countering the image of all grandparents as frail and dependent or known best for baking cookies after school.

The U.S. Bureau of the Census (1991) estimates that 3.2 million children under age 18 live with their grandparents (Minkler and Roe, 1993). This estimate refers only to homes maintained by grandparents and does not include grandchildren whose parents maintain the home even though a grandparent is coresident. It is important to note that these numbers vary as a function of race, with 12.3 percent of black children and 3.7 percent of white children living with their grandparents (U.S. Bureau of the Census, 1991).

A Historical Perspective

The passage to grandparenthood has been called a "countertransition" because it is brought about by the transition of another family member (Hagestad and Neugarten, 1985). Becoming a grandparent is often studied as a psychological variable related to possible changes in activities, relationships, and self-esteem. Early research on the grandparent role indicated that most grandparents enjoy their grandchildren and take pride in the grandchildren's accomplishments (Albrecht, 1954; Kahana and Kahana, 1970). Grandparents in these studies endorsed a "pleasure without responsibility" orientation toward the role of grandparent. During the 1960s and 1970s, various styles of grandparent-grandchild relationships were described (Neugarten and Weinstein, 1964; Robertson, 1977), and hypotheses were developed to account for differences in role type.

In the 1980s, greater attention to the grandparent role took two separate yet related courses. One focus has examined levels of satisfaction with the role itself, while the other has examined the relationship between grandparenting and broader, life-satisfaction issues (Roberto, 1990). Characteristics that have been associated with the psychological well-being of grandparents include timing of entrance to the role (Burton and Bengtson, 1985), gender (Thomas, 1986b), and the salience of the role for the individual (Kivnick, 1985).

Grandparents play various symbolic roles, including those outlined by Bengtson (1985) as "being there," the "national guard," "active participants in the family's social construction of its history," and "surrogate parent." Grandparents may also serve as historian, mentor, role model, wizard, or nurturer (Kornhaber and Woodward, 1981). Numerous writers (Baranowski, 1982; Bengtson and Robertson, 1985; Kivnick, 1982a, 1982b; Kornhaber and Woodward, 1981) underscore the reciprocal influence between grandparents and multiple generations.

Troll (1983) describes grandparenthood as a derived status only weakly regulated by social norms. As such, grandparent roles are ambiguous and vary in both form and function (see Bengtson and Robertson, 1985; Rosow 1976; Wood, 1982), and it is not at all clear what the social and legal rights and obligations of grandparents are (Bengtson, 1985). With few normatively explicit expectations for their role behavior, the type and level of involvement of grandparents are often matters for family negotiation.

One of the frequently disputed questions has been whether grandparenting roles have changed over the course of historical time. Kornhaber (1985) perceived a weakening role and asserted that grandparents have abdicated their responsibility by "turning their backs" on grandchildren both in terms of emotional investment and practical support (see also Gutman, 1985). Counterclaims have been made asserting that relations between grandparents and grandchildren remain strong, with both providing high levels of affection, feeling a strong sense of obligation, and providing extensive help to one another (Cherlin and Furstenberg, 1986b; Robertson, 1976). In a rare attempt to compare data over time, Kennedy (1990) found that compared to Robertson's (1976) findings twelve years earlier, contemporary young adult grandchildren were more likely than their earlier counterparts to turn to grandparents for advice and financial support.

Grandparenting and Adult Grandchildren in the Family Unit

Just as not all grandparents are old, not all grand-"children" are young. Bengtson and Harootyan (1994) found that 56 percent of people age 65 and older have at least one adult grandchild. What is the nature of the relationship between grandparents and their older grandchildren? Studies of such relationships over time have reported discrepant findings (Langer, 1990). Cross-sectional studies consistently indicate that older grandchildren are less involved with their grandparents than are younger grandchildren (Hodgson, 1992; Johnson, 1983; Kivett, 1991; Sprey and Matthews, 1982; Thomas, 1986a). In a longitudinal study, Field and Minkler (1988) found that frequency of contact with grandchildren declined over a fourteen-year period, but there was no corresponding decline in level of satisfaction with grandchildren. Investigating relationships between grandparents and teenaged grandchildren, Dellman-Jenkins, Papalia, and Lopez (1987) reported that over 80 percent of the teenagers viewed their grandparents as confidantes. Some researchers (Hagestad, 1981; Troll, 1980a) have speculated that the grandparent-grandchild bond may be even more significant in adult relations. Retrospective reports by adult children about the degree to which their childhood was influenced by grandparents strongly predict the quality of their contemporary intergenerational relationships (Lawton, Silverstein, and Bengtson, 1994; Matthews and Sprey, 1985). These findings support speculations that the quality of early attachment to a grandparent is sustained over time (Kornhaber and Woodward, 1981). Recently, Hodgson (1995) found that a large proportion of adult grandchildren maintain contact with their closest grandparents on a regular basis.

Finally, a new but increasing role is that of great-grandparent. The growth of four- and five-generation families has led a few researchers to explore the meaning and roles of great-grandparents in the lives of their families. Wentowski (1985), exploring the perceptions of nineteen great-grandmothers, found that great-grandmotherhood was significant for symbolic and emotional reasons. Doka and Mertz (1988) identified three aspects of the great-grandparent role, including personal and family renewal, diversion, and a mark of longevity. The vast majority of great-grandparents reported that great-grandparenthood renewed their zeal for life and reaffirmed the continuance of their families.

Custodial Grandparents

Recent national attention has focused on what is portrayed as an increasing number of grandparents who become surrogate parents for young grandchildren. Grandparents—especially grandmothers—may take on this role because of divorce (Ahrons and Bowman, 1982; Cherlin and Furstenberg, 1986a; Gladstone, 1988; Johnson, 1988), drug addiction (Burton, 1992; Minkler, 1991; Minkler, Roe, and Price, 1992), or adolescent pregnancy (Burton, 1995; Burton and Bengtson, 1985; Flaherty, Facteau, and Garver, 1987; Furstenberg, 1980; Ladner and Gourdine, 1984; Thomas, 1990). Related to the circumstances that may result in custodial grandparenting, a growing number of studies focus on grandparents beset with a myriad of problems. Shore and Hayslip (1990a, 1990b), for example, found that such grandparents had reduced scores on three out of four measures of psychological well-being, including satisfaction with the grandparent role, perceptions of grandparent-grandchild relationships, and overall well-being. Burton (1992) found that caring for grandchildren generated considerable stress for grandparents, with 86 percent of the 60 grandparents in the study reporting feeling "depressed or anxious most of the time." In a more recent report of these data, Burton and deVries (1993) highlight the rewards as well as challenges associated with surrogate parenting. Recently, the legal and economic difficulties experienced by grandparents rearing their grandchildren have come to the attention of both social scientists and the press (e.g., Chaloff, 1982; Creighton, 1991; Presser, 1989). In consideration of how custodianship affects grandchildren, Denham and Smith (1989), in their review of the literature, suggest both a direct and indirect positive influence. A recent study by Solomon and Marx (1995) found that children reared solely by their grandparents fared quite well relative to children in families with one biological parent present. Furthermore, they were not significantly different, except in academic performance, from children raised in traditional families.

Ethnicity and Social Class

Research on the intergenerational living arrangements, expectations, and circumstances of custodial grandparents has emphasized the need to examine ethnicity and social class in studies of grandparenting. Although studies of the grandparent role have included people from various ethnic groups (see, e.g., Bengtson, Rosenthal, and Burton, 1990), the different groups usually have been examined from very different perspectives. Studies of white grandparents have tended to focus on describing different typologies of grandparents and examining the meaning of the role of grandparents (McCready, 1985; Neugarten and Weinstein, 1964), while studies of black grandparents have focused on grandparents as parent substitutes (Burton, 1992; Burton, Dilworth-Anderson, and deVries, 1995; Flaherty, Facteau, and Garver, 1987; Minkler and Roe, 1993; Pearson et al., 1990) or on describing the traditional family structure of African Americans (Burton, 1995; Burton and Dilworth-Anderson, 1991; Dilworth-Anderson, 1992; Wilson, 1984). A study by Schmidt and Padilla (1983) found that Spanish language compatibility between grandparents and grandchildren predicted the amount of contact between them, underscoring the importance of cultural affinity in structuring intergenerational relations. The salience of the grandparent role in families of Hispanic elders has been described by Lubben and Becerra (1987) and Markides and Mindel (1987). Thomas (1994), contrasting the role of grandfathers across ethnic groups, found that grandparenting has a more central role for African-American men than for male members of other ethnic groups. Similarly, Kivett (1991) found grandparenthood to be more important among rural black grandfathers than among rural white grandfathers. Strom et al. (1995) investigated differences in performance and effectiveness of black and white grandparents.

One of the first studies to investigate the impact of social class on the role of grandparents was conducted by Clavan (1978). Cherlin and Furstenberg (1986b) report small class and ethnic differences among the whites in their sample, but substantial differences between black and white grandparents.

A Look to the Future

Generational research is currently a priority for many scientists involved in studies of aging, the family, and society. But important issues remain to be addressed, particularly if support for future investigations is to be secured. Three of these issues are prominent.

First, much remains to be done both in development of appropriate theory and in generation of empirical findings to test the theory. Current work is tentative, incomplete, and contradictory (Robertson, 1995). Methodological flaws limit how much studies can tell us about grandparents today (Werner, 1991), and the basic demographic picture is scanty (Aldous, 1995). Disciplinary differences may account for some discrepancies found in the grandparenting literature, since intergenerational research has been a topic for studies in psychology, sociology, social work, medicine, and law. Nevertheless, researchers are advised to look to theoretical frameworks—for example, generativity in later life, social support, family systems theory, role incongruence ("on- and off-time grandparenting"), or ethnic studies.

Second, the definition of grandparenthood and its boundaries is trickier for research than it might seem, given the biological ties. For example, what defines a custodial grandparent in a target population? Is it someone who serves as a family caregiver while the child's parent works? Or is it someone who cares intermittently for a grandchild, perhaps for the weekend or even for a year? Should only a grandparent with legal guardianship be regarded as a surrogate parent? What about the three-generation family in which the grandchild's parent is coresident but a teenager? And, how can research use innovative and cost-effective approaches to tap those families not experiencing problems?

Third, analysis issues must be carefully considered. Again, here are some questions often raised in research reviews. How is grandparenthood hypothesized to be related to, or causal, for a specific outcome, whether it is the grandparent's physical health, overall well-being, or self-concept? Does the research plan contain an assumption that custodianship is a burden? Will the unit of analysis be an individual grandparent, grandparent and grandchild dyad, or an entire family? Of importance also might be the ability to link research findings to the development of programs that enrich the lives of grandparents and their expanding families. . . .

Grandparents are an integral part of family life, yet they occupy an evolving family position. Only within the past half century has grandparenthood become a role that most older people will live long enough to enjoy. The challenge to aging research is to determine the impact of grandparenting for individuals, the family, and the larger society.

Discussion Questions

1. What symbolic roles are played by grandparents in the family?

2. In what ways and in what situations do you think that grandparents provide alternative role models for their grandchildren?

3. As about one in every two marriages now ends in divorce and remarriage, and second families are common, detail the issues grandparents are likely to encounter in maintaining their previous relationships with their grandchildren.

4. What social-class, ethnic, and racial variations in the types of issues described in the above question might be encountered?

5. Describe the roles that your grandparents have played in your life thus far and explain the reasons that you think they played these parts.

References

Ahrens, C. R., and Bowman, M. E. 1982. "Changes in Family Relationships Following Divorce of Adult Child: Grandmothers' Perceptions." *Journal of Divorce* 5: 49–68.

Albrecht, R. 1954. "The Parental Responsibilities of Grandparents." *Marriage and Family Living* 16: 201–4.

Aldous, J. 1995. "New Views of Grandparents in Intergenerational Context." *Journal of Family Issues* 16(1): 104–22.

Baranowski, M. D. 1982. "Grandparent-Adolescent Relations: Beyond the Nuclear Family." *Adolescence* 17: 575–84.

Baranowski, M. D. 1985. "Men as Grandfathers." In S. M. Hanson and F. W Bozet, eds., *Dimensions of Fatherhood*. Beverly Hills, Calif: Sage.

Bengtson, V. L. 1985. "Diversity and Symbolism in Grandparental Roles." In V L. Bengtson and J. F. Robertson, eds., *Grandparenthood*. Beverly Hills, Calif: Sage.

Bengtson, V L., and Harootyan, R., eds. 1994. *Hidden Connections: A Study of Intergenerational Linkages in American Society*. New York: Springer.

Bengtson, V. L., and Robertson. J., eds. 1985. *Grandparenthood*. Beverly Hills, Calif: Sage.

Bengtson, V. L., Rosenthal, C., and Burton, L. 1990. "Families and Aging: Diversity and Heterogeneity." In R. H. Binstock and L. George, eds., *Handbook of Aging and the Social Sciences*, 3d ed. San Diego, Calif.: Academic Press.

Burton, L. M. 1992. "Black Grandparents Rearing Children of Drug-Addicted Parents: Stressors, Outcomes, and Social Service Needs." *Gerontologist* 32: 744–51.

Burton, L. M. 1995. "Intergenerational Patterns of Providing Care in African-American Families with Teenage Childbearers: Emergent Patterns in an Ethnographic Study." In V. L. Bengtson, K. W Schaie, and L. M. Burton, eds., *Adult Intergenerational Relations: Effects of Societal Change*. New York: Springer.

Burton, L. M., and Bengtson, V. L. 1985. "Black Grandmothers: Issues on Timing and Continuity of Roles." In L. M. Burton and V. L. Bengtson, eds., *Grandparenthood*. Beverly Hills, Calif: Sage.

Burton, L. M., and deVries, C. 1993. "Challenges and Rewards: African-American Grandparents as Surrogate Parents." In L. M. Burton, ed., *Families and Aging*. Amityville, N.Y.: Baywood.

Burton, L. M., and Dilworth-Anderson, P. 1991. "The Intergenerational Roles of Aged Black Americans." *Marriage and Family Review* 16: 311–30.

Burton, L. M., Dilworth-Anderson, P., and Merri-wether-deVries, C. 1995. "Context and Surrogate Parenting Among Contemporary Grandparents." *Marriage and Family Review* 20(3/4): 349–66.

Chaloff, M. B. 1982. "Grandparents' Statutory Visitation Rights and Rights of Adoptive Parents." *Brooklyn Law Review* 49: 149–71.

Cherlin, A. J., and Furstenberg, F. 1986a. "Grandparents and Family Crisis." *Generations* 10(4): 26–28.

Cherlin, A. J., and Furstenberg, F. F. 1986b. *The New American Grandparent: A Place in the Family, A Life Apart*. New York: Basic Books.

Clavan, S. 1978. "The Impact of Social Class and Social Trends on the Role of Grandparents." *Family Coordinator* 27: 351–57.

Creighton, L. L. 1991. "The Silent Saviors." *U.S. News and World Report* Dec. 16: 80–89.

Dellman-Jenkins, M., Papalia, D., and Lopez, M. 1987. "Teenagers' Reported Interaction with Grandparents: Exploring the Extent of Alienation." *Lifestyles: A Journal of Changing Patterns* 3–4: 35–46.

Denham, T. E., and Smith, C. W. 1989. "The Influence of Grandparents on Grandchildren: A Review of the Literature and Resources." *Family Relations* 38: 345–50.

Dilworth-Anderson, P. 1992. "Extended Kin Networks in Black Families." *Generations* 16(3): 29–32.

Doka, K. J., and Mertz, M. E. 1988. "The Meaning and Significance of Great-Grandparenthood." *Gerontologist* 28: 192–97.

Field, D., and Minkler, M. 1988. "Continuity and Change in Social Support Between Young-Old and Old-Old or Very-Old Age." *Journal of Gerontology* 43(4): P100-06.

Flaherty S., Facteau, L., and Garver, P. 1987. "Grandmother Functions in Multigenerational Families: An Exploratory Study of Black Adolescent Mothers and Their Infants." *Maternal Child Nursing Journal* 16: 61–73.

Furstenberg, F. F. 1980. "Burdens and Benefits: The Impact of Early Childbearing on the Family." *Journal of Social Issues* 36: 64–87.

Gladstone, J. W. 1988. "Perceived Changes in Grandmother-Grandchild Relations Following a Child's Separation or Divorce." *Gerontologist* 28: 66–72.

Gutmann, D. L. 1985. "Deculturation and the American Grandparent." In V. L. Bengtson and J. F. Robertson, eds., *Grandparenthood*. Beverly Hills, Calif: Sage.

Hagestad, G. O. 1981. "Problems and Promises in the Social Psychology of Intergenerational Relations." In R. Vogel et al., eds., *Aging: Stability and Change in the Family*. New York: Academic Press.

Hagestad, G. O. 1985. "Continuity and Connectedness." In V. L. Bengtson and J. F. Robertson, eds., *Grandparenthood*. Beverly Hills, Calif: Sage.

Hagestad, G. O. 1986. "The Family: Women and Grandparents as Kin-Keepers." In A. Pifer and L. Broute, eds., *Our Aging Society*. New York: Norton.

Hagestad, G. O. 1988. "Demographic Change and the Life Course: Some Emerging Trends in the Family Realm." *Family Relations* 37: 405–10.

Hagestad, G. O., and Neugarten, B. 1985. "Age and Life Course." In E. Shanas and R. Binstock, eds., *Handbook of Aging and the Social Sciences*. New York: Van Nostrand Reinhold.

Hodgson, L. G. 1992. "Adult Grandchildren and Their Grandparents: The Enduring Bond." *International Journal of Aging and Human Development* 34: 209–25.

Hodgson, L. G. 1995. "Adult Grandchildren and Their Grandparents: The Enduring Bond." In J. Hendrick, ed., *The Ties of Later Life*. Amityville, N.Y.: Baywood.

Hooyman, N., and Kiyak, H. A. 1988. *Social Gerontology: A Multidisciplinary Perspective*. Boston: Allyn and Bacon.

Johnson, C. L. 1983. "A Cultural Analysis of the Grandmother." *Research on Aging* 5: 547–68.

Johnson, C. L. 1988. "Active and Latent Functions of Grandparenting During the Divorce Process." *Geronotologist* 28: 185–91.

Kahana, B., and Kahana, E. 1970. "Grandparenthood from the Perspective of the Developing Grandchild." *Developmental Psychology* 3: 98–105.

Kennedy, G. E. 1989. "College Students' Relationship with Grandparents." *Psychological Reports* 64: 477–78.

Kivett, V. R. 1991. "The Grandparent-Grandchild Connection." *Marriage and Family Review* 16: 267–90.

Kivnick, H. Q. 1982a. *The Meaning of Grandparenthood*. Ann Arbor: University of Michigan Research Press.

Kivnick, H. Q. 1982b. "Grandparenthood: An Overview of Meaning and Mental Health." *Gerontologist* 22: 59–66.

Kivnick, H. Q. 1984. "Grandparents and Family Relations." In W. Quinn and G. Hughston, eds., *Independent Aging: Family and Social Systems Perspectives*. Rockville, Md.: Aspen Systems Corp.

Kivnick, H. Q. 1985. "Grandparenthood and Mental Health: Meaning, Behavior, and Satisfaction." In V. L. Bengtson and J. F. Robertson, eds., *Grandparenthood*. Beverly Hills, Calif: Sage.

Kornhaber, A. 1985. "Grandparenthood and the 'New Social Contract.'" In V. L. Bengtson and J. E. Robertson, eds., *Grandparenthood*. Beverly Hills, Calif: Sage.

Kornhaber, A., and Woodward, R. 1981. *Grandparents/Grandchildren: The Vital Connection*. New York: Doubleday.

Ladner, J., and Gourdine, R. 1984. "Intergenerational Teenage Motherhood: Some Preliminary Findings." *A Scholarly Journal of Black Women* 1(2): 22–4.

Langer, N. 1990. "Grandparents and Their Adult Children: What They Do for One Another." *International Journal of Aging and Human Development* 31: 101–10.

Lawton, L., Silverstein, M., and Bengtson, V. L. 1994. "Affection, Social Contact, and Geographic Distance Between Adult Children and Their Parents." *Journal of Marriage and the Family* 56: 57–68.

Lubben, J. E., and Becerra, R. M. 1987. "Social Support Among Black, Mexican, and Chinese Elderly." In D. E. Gelfand and C. H. Barresi, eds., *Ethnic Dimensions of Aging*. New York: Springer.

Markides, K. S., and Mindel, C. H. 1987. *Aging and Ethnicity*. Beverly Hills, Calif: Sage.

Matthews, S. H., and Sprey, J. 1984. "The Impact of Divorce on Grandparenthood: An Exploratory Study." *Gerontologist* 24(1): 41–7.

Matthews, S. H., and Sprey, J. 1985. "Adolescents' Relationships with Grandparents: An Empirical Contribution to Conceptual Clarification." *Journal of Gerontology* (5): 621–26.

McCready, W. C. 1985. "Styles of Grandparenting Among White Ethnics." In V. L. Bengtson and J. E. Robertson, eds., *Grandparenthood*. Beverly Hills, Calif: Sage.

Minkler, M. 1991. "Health and Social Consequences of Grandparent Caregiving." Paper presented at Gerontological Society of America, San Francisco.

Minkler, M., and Roe, K. M. 1993. *Grandmothers as Caregivers: Raising Children of the Crack Cocaine Epidemic*. Beverly Hills, Calif: Sage.

Minkler, M., Roe, K., and Price, M. 1992. "The Physical and Emotional Health of Grandmothers Raising Grandchildren in the Crack Cocaine Epidemic." *Gerontologist* 32: 752–60.

Neugarten, B. L., and Weinstein, K. 1964. "The Changing American Grandparents." *Journal of Marriage and the Family* 26:199–204.

Pearson, J. L., et al. 1990. "Black Grandmothers in Multigenerational Households: Diversity in Family Structure and Parenting Involvement in the Woodlawn Community." *Child Development* 61: 434–42.

Presser, H. B. 1989. "Some Economic Complexities of Child Care Provided by Grandmothers." *Journal of Marriage and the Family* 51: 581–91.

Roberto, K. A. 1990. "Grandparent and Grandchild Relationships." In T. H. Brubaker, ed., *Family Relationships in Later Life*, 2d ed. Beverly Hills, Calif: Sage.

Roberto, K. A., and Stroes, J. 1992. "Grandchildren and Grandparents: Roles, Influences, and Relationships." *International Journal of Aging and Human Development* 34: 227–39.

Robertson, J. F. 1976. "Significance of Grandparents: Perceptions of Young Grandchildren." *Gerontologist* 16: 137–40.

Robertson, J. F. 1977. "Grandmotherhood: A Study of Role Conceptions." *Journal of Marriage and the Family* 39(I): 165–74.

Robertson, J. F. 1995. "Grandparenting in an Era of Rapid Change." In R. Blieszner and V. Bedford Hilkevitch, eds., *Handbook of Aging and the Family*. Westport, Conn.: Greenwood Press.

Rosow, I. 1976. "Status and Role Change Through the Life Span." In R. H. Binstock and E. Shanas, eds., *Handbook of Aging and the Social Sciences*. New York: Van Nostrand Reinhold.

Rossi, A. S., and Rossi, P. H. 1990. *Of Human Bonding: Parent-Child Relations Across the Life Course*. New York: Aldine de Gruyter.

Schmidt, A., and Padilla, A. M. 1983. "Grandparent-Grandchild Interaction in a Mexican American Group." *Hispanic Journal of Behavioral Sciences* 5(2):181–98.

Schwartz, J., and Waldrop, J. 1992. "The Growing Importance of Grandparents." *American Demographics* 14: 10–11.

Shore, R. J., and Hayslip, J. B. 1990a. "Comparisons of Custodial and Noncustodial Grandparents." Paper presented at Gerontological Society of America. Boston.

Shore, R. J., and Hayslip, J. B. 1990b. "Predictors of Well-Being in Custodial and Noncustodial Grandparents." Paper presented at American Psychology Association, Boston.

Smith, P. K. 1991. *The Psychology of Grandparenthood: An International Perspective*. London: Routledge.

Solomon, J. C., and Marx, J. 1995. "'To Grandmother's House We Go': Health and School Adjustment of Children Raised Solely by Grandparents." *Gerontologist* 35: 386–94.

Sprey, J., and Matthews, S. H. 1982. "Contemporary Grandparenthood: A Systemic Transition." *Annals of the American Academy of Political and Social Sciences* 464: 91–103.

Strom, R., et al. 1995. "Strengths and Needs of Black Grandparents." In J. Henricks, ed., *The Ties of Later Life*. Amityville, N.Y.: Baywood.

Thomas, J. 1986a. "Age and Sex Differences in Perceptions of Grandparenting." *Journal of Gerontology* 4I: 417–23.

Thomas, J. 1986b. "Gender Differences in Satisfaction with Grandparenting." *Psychology and Aging* 1: 215–19.

Thomas, J. L. 1990. "The Grandparent Role: A Double Bind." *International Journal of Aging and Human Development* 31: 169–71.

Thomas, J. L. 1994. "Older Men as Fathers and Grandfathers." In E. H. Thompson, Jr., ed., *Older Men's Lives*, vol. 6. Beverly Hills, Calif: Sage.

Treas, J., and Bengtson, V. L. 1982. "The Demogaphy of Middle and Late-Life Transitions." *Annals of the American Academy of Political and Social Science* 464: 11–21.

Troll, L. E. 1980. "Intergenerational Relations in Later Life: A Family Systems Approach." In N. Datan and N. Lohmann, eds., *Transitions of Aging*. New York: Academic Press.

Troll, L. E. 1983. "Grandparents: The Family Watchdogs." In T. H. Brubaker, ed., *Family Relationships in Later Life*. Beverly Hills, Calif: Sage.

U.S. Bureau of the Census. 1991. *Current Population Reports: Marital Status and Living Arrangements: March 1990*. Washington, D.C.: Government Printing Office.

Wentowski, G. 1985. "Older Women's Perceptions of Great-Grandmotherhood: A Research Note." *Gerontologist* 25: 593–96.

Werner, E. E. 1991. "Grandparent-Grandchild Relationships Amongst U.S. Ethnic Groups." In P. K. Smith, ed., *The Psychology of Grandparenthood: An International Perspective*. London: Routledge.

Wilson, M. 1984. "Mothers' and Grandmothers' Perceptions of Parental Behavior in Three-Generational Black Families." *Child Development* 55: 1333–39.

Wood, V. 1982. "Grandparenthood: An Ambiguous Role." *Generations* 7(2): 18–24.

Chapter 31
The Influence of Ethnicity and Culture on Caregivers

*María P. Aranda
and Bob G. Knight*

Much research on aging stresses the strains of caring for an elder. Priority and obligations for care in U.S. society are generally ranked; care for a spouse is obligatory, care for a disabled child necessary, care for a elderly parent note-worthy. Providing care to an infirm older person is complex and situation dependent, ranging from emotional support to help with everyday tasks to total care. María Aranda and Bob Knight apply an important corrective to the notion that caregiving is experienced by different ethnic and racial groups in the same way and point out that differences in morbidity among ethnic and racial groups affect the tasks caregivers may be expected to perform. Ethnicity and race also may influence the type of disability or disease of an elder as well as beliefs about appropriate treatment. Moreover, elders' infirmities may be regarded as "normal aging" in some subcultures and as burdensome diseases in others. Degree of acculturation plays a role, affecting not only beliefs about treatment but allocation of caregiving duties and use of community services.

Not only do caregivers' responsibilities differ, but ethnic and racial norms affect caregivers' coping skills, stress level, and availability and use of family supports. For example, the family support system in Latino families may reduce caregiver stress in some situations or increase it in other contexts where younger, more acculturated family members have views of caregiving very different from those of their less acculturated older relatives. As you read the following selection, consider the roles that cultural beliefs associated with racial and ethnic membership play in social supports, stress, definition of the self, and coping behavior among Anglos, Latinos, and African Americans. Think about the ways you might assess the strains and rewards of caregiving among each of these groups. Deliberate what sorts of culturally sensitive community social supports are most appropriate for each group to alleviate caregiver stress.

Population projections for the period between 1987 to the year 2000 indicate that the increase for older Latinos is expected to be nearly five times as great as the rate of growth for the entire Anglo older adult population (76.9 vs 15.9 percent; U.S. Select Committee on Aging, 1989). Increasing numbers of older persons in the Latino population places unforeseen long-term care demands on Latino caregivers, yet minimal attention has been given to the issue of caregiving in this group. Since there is a dearth of research related to the stress and coping process of Latino caregivers, we propose to review the extant literature on Latino caregivers and to suggest directions for future research on how ethnicity and culture play a role in the stress and coping model for caregiving distress in this population. We will also draw from literature on related social science research, other ethnic minority caregivers, and the literature on ethnicity and aging. Since the term "Latino" is somewhat problematic given the intragroup differences likely to exist, e.g., Mexican American, Puerto Rican, Cuban, Central and South American, caution should be taken in noting sources of variation among the subgroups studied (see Appendix, Note 1). Where available, specific ethnic qualifiers will be used to relate the review results to the group under study.

This leads to the important issue of definition of terms used throughout the article. Ethnicity refers to a group's shared sense of peoplehood based on a distinctive social and cultural heritage passed on from generation to generation (Gordon, 1964). In the United States, "the core categories of ethnic identity from which individuals are able to form a sense of peoplehood are race, religion, national origin, or some combination of these categories" (Mindel, Habenstein, & Wright, 1988, p. 5). Culture, on the other hand, is defined as a group's way of life: the values, beliefs, traditions, symbols, language, and social organization that become meaningful to the group members. Such terms as *acculturation* and *minority group status* will be defined in the context of the remaining sections of the article.

Stress and Coping Models of Caregiving

The understanding of caregiver distress has come from the literature on stress research (Folkman, Lazarus, Pimley, & Novacek, 1987, Lazarus & Folkman, 1984a, 1984b; Pearlin & Schooler, 1979) and the caregiver stress process (Lawton, Moss, Kleban, Glicksman, Rovine, 1991; Pearlin, Mullan, Semple, & Skaff, 1990; Zarit, 1989). A review of work on the impact of caregiving on families of functionally dependent older adults reveals that there is some agreement on the major components which comprise a multivariate theoretical model of caregiver stress and coping (Lawton et al., 1991; Pearlin et al., 1990; Poulshock & Deimling, 1984; Schulz, Tompkins, & Rau, 1988; Zarit, 1994). In general, stress and coping models include the following categories of variables: a) contextual or background variables such as age, gender, socioeconomic status, relationship of the caregiver to the patient, etc.; b) primary stressors and secondary strains on the caregiver as a result of directly caring for the impaired person, and the "spillover" effects into other domains of the caregiver's life such as family and work; c) the caregiver's appraisal of demands as stressful or satisfying; d) the potential mediators of burden: coping attitudes and behaviors and social support; and e) the consequences of those demands, i.e., quality of life and physical and mental health.

We propose that ethnicity and culture play a significant role in the stress and coping process of caregivers to the elderly as a result of a) a differential risk for specific health disorders and disability, b) variation in the appraisal of potential stressors, and c) the effect on stress-mediating variables such as social support and coping. First, we will explore the possibility that ethnicity and culture change the nature of caregiving by exposing the Latino population to different risks for specific illnesses and disability.

Health Stressors on Latino Caregivers: Illness-Specific Demands and Disability

If Latinos suffer from different patterns of illnesses as they age due to genetic, environmental, and lifestyle factors, then Latino caregivers may be caring for disabled elderly persons with different types and/or levels of complications and functional disabilities than the general aged population. We turn our attention to the literature on diabetes as an illustration of how the nature of a serious chronic illness can affect late-life caregiving needs. Later, we will conclude this section by reviewing functional disability and long-term care.

Diabetes

Non-insulin-dependent diabetes mellitus (or type II diabetes mellitus) is a significant source of morbidity in Latinos over the age of forty. Prevalence rates for non-insulin-dependent diabetes indicate that Latinos are two to five times more likely to develop diabetes than non-Latinos (Baxter et al., 1993; Hamman et al., 1989; Hanis et al., 1983; U.S. Select Committee on Aging, 1992). Obesity, socioeconomic factors, and a genetic contribution are implicated as possible explanations for the excess rates (Hazuda, Haffner, Stern, & Eifler, 1988; Marshall et al, 1993). The age-related deaths due to diabetes are especially high among Mexican Americans and Puerto Ricans, but lower for Cubans, who are only about half as likely to die from diabetes (U.S. Select Committee on Aging, 1992). Latina women are especially at risk, as evidenced by one population-based study showing that Latina females living in rural southern Colorado were 4.8 times more likely than Anglo females to have confirmed non-insulin-dependent diabetes (Hamman et al., 1989).

Reports from a study based on the same rural Colorado sample indicate that, not only do Latinos have higher diabetes prevalence rates, but that a pattern of earlier onset of approximately ten years may exist among both Latino men and women as compared with their Anglo counterparts (Baxter et al., 1993). Furthermore, once afflicted with diabetes, Latinos have a more severe form of the disease resulting in disproportionately higher rates of diabetes-related complications (U.S. Select Committee on Aging, 1992). Diabetes complications are considered medical problems that occur more often in people with diabetes than in others without diabetes. Categories of complications include: a) obesity, b) retinopathy (a diabetic eye disease which is the leading cause of blindness in the U.S.), c) peripheral neuropathy (nerve damage affecting the legs and feet), d) kidney disease requiring permanent hemodialysis, e) vascular disease resulting in stroke and heart disease, and f) amputations (American Diabetes Association, 1989; Pugh, Stern, Haffner, Eifler, & Zapata, 1988; U.S. Select Committee on Aging, 1992; Villa, Cuellar, Gamel, & Yeo, 1993). The fact that Latinos are identified at a later stage of the disease and have a more serious form of the disease once diagnosed has implications for the caregiver, as will be discussed.

Acculturation has also been found to have an effect on diabetes and obesity among Mexican Americans. For example, in a San Antonio, Texas-based study of Mexican Americans, Hazuda and her associates (Hazuda et al., 1988) found that higher acculturation, as measured by a multidimensional acculturation scale, had a protective effect against diabetes. More specifically, an increased level of acculturation was associated with a statistically significant decline in both obesity and diabetes for men and women alike. For women, socioeconomic status was also inversely related to obesity and diabetes, although the relationship was not as strong as that attributed to acculturation. Thus, for both sexes, "cultural factors play a more pervasive role in the development of obesity and diabetes among Mexican Americans than do purely socioeconomic factors" (p. 1298). Such findings underscore the importance that researchers address health stressors of specific subpopulations of "Latinos" (e.g., males, females, low/high acculturated, Mexican Americans, Puerto Ricans, rural/urban, etc.) and how these groups may pose similar or diverse challenges in the caregiving context as compared to the general population. Understandably, the preponderance of efforts in this area of Latino research is based on samples of Mexican Americans, who constitute almost 60 percent of the U.S. Latino population (Bean & Tienda, 1987).

Deserving of attention in the above-cited study is the multidimensionality of acculturation and how each dimension differentially influences various health outcomes. Specifically, of the three acculturation dimensions measured (i.e., functional integration with mainstream society, value placed on preserving Mexican cultural origin, and attitude toward traditional family structure and sex-role organization; see Hazuda, Stern, & Haffner, 1988), only attitude toward traditional family structure and sex-role organization was related to obesity in men, whereas all three scales were related to obesity in women. Furthermore, when the two remaining scales were included in the same multivariate analysis, only the effect of functional integration with mainstream society remained statistically significant in both gender groups. The findings that three separate dimensions of adult acculturation were measured and that these dimensions were differentially associated with obesity and diabetes in men and women underscore the importance of addressing multidimensionality in cultural mediators of health status.

The nature of caregiving for a family member with diabetes mellitus and its sequelae may present special challenges for the Latino caregiver. The caregiver is more likely to be caring for a diabetic family member who is corpulent, vision-impaired, having difficulties in stabilizing his or her blood glucose levels, and at risk for vascular disease, peripheral neuropathy, amputation, and end-stage renal disease (American Diabetes Association, 1989; Pugh et al., 1988; U.S. Select Committee on Aging, 1992; Villa et al., 1993).

Consequently, the caregiver may be more intensely involved in tasks related to providing tangible assistance in the following areas: a) home blood glucose monitoring, b) medication administration, including injections, c) patient weight control and diet compliance, d) exercise regimen, e) pain management (due to poor circulation or nerve damage in the legs or feet), f) wound and foot care (due to chronic diabetic ulcers and infections), g) body transfers (e.g., moving patient from bed to chair, etc.), h) transportation (to health care providers, including for frequent dialysis treatments).

Aside from the tangible tasks listed above, Latino caregivers are faced with the psychosocial challenges of providing care to the diabetes-affected older adult. Focus group findings based on a study of the health status and service utilization of 35 low income older Latinos receiving health services from a primary medical clinic in the East Los Angeles area have underscored typical sources of stress: role changes in the patient-caregiver dyad, interpersonal conflicts related to treatment compliance, increased anxiety over responsibility for prevention of complex medical emergencies and their management, and an increased sense of futility related to progressive deterioration of the patient's vital organs (Aranda & Galvan, 1993). To illustrate, let us turn our attention to a case vignette reported by the Sánchez family from this study.

> Mr. and Mrs. Sánchez, an elderly couple, were both born and raised in El Paso, Texas. Mrs. Sánchez cares for her spouse who was diagnosed with non-insulin-dependent diabetes mellitus 14 years ago, and who has since had one below-the-knee amputation. She gives her spouse daily injections of insulin. The patient has poor circulation and complains of tingling and burning pain in his remaining limb which causes him excessive pain during the night. Although he is taking pain medication, he reports minimal relief. Mrs. Sánchez wakes up frequently during the night to try to comfort her spouse. She complains of lost sleep and increased anxiety over her inability to attenuate his physical pain. Mrs. Sánchez also complains of back problems which she has developed as a result of transferring and re-

positioning her spouse in order to avoid the formation of bed sores.

It is important to note that although Mrs. Sánchez may be facing increased demands (or a different constellation of demands) due to the nature of the diabetes-related illnesses, she, like many other Latino caregivers, has decreased access to information on the prevention, pathophysiology, diagnosis, and management of diabetes in comparison to her non-Latino White counterparts (U.S. Select Committee on Aging, 1992). Second, pre-existing cultural beliefs regarding the nature, course, and treatment of diabetes may have a significant effect on stress and adaptational outcomes. For example, in the qualitative study cited above, anecdotal information from the focus group participants supported the notion that at least for this specific sample, Latinos equated being diabetic "with eating too many carbohydrates, e.g., refined sugar and sweets, and needing to be on a diet." Thus, patients may be encouraged by family and friends to skip meals with the goal of decreasing their caloric intake. This can precipitate a serious medical crisis such as a hypoglycemic reaction in the diabetic patient and increase the caregiving demands for the caregiver. Another example of a culture-bound belief expressed by the participants is that "injections of insulin cause blindness and need for amputations." Perhaps because Latinos are diagnosed with diabetes at a later stage, diabetes-related complications are already evident, and the initiation of insulin treatments is associated with the onset of serious complications. This could have deleterious effects on treatment compliance, resulting in increased morbidity and increased caregiver demands. Whether provision of timely, accurate information can dispel these and other ideas is yet to be determined empirically.

The focus in the previous section on diabetes is meant to illustrate the ways in which specific differences in morbidity can influence caregiving demands. Latinos are also susceptible to a broad range of diseases leading to functional disability such as heart disease, cancer, and stroke (Markides & Coreil, 1986; Mitchell, Stern, Haffner, Hazuda, & Patterson, 1990; U.S. Department of Health and Human Services, 1990), which also warrant further investigation into their effects on the well-being of the Latino caregiver. We would also like to note that for Anglo caregivers, dementing illnesses such as Alzheimer's disease constitute a major reason for caregiving and a central focus of study in the caregiving research literature (Light & Lebowitz, 1989) as will be noted in subsequent sections of this article. While ethnic differences in the rates of dementing illnesses have been examined, the rates for dementing illnesses in the Latino population are uncertain (Gurland, Wilder, Cross, Teresi, & Barrett, 1992). Clearly, more work is needed to establish the prevalence of dementing illnesses among the Latino population, the possible risk associated with Latino ethnicity and culture, and the effect on the experience of caregiving.

Functional Disability

In addition to differences in the types and nature of illnesses affecting older Latinos, the need for care due to illness may be more frequent among Latino older adults, and the obstacles delaying access to formal sources of care may be greater than those of the Anglo population. The need for long-term care appears to be greater among older Latinos as a result of their disadvantaged functional status: they report greater deficits in basic self-care activities (40 percent) than elderly people in general (23 percent), and in instrumental activities of daily living (54 percent vs 27 percent; Commonwealth Fund Commission, 1989). Latinos also have a higher incidence of restricted activity days (46.5 vs 38.7 for Anglos), and increased bed disability days (20.7 vs 12.9; see Villa et al., 1993; U.S. Select Committee on Aging, 1989). Furthermore, elderly Latinos report having been cared for by a family member following a hospitalization more frequently than the general elderly population (Commonwealth Fund Commission, 1989).

Although Latino elders report higher levels of impairment and a greater need for community-based services than the general population, the literature supports the conclusion that older Latinos under-utilize community-based, long-term care services (Greene &

Monahan, 1984; Torres, 1995; Wallace & Lew-Ting, 1992). Thus, past empirical efforts have shown that the Latino older adult has a lower functional status than the general population, requires higher levels of informal community care, and is less able to access and afford long-term care services when needed.

In summary, future research endeavors should test the hypothesis that caregivers of older Latinos may be facing special challenges in caregiving for an individual who is: a) at risk for specific diseases, such as diabetes and its numerous medical and psychosocial complications, b) disabled at an earlier age, and with a more severe form of the illness, c) afflicted with higher levels of functional disabilities, and d) less able to access long-term care services.

Appraisal of Stressors

Caregiving Burden

Ethnicity and culture can also influence the experience of caregiving vis-à-vis the culturally specific appraisals of the caregiving situation. While there is very little data on caregiver burden among Latinos per se, there exists a small yet growing empirical literature that compares how different cultural groups experience the strain or positive outcomes of caring for their functionally dependent elders. A study by Morycz and his associates (Morycz, Malloy, Bozich, & Martz, 1987) examined the differential impact of caregiving strain between Blacks and Whites in a sample of elderly patients from an urban geriatric assessment center. First, the data suggested that although ethnicity by itself made little difference in the amount and the experience of family burden between the Black and White groups studied, a significant interaction effect was found between ethnicity and care for a patient with a diagnosis of Alzheimer's disease: Black families were less burdened caring for a family member with dementia than were Whites and were much less likely than Whites to institutionalize a cognitively impaired family member. In fact, when the patient had Alzheimer's disease, only 12 percent of Blacks versus 82 percent of Whites institutionalized their family member.

Another important finding was that the two ethnic groups differed in terms of which caregiving tasks predicted burden. For example, Black caregivers were more burdened by the provision of assistance related to physical activities of daily living (ADLs; toileting, bathing, dressing, eating), while Whites experienced increased burden from the provision of instrumental activities of daily living, (IADLs; shopping, money management, taking medications, preparing meals). Morycz and his associates also reported that socioeconomic status, which is often confounded with ethnicity, was not a significant predictor of burden, but was a significant predictor of institutionalization in the Black sample. Thus for Blacks, having insufficient financial resources and social supports predicted the disposition to admit their family member to a nursing home. This finding may reflect the tendency for public support programs (e.g., Medicaid) to encourage institutional care by underfunding community-based, in-home care.

The finding that Blacks reported lower mean levels of burden than did Whites in the care of Alzheimer's disease patients was corroborated by two studies (Haley et al., 1996; Lawton, Rajagopal, Brody & Kleban, 1992) which found significant ethnic differences in caregiving appraisal between Blacks and Whites. In the work by Lawton et al. (1992), initial descriptive comparisons of means indicated that Black caregivers of Alzheimer's patients reported more favorable scores on traditional caregiving ideology, subjective burden, caregiving satisfaction, and caregiving as intrusion than White caregivers. When interactions were tested between background variables and ethnicity, it was found that the interaction terms of ethnicity by age and ethnicity by income significantly predicted caregiving burden and caregiving intrusion. First, older Black caregivers experienced less burden, while more burden was reported by White caregivers as their age increased. Second, higher income caregivers were more burdened than lower income caregivers in the Black sample, while Whites showed the reverse pattern. In terms of caregiving as an intrusion on life style, more highly educated Blacks reported intrusion than better educated Whites. A later study by Haley et al. (1996) showed that Black caregivers appraised caregiving as less stressful than did Whites and that this appraisal acted as a mediator of the relationship of race to lower depression. In other words, Blacks reported lower depression vis-à-vis their less distressed appraisals of the caregiving situation. The fact that intragroup as well as intergroup differences were found in terms of caregiver appraisal points to the need for formulating and testing hypotheses on interaction effects of age, income, education and other ethnic differences in the subjective caregiving experience of Latino caregivers. Such attention to subgroups of Latino caregivers can enrich our understanding of how caregiving may be appraised differently by those who are younger, better educated, and have higher incomes.

Research on Latino Caregivers

It is conceivable that ethnicity and culture may also help predict burden among other ethnic groups, including those of Latino origin. For example, in a cross-sectional comparative study, Valle, Cook-Gait, and Tazbaz (1993) found significant differences between Latino and Anglo caregivers to dementia-affected older adults living in the greater San Diego, California area in their reactivity to the caregiving role. The Latino sample ($n = 38$), which was mainly Mexican American, appeared to react more strongly than the Anglo sample ($n = 52$) both to the overall caregiving situation and to the overall tasks of caregiving, even though the caregiving responsibilities between both groups were similar. Not only did they report feeling generally more bothered, Latinos were more likely than the Anglos to report feeling bothered or upset by (a) such specific tasks as feeding, dressing, toileting, etc. and (b) the person's "problem" behaviors, such as hiding things and constantly reliving the past. No differences were found in response to "difficult or dangerous" behaviors such as incontinence, wandering, and combativeness.

Other research has supported the greater psychological distress in response to specific aspects of the caregiving context by Latino and Black caregivers (Cox & Monk, 1993; Hinrichsen & Ramírez, 1992; Mui, 1992;

Wykle & Segal, 1991). Cox and Monk (1990, 1993) undertook a comparative study of Latino ($n = 86$) and Black ($n = 76$) caregivers to dementia-affected older adults in New York City. Approximately half of the Latino sample was Puerto Rican and the remainder were from Cuba or Central or South America. The researchers found that Latino caregivers perceived their caregiving responsibilities to be a greater burden than did Blacks (mean scores on the Zarit Burden Interview of 36.6 and 23.4, respectively, which were roughly equal to that found for White samples in previous studies (30.8 and 33.6; Zarit, Reever, & Bach-Peterson, 1980; Zarit, Todd, & Zarit, 1986 respectively). It should be noted that the test of significant differences in levels of burden reported did not control for the degree of the older person's memory, behavior, and ADL impairment.

Empirical data available on the overall physical and mental health of Latino caregivers is limited and inconclusive. In a report based on statewide data about caregivers of brain-impaired adults served by the Caregiver Resource Centers in California, ethnic minority caregivers (the majority of whom were Latinos) were significantly more likely to be in fair to poor health than non-minorities (60 percent compared to 48 percent), and to report high levels of depressive symptomatology (73 percent vs 68 percent using a cutoff score of 16 on the Center for Epidemiological Studies Depression Scale [CES-D]; Friss, Whitlatch, & Yale, 1990). The researchers concluded that the ethnic minority caregivers were "younger, poorer, more likely to be in the labor force juggling multiple responsibilities, and in significantly worse physical and mental health" (p. 106).

Cox and Monk (1990) examined the caregiving experiences of Black and Latino families of dementia victims. Latino caregivers had significantly higher scores than Blacks on the CES-D (mean scores of 19.7 vs 9.74). In the only study found which compared both caregiving and noncaregiving Blacks and Whites, Haley and his associates (Haley et al., 1995) found that only White caregivers had elevated CES-D scores as well as similar patterns for psychological distress. Black caregivers did not differ significantly from either Black or White noncaregivers.

Mintzer and his colleagues (Mintzer et al., 1992), found no significant differences in the level of depression between Cuban American and Anglo daughters of dementia patients living at home in the greater Miami, Florida area. In a Santa Clara County, California study, Yañiz (1990) interviewed Latino caregivers of both physically and dementia-affected elderly and found that 40 percent of the Latino caregiver sample had CES-D scores in the clinical range. Valle et al. (1993) found significant differences in self-reported health, with Latino caregivers reporting lower perceived health than the Anglo caregivers. On the other hand, no significant differences were found in depression as measured by the CES-D.

Generalizability from the studies cited is limited due to nonrandom sampling, small sample size, and possible cultural biases of the CES-D. The use of the CES-D in Latino populations at times has resulted in exaggerated scores among Latinos, especially among groups characterized as poor, less educated, Spanish-speaking, and female (Aneshensel, Clark, & Frerichs, 1983; Roberts, 1980; Taussig, Harris, Cervantes, & Rosin, 1995; Vega, Kolody, & Valle, 1986; Vega, Warheit, Buhl-Auth, & Meinhardt, 1984), yet reasons for the elevated scores are still being debated. The existing research indicates that Latino caregivers experience significantly poorer health than their Anglo counterparts, while the data supporting differences in psychological distress is equivocal. It can be hypothesized that Latino caregivers experience at least similar and possibly higher levels of burden and depression as compared to Anglos.

It is important to note that the studies on Latino caregivers to date have been exploratory and based on relatively small, cross-sectional, convenience samples. The degree of representativeness and generalizability is therefore compromised. Future work should build on these previous efforts by utilizing larger, randomly selected samples in different regions of the U.S. and measured over time.

Differential Appraisal of Stressors Among Latinos

The issue of cultural differences in the perception of stressful events outside of the realm of caregiving per se has been examined in Latino populations. These studies have indirect implications for the appraisal of caregiving stress by Latinos. Cervantes and Castro (1985) reviewed studies from the life change event literature, which has implications for ethnic differences in the appraisal of stressful situations. One study, which utilized the Social Readjustment Rating Scale, looked at the difference between Mexican Americans, Blacks and Anglos in their assessment of the amount of adaptation required by certain life change events (Komaroff, Masuda, & Holmes, 1968). Overall, Blacks gave the life change items higher stress ratings than the other two groups, which may be explained by the lower rating given by Blacks to the criterion item of "getting married." The converse was true for Mexican Americans who responded with lower stress ratings for all other items than the criterion item of "getting married." As summarized by Cervantes and Castro, marriage may have been perceived as requiring more adjustment because of its concomitant changes in the family and extended kinship network.

Whether caregiving for a functional dependent older adult would also carry a higher stress rating by Latinos due to changes in that familial support network is still unclear and in need of empirical testing. As noted earlier, Latino caregivers for demented relatives appear to have levels of burden and depression that are higher than Black caregivers and equal to Whites. The processes that lead to these levels of distress might result from distinct appraisals of the nature and scope of caregiving. Empirical examination of the relative importance of caregiving life events and the appraisal of their benefits and/or consequences is clearly needed.

Another study examined differences between Mexican-origin respondents and Anglos in their perception of the change required on 95 specific life events (see Hough, 1985; Hough, McGarvey, Graham, & Timbers, 1981). The El Paso-Ciudad Juarez border area study found that the Mexican-origin sample (i.e., sample comprised of Mexican nationals in Ciudad Juarez and Mexican-origin Latinos living in El Paso) tended to rate events as requiring significantly more change if the event involved social advancement, e.g., social, economic, and geographic mobility. Anglos rated higher those events which involved negative social interactions within the nuclear family but not of others outside the immediate family, e.g., death of spouse, marital separation or divorce rated as of more concern to them than functional or instrumental events. It may be that changes in upward economic and geographic mobility may reflect "a move out of the larger social structure upon which the Mexican respondents depend and live and thus represent a crucial disruption of that support structure" (Hough, 1985; p. 117), which is less true of the social environment of other Anglo groups. It is unclear whether the same results would hold in other regions of the U.S. or with other Latino-origin groups.

Hough and his associates (Hough, 1982; Hough, McGarvey, Graham, & Timbers, 1981; Hough, 1985) in a follow-up survey, found that Mexican-origin respondents on both sides of the El Paso-Ciudad Juarez border area reported more illness symptoms if the event occurred to significant others in their environment. In this sample, those Mexicans living in Ciudad Juarez were more likely to be distressed by events happening to others than to themselves as compared to both Anglos and the Mexican Americans living on either side of the border. Perhaps, as summarized by Cervantes and Castro (1985)

> extended social support networks are of much greater importance for Mexicans relative to Anglo respondents and that the disruption of these networks is associated with a greater expression of illness by Mexicans. Such an explanation is consistent with the ratings by Mexican respondents that migratory and social mobility life events require more change since such events would obviously be disruptive of extended family networks. (p. 23)

Further attempts at analyzing the differential appraisals of life change events, their direct and indirect effects on the individual, and their examination across subgroups of

Latinos are sorely needed. However, the work summarized by Cervantes & Castro would seem to indicate that group differences in the appraisal of life change events may be due to ethnic and cultural background. Latino caregivers of frail elderly persons may be likely to experience the relative's illness as more distressing if it requires reorganization or relocation of the family system. It is also likely that the distress may reach beyond the "primary caregiver." If so, differences in culture and its associated world view between these groups and those Mexican Americans living further into the interior of the U.S. as well as those of later generation Latinos must be examined. Thus, key hypotheses requiring further testing are: a) Among Latinos, the family system, rather than a designated primary caregiver, is at risk of emotional distress and physical illness; b) Such factors as socioeconomic status, acculturation, and geographical and generational differences are likely predictors of the perception of life change events; and c) The relative importance attributed to caregiving in relation to other change events can be explained in part by the perception of the consequences to the existing social networks and the fulfillment of cultural norms and filial responsibilities.

Social Support From the Family

Care provided by family and friends, or what has been termed the informal support system, continues to be the traditional source of assistance for elderly persons even today. Previous writers have discussed Latino natural support structures and their viability for providing assistance during acute enduring stress (Becerra & Shaw, 1984; Bengtson, 1979; Sotomayor & Randolph, 1988; Valle & Vega, 1980). There is reason to believe that Latino social structures are at least as supportive as those of the mainstream culture, although many have criticized the over-romanticization of the Latino family (Korte, 1982; Leonard, 1967; Maldonado, 1975; Mendes de Leon & Markides, 1988; Rubel, 1966). In any case, most writers are in agreement that the Latino kinship network is an important source of social support for the Latino older adult and a key mediator of

stressful life events (Bastida, 1988; Cantor, 1979; Carp, 1969; Dowd & Bengtson, 1979; Sotomayor & Applewhite, 1988; Sotomayor & Randolph, 1988; Szapocznik & Hernández, 1988; Torres-Gil, 1978; Valle & Mendoza, 1978). However, special attention must be given to variations in social support: variation as a result of ethnic memberships in specific subgroups of Latinos, and as a result of multiple network members' exposure to caregiving events. The following review is based on social support provided solely by the informal support system comprised of spouses, children, and other relatives, in contrast to quasi-formal and formal support provided by civic and religious groups and government and private programs.

Latino older adults do rely on family members for functional support following health-related crises. For example, in a randomized national survey of 2,299 elderly Mexican Americans, Cuban Americans, and Puerto Ricans living in the U.S. (Commonwealth Fund Commission, 1989), evidence was found to corroborate previous studies and anecdotal accounts that elderly Latinos rely more heavily on informal sources of support after release from the hospital than they do on organized services: 77 percent of the Latino survey respondents with long-term impairments received help from a spouse or child, and only 14 percent cared for themselves. On the other hand, less than 60 percent of the general elderly population relied on family post-hospitalization support and up to 30 percent cared for themselves following hospitalization (Commonwealth Fund Commission, 1989; Louis Harris & Associates, 1987). Competing hypotheses to explain why older Latinos rely more on informal supports include cultural preferences, language limitations, and institutional exclusions. Hypothesis-driven empirical research is clearly needed to help clarify these complex issues relevant to the availability of and reliance on informal supports as well as the satisfaction with these supports.

Acculturation and Social Support

Subgroups of Latinos differ in terms of attitudes regarding support of the elderly. For example, groups that differ in terms of acculturation and recency of immigration play a role in the nature, quantity, and scope of social support from the Latino family. Acculturation refers to the process of cultural change resulting from continuous intergroup contact. In this change process, individuals whose primary cultural learning has been in one culture modify their beliefs, values, and behaviors and absorb the cultural behaviors and characteristic patterns of living from another host or mainstream culture. For example, Zuniga de Martínez (1980) reported on the attitudes of Mexican Americans in the San Diego area regarding support of the elderly and found that as acculturation increased, traditional attitudes regarding familial support of the aged decreased. Although beyond the scope of this article, more recent discussions on the dynamics of acculturation emphasize that acculturation does not occur along a simple continuum of traditional versus mainstream cultural norms, but is multidirectional and can occur differentially across several life domains, e.g., family, work, religion, etc. (Keefe & Padilla, 1987; Valle, 1989). In the Zuniga de Martínez study (1980), weakened reliance on the family was correlated with a departure from identification with Mexican cultural heritage, loss of contact with relatives in Mexico, longer U.S. residency, and English-language ability. Thus, Zuniga de Martínez posits that although Mexican culture is maintained by the closeness to Mexico for many Mexican Americans, for those most affected by acculturation processes, there will be a trend toward less familial support of elderly persons.

Immigration status and recency of immigration are approximate indices of acculturation factors that can potentially influence social support and social networks (Keefe, 1980; Keefe & Padilla, 1987; Sabogal, Marin, Otero-Sabogal, Marin, & Peréz-Stable, 1987). The preponderance of work in the area of Latino family relations has focused on the Mexican American experience, number of social ties, and the dynamics of the cultural value of familism. Keefe and her associates (Keefe, 1980; Keefe & Padilla, 1987) have found that usage of primary kin networks was positively correlated with generation level. Mexican Americans have the same cultural preference for interacting with relatives whether born in the U.S. or Mexico, but the potential number of local social ties increases with the length of stay in the U.S. Native-born individuals or immigrants living in the U.S. for an extended length of time can count on more primary and secondary kinship ties (Keefe & Padilla, 1987). Recent immigrants, on the other hand, may be vulnerable to stress given the geographical remoteness from their natural support networks in their country of origin. However, they may be held accountable by distant family members who have traditional notions on how the older adult should be cared for. Since these hypotheses have yet to be tested empirically, research is necessary in order to ferret out the effects of recency of immigration on the social networks and the experience of caregiving.

For Latinos, conflicts within the family may be indicative of stress due to variation in acculturation level across a) the multiple caregivers (the elder's spouse, adult children, siblings, other caregivers; b) the relevant life domains (family, work, school, religion, health, leisure); and c) the developmental family life cycle changes (child launching, retirement, death, and dying). To illustrate,

> Mr. Alarcón is originally from El Salvador and has been living in the U.S. for the past 20 years. The spouse of an Alzheimer's disease patient, Mr. Alarcón refused to give consent to his wife's physician for her brain to be autopsied upon death. According to Mr. Alarcón, such a procedure is considered offensive to the couple's long held cultural and religious beliefs. According to Mr. Alarcón, the body should be intact after death for the resurrection of the body into "el más allá" (the world after). Yet, he feels pressured by his more acculturated adult children to acquiesce to the request on grounds that it would provide more conclusive evidence regarding the diagnosis. He continues to express that respect for his wife's spiritual beliefs has greater primacy than obtaining information about the source of her memory loss. At times he feels both angry and guilty when his family accuses him of "being a stubborn, old-fashioned macho" (see Appendix, Note 2).

Other acculturation conflicts within the caregiving context can arise regarding who becomes identified as the primary caregiver, how serious is the impairment of the elder, which formal service or institution should be accessed for assistance, and when treatments should be implemented, to name only a few (Aranda, 1994). Indeed, more analytic efforts are needed to test the differential effects of acculturation on the perceived attitudes, availability of support, and enacted support toward care of elderly family members across Latino subgroups.

Familism and Social Support

Other researchers argue that Latinos hold familism values despite variations due to acculturation, recency of immigration, and sociodemographic variables (Sabogal et al., 1987; Keefe & Padilla, 1987). The cultural value of familism, or "a strong identification and attachment of individuals with their families (nuclear and extended), and strong feelings of loyalty, reciprocity and solidarity among members of the same family" (Sabogal et al., 1987, pp. 397-398), has been discussed in the literature and may have implications regarding family care for older Latinos.

Sabogal et al. (1987) measured familism values in a comparison sample of nonelderly Latinos in the San Francisco area (Mexican Americans, Cuban Americans, Puerto Ricans) and non-Latino Whites. The study identified three separate dimensions of familism and their relative resiliency to acculturation changes: 1) family obligations (the individual's perceived obligation to provide material and emotional support to the family), 2) perceived support from the family (the perception of family members as reliable providers of help and support to solve problems), and 3) the family as referent. Perceived support from the family showed the most resiliency to acculturation as compared to the other two dimensions. Nevertheless, even though the highly acculturated Latino groups' adherence to attitudes regarding family obligations and family as referents were lower than the low acculturated, they still had higher ratings than the non-Latino White group. The authors note that the results add support to the hypotheses that a) some familism values decrease in importance as acculturation and exposure to the U.S. culture increase, and b) the similarity in the level of adherence to familism values among the three Latino groups is consistent with the idea that familism is a central value for Latinos.

Ethnic differences in perceived caregiver availability were not supported in a San Antonio, Texas study using a random sample of young-old (65–74, years old) Mexican Americans (n = 309) and non-Latino Whites (n = 340; Talamantes, Cornell, Espino, Lichtenstein, & Hazuda, 1996). Also, there were no overall significant ethnic differences in perceived caregiver availability between Mexican Americans and non-Latino Whites in either middle- or upper-SES neighborhoods. Nevertheless, the authors report that the number of children modified ethnic differences in perceived caregiver availability among middle- and upper-SES Mexican Americans and non-Latino Whites, such that, among those with two or fewer children, Mexican Americans were more likely to have a perceived available caregiver. Conversely, among those with three or more children, Mexican Americans were less likely to report caregiver availability than non-Latino whites. In summary, future research must examine the complex cultural dimensions that influence social support-as-mediator of stress and the intragroup differences potentially influenced by acculturation and its correlates, i.e., recency of immigration, generational status, place of birth, language preference.

The study of informal social supports and social networks goes beyond the scope of consanguine ties and may help us understand the complexity of Latino network configurations (Talamantes et al., 1996; Valle et al., 1989). One dementia study commissioned by the federal Office of Technology Assessment (Valle et al., 1989), explored the social network/caregiver configuration of dementia-affected ethnic minority elderly from four groups: American Indian, Japanese Americans, African Americans and Latinos. Close to one-third of the primary caregivers sampled were "non-kin," such as friends, neighbors, and paid personal care workers. While Black caregivers had the highest rate of friends and neighbors, Latinos reported the highest rate of paid homemakers. Valle and his colleagues suggested that multiple network actors may mean a form of task distribution across caregivers and/or the absorption of more persons into the attendant stressors of caregiving. The stronger likelihood of relying on non-family caregivers has been found to increase as more children are present for young-old Mexican Americans in the San Antonio, Texas area (Talamantes et al., 1996). Although the family is still the primary category of caregiving individuals for Latinos, the idea that paid personal care workers may have a role in the caregiving of elder Latinos has not been addressed in the literature. It is still unclear, however, which factors influence the absorption of non-kin persons and personal care workers into the Latino family system and to what extent culture may exert a role.

Clearly, in other studies, non-kin caregivers were more prominent in Black samples (Lawton et al., 1992) as compared to their Anglo counterparts, which may indicate a greater tendency toward inclusiveness in the caregiving role of individuals outside the primary kin network. This inclusivity may extend toward paid homemakers or attendants who may be regarded as part of the family system as well. Future work should focus on comparing different population groups on the inclusivity of social networks to include nonconsanguine members, the type of care provided by these members in contrast to blood kin, the relative importance of each in mediating caregiving stress, and the realms of decision making (legal, financial, ethical) across these two types of kinship networks. Current models of informal support in caregiving are implicitly rooted in Anglo cultural norms and may place too much emphasis on nuclear family, blood ties, and the primary caregiver roles when applied to other cultures.

Coping Attitudes and Behaviors

Once the event is appraised as being stressful, the choice of specific types of coping may also be determined by the individual or group's previous coping experiences. The idea that caregivers differ in their coping at-

titudes and behaviors is not a new notion, yet few studies focus on the role of ethnicity and culture in explaining possible variations. An important exception is Haley et al. (1996) in which Blacks were found to use both less approach and less avoidance coping than White caregivers, a difference which the authors attributed to the lower appraisal of caregiving as a stressor. Valle and his associates (1993), studied the coping styles of Latino (mostly Mexican American) and Anglo caregivers in San Diego and found that significant differences remained in several categories after controlling for contextual variables such as age, income, and education: Latinos were less prone to talking about their situation or sharing their private feelings; they were less likely to obtain professional help; tended to keep others from knowing how bad things were with regard to their caretaking situation; and relied more on their faith or praying about their problems. Turning to one's religious faith has also been supported in studies of Black caregiver samples (Segall & Wykle, 1988-89; Wood & Parham, 1990).

Cultural definitions of the self may also influence the choice of coping behaviors. Landrine (1992) contrasts the "indexical" meaning of the self that is common among non-Western cultures (including U.S. American ethnic cultural minorities), with the Western "referential" concept of the self. She argues that

> the referential self of Western culture is construed as an autonomous entity . . . presumed to be a free agent . . . to make all sorts of choices and decisions of its own . . . construed as determining the actions—the behaviors—of the body in the world. The self is unconsciously assumed to be morally responsible: The self in Western culture is the final explanation for behavior, and is responsible for behavior. It is taken for granted that the self will claim responsibility for its actions and for the consequences of its actions in the world. (p. 404)

Using Landrine's definition, we can expect that the individual with this orientation will more likely rely on coping behaviors geared toward self-fulfillment, self-development, and self-actualization. In this process, Landrine argues, the self seeks to control its environment by changing situations and others to meet one's needs. Failure to take control and further the self is construed as a failure and a sign of helplessness, passivity, low self-efficacy, and poor self-esteem. This has implications for the caregiving role to the degree that the individual with a referential self-orientation may perceive the caregiving experience as a threat to his sense of control which then threatens the definition of an independent selfhood.

Conversely, non-Western cultures define the self as embedded in social roles and less likely to view individual control of others and situations as part of his or her coping repertoire. The indexical self of many U.S. ethnic cultural groups is seen as

> . . . constituted by social interaction, contexts, and relationships. . . . Because the indexical self exists only in and through interactions, it cannot be described per se, without reference to specific, concrete encounters with others. Thus, the indexical self has no enduring, trans-situational characteristics, no traits or desires or needs of its own in isolation from its relationships and contexts . . . the person is the role he or she occupies because family and community are prior to individuals. Families and communities—rather than individuals—have goals, desires, and needs. . . . Thus, these social-role-selves do not have rights (to privacy, autonomy, and self-determination), but duties and obligations to perform their role well for the larger units. . . . Role failure or violation is the loss of the self . . . the self tends to be seen as not responsible for behavior. (Landrine, 1992, pp. 406–408)

Thus, if the sociocentric self consists of different persons and forces (natural and supernatural), the individual may perceive that he or she has less control over actions and circumstances as determined by fate, God, spirits, and the social group. This self-concept would lead to different role-actualizing responses than the responses that are dictated by a Western notion of an independently existing self. Instead, behaviors toward self-fulfillment and self-actualization take on a new meaning: self-actualizations occur in social contexts or for the good of the group or ancestral family. Thus, Landrine's argument coupled with the previously discussed findings that Latinos may be more sensitive to network crises and disruption, pose certain possibilities: Does caregiving for a frail, functionally dependent older adult directly affect the socially-embedded self, the use of coping attitudes and behaviors, and the evaluation of success or failure in the role of caregiving? Does the absence of need to control situations and people give the caregiver the freedom to continue in the caregiving role by attenuating the pressures of responsibility for those things not under his or her control, and thus, experiencing less self-doubt and sense of failure?

Culture, Socioeconomic Status, and Minority Group Membership: A Cautionary Note

Sorting ethnic and cultural variables from other status variables is problematic given the underclass position and minority group status of certain ethnic groups in the U.S. (Valle, 1989). Many differences in stress outcomes among certain cultural groups can be attributed to socioeconomic and minority group status factors. Culture, as defined earlier, refers to a group's way of life as manifested by those elements of the group's history, tradition, values, and social organization that are meaningful to the individual members. For example, U.S. Anglos represent a number of diverse and distinct ethnic origins. Yet, certain non-Anglo groups, because of their shared cultural values and/or physical characteristics, are stigmatized, deemed inferior. and barred from equal access to power in U.S. society; thus they are considered a disadvantaged ethnic minority group (Greene, 1994). Historically, these groups have been identified as Blacks/African Americans, Asian Americans/Pacific Islanders, Latinos/Hispanics, and Native Americans/American Indians. Although disadvantaged minority group status is often intertwined with membership in ethnic groups, it is conceptually distinct as evidenced by the fact that many cultural groups are not presently identified as disadvantaged minority group members although they may have been in the past (groups of Irish, Italians, Eastern Europeans, etc.).

Latinos are considered an ethnic minority group in the U.S., which is partly evidenced by their disadvantaged status in the labor market. According to Bean and Tienda (1987), "most studies of ethnic variation in labor market position acknowledge the importance of ascribed characteristics, such as birthplace, national origin and race in determining the employment opportunities of non-white people (p. 282)." One result of ethnic stratification in labor market processes is the over-representation of Latino workers in unskilled and service jobs across the U.S. (Bean & Tienda, 1987). This has implications for Latino caregivers of functionally disabled older adults. For example, occupational role strain, which has been identified as a source of caregiving stress (Pearlin et al., 1990), may be greater among Latino caregiving families who are not covered by employee benefits such as sick leave, dependent leave, compensatory time, or even time off during the day to make phone calls related to the care of the elderly person. Such employee benefits can alleviate some of the cross-pressures of reconciling work and caregiving responsibilities. To illustrate, caregivers employed in the garment industry may get paid on a piecework basis which provides a built-in disincentive to take time off from work. Seasonal migrant workers do not have the physical, on-the-job amenities (e.g., access to telephones) to facilitate dialogue with formal care agencies and services which are frequently inaccessible during evening hours.

On the other hand, culture may have a beneficial impact on well-being, especially for the aged (Simic, 1985). If true for Latino caregivers, this effect may counterbalance in part the stresses of caregiving. For example, although clearly not conclusively settled at this time, the evidence cited in this review suggests that the effects of disadvantaged minority group status are outweighed by other factors for Blacks. To illustrate, in the Lawton et al. study (1992), Black caregivers tended to be less burdened than Whites even though they were disadvantaged economically and

educationally, while more advantaged Blacks reported more burden. This finding is reminiscent of Burnam's data indicating that higher levels of acculturation for Latinos are associated with higher six-month and lifetime prevalence rates of mental disorder. Also, U.S.-born Mexican Americans, who tended to have high levels of acculturation, experienced higher lifetime psychiatric prevalence rates than their immigrant counterparts (Burnam, Hough, Karno, Escobar, & Telles, 1987).

The effects of discrimination and oppression could also have far-reaching implications for the development of certain coping expectancies. For example, the choice of specific types of coping may also be determined by the individual or group's previous coping experiences. For U.S.-based ethnic minorities, the socio-historical-political realities may influence the coping strategies developed over time, such as perceived fatalism as an adaptive response to the severe stress faced by disadvantaged minorities and as enhancing self-efficacy in effecting positive outcomes (Varghese & Medinger, 1979). Varghese and Medinger propose that fatalism, or a generalized expectancy for external control of reinforcement in the form of fate, chance, or other forces outside the individual's control, may protect a person "from the severe depression and anxiety that would ensue were he or she to assume complete personal responsibility for the stressful, poverty-related circumstances present in his/her life (p. 96)." Thus, perceived fatalism over threatening circumstances may be functional given the socially imposed gaps in resources that exist for the Latino caregiver to counter these circumstances.

Further research is needed to analyze the confounding effects of ethnicity and culture, socioeconomic class, and minority group status and to clarify the relative contributions of each to be tested in predicting well-being among Latino caregiver groups. Key hypotheses can address how ethnicity and culture are likely to a) influence the differential risk for specific disorders and disability, b) affect the appraisal of illness and problem behaviors, c) influence coping attitudes and behaviors, d) set expectations regarding social support and filial care, and e) provide larger social networks of both kin and non-kin helpers. On the other hand, to the extent that caregiving Latinos are disadvantaged socioeconomically and subordinated within the larger society, caregiving is predicted to be complicated by lower income and education, restricted access to health care and employment benefits, and by institution-based exclusions from long-term care programs and services.

Summary: Ethnicity, Stress, and Coping

In summary, the stress and coping model has provided a framework for reviewing literature related to caregiving in the Latino population. This literature suggests that Latino caregivers are as distressed as are Anglo caregivers. In part, the sources and types of incapacity may be different since Latinos suffer from different chronic medical diseases. Rates of functional dependency are higher for Latinos as well. We have also seen that ethnicity and culture can influence whether cognitive impairment or physical impairment is perceived as being stressful between Blacks and Whites. It is hypothesized that caregiving may be compared to a different life event anchor point and evaluated differently by Latinos, specifically as it impacts on the social network. As a corollary, appraisal of stress in the Latino population may depend on the degree of disruption to the family rather than on the interference with the individual's perceived control over life circumstances. Latino social networks are likely to be larger, composed of more multigenerational households, extended family, and non-kin "family," including personal care workers. We hypothesize that these larger networks also lead to greater exposure to other stressors with the likelihood of receiving support from the network over time being unclear at this time. Another hypothesis is that social support from family may function differently from that among Anglos with the family members/systems acting as caregivers and experiencing distress. We would also hypothesize that coping behaviors differ, with less emphasis on control and greater emo-

tional regulation, although more evidence on specific differences is needed.

Empirical examination of the determinants of caregiver reactions and coping among ethnic minority groups is clearly in its infancy stage. Illustrations of caregiving by Latino families to older adults provide provocative areas of inquiry into potential sources of variation in the caregiving experience of other U.S. ethnic groups. As noted throughout this article, many conceptual and methodological issues remain. Future research must also focus on improvements in sampling, research design, and standardization of major study variables.

As service programs begin to address the growing ethnic and cultural diversity of this country (Aranda, 1990), there is a pressing need for cross-cultural research on caregiving to examine possible ethnic and cultural differences in terms of the illnesses which cause frailty and disability, the appraisal of stressors, and the use of specific coping behaviors and social support systems in moderating the impact of stressors. Such research is likely to show that ethnic and cultural differences affect many aspects of caregiving. Education, policy, and service delivery must address these differences using sound empirical research so that policies and programs are based on actual differences rather than assumptions, stereotypes, or the inappropriate generalizations of existing paradigms to other culturally distinct groups.

Discussion Questions

1. What morbidity patterns are found among Latino elders and how do specific diseases, such as diabetes, affect both hands-on caregiving and cultural beliefs about appropriate treatments for the elderly?

2. Social support is an important factor in relieving caregiver stress; paradoxically, larger social networks may lead to greater exposure to stress. Given the evidence presented in this selection, explain this apparently contradictory set of findings.

3. Describe the multidirectional nature of acculturation and its relationship to social support.

4. Different cultures have different definitions of the self that impact behavior. How may definition of the self as "referential" or as "sociocentric" affect caregiving and caregiver stress?

References

American Diabetes Association. (1989). *Complications of diabetes*. Alexandria, VA: American Diabetes Association.

Aneshensel, C. S., Clark, V. A., & Frerichs, R. R. (1983). Race, ethnicity, and depression: A confirmatory analysis. *Journal of Personality and Social Psychology, 44*, 385–398.

Aranda, M. P. (1990). Culture friendly services for Latinos. *Generations, 14*, 55–57.

Aranda, M. P. (1994, July). *The clinical/cultural assessment: Areas of inquiry for ethnic minority populations*. Paper presented at the Third Annual Education Conference of the National Alzheimer's Association, Chicago, IL.

Aranda, M. P., & Galvan, F. (1993). *The role of culture and SES on the utilization of health and social services: A focus group analysis of older Mexican Americans*. Unpublished manuscript, University of California, School of Social Welfare, Los Angeles.

Bastida, E. (1988). Reexamining assumptions about extended familism: Older Puerto Ricans in a comparative perspective. In M. Sotomayor & H. Curiel (Eds.), *Hispanic elderly: A cultural signature* (pp. 163–183). Edinburg, TX: Pan American University Press.

Baxter, J., Hamman, R. F., Lopez. T. K., Marshall, J. A., Hoag, S., & Swenson, C. J. (1993). Excess incidence of known non-insulin-dependent diabetes mellitus (NIDDM) in Hispanics compared with non-Hispanic whites in the San Luis Valley, Colorado. *Ethnicity and Disease, 3*, 11–21.

Bean F. D., & Tienda, M. (1987). *The Hispanic population of the United States: The population of the United States in the 1980's*. New York: Russell Sage Foundation.

Becerra, R. M., & Shaw, D. (1984). *The Hispanic elderly. A research reference guide* (2nd ed.). New York: Academic Press.

Bengtson, V. (1979). Ethnicity and aging: Problems and issues in current social science inquiry. In D. Gelfand & A. Kutzik (Eds.), *Ethnicity and aging* (pp. 9-31). New York: Springer.

Burnam, M. A., Hough, R. L., Karno, M., Escobar, J. I., & Telles, C. A. (1987). Acculturation and lifetime prevalence of psychiatric disorders among Mexican Americans in Los Angeles. *Journal of Health and Social Behavior, 28*, 89–102.

Cantor, M. (1979). The informal support system of New York's inner city elderly: Is ethnicity a factor? In D. Gelfand & A. Kutzik (Eds.), *Ethnicity and aging: Theory, research and policy* (pp. 153–174). New York: Springer.

Carp, R. M. (1969). Housing and minority group elderly. *The Gerontologist, 9*, 20–24.

Cervantes, R. C., & Castro, F. G. (1985). Stress, coping, and Mexican American mental health: A systematic review. *Hispanic Journal of Behavioral Sciences, 7*(l), 1–73.

Commonwealth Fund Commission. (1989). *Poverty and poor health among elderly Hispanic Americans*. Baltimore, MD: The Commonwealth Fund Commission on Elderly People Living Alone.

Cox, C., & Monk, A. (1990). Minority caregivers of dementia victims: A comparison of black and Hispanic families. *The Journal of Applied Gerontology, 9*, 340–354.

Cox, C., & Monk, A. (1993). Hispanic culture and family care of Alzheimer's patients. *Health and Social Work, 18*, 92–99.

Dowd, J., & Bengtson. V. (1978). Aging in minority populations: An examination of the double jeopardy hypothesis. *Journal of Gerontology, 33*, 427–436.

Folkman, S., Lazarus, R. J., Pimley, S., & Novacek, J. (1987). Age differences in stress and coping processes. *Psychology and Aging, 2*, 171–184.

Friss, L., Whitlatch, C. J., & Yale, R. (1990). *Who's taking care? A profile of California's family caregivers of brain-impaired adults*. San Francisco: The Family Survival Project.

Gordon, M. (1964). *Assimilation in American Life*. New York: Oxford University Press.

Greene, R. (1994). *Human behavior theory: A diversity framework*. New York: Aldine de Gruyter.

Greene, V. L, & Monahan, D. J. (1984). Comparative utilization of community based long-term care services by Hispanic and Anglo elderly in a case management system. *The Journals of Gerontology, 39*, 730–735.

Gurland, B. J., Wilder, D. E., Cross, P., Teresi, J., & Barrett V. W. (1992). Screening scales for dementia: Toward reconciliation of conflicting findings. *International Journal of Geriatric Psychiatry, 7*, 105–113.

Haley, W. E., West, C. A. C., Wadley, V. G., Ford, G. R., White, F. A., Barrett, J. S., Harrell, L. E., & Roth, D. L. (l995). Psychological, social, and health impact of caregiving: A comparison of black and white dementia family caregivers and noncaregivers. *Psychology and Aging, 10,* 540–552.

Haley, W. E., Roth, D. L., Coleton, M. I., Ford, G. R., West, C. A. C., Collins, R. P., & Isobe, T. L. (1996). Appraisal, coping, and social support as mediators of well-being in black and white family caregivers of patients with Alzheimer's disease. *Journal of Consulting and Clinical Psychology, 64,* 121–129.

Hamman, R. F., Marshall, J. A., Baxter, J., Kahn, L. B., Mayer, E. J., Orleans, M., Murphy, J. R., & Lezotte, D. C. (1989). Methods and prevalence of non-insulin-dependent diabetes mellitus in a biethnic Colorado population. *American Journal of Epidemiology, 129,* 295–311.

Hanis, C., Farrell, R. E., Barton, S. A., Aguilar, L., Garza-Ibarra, A., Tulloch, B. R., Garcia, C. A., & Schull, W. J. (1983). Diabetes among Mexican-Americans in Star County. *American Journal of Epidemiology, 118,* 659–672.

Hazuda, H., Haffner, S., Stern, M., & Eifler, C. (1988). Effects of acculturation and socioeconomic status on obesity and diabetes in Mexican Americans. *American Journal of Epidemiology, 128,* 1289–1301.

Hazuda, H. P., Stern, M. P., & Haffner, S. M. (1988). Acculturation and assimilation among Mexican Americans: Scales and population-based data. *Social Science Quarterly, 69,* 687–706.

Hinrichsen, G. A., & Ramírez, M. (1992). Black and white dementia caregivers: A comparison of their adaptation, adjustment, and service utilization. *The Gerontologist, 32,* 375–381.

Hough, R. L (1985). Life events and stress in Mexican American culture. In W. A. Vega & M. R. Miranda (Eds.), *Stress and Hispanic mental health: Relating research to service delivery* (pp. 110–146). Rockville, MD: U.S. Department of Health and Human Services.

Hough, R. L., McGarvey, W., Graham, J., & Timbers, D. (1981). *Cultural variation in the modeling of life change-illness relationships.* Working paper, Life Change and Illness Research Project. Neuropsychiatric Institute, University of California, Los Angeles.

Keefe, S. E. (1980). Acculturation and the extended family among urban Mexican Americans. In A. M. Padilla (Ed.). *Acculturation: Theory, models, and some new findings* (pp. 85–110). Boulder, CO: Westview, Press.

Keefe, S. E., & Padilla, A. M. (1987). *Chicano ethnicity.* Albuquerque: NM: University of New Mexico Press.

Komaroff, A. L., Masuda, M., & Holmes, T. H. (1968). The social readjustment rating scale: A comparative study of Negro, Mexican, and white Americans. *Journal of Psychosomatic Research, 12,* 121–128.

Korte, A. O. (1982). Social interaction and morale of Spanish-speaking rural and urban elderly. *Journal of Gerontological Social Work, 4,* 57–66.

Landrine. H. (1992). Clinical implications of cultural differences: The referential versus the indexical self. *Clinical Psychology Review, 12,* 401–415.

Lawton, M. P., Moss, M., Kleban, M. H., Glicksman, A., & Rovine, M. (1991). A two-factor model of caregiving appraisal and psychological well-being. *Journal of Gerontology Psychological Sciences, 46,* P181–Pl89.

Lawton, M. P., Rajagopal, D., Brody, E., & Kleban, M. H. (1992). The dynamics of caregiving for a demented elder among black and white families. *Journal of Gerontology: Social Sciences, 47,* S156–Sl64.

Lazarus, R. S., & Folkman, S. (1984a). Coping and adaptation. In W. D. Gentry (Ed.) *The handbook of behavioral medicine* (pp. 282-325). New York: Guilford.

Lazarus, R. S., & Folkman, S. (1984b). *Stress, appraisal, and coping.* New York: Springer.

Leonard, O. (1967). The older rural Spanish people of the Southwest. In E. Youmans (Ed.), *Older rural Americans* (pp. 239–261). Lexington, KY: University of Kentucky Press.

Light, E., & Lebowitz, B. D. (1989). *Alzheimer's disease treatment and family stress: Directions for research.* Rockville, MD: U.S. Department of Health and Human Services.

Louis Harris and Associates, Inc. (1987). *Problems facing elderly Americans living alone.* New York: Report for The Commonwealth Fund Commission on Elderly People Living Alone.

Maldonado, D. (1975). The Chicano aged. *Social Work, 20,* 213–216.

Markides, K. S., & Coreil, J. (1986). The health of Hispanics in the southwestern United States: An epidemiologic paradox. *Public Health Reports, 101,* 253–265.

Marshall, J. A., Hamman, R. F., Baxter, J., Mayer, E. J., Fulton, D. L., Orleans, M., Rewers, M., & Jones, R. H. (1993). Ethnic differences in risk factors associated with the prevalence of non-insulin-dependent diabetes mellitus. *American Journal of Epidemiology, 137,* 706–718.

McGarvey, W., Hough, R., Timbers. D., & Graham, J. (1981). *Sex and age variations in the modeling of life change-illness relationships*. Working paper, Life Change and Illness Research Project. Neuropsychiatric Institute, University of California, Los Angeles.

Mindel, C. H., Habenstein, R. W., & Wright, Jr., R. (1988). Family lifestyles of America's ethnic minorities: An introduction. In C. H. Mindel, R. W. Habenstein, & R. Wright, Jr. (Eds.), *Ethnic families in America* (3rd ed.) New York: Elsevier.

Mendes de Leon, C., & Markides, K. (1988). Depressive symptoms among Mexican Americans: A three generation study. *Journal of Epidemiology, 127*, 150–160.

Mintzer, J. E., Rubert, M. P., Loewenstein, D., Gámez, E., Millor, A., Quinteros, R., Flores, L., Miller, M., Rainerman, A., & Eisdorfer, C. (1992). Daughters caregiving for Hispanic and non-Hispanic Alzheimer's patients: Does ethnicity make a difference? *Community Mental Health Journal, 28*, 293–303.

Mitchell, B. D., Stern, M. P., Haffner, S. M., Hazuda, H. P., & Patterson, J. K. (1990). Risk factors for cardiovascular mortality in Mexican Americans and nonhispanic whites: The San Antonio Heart Study. *American Journal of Epidemiology, 131*, 423–433.

Morycz, R. K., Malloy, J., Bozich, M., & Martz, P. (1987). Racial differences in family burden: Clinical implications for social work. *Gerontological Social Work, 10*, 133–154.

Mui, A. (1992). Caregiver strain among black and white daughter caregivers: A role theory perspective. *The Gerontologist, 32*, 203–212.

Pearlin, L. I., Mullan, J. T., Semple, S. J., & Skaff, M. M. (1990). Caregiving and the stress process: An overview of concepts and their measures. *The Gerontologist, 30*, 583–594.

Pearlin, L. I., & Schooler, C. (1979). The structure of coping. *Journal of Health and Social Behavior, 19*, 2–21.

Poulshock, S. W., & Deimling, G. T. (1984). Families caring for elders in residence: Issues in the measurement of burden. *Journal of Gerontology, 39*, 230–239.

Pugh, J. A., Stern, M. P., Haffner, S. M., Eifler, C. W., & Zapata, M. (1988). Excess incidence of treatment of end-stage renal disease in Mexican Americans. *American Journal of Epidemiology, 127*(l), 135–143.

Roberts, R. E. (1980). Reliability of the CES-D scale in different ethnic contexts. *Psychiatry Research, 2*, 125–134.

Rubel, A. J. (1966). *Across the tracks: Mexican-Americans in a Texas city*. Austin, TX: The University of Texas Press.

Sabogal, F., Marin, G., Otero-Sabogal, R.. Marin, B. V. 0., & Peréz-Stable, E. J. (1987). Hispanic familism and acculturation: What changes and what doesn't? *Hispanic Journal of Behavioral Sciences, 9*, 397–412.

Schulz, R., Tompkins, C. A., & Rau, M. T. (1988). A longitudinal study of psychosocial impact of stroke on primary support persons. *Psychology and Aging, 3*, 131–141.

Segall, M., & Wykle, M. (1988-89). The black family's experience with dementia. *The Journal of Applied Social Sciences, 13*, 170–191.

Simic, A. (1985). Ethnicity as a resource for the aged: An anthropological perspective. *Journal of Applied Gerontology, 4*, 65–71.

Sotomayor. M., & Applewhite, S. (l988). The Hispanic elderly and the extended multigenerational family. In S. Applewhite (Ed.), *Hispanic elderly in transition* (pp. 90–104). New York: Greenwood Press.

Sotomayor, M., & Randolph, S. (1988). A preliminary review of caregiving issues and the Hispanic family. In M. Sotomayor & H. Curiel (Eds.), *Hispanic elderly: A cultural signature* (pp. 137–160). Edinburg, TX: Pan American University Press.

Szapocznik, J., & Hernández, R. (l988). The Cuban American family. In C. H. Mindel, R. W. Habenstein, & R. Wright, Jr. (Eds.), *Ethnic families in America* (3rd ed.; pp. 160–172). New York: Elsevier.

Talamantes, M., Cornell, J., Espino, D. V., Lichtenstein, M. J., & Hazuda, H. P. (1996). SES and ethnic differences in perceived caregiver availability among young-old Mexican Americans and Non-Hispanic Whites. *The Gerontologist, 36*, 88–99.

Taussig, I. M., Harris, J. N., Cervantes, O., & Rosin, D. (1995, August). *Measurement of the symptoms of depression: Comparisons of the utility of the Geriatric Depression Scale and the Center of Epidemiological Studies Depression Scale in the Spanish-speaking elderly population*. Paper presented at the 103rd Annual Convention of the American Psychological Association, New York.

Torres, M. S. (1995). *Accessibility and effectiveness of home- and community-based long-term care services used by Latino elderly*. Unpublished doctoral dissertation, University of Southern California, Los Angeles.

Torres-Gil, F. M. (1978). Age, health, and culture: An examination of health among Spanish-speaking elderly. In M. Montiel (Ed.), *Hispanic families: Critical issues for policy and programs in human services* (pp. 83–102). Washington, DC: National Coalition of Hispanic

Mental Health and Human Services Organizations.

U.S. Department of Health and Human Service. (1990). *Healthy people 2000: National health and promotion and disease prevention objectives (DHHS Publication No. PHS 91-50213).* Washington, DC: U.S. Government Printing Office.

U.S. Select Committee on Aging, House of Representatives. (1989). *Demographic characteristics of the older Hispanic population* (Comm. Pub. No. 100-696). Washington, DC: U.S. Government Printing Office.

U.S. Select Committee on Aging, House of Representatives. (1992). *Diabetes mellitus: An unrelenting threat to the health of minorities:* Hearing before the Select Committee on Aging, House of Representatives, 102nd Congress, 2nd Sess. (Comm. Pub. No. 102-864). Washington, DC: U.S. Government Printing Office.

Valle, R. (1989). Cultural and ethnic issues in Alzheimer's disease family research. In E. Light & B. D. Lebowitz (Eds.), *Alzheimer's disease treatment and family stress* (pp. 122–154). Rockville, MD: U.S. Department of Health and Human Services.

Valle, R., Cook-Gait, H., Tazbaz, D. (1993). *The cross-cultural Alzheimer' dementia caregiver comparison study.* Paper presented at the 46th Scientific Meeting of the Gerontological Society of America in New Orleans, LA.

Valle, R., & Mendoza, L. (1978). *The elder Latino.* San Diego: The Campanile Press.

Valle, R., & Vega, W. (Eds.). (1980). *Hispanic natural support systems: Mental health promotion perspectives.* Sacramento, CA: State of California, Department of Mental Health.

Varghese, R., & Medinger, F. (1979). Fatalism in response to stress among the minority aged. In D. Gelfand & A. Kutzik (Eds.), *Ethnicity and aging* (pp. 96–116). New York: Springer.

Vega, W. A., Warheit, G., Buhl-Auth. J., & Meinhardt, K. (1984). The prevalence of depressive symptoms among Mexican-Americans and Anglos. *American Journal of Epidemiology, 120,* 592–607.

Vega, W. A., Kolody, B., & Valle, R. (1986). Depressive symptoms and their correlates among immigrant Mexican women in the United States. *Social Science Medicine, 22,* 645–652.

Villa, M. L., Cuellar, J., Gamel, N., & Yeo, G. (1993). *Aging and health: Hispanic American elders* (3rd ed.). Stanford Geriatric Education Center Working Paper Series, Ethnogeriatric Reviews, No. 5. Stanford, CA: Stanford University.

Wallace, S., & Lew-Ting, C. (1992). Getting by at home: Community-based long-term care of the elderly. *The Western Journal of Medicine, 157,* 337–344.

Wood, J. B., & Parham, I. A. (1990). Coping with perceived burden: Ethnic and cultural issues in Alzheimer's family caregiving. *Journal of Applied Gerontology, 9,* 325–339.

Wykle, M., & Segal, M. (1991). A comparison of black and white family caregivers with dementia. *Journal of the National Black Nurses Association, 5,* 28–41.

Yañiz, M. J. (1990). *Geriatric assessment: Risks of functional disability, dementia, and depression among Hispanic elderly living at home with caregiver support.* Unpublished doctoral dissertation, Illinois Institute of Technology, Chicago.

Zarit, S. H. (1989). Issues and directions in family intervention research. In E. Light & B.D. Lebowitz (Eds.), *Alzheimer's disease treatment and family stress: Directions for research* (pp. 458–486). Rockville, MD: U.S. Department of Health and Human Services.

Zarit, S. H. (1994). Research perspectives on family caregiving. In M. H. Cantor (Ed.), *Family caregiving: Agenda for the future* (pp. 9–24). San Francisco: American Society on Aging.

Zarit, S. H., Reever, R., & Bach-Peterson, J. (1980). Relatives of impaired elderly: Correlates of feelings of burden. *The Gerontologist, 20,* 649–655.

Zarit, S., Todd, P., & Zarit, J. (1986). Subjective burden of husbands and wives as caregivers: A longitudinal study. *The Gerontologist, 26,* 260–266.

Zuniga de Martínez, M. (1980). *Los Ancianos: A study of the attitudes of Mexican Americans regarding support of the elderly.* Unpublished doctoral dissertation, Brandeis University, Waltham, Massachusetts.

APPENDIX

1. The term *Latino* is used here as an ethnic group label for several groups which share various commonalties such as Latin American origin, indigenous group ancestry, the Spanish language, religious and cultural values, etc. It is apparent that although many similarities exist, to some degree such a term sacrifices the individual identities of each Latino ethnic group comprised of its respective national and sociopolitical history, immigration patterns, class

structure, regional differences, customs and traditions, and the like.

2. The term *Macho*, as used in this stereotypical context, is the Spanish-language term given to patriarchal and male dominance in relationships and decision making. The original use of the word reflected a more positive view of male roles as encompassing honor, respect, and self-sacrifice for family members and others. The material for the vignette in which this term was used was taken from anecdotal accounts provided from the first author's clinical social work practice in the Los Angeles area.

Chapter 32
A Mother and Daughter

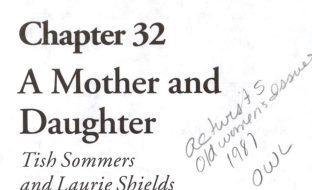

Tish Sommers
and Laurie Shields

An estimated 80 percent of informal care for frail and disabled older people is provided by family members, about three-fourths of it by women. There is a gender-linked hierarchy of caregiving, with wives most likely to provide hands-on care for a disabled spouse, followed by daughters, daughters-in-law, and other female relatives. Among aging couples, wives are almost twice as likely to be the primary caregiver, reflecting the greater life expectancy of women. Usually only when the spouse becomes incontinent is paid care sought. In the absence of a spouse or when the spouse is disabled, more hands-on care falls to daughters or other female relatives than to sons or male relatives. Males are more likely to provide financial management, household repairs, and other traditionally male forms of assistance. Not surprisingly, women report more stress associated with caregiving, as they are involved in more of the day-to-day physical care of an infirm elder than men are.

One aspect of care that has received attention is the "sandwich generation," people who find themselves caring for elderly parents while still caring for their own children. The following account, by Tish Sommers and Laurie Shields, both of whom have been leaders in calling attention to older women's issues, presents the experiences of two generations caring for an elderly relative. Dolores cared for her husband, who was dying with terminal cancer, until she became incapacitated; her daughter, Dorothy, then assumed the caregiver role despite pressing needs of her own family. This selection presents the perspective that women are likely to fall into "the compassion trap" where their gender-linked nurturing

skills make them more willing to take on demanding and often unrewarded caregiving. Socialized to be nurturers, they are trapped between a sense of obligation to spouse, parents, or other relatives and their own hopes for individuation and self-expression. As you read their experiences, pick out the major themes that emerge. Follow the sequence of events that led to Dorothy's participation in her father's care. Think critically about the role gender socialization played in the patterns of caregiving in this family. Consider the effects that caregiving had on Dolores' physical and mental health. Note effects that caregiving had on Dorothy's relationship with her brother and with her husband and children.

Dolores and Dorothy are a mother and daughter who cared for Dolores' husband (Dorothy's father) when he had terminal cancer. First, Dolores' story:

> My husband died at 75 of cancer, after a long and debilitating illness. It started as a prostate cancer, which surgery held in suspension for a few years, but it eventually developed into a widespread malignant invasion of his entire body. This process was spread over a period of eleven years, during which he had ups and downs. Gradually he turned into a bedridden invalid, totally dependent on me for his daily care.
>
> The last three years were the most demanding. I was 71 when he died. The last year was devastating; it became a 24-hour job and I got little sleep because of his extreme restlessness. The last few months of his life he was given Dilaudin, a morphine derivative, that caused him to have hallucinations. His sleeplessness caused my sleeplessness because he constantly called to me in his drug-laden state.
>
> My lack of sleep made deep inroads on my sense of reality. I have several gaps in my memory of that terrible time, probably because I was carrying on as I have been programmed to do, operating at full speed with vastly reduced amounts of energy. I doubt if I would have been able to last if my daughter hadn't been able to stay with us and help care for her father the last two months. What happened, however, is that there were now two of us who were going

without sleep, as my home is small and not soundproof. There was no escape from that constant and pathetic calling, "Honey. Honey. Honey, come and get me out of here."

I decided that he should die at home for several reasons. After his last short stay in the hospital, they said they had done all they could for him. The alternative of a nursing home seemed so unkind. It would have almost seemed inhuman. Even if I had been able to do it financially (which I was not), I would not have been able emotionally to let him die there alone. The care at nursing homes, while very expensive, is also uneven and unreliable. In some instances there is outright neglect. I could not do this to my husband. Throughout a long marriage, he had earned my love and respect. As long as I was still on my feet, I wanted to help him die.

I experienced emotional problems because I was coping with an unforeseen domestic crisis with a bare minimum of tools with which to solve it. Anxiety loomed large. At the last, the cancer destroyed the 7th nerve in his head, causing one eye to remain permanently open (it had to be bandaged shut). It also caused a malfunction of his jaw. He could not chew and could not wear his dentures. All his food had to be put through a blender so he had only to swallow it. As he got weaker, it became increasingly hard to get enough food down as I fed him. I became so afraid he was going to starve to death that on the few occasions when I could fall asleep, my sleep would turn into a nightmare that my husband was dying of starvation and I was to blame. I was never free of this free-floating anxiety.

Isolation was an important part of this stressful time. While I have what I consider good neighbors, I live in a rural area, and houses are not close. My neighbors are not the kind of people who "run in" as legends tell us rural people do. These people are all retired from large cities, where people tend to stay to themselves. They responded well when I asked, but I have a personal problem about asking for help. I have been socialized to remain independent as long as possible and this training does get in my way in a time of crisis.

The outstanding memory I have is of being abandoned by the institutions I formerly had a great deal of respect for. The last thing I remember of the hospital was being told they needed his bed and I was to take him out of there. No advice as to what I was to do with him, just take him away. By this time, I was beginning to suspect he was dying, although no one ever said as much to me.

I got no information from his doctor or the nurse in his office. I inadvertently heard of the Visiting Nurses Association from the alternate doctor in the office. The VNA saved what was left of my sanity by giving me information, as well as help three days a week. I was reassured that I was "doing it right." Also, they told me about *hospice*, which helped to give me (and eventually my daughter) occasional short respite times.

However, by the time I received this help, I was seriously near the breaking point myself. I had eye surgery just after my daughter came to help. My recovery has been very slow. My age has something to do with it, of course, but the emotional hurts of feeling lost and abandoned by society are not easily healed.

Like many caregivers, Dolores cared for her husband for a long time, and the demands on her accelerated as his condition worsened. Her story also illustrates some other common facets of the caregiving situation. She got little help or useful information from medical professionals, not even the information that her husband was dying. She was left to find services that could help on an almost random basis of luck.

She chose to provide care right up until the day of her husband's death, not wanting him to have to go to a nursing home. While there are good quality nursing homes, they are rare and, as Dolores notes, expensive. Many caregivers view them as the last possible resort; couples make pacts to avoid them. Many very stressed caregivers, like Dolores, simply refuse to consider the option.

Dolores' daughter, Dorothy, helped with her father's care for a much shorter period. Because her time as a caregiver was unexpected, she saw things much more sharply than did her mother. The experience was so deeply felt that five years later, as she told her story, she seemed to be reliving it. Dorothy's story:

> In April of 1981, at the request of my parents, I returned from Berlin, West Germany (where I was living with my husband and child) to help my parents during my mother's eye surgery, which she had needed for some time. I had planned to stay two weeks, until my mother was recovered enough to continue her long-term care of my father. I ended up staying two and a half months, until my father died.
>
> My mother's surgery went well, but my father's cancer got progressively worse day by day, right before my eyes. He was still eating well—although all the food had to be pureed—but he lost weight. He was, however, still able to get around by himself: to the bathroom, to the dinner table, and, occasionally, out on the beautiful deck surrounding their small home. Then, about three weeks after mother's surgery, his cancer began to spread fast throughout his body, causing him to become bedridden.
>
> When I first came, I became the caregiver for them both, with no respite. The emotional atmosphere of having two patients whom I loved very much, combined with the magnetic pull of my family back in Europe, was almost unbearable. The inconvenience was great for me. My parents and I discussed it many times, always coming up with the same answer: their need was greater than my inconvenience.
>
> My husband and our son, who was 17 years old, were left on their own in Germany during this desperate time in our lives. Our two daughters lived here in the states. One, 22, lived and worked in Sacramento, and the other, 19, was enrolled at San Francisco State University. It was a very stressful experience for all of us. As a family, we had always been close, no matter where we lived. Thank heaven for the telephone! We talked often, but the separation was traumatic. My parents lived in Penn Valley, California, so all calls were long distance.
>
> It was a time full of anxiety and guilt, mostly due to our inexperience. I was not prepared for the dying process, for our society does not teach us to die, only to be born and to be young and beautiful. It was appalling to watch the wasting of my father's body.
>
> At first, he was up several times each night, shuffling down the hall to the bathroom across from my bedroom, tapping his cane on the floor, disturbing my rest. Then, as the disease caused even more disintegration, he needed help getting to the bathroom and mother and I divided up the nights we were "on duty." Soon, he needed constant care and became bedridden, with a toilet beside his bed. The closeness of the situation, and the sudden need to be more than a daughter, stretched our relationship. Where was our God? I still remember the guilt. More than once I wished my father would die. A couple of times I even said so, out loud to my mother. I needed periodic *overnight* respite from this constant stress. So did my mother. My father was very concerned for my welfare, as I was for theirs. However, there was no such overnight relief.
>
> For four weeks I had two patients, 24 hours a day. My father's right eye had been destroyed and my mother had had eye surgery. I was dressing an eye on each three times a day as well as the general strenuous care for the terminal patient. In retrospect, I wonder how I survived. I am not a nurse, merely a human being with no choice in what was happening to me.
>
> My brothers apparently thought they had a choice, for they only dealt with it all by long distance. One brother even took his girlfriend on a two-week vacation on the day my mother got out of the hospital from eye surgery, leaving me alone with two patients. He had no steady job and hadn't for some time. He could have been of tremendous help to us. My brothers were very fearful of the death process. I was, too. However, I could not ignore it.
>
> My oldest brother called long distance and accused me of keeping our father out of the hospital. When I told him that the hospital had released Daddy because they needed the bed for someone they could help, my brother merely scoffed. I told him that the best way to find out about the condition of his father, and the way in which he was being care for, was to come up to Penn Valley and observe. I would also be glad to have the help and moral

support. He said he couldn't manage that, and that I ought to know better than to suggest such a thing, for after all, he had job commitments.

My older daughter would come up from Sacramento on weekends, when she could, to help with the cleaning and shopping. One weekend when I was really on the ragged edge and needed moral support, she called and said she "needed some time off." I very tersely asked her, "When do I get time off?" This resulted in her hiring a night nurse on two separate occasions so that Mother and I could get some much-needed rest. However, because of the thin walls in the house, we were still kept awake as Daddy talked with the nurse. He was constantly telling the nurse how to care for him, or was calling out "Honey" for my mother to show the nurse exactly what to do. It was a nightmare.

My other daughter was away from home for the first time. She was not able to come and help because of her school demands. Taking advantage of the habit of usually having my attention, she called one day to cry on my shoulder about breaking up with her boyfriend, only to have me say, "Don't bother me with your problems." I had suddenly become unavailable to her and to the rest of my family.

I went along with my mother's decision to keep my father at home until he died. But we made this decision at our own risk. My father's doctor was a real downer, as was his nurse. And, once checked out of the hospital, we received no additional help or information from hospital personnel or my father's doctor, his nurse, or office staff.

We were just lucky the day my mother stumbled on an informed person, Daddy's doctor's alternate. He told my mother, by telephone, of the Visiting Nurses Association, and they in turn told us of the Thrift Shop Cancer Aid Society of Grass Valley and, eventually, hospice. Except for these organizations, we were isolated.

Few of the neighborhood women came to visit us. When I asked neighborhood men to help keep cars running and the outside yard from going completely to seed, they were very guarded, but they were willing to help when contacted.

My father didn't want hospice around because he thought they were a religious group. We had them anyway at the very end, out of desperation. There was no one else to turn to for aid. As to counseling and education of the sick and dying, the information is there only if you know where to look. The Visiting Nurses Association was a blessing. They were convinced that my father was better off at home and was getting better care than in a convalescent home.

I had to educate myself about in-dwelling catheters so I could get past the doctor's nurse and convince the doctor that my father needed one (or rather, that I needed fewer wet bedclothes). The Visiting Nurses finally stepped in and called the doctor's office and we got the in-dwelling catheter. I wanted my parents to change doctors, but that was unthinkable to them, although they were not impressed with their doctor either. I discovered that debilitating diseases such as cancer can cause one to grow inward for protection. Anything or anyone new results in emotional trauma that one so ill hasn't the energy to deal with.

Every morning the last two or three weeks of Daddy's life, Mother and I would take our morning tea out on the sunny deck and discuss our situation. It always began with our feelings of inadequacy in caring for Daddy. We really were inexperienced, though we both had researched the disease so we could describe to the doctor what we felt we needed in caring for Daddy. We also discussed putting him in a "home" for the final weeks. This was only because we felt so helpless and exhausted. We both wondered how much longer we could go on keeping our head and our physical health, caring for him night and day with no respite.

My father talked all night, re-living his childhood, my childhood, and my children's childhood. He would sing vaudeville songs to me and tell bawdy jokes, a side of my father I had never witnessed. He was restless and awake most of the 24 hours. If he did sleep, he would awaken within an hour and begin talking again. It was as though a camera in his head had been speeded up, making him run instead of walk through life's memories and experiences.

One night very late, I had just fallen asleep and Daddy called to me to come help him to the toilet beside his bed. I wearily made my way down the hall. He was sitting on the side of the high hospital bed, very apologetic as usual. I assured him it was no problem and reached up and put my arms around him to help him lift himself off the bed, and position him to sit on the toilet. His knees just wouldn't hold him up, and I remember absolute fright that if I dropped him, he'd most likely break a bone or something equally as dangerous. We sort of both fell onto the toilet.

I developed a chronic back problem due to lifting and assisting my father in and out of bed and on and off the toilet. The countless household chores went on and on, keeping food not only in the larder but on the table, and keeping the garden outside from going to seed, which meant moving the hose and mowing the lawn once in a while.

Mostly, the outside work became a refuge from the dying process inside. My hands began to smell like my father's bowel movements. I just couldn't get the smell out no matter how or what I washed them with. It seems it never failed that the minute I sat down to a meal, he'd call and need to be cleaned up. The outside smelled so good. My eating habits also changed drastically, causing me to gain weight as never before. The less my father could eat, the more I ate. I lived with interrupted sleep and nightmares for several months after my father died. I still get tearful as I write this story. The frustration of trying desperately to help my parents, and to field the obstacles that were constantly being thrown from every conceivable direction, is still very vivid.

In looking back, I can't help but compare the birth of a newborn and the care it requires with the care of a terminal patient.

They are both very dependent on their mother/caregiver. Observe the networking that goes on when a newborn makes an entrance into our world. I was always surrounded with help and information when my babies were born. Comparing notes with other new mothers about a green bowel movement being the norm for a newborn was information gladly shared. On the other hand, the subjects of the bedridden cancer patient and the probable death are subjects that are avoided, even ignored. There is a definite need for information in dealing with death, no matter what the loved one's age. Death and dying are taboo subjects. No one wanted to talk to Mother and me, though we needed to talk about it. . . .

Discussion Questions

1. To what extent may have Dolores' care for her husband contributed to her own poor health?

2. Discuss the concept of "sandwich generation" using the illustration of Dorothy.

3. What problems did this mother and daughter experience in seeking formal care?

4. What formal care (i.e., paid help) would you advise for families in situations similar to that of Dolores and Dorothy?

5. What agencies providing formal home care are available in your home community? What are the eligibility requirements (including financial restrictions or costs) for such care? What, if any, publically financed programs would help meet the costs of such care?

Chapter 33

Gendered Caregiving of Husbands and Sons

Edward H. Thompson, Jr.

As the previous selection suggests, caregiving is usually viewed as a woman's task. The gender-linked patterns of caregiving mirror the persistence of traditional gender roles, where women are more likely to provide hands-on care. Men are more likely to contribute typically "masculine" services such as home repairs, transportation, financial management, and money. Moreover, some scholars have proposed that women have an ethic of care based on human connection while men are more likely to be concerned with abstract moral principles than with personal ties to others. How accurate is this picture?

*In the following selection, Edward Thompson examines social factors that have constructed the tradition of women as caregivers and explores common beliefs that men either do not provide adequate and dependable care or that they are incapable of providing it because of gender socialization. Examining a range of prior studies on caregiving, he argues that caregiving by men has not only been underestimated but devalued. By using an often tacit "feminine" caregiving model as the gold standard of care, researchers have been blind to the value of the managerial caregiving model used by many men. Moreover, those men who do provide elder care are portrayed as atypical "deviants" by the research community; while exemplary, they are an exception to the rule that truly "caring care" can only be provided by women. Think critically about his statement that many caregiving studies fail to distin-*guish between gender and sex; that is, the biological classification is used to label both men and women without consideration of the many meanings that gender identity may have. Here you may want to review the articles by Huyck and Turner and Silva in Section II of this volume. Consider also racial and ethnic variations in caregiving patterns and how these may relate to findings about gender roles and the meaning of caregiving.*

The issue of elder care is one of the more important policy and personal issues continuing to challenge the peoples of the United States and Canada. In both countries, the elderly population has doubled since World War II and population estimates forecast another doubling by 2030. By that time, at least one in five people will be age 65 and over, and many of these elders will be older than 85. Further, since World War II the principal causes of disability among elders, and eventually death, have become the chronic conditions of later life—dementia, stroke, chronic heart failure, and cancers, which are all ordinarily characterized by longer periods of frailty and dependency. These changes are the subject for debate among gerontologists (e.g., Binstock 1994; Callahan 1987) and material for a news magazine's cover story. Unquestionably the greater demand that elders place on a nation's resources will generate considerable discussion about *who* should be responsible for meeting the personal needs of this expanding population.

The research community has already documented that the task of caring for the nation's frail and cognitively impaired elders now falls disproportionately on spouses and adult children. And as R. L. Stone, G. L. Cafferata, and J. Sangl's (1987) national survey affirmed, the most consistent research finding is that the majority of caregiving responsibilities within the family network fall heavily, although not exclusively, to women (cf., Boaz and Muller 1992; Brody 1981; Guberman, Maheu, and Maille 1992; Ungerson 1983). Demographics are very telling. At present, elderly wives are more likely to be caregivers for their husbands because women generally marry older men, who have shorter life expectancies, and older men more frequently require family care earlier in the marital life cycle (Lee, Dwyer, and Coward 1993). Such men have surviving wives to provide it. By comparison, older women more often are widows before needing their family's assistance. And, for a variety of reasons their preference seems to be for gender consistency, which means they prefer care from the adult daughter (cf., Lee, Dwyer, and Coward 1993).

In addition to the demographic impetus, other social forces have helped construct a tradition of women as family caregivers. As is now popularly recognized (Finley 1989; Lee 1992; Miller and Cafasso 1992), the long-standing ideology of separate spheres and the division of labor by gender dictated that domestic labor was "women's work" and women were expected to receive minimal help from the men in the family. The readiness of present-day women to accept the role of caregiver for elders and the reluctance of men to become caregivers derives from a number of threads central to this traditional gender ideology. N. J. Finley (1989) distinguished four. One thread is women's exclusion from, and limited participation in, the labor market and their lesser rewards for paid work, which left women with greater perceived time to provide time-consuming caregiving (Walker, 1992).

A second thread is the argument that childhood socialization produces a "caring" perspective in which nurturing and interpersonal concerns become more central to a woman's identity than a man's (Gilligan 1982). This essentialist interpretation emphasizes women's proclivity to care and men's inadequacy. Women are considered suited for caregiving because they are seen as more interpersonally connected (Gilligan 1982), "more responsive to pain and suffering and more willing to take on arduous and often unrewarding personal duties" (Wilson 1990, p. 417). The fact that mothers bear children and nurture their infants also "may serve to identify nurturance with the female role and make nurturing an integral part of women's self-concepts" (Lee 1993, p. 124) rather than men's.

Partly consistent with this traditional ideology the reality is that caregiving follows a hierarchical pattern, which is more consistent with a norm of reciprocity (Dwyer, Folts, and Rosenberg 1994, p. 616). Elder wives of health-dependent husbands become caregivers because they are a co-resident spouse; co-residence and gender converge to make wives the so-called natural caregivers. Husbands of health-dependent wives, however, are equally expected to accept the role of caregiver, despite their presumed inexperience or aversion. The marriage contract and co-residence imply that "in sickness and in health" men, too, will provide care. Husbands are the first line of informal caregivers, followed by the reserves of adult daughters and sons. Simply put, as much as it might be taken for granted that women are "naturals" and men are "unnaturals" when it comes to caregiving, there is no easy, "separate spheres" explanation: A multitude of psychological, political, and social factors come into play to affect someone's availability and, then, decision to assume caregiving for a dependent adult relative.

Studies now document a substantial presence of men who are active caregivers (e.g., Arber and Gilbert 1989; Kaye and Applegate 1990; Stoller 1983, 1990; Stone, Cafferata, and Sangl 1987). An earlier study by the American Association of Retired Persons (AARP) and Travelers Companies Foundation found one quarter of the 7 million caregivers in the country are men (Kaye aand Applegate 1990). J. C. Cavanaugh and J. M. Kinney's (1998) recent sample of caregivers for those with dementia included 37 percent men; 35 percent of the W. S. Shaw et al. (1997) San Diego sample were husbands; and 36 percent of the spouse-caregivers and 34 percent of the adult-child caregivers in the 1994 Alameda County study were men (Strawbridge, Wallhagen, Shema, and Kaplan 1997). As this pattern suggests, one can expect one-third of family caregivers to be men. Estimates for 2020 (Himes 1992) also suggest that with declines in mortality and increases in rates of marriage, a greater proportion of men will be available to care for their wives in their old age.

Why is a review of the research examining men caregivers necessary? First, men caregivers are generally presumed to be peripheral. But as just suggested, appraisals of men as caregivers find they are frequently a primary caregiver; and the importance of men as secondary caregivers and helpers should not be dismissed (Tennstedt, McKinlay, and Sullivan 1989). The primary male caregiver is typically the husband or geographically close adult son, who provides routine care or is responsible for all of the care provided (Dwyer and Coward 1992; Kaye and Applegate 1990). Primary caregivers render a wide range of assistance, from the ordinary activities of daily living such as shopping and telephoning, money management, and medication management (Barusch and Spaid 1989) to the essential activities of daily living such as preparing meals and eating, dressing, and toileting. Their involvement is much more than supervising and offering limited instrumental assistance. The areas of companionship, emotional and psychological support, and maintaining a sense of dignity are considered "ordinary" parts of elder caregiving by men and women alike. Studies document that husbands report spending the greatest number of extra hours fulfilling caregiver responsibilities (Chang and White-Means 1991; Stone, Cafferata, and Sangl 1987), and over half of them receive no assistance from others.

Second, men are generally believed to be less capable caregivers. Caregiving has been defined as both the measurable and the immeasurable family work. It blends the instrumental and emotional spheres, and the absence of the full range of care can be viewed as neglect. Researchers have revealed a number of differences between men's and women's *types* and *amounts* of care provided. One often cited difference is that when men provide elder care they are more likely to provide help in such areas as home repair or maintenance and financial management and less likely to provide hands-on help with personal care such as bathing, dressing, and eating (e.g., Allen 1994; Coward and Dwyer 1990). Another proposed difference is that men provide less reliable care and are prone to request others to help provide care. Indeed, R. F. Young and E. Kahana (1989) stress that men spend fewer hours providing care than women do. E. P. Stoller (1990, p. 229, 235) suggests that "husbands may not be quite as dependable as wives in providing long-term

care" and "have lower tolerance thresholds for providing care." Yet other studies reveal that men caregivers are every bit as conscientious as professional caregivers (cf. Harris 1993; Hirsch 1996; Motenko 1988). This contradiction warrants systematic review.

Third, explanations of the participation by men in elder care have assumed that socialization predisposes men to provide a lesser quality of care (Finley 1989). The image conveyed is that men *as men* cannot cross-over to be accomplished caregivers, perhaps because they are expected to be oriented to market work (Boaz and Muller 1992; Stone and Short 1990) and because they are unaccustomed to providing family labor (Miller 1990; Ungerson 1983). There is a "skill malfit" (Allen 1994). However, the image of men's inadequate caregiving and malfit might be spurious. How fully individual men cross-over to become caregivers is not routinely separated from the broader question of whether men are incapable of providing quality care. A failure to distinguish between what men do and what they are capable of doing could well lead to misinterpretation. That is, structural arrangements might have more to do with how little or how much individual men crossover and render support: men who become primary rather than secondary caregivers are generally married to the care recipient or are a son without geographically close siblings. To illustrate, adult sons with local family members ordinarily choose to remain background supporters rather than primary caregivers (Matthews and Rosner 1988) and they do not "step up" until the elder parent is infirmed or in greater need (Matthews 1997; Stone, Cafferata, and Sangl 1987). By comparison, sons who get involved early in becoming central to their frail parent are geographically close (Lee, Dwyer, and Coward 1993), at a stage in their work career where they are unencumbered by the time demands of caring (Matthews 1997), and less likely to be married (Stoller 1983). The brute fact of *when* men step up to become the primary caregiver could largely determine the type and amount of care they render. Some studies suggest that men do not step up if another family member is available (Matthews and Rosner 1988). Thus, the issue of whether or not men could or do cross-over the traditional gender boundary is an important one. Perhaps more than socialization, structural arrangements and gender ideology determine who cares for whom and what types and amounts of support are provided.

Finally, after many men become primary caregivers, their style of caring is noted to be different from women's. Men's style is more managerial than women's. It is as if men distance themselves from the tasks of caregiving and distinguish "caring *for*" from "caring *about*" the care recipient (cf., Ungerson 1983). As M. Fitting, P. Rabins, M. J. Lucas, and J. Eastman commented, "Men *might* have a different model [of caring], derived from the work setting, in which delegation of responsibility and recognition of limitations necessary to do a good job are emphasized" (1986, p. 251, my emphasis). The question of whether men care differently is itself important.

Because the understanding of men caregivers and their caregiving is underdeveloped, a systematic review of the literature also ensures a detailing of the underlying assumptions researchers work with when men caregivers are discussed. As already suggested, contradictions about how and why men provide care may permeate the literature. The question is, What has the research literature to say about the experience of men who provide elder care? The purpose of this selection is critically to review studies of men caregivers. It asks the simple question, How are men caregivers envisioned? The working assumption is that they are viewed as odd, and the intent of this study is to chart how men have been studied and how men's caregiving is assessed. Is the caregiving men provide interpreted as valuable?

Methods

Data for this review were obtained from an extensive search for original material on men as caregivers to the elderly. An electronic literature search initially combed the data sets of AgeLine, Medline, PsychLit, and Social Work Abstracts and identified 41 studies. Unique references found within the first wave of articles that cited another study of men caregivers identified 12 additional studies for a total of 53. Many articles on caregiving were excluded because they never directly distinguished men caregivers (e.g., Cavanaugh and Kinney 1998); they only examined gender as a "census bureau category" using a dummy variable to distinguish females in a multivariate analysis (e.g., Shaw et al. 1997), or they were fundamentally review articles without an original research question (e.g., Gregory, Peters, and Cameron 1990; Miller and Cafasso 1992). Criteria for inclusion required that each study examine men as a distinct group or subgroup of caregivers and conduct its own analysis of men as caregivers from either qualitative or quantitative data. Studies were included because they addressed the following topics:

1. Men as a distinct category.

2. The type and amount of care men and women caregivers rendered.

3. The gendered style of caregiving.

After several rounds of reading the full set of studies, the way researchers viewed men's and women's caregiving seemed to convey that men's caregiving was inadequate in comparison to women's. A set of evaluative criteria was thus formulated by which to analyze each article. Three specific questions were asked: (1) Do authors examine the extent to which men provide a full range of services or discuss men's need for assistance in caregiving? (2) Are men presented as being comfortable in the role of primary caregiver and recognized as nurturing and caring *about* the care recipient? (3) Is men's approach to caregiving perceived as "masculine" and/or defined as managerial in contrast to women's integral caregiving? Finally, one summary question was asked about each study: Are the men caregivers discussed as if they are deviant? Collectively, the four questions track the extent to which men were considered deviant in their motivations for caring or in how they provide care.[1] The theoretical underpinning of each study was recorded in an effort to chart how men's caregiving is framed.

Findings

Men Caregivers Are Deviant

The principal finding is that men who provide elder care are portrayed as deviant by the research community. Most of the time men caregivers are described conventionally as inexperienced and unskilled in family labor, ill fit for the responsibilities to render high-quality elder care, poor substitutes for the gold standard set by women caregivers, or unable to cope with the arduous, daily drudgery of caregiving without purchasing outside services. The primary explanation for men's perceived incompetency was their prior socialization. Men were thought to be apt at meeting some of the instrumental needs of the elder, such as offering transportation or managing financial matters; but they failed at caring *for* the elder. The study by J. B. Enright (1991), for example, reported that husbands purchase outside help to manage their responsibility. The message is that men need and receive more outside assistance. More recently S. Allen (1994) implied that husbands sought more formal assistance when she observed that wives being cared for received more formal help. In a review article on elder husbands, D. Gregory, N. Peters, and C. F. Cameron stated that "husbands as caregivers were more likely than wives to seek the help of formal providers and receive more informal support" (1990, p. 23). This article contradicts the findings from a national survey that showed husbands depended less on outside help than wives did (Stone, Cafferata, and Sangl 1987).

Men Who Care Are Deviant

Ironically, some men caregivers (principally husbands) are recognized as extra-ordinary men who care for and unequivocally care about the care recipient; yet these extraordinary men are deviants too, because they do not appear to adhere to the masculinity standards or traditions that forecast marked gender differences in caregiving. It was routinely found that nearly one-half of spouse caregivers are men (Stone, Cafferata, and Sangl 1987) and their level of involvement in caregiving (as defined by the amount, type, and style) is approximately equal to wives' involvement. B. Miller (1987) found no difference between men and women in terms of the help given in daily living tasks. A. S. Barusch and W. M. Spaid (1989) report husbands perform more caregiving tasks than wives. Nonetheless, this pattern of men being deeply invested in caregiving is generally discounted as an anomaly or a methodological artifact (Stoller and Cutler 1992). These men emerge somehow as atypical men, which reaffirms the general finding that men who care are deviant.

The Pervasiveness of Stereotypes

In this sample of 53 research studies, more than two-thirds of the studies present men's caregiving as not measuring up to women's. This conclusion strongly suggests that a gold standard of caregiving exists, and caregiving is measured by a "feminine yardstick." At times it was implied that those cared for by men are "at risk," because they receive inadequate care; and without additional, outside assistance the care recipient is being neglected or under-benefitted. At other times, this yardstick emerges through the suggestion that men are not morally committed to providing good elder care. Men hire other service providers to fill in the gaps; they take respites; and they depend on their frail wives to help with the household chores. All but six articles out of the sample of 53 discussed this issue, and only a handful of articles concluded that men's caregiving meets the needs of the elder.

The Professional Model of Caregiving

There is limited but suggestive evidence that many men approach caregiving as if it were a profession. These men engage themselves in caregiving as if the responsibility was "work," and they take on a care-management orientation and thereby care *for* the elder. The professional model emphasizes control by the caregiver (Miller 1987) and the completion of caregiving in the most efficacious manner with the least engulfment of the person providing it (Skaff and Pearlin 1992). The "professional" caregiver is fully engaged in the tasks of caregiving yet emotionally distant from the often transient, personal feelings associated with the noxious tasks of caregiving. Thus, the managerial model helps men distinguish between caring *about* their wife or elder parent and caring *for* the person.

Efficacy of Management Style

Routinely, studies of caregiver distress report that men engaged in the tasks of caregiving report being less burdened (Miller and Cafasso 1992) by the "work" than women caregivers. Perhaps it is the professional model that men emulate, or the so-called managerial model that Fitting et al. (1986) described, which shelters men from symptoms of poor mental health and burnout (Braithwaite 1996; Skaff and Pearlin 1992). The managerial strategy provides the caregiver with greater perceived control, the sense of being in charge, feelings of self-efficacy, the ability to choose to act or not act, and the opportunity not to become engulfed in the caregiving relationships (Wallhagen and Kagen 1993). Men using a managerial approach appear not to experience difficulty with taking respite time for themselves (Motenko 1988; Perkinson 1995). They seem to avoid being engulfed by maintaining outside interests (Archer and MacLean 1993; Miller 1987) and, at times, by emotional withdrawal (Parks and Pilisuk 1991). This cognitive and behavior distancing from the demands of caregiving may well assist men temporarily to forget the heavy responsibilities and thereby reduce the distress of caring *for* and increase the perceived gains of caring *about*. Wives do not appear as able to "withdraw" until after a more prolonged period of caring (Zarit, Todd, and Zarit 1986).

A number of other conceptual and methodological observations were uncovered during the literature search for this review and in analyzing the 53 studies addressing men caregivers. Five are most pertinent:

Gender Is Never Considered

Years after scholars called attention to gender differences in elder caregiving (e.g., Litwak 1965; Ungerson 1983; Zarit, Todd, and Zarit 1986), many studies still do not identify the gender of the caregivers in the sample. It is frankly remarkable the number of published studies that indiscriminately lump caregivers together, e.g., adult daughters-in-law and elder husbands. When demographic characteristics of a sample are described and a sizeable proportion of men caregivers is reported, many studies fail to perform separate analyses of men's caregiving experiences.

Emphasis on Sex Difference, not Gender

As reflected across most theoretical orientations that frame the literature on caregiving, the research community's understanding of "gender" falls short. Too often gender is not distinguished from the variable "sex." Masculinity standards and men's experiences as men are treated as identical to being male. Consequently, men are not studied *as men* but as members of a class. Adult sons and elderly husbands; white men and men of color; auto assembly-line workers and financial planners are classified the same; they are all classified as males. The categorical variable in multivariate analysis is frequently coded "female," which is a label for a demographic characteristic. Ironically, "male" remains the background, contrast effect, and the distinctiveness of men's caregiving remains invisible.

Within Gender Variations Understudied

Because the differences between men's and women's caregiving efficacy is routinely measured, rarely investigated are the ways different men interpret the caregiving experience. Comparison between adult sons with and without sisters (Matthews and Rosner 1988), or husbands and sons (Archer and MacLean 1993), strongly suggests that men's experiences with caregiving are not uniform. When systematic variation among men is investigated, the prime basis for differentiating among men has been structural—e.g., men's relationship to the care recipient (elder husband v. adult son). Very seldom have researchers set out to assess how styles of interaction, such as controlling or not, might differently shape the caregiving experiences of husbands or sons (cf., Harris 1993; Motenko 1988) or how men's gender identity is related to their style of caregiving (Hirsch and Newman 1995).

Gendered Caregiving Observed, not Understood

Again based on the patterns noted across the 53 studies, the research community certainly recognized men's caregiving was uniquely gendered. That is, men's strategy of caregiving is often noted as different from that of women; husbands' "standard of care" differed from wives' standard and men's style of care was managerial. Yet research has been unable to trace clearly how gender influences elder care. Ad hoc explanations dominate (see the critiques by Lee 1993; Walker 1992). Distilled from this review, men's caregiving behavior is typically interpreted according to theories of gender socialization and task specialization (e.g., Allen 1994; Horowitz 1992; Montgomery and Kamo 1989), women's and men's internalized caring orientations (e.g., Dwyer and Seccombe 1991; Ungerson 1983), theories about later life development (e.g., Fitting, Rabins, Lucas, and Eastham 1986; Miller 1990), and a resource and time-available model which emphasizes men's differential costs and gains (e.g., Enright 1991; Stommel, Given, Given, and Collins 1995). The more prevalent "frames" present essentialist interpretations about men's behavior.

The Meaning of Caregiving

Collectively, the studies reviewed revealed several distinct reasons why men become active caregivers. Some men seem to assume their caregiver responsibilities as a sense of fulfillment of unmet family needs (Pruchno and Resch 1989); some men respond to their affection and feelings of interpersonal commitment (Fitting et al. 1986; Motenko 1988); others seek to replace the gratifications and intrinsic rewards formerly found in work (Archer and MacLean 1993; Vinick 1984); some men take the opportunity to experience nurturing (Hirsch 1996; Kaye and Applegate 1990); and some men extend their work-related experiences of "taking control" into caregiving (Miller 1987). Each of these explanations for why men are caregivers is an ad hoc explanation, and the meaning of caregiving for men has been given little *a priori* attention.

Discussion and Conclusions

The consensus within the research literature is that men caregivers are deviant. Men caregivers face a kind of double jeopardy. Either they are perceived as deviant because they do not care the way women do, or when they do match women's standard of care in terms of the amount and type of chores they perform, they are perceived as deviant because they are unlike other men. The long tradition of comparing women to men in terms of how much care men provide and what types of caregiving tasks are undertaken, has institutionalized the use of a single, feminine yardstick to measure caregiving. Should this convention of comparing men and women on a single standard continue, the stereotype that men caregivers will be deviant will not be shaken. These results may mean that, no matter what their findings, researchers will feel compelled to conclude that husbands and adult sons are not capable of crossing-over and performing "cross-gendered" tasks without being deviant. As S. Arber and A. Gilbert observed:

> Although at least a third of carers of frail elders are men, caring conflicts with norms of masculinity and appears to break fundamental gender roles. One way in which the literature has addressed this problem has been to ignore it, and another has been to suggest that men carers are not really doing much caring. . . . This argument dismisses male carers as an artifact; men are not considered "real" carers who suffer the same social, emotional and physical consequences which women carers have been demonstrated to suffer. (1989, p.80)

Indeed, according to L. W. Kaye and J. S. Applegate, "Conventional wisdom and stereotypical thinking have led us to assume that . . . men lack the inclination and capacity to meet the physical and emotional needs of another person" (1994, p. 218).

This quote is what is meant by the feminine yardstick, and this oversocialized view of men and women can have a number of ill effects. Two seem most important. First, this review has unearthed sufficient evidence to suggest that failure to abandon the feminine yardstick will undermine the understanding of men caregivers. Use of the yardstick certainly leads to stigmatizing men's unique participation in elder care. The active management of an elder's needs that some men direct via the recruitment of help from family members and professionals can be falsely dismissed as coldness and uncaring. Their decision to serve as a "case manager" and coordinate care is reinforcement for gender stereotypes (Miller and Cafasso 1992), but this style of care also is consistent with the individual men's gender identities (Hirsch 1996). It is the way these men think of gender and give care. Other men's management of an elder's needs demonstrates an effort to blend management and nurturing. Studies such as those by A. K. Motenko (1988), P. B. Harris (1993, 1995), S. H. Matthews (1997), C. Hirsch and J. L. Newman (1995), or B. H. Vinick (1984) readily indicate that for some men, caregiving is desirable and seems to be natural. These men use an original model of caregiving, one that combines traditionally masculine, workplace values with an affective provision of care. One must be cautious, however. The evidence for this joint management-nurturing approach to caregiving is principally found among older husbands and it is derived from in-depth, qualitative studies using small samples. Thus, what is known about the experiences of men caregivers is limited, in part because of the types of studies available. However, according to E. K. Abel, the conceptual constraints are more problematic than the methodological: we cannot continue to focus caregiving research on the "chores caregivers perform and the stress they experience" (1990, p. 140). The hegemony of the feminine yardstick that has been used has become so unnoticed that it constrains imagination and understanding. To envision the different ways men and women give care as no longer evidence of deviance and a gold standard, frees the research community to ask why men care in the variety of ways they do.

A second ill effect is when the feminine yardstick unwittingly becomes support for the continued classification of caregiving as women's work. Defining men caregivers as deviant, and trumpeting women's style of caregiving as "natural" and preferred, can excuse men from obligations as privilege has traditionally exempted them from family work. As A. J. Walker pointed out:

> Most of the studies that have focused on gender have simply described rates and/or the extent of caregiving for wives versus husbands and . . . daughters versus sons. . . . Most research has relied on psychological and sociological perspectives to account for the differences in behavior between women and men. Typically, in such an approach, caregiving by women is defined as normative. (1992, p. 45)

As long as caregiving to elders is defined by a single standard, and the variations among men are ignored, scholars are unlikely to appreciate N. Guberman, P. Maheu, and C. Maille's (1992) finding that family caregiving is not desirable or natural for all women. Nor are they likely to appreciate M. Bar-Yam's argument that "The orientation toward relationships and attachment is not necessarily feminine nor is the orientation toward autonomy and separateness necessarily masculine" (1991, p. 257). Instead, the persistence of a feminine yardstick serves as a basis for the barriers men experience in crossing over (Kaye and Applegate 1994) and the lack of assistance women experience with their accepted responsibilities (Abel 1990; Guberman, Maheu, and Maille 1992).

Several steps can be taken to develop a better understanding of men caregivers. One is to conduct studies that acknowledge the heterogeneity among men caregivers and begin to break down the tradition of studying men as a unitary bloc. Researchers know men step-up to become primary caregivers for different reasons. We know that men who become the primary caregiver are not all the same. Harris (1993) has already pointed to four different types of husbands. S. H. Matthews and T. T. Rosner (1988) distinguish among adult sons. The variations among the men who become caregivers may well be at the root of the reported contradictions in the literature. Although researchers have treated men as a homogeneous group and continue to lump together all men caregivers, some recent studies have begun to distinguish among men on the basis of participation in the labor market, family position (Dwyer and Seccombe 1991), and age and marital status (Marks 1995).

Attempts need to be made to understand under what conditions men agree to become caregivers. In doing so, studies need to understand the father-son and mother-son relationships, for there is sufficient evidence that parents are the ones who select the adult-child caregiver, and often the preference is for same-sex assistance (Barusch and Spaid 1989; Lee, Dwyer, and Coward 1993). In addition, the needs for encouraging and supporting men caregivers in terms of gender-sensitive services (Harris 1993; Miller 1987) and formulating public policies have not been thoroughly outlined and debated. Although there is evidence of the growing number of men who are providing elder care and some acknowledgment that men have a place in caregiving, many researchers still treat men's place in caregiving as less important than that of women and men's caregiving as a lesser quality of care. Until the conceptual blinders are removed, men caregivers will remain defined as deviant and odd men, and men as a class will retain their privilege to choose not to participate in such family work.

Discussion Questions

1. In what ways does Thompson feel that men caregivers are regarded as deviant?

2. Describe the feminine yardstick of caregiving and how this measure devalues the caregiving provided by men.

3. Assess the possible value of the "managerial" caregiving role in reducing caregiver stress among women caregivers.

4. In what ways does the feminine yardstick of care reinforce the designation of caregiving as women's work, and what effects does this have on both men and women as caregivers?

Note

Tables summarizing the studies reviewed herein are available upon request from the author.

References

Abel, E. K. 1990. "Informal Care for the Disabled Elderly: A Critique of Recent Literature." *Research on Aging* 12: 139–157.

Allen, S. 1994. "Gender Differences in Spousal Caregiving and Unmet Need for Care." *Journal of Gerontology* 49: S187–S195.

Arber, S., and Gilbert, N. 1989. "Transitions in Caring: Gender, Life Course, and the Care of the Elderly." In B. Bytheway, T. Keil, P. Allatt, and A. Bryman, eds., *Becoming and Being Old: Sociological Approaches to Later Life*, pp. 72–92. London: Sage.

Archer, C. K., and MacLean, M. J. 1993. "Husbands and Sons as Caregivers of Chronically-ill Elderly Women." *Journal of Gerontological Social Work* 21(1/2): 5–23.

Bar-Yam, M. 1991. "Do Women and Men Speak in Different Voices? A Comparative Study of Self-evolvement." *International Journal of Aging and Human Development* 32: 247–259.

Barusch, A. S., and Spaid, W. M. 1989. "Gender Differences in Caregiving: Why Do Wives Report Greater Burden?" *The Gerontologist* 29: 667–676.

Binstock, R. H. 1994. "Old-age-based Rationing: From Rhetoric to Risk?" *Generations* 18(4): 37–41.

Boaz, R. F., and Muller, C. F. 1992. "Paid Work and Unpaid Help by Caregivers of the Disabled and Frail Elders." *Medical Care* 30: 149–158.

Borden, W., and Berlin, S. 1990. "Gender, Coping, and Psychological Well-being in Spouses of Older Adults with Chronic Dementia." *American Journal of Orthopsychiatry* 60: 603–610.

Braithwaite, V. 1996. "Understanding Stress in Informal Caregiving: Is Burden a Problem of the Individual or Society?" *Research on Aging* 18: 139–174.

Brody, E. M. 1981. "Women in the Middle and Family Help to Older People. *The Gerontologist* 21: 471–479.

Callahan, D. 1987. *Setting Limits: Medical Goals in an Aging Society*. New York: Simon & Schuster.

Cavanaugh, J. C., and Kinney, J. M. 1998. "Accuracy of Caregivers' Recollections of Caregiving Hassles." *Journal of Gerontology: Psychological Sciences* 53B: P40–P42.

Chang, C. F., and White-Means, S. I. 1991. "The Men Who Care: An Analysis of Male Primary Caregivers Who Care for Frail Elderly at Home." *Journal of Applied Gerontology* 10: 343–358.

Coward, R. T., and Dwyer, J. W. 1990. "The Association of Gender, Sibling Network Composition, and Patterns of Parent Care by Adult Children." *Research on Aging* 12: 158–181.

DeVries, H. M., Hamilton, D. W., Lovett, S., and Gallagher-Thompson, D. 1997. "Patterns of Coping Preferences for Male and Female Caregivers of Frail Older Adults." *Psychology and Aging* 12: 263–267.

Dwyer, J. W., and Coward, R. T. 1992. "Gender, Family, and Long-term Care of the Elderly." In J. W. Dwyer & R. T. Coward, eds., *Gender, Families, and Elder Care*, pp. 3–17. Newbury Park, CA: Sage.

Dwyer, J. W., Folts, W. E., and Rosenberg, E. 1994. "Caregiving in Social Context." *Educational Gerontology* 20: 615–631.

Dwyer, J. W., and Seccombe, K. 1991. "Elder Care as Family Labor: The Influence of Gender and Family Position." *Journal of Family Issues* 12: 229–247.

Dwyer, J. W., Henretta, J. C., Coward, R. T., and Barton, A. J. 1992. "Changes in the Helping Behaviors of Adult Children as Caregivers." *Research on Aging* 14: 351–375.

Enright, R. B., Jr. 1991. "Time Spent Caregiving and Help Received by Spouses and Adult Children of Brain-impaired Adults." *The Gerontologist* 31: 375–383.

Farran, C. J., Keane-Hagerty, E., Salloway, S., Kupferer, S., and Wilken, C. S. 1991. "Finding Meaning: An Alternative Paradigm for Alzheimer's Disease Family Caregivers." *The Gerontologist* 31: 483–489.

Finley, N. J. 1989. "Theories of Family Labor as Applied to Gender Differences in Caregiving for Elderly Parents." *Journal of Marriage and the Family* 51: 79–86.

Fitting, M., Rabins, P., Lucas, M. J., and Eastham, J. 1986. "Caregivers for Dementia Patients: A Comparison of Husbands and Wives." *The Gerontologist* 26: 248–252.

Fuller-Jonap, F. A., and Haley, W. E. 1995. "Mental and Physical Health of Male Caregivers of a Spouse With Alzheimer's Disease." *Journal of Aging and Health* 7: 99–118.

Gilligan, C. 1982. *In a Different Voice*. Cambridge, MA: Harvard University Press.

Gold, D. P., Cohen, C., Shulman, K., Zucchero, C., Andres, D., and Etesadi, J. 1995. "Caregiving and Dementia: Predicting Negative and Positive Outcomes for Caregivers." *International Journal of Aging and Human Development* 41: 183–201.

Gregory, D., Peters, N., and Cameron, C. F. 1990. "Elderly Male Spouses as Caregivers—Toward an Understanding of Their Experience." *Journal of Gerontological Nursing* 16: 20–24.

Guberman, N., Maheu, P., Maille, C. 1992. "Women as Family Caregivers: Why Do They Care?" *The Gerontologist* 32: 607–617.

Hamon, R. R. 1992. "Filial Role Enactment by Adult Children." *Family Relations* 41: 91–96.

Harris, P. B. 1993. "The Misunderstood Caregiver? A Qualitative Study of the Male Caregiver of Alzheimer's Disease Victims." *The Gerontologist* 33: 551–556.

Harris, P. B. 1995. "Differences Among Husbands Caring for Their Wives With Alzheimer's Disease: Qualitative Findings and Counseling Implications." *Journal of Clinical Geropsychology* 1: 97–106.

Hibbard, J., Neufeld, A., and Harrison, M. J. 1996. "Gender Differences in the Support Networks of Caregivers." *Journal of Gerontological Nursing* 22(9): 15–23.

Himes, C. L. 1992. "Future Caregivers: Projected Family Structures of Older Persons." *Journals of Gerontology: Social Sciences* 47: S17–S26.

Hirsch, C. 1996. "Understanding the Influence of Gender Role Identity on the Assumption of Family Caregiving by Men." *International Journal of Aging and Human Development* 42: 103–121.

Hirsch, C., and Newman, J. L. 1995. "Microstructural and Gender Role Influences on Male Caregivers. *Journal of Men's Studies* 3: 309–333.

Horowitz, A. 1992. "Methodological Issues in the Study of Gender Within Family Caregiving Relationships." In J. W. Dwyer, and R. T. Coward, eds., *Gender, Families, and Elder Care*, pp. 132–150. Newbury Park, CA: Sage.

Ingersoll-Dayton, B., Starrels, M. E., and Dowler, D. 1996. "Caregiving for Parents and Parents-in-law: Is Gender Important?" *The Gerontologist* 36: 483–491.

Johnson, C. L. 1983. "Dyadic Family Relations and Social Support." *The Gerontologist* 23: 377–383.

Jutras, S., and Veilleux, F. 1991. "Gender Roles and Care Giving to the Elderly: An Empirical Study." *Sex Roles* 25: 1–18.

Kaye, L. W., and Applegate, J. S. 1990. *Men as Elder Caregivers to the Elderly*. Lexington, MA: Lexington Books.

——. 1994. "Older Men and the Family Caregiving Orientation." In E. Thompson, ed., *Older Men's Lives*, pp. 197–217. Thousand Oaks, CA: Sage.

——. 1995. "Men's Style of Nurturing Elders." In D. Sabo, ed., *Men's Health and Illness*, pp. 205–221. Thousand Oaks, CA: Sage.

Kivett, V. R. 1988. "Older Rural Fathers and Sons: Patterns of Association and Helping." *Family Relations* 37: 62–67.

Kramer, B. J. 1997. "Differential Predictors of Strain and Gain Among Husbands Caring for Wives with Dementia." *The Gerontologist* 37: 239–249.

Kramer, B. J., and Kipnis, S. 1995. "Eldercare and Work-role Conflict: Toward an Understanding of Gender Differences in Caregiver Burden." *The Gerontologist* 35: 340–348.

Lee, G. R. 1993. "Gender Differences in Family Caregiving: A Fact in Search of a Theory." In J. W. Dwyer, and R. T. Coward, eds., *Gender, Families, and Elder Care*, pp. 120–131. Newbury Park, CA: Sage.

Lee, G. R., Dwyer, J. W., and Coward, R. T. 1993. "Gender Differences in Parent Care: Demographic Factors and Same-gender Preferences." *Journal of Gerontology; Social Sciences* 48: S9–S16.

Marks, N. 1995. "Midlife Marital Status Differences in Social Support Relationships With Adult Children and Psychological Well-being." *Journal of Family Issues* 16: 5–28.

Mathew, L. J., Mattocks, K., and Slatt, L. M. 1990. "Exploring the Roles of Men: Caring for Demented Relatives." *Journal of Gerontological Nursing* 16: 20–25.

Matthews, S. H. 1997. "Older Sons' Relationships with Very Old Parents." Paper presented at the annual meeting of the Gerontological Society of America, Cincinnati.

Matthews, S. H., and Rosner, T. T. 1988. "Shared Filial Responsibility: The Family as the Primary Caregiver." *Journal of Marriage and the Family* 50: 185–195.

Miller, B. 1987. "Gender and Control Among Spouses of the Cognitively Impaired: A Research Note." *The Gerontologist* 27: 447–453.

Miller, B. 1990a. "Gender Differences in Spouse Caregiver Strain: Socialization and Role Explanations." *Journal of Marriage and the Family* 52: 311–321.

Miller, B. 1990b. "Gender Differences in Spouse Management of the Caregiver Role." In E. Abel and M. K. Nelson, eds., *Circles of Care: Work and Identity in Women's Lives*. Albany: SUNY Press.

Miller, B., and Cafasso, L. 1992. "Gender Differences in Caregiving: Fact or Artifact?" *The Gerontologist* 32: 498–507.

Miller, B., and Montgomery, A. 1990. "Family Caregivers and Limitations in Social Activities." *Research on Aging* 12: 72–93.

Miller, B., and McFall, S. 1992. "Caregiver Burden and the Continuum of Care." *Research on Aging* 14: 376–398.

Montgomery, R. J. V., and Kamo, Y. 1989. "Parent Care by Sons and Daughters." In J. A. Mancini, ed., *Aging Parents and Adult Children*, pp. 213–230. Lexington, MA: Lexington Books.

Motenko, A. K. 1988. "Respite Care and Pride in Caregiving: The Experience of Six Older Men Caring for Their Disabled Wives." In S. Reinharz and G. D. Rowles, eds., *Qualitative Gerontology*, pp. 104–127. New York: Springer-Verlag.

Mui, A. C. 1995. "Perceived Health and Functional Status Among Spouse Caregivers of Frail Older Persons." *Journal of Aging and Health* 7: 283–300.

Mui, A. C., and Morrow-Howell, N. 1993. "Sources of Emotional Strain Among the Oldest Caregivers." *Research on Aging* 15: 50–69.

Parks, S. H., and Pilisuk, M. 1991. "Caregiver Burden: Gender and the Psychological Costs of Caregiving." *American Journal of Orthopsychiatry* 61: 501–509.

Perkinson, M. A. 1995. "Socialization to the Family Caregiving Role Within a Continuing Care Retirement Community." *Medical Anthropology* 16: 249–267.

Pruchno, R. A., and Resch, N. L. 1989. "Husbands and Wives as Caregivers: Antecedents of Depression and Burden." *The Gerontologist* 29: 159–165.

Semple, S. J. 1992. "Conflict in Alzheimer's Caregiving Families: Its Dimensions and Consequences." *The Gerontologist* 32: 648–655.

Shaw, W. S., Patterson, T. L., Semple, S. J., Grant, I., Yu, E. S. H., Zhang, M. Y., He, Y., and Wu, W. Y. 1997. "A Cross-cultural Validation of Coping Strategies and Their Associations With Caregiving Distress." *The Gerontologist* 37: 490–504.

Skaff, M. M., and Pearlin, L. I. 1992. "Caregiving: Role Engulfment and the Loss of Self." *The Gerontologist* 32: 656–664.

Stoller, E. P. 1983. "Parental Caregiving by Adult Children." *Journal of Marriage and the Family* 45: 851–858.

——. 1990. "Males as Helpers: The Role of Sons, Relatives, and Friends." *The Gerontologist* 30: 228–235.

Stoller, E. P., and Cutler, S. J. 1992. "The Impact of Gender on Configurations of Care Among Married Elder Couples." *Research on Aging* 14: 313–330.

Stoller, E. P., Forster, L. E., and Duniho, T. S. 1992. "Systems of Parent Care Within Sibling Networks." *Research on Aging* 14: 28–49.

Stommel, M., Given, B. A., Given, C. W., and Collins, C. 1995. "The Impact of Frequency of Care Activities on the Division of Labor Between Primary Caregivers and Other Care Providers." *Research on Aging* 17: 412–433.

Stone, R. I., and Short, P. F. 1990. "The Competing Demands of Employment and Informal Caregiving to Disabled Elders." *Medical Care* 28: 513–526.

Stone, R. I., Cafferata, G. L., and Sangl, J. 1987. "Caregivers of the Frail Elderly: A National Profile." *The Gerontologist* 27: 616–626.

Strawbridge, W. J., Wallhagen, M. I., Shema, S. J., and Kaplan, G. A. 1997. "New Burdens or More of the Same? Comparing Grandparent, Spouse, and Adult-child Caregivers." *The Gerontologist* 37: 505–510.

Tennstedt, S. L., McKinlay, J. B., and Sullivan, L. M. 1989. "Informal Care for Frail Elders: The Role of Secondary Caregivers." *The Gerontologist* 29: 677–683.

Ungerson, C. 1983. "Why Do Women Care?" In J. Finch and D. Groves, eds., *A Labour of Love: Women, Work, and Caring*. London: Routledge & Kegan Paul.

Vinick, B. H. 1984. "Elderly Men as Caretakers of Wives." *Journal of Geriatric Psychiatry* 17: 61–68.

Walker, A. J. 1992. "Conceptual Perspectives on Gender and Family Caregiving." In J. W. Dwyer, and R. T. Coward, eds., *Gender, Families, and Elder Care*, pp. 34–46. Newbury Park, CA: Sage.

Wallhagen, M. I., and Kagan S. H. 1993. "Staying Within Bounds: Perceived Control and the Experience of Elderly Caregivers." *Journal of Aging Studies* 7: 197–213.

Wilson, V. 1990. "The Consequences of Elderly Wives Caring for Disabled Husbands: Implications for Practice." *Social Work* 35: 417–421.

Young, R. F. , and Kahana, E. 1989. "Specifying Caregiver Outcomes: Gender and Relationship Aspects of Caregiving Strain." *The Gerontologist* 29: 660–666.

Zarit, S. H., Todd, P. A., and Zarit, J. M. 1986. "Subjective Burden of Husbands and Wives as Caregivers: A Longitudinal Study." *The Gerontologist* 26: 260–266.

Edward H. Thompson, Jr., "The Gendered Caregiving of Husbands and Sons and the Social Construction of Men Caregivers as Deviants." Printed by permission of the author.

Chapter 34

Hand-Me-Down People

Jennifer Hand and Patricia Reid

When we think of caregiving relationships in later life, we usually think of a spouse, child, or other relative caring for an older relative. Increasingly, however, older family members may be caring for a developmentally disabled adult relative. In many nations, the developmentally disabled have traditionally been placed in institutions, most often state schools or mental hospitals, where they spend most of their lives. As deinstitutionalization has occurred in both the United States and other countries, more developmentally disabled people either are being released from these facilities or are never institutionalized. As life expectancy has also increased among the developmentally disabled, many now live into old age, presenting specific issues about who will care for them and what kinds of care are most appropriate.

In the following selection, Jennifer Hand and Patricia Reid examine the experiences of a small number of New Zealand families caring for a developmentally disabled relative and the dilemmas they encounter. An exceptional group for their generation, most of these families provided round-the-clock care for their developmentally disabled relative from childhood to old age. Although occurring in a much smaller country than ours, the New Zealand experience is highly relevant because of present-day trends towards community-based and family-based care throughout industrialized nations, including the United States. The issues confronted are the same. Pay attention to the concerns raised by the various family members as you read. To what extent are the middle-aged and old developmentally disabled at risk of being "hand-me-down" people in their families? What are the likely results for family members and for the disabled individual?

Introduction

In earlier decades, most developmentally disabled people simply did not live past young adulthood, owing mostly to poor medical care. In recent decades, however, developmentally disabled individuals enjoy a life expectancy approaching that found in the general population, except for people with Down's syndrome, who continue to experience the higher mortality rates associated with this condition. People with developmental disabilities (DD) require support over their entire lifetime. They are likely to experience transitions from one caregiver to another, whether from one family member to another, from parental home to institution and back, or from family to private agency. This fragile living situation generates important and often emotional discussion about their needs and who should be responsible for their care and support. The aim of this selection is to contribute to this discussion by focusing on the transition from one caregiver to another in families with an older, developmentally disabled member.

This selection draws on data from a series of studies conducted in New Zealand from 1989 to 1996. The population studied was not a sample but the nationwide universe of older people with a developmental disability. In this study, 1,063 older individuals were identified, a prevalence rate of 1.43 per 1,000 people in this age group living in New Zealand in 1990 (Hand 1994). Data collected included national demographic, health-status, and health-service statistics (Hand 1994; Hand 1996; Hand and Reid 1996); transcripts and audiotapes of personal interviews with research subjects and some family members (Hand and Reid 1989; Hand, Trewby and Reid 1994; Hand and Trewby 1996); and photographs focusing on the relationships between the person with DD and the caregiver (Noble 1994).[1] Of the more than 1,000 individuals studied, half were men and half were women, and 42 percent were Maoris, the indigenous people of New Zealand. Thirteen percent had been diagnosed with Down's syndrome. Half of the group were aged between 50 and 60; the oldest person was a man of 88. Slightly more than 40 percent of people with developmental disabilities in New Zealand lived in institutions in 1990; 38 percent lived in community-based residences; 13 percent were in nursing homes; and 7 percent lived with their families. Only 1 percent lived independently.

In 1996, the authors conducted a follow-up study of family caregivers. By that time, only 3 percent (33 people) of those initially identified in 1990 were living with relatives; the remaining 32 people had moved to agency care or private rest homes or had died. This group of 33 comprised 20 men and 13 women, ranging from 55 to 84 years. About 3 in 4 were aged between 55 and 64. Eight had Down's syndrome; 5 had been injured at birth. For the remainder, the cause of disability was unknown. Although over half had generally good or excellent health, over 1 in 4 of the group living with a family member had eyesight problems; 1 in 3 were forgetful, vague, or slightly mentally impaired from time to time; and another 1 in 4 were confused or disturbed on an on-going basis. Most were able to converse with caregivers. A quarter of the group, however, had little or no speech; in these instances, the vigilance and dedication of the caregivers enabled their relatives with DD to remain at home.

The Caregivers

In the 33 families living with an aging developmentally disabled relative, life at home—for both the caregiver and the person with DD—was characterized by mutual caring and help. The Caregivers often provided 24-hour supervision of their disabled loved ones for 40 to 50 years or more. In addition to attending to physical needs such as shelter, meals, and personal care, they provided skills training and advocacy with teachers, the health-care system, employers, and neighbors. They also shielded their relative from the negative comments and actions of an insensitive public.

The caregivers ranged in age from a sister of 44 to a mother [of] 96 years. On the average, caregivers were 69, and most were older than the relatives they cared for. Despite their own advancing age, two-thirds of the caregivers reported their health to be good or excellent. A few caregivers, however, were in very poor or fair health, and several were younger siblings. Caregivers reported difficulties with many of the same health problems affecting their aging DD relative: vision problems, difficulty with mobility, arthritis, heart problems, and diabetes.

Caregiving resulted in drastic lifestyle changes for some caregivers. Some women were able to continue with full-time paid work while their DD relative attended day programs. Some, however, had to give up paid work or retired early to look after their relative, who could not be left alone and had no access to day-care services.

Family Composition

Families providing care showed a variety of members. Some families included siblings and their spouses, or several siblings, or siblings and relatives from older or younger generations. Twenty families consisted only of a single caregiver and a developmentally disabled relative. Over half of this single-caregiver group were widowed mothers or stepmothers. Other single caregivers were brothers, sisters, and a widowed father. In this study, 13 developmentally disabled adults lived with their parents. In the other 20 families, the adults lived with relatives, who were mostly siblings; in one instance, a nephew had assumed care. Thirteen of the caregiving siblings were sisters of the DD person; two of the sisters had taken in an elderly parent as well as the sister or brother with the developmental disability. In some families, caregiving was shared to the point that it was not possible to identify a primary caregiver, with each insisting that caring was shared among all the family members.

In addition to the family members under one roof, 3 out of 4 (25) caregivers reported that they had other family members who lived nearby. Of these, the overwhelming majority (22) said that they had person-to-person contact with those relatives at least once every two weeks. Several caregivers reported daily personal contact or telephone calls.

This contact was highly valued. Among the three caregivers with no contact between themselves and nearby relatives, one reported he had one sister in the same town and one sister in a city about three hours' drive away. It was the latter sister with whom he had more contact and on whom he relied for support. The sister who lived nearby, although helpful at times, did not offer him help for respite and only responded to requests for assistance. In contrast, his other sister was willing to be involved in whatever way needed, and she offered help and frequently invited their developmentally disabled brother to stay. For another family, other siblings lived in the same city but for many years had chosen not to be involved in the welfare of their DD relative and there was little or no contact between the families. The remaining families said they had no relatives nearby; these families were very much on their own. One caregiver reported his only relatives were overseas, and another family said they had no relatives who were interested: "We don't mind," one commented. " . . . [It is] their loss." This family had become divided over issues of care and responsibility for their sister with Down's syndrome many years ago, and the current caregivers believed reconciliation was impossible.

Caregivers were asked about the abilities and disabilities of their DD relatives and about the amount and kind of care provided. Caregivers did not usually describe their relatives in the terms of levels of functioning, such as "mild" or "severe." Indeed, 19 caregivers had never been given that type of information, even from health professionals. Instead, caregivers preferred to describe the abilities and disabilities of their relatives in terms of the care they needed, for example, "He can't be left at all" or "[She] can make a cup of tea." An indication of skills and abilities was also obtained from a question about how long their DD relative could be left alone.

Just more than a third of the caregivers said they could not leave their relative alone at all. One mother described how "if she had to," she would instruct her son to stay in his chair, lock him in the house, go over to the shop, and return straight away. One sister said she could be in another room for a brief period of time, but if her brother, who was chair bound and had no sense of balance, should fall then she would be unable to steady him again; she was not strong enough to lift him by herself, and her solution to the problem was to be always on hand.

History of Care and Residence

The adults with developmental disabilities in the New Zealand study were born at a time when hospitalization was the only form of support available to their families. It was usual, before policies of deinstitutionalization and community-based care were implemented, to admit children to institutions. However, only 4 of the 33 families studied here had followed this path. Several other families remembered considering hospitalization but had rejected that service.

Of the four families in which the DD relative had lived in a large state institution at one time, one sister said her brother had been "a bit of a handful" when he was young and had been admitted to "hospital"; however, he became ill and his mother brought him home again. Another caregiver said that their mother had brought their brother home from a hospital when the family's financial circumstances had improved; he had lived in an institution from the age of 7 until his mid-20s. One woman reported that she had to choose between caring for an elderly parent and her developmentally disabled sibling: when her mother was unable to continue caring for her brother, she chose to care for her mother and her brother was hospitalized. After their mother died, the hospital asked if she would take over care for her brother; she agreed, on a trial basis, and he had lived with her ever since. The fourth caregiver, a mother, said her daughter lived in a "government-run home" until she was 17 and returned home when other siblings had left.

Transitions

Most of the developmentally disabled group had always lived with relatives, and 13 still lived in parental households. When considering who might be available when a new caregiver was needed, the majority of current nonparental caregivers felt they were the only ones available to provide 24-hour care. In only three cases were other relatives nominated; in the remaining instance, the answer was "don't know." Relatives' reasons for not being available included work-related transfer to another city or not enough room in the house. Unwillingness to care was another reason. As one sister said, "Others could have shared but no one wanted to." She explained that both she and her husband chose to live an "ordinary" way of life with no big ambitions. Other family members had become business or career people without time to care, "so it was just expected of me." A brother who was the youngest in his family explained that older family members "all married and went away." Transitions where a person has been "handed down" from parent to siblings and transitions among siblings are described below.

Parents to Sibling

Comments about the transfer of relatives with developmental disabilities from parents to siblings were obtained from the 20 families in which this transfer had occurred. For these families, parents had either died or moved into care themselves, or both the parent and the relative with DD had moved to the care of siblings. Nine of the sibling caregivers said they were unaware of the plans or wishes of their parents. One woman said she "just knew" she would continue care and that nothing was explicit; she said that she and another sister had always been involved in daily care because one of them had always lived at home, and that there was no clear point of transition. One brother said that talking to his mother about what would happen in the future was too painful, and that she had hoped her developmentally disabled son would die before she did; in contrast, his siblings acknowledged that their brother might outlive them all and therefore there was the possibility that care might have to be passed on to the next generation, to their own children. In one single-caregiver household, a mother stressed the reciprocal nature of care and said that her developmentally disabled son had an equal role in the household because he did many chores, such as shopping,

putting out the garbage, and making sure the house was locked at night and when they went out. She added that her friends thought she was lucky to have her son as company.

After their parents died, three of these nine families found that formal plans had been made without their knowledge. One woman, a nurse and the youngest in the family, discovered that her mother had left written instructions naming her to look after her sister. In the two other cases, parents had left the family home to the person with DD so that he or she would have somewhere to live; they had not specified who might provide care but merely that their DD child would have a home. In these three cases, family lawyers were aware of the plans, but those most affected by parental instructions were not.

Ten families said they had some knowledge of what their parents had hoped would happen in the future and knew parents wanted the son or daughter to live in a family atmosphere; however, no particular family member had been identified as caregiver. Two daughters said they realized the issue of long-term care would remain unspoken unless they raised it with their parent themselves, and they said that the wishes of the parent would never have been known unless this action had been taken. Both daughters told their parent they would continue to look after their sibling, although the exact nature of "look after" was not defined.

Although half of the caregivers said they did not recall specifically discussing future-care issues with parents, eight people said they had made a verbal commitment to look after their developmentally disabled brother or sister in the future. Several people said that their offer was made informally and included a range of possible supports, such as "keeping an eye on" or making sure the sibling would be "all right." One caregiver, who said his family had a history of "not talking," had retired early to continue to care for his brother, although this had never been discussed with any other family member.

Eight of the 10 caregivers who had some knowledge of what their parents hoped would happen recalled they felt a duty to continue care. They made comments such as it was "just expected of me" or "moral obligation to care." One caregiver said that it was very hard to say "you do not want to look after your own family," and because she was the only other person in the family, there was no discussion about it.

Sibling to Sibling

Some developmentally disabled people had moved among different family members several times. Family members had organized who should continue care, although the reasons for the moves varied. In one family, the DD person had been living with his brother and sister-in-law, but their transfer to another city was seen as too disruptive for him. He moved in with his sister, who remained in the same city, at a time when she had four small children; she was "devastated" when he came to live with them, she said. It was a situation she had not expected but one she found herself unable to reject. In another instance, a brother had gone to stay with his sister, brother-in-law, and their small children for a holiday 25 years ago and had never left. He continued to live most congenially with this family in the different places to which they had moved.

In two other families, sisters lived together and shared responsibilities of caring for several decades, each alternating caring with paid work. The lives of these women had revolved around their relative with developmental disabilities. In another family, a sister wanted to provide care for her brother, but when her health deteriorated another sister volunteered to continue care. In the fifth family, the mother had died while the children were young and the whole family had moved in with cousins. Someone from this extended family had always provided care.

Three people with developmental disabilities had lived on their own before moving in with siblings. One of them, a woman, had lived in an apartment adjacent to her parents. After the parents died, she was not able to continue living alone because, as her sister explained, "she was being ripped off by those she sort of depended on in the community and that was dreadful." This sister had promised their mother that she would look after her sibling, and although she delayed the move for as long as she could, she found little

choice but to move her sister into her own home. In another family, after parents died, living alone lasted only a few months before concerns about hygiene arose, and a brother moved in to live with his developmentally disabled sister.

Future Plans of Families

There has been much discussion in recent years about long-term residential-care plans made by parents (Freedman, Krauss, and Seltzer 1997; Noonan-Walsh, Conliffe and Birkbeck 1993; Heller and Factor 1991; Grant 1990), about the roles of siblings in future care (Seltzer and Krauss 1989; Krauss et al. 1996), and about the responsibilities of, and boundaries between, family and state (Opie 1992; Green 1993).

In the New Zealand study, less than one-quarter of the families had made formal, specific, on-going residential-care plans. In all, three parents and four siblings were the only caregivers clearly to nominate a key person or people to resolve future care issues. Six of these key people were family members and one was a social worker. It has been suggested that those people nominated in key-person succession plans may find discussing future plans "less emotionally challenging than parents who tend to avoid confronting issues" (Bigby 1996).

The inclusion of the person with developmental disabilities in these discussions was unclear. Twelve caregivers had not discussed the future, and most of them said it was because their DD relative did not have the verbal or comprehension skills, "would not register," or "wouldn't understand." Another 12 families said that the topic had been raised but that their relative had not responded in any way. One developmentally disabled daughter spoke up during the interview with her caregiver and suggested that "some would be too thick to make a decision." However, according to the caregivers, few people with DD had raised concerns about their future. One woman had nominated a rest home in which she wanted to live in the future. One man had insisted that he wanted to live with another sister and he would have preferred to be living with her already. After discussion with caregivers, another three people developed their own ideas about where they wanted to live in the future. One of them, for instance, wanted to stay in the family home and have someone come and live there with her.

It has been demonstrated in several countries that parents are often reluctant to make explicit plans for a transition to nonparental care. One American study (Heller and Factor 1991) found that less than one-third of the families made future living plans for their DD relatives; another study in Australia found that only 15 percent of parents had planned comprehensively (Bigby 1996). In a large, multiphase study of 340 mothers, it was found that less than half of mothers had specific plans for where their son or daughter would live in the future (Freedman, Kraus, and Seltzer 1997).

As reported elsewhere, parents intended to carry on for as long as possible (Heller and Factor 1991). The 13 New Zealand parents who still provided daily care were asked about their thoughts for the future. Two parents were planning that their son or daughter would be "all right" by themselves, and another two parents had willed the family homes to their developmentally disabled children. One mother wondered if she might leave the house to an agency on the condition that the agency would support her daughter. Four parents had thought about either generic or specialist rest-home care. One mother wanted both her developmentally disabled son and herself to move to a rest home and continue to be together. Although all parents said they had *thought* about the future, they intended to carry on as long as they could and had no plans ready to hand on care if necessary.

None of the 13 parents reported that their other children would look after their DD sibling on a long-term basis, although 9 said their families would give temporary care if required. However, 10 siblings, now caregivers, acknowledged making general commitments but not specifically agreeing that they would provide the ongoing 24-hour care they felt their parents wanted. Eight of these siblings recalled making verbal commitments to look after the DD person in the fu-

ture; however, to "look after" was intended to mean any of a range of possible care supports, from 24-hour care to "keeping an eye on" their sibling from a distance. One sister had assured her mother she would "make sure her brother was all right" but had not expected that he would move in to live with her at a later stage.

One parent had made inquiries about alternative residential care, but his other son, who was overseas, made it clear he would come home and sort everything out when "the need" arose. Another parent refused to comment on future plans, which she had left to her two daughters; however, the daughters could not agree and so plans did not progress. Five parents said they were leaving "it"—that is, ongoing care—to their children.

Some of the next generation of caregivers, the brothers and sisters of those with developmental disabilities, had considered who would assume responsibilities of care after them. Several of these families said they already involved relatives from the second generation; one DD person in the study group was currently living with the next generation. In one family, the current caregiver wanted her DD sister to go to a particular rest home, which she had already identified; however, her daughter and son-in-law wanted their aunt to live in a flat they owned, and the caregiver felt she had to agree. Five other sibling caregivers felt their own children, four of whom were daughters, would help out if needed. In one instance, one sister had a formal, paid agreement with a niece, who did housework and advocated for services and information as required. Another three siblings had involved daughters, nieces, or nephews in family conferences about the future, along with lawyers; they had explicitly nominated key people, all family members, to be part of future planning efforts.

Discussion

Most of the families in this study had provided 24-hours-a-day care for their relative with a developmental disability from childhood to old age. This fact makes them an exceptional group for their generation. Nonetheless, because of present-day trends toward community-based, and particularly, family-based ongoing care in industrialized countries, this experience is highly relevant. This study of family caregiving has provided valuable insights into decision-making processes of family-based ongoing care, but the future environment, including the values and motivation of people able to provide care, may be quite different. The circumstances surrounding the transition from parental to nonparental care (Seltzer, Krauss, and Heller, 1991), and from family to nonfamily care, need to be better understood. The decisions leading to a move from parent to another caregiver or from one caregiver to another caregiver are relatively unexplored.

The New Zealand families surveyed demonstrated a variety of motives and capacity for continuing 24-hours-a-day care. Some family members wanted to, and volunteered to, continue; some felt they had no choice but to continue care, and some never made a choice or identified a particular point of transition because they had always been involved in daily care.

The hopes of parents for 24-hour family care rested on assumptions about the availability and willingness of the next generation. As the present-day society is characterized by smaller households, a higher proportion of women in paid work, and dispersed and mobile families, in a climate where there is a general failure of governmental policy and bureaucracies to help family and community caregivers adequately or to acknowledge the costs they bear, the next generation may be less able and less willing to accept the "handing down" of a person, particularly an older one, who needs ongoing care (Hand 1996). These are worldwide trends.

The study of family care in New Zealand showed that plans for future care were often not articulated clearly by parents or other caregivers, and that resulting implicit assumptions provided some individuals with unexpected responsibilities to provide 24-hour care. The authors suggest here that the positive force and value of "weak" promises and tacit understandings should not be underestimated. Informal arrangements within families have the advantages of flexibility and maintenance of support networks. However,

the study showed that parents' assumptions may have negative effects and the implicit and unexpected nature of the transfer from parent to nonparent care meant that some sibling caregivers had to give up paid work or faced exhausting workloads or living a relatively isolated lifestyle with little respite. But it is also worth considering the functions of such assumptions.

On the one hand, for parents, the avoidance of discussion means that future-care issues are not forced on their other children, informal support relationships remain flexible, unnecessary family conflict is avoided, and hopes for the desired future arrangement remain intact. In an environment where the options are unclear or there is a lack of choice, such avoidance may be positive for the parent but does not address the underlying issues.

On the other hand, discussion and better knowledge about options may result in future arrangements that are satisfactory to all concerned. For example, brothers and sisters may find that roles as advocates and friends to their DD sibling are more practical and acceptable than full-time caregiving. One study examined informal plans and suggested the advantages of having a key person to relieve parents from confronting dilemmas that future planning invariably involves (Bigby 1996). The involvement of key people ensured that there was advocacy for gaining access to services and making decisions in the interests of the person with DD. In general, it is both possible and desirable to identify an individual or a group of individuals who are expected, and willing, to take a role in future care. Planning for the future need not be prescriptive. Indeed, under some circumstances, the most that can be expected may be discussion of possible roles and the identification of alternatives.

Such discussion can only be useful, however, in contexts where options are available or can be created. Public policy, sometimes in concert with community initiatives, is the major player in setting this context. To date, planning for the future has been complicated by the lack of options. Certainly some families in the New Zealand studies did not perceive a set of possibilities and therefore operated in an environment without choice and where avoidance of succession issues was a common and reasonable phenomenon. Discussion of a range of options is fruitful because it encourages the involvement of a number of possible caregivers, sensitizes families and communities to the types of options available, encourages new solutions, and provides support to advocates. This situation benefits the families directly involved and increases resources available to all.

The person with developmental disability needs to be involved in this process, for both practical and human-rights reasons (Larnaca Resolution 1998). In planning or in research, there is often no provision for their voices to be heard directly. Their views are necessary for a full discussion relating to preferences for their future care, and they may well challenge the comments from caregivers or advocates who speak on their behalf. It is apparent that decisions about where people with developmental disabilities will live and who their caregivers will be are contingent on complex sets of personal, family, and public-policy circumstances. These decisions should also take into account the desires and preferences of the people whose lives are most intimately affected. People with DD do have preferences and wishes, and many can communicate them effectively (Hand and Reid 1989; Rioux and Bach 1994; Donald Beasley Institute 1996). They may not wish to be "hand-me-down" people.

Discussion Questions

1. From your understanding of caregiver stress thus far, do the strains of caring for a developmentally disabled older relative differ from those of caring for an elderly spouse, parent, or other relative?

2. Describe the difficulties and gaps in the family decision-making process about planning for the future care of a developmentally disabled relative.

3. What are the advantages and disadvantages for the family members and for the developmentally disabled individual of postponing discussion about his or her future care?

4. Since fewer developmentally disabled people are currently being placed in institutions and more women are in the labor force, what social policies may be needed to ensure adequate care and quality of life for both the disabled and their caregivers in the future?

References

Bigby, C. 1996. "Transferring Responsibility: The Nature and Effectiveness of Parental Planning for the Future of Adults With Intellectual Disability Who Remain at Home Until Mid-life." *Journal of Intellectual and Developmental Disability* 21(4): 295–312.

Donald Beasley Institute. 1996. *Women With Disabilities: Speaking Out for Ourselves*. Dunedin, New Zealand: Donald Beasley Institute.

Freedman, R. I., Krauss, M. W. and Seltzer, M. M. 1997. "Aging Parents' Residential Plans for Adult Children With Mental Retardation." *Mental Retardation* 35(2): 114–123.

Grant, G. 1990. "Elderly Parents With Handicapped Children: Anticipating the Future." *Journal of Aging Studies* 4(4): 359–374.

Green, T. 1993. "Institutional Care, Community Services, and the Family:" In P. Koopman-Boyden ed. *New Zealand's Ageing Society*. Wellington: Daphne Brasell Associates Press.

Hand, J. E. 1994. "Report of a National Survey of Older People With Lifelong Intellectual Handicaps in New Zealand." *Journal of Intellectual Disability Research* 38: 275–287.

——1996. Health Research: Reflections on Ontology and Practice in the National Survey of Older People With Lifelong Intellectual Handicap in New Zealand.— In P. Norris ed. *Health-Related Papers From the Sociological Association of Aotearoa Annual Conference, Akaroa, December 1995*, working paper 16, pp. 99–110. Wellington: Victoria University Health Services Research Centre.

Hand, J. E., and Reid, P. M. 1989. "Views and Recollections of Older People With Intellectual Handicaps in New Zealand." *Australian and New Zealand Journal of Developmental Disabilities* 15(3 & 4): 231–240.

——1996. "Older Adults With Lifelong Intellectual Disability in New Zealand: Prevalence, Disabilities, and Implications for Regional Health Authorities." *New Zealand Medical Journal* 109: 118–121.

——1998. "Ageing and Lifelong Intellectual Disability: Implications for Policy." *New Zealand Journal of Psychology*, in press.

Hand, J. E., and Trewby, M. 1996. "Older People With Lifelong Intellectual Disabilities and the Medical Profession." *Revista de Gerontologia* 6(2): 124–130.

Hand, J. E., Trewby, M., and Reid, P. M. 1994. "When a Family Member Has an Intellectual Handicap." *Disability and Society* 9(2): 167–184.

Heller T. and Factor A. 1991. "Permanency Planning for Adults With Mental Retardation Living With Family Caregivers." *American Journal on Mental Retardation* 96(2): 163–176.

Krauss, M. W., Seltzer, M. M., Gordon, R., and Friedman, D. H. 1996. Binding Ties: The Roles of Adult Siblings With Mental Retardation. *Mental Retardation* 34(2): 83–93.

Larnaca Resolution. 1998. The Larnaca Resolution was passed by delegates of the International Conference on Intellectual and Developmental Disabilities, held at Larnaca, Cyprus. New York: United Nations.

Noble, A. 1994. *Hidden Lives: The Work of Care: A Photographic Installation* Wellington: National Library of New Zealand.

Noonan-Walsh, P., Conliffe, C., and Birkbeck, G. 1993. "Permanency Planning and Maternal Well-being: A Study of Caregivers of People With Intellectual Disability in Ireland and Northern Ireland." *The Irish Journal of Psychology* 14(1): 176–188.

Opie, A. 1992. *There's Nobody There: Community Care of Confused Older People.* Auckland: Oxford University Press.

Reid, P. M. and Hand, J. E. 1995. "The Process, Problems, and Rewards of Identifying Older Adults With Intellectual Handicap in New Zealand," *Australia and New Zealand Journal of Developmental Disabilities* 20(1): 1–14.

Rioux, M. and Bach, M. 1994. *Disability Is Not Measles: New Research Paradigms in Disability.* York, Ontario: Roeher Institute.

Seltzer M. and Krauss M. W. 1989. "Aging Parents With Adult Mentally Retarded Children: Family Risk Factors and Sources of Support." *American Journal on Mental Retardation* 94(3): 303–312.

Seltzer M., Krauss M. W. and Heller T. 1991. Family Caregiving Over the Lifecourse. In M. Janicki and M. Seltzer eds. *Aging and Developmental Disabilities. Proceedings of the Boston Roundtable on Research Issues and Aging in Developmental Disabilities.* Boston: American Association on Mental Retardation.

Note

1. A photographic installation of participants in this study, "Hidden Lives" by Anne Noble, is now in the Collection of the Gallery of the National Public Library of New Zealand. It is available for art museum exhibition. Write or call The National Library of New Zealand Te Puna Matauranga Aotearoa, P. O. Box 1467, Wellington 1, New Zealand, tel 64-4-474 3000. Also available is an exhibition, "Sharing and Caring: Older People Taking Care of Older People" authored by Hand and Reid and photographed by Anne Noble, that consists of photographs and text on folding display boards. Loan is free but borrowing agency pays freight costs. Contact: Donald Beasley Institute, e-mail NZIMR@otago.ac.nz.

Jennifer Hand and Patricia Reid, "Hand-Me-Down People: Aging Families Caring for a Developmentally Disabled Aging Relative." Printed by permission of the authors.

Section V

Health and Illness in Later Life

Since 1900, patterns of illness among all age groups in the United States have changed dramatically. In the past, people were more likely to develop acute illnesses that came on quickly, and they either died or recovered. Today many acute infectious diseases, such as smallpox, polio, diphtheria, scarlet fever, plague, and measles, have largely been eradicated or checked through immunizations, public health measures, and improved medical treatment. Infectious diseases thus are far less common, while chronic conditions, ranging from sinus problems to heart diseases, cancer, arthritis, and diabetes, have escalated. Chronic conditions affect people of all ages, from the very rich to the very poor. In 1995, approximately one in every three Americans had one or more chronic conditions, and one-third of these had some limitation in a major activity (Robert Wood Johnson Foundation 1996).

Contrary to popular belief, however, only one in four people living outside a long-term care setting with a chronic condition is 65 or older. Some chronic conditions are more common among specific age groups. For example, asthma is most frequent among those under the age of 45, while diseases such as arthritis, hypertension, and heart disease may begin in midlife but progress with age. Arthritis and heart disease most often develop among the elderly; hypertension (a major risk factor for heart disease and stroke), and diabetes strike both middle-aged and old people. Among those 65 and over, nearly one

in four people has one chronic disease, and over 2 in 3 (69 percent) have two or more (Robert Wood Johnson Foundation 1996).

One of the major challenges confronting researchers in the twenty-first century is to distinguish processes that are inextricably tied to growing old from aging-associated processes that some, but not all, people experience as they grow old. Numerous studies, usually cross-sectional observations at points across the life span, have detected negative changes in health or behavior and attributed it to the "aging process," that is, an inevitable feature of "normal aging." Within the past decade or so, however, the effects of chronological age have been examined much more carefully. What scholars had generally assumed to be "normal aging" turns out to be associated with environmental, lifestyle, and disease states that themselves are related to or change with aging. Thus, changes in many events are *not* directly caused by aging itself but rather by *processes*, which may change with age but are not intrinsic parts of "normal aging."

Normal aging thus describes those events that are inevitable as we grow older. *Usual* aging, in contrast, is a more statistical definition or average: what many people do or experience as they grow older but not part of our inevitable fate as we age. For example, many of us think of arthritis as part of "normal" aging. But many people grow very old without ever developing this disease. Arthritis thus is "usual" but not "normal" aging. In short, while some slowing down of the body always occurs with age, age is not a synonym for decay. Even in advanced old age, chronological age and disease do not necessarily go hand in hand. Some centenarians are mentally alert and physically active; others are mentally confused and bedridden (Palmore 1995). Even within the same person, decrements in functioning occur at different rates. A college student, for example, can have the kidney function of a 30-year-old, the memory retention of an 18-year-old, the muscles of a 40-year-old, and so on.

How do ageist prejudices and misconceptions about the elderly affect health care, medical treatment, and the lives of the elderly? Research indicates that medical students, for example, view older people as disagreeable, dull, inactive, and economic burdens (McCray 1998), attitudes that carry over into actual health-care practice. In her selection, Lynda Grant studies the effects of ageist beliefs on both the training of health-care professionals and patient outcomes. Healthcare professionals receive little training about normal aging processes; rather, old age is viewed as a downward journey to the grave. The concept of old age as disability and decline can become a self-fulfilling prophecy, where the expectation of disability creates frailty, loss of self-esteem, and a diminished sense of control over one's life. At the broader social level, ageist beliefs about the capacities of older people shape social policies that neglect their mental as well as physical needs.

Not only does ageism affect health procedures in later life, but racism and economic inequality interact with ageism to affect remedies offered. For example, African Americans who suffer a heart attack are significantly less likely to undergo bypass surgery and other procedures than whites with similarly severe heart disease. These treatment differences relate to the poorer survival rate among African Americans, who are more likely to die than whites within five years after a heart attack (Peterson, Shaw, DeLong, et al. 1997). And clot-busting heart medications are used less often among elderly African Americans (9 percent) than whites (17 percent) (Allison, Kiefe, Centor, et al. 1996).

Lack of cultural sensitivity, too, presents a barrier to effective treatment. The white majority model of health care often fails to take into account the value system of different racial and ethnic groups. Among Native Americans, the need for health-care services is extensive but largely unmet; excessive regulations, bureaucratic procedures, and fragmented services are but a few of the barriers (Administration on Aging 1996). Using a life history approach, Judith Bunnell Sellers studies cultural differences between elderly white Anglos and Navajos and their implications for health care delivery. The Anglo emphasis on self-expression, futurity, and technological progress is alien to Navajo elders, who value silence and harmony with nature and distrust technological intervention. If Anglo outlooks are used by health-care professionals to assess or treat Navajos, they are likely to be unsuccessful.

The importance of an accurate assessment of the whole person is underscored in the selection by Patricia Barry, a geriatric physician. Often overlooked in treating older people is the importance of their ability to perform everyday activities and ways in which their capacities to enjoy life can be improved. Chronic disease and functional disability can be reduced or postponed through lifestyle changes, and healthy behaviors are especially beneficial for the elderly. According to Barry, a complete assessment should encompass not only functional capacity to perform activities of daily living but a mental health assessment including depression, a commonly missed problem in later life, and cognition. Only then can effective intervention to restore or improve performance become a reality.

One of the most feared chronic diseases in later life is Alzheimer's Disease, the most common cause of dementia in old age. Alzheimer's is *not* a part of normal aging but a disease affecting the parts of the brain controlling thought, memory, and language. It is characterized by abnormal clumps and tangled bundles of fibers in the brain. Scientists now believe that genetic factors may be involved in more than half of the cases of Alzheimer's. A protein called apoliproprotein E (ApoE) may be a factor. Although all of us have ApoE, which helps carry cholesterol in the blood, the gene has three forms, including one that seems to protect people from Alzheimer's Disease and another that seems to make people more likely to develop it. Genetic factors alone, however, may not be enough to cause the disease, and other risk factors may combine with an individual's genetic makeup to increase his or her chances of developing it. What is it like to know that you have Alzheimer's Disease? The selection by Morris Friedell describes his reactions and current life after finding out he was a sufferer. A former college professor, he first became aware that something was amiss when he began to have memory lapses. Younger than the usual Alzheimer's victim, he was initially misdiagnosed. His experiences give a firsthand glimpse into the world of an individual coping with this disability.

Perhaps because of ageist myths, Alzheimer's Disease has been widely publicized as a scourge of late life, and many middle-aged people fearfully forecast that they will develop this form of dementia. Lynne Gershenson Hodgson and Stephen Cutler analyze anticipatory fears of dementia among adults who have a family member with Alzheimer's and compare their apprehensions with a group of adults whose families do not have a demented elder. Because of the genetic evidence linking the ApoE gene to Alzheimer's, adult children who have parents with the disease are particularly alarmed when they notice any memory lapses in themselves. Whether such people will ever develop the disease is uncertain, for there is currently no test that can detect or predict the likelihood of its onset.

Another myth in American society is that most elders live in nursing homes or other long-term-care facilities. The opposite is true. Only about 5 percent of old people are in such facilities at any given time. The typical nursing-home resident is not an individual abandoned by unfeeling children or other relatives but an 85-year-old white woman, most often widowed, with multiple disabilities that require round-the-clock monitoring or attention. How good is the care provided in nursing homes and board-and-care facilities. And what are the stresses and strains associated with providing care to severely impaired residents? Leslie Morgan and Kevin Eckert, focusing on small long-term-care facilities, where the operator is most likely to be on duty 24 hours a day, explore the little-considered emotional and psychological burdens experienced by these paid care providers. Rather than finding indifferent, insensitive, or stressed personnel, they note the caring and commitment of the workers and their closeness and feelings of responsibility for their residents, many of whom are severely impaired or have terminal illnesses.

As life-extension technology has increased, management of terminal illness and how and when we die have emerged as both medical and ethical issues. In a society such as ours where chronic, debilitating illness and death are feared and activity valued as an end in itself, death is a dreaded foe, to be vanquished whenever possible. Yet dying has become increasingly an act surrounded by costly, often futile, technology; for example, even when cardiopulmonary resuscitation (CPR) is successful, only about 15 percent of hospital patients younger than age 70 and almost nobody older than that can expect to live to be discharged (Nuland 1993). Living wills have emerged as one way in which to exert choice over the manner of one's death. A living will is a written declaration, signed by a mentally competent person, that instructs one's physicians to withhold or withdraw life-sustaining treatment if one is suffering from an incurable and terminal illness. In the selection by Philip Roth, whose father is suffering from an inoperable tumor, discusses his father's gradual decline, his own difficulties in discussing the topic of a living will with him, his hesitancy in honoring the living will, and his father's death and burial.

Faced with pain and the emotional and financial burden that can accompany life extension during terminal illness, physician-assisted suicide is advocated by some as an alternative. Publicity surrounding physician-pathologist Jack Kevorkian and his participation in numerous assisted suicides, including one subsequently shown on television, have stimulated discussion of the right to die. The experience of the Netherlands, where physician-assisted suicide is legal, has been heralded both as a model for "good death" and as an example of differential, sometimes involuntary use of the practice. In 1997 the United States Supreme Court ruled that individuals did not have a constitutional right to assisted suicide but that no constitutional bar prevented states from enacting legislation that permits it, thus leaving the debate about its legal status open. Although no one knows how many patients actually request help in dying, surveys report numerous requests to medical personnel for euthanasia. The selection by psychiatrist Philip Muskin addresses not the legality of assisted suicide but the psychodynamic issues involved in the request. All too often, he suggests, the simplistic evaluation of a patient's mental competence is considered rather than the emotions behind the wish. Is the request due to depression, guilt, a desire for self-punishment, or rage? Suicide is among the 10 top causes of death in the United States and a serious outcome of depression, stress, and other mental conditions. Some individuals requesting assisted suicide do not want to die but are expressing rage, despair, helplessness, or other feelings that should receive attention. Muskin stresses that understanding an individual's request to die can be understood only through careful, expert exploration rather than taken at face value.

The costs of terminal, intensive, or long-term care have played a role in consideration of assisted suicide as an alternative. Whatever the age of the patient, chronic illness and terminal care cost money. Many chronically ill people "cycle through the hospital, then go to the clinic or doctor's office, return home, go back to the hospital during acute episodes and again back to their homes"—all contributing to higher health costs (Wiener, Fagerhaugh, Strauss, and Suczek 1997, p. 26). Health care for older people remains a major cost to the nation, which has led some to suggest age as a criterion for rationing medical treatment. Daniel Callahan maintains that the growth of the elderly population has resulted in too many resources devoted to their care at the expense of the young. Health-care costs for the elderly are simply out of control. Taking an alternative view, Robert Binstock examines international data to explore whether a high proportion of elderly in the population is associated with higher health-care costs. In an analysis of 12 countries, he finds little relationship in the percentage of the gross domestic product (GDP) that a nation spends on health care and its percentage of elderly in the population. The United States, for example, spends more of its GDP on health care than the other 11 nations but has the smallest proportion of people aged 65 and over. Rather than predicting rising health costs using the "voodoo demography" of the specter of an elderly population, he calls for a consideration of the characteristics of the health-care system and the values upon which it is built.

Dramatic breakthroughs in public health, medicine, and technology such as the development of antibiotics and organ transplants have increased average life expectancy and reduced acute illness. Yet chronic diseases remain the leading causes of death, severe illness, and disability. The indirect costs of chronic illness are high to patients and their families. Work and daily activity may be limited, special care and equipment needed, and drugs, medical, and technical equipment required to maintain the chronically ill person at home. Although difficult to measure, the emotional costs, both to the chronically ill person and her or his family, are also high. Every nation rations health care in one way or another; in the United States, for example, health care is generally limited by what an individual can afford. Those without health insurance or the ability to pay for deductibles and co-payments are less likely to receive care than the well-off. In other nations with national health insurance, procedures may be allocated in various ways, including likelihood of success. Meting out health care on the basis of age is one possible solution already used in some nations such as Great Britain to contain costs. Explicit rationing, however, raises a number of both practical and ethical issues. An age cutoff is simple and objective, but is age alone a suitable criterion considering the enormous variation within the broad category of older people or even among those 80 years old and over? If age is used as a standard, what other touchstones could also be introduced?

Health and illness patterns in later life cannot be understood without taking into account the social context in which people grow old and their position in social hierarchies that have shaped their life course. Regardless of gender, race, ethnicity, or social class, the cultural construction of old age for both men and women in postindustrial society encourages elders to internalize their own limitations and to settle for less than their actual capacities (Philipson 1982). As you read through the following selections, think about the ways in which ageism affects decisions about health-care policies and funding priorities. Appraise possible strategies for today and tomorrow that older people, health professionals, and communities can use to promote health and delay disease in later life. What do you want to do to enable your parents, and someday yourself, to enjoy a healthy and good old age?

References

Administration on Aging. 1996. *Home and Community-based Long-term Care in American Indian and Alaska Native Communities*. Washington, DC: U. S. Department of Health and Human Services, Administration on Aging.

Allison, J. J., Kiefe, C. I., Centor, R. M., Box, J. B., Farmer, R. M. 1996. "Racial Differences in the Medical Treatment of Elderly Medicare Patients with Acute Myocardial Infarction." *Journal of General Internal Medicine* 1: 736–743.

McCray, C. C. 1998. "Ageism in the Preclinical Years." *Journal of the American Medical Association* 279: 1035.

Nuland, S. 1993. *How We Die*. New York: Knopf.

Palmore, E. 1995. "Centenarians." In G. L. Maddox, R. C. Atchley, J. G. Evans, C. E. Finch, D. F. Hultsch, R. A. Kane, M. D. Mezey, and I. C. Siegler, eds., *Encyclopedia of Aging*. 2nd ed., pp. 165–166. New York: Springer.

Peterson, E. D., Shaw, L. K., DeLong, E. R., Pryor, D. B., Califf, R. M., and Mark, D. B. 1997. "Racial Variation in the Use of Coronary Revascularization Procedures." *New England Journal of Medicine* 336(7): 480–486.

Philipson, Chris. 1982. *Capitalism and the Construction of Old Age*. London: Macmillan.

Robert Wood Johnson Foundation. 1996. *Chronic Care in America: A 21st Century Challenge*. New York: Robert Wood Johnson Foundation.

Wiener, C. F., Fagerhaugh S., Strauss, A., and Suczek, B. 1997. "What Price Chronic Illness?" In C. L. Wiener and A. L. Strauss, eds., *Where Medicine Fails*, pp. 25–42. New Brunswick, NJ: Transaction.

Chapter 35

Ageism and Its Impact on Healthy Aging

Lynda D. Grant

How would you feel if you went to your physician or other health-care professional and your complaints were brushed aside as just part of your age rather than a bonafide health concern? Unfortunately, this scenario is not uncommon for many older people. Physicians and others see the age of the patient rather than the patient. The elderly are stereotyped, where health-care providers fill in the picture of an older person with an ageist brush after knowing only one characteristic: age.

Although chronic disease is not a part of normal aging, many health professionals assume that chronic disease is inevitable in later life. Depression, one of the most common problems of older adults, may also be mistaken as "normal aging." Reluctant to spend the time required for an understanding of the elder and his or her health condition, physicians who stereotype the elderly not only disregard their concerns but convey attitudes that lessen older people's sense of self-esteem. Ageist preconceptions by health-care personnel may even lead to inappropriate and unnecessary institutional placement of individuals suffering from a reversible or treatable illness. In the following selection, Lynda Grant addresses ways in which health-care personnel stereotype the elderly and the negative impact of ageism on the elderly's self-assurance and competence. Grant's observations raise questions about the ways in which relatively healthy elders are regarded as well as about the allocation of social resources to treat mental health problems in later life.

Ageism has been described as "thinking or believing in a negative manner about the process of becoming old or about old people" (Doty, 1987, p. 213). Society's attitudes and beliefs about aging are culturally embedded and can have a profound effect on how people view themselves and others who are aging. Unfortunately, negative stereotypes about aging are still quite prevalent (Rowe & Kahn, 1987). Health care providers are not immune to these insidious stereotypes. This article reviews a number of ageism stereotypes in society generally and in the health care field. The aim is to demonstrate that ageism can negatively affect health care providers' professional training and service delivery and, ultimately, their clients' behavior and health outcomes.

For many years service providers used the World Health Organization (WHO, 1947) definition of health: "Health is a state of complete physical, mental, and social well-being, and not merely the absence of disease" (p. 16). This concept of health was a radical departure from the traditional model that saw health only as the absence of disease. WHO recognized that psychosocial well-being is an all-important component of health. However, health remained an abstract concept and, therefore, an ideal difficult to achieve. More recently, *Achieving Health for All* (Health and Welfare Canada, 1986) defined health in terms of "quality of life" and included in the definition the opportunity to make choices and to gain satisfaction from living despite functional limitations. This document suggested that health is a dynamic process of interaction between communities and individuals. Health involves freedom of choice: Communities (including health care providers) and individuals choose to take deliberate action to make the changes necessary for healthy aging.

Unfortunately, ageism can often affect the choices people are presented with and the decisions they make about those choices. If people believe that some of the "inevitable deterioration" of aging is preventable, they are likely to be more active in their own self-care. If health care providers believe that elderly people are valuable equal members of society, then this belief should be reflected in professional training and service provision. Consequently, confronting ageism by enhancing positive beliefs about aging is a vital component of health promotion training and programming.

Effect of Ageism on Factors in Aging

Sociological Factors

Traditionally, aging has been viewed as a continual process of decline. Unfortunately, this stereotyping results in systematic discrimination that devalues senior citizens and frequently denies them equality (Butler, 1987).

In his review of the attitudes toward aging shown by humor, Palmore (1986) found that elderly people were often portrayed negatively. The humor tended to focus on physical and mental losses, as well as on decreases in sexual attractiveness and drive. Jokes about older women tended to be more negative than those about older men.

In North American culture, employability is often viewed as a primary measure of one's ability to contribute meaningfully to society and as a source of self-identity and self-esteem (Moody, 1988). Botwinck (1984) reviewed the literature on the effects of ageism on employment. He found that although age was not an important factor in the evaluation of work competence, older age was given as one of the reasons for poor applicant quality if the person was not hired. When a younger applicant was not hired, lack of effort or inability was given as the reason.

Snyder and Barrett (1988) reviewed 272 federal court cases dealing with age discrimination and employment filed between 1970 and 1986. Sixty-five percent were decided in favor of the employer. The researchers found a number of problems with how these cases were decided. First, there was frequent use of generalities about the differences between older and younger workers' abilities, despite the fact that there was no documented evidence of consistent group differences in actual job performance. Often neither the employers nor the expert witnesses were asked for specific evidence concerning the plaintiff's actual physical capabilities and the specific job requirements. Second, the variabil-

ity of decreased physical strength and fitness with age was frequently not addressed. Third, the possible effects of redesigning the workplace to accommodate older workers was often not considered.

These societal attitudes can affect not only how elderly people are perceived but also how they view themselves. Bodily (1991) surveyed inactive nurses to find out why they were not working. She was surprised to find that many respondents cited their age as the reason for not working without giving any other qualifiers. As Bodily stated,

> What concerned me the most about the ways respondents were using "age" was that its meaning was being taken for granted; that is, as if the implications of phrases like "because of my age" or "I'm too old" were sufficiently obvious to require nothing more than a sympathetic nod on the part of the reader. While I was sympathetic, it was not because respondents were in fact too old, but because they were using "age" to disqualify themselves or otherwise limit their range of choices. (p. 248)

The quotation demonstrates the reciprocal nature of ageism. Negative stereotyping in society can lead to viewing elderly people in a depreciatory manner and as less valuable members of society. Elderly people who adopt these aging myths may see decline as inevitable and becoming more passive members of society as the only option available (Rodin & Langer, 1980). Unfortunately, when elderly people act according to these stereotypes, society's misperceptions about the aging process can be reinforced (Butler, 1987).

Physical Factors

Long-held beliefs in the health care field about the aging process are now being seriously questioned. Rowe and Kahn (1987) pointed out that much of what was considered to be inevitable deterioration is the result of individual behavior and environmental conditioning. They criticized researchers for perpetuating a narrow view of aging by concentrating on the central tendencies within a group and ignoring the substantial differences in functional aging (Troll, 1989).

Although changes in physiology are a part of aging, accumulated evidence indicates that many so-called usual disease processes can be modified and minimized (Rowe & Kahn, 1987). Diet and exercise have significant effects on carbohydrate metabolism, osteoporosis, cholesterol levels, diabetes, blood pressure, respiratory functioning, and hydration (Rowe & Kahn, 1987). Other studies have found that chronic pain can be greatly reduced through increased exercise and decreased medication use (Fordyce, 1976). Because musculoskeletal diseases account for 37 percent of all disabilities in the aged population (National Advisory Council on Aging, 1989b), increased mobility can have a significant effect on functional abilities and quality of life.

The lack of understanding about the aging process or the belief that continual decline is inevitable can lead to disease management as opposed to proactive intervention. Elderly people receive more medication prescriptions than younger people for equivalent symptoms (Rodin & Langer, 1980). Anxiolytic use more than doubles from 65 years of age and hypnotic medication use more than triples (Health and Welfare Canada, 1989). These statistics are quite disturbing given that 40 percent of all emergency department visits by elders are medication related.

Emotional Factors

It is well established that psychological well-being plays a significant role in the preservation of physical health and functional capacity (Zautra, Maxwell, & Reich, 1989). However, it has only recently been recognized that many of the variables that put elderly people at risk emotionally are responsive to intervention. In their review of the literature, Rowe and Kahn (1987) showed that lack of or decrease in social support increases elderly people's mortality and morbidity rates and decreases adherence to health-promoting regimens. As an example, they cited studies showing that moving from familiar surroundings to a nursing home or institution increased mortality rates. Longitudinal studies in Sweden revealed that death rates increased by 48 percent for men and 26 percent for women within the first three months after losing a spouse (Svanborg,

1990). Other risk factors include the stress of managing on a fixed income, elder abuse, isolation, perceived health limitations, and the strain of being a caregiver (National Advisory Council on Aging, 1989a).

Unfortunately, psychological problems in older people can go untreated for a number of reasons. Emotional difficulties in elderly people can be difficult to diagnose because they are often masked by physical symptoms that can lead to further isolation and decreased activities. These important symptoms may be misdiagnosed and written off as part of the "normal aging process" (Katz, Curlick, & Nemetz, 1988). Compared to younger adults presenting with the same symptoms, elderly patients are referred less frequently for psychiatric assessments (Hillerbrand & Shaw, 1990). Elderly people themselves are often reluctant to seek assistance for emotional difficulties, even though there are many ways of relieving psychological distress and helping elderly individuals achieve a greater sense of well-being. Whether they attach a stigma to such help or lack knowledge about what type of help is available is unclear.

Cognitive Factors

There is strong evidence to suggest that a sense of well-being is in large part determined by a person's belief systems (Beck, 1991; Persons, 1989). Although a system involves a number of beliefs, two are seen as crucial: belief about control and belief about self-worth (that is, self-esteem). Although discussed separately, they are very much interrelated.

Sense of Control. The belief in the ability to exert control over an event influences how that event is appraised and subsequent coping activity (Lazarus & Folkman, 1984). A sense of control results from the belief that certain actions will lead to certain results and the conviction that one has the capacity to take the action necessary to produce those results (Bandura, 1977, 1982). This is an important concept when considering the aging process because sense of control can often be compromised in elderly people. If they see physical and mental deterioration as uncontrollable, the perceived lack of control is likely to reduce active coping behaviors (Rodin & Langer, 1980). A sense of helplessness in elderly people has been shown to decrease responsiveness, motivation, and self-esteem and eventually to increase illness, mortality rates, and memory problems (Parnham, 1987). Unfortunately, research has shown that increased contact with helping professionals can reinforce this sense of helplessness (Rodin, 1986).

Providing elderly people with the opportunity to increase perceived control over the environment leads to improved memory, alertness, activity, and physical health and decreased morbidity and mortality (Rodin, 1986). In one noteworthy study, alterations that increased residents' control of the environment in a nursing home demonstrated that even small changes can have a profound effect (Langer & Rodin, 1976). When the researchers returned 18 months after the intervention, they found that the experimental group (with increased control) had a 48 percent increase in subjective happiness; were increasingly active, alert, and social; and, perhaps most surprisingly, had a 50 percent lower mortality rate than the control group.

Successful aging cannot be equated with total independence and lack of reliance on others. Everyone maintains a balance between dependence and independence. The need for self-determination encompasses the right to choose not to exercise control. Therefore, service providers must be sensitive to the fact that it is the individual who chooses his or her level of dependence (Clark, 1988).

Self-Esteem. *Self-esteem* is a basic feeling of self-worth and a belief that one is fundamentally a person of value. In George's (1987) review of the literature on self-esteem and older adults, she suggested that the same factors that predict self-esteem in younger adults apply to elderly people: measures of personal achievement, success in interpersonal relationships, and meaningful leisure activities. However, correlates of self-esteem that were unique to older adults were health status and attitudes toward aging.

If aging is seen only in terms of the negative side of growing old and not as another stage of development, self-esteem can be seriously compromised. Rodin and Langer (1980) studied actions commonly seen as characteristic of older people. The young and middle-aged participants saw elderly people as primarily involved in nonsocial behavior and passive activities and attributed to them unpleasant personal characteristics to a much greater extent than positive ones. They also found that all respondents, including the older ones, appeared to have a stereotype of elderly people that included the idea of senility. Ninety percent of the elderly respondents believed that there was a strong possibility they would become senile. However, medical estimates indicate that only 4 percent of people over 64 years of age suffer from a severe case of senility, and only another 10 percent suffer from a milder version (Katzman & Carasu, 1975).

Purpose and meaning in life influence self-esteem (George, 1987). For elderly people, this component is related to whether growing older is viewed as a time for continued contribution, goal setting, and purpose (Baltes, 1990). A perceived meaningless existence can lead to anxiety, depression, hopelessness, and physical decline, whereas meaning and purpose in life are associated with positive mental and physical health (Reker, Peacock, & Wong, 1987). Although meaning in life changes with each developmental phase, the need to be challenged and valued remains the same (Troll, 1989).

Effects of Ageism on Health Care Training and Service Delivery

Gatz and Pearson (1988) stated that although global negative attitudes of aging may not exist in the health care field, specific biases may. Part of the responsibility for health care professionals' biases belongs to the educational institutions. Santos and VandenBos (1982) pointed out that few graduate programs in the social sciences offered training in gerontology. Whitbourne and Hulicka (1990) analyzed 139 psychology textbooks written over 40 years for evidence of ageism. They found that aging issues received little attention even in the later editions. When aging was addressed the texts tended to focus on problems rather than successes and described older adults as suffering from multiple deficits and handicaps that were attributed entirely to the aging process. The texts also only infrequently mentioned intellectual plasticity, the difference between normal aging and disease processes, and the ways in which individuals can compensate for losses associated with aging. The authors concluded that these texts exposed students to a narrow and permanently fixed view of the aging process.

Researchers argue that when others believe that an older person's range of physical and cognitive abilities is narrowing, there is a tendency to restrict individual freedom even further (Clark, 1989). These restrictions can lead to reinforcement of dependent rather than independent behavior by the helping professions (Baltes & Barton, 1979) and to symptom management rather than health promotion (Rodin & Langer, 1980). This behavior may best be conceptualized as "disabling support" versus "enabling support" (Rowe & Kahn, 1987).

One study exemplifies the impact of the two approaches. Avorn and Langer (1982) divided residents in a nursing home into three groups and gave them a jigsaw puzzle to complete. One group was actively assisted by the staff to complete the puzzle (helped group), one was encouraged but received only minimal assistance (encouraged group), and one was left to complete the puzzle on its own (control group). All three groups were tested before and after puzzle assembly on ability to complete the task and on self-confidence ratings. The "helped" group's performance deteriorated post test and they rated the task as more difficult, compared with the "encouraged" group, who improved their performance and felt more confident in their abilities. Even the control group, who received no help at all, increased their speed of performance slightly. It may be that the expectation of disability becomes disabling in and of itself. It could be argued that what has been termed "helpless behavior" in elderly people is an active attempt to cope with a system that reinforces adherence to stereotypes and dependent behavior.

Clarfield (1989) also pointed out that established practice defines physical diseases and psychological difficulties according to the way they typically present in 20- to 40-year-old individuals. Diagnosis and treatment of a more complex presentation in older people generally has received only minimal attention. Behavior that would warrant fur-

ther investigation in a younger person may be less rigorously investigated in an elderly person. Elderly people are also more likely to receive less long-term therapy and to be institutionalized for the same symptoms that would be treated more aggressively in a younger population (Rodin & Langer, 1980). A study of age bias in a general hospital (Hillerbrand & Shaw, 1990) found that compared to younger patients, geriatric patients were less likely to be referred for psychiatric consultation. The study also found that the suicidal ideation and past psychiatric history evaluations were not as complete for older patients. The authors found this oversight disturbing because the suicide rate for the elderly population is 50 percent higher than for younger populations.

Schaie (1988) criticized psychological research for having ageism undertones. He listed a number of methodological mistakes, including failing to operationalize the concept of the aging variable (that is, grouping everyone over 60 together as if they were a homogeneous group), not providing reasonable estimates of effect size in age comparisons, confounding findings with other concomitant age changes (for example, uncorrected peripheral sensory deficits), using test materials that are normed on young adults, and not considering the range of individual differences that result in overlapping distributions. He concluded that to avoid being accused of inadvertently supporting ageist biases, researchers in psychology need to address the above concerns and be as sensitive to these issues as they would to issues of race and gender.

Effects of Ageism on Health Care Policy

Subtle ageism may be partly to blame for the deficits in service delivery to the elderly population. In his review of the effects of ageism on public policy, Kimmel (1988) stated that 45 percent of U.S. community mental health centers reported having no specific programs for elderly people and that 41 percent did not have any clinical staff members trained to deliver geriatric services. Roybal (1988) called for an expansion of the federal response to mental health and aging. He pointed out that even though elderly people make up 12 percent of the U.S. population, only 6 percent of people served by mental health centers are older Americans.

The American Psychological Association and the American Psychological Society were cosponsors of a recent report entitled *Vitality for Life: Psychological Research for Productive Aging* (Adler, 1993). This report recognized that elderly people have been poorly represented in research and funding priorities. It lists four priorities in the area of aging: (1) learning how best to maximize elderly people's productivity at work, (2) developing mental health assessment and treatment strategies to enhance vitality, (3) learning how to change older people's health behavior, and (4) increasing research on how to optimize the functioning of those over 75. The report's sponsors will use the report to demonstrate to Congress the importance of providing more funding to agencies that support behavioral science research on aging.

Discussion

The recent acknowledgment that society needs to examine the whole concept of the aging process is long overdue. Studies demonstrating the effect of individual behavior and environmental conditioning on the aging process are exciting and challenging. Such research supports the contention that there is a strong interaction between individuals and their environment about health choices and responsibilities. There are a number of implications for professionals working with the elderly population. The first concern is individual professional responsibility. Because ageism can be quite subtle, service providers need to continually examine their own attitudes toward aging and elderly people. Health care professionals need to move away from using the term "age" as an explanatory variable and the assumption that after enough time certain "things" will happen to people. As Bodily (1991) pointed out, this assumption moves away from actual causes to the view that time is a sufficient cause and places the profession squarely in the biomedicalization model of aging. Instead, social workers and other health professionals need to focus on the causes of functional impair-

ments, even the impairments that occur more frequently among older adults.

Professionals can also combat ageism through the types of programs offered and the way these programs are developed. Service providers need to actively involve elderly people in identifying what programs are needed and in designing, implementing, and managing the programs. Examples of such programs are Peer Counseling and Mentor Programs, where older people "buddy up" with high school students who are at high risk of dropping out. Programs could also be designed to target misconceptions about aging more directly in elderly people themselves. These Programs would encourage them to examine how aging myths may be affecting their behavior and to experiment with acting differently. Such programs could have three main components: (1) direct challenge of aging myths, (2) skill-developing practice, and (3) a supportive environment for testing the new behavior. The advantage of this approach is that not only do participants learn new ways of responding, they also become more attuned to the manifestations of aging in society and the subtle effect they may be having on their own responses to aging and sense of well-being.

The second concern is professional training. Exposure to elderly people and to aging issues has been shown to reduce ageism, (Gatz, Popkin, Pino, and VandenBos, 1984). Educational institutions in the health care and social sciences need to establish departments with sub-specialties in gerontology, particularly at the graduate level (Storandt, 1983). These same educational institutions need to include aging issues in their continuing education programs, thus allowing working professionals to keep up to date on the gerontological literature and new trends in the field. Schaie (1988) criticized researchers and professionals working in gerontology for having a lack of awareness of relevant work in the existing aging literature.

The third area of concern is research. More research needs to be conducted on the issues such as work and aging, individual differences in age-related change in behavior and performance, the magnitude of age changes and age differences, how to enhance health behaviors, and how to optimize the functioning of very old people. Research also needs to be aimed at identifying aging stereotypes and their effect on individuals and society, factors that contribute to their development and maintenance, and ways they can most effectively be changed. Researchers need to be educated about the biases that may be influencing their own research. As Schaie (1988) pointed out, much of the current aging literature can be dismissed because of these biases.

Finally, professionals working with the elderly population have an obligation to make a concerted effort to confront ageism in society as a whole. Older people's failure to make health changes may often be the result of the barriers society creates to block successful change. The stereotypes of aging discussed in this article may prevent elderly people from initiating change or may defeat them before they start. Much can be learned from other groups, such as the women's movement, about how to raise awareness of stereotyping and unfair practices, including concerted lobbying efforts to change government policy at all levels. And service providers must actively target stereotypical beliefs in themselves, their professional organizations, and their communities to bring about lasting change.

Discussion Questions

1. What sort of role should health-care professionals play in working with healthy elderly patients?

2. What sorts of aging-related issues need to be addressed in the training of health-care professionals?

3. Describe what is meant by "learned helplessness" and how it relates to ageism.

4. Assume that you were planning community mental health services for your area. What kinds of information would you want in order to develop appropriate services for the population 65 and over?

References

Adler, T. (1993). Experts in aging outline research, funding focus. *APA Monitor, 4*(10), 18.

Avorn, J., & Langer, E. (1982). Induced disability in nursing home patients: A controlled trial. *Journal of the American Geriatrics Society, 20*, 297–300.

Balles, M., & Barton, E. (1979). Behavioral analysis of aging: A review of the operant model and research. *International Journal of Behavioral Development, 2*, 297–320.

Baltes, P. B. (1990, October). *A psychological model of successful aging*. Paper presented at the 19th Annual Scientific and Educational Meeting of the Canadian Association on Gerontology, Victoria, British Columbia.

Bandura, A. (1977). Self-efficacy: Toward a unifying theory of behavioral change. *Psychological Review, 84*, 191–215.

Bandura, A. (1982). Self-efficacy mechanism in human agency. *American Psychologist, 37*, 122–147.

Beck, A.T. (1991). Cognitive therapy: A 30-year perspective. *American Psychologist, 46*, 268–375.

Bodily, C. L. (1991). "I have no opinions. I'm 73 years old!" Rethinking ageism. *Journal of Aging Studies, 5*, 245–264.

Botwinck, J. (1984). *Aging and behavior* (3rd ed.). New York: Springer.

Butler, R. N. (1987). Ageism. In G. L. Maddox & R. C. Atchley (Eds.), *The encyclopedia of aging* (pp. 22–23). New York: Springer.

Clarfield, A. M. (1989, November). *The geriatric imperative*. Paper presented at the 75th Annual General Meeting of the Pharmaceutical Manufacturers Association of Canada, Ottawa.

Clark, B. (1989, November). *The aging of North America: The shape of things to come*. Paper presented at the 75th Annual General Meeting of the Pharmaceutical Manufacturers Association of Canada, Ottawa.

Clark, R G. (1988). Autonomy, personal empowerment, and quality of life in long term care. *Journal of Applied Gerontology, 2*, 279–297.

Doty, L. (1987). *Communication and assertion skills for older persons*. New York: Hemisphere.

Fordyce, W. E. (1976). *Behavioral methods for chronic pain and illness*. St. Louis: Mosby.

Gatz, M., & Pearson, C. G. (1988). Ageism revised and the provision of psychological services. *American Psychologist, 11*, 184–188.

Gatz, M., Popkin, S. J., Pino, C. D., & VandenBos, G. R. (1984). Psychological interventions with older adults. In J. E. Birren & K. W. Shaie (Eds.), *Handbook of the psychology of aging* (2nd ed., pp. 755–787). New York: Reinhold.

George, L. (1987). Self-esteem in later life. In G. L. Maddox & R. C. Atchley (Eds.), *The encyclopedia of aging* (p. 593). New York: Springer.

Health and Welfare Canada. (1986). *Achieving health for all: A framework for health promo-*

tion (Catalog No. 1139-102/1986E,). Ottawa: Ministry of Supply and Services.

Health and Welfare Canada. (1989). *The active health report on seniors* (Catalog No. 11-39-124/1988E). Ottawa: Minister of Supply and Services.

Hillerbrand, E. T., & Shaw, D. (1990). Age bias in a general hospital: Is there ageism in psychiatric consultation? *Clinical Gerontologist, 2*(2), 3–13.

Katz, I. R., Curlick, S., & Nemetz, P. (1988). Functional psychiatric disorders in the elderly. In L. W. Lazarus (Ed.), *Essentials of geriatric psychiatry* (pp. 113–137). New York: Springer.

Katzman, P, & Carasu,T. (1975). Differential diagnosis of dementia. In W. S. Fields (Ed.), *Neurological and sensory disorders in the elderly* (pp. 103–104). Miami: Symposium Specialist Medical Books.

Kimmel, D. C. (1988). Ageism, psychology, and public policy. *American Psychologist, 11*, 175–178.

Langer, E., & Rodin, J. (1976). The effects of choice and enhanced personal responsibility for the aged: A field experiment in an institutional setting. *Journal of Personality and Social Psychology, 34*, 191–198.

Lazarus, R. S., & Folkman, S. (1984). *Stress, appraisal and coping.* New York: Springer.

Moody, H. (1988). *The abundance of life: Human development policies for an aging society.* New York: Columbia University Press.

National Advisory Council on Aging. (1989a). *1989 and beyond: Challenges of an aging Canadian society* (Catalog No. H37-3/10-1989). Ottawa: Ministry of Supply and Services.

National Advisory Council on Aging. (1989b). *Understanding Seniors' independence Report No. 1: The barriers and suggestions for action* (Catalog No. 1137 3/11-1-1989E). Ottawa: Ministry of Supply and Services.

Palmore, E. B. (1986). Attitudes toward aging shown by humor: A review. In L. Nahemow, K. McCluskey-Fawcett, & P. McGhee (Eds.), *Humor and aging.* (pp. 101–119). New York: Academic Press.

Parnham, I. (1987). Perceived control. In G. L. Maddox & R. C. Atchley (Eds.), *The encyclopedia of aging* (pp. 454–455). New York: Springer.

Persons, J. B. (1989). *Cognitive therapy in practice: A case formulation approach.* New York: W. W. Norton.

Reker, G. T., Peacock, E. J., & Wong, T. P. (1987). Meaning, purpose in life and well-being: A life

span perspective. *Journal of Gerontology, 11*(1), 44–49.

Rodin, J. (1986). Aging and health: Effects of the sense of control. *Science, 233,* 1271–1276.

Rodin, J., & Langer, E. (1980). Aging labels: The decline of control and the fall of self-esteem. *Journal of Social Issues, 36*(12), 12–29.

Rowe, J. W., & Kahn, R. N. (1987). Human aging: Usual and successful aging. *Science, 237,* 143–149.

Roybal, E. R. (1988). Mental health and aging. *American Psychologist, 43,* 189–194.

Santos, J. F., & VandenBos, G. R., (1982). *Psychology and the older adult: Challenges for training in the 1980s.* Washington DC: American Psychological Association.

Schaie, K. W. (1988). Ageism in psychological research. *American Psychologist, 43,* 179–183.

Snyder, C. J., & Barrett, G. V. (1988). The Age Discrimination in Employment Act: A review of court decisions. *Experimental Aging Research, 14*(1), 3–47.

Storandt, M. (1983). Psychology's response to graying in America. *American Psychologist, 38,* 323–326.

Svanborg, A. (1990, October), *Aging, health and vitality: Results from the Gothberg longitudinal study.* Paper presented at the 19th Annual Scientific and Educational Meeting of the Canadian Association of Gerontology, Victoria, British Columbia.

Troll, L., (1989). *Continuations: Adult development and aging.* College Park: University of Maryland, International University Consortium.

Whitbourne, S. K., & Hulicka, I. M. (1990). Ageism in undergraduate psychology texts. *American Psychologist, 11,* 1127–1136.

World Health Organization. (1947). The constitution of the World Health Organization. *WHO Chronicles, 1,* 16.

Zautra, A. J., Maxwell, B. M., & Reich, J. W. (1989). Relationship among physical impairments, distress, and well-being in older adults. *Journal of Behavioral Medicine, 12,* 543–557.

Chapter 36
Rural Navajo and Anglo Elders Aging Well

Judith Bunnell Sellers

How people view their health and use health-care facilities are affected by cultural values and beliefs. Although the majority of people turn to medical doctors or nurses for help when they are sick or injured, other people seek treatment elsewhere through folk healers. There are relatively few studies comparing the approaches to life among specific tribes of older Native Americans and Whites and the relationship between values and reliance upon folk medicine versus conventional modern medicine. The following selection by Judith Sellers examines connections between lifelong themes and health among two small samples of elders: Navajo and Anglo (White) Americans in Arizona. A case study, its purpose is to identify themes persisting throughout the life course that influence health and the use of health care. The rituals associated with traditional Navajo religion are predominantly health oriented and stem from an emphasis on enhancing well-being. Diseases, according to traditional belief, are caused by witchcraft, spirits, or violating tribal taboos. As you read, think about the ways in which Navajo beliefs differ from Anglo beliefs. What values emerge as most important to each group and how might these affect health and illness?

Most American health care is based on the norms and values of the dominant White culture. Population projections show, however, that elders in minority groups will increase dramatically by 2020. Many are the "new immigrants" of the past two decades; others, often forgotten, are Native Americans. Between 1980 and 1990, the proportion of Na-

tive Americans age 60 and over increased 35 percent faster than the proportion in the total American population in the same age group, and their numbers are expected to increase even more dramatically by 2020. Native Americans are diverse, representing many different tribes. Half of all Native Americans live in four states, one of which is Arizona, the site of the present study. If high-quality health care is to be provided, it is important to understand the ways in which cultural values and beliefs about health and illness differ among ethnic groups and their implications for care. This case study, the purpose of which is to identify themes persisting throughout the life course that influence health and the use of health care, focuses on two groups of elders: Native American Navajo and Anglo (White).

The respondents in this study were 10 Navajo and 10 Anglo elders aged 75 and older who volunteered to be interviewed. Additional sample characteristics are shown in Table 36.1. The average (mean) age of Navajo participants was 77; the average age for Anglos was 82. Although a small sample, the educational level is strikingly different: half of the Navajos never attended school; an-

Table 36.1

Respondent Characteristics

Characteristic	Navajo		Anglo	
Age range	75–83		75–92	
Mean age	77		82	
Male	4		5	
Female	6		5	
Marital Status				
Married	3		6	
Widowed	6		4	
Never married	1		0	
Educational level attained	**Male**	**Female**	**Male**	**Female**
Never attended or < 1 year	2	3	0	0
< 7 years	1	1	0	0
Some high school	0	1	1	0
High school graduate	1	0	2	3
Technical or college	0	1	2	2

Table 36.2

Major Themes in Anglo and Navajo Life Reviews		
Period of Life	**Anglo**	**Navajo**
Childhood	school as positive farm chores religion	school as negative seasonal moves with chores traditional ways/clan
Adulthood	military service work as achievement romance and marriage friendships relocation nuclear family	work as a traditional way of life arranged marriage outside clan constancy of life/tradition remaining on the land extended family and clan
Old age	family as companionship independence retirement/work/chores friends	family as respect from younger and as caregivers wisdom and tradition traditional work as way of life clan
Lifelong themes	religion work future orientation change and progress pro-technology	traditional beliefs work present orientation balance and harmony with nature anti-technology

other two attended school only to the third grade. In comparison, all Anglos had completed at least the sixth grade. All Navajo participants resided on the Navajo Nation Reservation land in northern Arizona. Anglo participants also resided in northern Arizona, grew up on farms or ranches, and were selected because of possible similarities associated with growing up in rural areas and living off the land. Interviewers conducted focused life-review interviews lasting from two to six hours. Seven of the Navajo participants spoke only their native language; interviews with them were conducted by native Navajo speakers.[1]

Recollections and Lifelong Themes

Major themes elicited during the interviews are summarized in Table 36.2. As may be seen, Anglo and Navajo elders share beliefs about the importance of work, the family, and independence. They differ in their opinions about the use of technology, tradition, silence, and orientation to time. The following section elaborates on specific topics

to outline their importance for health practices and organization of health care.

Education

Among the Anglo elderly, formal education was highly valued, and respondents recalled walking many miles to school. Those who were not able to complete high school had regrets and cited economic necessity as the reason. In bleak contrast to the Anglo recollections, Navajo elders looked back on formal education as entirely negative, an institution imposed by the Whites to destroy their traditional ways of life. Established by the Bureau of Indian Affairs (BIA), the only available schools were boarding facilities that did not permit cultural traditions. One respondent recalled that the first thing children were taught was not to speak Navajo; those who were caught speaking their language were punished and had to mop and scrub the school floors. Most ran away from school, returned home, and were hidden by their families whenever the school representatives appeared. As another respondent recalled a BIA recruiter of Navajo children:

It was said that he would ride up to the homes of Navajo families on his horse to find children to take to school. When hearing the horse tromping up to the hogans through the mud, many Navajo families would hide their children to keep them from being taken away.

Work

Among the Anglos, expectations for work began in childhood when boys were socialized in the traditional masculine role of family provider, and girls into the feminine role of caring for the family and household. Both Anglo men and women recalled working hard on the farm, doing chores before and after school. Chores encompassed taking care of the animals, bringing in wood, and, for girls, preparing breakfast for the farm hands. Helping with the harvest and animal care were other typical childhood chores. As one respondent summed it up: "I always had to milk them damn cows." In adulthood, the work ethic continued to dominate the lives of Anglo males as central. Military service during World War II was also prized: "I flew 91 missions and did two tours of duty, one in the South Pacific and one in Europe. This was a happy time, mostly because of my lasting friendships." "Service to my country was an important part of life that I took pride in." Others recalled the importance of contributing to the war effort, 50-year friendships forged in the military, and opportunities to act as lay ministers to soldiers in action.

After World War II, none of the Anglo respondents remained on farms or ranches; men moved to find employment, and women followed their husbands. In old age, work remained salient; albeit retired, men described their many home-related projects, including painting, repairs, construction, and gardening. Anglo women, however, seldom mentioned paid employment as part of their current or past lives unless it related to "helping out" economically.

The recollections of Navajo elders also emphasized the lifelong significance of work. Part of the Navajo Nation reservation is located on the Northern Arizona Colorado plateau, where the land is stark and rocky, rising to an elevation of 6,000 feet. Because winters are snowy and cold and summers warm and dry, seasonal moves during childhood to care for the sheep which form the economic base of Navajo culture were a common event. For the Anglo elders interviewed in this study, work represented productivity and a way to accrue material things and comforts. For the Navajo, work was a way of life, part of a tradition, a way to respect the land and to maintain harmony and the balance of nature. Girls learned to weave, cook, grind corn, and care for the sheep; boys herded sheep by the age of five. In old age, Navajo men continued to herd sheep, sometimes from horseback, sometimes from trucks. Women continued to cook, grind corn, weave rugs, and help herd sheep. For example, one respondent and his wife of 50 years still tended sheep, cows, and horses, and although neither herded on horseback, they used a truck to drive among the cows to check and count them.

Marriage and Family

Although both ethnic groups indicated the lifelong importance of family and kinship ties, their expectations and experiences differed. Navajo kinship systems are more elaborate than Anglo kin networks as the Navajo have both immediate family and clan family. Clan members provide support and guidance. The clan family were as important in recollections as immediate family and remained important in old age: "My grandmother is of the Mexican People clan, born of the Bitter Water People clan. My maternal grandfather is the Rock Gap People clan and [my] paternal grandfather is the Edgewater People clan."

Seven of the 10 Navajos had arranged marriages. Arranged marriages assure affiliations outside one's clan; matrimony within the clan is regarded as marrying a brother or sister would be in Anglo culture. Unlike the Navajos, Anglo respondents emphasized falling in love prior to marriage: "My most vivid memory is meeting and marrying my sweetheart." "Upon returning from the war, I met the love of my life. My wedding day was the happiest of my life."

Integral to Anglo discussions of family and kin among both men and women in later life were two themes: companionship and independence. Men emphasized the increasing importance of family in old age: "Because I was so busy working to raise money for my family, I feel this is my time to make up for it by spending time and supporting my grandchildren as much as possible." "I have a nice home, my children are all grown and successful, and my better half I love more than ever." In old age, Anglo women described constancy in familial roles, where they remained involved with their children and continued as caregivers, particularly of grandchildren, including being "Grandma to the neighborhood children."

Both Anglo men and women valued caring for oneself and one's family as well as productivity as integral to their self-image in old age. None wanted to be cared for by children; all were proud that they lived independently and remained active. Independence and health were closely related; remaining self-reliant despite illness was a sign of good health. For example, one respondent reported that during the previous week, he was up on his roof fixing some shingles despite eye problems and arthritis in his shoulders and knees. Another respondent, age 76, noted that he did not find his health a problem until he had some work. He used to be able to paint houses all day long; now he had to slow down to about four hours a day.

In later life, Navajo elders, unlike the Anglos, expected respect and, when required, care from their families, and they expressed anger when children were not there to help with chores. Navajo elders are regarded as wise teachers and mentors of traditional customs. As one respondent noted: "In the community, the 'elderlies' are respected and looked up to for advice by younger generations. As Navajos, everyone is taught to respect their 'elderlies' and look after them in time of need."

Most of the men interviewed were leaders in traditional ceremonies that involved family and clan members:

> The children visit once a month. When he needs help with a ceremony or with the cattle, his children help. When there is a need for a family meeting, they all sit and discuss the matter and come to a decision. They also have clan family who he sometimes asks for help with a ceremony.

Because the Navajo family structure includes a large extended kin network, both clan family and immediate family help with decisions. Among Anglos, elders either made decisions independently or called upon immediate family members.

Belief Systems

Among the Anglos, religion played a major role; church attendance was a part of life whenever weather and other conditions permitted. During childhood and adolescence, Sundays were special days when work was suspended; informal religious services were held on some farms too far from the nearest town to allow easy attendance at church. In old age, religion remained a major theme. Some Anglo respondents were active in churches; others simply gave thanks to a higher being for every day and all the good bestowed upon them. As one 92-year-old woman said: "I wake up with a smile and thank God for all He's given me and that He's given me another day." A similar theme was echoed by an 80-year-old man: "I am thankful to God that I have reached the age of 80 in good health of mind and body."

Also important were Anglos' beliefs in progress, technology, and change. Anglo respondents grew up in rural areas where they lacked "modern conveniences" but subsequently moved into modern houses where indoor plumbing, central heat, appliances, television, telephones, and cars were taken for granted as symbols of success in life and ability to provide for one's family. Technology and material possessions were means to maintain independence and to go along with social change. A common theme was the necessity to change with the times. Technology was described as "good and wonderful" and as needed for "change and improvement."

In sharp contrast, among Navajos, learning the traditional ways from one's family, including ceremonies, taboos, and use of the land, water, and sun, formed the basis for belief systems and were considered far more important to master than other aspects of life. Respondents expressed concern about the erosion of tradition: "Our children are not dependent on the livestock anymore. They have become lazy. They don't understand my language or my way of life. Tradition has contributed to my survival."

Important in traditional Navajo life are four concepts: Mother Earth, Father Sun, balance or harmony with nature, and silence and acceptance. Father Sun watches over Mother Earth, who brings good things from the land. The land is to be tended carefully and respected; if one takes more from the land than what is needed, illness and bad luck will follow. Father Sun also brings goodness, and it is important to welcome him before starting the day. For that reason, the hogan door always faces east: "All good things are out early in the morning as the sun rises." "At dawn the morning spirits are checking you and your place out. If everything is great, spirits send good dreams and feelings and happiness your way."

Balance and harmony with nature are intrinsic to Navajo belief systems. Maintaining and restoring balance and harmony is the province of the medicine man, a powerful figure who learned healing from his family. Navajos may seek a medicine man to find the causes of a loss of balance with nature, and a ceremony to restore balance will be conducted. Ceremonies also ward off evil spirits, assure evil spirits will not enter, and restore health. Silence and acceptance of life events is a tacit expectation; discussion of feelings, emotions, or negative events is discouraged. As one respondent commented "Listen and learn as much as you can while growing and live in the world." Although each respondent had experienced multiple tragedies, including death of siblings in childhood, death of children from meningitis or other diseases, motor vehicle accidents, violence and falls; alcoholism of spouse or children; and child and spousal abuse, Navajos neither complained nor blamed. Rather, prayers were offered daily as thanks for life's goodness. Speaking of negative events is likely to bring the event about: "He keeps his feelings, emotions, and true thoughts to himself. He believes that if you don't think about it, it will go away." "She says that she thinks about death but does not really want to talk about it. In a traditional setting one is not supposed to talk about death unless they want death to take place."

Beliefs about technology and social change also differ widely between the two ethnic groups. Anglos are proud of their participation in a technological world that includes space travel, computers, and conveniences for comfort and support. Navajos are ambivalent, for while some individuals use modern conveniences while conserving traditional lifestyles, elders worry about young people abandoning their cultural roots. These two different approaches to technology mirror their approaches to social change. Anglos almost unanimously welcomed change, and their advice was that "you just have to change with the times." In contrast, Navajo respondents feared change as a loss of cultural identity and an attempt to negate their way of life.

Implications for Health Care

As noted earlier, the American health-care system is based on the values of the dominant White culture. Because of different life orientations, the concept of "healthy aging" differs between the Anglo and Navajo respondents participating in this study. When health issues were discussed, Anglos reported that they relied upon Western medicine, using resources and medications as directed by health-care providers. None relied upon herbal medications or alternative therapies. How appropriate is this model for elderly Navajos? The answer would appear to be "not very." While Anglos are likely to view illness as impersonal and as caused by germs, Navajos view health and illness as related to one's interpersonal relationships, tradition, and religion. Navajos emphasize health and harmony as the same thing and employ ceremonies with the medicine man to diagnose and heal to restore proper balance. The singer, who is the most eminent person among Navajo healers, may lead rituals lasting several days that are designed to drive out of the body whatever is causing the illness (Levy 1983). Diseases are thought to be due to various causes, including witchcraft, spirit possession, soul loss, or bad behavior such as violating a tribal taboo. Only when traditional Navajo approaches to healing are not effective does one turn to Western medicine, usually combining both approaches. As one elderly Navajo expressed his scepticism about modern American medicine: "My problem stems from what I have encountered over my life. I believe I have broken some cultural taboos or beliefs and practices in the past and it surely affected my health. That's why the Western medicine doctors can't diagnose or treat my illness."

Not only is modern American medicine distrusted, but current assessment and diagnostic techniques lack cultural sensitivity to Navajo worldviews and modes of self-expression, thus further erecting barriers to its use. For example, because silence is highly valued in Navajo culture and complaints or discussion of negative or anxiety-laden health possibilities discouraged, taking a health history using open-ended questions will result in little or no information. Moreover, the quietude of Navajos may be misinterpreted as apathy or depression, leading to inappropriate prescriptions for medication. Questions about health and illness need to be framed using yes-no responses or should permit the individual to tell a story—a kind of morality tale that does not reflect on the narrator but is rather regarded by him or her as a way to teach.

Traditional questionnaires developed to assess White adults can present difficulties as well. Elderly Navajo respondents may be unable to read English or have limited English vocabulary, making their results difficult to interpret correctly. If questionnaires are translated into Navajo, care must be taken to ensure that the meaning of the item has not changed in conversion, and, equally important, the item must be culturally appropriate. Any item that is construed as likely to bring on bad things will not be acceptable—or answered—by the Navajo patient.

Health-care providers also need to be aware that their Navajo patients will use both their own traditional medicine plus Western medicine. Assessments of health and illness must thus elicit information on all types of care and medications received. Attention needs to be paid to the elders' beliefs about the possible causes of an illness. When sick, the traditional Navajo elder will consider taboos that he or she might have broken and try a variety of methods to restore harmony,

modern medicine being only one. For treatment to be effective, the health-care provider must not only understand traditional concepts of causality but be prepared to work with these concepts, proposing additional treatments that do not challenge or downgrade underlying traditional beliefs. As J. E. Levy has pointed out:

> No Navajo disease is known by the symptoms it produces or by the part of the body it is thought to affect. Rather, there is bear sickness and porcupine sickness, named for the agents thought to cause them. . . . Because the traditional health culture does not rely upon a knowledge of symptoms in the diagnostic process, Navajo patients often have difficulty understanding the purpose of history taking and physical examination. (1983, p. 132)

Provision of health care also represents a challenge. Access is a real issue, as Navajo homes are far apart and roads often impassable during the winter and spring. The family may have only one vehicle, which is in use for sheep herding; there is little or no public transportation; and many elders have never learned to drive as they relied upon horses for transportation. Moreover, appointments with a health-care provider are regarded as less important than other life events; care of sheep, cattle, goats, and family will take priority over scheduled medical appointments.

Even receiving adequate nutrition can present difficulties for many elders living on the reservation. Local stores are at least 30 miles away, and fresh foods are easy neither to find nor keep fresh. Because many Navajo elders remain in hogans without central heating, water, or electricity, risk of infection from unrefrigerated food is likely, leading many people to rely on processed foods. Although these foods need neither cooking nor refrigeration, they are high in sodium and fat, thus increasing the likelihood of hypertension and heart disease.

Clearly, Navajo values and beliefs differ from those of their Anglo contemporaries in the same general geographic area, and these differences are likely to affect both health and use of health-care facilities. It should also be kept in mind that each tribe of Native Americans is distinct in its values and beliefs. Thus the care acceptable and appropriate for Navajo elders living on a reservation is likely to be very different from that applicable to elders in another tribe. Moreover, cohort differences are important to consider when planning health care in the twenty-first century. Future cohorts of more assimilated Navajos, for example, may resemble their Anglo age peers much more closely when they reach old age than did the respondents in this study. Further information about the similarities and differences between and within racial and ethnic groups, including Native Americans of different tribes, and in different birth cohorts is needed if culturally sensitive care is to be provided to ensure a healthy old age. A "one size fits all" approach to designing elder health care is doomed to be only inappropriate and ineffective.

Discussion Questions

1. What similarities do you see in the themes elicited from Navajo and Anglo elders?

2. What roles do tradition and nature play in the health system of Navajo elders?

3. Suppose you were asked to design a screening tool or initial interview to assess the health of older Navajos who hold traditional beliefs. What would you want to include? What would you want to avoid?

Note

1. Because interviewers translated from the Navajo, many quotations from respondents are in the third person rather than the first person.

References

Levy, J. E. 1983. "Traditional Navajo Health Beliefs and Practices." In J. Kutznitz, ed., *Disease Change and the Role of Medicine: The Navajo Experience*, pp. 118–178. Berkeley: University of California Press.

Judith Bunnell Sellers, "Rural Navajo and Anglo Elders Aging Well." Printed by permission of the author.

Chapter 37

Assessment of Geriatric Patients

Patricia P. Barry

At any age, an individual's level of physical and psychological functioning is important because it affects quality of life. Physical and mental disabilities impairing one's ability to perform tasks of everyday living usually increase with age, influencing the need for care from others, living arrangements, and life satisfaction. The less they are able to function independently, the more likely are older people to live with others or to be admitted to a hospital or nursing home. According to data from the National Center for Health Statistics, three-fourths of people age 65 or over who had one or more limitations in their ability to perform basic self-care activities, such as bathing, dressing, eating, and walking, were admitted to a hospital or nursing home at least once during the following five years. Only 55 percent with no such limitations were admitted during the same time period.

Researchers, health practitioners, and physicians routinely assess the health of older people through standardized measures. Information from such assessments is useful in numerous ways: to determine needs for assistance, to determine what environmental modifications may enable the individual to cope more effectively in the community, to determine needs for long-term care, and to determine eligibility for services reimbursable through Medicare or Medicaid. In the following selection, Patricia Barry, a geriatric physician, discusses how functional status, dementia, and depression are ascertained and calls attention to their relationship to quality of life. As you read, think about the relationship of functional status and mental health to aging well. You may also want to review the article by Baltes and Carstensen in Section I of this book to consider

ways in which "successful aging" has been defined as you think about health assessments for older people.

People who reach the age of 65 can now expect to live into their 80s. Among the elderly, improving functional independence is important in promoting health. One measure of health that considers quality as well as quantity of life is years of healthy life—the number of years that an older person can expect to be active. Although people age 65 and over have on the average 16.4 years of actual life remaining, they have only about 12 years of healthy life because prevalence rates of most chronic conditions raise with age. Another quality-of-life index is functional capacity, the ability to perform activities required and usual in everyday living. Although most elderly people are relatively independent, many develop multiple chronic illnesses and disabilities that require management. Nonfatal, chronic conditions often cause prolonged disability, which limits roles and activities. Although chronic diseases do not lend themselves to "cure," their disabling impact may be reduced in order to improve or maintain elders' functional independence.

Since the physical, mental, and social aspects of illness are closely interrelated, the diagnosis-oriented approach has important limitations and may not correlate well with overall health and functional status. In order to evaluate and plan appropriately for the long-term health care of frail older persons, information must be obtained and organized in five basic areas: (1) performance of activities of daily living, (2) physical health, (3) mental health, (4) socioeconomic resources, and (5) environment. Since the interrelationship among these areas is especially important, a coordinated, multidimensional evaluation referred to as comprehensive geriatric assessment (CGA) has evolved in order to collect such information systematically.

Geriatric Multidimensional Assessment

In 1988 the National Institutes of Health sponsored the Consensus Development Conference on Geriatric Assessment Methods for

Clinical Decision Making (Consensus Development Panel 1988). The Consensus Statement issued by the conference noted that the goals of assessment are often interdependent, so that diagnostic accuracy leads to appropriate interventions and better use of available services, resulting in improved level of function and optimal placement. Two aspects of geriatric assessment are particularly important. The first aspect is to target assessment to those persons most likely to benefit, specifically, the "frail" but not terminally ill; those at critical transition points, such as entering a nursing home, and those in decline in health or function. Second, and equally important, is the need to link assessment with care management and follow-up services. CGA is thus a *process* involving referral, collection of information, assessment, development and implementation of a care plan, and periodic reassessment.

Although several studies have demonstrated that geriatric assessment in the office and hospital practice of the individual physician can identify previously unsuspected problems, its effect depends on targeting appropriate patients and the ability to identify resources and services necessary for follow-up care (Applegate, Blass, and Williams 1990; Barry 1994; Beck, 1991; Campion 1995; Reuben 1991; Rubenstein and Rubenstein 1991). A recent meta-analysis of 28 controlled trials of five different types of CGA concluded that CGA programs linking evaluation with strong long-term management are effective for improving survival and function in older persons (Stuck, Siu, and Wieland et al. 1993).

Assessing Functional Independence

Key to planning ways to maintain independence is an assessment of functional status, often a better indication of the patient's capacity for independent living than chronological age and diagnoses alone. Measures of functional status focus on two areas of activity: personal care (called activities of daily living) and household management (called instrumental activities of daily living). Activities of daily living (ADL) include bathing, toileting, feeding, dressing, ambulating,

continence, and transferring. Instrumental activities of daily living (IADL) include management of finances, preparation of food, housekeeping, shopping, ability to use a telephone, and ability to arrange transportation. Inability to perform ADL and IADL independently reduces an elderly person's autonomy and quality of life. It also increases dependency upon others, often adding a burden on family members. Functional status may be measured in two main ways:

- By asking the patient or someone else how well she or he can perform given activities.
- By having the patient perform an activity and scoring it.

The former technique is usually called a reported measure, the latter a performance-based measure. Many instruments have been developed to measure physical function; they vary primarily in level of detail. Standardized, quantifiable, report or performance instruments should be used to assess ADL and IADL. The choice of standardized instruments (1) increases the likelihood that the assessment will be comprehensive, (2) facilitates comparisons of an individual over time, and (3) improves communication among care providers by using a common yardstick. The instrument selected should be reliable (give the same result when measurement is repeated in the absence of real change) and valid (reflecting the characteristic that is being measured), sensitive, and specific. The length and complexity of the measurement process should be acceptable both to the evaluators and to frail elderly patients. The attributes measured should be clinically important and amenable to intervention.

Uses of Functional Assessment

Evaluation of ADL and IADL has many uses. Knowledge of a patient's capacity to perform ADL and IADL may be helpful in diagnosing numerous disease states, ranging from arthritis to dementia, and in estimating patient risk of falls and of possible hip fracture. The incidence of falls among elders living in their own homes or those of friends and relatives increases from 25 percent at age 70 to 35 percent after age 75, and half of those who fall do so repeatedly. Although falls occur for many reasons, ADL problems in ambulation and moving from bed to chair add significantly to the likelihood of falling. Fear of falling may inhibit a frail person's walking. The resulting immobility can reduce muscle strength and increase the danger of falling. Injury is the sixth leading cause of death among seniors; the majority of these fatal injuries are due to falls.

Functional assessment can be useful in measuring not only a patient's level of functioning at a given point but also in prescribing interventions. Interventions buffer the links between pathology and impairment, and impairment and limitation. Functional assessment is also useful to monitor the effectiveness of a treatment, follow the progress of a disease, and even predict the outcome. Disability due to chronic conditions is a variable process, sometimes improving, sometimes declining. A one-time assessment provides a snapshot of an individual but not a picture of the fluctuations, which may require periodic assessment to monitor changes in functional status. Assessment should also be performed at critical transition points, such as a decline in health or function, a change in living situation, and a period of rehabilitation.

Although important for survival and independent living, ADL and IADL are just two aspects of human activity. A variety of other activities are part of optimal functioning. Ability to carry out social activities, hobbies and leisure activities, participation in paid or unpaid work, and maintenance of socioeconomic status and social supports—all are important areas of life about which a healthcare provider should seek information when undertaking a functional assessment.

Alzheimer's Diseases Tables 37.1 and 37.2 present two commonly used tools for geriatric assessment of functional status. Alzheimer's Disease Table 37.1 summarizes items used to assess basic ADLs. Alzheimer's Disease Table 37.2 presents an informant-based measure of functional abilities (Pfeffer, Kurosaki, and Harrah et al. 1982). Informants provide performance ratings of the target individual on 10 complex, higher-order activities. A total score for the Table 37.2 questionnaire is computed by simply summing the scores across the 10 items. Scores range from 0 to 30. On both scales, the higher the score, the more dependent the person.

Assessing Dementia

Diagnosis and management of dementia are increasingly recognized as important skills in care of the elderly. Dementia may be irreversible and progress relentlessly, as in Alzheimer's disease, or it may be potentially reversible, as in vitamin B12 deficiency. Ability to perform ADLs and IADLs is also important in any assessment of dementia. Dementia may be classified as mild, moderate, or severe. In mild dementia, IADL is impaired but ADL usually intact, and the capacity for independent living remains relatively intact. In moderate dementia, elders may be unable to perform any IADLs but perform ADLs independently or with assistance. Independent living is hazardous, and some supervision is required. In severe dementia, the individual is usually unable to perform most ADLs, including maintaining personal hygiene. The patient may be incoherent or mute and incontinent.

To screen for possible dementia, a short, structured mental-status exam is vital. The Mini-Mental State Exam (MMSE) takes 5 to 10 minutes to complete and is a useful and reliable screening tool (Folstein, Folstein, and McHugh 1975). Points, scored on a 30-point scale, are awarded for correct responses.

It is important, however, to take into consideration not only the level of education of the patient but his or her familiarity with the English language, as many elders who are foreign born or have lived all their lives in ethnic enclaves may have difficulty in responding due to language problems. Low levels of education or unfamiliarity with English obviously affect the patient's scores on registration, attention, and calculation and should be taken into account. Hearing impairments may also affect scores, as hearing loss most commonly affects ability to distinguish consonants. The examiner must guard against these effects by (1) ascertaining level of education and its probable impact on the score,

(2) paying careful attention to any possible hearing loss (denied by many auditorily impaired elders) and speaking clearly in a lower register (not shouting), and (3) considering use of an interpreter with an elder whose comprehension of English is limited. In short, it is important to seek as much information as possible about the education, comprehension of English, and hearing of the respondent prior to testing.

In the early phases of dementia, elders may be aware that their cognitive functioning is impaired and may be anxious or depressed. They may try to conceal or compensate for these losses by extreme orderliness, withdrawal from social contacts, or a tendency to relate events in great detail to hide gaps in memory loss. In later stages of dementia, however, awareness of intellectual impairment usually disappears. Paranoid delusions are common in moderately and severely demented patients. Beliefs that neighbors, friends, or relatives are stealing from them; hallucinations; confusion; and inability to recognize family members—or their own reflections in the mirror—may also occur.

Dementia and Depression

The most frequently missed psychiatric cause of cognitive impairment is depression. Depressed older people are often distressed about memory loss. In younger people, changes in attention span, concentration, and memory are usually recognized as signs of depression; but among older people such changes are often misdiagnosed as dementia. In depression, however, loss in cognitive function is often spotty and changeable, occurring over a relatively short period and beginning with mood changes or false beliefs about parts of the body. The "pseudodementia" of severe depression is a common, treatable cause of cognitive impairment. In dementia, declines in cognitive function are usually more gradual than in a major depression; dysphoric mood is less frequent. People with dementia can also be depressed, especially if they have insight into their condition. If symptoms suggesting a major depressive episode are at least as prominent as memory impairment and there are no signs of a specific organic cause, a diagnosis of major depressive episode should be made.

Major depression differs from uncomplicated bereavement or grief, although the same behavioral symptoms may be present. Reactions to a specific loss, such as death of spouse, family member, or friend, or declining physical functioning and inability to perform activities of daily living, are frequently characterized by feelings of depression, weight loss, poor appetite, and insomnia. However, preoccupation with worthlessness, prolonged and marked functional impairment, and notable psychomotor retardation are uncommon. In uncomplicated bereavement, guilt, when present, is mainly about things done or not done by the survivor. Thoughts of death are usually limited to thinking one would be better off dead or should have died with the deceased. The onset of an uncomplicated bereavement reaction varies but usually occurs within one to three months of the loss. The duration of uncomplicated bereavement varies considerably, according to cultural and subcultural norms, but is self-limiting. If depressive symptoms continue beyond the culturally accepted period and the individual is unable to resume normal activities, bereavement may have given way to a major depression.

In interviewing elders with possible symptoms of depression, it is important first to consider physical causes for symptoms through a careful history and examination, including use of alcohol and medications (both prescription and over-the-counter medicines), as both can contribute to depression. A careful history, including any family history of depression or "nervous breakdown," any previous history of depression, missed periods of work due to undiagnosed illness, and any prior treatment, is very important.

Physical illness or disability often causes older people to report more somatic complaints that may be confused with depressive symptoms. When there is an acute deterioration of functioning without obvious physical causes, a diagnosis of depression should be considered. However, chronic disease may coexist or precipitate a depression that worsens functioning and causes significant decline in a patient's quality of life. In the absence of a physical cause, tactful but pointed

Table 37.1

Activities of Daily Living	
Bathing	Dressing
Grooming	Feeding
Toileting	Continence
Transferring	Ambulating

The levels of performance assigned range from dependence to independence and are rated as follows:

Dependent = 3
Requires assistance = 2
Has difficulty but does by self = 1
Normal [independent] = 0

Table 37.2

Functional Activities Questionnaire

1. Writing checks, paying bills, balancing checkbook
2. Assembling tax records, business affairs, or papers
3. Shopping alone for clothes, household necessities, or groceries
4. Playing a game of skill, working on a hobby
5. Heating water, making a cup of coffee, turning off stove
6. Preparing a balanced meal
7. Keeping track of current events
8. Paying attention to, understanding, discussing TV, book, magazine
9. Remembering appointments, family occasions, holidays, medications
10. Traveling out of neighborhood, driving, arranging to take buses

The levels of performance assigned range from dependence to independence and are rated as follows:

Dependent = 3
Requires assistance = 2
Has difficulty but does by self = 1
Normal [independent] = 0

Two other response options can also be scored:

Never did [the activity] but could do now = 0
Never did and would have difficulty now = 1

Source: Pfeffer, R. I., Kurosaki, T. T., Harrah, C. H., et al. 1982. "Measurement of Functional Activities of Older Adults in the Community." *Journal of Gerontology* 37:323–329.

questions on their beliefs about what is wrong with them physically may be useful in eliciting information in diagnosis. Standardized screening instruments, such as the Geriatric Depression Scale, may also be useful (Sheikh and Yesavage 1986).

Once an older person has been diagnosed as depressed, it is important for that person to be reassured and supported. Underlying physical causes should be treated. If medications are precipitating the depression, these should be withdrawn and substitutions made if necessary. Psychotherapy, social supports, and antidepressants may be used. If antidepressants are prescribed, their risks and benefits should be carefully weighed, along with possible drug interactions and drug effects in elderly patients.

The importance of comprehensive assessment of elderly patients by their health-care providers cannot be overestimated. Assessing functional independence, dementia, and depression is vital for an adequate understanding of the present condition and future potential of elders. Only then may they be treated most effectively and their quality of life improved.

Discussion Questions

1. Describe the basic functions assessed by ADL and IADL measures.

2. Explain the uses of functional assessment.

3. In screening for possible dementia, what safeguards are necessary to avoid false results?

4. Describe the ways in which major depression may be confused with dementia.

5. Explain why health-care professionals need to assess the "whole person," not just look at disease states. How often do you think such assessments occur in routine medical practice?

References

Applegate, W. B., Blass, J. B., Williams, T. F. 1990. "Instruments for the Functional Assessment of Older Patients." *New England Journal of Medicine* 322: 1207–14.

Barry, P. P. 1994. "Assessment of Geriatric Patients." In F. Homburger, ed. *The Rational Use of Advanced Medical Technology with the Elderly*. New York: Springer.

Beck, J. C., ed. 1991. *Geriatrics Review Syllabus, 1991–92*. New York: American Geriatrics Society, pp. 36–44, 218–224.

Campion, E. W. 1995. "The Value of Geriatric Interventions." *New England Journal of Medicine* 332: 1376–1378.

Consensus Development Panel. 1988. "National Institutes of Health Consensus Development Conference Statement: Geriatric Assessment Methods for Clinical Decision-Making." *Journal of the American Geriatrics Society* 36: 342–47.

Folstein, M. F., Folstein, S. E., McHugh, P. R. 1975. "Mini-Mental State: A Practical Method for Grading the Cognitive State of Patients for the Clinician." *Journal of Psychiatric Research* 12: 196–198.

Pfeffer, R. I., Kurosaki, T. T., Harrah, C. H., et al. 1982. "Measurement of Functional Activities of Older Adults in the Community." *Journal of Gerontology* 37: 323–9.

Reuben, D. B., 1991. "Use and Abuse of Assessment Instruments." In *Geriatrics Review Syllabus, 1991–92*, pp. 463–468. New York: American Geriatrics Society.

Rubenstein, L. Z., Rubenstein, L. V. 1991. "Multidimensional Assessment of Elderly Patients." *Advances in Internal Medicine* 36: 81–108.

Sheikh, J. I., Yesavage, J. A. 1986. "Geriatric Depression Scale: Recent Evidence and Development of a Shorter Version." *Clinical Gerontology* 5: 165–172.

Stuck, A. E., Siu, A. L., Wieland, G. D., et al. 1993. "Comprehensive Geriatric Assessment: A Meta-Analysis of Controlled Trials. *Lancet* 342: 1032–36.

Patricia P. Barry, "Assessment of Geriatric Patients: A Physician's View." Printed by permission of the author.

Chapter 38

Incipient Dementia: A Victim's Perspective

Morris Friedell

Dementia is caused by different illnesses that affect the brain. Alzheimer's Disease, named after the German physician, Alois Alzheimer, who first identified it in 1906, is the most common form of dementia and affects the parts of the brain controlling thought, memory, and language. Other causes of dementia include frontal-lobe dementia (Pick's disease), which affects personality and memory, and vascular dementia, which may follow a stroke or a series of small strokes. Although younger people may develop Alzheimer's, the risk increases with age. Among those age 65 to 74, about 3 percent of men and women have Alzheimer's and by age 85 or older, nearly one half may have the disorder. It is important to know, however, that Alzheimer's is not a part of normal aging.

Alzheimer's Disease begins slowly, and the initial symptom may be mild forgetfulness for recent events, activities, or the names of familiar people or things. As the disease progresses, symptoms become more serious. For example, people may forget how to do simple everyday activities, such as combing their hair or dressing. They can no longer think clearly, have problems communicating, and may become anxious or aggressive, or may wander. Eventually, people with Alzheimer's may need total care. In the following selection by Morris Friedell, a former college professor who was initially misdiagnosed as having frontal-lobe dementia (Pick's Disease), the author steps out of the frame of "dementia patient" to explain how becoming a victim of the disease has in-

fluenced his current life and his hopes for the future. Listen to him discuss his feelings of helplessness and ways of dealing with depression and despair. Pay attention to his use of rituals and ways of finding meaning in the face of uncertainty.

I am 58. I am a retired sociology professor. I live alone.

I first got worried in the fall of 1997 when I couldn't remember my mother's conversation and could not brush off this failing as undisciplined attention. Maybe this was a merely Freudian matter, but I didn't think so. In February 1998 I wound up at a neuropsychologist's and had the damnedest time trying to tell her about a movie I'd seen and enjoyed the night before. I knew it was in there, but it wouldn't come out. Later I wrote her a letter about it. In April she gave me her preliminary report and described to me the repetitiveness of words or actions indicating right frontal-lobe dysfunction. I knew little about neurology, and it had never occurred to me that anything could be wrong with my frontal lobes—I considered myself a decisive person rather than an apathetic zombie. However, I started learning, and in May, when I discovered on the Internet frontal-lobe dementia and its faint early signs as recalled by caregivers, I felt "uh-oh." I called my neurologist, and in June he told me that my MRI showed atrophy in the frontal lobes.

At this time benign alternatives to frontal-lobe dementia have not been ruled out, but I feel that's what I have. My philosophy of life is that in order to live fully one has to respect what one feels (barring irreversible decisions). That is what I'm doing. I also believe in reality testing, and I'm going to get a PET scan. [In September 1998 the PET and a QEEG showed an atypical Alzheimer's.[1]] (What was and is atypical is the clinical manifestation, not the PET scan.)

Now, how do I live? I have lost the normal feeling of moving forward in life, which I used to take for granted except when I was depressed, but I continue to desire quality of life. I now, as it were, paint a picture of what I'd like to see happen, and then act to realize the picture—sort of in the spirit of doing a jigsaw puzzle.

Oliver Sacks has a nice description of the way I sort of am now in contrast to the way I remember having been from age eight to last September. Speaking of the "The Last Hippie" in *An Anthropologist on Mars* (1995) he writes, "He lacked the constant dialogue of past and present, of experience and meaning, which constitutes consciousness and inner life for the rest of us. He seemed to have no sense of 'next' and to lack that eager and anxious tension of anticipation, of intention, that normally drives us through life." My Inner Computer will no longer open more than one window at a time—Past, Present, and Future won't open simultaneously.

When I finish this essay, even if I value it highly, I will not have the feeling of mastery or achievement that I formerly would have. However, I can hope, in looking back on this essay when it is in the past, to have the feeling of having achieved something worthwhile. My sense of the future has radically changed; my sense of the present is substantially altered; but my sense of the past has not only remained essentially the same but has somewhat deepened, I think.

I want, as long as possible, to maintain a quality of life that is characterized by (1) dignity, integrity, and responsibility; (2) meaningful human connection; and (3) individuality, creativity, and a sense of humor. In particular, I want deep communication and closure with those I love, and to make well the decisions leading to a "good death."

Inspiring Examples

As far as I know I am the first victim of Pick's (synonym for frontotemporal dementia, or FD) to write "de profundis," except for Ralph Waldo Emerson, whose progressive aphasia and leveling of affect suggest this condition. He wrote "Terminus":

It is time to be old,
To take in sail:
The god of bounds,
Who sets to seas a shore,
Came to me in his fatal rounds,
And said: 'No more!
No farther shoot

Thy broad ambitious branches, and thy
    root,
Fancy departs: no more invent,
Contract thy firmament
To compass of a tent.
There's not enough for this and that,
Make thy option which of two;
Economize the failing river,
Nor the less revere the Giver,
Leave the many and hold the few.
Timely wise accept the terms,
Soften the fall with wary foot;
A little while
Still plan and smile,
And, fault of novel germs,
Mature the unfallen fruit.
Curse, if thou wilt, thy sires,
Bad husbands of their fires,
who, when they gave thee breath,
Failed to bequeath
The needful sinew stark as once.
The Baresark marrow to thy bones,
But left a legacy of ebbing veins,
Inconstant heat and nerveless reins,—
Amid the Muses, left thee deaf and dumb.
Amid the gladiators, halt and numb.
As the bird trims her to the gale,
I trim myself to the storm of time,
I man the rudder, reef the sail,
Obey the voice at eve obeyed at prime:
'Lowly faithful, banish fear,
Right onward drive unharmed:
The port well worth the cruise, is near,
And every wave is charmed.'

Like me, Emerson experienced the loss of a taken-for-granted ability to do two things at once and, correlative with this, distressing helplessness. His poem ends humbly but nobly—dementia does not necessarily mean an incapacity for spiritual growth.

I find inspiration from authors suffering from Alzheimer's Disease (AD) or brain trauma,—Diana McGowin, Robert Davis, Claudia Osborn,—with symptoms far more severe than mine at this time. Morrie Schwartz wrote *Letting Go* (1997), when he was dying of ALS[2]—I sense mild frontal-lobe dysfunction and identify with his search for composure, his caring about human warmth, and his tendency to write aphoristically (logopenia) and expand from there.

My Background

Atypically, I've always had a little of the dysfunction I suffer. I couldn't solve the problem of which shoe went on which foot until someone wrote R and L in my shoes. I didn't enjoy playing bridge because the memorizing was onerous. I couldn't follow a basketball game, let alone play it. I was no good at small talk. Hopefully, all this now will help me cope. Robert Murphy, *The Body Silent* (1987), who became paralyzed by a spinal tumor, feels that his long-term sense of being scrawny and not happy with his body helped him cope.

I taught a course on human dignity. The first book was Viktor Frankl's *Man's Search for Meaning* (1959). Frankl had written a manuscript claiming that even in the most extreme situations man could keep his dignity and find meaning. Then he was thrown into Auschwitz. Could he live his theory? The first film in the course was of a teenager with (high-functioning) Down's syndrome. Though he was slow, he had caring, character, self-awareness, and a sense of humor. Whether challenged inwardly or outwardly, human beings are not the pawns of instincts or environment but have an inner worth. I now see I thought that teaching this stuff meant, magically, that I'd die by being run over by a truck and never have to face a dramatic challenge to my own human dignity. Oh, well . . .

Coping

Clinton Erb's *Losing Lou-Ann* describes what might lie ahead. Erb's wife lingered incommunicatively for five years in a nursing home, becoming mute three years before she died and losing facial expressions a year before that. I consider her fate worse than death. On the other hand, I care that the worth of a life not be judged by its normality or productivity. Religiously eclectic, my strongest affiliation is with liberal Judaism. Rabbi Rami Shapiro would say to someone terminally ill:

The Rituals

Why do I take the same long bike ride to the same destination and back almost every day? Why not vary it as I used to do? It's not because I'm anxious and compulsive à la "did I turn off the stove?" It's not that I've a special pleasure in consistency. So I made myself vary it—to observe my feeling. There was an uncomfortable absence of the familiar inner discussion (about losing weight, other possible physical activities, other uses of my time, etc.). It was as if I'd looked out the window and seen ominous clouds (suggestive of the aftermath of a nuclear war) rather than the familiar landscape. To ritualize my activities is to avoid looking out that window and to avoid the awareness of change.

Dietary Changes

I noticed that I'd stopped buying oranges. So I bought two, to note my feelings. To peel and eat the orange, what with its segments, unpleasantly absorbed my attention. I peeled and ate the other orange distractedly, when some issue from a phone conversation was reverberating in my mind. It was fine.

Interpersonal Relations

Patients suffering from Pick's disease and other frontal lobe syndromes [FLS] often provide some of the greatest caregiving challenges encountered. . . . These patients often have little insight into their limitations, make poor choices, and can be disruptive, posing risks to themselves and others. . . . Many are disinhibited and act on impulse seemingly without reason. . . . The patient with FLS may refuse to stop driving, make unusually large purchases, use power tools inappropriately, have social outbursts, or eat nonfood items such as glass ornaments. Their lack of insight and disinhibition may produce inconsistent behavior despite making verbally appropriate statements, constantly catching caregivers off guard. (Richard J. Caselli)

They can be apathetic too.

I've always felt something of a misfit and outsider, but compared to this picture I feel pretty normal. Of course that statement (and this whole essay) may be (at best) a "verbally appropriate statement." Be that as it may, I want to maintain insight and resist Caselli's picture as long as I can.

I was interrupted while writing this by a door-to-door salesman who had the effrontery to block my door with his foot, as I was politely telling him no. I instantly had a "social outburst," screaming at him. It was effective and, I believe, appropriate. But I find myself carefully reviewing any behavior of mine that might represent the nastier aspect of Pick's.

I also meditate on an essential core of human connection I can cleave to. Here Buddhist spirituality helps me. One can cultivate nonattachment to craving and impulse. Lou-Ann was for a long time able to resist her craving for snacks and desserts. Similarly, one ought to be able to resist impulses that are annoying to those around one. Then Buddhism identifies three basic interpersonal emotions that even young children enjoy but that have great spiritual value. One is compassion. This is the core of human feeling. Elie Wiesel wrote, "You suffer, therefore I am." It is gratifying to read about the response to distress of the 18- to 24-month-old child: "patting the head, fetching a toy, offering verbal expressions of sympathy, finding an adult to help, and so forth." When I deteriorate to this level, I too can keep my compassion, and hence my humanity.

The second basic emotion of Buddhism, closely allied to compassion, is loving-kindness, expressed in helping. It is gratifying to read that, eight years after diagnosis, a former family therapist reaches out to encourage others at his adult day-care center to talk and participate, "just like he did in the days when he was running things."

The third basic emotion is sympathetic joy. And even the infant is capable of this. Yet it is so often lost to envy and competition in the "normal" adult.

As a social psychologist, I can't help wondering if some of the self-centeredness of people with FD is due to their being given the role of pitiable victim or, alternatively, due to their losses being denied. Without denying their tragedy, suppose they were seen as people having a special opportunity to become the little child who enters the Kingdom of Heaven. According to Rabbi Harold S. Kushner, "There is a tradition in both Judaism and Christianity of the 'holy fool,' the simple, uneducated, unsophisticated person who serves God spontaneously and enthusiastically, without stopping to think about what he is doing. His serving is especially beloved because no intellectual barriers come between him and his God." With this thought I can hopefully face the prospect of disinhibition with the serenity of the 23rd Psalm.

Update in February 1999

I wrote "Incipient Dementia" in late July 1998, about a month after my first personal experience of the likelihood of catastrophic illness (triggered by the abnormal MRI). It was then titled: "Frontotemporal Dementia—A Victim's Perspective." I had just seen the head of the FD clinic at the University of California, Los Angeles, who told me the FD was "not unlikely." She had mentioned Alzheimer's Disease, but as an improbable alternative—later she admitted surprise at the PET results. She had mentioned some benign alternatives but without enthusiasm. Essentially, her examination seemed to confirm the impression I'd gotten from my reading and from the neurologist I had seen in June. Of course, my lucid "insight" spoke against an FD diagnosis but hardly conclusively.

In order to conquer depression and to assert my human dignity, I chose for myself the role of being perhaps the first FD victim ever to maintain awareness and to tell the story. One of the most impressive experiences of my life had been to talk with Thomas Blatt, a Holocaust survivor who had escaped from the Sobibor death camp. I would try, in my way, to emulate him.

Not only his courage but his humility impressed me. He had explained that he was not basically a hero, and if he had "merely" been in Auschwitz he would have perished. It was only the certainty of death that brought out the extreme of daring in himself and his comrades.

My UCLA neurologist was happy to tell me that the PET showed AD, because it was "treatable," but the news depressed me again. I thought "Auschwitz"—that I'd now be one of a gray horde of prisoners who would slowly, painfully, and ignominiously perish. So far, thank God, it hasn't turned out that way, even though there is no substantial reason to doubt the diagnosis (UCLA reinterpreted the MRI). I have not observed any further cognitive decline since I wrote "Incipient Dementia," but that's due, I think, to my starting on Aricept, which can retard AD by six months.[3]

In hindsight, I think the experience I reported in "Incipient Dementia" resulted from a mixture of congenital nonverbal learning disorder with a touch of Asperger's syndrome,[4] AD, anxiety, and taking the role of the FD victim. I'm less conscious of what I eat and how I eat it, now that I'm not worried that this reflects the first signs of the dreaded Kluver-Bucy syndrome[5]. I'm less anxious about my quietness in social situations as a measure of the atrophy of my frontal lobes, and this of course makes it easier to converse.

I have become more confident that I can usually pass for normal. An interlocutor would take me as some combination of shy, wanting to be a good listener, deep (unconcerned with mundane detail), self-centered, and absent-minded, and would rarely guess that I have an organic memory impairment.

I have joined the tiny community of early AD victims who communicate by chatting on the Internet. It is a great medium for us because it is relatively slow and provides an instantaneous written record of the conversation. We swap jokes. For instance: As a senior citizen was driving down the freeway, his car phone rang. Answering, he heard his wife's voice urgently warning him, "Herman, I just heard on the news that there's a car going the wrong way on 280. Please be care-

ful!" "Hell," said Herman, "It's not just one car. It's hundreds of them!"

In conclusion, "life goes on," even though it is not the same.

Discussion Questions

1. Describe the coping mechanisms Friedell uses to deal with early-onset Alzheimer's disease.

2. Explain how rituals may be useful coping tools for someone with Alzheimer's disease.

3. Does Friedell seem relieved or distressed to learn that he is suffering from Alzheimer's rather than Pick's Disease? Why?

4. Using the postscript to Friedell's selection, explain how he and other people with Alzheimer's disease are managing their disorder.

Notes

1. MRI (magnetic resonance imaging), PET (positron emission tomography), QEEG (a type of electroencephalogram), are medical tests to help in diagnosis of brain dysfunctions.

2. ALS, sometimes known as Lou Gehrig's disease, is a progressive and fatal neurological disorder.

3. Aricept is a drug used to retard the progression for AD but does not cure it.

4. Asperger's syndrome is a neurobiological disorder that describes people with normal or gifted intelligence but who lack skills in social interaction.

5. Kluver-Bucy syndrome is a disorder of the temporal lobes of the brain.

Morris Friedell, "Incipient Dementia: A Victim's Perspective." Printed by permission of the author.

Chapter 39
Anticipatory Dementia and Well-being

*Lynne Gershenson Hodgson
and Stephen J. Cutler*

As *Alzheimer's Disease has received more and more attention in the popular media as well as by scientists, increasing numbers of people are anxious that they might develop the disorder. Minor memory changes that normally occur as we grow older may cause alarm as signs of impending dementia. In the following selection, Lynne Hodgson and Stephen Cutler focus on how parent-child relations can affect a son's or daughter's perceptions of well-being in anticipation of future aging. Half of their subjects are the adult children of a living parent with Alzheimer's disease, and half are a matched group with no family history of the disease. This is an interesting examination of how intergenerational relations influence people's personal images of their future aging, even though these perceptions might be inaccurate. Look carefully at the measures of well-being used and their association to the fear that normal, age-associated memory loss is the forerunner of dementia. Pay attention to the ways in which the subjects manage their anxieties.*

Introduction

"I used to have an excellent memory, a phenomenal memory. . . . But lately I'm becoming frightened . . . that I can't remember things. . . . I'm going to the doctor on Monday and I'm definitely going to ask him. It'll make me feel a lot better because it's scary, very scary . . . and it's embarrassing . . . not remembering people's names that I see quite often. . . . It's very embarrassing. . . . Even with my job lately, I noticed it. . . . Normally, I'd just look at [the codes] and for the next six weeks I would know. Now I have to keep opening my book to see 'Now what was it for this? What is it for that?' Yeah, it's affecting my job. This is scary. . . . I'm very upset about it. I'm very concerned about it. Maybe in the back of my mind it is because of Alzheimer. . . ."

—49-year-old woman who has
a mother with dementia.

The concern voiced in this quotation illustrates a phenomenon we have labeled "anticipatory dementia," or the fear that normal, age-associated memory change is the harbinger of dementia. The phenomenon has two components—a person's concern about developing Alzheimer's disease and the extent to which perceived memory change affects that concern. Previous research has shown that middle-aged individuals sometimes interpret their normative memory changes as the onset of Alzheimer's disease or other dementias. The children of parents who have Alzheimer's disease are particularly susceptible to this anxiety when they acknowledge the genetic basis of the disease. Levels of anticipatory dementia vary not only by family history, but also by gender, marital status, and occupation.[1] The quotation not only points up anticipatory dementia, but it also offers a glimpse of its consequences for this 49-year-old woman who describes the effects of her anxiety on her job performance. This article focuses precisely on the consequences of anticipatory dementia and asks the question, is there an association between anticipatory dementia and well-being?

Although the concept of anticipatory dementia is a new focus of research, various components of the phenomenon have been previously studied. Memory functioning, for example, is an area which has been explored by many disciplines and much literature exists to establish the link between memory change and various measures of well-being. Most frequently studied is the relationship between cognition and depression, and although the robustness of the association varies by study, recent work tends to confirm the salience of the link.[2-5] In particular, there is evidence that subjective perception of memory (and memory concerns) is linked with depression.[2,3] Additionally, although there is no systematic scientific literature on the association between concern over developing Alzheimer's disease and well-being, there are anecdotal and first person accounts which make this connection.[6] Similarly, the growing body of research on the families of Huntington's disease sufferers offers a parallel, though not an exact picture of the relationship between concern about inheriting the disease and well-being.[7] As more and more diseases are linked to genetic endowments (for example, the discoveries of the genetic predispositions towards breast cancer and heart disease), the psychosocial consequences of problematic familial health histories are being explored.[8] Thus, based on past research evidence, we expect to find that those who exhibit higher levels of anticipatory dementia will report lower levels of well-being and will engage in a greater variety of help-seeking behaviors.

We would also expect that certain group memberships would alter the relationship between anticipatory dementia and well-being. For example, it is likely that the children of parents with Alzheimer's disease would be susceptible to different consequences than the control group sample, reflecting their differing experiences with the disease and concerns with regard to inheritability. Similarly, the literature reports that men and women have distinct patterns of health behaviors and symptom perceptions[9] and we would, therefore, expect to find that women experience more assaults on their well-being when they exhibit higher levels of anticipatory dementia.

Methods

During the Spring of 1994, a pilot study to examine the phenomenon of anticipatory dementia was conducted: Three community agencies serving persons with Alzheimer's disease and their families assisted with the recruitment of a purposive sample. Twenty-five men and women, between the ages of 40 and 60, all of whom had a living parent with a probable diagnosis of Alzheimer's disease or other dementia, were selected. A control group of 25 men and women who did not have a parent with dementia was recruited from the friendship networks of the original sample, so that they would be matched on a variety of social structural characteristics. The instrument format, which combined elements of a directed interview and a structured questionnaire, yielded both quantitative and qualitative data.

The sample is predominantly female, white, married, Catholic, white-collar, and well-educated. Seventy percent of those interviewed are women and 68 percent are currently married. Their average age is 45. Eighty-eight percent of the sample are white. The overwhelming majority of the men and women work outside the home, 66 percent full time and 22 percent part time. Almost half of the sample have completed college and 30 percent have continued their education beyond a four-year college. Fifty-four percent of the men and women are Catholic, 18 percent are Jewish, and 18 percent are Protestant. When the profiles of the two sub-samples—the 25 adult children of Alzheimer parents and the 25 control group respondents—are compared, there are no statistically significant differences on any of these background characteristics. The groups are, therefore, matched demographically.

Measures

To measure concern about developing Alzheimer's disease, we used a single closed-ended item: "I'd like to ask how concerned you are about personally developing Alzheimer's disease. Would you say you're very concerned, somewhat concerned, not very concerned, or not at all concerned about developing Alzheimer's?" We then followed up the response with a number of open-ended questions which probed the respondent's answer, including "could you tell me why it is that you (are/are not) concerned about developing Alzheimer's?"

For purposes of the present study, we used a measure of subjective memory functioning which is based on six questions developed for this study: four closed-ended items asking whether respondents think their memory has changed in recent years, whether others have noticed memory changes, whether the respondent's ability to remember causes them any worry, and whether respondents have ever spoken to anyone about their memory; and two open-ended questions probing overall evaluations of memory and feelings about the respondent's ability to remember. Scores on each of the six items were dichotomized and summed, resulting in a composite Memory Assessment Index (MAI) with a possible range from zero to six, with higher scores indicating a more negative assessment of memory. For the respondents in this study, the reliability coefficient (Cronbach's alpha) is .805.

A 12-point composite measure of anticipatory dementia was constructed from the MAI and responses to the single closed-ended item measuring concern about developing Alzheimer's disease. Scores on the two measures were summed, yielding a measure with a range from zero (indicating no memory problems and not at all concerned about developing the disease) to 12 (indicating negative perceptions of memory and very concerned about developing the disease).

Several measures of well-being were used, including:

- Radloff's 20-item Center for Epidemiological Studies Depression Scale (CES-D)[10] with a reliability coefficient of .847; and
- Pfeiffer's Short Psychiatric Evaluation Scale[11] with an alpha of .698;
- A single item, dichotomized measure of life satisfaction; and
- A dichotomized measure of self-reported health.

Finally, it should be noted here that, although it is not used in the following analysis, the six-item Orientation-Concentration-Memory Test[12] was administered to all respondents as a screen for the possible presence of dementia. Eighty-eight percent of the respondents in both samples had weighted error scores of four or lower, and none of the respondents had a weighted error score of greater than 10, which would be indicative of the presence of dementia.

Results

The results of the analysis provide evidence to support our general hypothesis, that

Table 39.1

Association Between Anticipatory Dementia and Well-being (n=50)

	Anticipatory dementia	
	Coefficient r	Significance p
CES-D	.329	.020
Psych symptoms	.403	.004
Life satisfaction	−.368	.009
Health status	−.297	.036

well-being—as measured by depression, psychiatric symptomatology, life satisfaction, and subjective health—is related to our measure of anticipatory dementia (see Table 39.1). For the total sample (n=50), higher levels of concern about one's memory and developing Alzheimer's, as indicated by the composite measure, are associated with higher levels of depression (r=.329, p .02) and psychiatric symptomatology (r=.403, p .005). Those respondents who report higher levels of anticipatory dementia also reported lower levels of life satisfaction (r=.368, p .01) and poorer self-reported health (r=.297, p .05).

As our initial hypotheses predicted, differential associations exist depending on group membership (Table 39.2). Among the adult children of parents with Alzheimer's disease (n=25), life satisfaction is significantly related to anticipatory dementia (r=.416, p .05) and depression and psychiatric symptomatology are marginally related (r=.352, p .10 and r=.341, p .10, respectively). Relationships among the control group sample (n=25) are significant for levels of psychiatric symptomatology (r=.433, p .05) and for self-reported health (r=.446, p .05).

Significant differences in these relationships also exist between men and women (Table 39.3). The data show that women who exhibit anticipatory dementia report higher levels of depression (r=.318, p .10) and psychiatric symptomatology (r=.405, p .02), and lower levels of life satisfaction (r=.433, p .01) and self-reported health (r=.355, p .05). For the men in the sample, no significant relationships were found.

Anticipatory dementia appears to relate to a variety of help-seeking behaviors. Respon-

Table 39.2

Association Between Anticipatory Dementia
and Well-being by Sample Group

	Anticipatory dementia	
	Adult children (n=25)	Control (n=25)
CES-D		
r	.352	.266
p	.085	.200
Psych symptoms		
r	.341	.433
p	.095	.031
Life satisfaction		
r	−.419	−.283
p	.037	.171
Health status		
r	−.173	−.446
p	.409	.026

Table 39.3

Association Between Anticipatory
Dementia and Well-being by Sex

	Anticipatory dementia	
	Males (n=15)	Females (n=35)
CES-D		
r	.066	.318
p	.815	.063
Psych symptoms		
r	.081	.405
p	.774	.016
Life satisfaction		
r	−.116	−.433
p	.680	.009
Health status		
r	−.062	−.355
p	.826	.036

dents were asked whether or not they ever took any actions given their concerns. Those men and women who reported higher levels of anticipatory dementia were significantly more likely to speak to friends and to family about their concerns (r=.664, p .001 and r=.587, p .01, respectively). More specifically, they tended to talk to family members and friends regarding their fears about Alzheimer's disease and subjective assessments of their memory functioning. They were also marginally (r=.380, p .10) more likely to speak to professionals (such as doctors, social workers, and counselors) about their memory concerns.

Analysis of the qualitative data reported in the open-ended questions provides additional and powerful evidence of the relationship between anticipatory dementia and well-being. The significant relationships reported in the quantitative analyses are corroborated by the commentary of these men and women who speak to the specific day-to-day consequences of their anxiety. Those respondents who exhibit the highest levels of anticipatory dementia frequently acknowledge the extent to which their worries affect their day-to-day lives. At one extreme are respondents (exclusively the children of parents with Alzheimer's disease) who are mind-

ful of every instance of forgetfulness and for whom these memory lapses take on ominous meanings. They take their fears into the workplace, the home, and occasionally, into the doctor's office. The themes surrounding the workplace deal with anxiety about job performance, lapses which are apparent to employers, and fears of dismissal. For example, the words of this 41-year-old woman whose father has dementia illustrate the themes of the workplace worries:

. . . when I'm out interviewing a client, I'll record a case right away because I know if I don't I'll lose it. It does worry me because if something happens later and I need to recall, a detail that I haven't written down, there's a good chance I won't remember it . . . sometimes I'll forget people's names, or if they tell me they're related, I'll forget that. That's important in my field. I have to remember who's who . . . I can see a genetic pattern between my father and his mother and I know what my memory is like now . . . I'm very concerned about developing Alzheimer's.

In the home, those respondents with high levels of anticipatory dementia offer glimpses of forgetfulness in family chores, such as appointments and shopping, even forgetting to "take the roast out of the oven." And, some of these men and women have taken their concerns into the doctor's office, bringing to the health professionals complaints about issues which they relate to Alzheimer's disease. For example, one 51-year-old woman in our sample, whose mother has Alzheimer's disease, brought her concerns to her doctor and to a support group:

> When Mom was first diagnosed, I was afraid that I was going to have it . . . and therefore every time I forgot something I thought, 'Ah, it's coming, I'm going to get it now.' You know, that's just fear. . . . After talking with the doctor, after being part of a support group, that's no longer a fear.

For this group, then, anxieties are often discussed openly with friends, family, professionals, though no one in the sample reports talking to employers about their fears. Several of the respondents have gone so far as to instruct their families about their wishes regarding housing and health care should they develop the disease, and several others have talked to their doctors about diagnostic testing. More common are the men and women of the sample who are willing to admit their fears to themselves, but who do not outwardly live their lives in anticipation of the disease. They are concerned about the possibility of developing Alzheimer's disease and cognizant of their memory changes, but in questioning, do not dwell on the consequences of these concerns.

Discussion

Research conducted on a sample of 25 adult children of a parent with Alzheimer's disease and a matched sample of 25—men and women with no family history of the disease, established the existence of anticipatory dementia—a concern that normal age-associated memory change is the first indication of incipient Alzheimer's disease. The present analysis extends that finding by focusing on one particular aspect of the phenomenon, the association between anticipatory dementia and well-being. Results show that the well-being of our respondents, as measured by life satisfaction, depression, psychiatric symptomatology, and self-reported health status, is related to anticipatory dementia. Although

the direction of the causal relationship cannot be established in this study, the results indicate that those who report higher levels of anticipatory dementia are likely to be more depressed, show more psychiatric symptoms, have lower life satisfaction, and claim poorer health than those for whom memory problems and Alzheimer's disease are not a concern. These findings confirm the hypotheses with which we started the research. People who have a high level of anxiety about developing Alzheimer's and who are experiencing some decline in their subjective evaluation of memory functioning might very well perceive their lives more negatively and that negativity may manifest itself in a variety of ways—worries on the job, help-seeking behavior, stress symptoms, depression, and a general low level of life satisfaction.

The differences observed in the significance of the relationship between anticipatory dementia and well-being provide some interesting avenues for further exploration. The adult children of parents with Alzheimer's disease reported an association in three out of the four measures of well-being (compared to two out of four of the measures for the matched sample), and were much more likely to mention tangible consequences of their anxieties about developing the disease. That their worries are explicit and consequential is not surprising, since they are living with the manifestations of the disease and have concrete experience on which to base their concerns. Similarly, the finding that the women of the sample, and not the men, exhibit the relationship between anticipatory dementia and well-being might be attributed to the differential patterns of symptom perceptions and reporting of women or it might be the result of their experience with the disease. It is more likely that the women are either primary or secondary caregivers for their afflicted parent, or at the very least, they might act as confidants for the caregivers, so they would be more likely to be close to the source of their fears.

In an exploratory study such as this one, the generation of hypotheses is one desired outcome. The ability to generalize and to offer conclusive findings is limited by the size of the sample, but the strength and direction of the relationship between anticipatory dementia and well-being opens up many possible lines of inquiry. For example, further research on a larger scale is needed to establish the direction of the relationship of these variables, but these findings suggest a possible hypothesis—that anxiety over the imminent development of Alzheimer's brought on by perceived memory change leads to assaults on a person's global well-being. If further study confirms this hypothesis, a better understanding of the phenomenon would be important in order to mitigate its negative consequences.

Discussion Questions

1. Do you see a connection between what Friedell says about Alzheimer's Disease and what Hodgson and Cutler say about anticipatory fear of dementia?

2. How do the control group and adult children differ in their feelings of well-being and fears of dementia? Does gender also play a role?

3. Outline the help-seeking and social supports that adult children of parents with Alzheimer's disease use to lessen their anxieties about dementia.

4. How do you think that observing, and perhaps caring for, a parent with Alzheimer's contributes to their adult children's lower feelings of well-being?

Acknowledgments

Funding for this project was provided by an Alzheimer's Association—F.M. Kirby Pilot Research Grant. The authors wish to acknowledge several individuals for their contributions to the project: Stacey Bjornberg, Amy Elkins, Paul Falcigno, Sarah Gilmore, Theresa Jeffries, Marilyn Kline, Michelle Merrill, April Radocchio, and Cynthia Schultz.

Notes

1. Cutler SJ, Hodgson LG: Anticipatory Dementia: A Link Between Memory Appraisals and Concerns About Developing Alzheimer's Disease. *The Gerontologist*. 1996; 36: 657–664.

2. La Rue A, Swan GE, Carmelli D: Cognition and Depression in a Cohort of Aging Men: Results from the Western Collaborative Group Study. *Psychology and Aging*. 1995; 10: 30–33.

3. Lichtenberg PA, Ross T, Millis SR, *et al*: The Relationship Between Depression and Cognition in Older Adults: A Cross-validation Study. *Journal of Gerontology: Psychological Sciences*. 1995; 50B: P25–P32.

4. O'Hara MW, Hinrichs JV, Kohout FJ, *et al*: Memory Complaint and Memory Performance in the Depressed Elderly. *Psychology and Aging*. 1986: 1: 208–214.

5. Rabbitt P, Donlan C, Watson P, *et al*: Unique and Interactive Effects of Depression, Age, Socioeconomic Advantage, and Gender on Cognitive Performance of Normal Healthy Older People. *Psychology and Aging*. 1995; 10: 307–313.

6. Konek CW: *Daddyboy: A Memoir*. St. Paul, MN: Graywolf Press, 1991.

7. Hunt V, Walker FO: Learning to Live At Risk for Huntington's Disease. *Journal of Neuroscience Nursing*. 1991; 23: 179–182.

8. Siebert C: The DNA We've Been Dealt. *New York Times*. September 17 1995; 50–57, 64, 74, 93-94, 104.

9. Verbrugge LM: Gender and Health: An Update on Hypotheses and Evidence. *Journal of Health and Social Behavior*. 1985; 26: 156–182.

10. Radloff LS: The CES-D Scale: A Self-Report Depression Scale for Research in the General Population. *Applied Psychological Measurement*. 1977; 1: 287–401.

11. Pfeiffer E: A Short Psychiatric Evaluation Schedule: A New 15-Item Monotonic Scale Indicative of Functional Psychiatric Disorder. *Proceedings of the Bayer-Symposium VII, Brain Function in Old Age*. 1979; New York: Springer-Verlag.

12. Katzman R, Brown T, Fuld P, *et al*: Validation of a Short Orientation-Memory-Concentration Test of Cognitive Impairment. *American Journal of Psychiatry*. 1983; 140: 734–739.

Chapter 40
Burdens and Boundaries

*Leslie A. Morgan and
J. Kevin Eckert*

One myth in American society is that most elders live in nursing homes or other long-term-care facilities. The opposite is true: only about five percent of old people are in long-term-care facilities at any given time. The large increase in numbers (but not percentage) of elderly in nursing homes is due both to greater numbers of elders surviving into old age and to the rapid growth of the nursing-home industry, which supplanted other long-term-care facilities such as almshouses and state mental hospital geriatric wards. Board-and-care homes, also known as adult foster care, are small facilities, often with few staff except the operator. It is thus most often the operators who are responsible for seriously impaired elders with both cognitive and physical impairments; they do the day-to-day "body work"— bathing, cleaning, dressing, toileting, and feeding—of impaired older people, many of whom have no close family.

*Yet aside from occasional horror stories about abusive care given in board-and-care homes and other long-term-care facilities, surprisingly little attention has been paid to either the strains of caregiving these paraprofessionals feel or to the coping strategies they use in dealing with their patients. In the following selection, Leslie Morgan and Kevin Eckert examine various dimensions of caregiver burden and the level of job-related burden that these paid caregivers, many of whom are "on duty" 24 hours a day, experience. As you read, consider the areas in which these formal caregivers feel most weighed upon. Think about the extent to which they find caregiving gratifying. Notice the different types of operators of board-and-care homes and the extent to which per-*sonnel draw boundaries between themselves and those for whom they care.*

Among the oldest old (85 and over), where rates of disability increase and more people require assistance with various tasks of health maintenance and daily living, care is typically provided by individuals from one of two groups—family members and friends (often referred to as the informal sector of care) and professional or paraprofessional workers (sometimes called the formal sector). In many cases, especially among those who are severely impaired, care may involve aid from both informal and formal sectors simultaneously, providing a mix of skills and efforts to meet complex needs (Miller, McFall, and Campbell 1994).

The Nature and Extent of the Informal-Sector Care

Family members and friends provide the largest volume of care, including some very intensive and medically complex care to older spouses, parents, or siblings who have physical or cognitive limitations (Glazer 1993; Stone, Cafferata, and Sangl 1987). In the last two decades the research on caregiving has focused heavily on the informal sector, the care provided by family, friends, and neighbors (George and Gwyther 1986; Vitaliano, Young, and Russo 1991). Indeed, it is often found that the care has been—or could be—reciprocal. Spouses usually care for each other on an "as needed" basis, and often this reciprocity extends to the bonds between parent and child. The fact that women marry older men and that men tend to die at younger ages than women means that, more often than not, the care provider in an older couple is a wife (Stone, Cafferata, and Sangl 1987). Husbands also provide care when called upon, but they may not perceive this work to be a "usual" part of their gender role, and they may act differently as caregivers (Kramer 1997b). With children as caregivers, there is often the acknowledgment of a responsibility to return the care that parents provided, should it be needed (Finlay, Roberts, and Banahan 1988). Not all children are equally likely to be caregivers, and often one out of a sibling group comes to be designated as the primary caregiver, who does much of the work and organizes the contributions of others (Matthews and Rosner 1988).

Whether it is a spouse, a child, or some other relative or friend, informal caregivers are presumed to be knowledgeable about the wants and needs of the person receiving care. Their care is mostly of high quality, since bonds of affection and lengthy personal relationships connect those giving and receiving care. As with most things about society that work well, we tend not to hear about the substantial effort that family members and others in the informal sector make around the clock to provide care for older kin, neighbors, and friends.

We do, occasionally, hear about cases when there are problems in the care given by the informal sector. Such a situation is typically labeled as "elder abuse or neglect" and can involve spouses or children, typically those serving as primary caregivers (Steinmetz 1988). Although abuse or neglect occurs in only a minority of cases, concerns regarding how to avoid these situations have led to examination of the dynamics of informal care. One of the issues most intensively studied in the last few decades has been the psychosocial strain among caregivers, or "caregiver burden" (Vitaliano, Young, and Russo 1991). This research has documented that, to varying degrees depending on relationship, type, and severity of impairment, and a variety of caregiving context variables, informal caregivers may experience strain, burden, and associated problems with physical and emotional health. In the last few years there have been efforts to balance this picture by examining the positive outcomes of caregiving for family and friends who undertake these roles (Kramer 1997a). An interesting point about these studies is that they examine the caregiver and seldom include the effects on the care recipient of being dependent (Pruchno, Burant, and Peters 1997).

Contrasting Informal and Formal Care

For many years, both researchers and practitioners have emphasized the differences between formal-sector and informal-sector caregivers, focusing on the strengths and limitations of each group in meeting elders' needs (Sussman 1977). A distinct body of research examines the professionals and paraprofessionals who specialize in caring for frail elders, either at home or in supportive environment, such as board-and-care (foster) homes or nursing homes. Professionals include physicians, nurses, social workers, occupational therapists, and others who are specially trained and certified at a high level of skill. Paraprofessional caregivers are those individuals who work as hands-on providers of health care and daily assistance for pay but who lack nursing or other advanced, professional credentials. It is usually the paraprofessionals in the formal-care sector who have the most intensive levels of contact with dependent adults, spending more time and providing more types of care than the professionals. Paraprofessional health-care workers occupy the lowest rung on the career hierarchy in health care, receiving minimal pay and prestige for their work, despite its importance to those in their care (Foner 1994; Institute of Medicine 1986; Oktay and Palley 1991).

Paraprofessional caregivers (such as home health aides, nursing assistants, and foster-care providers) work in a wide variety of settings, from private homes to residential-care facilities and more traditional nursing-home and special-care units. In some of these settings paraprofessional workers are in a tightly organized, shift-work setting where their activities are structured and monitored. A paraprofessional in a nursing home, for example, often has a set number of individuals for whom he or she is responsible for dressing, bathing, feeding, and assisting with mobility during an eight-hour shift.

In other situations (such as home health care or board-and-care facilities), paraprofessionals providing care may have considerably more autonomy and flexibility. An operator of a small board-and-care home who resides with her residents, for example, may have as few as two or three older adults in her care, may serve meals "family style," and may permit people to get up in the morning, eat, and undertake activities when they wish, rather than according to a strict schedule. Home health-care workers typically spend limited time with those in their care but can perform a wide range of helping tasks within that time, from assisting with meals, mobility, or bathing to attending to health needs.

People tend to think of professionals or paraprofessionals in the formal sector as differing in important ways from family and friends providing care in the informal sector. The relationships of the former have fairly short histories and are of limited scope, focusing on the care and assistance tasks required. These providers are believed to lack the strong emotional bonds that serve to link provider and recipient in the informal sector, and they have not witnessed the cognitive and physical losses that led to the need for care. The fact that the care is provided for money is believed by many to create a bulwark against the emergence of a personal, emotional relationship for paraprofessionals working in the formal sector.

The view of quality of care in the formal sector is also much different. Most of the attention addresses the quality of life of the care recipient rather than the well-being of the paraprofessionals giving care (Chappell and Novak 1992). When the impact of providing intensive levels of care to impaired and sometimes difficult elders is assessed, it tends to be explored in terms of negative behaviors of the paraprofessionals, such as high job turnover (Banaszak-Holl and Hines 1996) and inadequate job performance (Foner 1994), including neglect and abuse. As with family caregivers, the only situations that come to the attention of the public are those where poor care, theft, or neglect resulted in severe negative outcomes for older adults. Seldom does the stress of the paraprofessional worker, including her or his subjective well-being, come directly into the spotlight (Tellis-Nayak and Tellis-Nayak 1989).

The intention in this selection is to address two issues raised by the literature on the formal and informal sectors of care. First, do paraprofessional caregivers experience strain or burden from caregiving that is comparable to that found in family caregivers? Second, do paraprofessional caregivers draw firm boundaries between themselves and those in their care, creating a distance that may serve as a sort of defense against some of the pres-

sures that family caregivers experience? Do paraprofessionals, in fact, maintain through psychological boundaries a "distant" and "businesslike" relationship with those to whom they give assistance?

Prior Research on Paraprofessionals' Burden and Boundaries

Caregiver burden has been seen as having multiple dimensions, such as physical, psychological, financial, and social strains, which arise from the added responsibilities and role overload of family caregiving (Novak and Guest 1989; Stull, Kosloski, and Kercher 1994). Usually multiquestion scales are used to assess the level of burden on caregivers, and variations have been found depending on the characteristics of the caregiver (spouse versus child, co-resident versus separate household, etc.) and the traits of the recipient (Vitaliano, Young, and Russo 1991). Especially problematic in terms of burden is the loss of cognitive functioning in an older relative, as occurs in dementia, where the interpersonal relationship and emotional bond is strained, and disruptive behaviors (e.g., violence and wandering) appear (Ory et al. 1985; Poulshock and Deimling 1984; Quayhagen and Quayhagen 1988).

Surprisingly little attention has been paid to stress or burden among paraprofessional caregivers, given their central role in the hands-on work of caregiving (Chappell and Novak 1992). Most often when issues of stress or burden are raised, they are related to outcomes, such as high job turnover and failures in job performance documented for some paraprofessional workers (Banaszak-Holl and Hines 1996; Foner 1994; Tellis-Nayak and Tellis-Nayak 1989; Waxman, Carner, and Berkenstock 1984: Yu and Kaltreider 1987). In other words, burden is not defined in terms of the negative implications for the care provider (the paraprofessional) but instead in terms of outcomes for care recipients. When burden has been examined directly, the results have been mixed. N. L. Chappell and M. Novak (1992) found burden, burnout, and stress common in their Canadian sample of nursing assistants, but C. Tompkins (1995) found a low to moderate level of stress among home health-care workers, which was balanced by a sense of accomplishment for the importance of the work they performed. As with families, traits of those receiving care (e.g., cognitive impairment, violent behaviors) influence the degree of stress or burden reported by paraprofessionals (Heim 1985; Yu and Kaltreider 1987; Williams 1986).

Relatively little attention has been given to the issue of boundaries, doubtless because it is believed not to be important in informal care. Affection for and identification with the care recipient is presumed in the informal sector but not necessarily in the formal sector—including paraprofessional workers. Professionals in health care are encouraged to maintain an objective distance from those they treat. But are such boundaries equally relevant for those giving day-to-day care, which is often physically intimate? Motivated by money instead of love or a sense of duty, such distance is recommended in some contexts as a self-protective mechanism, to avoid emotional connections that might be severed when the worker changes jobs or patient load, or the older adult dies. Despite the differences in the nature and duration of relationships in the formal and informal sectors, there has been relatively little investigation of the quality or depth of the relationships between provider and recipient or in interpersonal boundaries that are established there.

The Research Subjects and Their Work Sites

The analysis that follows draws its data from two, related studies carried out by the authors. The first was a longitudinal study of 108 paraprofessional operators of small board-and-care homes in Maryland. Four interviews with these operators included both structured and open-ended questions and included a 23-item measure of several dimensions of burden. The homes were small (82 percent had three or fewer residents), had limited staff (if any) in addition to the home operator, and nearly all (97 percent) of the operators resided with those in their care 24 hours a day. Rather than being large and in-stitutional, as many nursing homes are, these facilities are homelike, and residents often bring personal belongings and furniture to use in their bedrooms. Older adults residing in such settings are seriously impaired by both cognitive and physical problems (typically less impaired than nursing-home residents, however); many are poor; and many lack close kin who might otherwise serve as their caregivers (Morgan, Eckert, and Lyon 1995).

A follow-up to this study involved in-depth interviews with a subset of the board-and-care operator sample ($N=36$), focusing on the operators' conceptualizations of caring. Questions were based on S. M. Albert's (1990) dimensions of family caregiving to see how paraprofessionals in board-and-care houses differed from family members in defining care. Albert argued that for family caregivers, the effort is organized into a cultural system driven by collective ideas about parental obligations, family loyalty, and other psychological and sociological variables. Following Albert's approach, the goal of these interviews was to tap the views of paraprofessional board-and-care operators, many of whom had also worked in nursing homes, hospitals, or other facilities, regarding their work.

The second source of information was an interview study with 48 individuals working as hands-on paraprofessional care providers for nursing homes or home health agencies. The respondents came from six nursing homes and five home health agencies, but most had worked in multiple settings (e.g., a home health worker often had worked in a nursing home at some time). Their discussions reflected the perspectives of experienced paraprofessionals on selecting and remaining in this type of work. Although it may seem questionable to weave together information from these different samples and settings, it was surprising to the authors to find that most had worked in multiple settings across the health-care spectrum, and some who now worked in one setting planned to move to another in the future. In a sense, these individuals mirror the mobility and changing trends in health-care delivery, moving as job opportunities change and their own experiences direct them to a particular setting or environment that best fits their lifestyle or caregiving style.

The Burden Among Paraprofessional Caregivers

At the time the authors were conducting the initial study, no scale existed to evaluate burden among paraprofessionals. As Chappell and Novak subsequently did, we adopted and modified the fundamentals of measuring burden used in studies of family caregiving—a multidimensional scale consisting of a number of items to reflect each dimension. Four dimensions (areas) of burden were identified as potentially relevant to paraprofessionals: psychological burden, financial burden, physical burden, and social or temporal burden (Novak and Guest 1989). We initially anticipated that operators with a larger number of residents in their care and those caring for more impaired elders would report greater burden.

The burden scale consisted of 23 questions to which the person could respond on a five-point scale from "strongly agree" to "strongly disagree". We summed the responses to gain an overall sense of burden (total burden) or by the four dimensions outlined above, to determine whether any burden experienced was focused in particular aspects of their lives. Items for the area of physical burden included statements such as, "I am generally very tired as a result of caring for the clients," or "Running a board-and-care home sometimes takes more physical effort than I can give." Items tapping the psychological or emotional aspects of burden included, "The work I do is mentally draining or exhausting," and "Taking care of these people causes me a lot of aggravation." Burden related to limitations on time and privacy included items such as, "It sometimes seems as if I have lost control of my time since I started taking people into my home," "This work would be easier if I could take some time off now and then," and "Caring for the people living here doesn't give me as much privacy as I would like." The final dimension, financial burden, was tapped with items such as "There are a lot of unexpected costs in running a board-and-care home" and "I don't earn enough money for the amount of work

that I do." Scores for the various items were added together, so that higher scores indicated a greater level of burden.

Contrary to our initial expectations, statistical analysis of the 23-item burden index for the 108 operators of small board-and-care homes revealed relatively low to moderate amounts of burden. For total burden scores, which ranged from 0 to 92, 82 percent of the operators interviewed had scores below the mid-point of that range, indicating that most of them disagreed with our statements indicating that their lives were burdened. The degree of burden varied across the four areas, however. More of the operators reported burden in the dimensions of finance (where 59.5 percent of operators scored above the mid-point of the range) and time constraints and intrusions on privacy, (where 29 percent of operators scored above the mid-point of the scale's range).

For physical burden, in contrast, 94 percent of operators were in the bottom half of the burden scale and 82 percent reported themselves experiencing limited burden with regard to the emotional strains of caregiving. Less formal discussions with the operators in the interviews confirmed that they experienced a high level of gratification from their work and that most of them viewed their caregiving activities as nonproblematic. The financial dimension was the one exception, probably because operators in small homes are receiving very modest amounts of money to provide complete care for the frail elders in their charge.

The reports of relatively low levels of burden raised some important questions. If most of these operators were caring for multiple individuals in their homes (as many family caregivers do), how did they escape burden? These unexpected results, which were confirmed in subsequent interviews with these same operators, suggest that there are some important differences between how informal-sector and formal-sector caregivers respond to the similar tasks they face. One possibility, of course, is that the boundaries that formal-sector paraprofessionals draw between their work and their families enable them to maintain that emotional distance that protects them from some of the strains faced by families watching a loved one in failing health. In order to examine this issue further, we draw on materials from interviews with paraprofessionals regarding how they conceptualize their relationships with those in their care to see whether distance is protective against feeling burden.

Evidence on Boundaries for Paraprofessional Caregivers

Do the paraprofessional workers draw clear boundaries between their personal lives and those in their care? Evidence from the interviews with operators of board-and-care homes, as well as the interviews with nursing-home and home health workers, suggest that many of them do not. In the sample of 108 board-and-care home operators, 76 percent strongly agreed with a statement that the relationships with their clients were warm and close, and 78 percent strongly agreed with a statement that their residents were like a part of their family. A majority disagreed with statements that they tried to avoid becoming attached to their clients, suggesting that they did not take the advice of some to keep their emotional distance (Skruch 1993). As evidence that more than a pay-for-care relationship is occurring, three-fourths of the board-and-care sample reported at some time having continued to care for a resident who could not afford to pay the usual fee (Skruch 1993). This closeness means that operators often grieve when a resident in their care dies, suggesting a permeable boundary rather than a firm one for some paraprofessional caregivers.

These homes were also characterized by a family-like environment, where activities typically shared by kin include the caregiver and her recipients. Nearly three-fourths of board-and-care home operators took residents on day trips or outings, and 90 percent shared holidays or family parties with residents (Skruch 1993). Again, there is a blurring between the roles of paraprofessionals when they share a household with those in their care, such that they establish what might be called quasi-kin relationships. A final indicator of this blurring from the initial interview study is response to a question asking operators if they thought of what they

were doing as running a business. Only one home operator out of five agreed with this statement, confirming that the majority of the paraprofessionals operating these small "mom and pop" homes do not think of what they do in formal-sector, payment-for-services terms.

Analysis of the qualitative interviews with 36 operators of small board-and-care homes examined in greater detail the meanings that they attached to their caregiving and how they organized it within their family and personal lives. This analysis (Eckert and Cox 1997) suggests a typology of operators with varying degrees of boundary permeability with regard to their clientele. Those with the most permeable boundaries (who drew the fewest distinctions between familylike feelings and caregiving for their paying clients) were described as "fully integrated households," where caregiving seemed a natural part of everyday life. These caregivers described altruistic motivations for their work that superseded recognition or financial compensation. "I do it because I know that is what I am supposed to do." "I was born . . . with it." Operators integrated their residents completely into their domestic and family lives, sharing meals, living space, and both routine and special events; emotional bonds seemed a natural part of this overall orientation to providing care, and they tended to discuss the residents as family members. "I don't see where they are not like family. I don't see the difference."

The second type, "partially integrated households," involved operators who drew some boundaries between their personal and family lives without thinking of what they did as a "business." They appreciated both the gratifications of caring for their residents and the importance of the financial side of their work. "I have a big house and these people don't have anybody. If I can help somebody as I go through, yes. This gives me money for doing it, but I feel like my time is worth it." "One thing that bolsters me is that I am doing pretty well financially and I actually like the clients." Residents tended to be viewed as "fictive kin" in these households, rather than full-fledged family members, and some emotional distance was acknowledged. "You are protecting them and you are taking care of them and grow to love them. It is a very fine line. It is still a business too. . . . I don't own these people. They are not mine." "If they decide they want to move, they move and you get another one. So you couldn't get close to them like you would your family. If you did, it would hurt too much."

The third type, "nonintegrated households," drew fairly strict boundaries between what was private and personal and the business of caregiving. The home operators spoke of their work as a marketable service, a job requiring particular skills and qualities. "It is just a job, like anything else." "You need to know some medical skills. Health skills. . . . A person off the street just could not walk up and do this." This group described their purposeful detachment from residents yet maintained positive sentiments toward them. "I don't think that you have to love somebody to take such good care of them. . . . I have my own family." "If they choose to talk, I will listen, but I don't ask too many questions." These three styles indicate that there are some real differences in how the operators define boundaries between their personal lives and their caregiving work. Some draw no real boundaries, while for others the boundaries are firm. Perhaps there are varying approaches that work to enable paraprofessionals in caregiving roles to avoid burden and burnout in their work.

The Role of the Setting

It should be somewhat easier for operators of small board-and-care homes to define what they are doing as an extension of family than it would be for those working in more formal-sector settings, such as nursing homes. After all, the former share a residence and often a breakfast table with those in their care, ride together to the pharmacy, and celebrate holidays together. But what about paraprofessional caregivers working in more structured, formal environments, such as home health care or nursing homes? Do these types of arrangements, where tasks and time schedules are monitored, result in clearer boundaries being drawn by paraprofessionals between themselves and those in their care? Interviews with 48 nursing assistants

from these two settings shed some important light on similarities and differences from the operators of board-and-care homes.

Comments from the nursing assistants reflected the same permeable boundaries described by the paraprofessionals operating board-and care-homes. "With her, anything that needed to be done, I did. I was her companion, I was her friend, I was her daughter." "I feel like when I am here, these people, they are my family and as far as I am concerned. I care about all the residents, but you do have residents that you care about more so than others. It is like a family atmosphere. You know, you love your family members . . . and you care about the residents." "I've got my mother out there. She is not my mother, but she thinks she is my mother." "You share yourself with several people. It is like family away from a family. . . . Right now this is my love. I look forward to it." Although some reported being told to maintain an emotional distance, most became attached to those in their care, grieved when they died, and recollected special aspects of their relationships. In sum, the paraprofessionals working in formal-care settings, even with a load of several people to care for and an eight-hour shift, often developed quasi-familial relationships and extended their emotional and interpersonal boundaries to include their patients. The gratifications received from these personal linkages were mentioned as critical, compensating somewhat for the low salary and lack of prestige in their occupations.

An Alternative Explanation

How do the authors account for the findings of low levels of burden and permeable boundaries among many paraprofessional caregivers? Our research does not provide definitive answers but raises some tantalizing questions requiring further examination.

First, the respondents in these studies were, in essence, volunteers from among the ranks of paraprofessionals. It is likely that those who were most stressed by their work refused to participate in our interviews, preferring to avoid thinking further about the demands of their occupations. We cannot gauge, due to limitations in the way we located respondents, the degree to which we may have missed the more "burned out" paraprofessionals currently working, hence underestimating the burden among paraprofessionals in general.

Second, the research literature describing high job turnover and comments from those we interviewed suggest that many people who start out doing this type of work discover that they are not well suited to it. Many drop out and find other occupations better suited to their skills, abilities, and orientations. This process of self-selection leaves behind a group of paraprofessional workers who may be better attuned—motivationally, physically, and emotionally—to this type of work. When we contrast family caregivers with the paraprofessionals, the importance of this self-selection process becomes clear. Family members often lack choice about undertaking the caregiving role. When a spouse becomes ill or disabled, it is incumbent upon the wife or husband to undertake caregiving if she or he is able. Adult children also feel a keen sense of responsibility, although the responsibility falls unevenly on sons and daughters and within a set of siblings (Horowitz 1985). Lacking sufficient income to hire assistance from the formal sector or afford a nursing home or a residential-care facility, family members must provide care themselves (Estes, Swan, and Associates 1993). Only those sufficiently frail to qualify for nursing-home care under Medicaid manage to avoid this cost dilemma. Even though parent care is becoming more common, it still remains an unexpected burden in many families, creating the potential for an overload or burden situation to arise (Rosenthal, Matthews, and Marshall 1991). Thus, one question that needs to be examined in future research is whether the lower level of burden we found is characteristic of paraprofessionals overall and, if not, whether self-selection into the work accounts for this difference from informal caregivers.

For many of the experienced paraprofessionals we interviewed, E. Friedson's concept of "labors of love" seems appropriate (1990). In discussing the concept of work, Friedson argues that it is possible for work to be creative and satisfying, providing satisfactions reaching well beyond the monetary rewards of the paycheck. In the case of "labors of love," he argues that the task is freely chosen and motivated by factors other than purely economic. Certainly the notion explains the persistence of some paraprofessionals in their work despite poor pay, heavy work loads, and frequently difficult working situations. The permeable boundaries created by many (certainly not all) of these paraprofessionals enable them to gain gratifications other than purely financial ones from the work that they do by emphasizing the interpersonal relationships and the importance of being needed and doing vital work. Such altruistic motivations are reflected in the descriptions of their work and their relationships with care recipients among some of the more experienced paraprofessionals we studied. For these paraprofessionals, the strict distinction between a personal and a for-pay relationship did not maintain emotional distance from those in their care.

Summary

In care provided for frail elders, both the informal and the formal sectors play a critical role. Family members provide by far the bulk of the care to older relatives, with both spouses and adult children playing pivotal roles. The great majority of the care is of good quality, but one does hear of occasional failures of the kinship norms of reciprocity, resulting in neglect or abuse. Although caregiving is often stressful to the caregiver (and sometimes to the care recipient), the bonds of affection that link the two are perceived to be essential to the assurance that care is timely, personalized, and responsive to needs.

Paraprofessionals, although typically described as occupying very different structural positions toward those in their care, are surprising in two regards. First, many of them report relatively little stress or burden deriving from the care they provide to very frail elders. This seems to be true despite the fact that some have 24-hour responsibilities or provide assistance to several multiply impaired adults. Second, presumptions of poor motivation, emotional distance, and perfunctory performance seem to be characteristic of some, but certainly not all, of the paraprofessionals working in the field. As with family caregivers, one tends to hear about instances where the system fails and abuse or neglect takes place at the hands of a paraprofessional. Some of the best and most motivated paraprofessionals, however, view their work as a labor of love, a calling to serve others. When motivations go beyond monetary reward or status, and when self-selection to this "calling" occurs, both the limited levels of burden and the absence of firm boundaries between the personal and the professional make sense. Clearly for many of these paraprofessionals, these boundaries are highly permeable, and it is likely that the care they provide is better as a consequence. Given the importance of such interpersonal motivations to quality of care, this raises the question of whether a "professional distance" should be advocated for paraprofessionals.

Care provided by the formal sector is moving in the direction of stricter regulation and more rules and requirements for professionals and paraprofessionals alike. Currently paraprofessionals operate in an ambiguous environment, somewhere between the strong bonds and emotional closeness of the family and the distant and objective position advocated for professionals. If care continues to move in the direction of standardization, routinization, and rationalization as regulations become stricter, the options to maintain flexible boundaries in relationships between paraprofessional care providers and formal-sector care recipients may diminish. Paraprofessionals who have pursued their labor of love in care of the frail elderly may find one of their central sources of gratification removed from them.

Discussion Questions

1. Did the majority of board-and-care operators report high levels of caregiver burden?

2. In what areas was caregiver burden most likely to be felt? Does this surprise you?

3. Describe the differences in psychological boundaries used by "fully integrated

households," "partially integrated households," and "nonintegrated households."

4. What implications do you think stricter regulation and more rules and requirements for board-and-care homes will have on the "labor of love"?

Note

Support for this research was provided by NIA Grant RO1-AG04895-04 and NIA Fellowships F33 AG05584 and F33 AG05620 awarded to the authors.

References

Albert, S. M. 1990. "Caregiving as a Cultural System: Conceptions of Filial Obligation and Parental Dependency in Urban America." *American Anthropologist* 93: 319–331.

Banaszak-Holl, J., and Hines, M. A. 1996. "Factors Associated with Nursing Home Staff Turnover." *Gerontologist* 36: 512–517.

Chappell, N. L., and Novak, M. 1992. "The Role of Support in Alleviating Stress Among Nursing Assistants." *Gerontologist* 32: 351–359.

Eckert, J. K., and Cox, D. 1997. "The Meaning of Family-Like Care Among Operators of Small Board and Care Homes." Paper Presented at the 50th Annual Scientific Meeting of the Gerontological Society of America, Cincinnati.

Estes, Carroll L., Swan, James H., and Associates. 1993. *The Long Term Care Crisis: Elders Trapped in the No-Care Zone.* Newbury Park, CA: Sage.

Finlay, N. J., Roberts, M. D., and Banahan, B. F. 1988. "Motivations and Inhibitors of Attitudes of Filial Obligation Toward Aging Parents." *Gerontologist* 28: 73–78.

Foner, N. 1994. "Nursing Home Aides: Saints or Monsters?" *Gerontologist* 34: 245–250.

Friedson, E. 1990. "Labors of Love in Theory and Practice: A Prospectus." In *The Nature of Work: Sociological Perspectives,* K. Erikson and S. P. Valas, eds. New Haven: Yale University Press.

George, L. K., and Gwyther, L. P. 1986. "Caregiver Well-Being: A Multidimensional Examination of Family Caregivers of Demented Adults." *Gerontologist* 26: 253–259.

Glazer, Nona Y. 1993. *Women's Paid and Unpaid Labor.* Philadelphia: Temple University Press.

Heim, K. M. 1986. "Wandering Behavior." *Journal of Gerontological Nursing* 12: 4–7.

Horowitz, A. 1985. "Sons and Daughters as Caregiver to Older Persons: Differences in Role Performance and Consequences." *Gerontologist* 25: 612–617.

Institute of Medicine. 1986. *Improving the Quality of Care in Nursing Homes*. Washington, DC: Academy.

Kramer, B. J. 1997a. "Gain in the Caregiving Experience; Where Are We? What Next?" *Gerontologist* 37: 218–232.

———. 1997b. "Differential Predictors of Strain and Gain Among Husbands Caring for Wives with Dementia." *Gerontologist* 37: 239–249.

Matthews, S. H., and Rosner, T. T. 1988. "Shared Filial Responsibility: The Family as the Primary Caregiver." *Journal of Marriage and the Family* 50: 185–195.

Miller, B., McFall, S., and Campbell, R. T. 1994. "Changes in Sources of Community Long-Term Care Among African American and White Frail Older Persons." *Journal of Gerontology* 49: S14–S24.

Morgan, L. A., Eckert, J. K., and Lyon, S. M. 1995. *Small Board-and-Care Homes: Residential Care in Transition*. Baltimore: Johns Hopkins University Press.

Novak, M., and Guest, C. 1989. "Application of a Multidimensional Caregiver Burden Inventory." *Gerontologist* 29: 798–803.

Oktay, J. S. and Palley, H. A. 1991. "The Medicaid Personal Care Services Program: Implications for Social Work Practice." *Health and Social Work* 16: 110–117.

Ory, M. G., Williams, T. F., Emr, M., Lebowitz, B., Abins, P., Salloway, J., Sluss-Radbaugh, T., Wolff, E., and Zarit, S. 1985. "Families, Informal Supports, and Alzheimer's Disease." *Research on Aging* 7: 623–644.

Poulshock, S. W., and Deimling, G. T. 1984. "Families Caring for Elders in Residence: Issues in the Measurement of Burden." *Journal of Gerontology* 39: 230–239.

Pruchno, R. A., Burant, C. J., and Peters, N. D. 1997. "Understanding the Well-Being of Care Receivers." *Gerontologist* 37: 102–109.

Quayhagen, M. P., and Quayhagen, M. 1988. "Alzheimer's Stress: Coping with the Caregiving Role." *Gerontologist* 28: 391–396.

Rosenthal, C., Matthews, S., and Marshall, V. 1991. "Is Parent Care Normative? The Experiences of a Sample of Middle-Aged Women." In *Growing Old in America*. B. Hess and E. Markson, eds. New Brunswick: Transaction Books.

Skruch, M. K. 1993. "Family-Likeness in Small Board and Care Homes: The Measurement and Prediction of the Interpersonal Environment." Ph.D. dissertation, University of Maryland.

Steinmetz, Suzanne K. 1988. *Duty Bound: Elder Abuse and Family Care*. Newbury Park, CA: Sage.

Stone, R., Cafferata, G. L., and Sangl, G. 1987. "Caregivers of the Frail Elderly: A National Profile." *Gerontologist* 27: 616–626.

Stull, D. E., Kosloski, K., and Kercher, K. 1994. "Caregiver Burden and Generic Well-Being: Opposite Sides of the Same Coin." *Gerontologist* 34: 88–94.

Sussman, M. B. 1977. "Family, Bureaucracy, and the Elderly: An Organizational/Linkage Perspective." In E. Shanas and M. B. Sussman, eds. *Family, Bureaucracy, and the Elderly*, pp. 2–20. Durham, NC: Duke University Press.

Tellis-Nayak, V., and Tellis-Nayak, M. 1989. "Quality of Care and the Burden of Two Cultures: When the World of the Nurse's Aide Enters the World of the Nursing Home." *Gerontologist* 29: 307–313.

Tompkins, C. 1995. "The Effects of Stress, Role Ambiguity, and Social Support on Burnout among Home Health Aides Caring for the Frail Elderly: Toward the Prevention of Maltreatment." Paper presented at the 48th Annual Scientific Meeting of the Gerontological Society of America, Los Angeles.

Vitaliano, P. P., Young, H. M., and Russo, J. 1991. "Burden: A Review of Measures Used Among Caregivers of Individuals with Dementia." *Gerontologist* 31: 67–75.

Waxman, H. W., Carner, E. A. and Berkenstock, G. 1984. "Job Turnover and Job Satisfaction Among Nursing Home Aides." *Gerontologist* 24: 503–509.

Williams, L. 1986. "Alzheimer's: The Need for Caring." *Journal of Gerontological Nursing* 12: 20–28.

Yu, L. C., and Kaltreider, D. L. 1987. "Stressed Nurses: Dealing with Incontinent Patients." *Journal of Gerontological Nursing* 13: 27–29.

Leslie A. Morgan and J. Kevin Eckert, "Burdens and Boundaries: Paraprofessional Care to Frail Elders." Printed by permission of the authors.

Chapter 41
Patrimony

Philip Roth

I*n the following selection, Philip Roth recounts scenes with his terminally ill father. His relationship with his father was part of the younger Roth's patrimony, his inheritance. Diagnosed with a rare, radiation-resistant brain tumor a year or so prior to the following excerpts, the senior Roth, a retired insurance agent, was noted for his energy, dynamism, feistiness, and endless repertoire of stories. After the diagnosis, he remained vigorous and spirited despite the tumor-related facial paralysis and blindness in one eye and an operable cataract in the other eye; he even took his annual trip to Florida with his friend Lil.*

Surgery for the brain tumor promised little hope of recovery; thus, only cataract surgery was performed. The following selection focuses first on an interchange between father and son following the surgery. The second describes the senior Roth's death. As you read, think about the following questions: To what extent does Philip Roth's role reflect the "gendered caregiving" described by Thompson in Section IV? How did Roth approach the topic of a "living will" with his father, and what were his father's reactions? What is the emotional backdrop that colors end-of-life decisions for an adult child? See if you can detect the ethnic ties associated with Philip Roth's decision to bury his father in a shroud.

Just about a year passed before he began, all at once, to lose his equilibrium. In the meantime, he'd had the cataract removed—restoring to his left eye practically 20/20 vision—and he and Lil had gone to Florida for their usual stay of four months. In December, in Palm Beach, they even attended the wedding that Sandy Kuvin had invited him to the previous spring, back when the brain surgeon had told me that unless we okayed the operation, in a relatively short time he'd be much

worse off—back when I thought that he'd never see Florida again.

When he returned to Elizabeth [NJ] at the end of March and I went over to welcome him home, I saw that his condition had already worsened since I'd visited him in Florida the month before. His head was beginning to hurt him practically every day, the facial paralysis seemed to have got worse, causing his speech to thicken now nearly to the point of unintelligibility, and he had become alarmingly unsteady on his feet. Late one night, a few weeks after coming home, when he got out of bed to go to the bathroom, he lost his balance (or momentarily blacked out) and fell. He was on the bathroom floor some ten minutes before Lil woke up and heard him calling. He came away with nothing worse than some badly bruised ribs, but the damage to his morale was enormous.

At about this time, a friend told me about a living will, a legal document that—in its own phraseolgy—enables you to declare in advance that in the event of extreme physical or mental disability from which there's no reasonable expectation of recovery, you refuse any sort of life-support system. The signer designates who will make the necessary medical treatment decisions if he or she is incapable of doing so. I called my lawyer to ask if living wills were valid in New Jersey, and when she said yes, I instructed her to draw up two living wills, one for my father and another for me.

The next week I drove over to New Jersey to have dinner with my father, Lil, and Ingrid, who was working as his housekeeper again now that he was home—she'd begun the previous July, just after he'd had the cataract removed. I brought with me my own living will, signed and notarized at a local luncheonette that afternoon, and the living will that had been prepared by my lawyer for him, which assigned the power to make medical decisions—if he was not able—to my brother and me. I was hoping that if I showed him that I'd had a living will drawn up for myself, signing his might seem to him not so much portentous as commonsensical, something any adult ought to do regardless of age or physical condition.

But when I got there and discovered how depressed he still was as a result of the bathroom fall, I found it was even harder for me to talk about the living will than it had been to tell him about the brain tumor the year before. In fact, I couldn't do it. Ingrid had prepared a big turkey dinner and I had brought some wine and we sat a long time at the dining table, where, instead of explaining what a living will was and why I wanted him to have one, I tried to get his mind as far from death as I could by telling him about a book that I'd just finished reading. I'd picked it up while browsing in a Judaica store on upper Broadway when I'd been out taking a walk a few days before. It was called *The Jewish Boxers' Hall of Fame*—old archive photographs and chapter-long biographies of thirty-nine boxers, a number of them world champions or "title claimants" who had been active in the ring when my father was young. As a boy, along with my brother, I had been taken by him to the Thursday night fights at Newark's Laurel Garden, and though I for one no longer had an interest in the sport, he still enjoyed enormously watching boxing on television. I asked him how many of the old-time Jewish fighters he thought he could name.

"Well," he said, "there was Abe Attell."

"That's right," I said. "You were just a little kid when Attell was featherweight champ."

"Was I? I thought I saw him fight. There was what's-his-name, the big lug . . . Levinsky—Battling Levinsky. He was champ—right?"

"Light heavyweight champ."

"Benny Leonard, of course. Ruby Goldstein. He became a referee."

"So did Leonard. He dropped dead refereeing a fight at the old St. Nick's Arena. Remember that?"

"No, I don't. But there was Lew Tendler. He finally opened a restaurant. I used to go to it, in Philadelphia. A steak house. They were terrific characters. They were poor boys, just like the colored, that made the grade in boxing. Most of them wasted their money, they died poor men. The only one who I think made money was Tendler. I remember the era very vividly of Tendler, Attell, and Leonard. Barney Ross. He was a helluva fighter. I saw him fight in Newark. There was

Bummy Davis—he was a Jew. There was Slapsie Maxie Rosenbloom. Sure, I remember them."

"Did you know," I said, "that Slapsie Maxie fought another Jew for the light heavyweight title?" I'd learned this myself only the night before, skimming through an appendix to the *Hall of Fame* book titled "Jews Who Fought Other Jews for the World Title." The list, a longer one than I would have expected, came just before the appendix listing "Lester Bromberg's 10 Great Jewish American Boxers of All Time." "He fought a guy named Abie Bain," I said.

"Sure. Abie Bain," my father said, "he was a nut from Jersey here—Newark, Hillside, around these parts. And he was a bum. They were all bums. You know how it was: these kids grew up, they had a tough life, the slums, no money, and they always had an adversary. The Christian religion was an adversary. They fought two battles. They fought because they were fighters, and they fought because they were Jews. They'd put two guys in the ring, an Italian and a Jew, an Irishman and a Jew, and they fought like they meant it, they fought to hurt. There was always a certain amount of hatred in it. Trying to show who was superior."

This line of thinking led him to remember a childhood friend, Charlie Raskus, who, after he left the neighborhood, became a killer for the kingpin Newark mobster Longie Zwillman.

"Charlie was no good even as a kid," my father said.

"How so?" I asked.

"He tied his teacher to her desk in grade school."

"No kidding."

"Sure. They threw him out and put him in an ungraded school and he wound up killing people for Longie. They were a bad bunch, Charlie and his friends. They were all Jewish boys around the Third Ward. The Polocks used to kill the Jews who had beards, in the Third Ward I'm saying, not just in the old country, and so the Jewish boys started a gang—it had a name but it doesn't come to me right away—and they'd kill the Polocks. I mean personally kill them. They were all no good. My father used to call them 'Yiddische bums.'"

"What happened to Charlie Raskus?"

"He's dead. He died. Natural causes. He wasn't that old. Even the bastards die," my father said. "That's about the only good thing you can say for death—it gets the sons of bitches, too."

About ten-thirty, after we'd caught the Mets score on the news and he seemed, at least for the moment, to have been distracted from his gloom, I took the living wills, his and mine, which I'd carried rather officially with me in something I rarely ever use—my ancient briefcase—and drove with them back to New York, thinking maybe it was a mistake to force him to face the most bitter of all possibilities. "Enough," I thought, and went home, where, unable to sleep, I passed the night studying, in Appendix V, the won-and-lost records of some fifty Jewish world champions and contenders, including Jersey's own Abie Bain, who'd won forty-eight—thirty-one by knockout—lost eleven, and, strangely, according to this book, had thirty-one no decisions.

Early the next morning, however, before he'd begun to have a chance to be worn down by worrying, I telephoned my father and launched into my spiel: I told him how my lawyer had suggested that I ought to have a living will, how she had explained its function to me, how I had said it sounded like a good idea and had asked her, as she was preparing one for me, to draw up one for him as well. I said, "Let me read you mine. Listen." And of course, his reaction was nothing like what I'd feared it would be.

How could I have forgotten that I was dealing with somebody who'd spent a lifetime talking to people about the thing they least wanted to think about? When I was a small boy and would go with him to his office on a Saturday morning, he used to tell me, "Life insurance is the hardest thing in the world to sell. You know why? Because the only way the customer can win is if he dies." He was an old and knowledgeable expert in these contracts dealing with death, more used to them by far than I was, and as I slowly read him each sentence over the phone, he responded as matter-of-factly as if I were reading the fine-print boilerplate prose off an insurance policy.

" 'Measures of artificial life support in the face of impending, death,'" I read, " 'that I specifically refuse are: (a) Electrical or mechanical resuscitation of my heart when it has stopped beating.' "

"Uh-huh," he said.

" '(b) Nasogastric tube feeding'—that's feeding through the nose—'when I am paralyzed or unable to take nourishment by mouth.' "

"Uh-huh, yeah."

" '(c) Mechanical respiration when I am no longer able to sustain my own breathing.' "

"Uh-huh."

I continued on through to where my brother and I were named as the people who should make his medical decisions for him if he became unable to do so. Then I said, "So? How does it strike you?"

"Send it over and I'll sign."

And that was it. Instead of feeling like the insurance man's son, I felt like an insurance man myself, one who'd just sold his first policy to a customer who could win only if he died. . . .

. . . He died three weeks later. During a twelve-hour ordeal that began just before midnight on October 24, 1989, and ended just after noon the next day, he fought for every breath with an awesome eruption, a final display, of his lifelong obstinate tenacity. It was something to see.

Early on the morning of his death, when I arrived at the hospital emergency room to which he had been rushed from his bedroom at home, I was confronted by an attending physician prepared to take "extraordinary measures" and to put him on a breathing machine. Without it there was no hope, though, needless to say—the doctor added—the machine wasn't going to reverse the progress of the tumor, which appeared to have begun to attack his respiratory function. The doctor also informed me that, by law, once my father had been hooked up to the machine he would not be disconnected, unless he could once again sustain breathing on his own. A decision had to be made immediately and, since my brother was still en route by plane from Chicago, by me alone.

And I, who had explained to my father the provisions of the living will and got him to sign it, didn't know what to do. How could I say no to the machine if it meant that he needn't continue to endure this agonizing battle to breathe? How could I take it on myself to decide that my father should be finished with life, life which is ours to know just once? Far from invoking the living will, I was nearly on the verge of ignoring it and saying, "Anything! Anything!"

I asked the doctor to leave me alone with my father, or as alone as he and I could be in the middle of the emergency room bustle. As I sat there and watched him struggle to go on living, I tried to focus on what the tumor had done with him already. This wasn't difficult, given that he looked on that stretcher as though by then he'd been through a hundred rounds with Joe Louis. I thought about the misery that was sure to come, provided he could even be kept alive on a respirator. I saw it all, all, and yet I had to sit there for a very long time before I leaned as close to him as I could get and, with my lips to his sunken, ruined face, found it in me finally to whisper, "Dad, I'm going to have to let you go."

He'd been unconscious for several hours and couldn't hear me, but, shocked, amazed, and weeping, I repeated it to him again and then again, until I believed it myself. After that, all I could do was to follow his stretcher up to the room where they put him and sit by the bedside. Dying is work and he was a worker. Dying is horrible and my father was dying. I held his hand, which at least still felt like his hand; I stroked his forehead, which at least still looked like his forehead; and I said to him all sorts of things that he could no longer register. Luckily, there wasn't anything I told him that morning that he didn't already know.

Later in the day, at the bottom of a bureau drawer in my father's bedroom, my brother came upon a shallow box containing two neatly folded prayer shawls. These he hadn't parted with. These he hadn't ferreted off to the Y locker room or given away to one of his great-nephews. The older tallis I took home with me and we buried him in the other.

When the mortician, at the house, asked us to pick out a suit for him, I said to my brother, "A suit? He's not going to the office. No, no suit—it's senseless." He should be buried in a shroud, I said, thinking that was how his parents had been buried and how Jews were buried traditionally. But as I said it I wondered if a shroud was any less senseless—he wasn't Orthodox and his sons weren't religious at all—and if it wasn't perhaps pretentiously literary and a little hysterically sanctimonious as well. I thought how bizarrely out-of-character an urban earthling like my insurance-man father, a sturdy man rooted all his life in everydayness, would look in a shroud even while I understood that that was the idea. But as nobody opposed me and as I hadn't the audacity to say, "Bury him naked," we used the shroud of our ancestors to clothe his corpse. . . .

Discussion Questions

1. What does the prize fighting interchange between Philip Roth and his father tell you about his father's cultural identification as a Jew and its relationship to his hold on life?

2. Philip Roth states: "Instead of feeling like the insurance man's son, I felt like an insurance man myself, one who'd just sold his first policy to a customer who could win only if he died." How does this statement relate to the difficulties of asking a parent or spouse to sign a living will?

3. What kinds of dilemmas and tensions did Philip Roth report when his father was dying?

4. What cultural and personal factors motivated Roth's decision to bury his father in a shroud?

5. How difficult would you find it to ask a parent or other family member to sign a living will?

Reprinted from: Philip Roth, *Patrimony*. Copyright © 1991 by Philip Roth. Reprinted with permission of Simon & Schuster, Inc.

Chapter 42
Psychodynamic Perspective: Physician-Assisted Suicide

Philip R. Muskin

I*n the preceding selection, Roth faces the issue of asking his father to indicate his preferences for end-of-life care. The following article by Philip Muskin takes a further step about end-of-life decisions to examine patients' requests for physician-assisted suicide. The sociologist Emile Durkheim, in his classic book Suicide (1897), proposed that suicides are of three types: "anomic," or due to normlessness as when rapid social change occurs, such as a massive economic upheaval; "altruistic," where an individual sacrifices life for the greater good of the group or society; and "egoistic," associated with lack of integration into work, friendship, and family roles. The high public attention paid to physician-assisted suicide makes Durkheim's formulation particularly relevant. Between two and three percent of all deaths in the Netherlands are physician-assisted suicides, a legal procedure in that nation. Dutch patients whose lives will be medically terminated must be rational and request death repeatedly; their request must be certified by two physicians as reasonable; and they must be suffering from unbearable pain without hope of relief. Illness does not have to be terminal, however, as psychologic suffering, potential disfigurement of personality, and necessity have also been noted by courts in the Netherlands as sufficient grounds. Muskin argues that it is important for medical personnel to go beyond the individual's legal competence to make a decision about his or her own death and consider the motivations a person may* have to request assisted suicide. *As you read the following selection, think about the motives for assisted suicide he discusses. Ask yourself whether some chronically ill older people may feel obligated to commit "egoistic" suicide due to their apparently "role-less role" where there is a lack of clear guidelines for behavior and social support after the death of significant others. Also ponder whether the future primacy of a "social good"—reduced health-care costs for expensive hospital or long-term care—might prompt some elders to choose "altruistic" physician-assisted suicide in order to spare their families financial expense and anguish.*

The issue to be addressed in this article is not one of ethics or law. The focus is on the variety of potential psychodynamic meanings contained within a patient's request for assistance in bringing about his or her death, and the important role a psychodynamic understanding can play in the physician's response to the patient. Some treatment refusals will result in the death of the patient and, thus, should also be carefully assessed.[1] The principle that every request to die should be subjected to careful scrutiny of its multiple potential meanings has not been part of the standard response to such requests. . . .

A psychodynamic approach to a patient's communication attempts to understand both the manifest content and also to explore unconscious meanings. Critics of this approach label the search for meaning reductionist, indicating that it entails seeking a different origin or a "true" meaning hidden from that apparent on the surface, without acknowledging the importance of the manifest content. A modern view of psychodynamics is expansionist, i.e., seeking to find other important hidden meanings within emotion, thought, and behavior rather than searching for a singularity, a core unity, or a "truth." The premise that follows from this conceptual framework is that every case of a patient requesting to die should be explored in depth by the physician primarily responsible for the care of the patient, mindful of the complex psychodynamics that might be involved. No action should be taken prior to such close scrutiny. Discussions of the psychiatric evaluation of a patient's request to die often focus on whether the patient is "competent," which is too simplistic an approach for so complex a matter. This article is designed to explore some of that complexity using general categories of thoughts and emotion present in patients who express suicidal ideation. This may shed light on the significance to the patient and to the physician of conscious and unconscious meanings in a medically ill patient's request to die.

The Request to Die as a Communication

When a person commits suicide, the note left behind communicates (overtly and symbolically) the reasons for the choice of death. Of greatest importance is the fact that this communication follows the death. There must be a difference between patients who commit suicide, with no communication save the note left behind, and patients who say to their physicians "Would you assist me in my death?" or "Would you kill me?" The very fact that there is a communication while the person is alive suggests the expectation of an interaction with the physician. What could such a request mean to the patient and what does the request signify as a communication to the physician? There are many possibilities, but one that should be considered is that the request to die is an attempt to be given a reason to live[2]; i.e., the patient is asking, "Does anyone care enough to talk me out of this request, to want me to be alive, to be willing to share my suffering?" Acting on a patient's wish because he or she is judged to be rational and competent ignores the unspoken or unconscious meaning(s) of the request. Acknowledging this dynamic without stating it overtly, a physician might respond to the patient, "I want to try to do everything I can to work with you and provide you with the best care I can offer. If you die, you will be greatly missed; how can we understand together why you want to die right now?"

Control

"It is always consoling to think of suicide: in that way one gets through many a bad night."[3] Nietzsche's comment suggests that one possibility contained within a patient's request to die may be an effort to take control over life, even if this control is illusory and paradoxical. When a patient has lost control over every aspect of life, the only place control may be established is by asking for death. Many patients find great solace in knowing they can kill themselves at any time by hoarding a lethal dose of medication, even though the medication is never used. Is the person actually seeking death or a magical protection in the form of the pills, a talisman against the agonizing helplessness of having no control? A discussion with the physician could provide the patient with the reassurance that the ability to control his or her destiny is maintained without requesting to die.

A patient awaiting a heart for transplant informed the physician that patients had the "right" to request physician-assisted suicide. A psychiatric consultation was requested to evaluate the patient's "suicidality," and there was great concern on the ward that the patient might remove the battery from the left ventricular assist device (LVAD). When interviewed, the patient was lively and engaging, clearly enjoying the back-and-forth discussion of a patient's right to end his or her life. There were no symptoms of depression, and the patient was hopeful about obtaining a new heart. The patient came from a tradition of argument as a way of interaction with others, and physician-assisted suicide was a topic of personal importance. The discussion made clear the patient's need to feel in control of every aspect of life, control that the idiopathic cardiomyopathy had taken away. In talking about the "right to die," the question of the LVAD arose, especially the fact that this individual could end life at any moment by removing the batteries. The patient responded instantly and passionately that a major concern was that there would not be an adequate supply of batteries to guarantee a charged battery be available every moment of the day, at work, at home, or while traveling. The patient looked directly at the interviewer and said, "Do you think I am crazy, if I did that I would die! We're not talking about death here, we're talking about my rights."

Split in the Experience of the Self

A cognition found in suicide and in some medically ill patients' request to die is the wish that the bad, i.e., medically sick, part of the self be killed, leaving the healthy self to survive. This fantasized split may be unconscious; however, some patients may have a conscious experience of another, "sick self," who feels like an alien within the patient. Such patients make comments such as "I don't know the person I've become" or "This isn't how I usually act." Patients may complain that they feel "taken over" by their physical, medical, or emotional needs to the exclusion of their "normal" personality. Conscious or not, the wish to kill off a part of the self in order to survive or to be willing to die along with the sick self with the fantasy that the healthy self will be reborn may be a motivation contained within the request to die. In such a situation a psychological intervention could enable the individual to resolve this split so that there is no longer a healthy and sick self but one self who is suffering and ill. The physician might make a comment such as "It may feel at times as if you don't recognize yourself, particularly when you have many complaints or when you have a great deal of physical discomfort. But the 'real' you still comes through. It's okay to complain and okay to have needs." Such patients, after an initial discussion with their physician, should be referred for psychological treatment if the split in self-experience persists.

Rage and Revenge

Patients who are desperately ill may feel some degree of rage: rage at themselves, rage at their doctors, rage at the world, rage at God for their illness and for their suffering. Rage, caused by physical suffering, psychological suffering, or both, may induce wishes to kill. The impact of hopelessness, the experience of being helpless, the agony of experiencing oneself as out of control, the terror of the unknown, and the physical suffering from inadequately treated pain may cause the patient to seek revenge by demanding death. To kill whom? Along with the emotion of rage comes the wish for revenge. A psychodynamic understanding of some suicidal patients indicates they are seeking revenge by murdering what is an unconscious image of an important person who is simultaneously loved and hated. Atonement for the murder is achieved by the person's death via suicide. This mental mechanism is presumed to be unconscious, though patients with severe character disorder are often aware of the wish to seek revenge on others via their own death. These are patients for whom a psychiatric consultation is necessary. Patients can have fantasies of harming the doctor or of harming significant others by dying. A successful psychotherapeutic intervention could lead to the realization on the part of the patient that there is no actual revenge that will accrue from his or her death. The patient arrives at an understanding that the focus of this love and hatred is a psychological creation. Suicide will end his or her life and potentially have an emotional impact on people who care about the person, but not the impact the patient desires.

Hopelessness and Suffering

Beck et al.[4] note that the seriousness of suicidal intent correlates better with the degree of hopelessness about the future than with any other indicator of depressive severity. When a patient is hopeless, the physician should investigate whether the patient is depressed. Hopelessness, desperation, and despair are also emotions that accompany suffering. Suffering poses a great challenge to patient and physician. Is it the prospect of death some days, weeks, months, or years in the future that causes the patient to feel despair, hopelessness, and desperation and request death now? Or is it the patient's prospect of suffering unremitting physical pain that prompts the request for death (see below)? Patients' experience of hopelessness or hopefulness is associated with what they have been told by their physician. Informing patients about their illness and treatment necessitates that the physician strike a balance between giving too little or too much information. Inadequate information fosters a situation of hopelessness because patients have no facts with which they can make decisions. Patients can usually sense when information is withheld or is slanted. This creates distrust of the physician and seriously damages the potential effectiveness of the patient-physician relationship. At the other end of the communication spectrum is "truth dumping," which takes away all hope by telling patients morbid statistical "facts" without balancing the seriousness of the illness with a basis for hope. The physician's evaluation of the patient's hopelessness relies on his or her understanding of what information has been provided to the patient, and how that information has been communicated. The physician of a patient with diabetes, hypertension, and renal disease received a call when the patient regained consciousness after an unsuccessful suicide attempt. The patient requested that the physician assist in suicide because the diabetes and renal dysfunction were experienced as intolerable. The physician arranged for the patient to be taken to an emergency room of another hospital, where the patient was admitted in mild diabetic ketoacidosis and uncontrolled hypertension. The patient described a state of despair and felt physician-assisted suicide was a reasonable plan given the hopelessness of the renal disease. The ketoacidosis and hypertension were quickly stabilized. The family was contacted, and the patient's mother flew from out of state to bring her adult child home. History from a friend and the mother and some from the patient revealed the onset of juvenile onset diabetes 20 years previously. The patient had recently sent all personal effects to the parents' home, simultaneously refusing to talk with them or with friends. This occurred after the physician had informed the patient of the need for dialysis (and likelihood of a kidney transplant) within the next year at the rate the renal function was declining. It was also revealed that the physician had presented the "facts" that there was little long-term hope for a successful transplant 2 days before the suicide attempt and the request for physician-assisted suicide. The patient's mother, having contacted a group investigating renal and pancreatic transplants, came ready to take the patient home for such an evaluation. The despair disappeared when this news was received. The patient spoke about the "important things left to do with life" and was "glad" that the suicide attempt had been unsuccessful.

Pain

Pain is a physical experience that also creates emotional suffering. Inadequate pain control may cause rage, sadness, and hopelessness or contribute to the development of an affective illness. Some patients suffer from ineffective treatment of physical pain as a result of insufficient analgesia, the product of inadequate physician education and moralistic views regarding narcotics.[5,6] The situation has not been remedied by journal articles, textbooks, newspaper articles, or guidelines.[7-10] In the Netherlands the request for "hastened death" is withdrawn in 85% of patients when their symptoms are better controlled.[11] The availability of reliable and effective palliative care may reduce dramatically the requests for physician-assisted suicide.[12] Without optimal treatment, we cannot be sure that the request for death does not derive from an attempt to escape from physical pain. No more powerful statement can be made to a patient who is in pain than that of the physician who says, "I will do everything that can be done to alleviate your pain, and I guarantee that nothing will be withheld from you unless you tell me to do otherwise."

Sadness and Depression

Distinction must be made between depression, a treatable medical illness, and the experience of sadness. "Periods of sadness are inherent aspects of the human experience. These periods should not be diagnosed as a Major Depressive Disorder."[13] Arriving at a diagnosis of depression in physically ill patients may be complicated by the somatic symptoms that accompany illness and medical or surgical therapies.[14-16] Nonpsychiatric physicians frequently miss the diagnosis of depression,[17-19] particularly where "depression" is presumed to be a normal response to the situation. This "pseudoempathy" prevents physicians from distinguishing sadness from depression.[1] Physicians are not convinced that they could recognize depression in terminally ill patients.[20] As the patient's request for death may arise from a depression, the evaluation should be performed by physicians skilled in making the diagnosis. The judge who ruled that the Oregon physician-assisted suicide law was unconstitutional commented, "The very lives of terminally ill persons depend on their own rational assessment of the value of their existence, and yet there is no requirement that they be evaluated by a mental health specialist."[21] The physician should ask for a psychiatric consultation in every case where he or she is unsure whether the patient's request for death arises from a depression.

That does not mean that every patient who is depressed is suicidal or that the depression is the source of every patient's request to die. Ganzini et al.[22] note, "When depression influences decision making, this influence is evident to a trained observer on clinical interview." While it may be difficult for physicians always to be sure of the diagnosis of depression, Chochinov et al.[23] recently demonstrated that the easiest and best method for quickly assessing depression in terminally ill patients is to ask the question, "Are you depressed?" A 90-year-old woman was admitted to the hospital after a fall. Though she did not sustain a fracture, she was found to be in congestive heart failure, with pitting edema of her legs. She was anemic and had heme-positive stools. She had been widowed several years and complained that all of her friends had passed away. All of her family lived out of state except for a grandchild attending a local college. It was expected that she would fully recover with medical treatment. From the beginning of her admission she asked if she could die, and she was uncooperative with the medical evaluation. Ambulation had become increasingly difficult for her, and she stated strongly that she was "old and had lived long enough." A piece of history casually revealed during the psychiatric consultation was that she was once a professional dancer with a famous dance troupe. The many losses in her life, including the recent loss of the use of her legs, suggested a clinically significant depression, and a psychostimulant was prescribed. She was disappointed in the doctor's decision not to end her life but reluctantly complied with the continuation of the medical evaluation and with

taking medication. After a week of treatment, realizing that she would regain the ability to walk, she began to press for more aggressive physical therapy. When a nursing home placement was obtained, she refused the transfer because she believed the physical therapy offered in the hospital was superior to the nursing home, and she was anxious to regain full use of her legs and return home.

Guilt, Self-Punishment, and Atonement

Guilt is a potentially destructive emotion that may occur in both patient and physician. Patients may attribute their cancer to unacceptable emotions and bad deeds.[24] Some patients may conclude, "If I was not bad, I would not have gotten this terrible illness. I don't love people who are bad; thus, nobody could love me. Now I have been a bad patient because I have not recovered from my illness. My failure has made my doctor fail and my doctor must hate me. If I die, it will make amends for being a bad person." Self-punishment and the desire to atone can thus become a motivation for the request to die. In patients for whom illness is equated with a personal failure, death is equated with deserved punishment. Such thoughts may seem logical to patients influenced by the regressive pull of physical illness, by pain, by the threat of loss of body parts or functions, by the chaos of the hospital, and by the intrusive nature of being a patient.[25]

Patients' feelings of guilt may be stimulated or exacerbated by interactions within the patient-physician relationship. Physicians are imbued with omnipotent powers by patients, derived from the child's experience of the parent as omnipotent.[26,27] One has only to witness or participate in the "kissing of a boo-boo" to perceive the power of the child's belief in the parent's omnipotence to heal. Powerful fantasies about the physician, deriving from the patient's childhood experiences, often remain unknown. The patient may perceive that his or her physical and emotional suffering causes the physician to suffer, accompanied by the patient's perception of the physician's wish to end his or her own emotional suffering. This wish may be interpreted by the patient as the physician's wish that the patient be dead. The patient's request to die can therefore be an attempt to accede to what the patient believes is the "doctor's wish."

When the physician cannot accept that some patients do not respond to treatment, he or she may experience guilt for having failed. Some physicians blame the patient for having the illness or for the poor treatment response. The patient's guilt influences the physician's response to the patient's request to die.[28] The patient's experience of the physician's guilt and the physician's unchallenged acquiescence to the patient's request to die confirm the patient's guilty experience of being bad and unworthy of the physician's healing power. Where there is no avenue for a discussion that will uncover these complex dynamics, action may replace affects and words. The patient's death thus replaces the opportunity for understanding and life. Miles[29] has stated, "Openness to my distress at a patient's suffering improves therapeutic insight into a patient's pain, demoralization, and depression." There are times that the physician might benefit from a discussion with a psychiatric colleague about thoughts and feelings encountered in the relationship with a particular patient.

The Living Dead

Some patients who request to die seem to experience themselves as already dead. This may occur more readily in individuals rendered vulnerable by a childhood devoid of a warm, nurturing parent. This self-experience may also occur as the result of physical suffering, emotional suffering, or both, the fear of unremitting agony, the loss of social support that accompanies catastrophic illness for some patients, and the impact of significant depressive and/or anxiety disorders. While not a diagnosis in the Diagnostic and Statistical Manual of Mental Disorders, Fourth Edition, this self-experience takes the form of a condition that might be called "the living dead," and it robs the person of all hope for recovery or for a more comfortable existence. The person "knows" that he or she is going to die, which leads to the decision to attempt to get it over with quickly. It is extremely challenging for the physician to work with such a patient, as the physician too may have the experience that the person, though alive, feels already deceased. The physician's confrontation of the patient's self-experience requires skill, tact, and the belief that there remains life worth living for this patient. Therapeutics for pain, insomnia, anxiety, and depression, as well as recommending and instituting psychological treatments, can effectively treat this condition. The patient is restored to the living, able to acknowledge the seriousness of the illness, without feeling overwhelmed. An emergency consultation was requested for a woman in her mid-40s who decided she was unable to continue with chemotherapy. She complained of severe pain, nausea, and fear of the pain associated with each treatment. Aware that she had a rare cancer that carried a poor prognosis, she questioned continuation of the treatment that had just begun. During the consultation, which lasted 3 hours, she cried continuously, referring frequently to the fact she would never see her garden bloom again, though spring was only a few months away. "I have no reason to go on with this," she stated, simultaneously listing all of the things and people that were important to her, especially her impending graduation from professional school, while repeatedly emphasizing the pain of not seeing her garden again. The comment was made to her that she acted as if she were already dead, in spite of the fact that the indications were that she had many months to live, and live comfortably, even if the therapy was ultimately unsuccessful. Her response was dramatic and instantaneous, her tears dried up, she looked at the consultant and took his hand, "You mean I have something to live for?" she asked; "I will see my garden bloom again, won't I." This was not asked as a question. She never again, through her difficult course and her death a year later, stopped being alive, often reminding the consultant and herself of the importance of "not being dead until your time comes."

The Role of the Psychiatrist

Psychiatrists bring the potential for expert exploration and understanding of the issues involved in a patient's request to die. In the evaluation of the patient's request, psychiatrists help identify both the psychodynamic issues and psychiatric disorders, particularly depression, that would benefit from treatment.[1] These evaluations should not be limited to the determination of a patient's capacity to make decisions.[30] Nor should the evaluation be a single diagnostic visit. Only a small number of psychiatrists surveyed in the Oregon study felt confident that they could determine whether a psychiatric disorder impairs a patient's judgment in a single visit.[31] There is an additional significant role for the psychiatrist, who, through the psychotherapeutic process, can offer relief from psychological suffering in a terminally ill patient.[32,33] This is not the tendering of foolish optimism or naive hope, but offers an expectation of self-understanding that can lead to a reduction of the individual's suffering. It is a coming to terms with oneself and with the significant people in one's life, both those who are living and those who are dead but with whom the patient continues an active relationship. In concert with the physician responsible for the person's medical care, psychiatrists can assist in assuring the patient that his or her suffering will be reduced to a minimum with appropriate treatment. This includes a frank discussion of the possibility that the person's consciousness might be compromised by maximal analgesic treatment.

There may be times that the psychiatrist's role in the process requires that he or she tell a colleague "You are overinvolved, it is time to let this patient die" or "You are not adequately treating this patient's pain" or "You have given the patient information in such a way as to rob him or her of hope." In each of these and other communications, the psychiatrist must make it clear that these observations do not reflect on the colleague's competence or ideals, but rather that the psychiatrist's focus is on different needs of the patient that may have gone unrecognized.

In speaking with patients, I (and psychiatrists who have described their experiences to me) have encountered the criticism from patients and families that, under the guise of investigating the meaning of a patient's communication, we are violating the patient's basic human rights, i.e., "the right to die." I contend that not discussing a patient's motivation is the real violation of his or her rights, as there exists the possibility that the role of psychological factors has been underestimated.[34] Some of the skills in communication required for this exploration are those that every physician should possess[35-37]; however, some of the skills required for the in-depth exploration are not those of the primary care physician, the oncologist, or the surgeon. These are the skills of the psychiatrist who has the training and skills in both psychodynamic exploration and interaction with medically ill patients. Not all psychiatrists are comfortable in this arena, nor do all psychiatrists have clinical experience with medically ill and dying patients. The psychiatrist in these cases should have the training and experience to provide patient and physician with a meaningful consultation. There are some psychologists and social workers who have clinical expertise from their work with patients who have medical illness. Such consultants would also be appropriate to conduct this type of psychological exploration.

Policy, Physician-Assisted Suicide, and the Role of the Physician

In every situation where a patient makes the request for his or her physician to end the person's life, the physician's answer should not be a simple yes or no. Answering yes without exploring the meaning of the request, while seemingly giving the patient what he or she asks for, in actuality may abolish the opportunity for patient and physician to more fully understand and know one another. Answering no leaves the patient in a situation of helplessness to control his or her destiny and closes off further communication. Inquiring about the patient's emotional state, validating the patient's experience, and helping the patient identify the motivations for the request to die allow the physician to engage in a truly meaningful communication at a crucial time in the patient's life. An initial response might be, "That is a serious request. Before we can know what would be the best way to proceed, let's talk about why you are asking me to help you die now." Not every request for physician-assisted suicide indicates complex unspoken psychodynamics, but that cannot be known until the physician and the patient talk. A psychiatric consultation is necessary in cases where there is complexity regarding the psychological motivations, cases where the physician feels there is a psychiatric disorder, cases where there is a suggestion that the patient is clinically depressed, and cases where the physician has intense emotions regarding the patient (particularly feelings of guilt, anger, or inadequacy). The request for suicide may be found to be "rational" but not until there has been an adequate exploration of its meaning.[38] The willingness of a physician to enter into such a dialogue with patients is not without an emotional impact on the physician, but it is what is required if physicians are to appropriately respond to such requests.[29]

The U.S. Supreme Court decision on physician-assisted suicide has not ended the debate. Decriminalizing physician-assisted suicide is insufficient as there is no requirement to explore the patient's request. It is our professional responsibility to make provision for an exploration of the motivation in patients who make such a request. Regardless of the outcome of the societal and legal debate regarding physician-assisted suicide, physicians should recognize that patients who make a request to die deserve a compassionate and comprehensive evaluation.

Discussion Questions

1. Why should the role of the physician be more than assessing the competence of a patient's request to die?

2. In what ways is the patient's request for assisted suicide an attempt to maintain control over his or her life?

3. What relevance does this selection have to the evaluation of depression among older people? Apply your answer to the case of the 90-year-old woman described by Muskin.

4. Explain Muskin's statement, "decriminalizing physician-assisted suicide is insufficient."

5. Are there any potential misuses of assisted suicide? How might these abuses relate to minority-group membership or to membership in other social hierarchies?

Acknowledgment

I am indebted to Donald Kornfeld, MD, and Karen Antman, MD, for their encouragement and invaluable assistance in the preparation of this article.

Presented at the American Academy of Psychoanalysis, New York, NY, May 3, 1996.

Notes

1. Sullivan, M.D., Youngner, S.J. "Depression, Competence and the Right to Refuse Lifesaving Medical Treatment." *Am J Psychiatry.* 1993;151:971–978.

2. Block, S.D., Billings, J.A. "Patient Requests for Euthanasia and Assisted Suicide in Terminal Illness: the Role of the Psychiatrist." *Psychosomatics.* 1995;36:445–457.

3. Nietzsche, F. *Beyond Good and Evil.* (1886). Quoted in: *The Columbia Dictionary of Quotations.* New York, NY: Columbia University Press; 1993.

4. Beck, A.T., Steer, R.A, Kovacs, M., Garrison, G. "Hopelessness and Eventual Suicide: a 10-year Prospective Study of Patients Hospitalized With Suicidal Ideation." *Am J Psychiatry.* 1985;142:559–563.

5. Marks, R.M, Sachar, E.S. "Undertreatment of medical inpatients with narcotic analgesics. *Ann Intern Med.* 1973;78:173–181.

6. Foley, K.M. "The Relationship of Pain and Symptom Management to Patient Requests for Physician-assisted Suicide." *J Pain Symptom Manage.* 1991;6:289–297.

7. Cleeland, C. "Barriers to the Management of Cancer Pain." *Oncology.* 1987;1(April suppl):19–26.

8. Massie, M.J., Holland, J.C. "The Cancer Patient With Pain: Psychiatric Complications and Their Management." *Med Clin North Am.* 1987;71:243–258.

9. Max, M.B. "Improving Outcomes of Analgesic Treatment: Is Education Enough?" *Ann Intern Med.* 1990;113:885–889.

10. Jacox, A., Carr, D.B., Payne, R., et al. *Management of Cancer Pain: Clinical Practice Guideline No. 9.* Rockville, Md: Agency for Health Care Policy Research, U.S. Dept of Health and Human Services; March 1994. AHCPR publication 94-0592.

11. Admiraal P. Personal communication. Cited in: Lo, B. "Euthanasia: The Continuing Debate." *West J Med*. 1988;49:211–212.

12. McKeogh, M. "Physician-assisted Suicide and Patients With HIV Disease." *N Engl J Med*. 1997;337:56.

13. American Psychiatric Association. *Diagnostic and Statistical Manual of Mental Disorders, Fourth Edition*. Washington, DC: American Psychiatric Association; 1994:326.

14. Cavanaugh, S. "The Diagnosis and Treatment of Depression in the Medically Ill." In: Guggenheim, F., Weiner, M.F., eds. *Manual of Psychiatric Consultation and Emergency Care*. New York, NY: Jason Aronson; 1984:211–222.

15. Ormel, J., Van Den Brink, W., Koeter, M.W.J., et al. "Recognition, Management and Outcome of Psychological Disorders in Primary Care: A Naturalistic Follow-up Study." *Psychol Med*. 1990;20:909–923.

16. Sherbourne, C.D., Wells, K.B., Hays, R.D., et al. "Subthreshold Depression and Depressive Disorder: Clinical Characteristics of General Medical and Mental Health Specialty Outpatients." *Am J Psychiatry*. 1994; 151:1777–1784.

17. Schulberg, H.C., Saul, M., McCelland, M., et al. "Assessing Depression in Primary Medical and Psychiatric Practices." *Arch Gen Psychiatry*. 1985;42:1164–1170.

18. Eisenberg, L. "Treating Depression and Anxiety in Primary Care: Closing the Gap Between Knowledge and Practice." *N Engl J Med*. 1992;326:1080–1084.

19. Badger, L.W., deGruy, F.V., Hartman, J., et al. "Patient Presentation, Interview Content, and the Detection of Depression by Primary Care Physicians." *Psychosomat Med*. 1994;56:128–135.

20. Lee, M.A., Nelson, H.D., Tilden, V.P., et al. "Legalizing Assisted Suicide: Views of Physicians in Oregon." *N Engl J Med*. 1996;334:310–315.

21. *Lee v State of Oregon*, 891 F Supp 1429, WL 471792 (D Or 1995).

22. Ganzini, L., Lee, M.A., Heintz, R.T., et al. "The Effect of Depression Treatment on Elderly Patients' Preferences for Life-sustaining Medical Therapy." *Am J Psychiatry*. 1994; 151:1631–1636.

23. Chochinov, H.M., Wilson, K.G., Enns, M., Lander, S. "'Are You Depressed?' Screening for Depression in the Terminally Ill." *Am J Psychiatry*. 1997;154:674–676.

24. Sontag, S. *Illness as Metaphor*. New York: Farrar Straus & Giroux; 1978.

25. Muskin, P.R. "The Medical Hospital." In: Schwartz, H.J., Bleiberg, E., Weissman, S.H., eds. *Psychodynamic Concepts in General Psychiatry*. Washington, DC: American Psychiatric Press; 1995:69–88.

26. Kohut, H. *The Analysis of the Self*. New York, NY: International Universities Press; 1971.

27. Kohut, H. *The Restoration of the Self*. New York: International Universities Press; 1977.

28. Goldstein, W.N. "Clarification of Projective Identification." *Am J Psychiatry*. 1991;148: 153–161.

29. Miles, S.H. "Physicians and Their Patients' Suicides." *JAMA*. 1994;271:1786–1788.

30. Huyse, F.J., van Tilburg, W. "Euthanasia Policy in the Netherlands: The Role of Consultation-liaison Psychiatrists." *Hosp Community Psychiatry*. 1993;44:733–738.

31. Ganzini, L., Fenn, D.S., Lee, M.A., Heintz, R.T., Bloom, J.D. "Attitudes of Oregon Psychiatrists Toward Physician-assisted Suicide." *Am J Psychiatry*. 1996;153:1469–1475.

32. Eissler, K.R. *The Psychiatrist and the Dying Patient*. New York: International Universities Press; 1955.

33. Druss, R.G. *The Psychology of Illness*. Washington, DC: American Psychiatric Press; 1995.

34. Ganzini, L., Lee, M.A. "Psychiatry and Assisted Suicide in the United States." *N Engl J Med*. 1997;336:1824–1826.

35. Cohen-Cole, S.A. *The Medical Interview: The Three-Function Approach*. St Louis, MO: Mosby-Year Book Inc; 1991.

36. Roter, D.L., Hall, J.A. *Doctors Talking With Patients/Patients Talking With Doctors*. Westport, CN: Auburn House; 1992.

37. Roter, D.L., Hall, J.A. "Strategies for Enhancing Patient Adherence to Medical Recommendations." *JAMA*. 1994;271:80.

38. Battin, M.P. "Rational Suicide: How Can We Respond to a Request for Help?" *Crisis*. 1991;12:73–80.

Chapter 43
Health Care Struggle Between Young and Old

Daniel Callahan

Medical Ethicist

Setting Limits

A *major issue related to the organization and use of health care is how it is financed. Medical care now accounts for about 14 percent of the gross domestic product of the United States. In part, these expenditures reflect the aging of the population as most health-care dollars are spent on the treatment of diseases in later life and terminal care. Taken as a group, those 65 and over, who represent about one in eight Americans, account for about 36 percent of the total national health expenditures, more than four times the amount spent on younger people. According to federal government statistics, when ill, the elderly enter hospitals twice as often and stay one or two days longer than the national average. Spending for Medicare, the public insurance program providing coverage to about 97 percent of the population 65 and over, increased from $36.4 billion in 1980 to $184.2 billion by 1995 and continues to increase. The demand for health-care services is also increasing. As the baby boom ages, the population 65 and over will grow from about 13 percent of the total to an estimated 21 percent by 2030. The costs of health care are likely to increase as the population ages, especially for those age 75 or over who are at the greatest risk for disabilities. Nonetheless, the major portion of Medicare spending is on a very small proportion of the elderly; again according to federal government reports, about five percent of Medicare recipients account for 50 percent of the expenditures and 10 percent account for 70 percent of expenditures. In the following selection, Daniel Callahan argues that expensive medical technology has played a major role in health-care ex-*penditures in old age. Every nation rations health care; in the United States it is rationed on the basis of ability to pay rather than other criteria such as age. As you read the following selection, think about the allocation of funds for health care for people of all ages, not just the elderly. Ask yourself what kind of care you expect your parents to have in old age should they become seriously ill. Consider what kinds of health-care policies you will support now and in the future and why.*

One of the most important moral principles in any society is that of the reciprocal obligations of young and old. The old are bound to care for the dependent young, and the young, when able, to care for the dependent old. When life expectancies were short, medicine primitive and ineffective, and illness brief, there was no special problem with this principle. Each age group could do its duty. This once common situation has given way to a different situation: health care for the elderly threatens to destroy the earlier symmetry, placing new and unprecedented demands on the young.

Why is this happening? The answer is not necessarily found in a change of the ratio of young to old (although that is a factor), or in the costs for an aging population as such (also a factor), but in an intensification of expensive technological treatments for the elderly. The combination of a growing number and proportion of the elderly and the application of constant medical progress to them is the main engine of rising costs for the elderly. The fastest growing group of those on kidney dialysis, for instance, are over age seventy. Also, complex surgical procedures are now performed on the elderly in a way that would have been unthinkable even a decade ago.

As consequence of these developments, some 30 percent of the federal health budget now goes to the elderly (with a predicted increase to 50 percent in the next ten to twenty years). Seven to eight times more government money is spent on health care for the old than for the young. The contrast, say, between what we pay a primary school teacher to teach the young and what we pay a physician to take care of the old is striking.

These are unpleasant facts. Great leaps of hope and faith have been made to tame them. It is said, for instance, that since we will all age, everyone will eventually benefit from present policies. This may be true, provided the young are able to make it to old age in a society as affluent as the one in which their parents grew up. In our present society the young are, in fact, losing many opportunities of growing old in the best possible fashion; and the country can hardly afford poorly educated or socially maladjusted young people. It has also been said that, if we simply had a more efficient health care system and assessed the efficacy of the care provided for the elderly more carefully, we could hold down the costs to a more tolerable level.

However, we have not learned to hold down costs, and the experience of European countries is now beginning to suggest that, even with a far more cost-effective health care system, the problem of the elderly is still enormous and daunting. Or it has been claimed that more research money will lead to a cure of those increases rather than reduces costs. Usually it is more expensive than inexpensive ways of sustaining life that are found. This is hardly surprising in the face of the chronic and degenerative diseases of aging people. It is a fallacy, however understandable, to extrapolate from past medical success with infectious diseases to equal success with the diseases of aging. Simple immunization against Alzheimer's disease, or cancer, might someday be possible—but it is not probable. In the former case, the struggle was with exogenous pathological forces; with the latter, the struggle is with the endogenous biology of aging.

If these hopeful ways out of the technological trap are not in fact likely to yield a solution, then we have a terrible situation on our hands, not easily amenable to a happy economic or political outcome. The problem may be posed this way. If we continue to believe the elderly are entitled to whatever medical progress might bring in the way of saving and extending life, then there are an infinite number of future medical possibilities and a no less infinite number of ways to spend money in pursuing them; that is, a struggle against mortality itself. If, however, we recognize that we may have to set some boundaries in that struggle, then it can easily appear as if we hold the lives of the elderly in low regard, as somehow less valuable than the lives of the young. If we choose to ignore age altogether in allocating resources—meeting legitimate medical needs only in an age-blind way—then the elderly will inevitably have greater needs; those needs will necessarily trump the needs of other age groups.

Is there an escape from these problems? Yes, but only if we are willing and able to rethink some moral and social assumptions about our obligations to the elderly. Three ingredients of a possible approach can be suggested. Neither the elderly nor any other age group can make unlimited claims on resources, nor can the old make unlimited claims on the young. I do not think anyone would really disagree with this idea, but we have been affluent enough in the past so that we never had to invoke it. Now we do. Some relative priority has to be established between the needs of the young and those of the old; a pure age-egalitarianism makes neither economic nor moral sense. I would state the priority this way: Every young person should have an opportunity to become an old person, and it is only fair to limit assistance to those already old to make that possible—the elderly already have that which the young lack.

Given a whole range of social needs—housing, education, economic development, and so on—it makes no sense to jeopardize meeting them to find and pay for endless ways of improving the health and lengthening the lives of the elderly. If we must set limits on health care for the elderly then we need to fashion a fresh view of old age, and a range of services appropriate to the needs of the elderly. Such a view should encompass a far better balance, than exists at present, between caring and social services and high-technology curative medicine. Our present system is enormously biased toward the latter, as the Medicare program makes obvious.

What I suggest would also encompass a perception easily obtainable: There is no necessary correlation between length of life and human happiness (at least once an early, premature death has been avoided). The fact that some people want to live to 100 does not mean that we are obliged to shape public policy to help them obtain that goal. A long life, yes; a very long life, no.

Probably the worst legacy of medical progress has been to transform our view of old age into a kind of medical accident. Since it is true that many diseases once associated with aging can be treated effectively, it has become common to think that there is no necessary correlation between becoming sick and getting old; medicine constantly works to separate the two categories.

At the same time, the notion is conveyed from many sources that a good old age is one that preserves the physical and mental vitality of middle age; if age takes its toll it is only because we have yet to learn how to control the illnesses and infirmities that seem go with it. They can all be eradicated given enough ingenuity and money for science.

An important result of this kind of thinking, combined with a cultural proclivity for glorifying youth, has been to rob old age of meaning and significance. How can it have those values if it is nothing more than a reflection of the present state of the medical arts, not something intrinsic to the condition itself.

Perhaps the deepest question that must be faced here is this: How should we allocate our resources between the present and the future? The elderly are with us, here and now. They have serious health needs and they most likely will always have such needs regardless of future medical advances. Yet, it is also true, however unappealing to say so, that the future lies always with the young rather than the old. The primary duty of a society is to make certain that it has a future, and that those who will inherit that future are well prepared to do so. In the struggle between young and old for resources, the young should be given the advantage. If they are not, then there will be no decent future for them or for the elderly people they will become.

The elderly themselves should be the first to understand this. Their own youth, and much of their welfare, rested upon the work and contributions of earlier generations, upon those who were once their elders. The young should not be put in the position of forcing the elderly to make sacrifices or to give way to the young. The elderly should lead the way. They should be the first to say that the needs of the young must take precedence over their own needs. This is being both gracious and fair.

Discussion Questions

1. What is the problem of allocation of resources as described in this selection?

2. What is the "endogenous biology of aging" that Callahan views as a health-care challenge?

3. What social and political changes would be necessary to reallocate resources as Callahan suggests?

4. Should age be a criterion for health care? Using the same line of reasoning regarding allocation of resources, what other criteria for health-care rationing might be introduced in the future?

5. What, if any, ethical dilemmas does the suggestion that the elderly should be "both gracious and fair" present?

Chapter 44

Healthcare Costs Around the World

Robert H. Binstock

The preceding selection proposed that the health-care costs for the elderly are out of control. The expansion of the older population has not only increased health-care costs but has resulted in lessened opportunities for younger people, affecting their opportunities for education and upward mobility. How true is this apocalyptic view of the result of population aging and what are the implications of a rapidly increasing proportion of the old-old, who now comprise the most rapidly growing segment of the population? Will health care for older people bankrupt the nation in the future?

Robert Binstock addresses these questions in the following selection. He examines international data to explore whether there is a close relationship between the proportion of people 65 and over or 80 and older to health-care expenditures. The amount of the gross domestic product (GDP) spent on health care within a nation is a commonly used way to assess total health care expenditures. Is the amount of GDP spent on health care a result of the percentage of elders in a nation, or are the characteristics of health-care systems more important? As you read the following selection, think about the effects of an older population on health-care expenditures and weigh the evidence he presents. What social values are reflected in American health-care expenditures? Why, when we spend more on health care than other nations, is average life expectancy shorter than in Japan or Sweden? What would be the effect of limiting high-technology interventions not only in old age but throughout the life course?

Among the many possible challenges that population aging poses for industrialized na-

tions is an enormous increase in healthcare expenditures. The specter of this prospect is especially ominous in the United States, which already spends more on healthcare—absolutely and in proportion to its wealth—than any other country and experiences the fastest rate of growth in spending (Schieber, Poullier and Greenwald, 1992).

Persons aged 65 and older, 12.6 percent of the U.S. population, account for one-third of the nation's annual healthcare expenditures, or about $300 billion of an estimated total of $900 billion in 1993 (Burner, Waldo and McKusick, 1992). Per capita expenditures on Americans 65 and older are four times as much as on those under the age of 65 (Waldo et al., 1989).

Because the older population is growing, absolutely and proportionately, healthcare costs for older people have frequently been depicted as an unsustainable burden in the future, or as one observer has put it, "a great fiscal black hole" that will absorb an unlimited amount of national resources (Callahan, 1987, p. 17). Already, a number of U.S. academicians and public figures have proposed that the health care of older people be rationed (for a discussion of such proposals offered by Daniel Callahan, Richard D. Lamm, and others, see Binstock and Post, 1991).

Although population aging is frequently cited as a major pressure causing growth of healthcare spending both in the United States and abroad (e.g., see U.S. General Accounting Office, 1991, p. 7), empirical studies attempting to identify such a relationship have been rare. The few analyses that have focused on aging as a factor in U.S. healthcare cost increases have found that the impact of aging and other demographic changes on expenditures in recent decades has been dwarfed by the combined effects of such factors as increases in the intensity and utilization rates of health services, health-sector-specific price inflation, and general inflation.

A recent U.S. study by Mendelson and Schwartz (1993), for instance, indicated that while population aging accounted for about one-fifth of the annualized rise in real expenditures for long-term care from 1987 through 1990, it was a relatively negligible factor in the rise of spending on hospitals, physicians, and other forms of healthcare. Moreover, this analysis found a steady reduction in the contribution of aging to healthcare costs between 1975 and 1990, and projected little impact of aging on costs through 2005. Earlier analyses (Arnett et al., 1986; Sonnefeld et al., 1991) yielded similar findings regarding the minimal impact of aging and other demographic changes on increases in healthcare expenditures through the end of this century. Yet, the authors of these studies boldly state that they expect population aging to be a major factor in increasing U.S. healthcare costs in the early decades of the twenty-first century. Their explanation for this prediction is that as the baby boom generation enters the ranks of the old, the proportion of the population that is aged 65 and older will increase rapidly, projected to reach 20.2 percent by 2030 (U.S. Bureau of the Census, 1992). Intuitively such predictions seem to be sound, particularly for a nation where per capita expenditures on older people are 400 percent greater than on other people. But they may be unwarranted.

This article examines some data from around the world to explore whether a comparatively high proportion of older people and/or a rapid increase in their percentage of the population contribute substantially to healthcare expenditures. First, it compares population aging and total spending on healthcare for a dozen countries; then it considers how relations between aging and healthcare spending may be affected by the complex and varying features of different healthcare systems.

These cross-national explorations do not at all indicate a clear relationship between population aging and increased national healthcare expenditures. To the extent that the changing demographics of an aging population may have a potential impact on aggregate national spending, their effects may be vitiated or exacerbated by many features of national healthcare systems—particularly the structures of healthcare financing, organization, and delivery, and their influence, in turn, on the behavior of consumers and providers of healthcare.

Cross-National Overview of Aging and Expenditures

Simple cross-national comparisons of expenditures and selected aspects of population aging suggest that little if any direct relationship exists between these factors. A comparison of aging and healthcare spending in 1990 is displayed in Figure 44.1 where 12 advanced industrial nations are ranked by their percentages of population aged 65 and older. Their respective proportions of gross domestic product (GDP) spent on healthcare in that year indicate no pattern of comparable ranking or relation to their proportions of elderly people. It is worth noting that the United Scates, the highest spending country at 12.1 percent of GDP, is one of the lowest ranking of the dozen countries in percentage aged 65 and older (at 12.6 percent). In contrast, Sweden, which ranks highest in proportion of population aged 65 and older (at 17.8 percent), spent just over two-thirds as much of its GDP on healthcare as the United States.

Changes in aging and expenditures over time are shown in Figure 44.2, which ranks the 12 nations in accordance with their rates of change from 1980 to 1990 in proportion of population aged 65 and older. Again, the rates of change in national health expenditures for that period of time show no pattern of relations to change rates in the percentage of persons aged 65 and older. Perhaps the most striking illustrations of the absence of relationships between the two variables are provided by the cases of Japan and the United States. Japan is notable among the industrial nations of the world for its extremely rapid contemporary rate of population aging, with its proportion aged 65 and older increasing by 31.9 percent from 1980 to 1990. Yet, it experienced only a 1.6 percent increase in the proportion of GDP spent on healthcare during the decade. In contrast, the United States is notable for its high rate of increase in healthcare costs, 31.5 percent during the ten-year period, or about 20 times the increase in Japan. But its population aged 65 and older increased at a rate of about one-third that of Japan's.

One might argue that an older age group—say, age 80 and older—should be used for

Figure 44.1
*Selected Nations Ranked by Percentage of Population Aged 65 and Older, Compared
With Percentage of Gross Domestic Product (GDP) Spent on Healthcare, 1990*

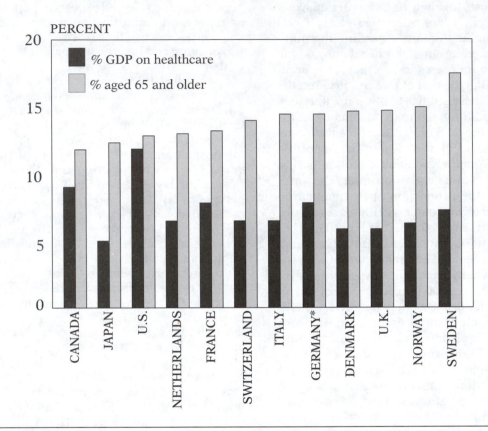

Source: Assembled by author from data in Schieber, Poullier and Greenwald, 1992. "U.S. Health Expenditure Performance: An International Comparison and Data Update." *Health Care Financing Review* 13(4): 1–15.
*Both percentages are for the Federal Republic of Germany, 1988.

such cross-national comparisons. After all, it is well established that this and other older age groupings within the age population have higher rates of morbidity and healthcare utilization than persons aged 65-79 (see Binstock, 1993). Hence, the proportion of persons aged 80 and older, and their rates of proportional increase in a nation's population, might be more salient dimensions for examining relations between aging and national health expenditures than comparisons based on age 65 and older.

But Figures 44.3 and 44.4, depicting cross-national comparisons based on age 80 and older, show no more salient relations with expenditures on healthcare than the comparisons based on age 65 and older. Once again, specific cases underscore the absence of relations between population aging and healthcare spending. In Figure 44.3, for example, Sweden's proportion of population aged 80 and older is 55 percent greater than that in the United States. Yet, Sweden's proportion of GDP spent on healthcare is but three-quarters of the U.S. proportion. Similarly, in Figure 44.4, one can note that the United States shows the highest rate of spending increase and the lowest rate of in-

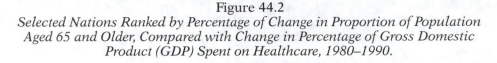

Figure 44.2
Selected Nations Ranked by Percentage of Change in Proportion of Population Aged 65 and Older, Compared with Change in Percentage of Gross Domestic Product (GDP) Spent on Healthcare, 1980–1990.

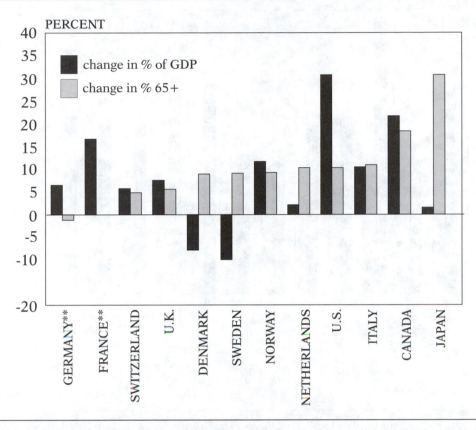

Source: Author's calculations based on data from Schieber, Poullier and Greenwald, 1992. "U.S. Health Expenditure Performance: An International Comparison and Data Update." *Health Care Financing Review* 13(4): 1–15.
*Both percentages are for the Federal Republic of Germany, 1980–1988.
** No change, 1980–1990, in % 65+

crease in proportion of population aged 80 and older. In contrast, Japan has the highest rate of increase in the proportion aged 80 and older (370 percent greater than the rate for the United States), and a low rate of expenditure increase (only 12 precent of that for the United States.)

The Salience of Healthcare System Characteristics

Before abandoning the notion that there is a definite relation between population aging and pressures on national healthcare expenditures, it is worth considering that specific features of various healthcare systems may account for some of the counter-intuitive comparisons that appear in the cross-national data above, because they mask the impact of aging, per se. Consider, for instance, certain contrasting characteristics of the healthcare systems of great Britain and the United States.

In Great Britain people of all ages are publicly insured through the British National Health Service. But, as chronicled by Aaron

Figure 44.3
*Selected Nations Ranked by Percentage of Population Aged 80 and Older, Compared
With Percentage of Gross Domestic Product (GDP) Spent on Healthcare, 1989*

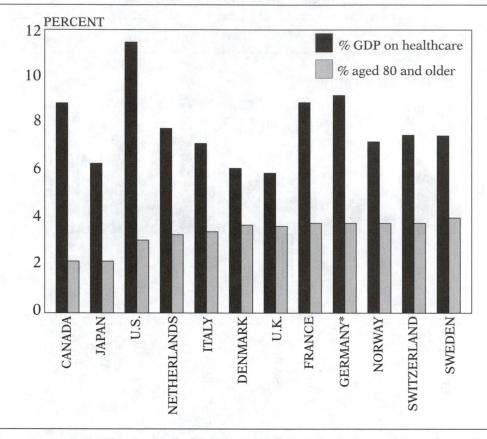

Source: Assembled by author from data in Schieber, Poullier and Greenwald, 1992. "U.S. Health Expenditure Performance: An International Comparison and Data Update." *Health Care Financing Review* 13(4): 1–15.
*Both percentages are for the Federal Republic of Germany, 1988.

and Schwartz (1984) and others, customary practices within the Health Service lead to the rationing of care for older persons. In the United States, by virtue of the Medicare program, people aged 65 and older are the *only* age group that has universal public insurance for—and thereby, universal access to—healthcare; meantime, some 35 to 40 million younger Americans are estimated to be uninsured, publicly or privately, and have limited access. These characteristics of the two systems could at least partially account for the contrast between the two nations in average spending on healthcare for elderly as compared with nonelderly citizens. In Britain the

elderly/nonelderly per capita spending ratio is 2.8; the U.S. ratio is 4.1, or 46 percent higher (Chollet, 1991).

Referring back to Figure 44.1, the practice of rationing care for the aged might also partially explain the seeming anomaly that Great Britain has a high proportion of older people but the lowest overall healthcare bill. (Probably stronger explanations are that the Health Service operates within a global budgetary allocation and makes comparatively limited use of high technology interventions.)

Similarly, the existence of the Medicare program might contribute to the fact that the

Figure 44.4
Selected Nations Ranked by Percentage of Change in Proportion of Population Aged 80 and Older, Compared With Change in Percentage of Gross Domestic Product (GDP) Spent on Healthcare, 1980–1989.

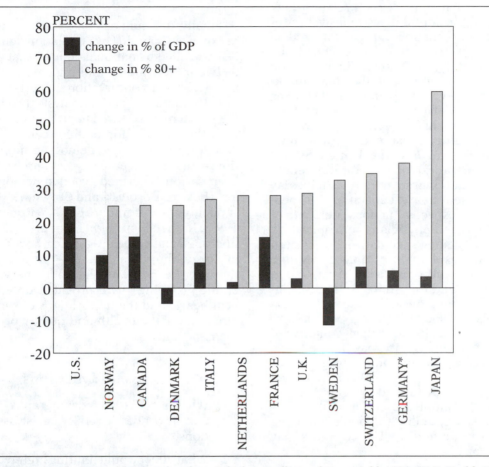

Source: Author's calculations based on data from Schieber, Poullier and Greenwald, 1992. "U.S. Health Expenditure Performance: An International Comparison and Data Update." *Health Care Financing Review* 13(4): 1–15.
*Both percentages are for the Federal Republic of Germany, 1980–1988.

United States, with a relatively low proportion of aged persons, is the highest spender for healthcare, overall. (Heavy U.S. reliance on the marketplace and high technology interventions, however, are probably much more important factors.)

An effort to move beyond such speculations toward more comprehensive and systematic interpretations regarding the effects of health system features was undertaken by Chollet (1992) in an analysis of the relative impact of aging on per capita healthcare

spending in six nations (Canada, France, Germany, Great Britain, and the United States). She undertook this difficult challenge by constructing an econometric model that used a variety of independent variables for each nation—measures of health system administrative centralization, system capacity, system use, per capita gross domestic product, and proportion of population aged 65 and older. Although a detailed account of this analysis is beyond the scope of this discussion, her findings are of interest.

In the context of her particular model, Chollet provided evidence that population aging in selected countries may have an impact on levels of national healthcare spending, but the dynamics of such relationships are unclear. She found the responsiveness of spending to population aging (expressed as "age elasticity" of national spending) to be high in Great Britain and still higher in the United States, even though they have markedly different levels of spending and systems of healthcare. The other four countries showed some slight expenditure sensitivity to population aging, substantially lower than for Great Britain and the United States. Chollet's general explanation for differences in aggregate national spending elasticities lay in varying healthcare capacities, as measured by the respective nations' numbers of hospital beds and physicians per capita.

Chollet remained speculative, however, in attempting to explain the comparatively high but different levels of age elasticity found in Great Britain and the United States. She interpreted Britain's low aggregate national expenditures as associated strongly with its limited system capacity, and then conjectured that its high age elasticity may be due to the possibility that population aging generates successful "public pressure" for increased services from that limited system. And she concluded by simply observing that the dynamics of susceptibility to population aging in Great Britain and the United States may "differ greatly."

Concluding Observations

Several observations seem warranted from the evidence presented in this discussion. First, simple cross-national comparisons—inevitably involving healthcare systems with markedly different features—do not provide convincing evidence that substantial and/or rapid population aging causes high levels of healthcare spending. Second, healthcare costs are far from "high" or "out of control" in many nations that have comparatively large proportions of older people or have experienced rapid population aging. Third, the structural features of healthcare systems—and behavioral responses to them

by citizens and healthcare providers—are probably far more important determinants of a nation's healthcare expenditures than population aging and other demographic trends.

Finally, it should be noted that the amount of expenses "caused" by population aging can be controlled by national policies that are effective in denying or limiting care for older people. This last observation suggests that political leaders and policy analysts throughout the world might do well to give less attention than they have to foreboding scenarios generated through simple demographic projections—that is, to cease engaging in what has been variously termed "voodoo demographics" (Schulz, Borowski and Crown, 1991) and "apocalyptic demograpby" (Robertson, 1991). Rather, they might focus greater attention on social values regarding how various groups within their nations—the young and the old, the rich and the poor, the various ethnic groupings—are provided differential healthcare, and the implications of such differences for the health and quality of life in their societies.

Discussion Questions

1. What does "voodoo demography" mean and how does it reflect ageist assumptions?

2. What effect would limiting high-technology interventions be likely to have on health-care costs in the United States?

3. Explain the effect adjusting for the proportion of people 80 years of age and over has upon health-care expenditures.

4. Should patients receive the maximum care possible for any given medical condition? Why or why not?

5. What services would you be willing to give up to control health-care costs?

6. If national health insurance were enacted in the United States, how would health-care patterns and costs be likely to change?

References

Aaron, H. J., and Schwartz, W. B., 1984. *The Painful Prescription: Rationing Hospital Care*. Washington, D.C.: Brookings Institution.

Arnett, R. H., III, et al., 1986. "Projections of Health Care Spending to 1990." *Health Care Financing Review* 7(3): 1–36.

Binstock, R. H., 1993. "Health Care Reform and Older People." *American Behavioral Scientist* 36(6): 823–40.

Binstock, R. H. and Post, S. G., eds., 1991. *Too Old for Health Care?: Controversies in Medicine, Law, Economics, and Ethics*. Baltimore, Md.: Johns Hopkins University Press.

Burner, S. T., Waldo, D. R. and McKusick. D. R., 1992. "National Health Expenditures Projections Through 2030." *Health Care Financing Review* 14(l): 1–29.

Callahan, D., 1987. *Setting Limits: Medical Goals in an Aging Society*. New York: Simon & Schuster.

Chollet, D. J., 1991. *Health Care Spending by the Elderly Population: A Comparison of Selected Countries and the United States*. Atlanta, Ga.: Center for Risk Management and Insurance Research, Georgia State University, Research Report No. 91-4.

Chollet, D. J., 1992. "The Impact of Aging on National Health Care Spending: Cross-National Estimates for Selected Countries." Paper presented at the annual meeting of the American Risk and Insurance Association, Washington, D.C., August 16–19.

Mendelson, D. N. and Schwartz, W. B., 1993. "The Effects of Aging and Population Growth on Health Care Costs." Health Affairs 12(1): 119–25.

Robertson, A., 1991. "The Politics of Alzheimer's Disease: A Case Study in Apocalyptic Demography." In M. Minkler and C. L. Estes, eds., *Critical Perspectives on Aging: The Political and Moral Economy of Growing Old*. Amityville, N.Y.: Baywood, pp. 135–50.

Schieber, G. J., Poullier, J.-P. and Greenwald, L. M., 1991. "Health Care Systems in Twenty-four Countries." *Health Affairs* 10(3): 22–38.

Schieber, G. J., Poullier, J.-P. and Greenwald, L. M., 1992. "U.S. Health Expenditure Performance: An International Comparison and Data Update." *Health Care Financing Review* 13(4):1–15.

Schulz, J. H., Borowski, A. and Crown, W. H., 1991. *Economics of Population Aging: The "Graying" of Australia, Japan, and the United States*. New York: Auburn House.

Sonnefeld, S. T et al., 1991. "Projections of National Health Expenditures Through the Year 2000." *Health Care Financing Review* 13(l): 1–27.

U.S. Bureau of the Census, Current Population Reports, Special Studies, P23–178, rev., 1992. *Sixty-Five Plus in America*. Washington, D.C.: Government Printing Office.

U.S. General Accounting Office, 1991. *Health Care Spending Control: The Experience of France, Germany, and Japan*. Washington, D.C.: Government Printing Office, GAO HRD-92-9.

Waldo, D. R. ct al., 1989. "Health Expenditures by Age Group, 1977 and 1987." *Health Care Financing Review* 10(4): 111–20.

Section VI

Future Directions for Older Americans and for Gerontology

The four selections in this concluding section address very different issues but share a similar theme: The next century will present new and different types of challenges to the elderly and to the ways in which we think about aging and deal with the needs of a growing proportion of the population. Although the term *postmodern* has been in our vocabulary for several decades, it will most assuredly apply to the twenty-first century, when established ideas and policies and institutions will undergo extreme scrutiny. The old truths and established ways will no longer fulfill the functions for which they were created. For example, the U.S. system of income maintenance in old age, the provision of health care, the capacities of older people and societal expectations, the very patterning of the stages of the life course—all will be subject to revision and new visions. Behind much of this flux is the demographic reality of the sheer number of people who will be age 65 and older in a society with relatively low birth rates, producing cohort imbalances that, in turn, affect programs for income security, the health-care system, the study of aging, and the fit between people and their social environment in general.

For an older person, the two most salient issues are income and health. Unlike most other modern industrial societies, the United States does not consider sufficient income or health care a right of citizenship to be available across the life course. Rather, in response to the widespread economic dislocations of the Great Depression, Congress passed the Social Security Act in 1935 to encourage older workers to leave the labor force in favor of younger men with families, as well as to provide minimal income support to disabled workers and to the unpaid survivors of deceased workers. The Old Age, Survivors, and Disabled Trust Fund was funded by a payroll tax equally divided between employers and employees. Later amendments, most notably in 1965 with the introduction of Medicare, a system for reimbursing providers of health care to the elderly, and in 1972 with a liberalization of the benefit formula for widows, enhanced the importance of Social Security as the guarantor of well-being for America's aged.

In turn, until the last few years, public support for Social Security was also very high. Because it embraced the nonpoor as well as the poor, it was not perceived as "welfare"; and because it relieved offspring of the burden of supporting older parents, it had multigenerational backing. But, as Eric Kingson reports in his selection, fears that the aging of the large baby boom cohort (persons born between 1947 and 1967) will bankrupt the Social Security system have been advanced by conservative political figures who seek the end of all government programs in favor of the private sector. As Kingson notes, if Social Security, the most popular federal initiative, can be dismantled, less popular programs can easily be terminated, as we have already seen with respect to income supports for poor mothers. Kingson leads us through a careful explanation of the origins, logic, values, and politics of the new Social Security debate, one in which you will be engaged as a citizen, as child or grandchild of an older American, and ultimately as an elder yourself.

In his selection, Charles Longino looks at the health-care needs of the elderly from the point of view of how the practice of medicine and the training of physicians must change, not only in response to older patients but for the well-being of all patients. He suggests that geriatric medicine, with its reliance on inter-disciplinary teams, is actually in the van-guard of the necessary changes toward a medical model that incorporates social and other environmental variables in assessing the causes of and cures for various maladies. Old people rarely suffer from only one dis-ease, and much in the origins and treatments for their ailments depends on their social net-works and physical environment. Yet, as Longino discusses, the new geriatric ap-proach—a biopsychosocial paradigm—is in stark contrast to the traditional biomedical model in which the body and its symptoms are treated in isolation from the social and psychological forces that affect the individ-ual. However, medical education as well as the worldview of most physicians must be changed before the new paradigm becomes the basic model for health care for persons of all ages sometime in the next century.

The postmodern spirit also informs the se-lection by Meredith Minkler on how the edu-cation and worldview of gerontologists will have to change in order to understand the multifaceted nature of aging within a diverse population. As with physicians, gerontolo-gists seeking insight into universal processes of aging sometimes tend to view "the older person" in the abstract in some timeless soci-ety. Over the past few decades, however, other perspectives have entered the geronto-logical literature, perspectives that expand the traditional view in two ways. At one end

of the methodological continuum, the "politi-cal economy of aging" paradigm examines trends and political considerations at the so-cietal level that determine social policy, to explain the distribution of resources among groups within the society. At the other end, the "humanistic" approach attempts to enter the world of experience of the older person, to see through the eyes of the other.

Minkler also describes two additional in-tellectual trends that contribute to the critical perspective: feminism and culturally relevant ways of thinking about aging. The four ap-proaches are linked by the concept of empow-erment, that is, returning to older people a sense of agency as actors rather than subjects of societal interventions. Such a perspective, she claims, is particularly relevant, even a necessity, for those who study and provide services to the elderly in the decades ahead. These professionals will be working in a so-ciety characterized by ever greater diver-sity—the baby boom elderly will themselves span a twenty-year age difference; the two largest pools of immigrants in the late twen-tieth century—Hispanic and Asian—will en-ter old age; differences by income continue to widen; and the proportion of very old who are women grows rapidly. Such a diverse population should be studied by practitioners sensitive to and empathetic with these differ-ences.

Diversity is also a theme of Matilda White Riley's picture of aging in the twenty-first century, as the growing number of elderly bring a diversity of life experiences into old age. Her major concern, however, is the mis-match between these diverse individuals and the social structures that influence the course of aging—a phenomenon she terms "struc-tural lag." Because such a lack of fit between individual needs and capacities, on the one hand, and the policies of employers, govern-ment, and health-care providers, on the other hand, is a product of social forces, Riley notes the many ways in which policies can be redi-rected to minimize the lag.

It is in the very nature of human aging and social systems that the two are never "in sync," but there are feasible interventions that can reduce the problems caused by structural lag. Some of these interventions

Figure 1
Segments of the Life Course: Now and in the Future

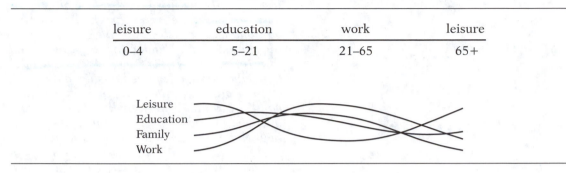

leisure	education	work	leisure
0–4	5–21	21–65	65+

Leisure
Education
Family
Work

can be made by employers, others by legislators, still others by service providers, and, often overlooked, by older persons themselves. Riley foresees a future in which segments of the life course that, in modern industrial societies, have been more or less exclusively devoted to one set of activities— education in childhood and youth, work in adulthood, and leisure in retirement—will become more internally diverse and interwoven. This image is very similar to a view of the future presented 20 years ago by B. B. Hess and E. W. Markson (1980), as seen in the figure above.

Recognizing that the current pattern of life stages is a product of the needs of an industrial economy, and that the postmodern era will be characterized, at least in the West, by service employment, much of which can be done at a distance thanks to computers and the Internet, the new view of the intertwined life course will be most suited to the new era. At the individual level, it will be your challenge, as well as potential liberation, to engage in a flexible mix of activities across the life course, a mix that permits or encourages optimal development of your talents at different points in time. Welcome to the twenty-first century!

References

Hess, B. B. and Markson, E. W. 1980. *Aging and Old Age.* New York: Macmillan.

Chapter 45

Social Security and Aging Baby Boomers

Eric R. Kingson

As you read the following selection by Eric Kingson, think about the debate between those ideologically committed to ending all entitlement programs (i.e., those for which people are automatically eligible by virtue of some defining characteristics such as age or poverty) and those who believe that some "social goods" (e.g., education, adequate housing, old age income security, family supports, and health care) are rights of citizenship and therefore must be protected by government. Consider how Kingson elaborates on the theme of the basic political argument of private versus public responsibilities that runs like a thread through American history.

In the first five decades after the passage of the Social Security Act in 1935, despite the fact that Republicans occupied the White House for much of that time, a "liberal consensus" about the obligations of government to its less fortunate citizens existed. By the late 1980s, however, as memories of the Great Depression faded and new generations grew up in periods of relative prosperity, support for social-welfare programs in general began to wane. The attack on Social Security, which began in the mid-1980s, took on increasing force in the 1990s, as control of Congress passed to men and women committed to reducing the size of government by turning as many functions as possible over to the private sector.

True conservatives and their Wall Street supporters had long looked to the Social Security Trust Fund, by statute invested in U. S. Treasury notes, as a potential source of billions of dollars for the financial markets. The problem for them was the widespread support that Social Security enjoyed; members of all social strata benefitted, as did the adult children of elderly relatives. Therefore, rather than attack Social Security on ideological grounds, it was necessary to create a sense of crisis over the financial viability of the Trust Fund by convincing younger workers that when they retired, there would be too few people paying in to support them. The demographics of an aging population, especially when the baby boomers hit 65, compared to the number of persons anticipated to be in the labor force by the middle of the twenty-first century, lent some support to the claim of potential insolvency.

A new debate has emerged about the future of Social Security, the Old-Age, Survivors and Disability Insurance program (OASDI), and the aging of the baby boom cohorts—76 million persons born between 1946 and 1964. Unlike the financing debates of the mid-1970s and the early 1980s, which led to the 1977 and 1983 amendments, today's debate is not based on a consensus among policy elites that is deeply supportive of the program or of social-insurance principles. Serious consideration is being given to proposals that could substantially alter the program as the baby boom cohorts reach traditional retirement ages. Questions are being raised about the value of a universal approach to retirement, disability, and survivorship protection. Questions are also being asked about whether the nation can afford to meet the needs that will arise as the baby boomers age. Some influential voices are advocating means testing and privatizing (mandating contributions into IRA-like accounts) Social Security to meet the challenge. These and other proposals are being discussed amidst claims that OASDI is not sustainable and is undermining the future well-being of today's young.

Those believing that certain public benefits (e.g., Social Security, health care, and public education) should be provided to all members of the national community are challenged to disentangle the debate surrounding OASDI and the aging of the baby boom cohorts, clarifying the values at stake, offering realistic approaches to reforming Social Security, and identifying themes for conveying their ideas.

While recognizing that there is room for disagreement, this selection makes the case for reform of Social Security within the existing structure of the program. A real—though quite manageable—financing problem needs to be addressed within the next few years through some combination of moderate reforms. But more is needed to sustain and strengthen the program and prepare for the aging of the baby boomers—including a better understanding among policy elites and the public of the values served by OASDI; better understanding of the challenges and opportunities posed by the baby boom cohorts; more recognition in the reborn process of those who are at greatest risk, and more attention to the link between investing in *all* of the nation's young people and maintaining a sound Social Security program.

In other words, it is neither desirable nor strategically feasible (over the long run) to address the future of Social Security in an aging society in solely technical terms. The moral basis and the distributive and cross-generational implications of OASDI (and related policies) need to be communicated in forthcoming public discourse. Thus, the emphasis on definition of the problem, values, and themes in addition to the various implications of technical fixes.

The Boundaries of the Debate

From a technical point of view the growing pressures on Social Security financing are primarily a result of population aging (especially the anticipated retirement of baby boom cohorts), increases in life expectancy, the changing ratio of working-age persons to elderly persons, the growth of disability rolls, slowed growth of the economy since the mid-1970s, and stagnating real wages. Increasingly, the OASDI long-term financing issue is tied to concerns over the federal deficit, a questioning of the 60-year role of government in promoting individual and family well-being, and a raising of the question of whether the program is "generational equitable."

Technical Boundaries

The technical boundaries of the debate can be summarized relatively easily. Under the most commonly accepted (economic and demographic) assumptions, the Social Security Office of the Actuary projects that tax returns (payroll-tax receipts and receipts from taxation of benefits) will exceed outlays until 2012. Yearly OASDI surpluses are projected through 2018 ($60 billion in 1995). Projected funds are sufficient to meet all benefit obligations until 2029, with sufficient revenues to meet 76 percent of all benefits promised thereafter (Board of Trustees 1996). The actuaries project a 2.19 percent of payroll shortfall; that is, a roughly 14 percent shortfall in anticipated revenues (relative to anticipated expenditures) over the 75-year period that is covered in the estimates. Although some analysts and political figures question these projections, most agree that they provide a reasonable basis for policy development. Of course, the projected shortfall may be larger or smaller, depending on economic and demographic changes.

Ideological Boundaries

The ideological boundaries of debate are more interesting and more difficult to summarize. To some budget hawks (e.g., Concord Coalition) and especially to some on the right, OASDI's financing problems present an opportunity to tug at the cornerstone of social welfare in the United States by framing the projected long-term Social Security financing problem as a central part of today's budget problems and as unsolvable without radical reform of the program (i.e., extremely large benefit cuts, privatization, or means testing). This approach is tied to a strategy of suggesting that OASDI is undermining savings and the well-being of younger cohorts and to an effort to delegitimize the program. It is also tied to a strategy of describing Social Security's financing as part of a large, homogeneous entitlement problem, which includes Medicare, Medicaid, and all other entitlement programs.

Those favoring the preservation of the existing program tend to frame the financing issue as a problem that can be addressed through prudent planning and some reasonable combination of payroll-tax increases and benefit cuts. As for other problems related to population aging and rising health-care costs, they are obviously important and relevant but best addressed separately from OASDI financing. This approach tends to be tied to a strategy of preserving and strengthening a universal approach by responding to real problems posed by demographic and economic change. But unfortunately, it is often defensive and technical in nature and does not proceed with sufficient attention to clarifying the values that are at stake in the debate, thus avoiding important questions about the kind of society the United States wishes to be.

The Changing Political Boundaries: A Tale of Two Commissions

A short digression, here, exemplifies the stretching of the political boundaries of the OASDI policy debate.

There are many superficial parallels between the 1982 National Commission on Social Security Reform (chaired by Alan Greenspan) and the 1994 Bipartisan Commission on Entitlement and Tax Reform (chaired by Senator Bob Keffey). Both were structured similarly and dealt with comparable subjects. Both were high profile and operated in politically charged environments. Both included major actors in the Social Security policy arena. Both were ably staffed. And both managed to gain consensus on the existence of a problem. But here the parallels stop.

The 1994 commission was, first and foremost, a marketing device. Through media relations, the commission's leadership sought to turn the word *entitlement* into a "four letter word" (Bechtel 1994); that is, it advanced the idea that the growth of Social Security and other programs directed at the old was undermining our children's futures and directing benefits to many who are undeserving. Reduction of the deficit, though very much a part of the focus of the commission, was not viewed by its leadership as politically salable and so they and the staff sought to frame the deficit-reduction goal in terms of restoring the American Dream. Advice and insights were sought from political polling consultants on how best to cut into the support of

the young for Social Security. One-sided information was disseminated through press efforts and commission reports about the value of Social Security and related programs (see Quadagno 1996; Kingson and Quadagno, forthcoming).

The 1982 commission represented a more serious analytic and political effort to arrive at an agreement about how to address an impending financing problem. The 1982 commission and its staff functioned with more technical knowledge of the program and was broadly supportive of the social-insurance approach to economic welfare. Once agreement was reached on the existence and the size of the financing problem, the battle lines formed around the question of whether tax increases or benefit reductions should be the primary vehicles for reform (Light 1995). As the final report of the commission made clear, there was unanimous agreement that Congress "should not alter the fundamental structure of the Social Security program or" means test or privatize the program (National Commission on Social Security Reform 1983, p. 22).

In contrast, the leadership and most of the staff of the 1994 commission felt no such commitment and had little knowledge of the history or structure of Social Security. They saw little value in maintaining a system whose widespread and effective protections are based on the inclusion of all Americans. Hence, the chair and vice-chair of the commission advocated a partial privatization of Social Security and the means testing of two other social-insurance programs—Medicare and Unemployment Insurance (Bipartisan Commission on Entitlement and Tax Reform 1995).

Where serious analytic attention was also given to the consequences of reform options for various middle-income and low-income groups, the 1994 commission process was virtually devoid of interest in the distributional impact of various policy options (Quadagno 1996). This lack of interest is best exemplified by the elaborate computer game that the commission produced. Here was an exquisitely developed piece of software that claimed to be simply a tool to inform Americans about policy options for reducing the federal deficit. Unfortunately, there are many unexamined assumptions. The game is structured so that its players cannot touch defense or general taxation! But they are encouraged to consider means tested Social Security and radically reducing benefits through changes in the benefit formula or large cuts in inflation protection. And such options are presented and explained in a most antiseptic—and one-sided—fashion, as if all problems could be solved by just pushing a few buttons. Nowhere in this computer game or in any of the commission documents is there any serious recognition of the people who will be affected (Trumka 1995).

Now if this situation were just an isolated instance of attacks on Social Security driven by one-sided analysis and politics, there would be little need to be terribly concerned. But, almost without regard for the facts, the mantra of generational conflict and inequities is slipping into the daily discourse about the federal deficit, the baby boom, and the future of Social Security and Medicare. Early in 1995, Republican pollster Frank Luntz (1995) circulated a memo to the newly elected Republican members of the House warning them to present their political agenda in moral terms, that is, to talk about fairness to the young requiring a balanced budget; to suggest that Medicare is unfair because some elders have better health-care protection than many of today's workers who help pay for Medicare. Groups such as the Concord Coalition and the Third Millennium regularly engage in the rhetoric of crisis mongering and the promotion of generational conflict.

Rather than explore the complexities surrounding important questions such as the declining living standards of many among today's young, such groups offer as the cause the pabulum of federal deficits and spending on the old. Whatever the problem, they have the answer—cutting entitlement spending and "privatizing Social Security," which will lead to increased savings, economic growth, and a better future for all. And so they ignore important concerns such as the reality that the gap between rich and poor and between the middle class and the very well-off increased even during the economic expansion of the 1980s. They fail to acknowledge the evidence that economists Sheldon Danziger and Peter Gottschalk present that "economic growth in itself" will not necessarily "benefit the average American family and solve the problems of poverty and economic hardship" for others (1995, p. 10).

What's at Stake?

The point of this little diversion is not to argue that Social Security and related programs should never be touched or to suggest that financing reforms are not needed. Rather it is to suggest those concerned with maintaining a progressive Social Security program should take care to assure that the debate about its future "should not move forth with numerous unexamined assumptions about the implications of population aging . . . and the societal goals we seek to achieve through public policies" (Cornman and Kingson 1996, p. 14). If it does, there is the worry that policy makers will intensify the poverty of low-income baby boomers and undermine the economic security of many middle-income boomers during their retirement years, while doing little to promote the well-being of low-income and middle-income young Americans.

Much is at stake in this debate. Most fundamentally, the broad principle that Americans, as members of a community, have responsibility for the well-being of their neighbors is being called into question. If we are unable to make the argument of communal responsibility as it relates to the nation's largest (and arguably most successful and popular) program, then it will be all the more difficult to extend health protections and strengthen public education and more targeted services. Similarly, the value of respect and dignity for each person (and family), which is given expression through and reinforced by a universally available set of benefits, is at risk. A powerful vision of providing basic protection against risks to which all are subject informs Social Security and related programs. Stagnant wages and growing job insecurity have fueled public cynicism about the role of government, yet these same concerns can also provide increased rationale for Social Security as a mechanism that helps stabilize families and society in a time of change.

The economic security of the old, the long-term severely disabled, and survivors (e.g., young children, aged widows) is also at stake, especially for those with moderate or low incomes. Social Security is the heart (such as it remains) of the U.S. welfare state. In concrete terms, it translates into benefit payments to about 43.6 million Americans each month of 1995—including some 29.7 million retired workers and spouses, 4.2 million disabled workers, 3.8 million children, 5.6 million widows and widowers, and 0.3 million spouses of disabled workers. Because of the adequacy of the program, these benefits are especially important to persons of low and moderate income. For example, Social Security provides roughly three-fourths of the aggregate income to elderly households with less than $10,000 a year but one-fifth for those with $50,000 to $74,0004. . . .

How Not to Reform OASDI

Two major proposals for reforming OASDI are ill-advised, means testing and privatizing.

Means Testing

The author shares Alvin Schorr's view that OASDI should remain a universal program and that means testing would undermine the program, with especially deleterious effects in the long run on low-income populations. Two points may be added to Schorr's discussion. First, in arguing for a universal approach, we need to acknowledge that the new approach to the means test (see Concord Coalition 1993)—sometimes called an affluence test—responds to some of the earlier criticisms of means testing, notably that such programs are expensive to administer and deeply stigmatizing (Kingson and Schulz 1997). By using the tax system to exclude the affluent from benefit receipt, this approach substantially addresses these concerns. However, as a program that derives much of its support from the fact that all classes participate in it and benefit, an "affluence test" would erode this political base. Second, it is important to note that means testing for Social Security would create a disincentive for

retirement income savings and would penalize the prudent, outcomes that run counter to the need to encourage private savings.

Privatizing

During the past [few] years, the idea of partially privatizing Social Security has "taken on political legs." In 1994 Senator Bob Kerrey (D-NE) and former Senator John Danforth (R-MO) proposed huge reductions—an average of 43 percent—in the basic Social Security benefits for future beneficiaries in order to address the long-term financing problem and to make room for a mandatory 1.5 percent contribution of workers into private retirement accounts. Later Senator Kerrey teamed up with former Senator Alan Simpson (R-WY) to submit a bill that would allow for partial privatization. The Kerrey-Simpson plan would rely very heavily on large reductions in cost-of-living protections, greatly undermining the economic security of elderly persons, especially formerly middle-income women, living to advanced old age. The CATO Institute has its own privatization project and is advocating consideration of the total privatization of Social Security, as was done in Chile at a time when the Chilean system *really* was bankrupt, and that nation had a large federal budget surplus and a military dictatorship that mandated an 18 percent pay raise for workers to cover the cost of requiring them to contribute to personal retirement accounts (Rix 1996).

Interestingly, two plans are emerging out of the 1996 Advisory Council on Social Security—the Individual Account (IA), supported by 2 (out of 13) members, and the Personal Security Account (PSA), supported by 5 members—that would introduce mandatory private savings through individual accounts into Social Security.

The IA plan would raise the normal retirement age, scaling back replacement rates for higher-income workers (Gramlich, forthcoming). The PSA plan would phase in a two-tier system—a universal flat benefit equal to two-thirds of the poverty line and individual accounts whose value would reflect the outcome of individual contributions and the investment decisions of workers. Both plans reduce benefit commitments under the basic

Social Security program while also increasing revenues. The IA plan would mandate a 1.6 percent payroll charge, and the PSA plan incorporates a 75-year transition payroll tax of 1.5 percent. It also relies on additional borrowing from general federal revenues during the first third of the twenty-first century. The proponents of these plans see them as promoting the savings habit, addressing the financing problem, and assuring younger workers that their Social Security investments will come to fruition.

But those opposing these and related privatization plans criticize them for undermining the political base of Social Security, shifting additional risks onto individuals, and compromising the redistributive role of Social Security (Quadagno 1996; Kingson and Quadagno, forthcoming). Significantly, such plans shift much of the risk of inflation and economic uncertainty from the government (i.e., the social-insurance risk pool) to workers and retirees. By explicitly separating out the individual equity and adequacy components of OASDI, these private schemes, like means testing, threaten to fracture political support for the program (see Ball 1997; Gramlich, forthcoming: Quinn and Mitchell 1996) and risk undermining the poverty-reduction and communal features of Social Security. Moreover, their transition costs would place additional pressures on the federal goverment's revenues, since it would be necessary to pay off benefits promised to today's current beneficiaries and older workers, while also pre-funding the retirement accounts of current workers. But, the most important point to make is that such drastic changes are not necessary to address the OASDI financing problem.

What to Do

Perhaps most important, the policy discourse about Social Security and the aging of the baby boom cohorts needs to be broadened.

Recognize the Diversity of Baby Boom

A good place to start is by recognizing how diverse the baby boom cohorts are. As Paul Light (1988) notes, there are numerous differences among groups of baby boomers, and these differences must be taken into account when developing public policy.

For example, baby boomers differ by 19 years of birth, with the younger members of the boom more likely to feel the pinch of benefit reductions (Bouvier and DeVita 1991; Congressional Budget Office 1993; Light 1988) and, conversely, to reap greater returns from long-term economic growth. They differ by race and ethnicity, with the roughly 18 million baby boomers currently among "minorities at risk" more likely to enter old age with limited financial resources (Kingson 1992). They differ by employment, income, and preparation for their retirement. Having experienced a more favorable labor market, the older ones are more likely to accrue higher rates of retirement savings in the form of employer-pension, Social Security, housing wealth, and other assets (see Apgar et al. 1990), although this situation may change for some given the current rash of downsizings.

Hence, while stereotypes of baby boomers as a homogeneous group may make for a good news story, such stereotypes provide an inaccurate basis for public policy. Therefore, it is important to recognize and plan for the diversity of the baby boom cohorts (Light 1988; Kingson 1992; National Academy of Aging 1994), especially if Americans wish to address the needs of those who are likely to be at greatest economic and social risk.

Acknowledge Uncertainties and Complexities

Social scientists must present a realistic view of the implications of population aging, one that acknowledges its complexities and uncertainties and society's inability to precisely forecast Social Security income, other retirement income, and health-care costs. Certainly, there will be a large increase in the old and eventually in the very old as baby boomers age. No doubt their aging will strain public and private health and retirement institutions and the ability of family members to provide care for those who are disabled. But it should also be recognized that their aging presents new opportunities and represents some significant societal successes— the outcome of century-long investments in nutrition, public health, biomedical research, and improved living standards.

It is very important to recognize that the baby boomers will not all turn 65 or 85 at once. There is a roughly 60-year transition as they move into and eventually through old age, so there will be differences in the timing and tempo of the challenges posed by their aging (Soldo and Agree 1988). In other words, there is some time to plan for their aging.

It must also be recognized that the baby boomers will age in a society that is more diverse. Older populations will be more diverse, younger ones even more so. By 2045, about 50 percent of the nation will be composed of populations that are today often referred to as minorities. Anticipating this possibility provides further rationale for investments in education and training that will expand employment opportunities for today's children and younger workers. After all, today's young are the workers of the future, who will be called on to support baby boomers during their retirement years.

Yet another complexity: Just as it is important to recognize that the ratio of elders to workers will change, so is it important to recognize that this change may be partially offset by the relative decline in the number of children, economic growth, and lengthened work lives. In other words, by itself, the changing aged dependency ratio tells only a part of the story of the implications of population aging. Things are really not as bad as those who prefer to focus only on one side of this equation like to suggest.

Also, in entering a new era, Americans must be flexible. For example, the ability to monitor changing economic and demographic trends and anticipate the implications of such changes is a strength of Social Security. Projections provide useful indicators of probable experience, even 40, 50, or 75 years into the future, and are a useful tool for making necessary mid-course corrections. But because the contours of the future are uncertain, it is important to educate the public that changed adaptation are to be expected, and it is important to plan for a variety of contingencies.

There is much Americans do not know. We do not know whether people will be able to work longer, or whether there will be jobs for those that can. We do not know what advances in biomedical technology await us, nor can we accurately anticipate the course of the economy 20, 30, or 50 years in the future. What we do know with near certainty is that nothing will be precisely as we forecast, and so there is reason to proceed cautiously, making adjustments as we go along.

Reform Social Security

The well-being of the great bulk of baby boomers will depend, first and foremost, on how the nation reforms Social Security.

The Maintenance of Benefits Plan. One realistic plan for reforming Social Security, the Maintenance of Benefits plan (MB), is supported by 6 of the 13 members of the 1996 Advisory Council on Social Security. This plan begins with four proposals essentially supported by almost all members of the council:

- Extending coverage to new state and local government employees (most are already covered).

- Reducing benefits by roughly 3 percent by computing average earnings of future beneficiaries based on 38 years of earnings (instead of 35)—an approximately 3 percent cut in benefits.

- Taxing Social Security benefits in roughly the same manner as income from contributory defined-benefit plans.

- Adjusting the cost-of-living allowance to reflect the Bureau of Labor Statistics estimate that the consumer price index overadjusts for inflation by 0.21 percent.

Together, these changes would reduce the projected financing problem by 1.06 percent of taxable payroll—that is, they would address nearly half of the projected 75-year average annual deficit of 2.19 percent of taxable payroll.

Additionally, the MB plan would:

- Direct (by 2020) all income generated from taxing OASDI into the combined OASDI trust fund. (A portion of these receipts are credited currently to the Medicare Hospital Insurance trust fund.)

- Schedule a 1.6 percent payroll-tax increase (0.8 percent on employer and employee) near the middle of the twenty-first century.

Very notably, the plan would seek a higher rate of return on trust-fund investments. Now that Social Security is building large assets, it makes sense to consider some form of investment in the private sector, which historically provides a real rate of return of 6.3 percent where investments in government bonds have historically provided a real rate of return around 2 percent. The MB plan proposes gradually investing two-fifths of OASDI trust-fund assets in broad, passively managed index funds (e.g., Wilshire 5000). This change would indirectly increase rates of return to individuals while also eliminating 40 percent (+.90 percent of taxable payroll) of the projected financing problem.

Other Reasonable Reforms. Of course, there are many other ways of addressing the financing problem without introducing large benefit cuts, large tax increases, means testing, or private accounts. For instance, some approaches to financing are built around substantial increases in the age of eligibility for full benefits (the normal retirement age), beyond those already scheduled in the law. (Under current law the normal retirement age [NRA] is scheduled to be increased essentially over a 27-year period to age 67 by 2027.) Other proposals include significant alterations in the benefit formula so that future beneficiaries would receive a smaller, although still substantial, monthly benefit than promised under current law. Yet another approach would eliminate the taxable maximum ceiling for the employer, set at $62,700 in 1996, thereby requiring the employer to pay the Social Security payroll tax on all wages that are paid. (As the income distribution has become more unequal, the proportion of wages covered by the payroll tax dropped from roughly 90 percent to 88 percent, and it is projected to drop to 85.5 percent 10 years from now.) Subjecting 100 percent of the employers' payroll to FICA taxation would effectively eliminate almost half of the projected financing problem (about 1.0 percent of taxable payroll). Yet another tax-ceiling approach would restore and maintain the proportion of wages covered by the pay-

roll tax at the 90 percent level by 2000, addressing about 14 percent of the projected financing problem (0.31 percent of taxable payroll). And there are many other possibilities.

Assuming the nation is not stampeded into radical reforms of this most basic institution, then there is every reason to think that the Congressional Budget Office and others are right in their assessment that the retirement-income circumstances of baby boomers will not be radically different from those of today's old (Congressional Budget Office 1993; Lewin-VHI Inc. 1994). But if Social Security protections are greatly reduced, then all bets are off because no feasible public, or private alternative can provide as much basic protection to as many people.

Highlighting Distributive Consequences

As the discussion of OASDI and related reforms unfolds, it will be important to make explicit the distributive consequences of various options and offer mechanisms to offset (or ameliorate) the effects of these reforms in some cases. Reliance on a simplistic time-freeze perspective of who benefits and who pays for public and private transfers should be avoided. Such a perspective suggests that it is children and the old who receive transfers and the young adult and middle-aged who give. This perspective is often implicit in claims of inequities between cohorts and age groups with respect to the costs and benefits of Social Security and Medicare. In contrast, a longitudinal perspective does more to highlight the reciprocity over time. From this perspective, the prior contribution of older family members and older cohorts to the young and to society can be seen as justifying the claims of older cohorts to a reasonable return in the form of retirement and health benefits (National Academy on Aging 1994) and caregiving.

Certain reforms would be particularly deleterious to low-income and moderate-income households, thereby undermining the program's goal of adequacy. For example, proposals to reduce the annual cost-of-living adjustments (beyond what is justified under a technical revision of the CPI) would guarantee a declining purchasing power for those who live the longest—a group already at great risk for poverty—and who generally receive a larger portion of their incomes from Social Security.

Proposals to raise the NRA provide another example of the need to carefully assess distributive consequences. In many respects this type of benefit reduction represents a fair and understandable way of reducing expenditures. Life expectancies, and hence the number of years beneficiaries receive retirement benefits, have increased and are expected to increase even further. Even after age 67 is phased in as the new normal retirement age beneficiaries of the future will generally receive retirement benefits for more years than current beneficiaries. The real value of Social Security benefits in the future will be greater than it is today even with the changing age provisions. Moreover, this change, some suggest, will encourage work effort on the part of the old. There is little evidence, however, that people will substantially increase their work effort, even if employment opportunities are available.

Of most concern, a change in the NRA compromises the adequacy goal of Social Security in the pursuit of strengthened financing, with the long-term savings coming disproportionately at the expense of future lower-income persons, who may be unable to work due to limited employment opportunities and health problems. Among both proponents and opponents of changes in the retirement age, there is recognition that such changes will have potentially deleterious effects on some marginally employable older workers of the future, leading many to suggest the need to consider ameliorative policy interventions if the normal retirement age is increased. For example, Congressman Jake Pickle (D-Texas) proposed pairing an increase in the Social Security retirement age to 70 with a reduction in the SSI eligibility age to 62. Similarly, the effects of unemployment among future older workers might be mitigated by a provision that would reduce the reduction for early retirement for periods of unemployment occurring at age 60 or later. And as the NRA is increased, it may be prudent to consider increasing the early retirement age (to remove the temptation for retir-

ing workers to accept very large permanent reductions in monthly benefits).

Reforms Addressing the Needs of the Economically Vulnerable

Very significantly, as Schorr notes, there is need to respond to those beneficiaries at the low end of the income distribution. For instance, the transition from marriage into widowhood carries a substantial risk of poverty and substantial drops in living standards in old age. This risk will be exacerbated by two factors: (1) raising the NRA with its corresponding benefit reductions for those first accepting aged-widows' benefits before the NRA and (2) the trend toward dual entitlement of retirement benefits for future elderly couples. (Poverty rates among elderly couples are quite low and expected to continue as such.) One proposal calls for a revenue-neutral reduction in the PIA of all retired workers combined with an increase in aged-survivor benefits. Another revenue-neutral approach would pair reductions in aged-spouse benefits to increases in widows' benefits (see Burkhauser 1994). Consideration could also be given to other incremental approaches to strengthening the targeting of OASDI to beneficiaries at greatest risk; for example, introducing some sharing of earnings at divorce, improving the OASDI special minimum benefit for long-term, low-income workers, and counting time lost in the labor force as a result of giving care to young children or disabled family members toward the special minimum benefit for low-income workers.

Also, some remedies can be found outside OASDI by, for example, reforming SSI (e.g., elimination or liberalization of the assets test) and by maintaining and improving the Earned Income Tax Credit.

Reforms to Address the Skepticism of the Young

Reform of OASDI also needs to address the skepticism of younger taxpayers, a group that, while remaining supportive of the program, expresses little confidence that the program will be there for them. Most often, Social Security is portrayed to the public, especially the young, as a program in crisis, one that will be difficult to sustain under the press of the demographic onslaught of the baby boom cohorts. Inaccurate and negative media presentations of program issues lay the groundwork for regressive reforms while arguably also increasing cynicism about the role of the national government.

Bringing the program back into actuarial balance should help to restore confidence, as could educational efforts to strengthen public understanding of the program. Perhaps more needs to be done? The time horizons of young adults are relatively limited. OASDI may be valued because it helps (or will help) their parents or older relatives, but it is generally not greatly valued by people in their 20s because of the disability and survivors' protections it offers. After all, most of us do not really think such things will happen to us when young. Moreover, reforms such as increases in the NRA, which reduce the value of future benefits, can be viewed as taking something away from the young. Given this attitude, it may be worth considering pairing reduced benefits with some type of *small* new benefits for today's and tomorrow's young that respond to contingencies workers are likely to experience earlier in the life course than retirement. For example, at some future period it may be possible to explore phasing in a one-month benefit on the birth or adoption of a child or a retraining benefit for tomorrow's middle-aged workers in tandem with NRA increases.

Encourage Social and Economic Investment

Besides encouraging increased personal and social savings and parallel investments, it is imperative that society make prudent social investments in education and employment training of the young, in biomedical research, and in a policy that encourages human development throughout life. The nation cannot afford to cast aside its low-income children and the poor, nor should today's and tomorrow's old be treated as bundles of needs. Each group should be acknowledged as individuals and treated with dignity—with the capacity to grow; with the ability (and expectation) to give to their families, their communities, and the economy; and with needs that are likely to vary as they move throughout their course of life. To discuss some as part of superfluous populations or to discuss the disabled and old primarily in terms of dread for the economic burden they will impose, diminishes the value of life and undermines human potential.

Conclusion

The reluctance of many people to talk about the values served by Social Security and related programs may contribute to the defensive position of many of its supporters and to the increasingly narrow framing of issues surrounding the aging of the baby boom cohorts. Too often the policy discussion is cast in technical terms. Policy makers have shied away from discussing the moral basis of these programs, how they are grounded in the desire to carry out the biblical injunction that we honor our fathers and mothers and care for ourselves and our neighbors. The press reports often sensationalize financing problems but do little to show what Social Security has meant to the nation's families. Rarely are the life insurance and disability-insurance protections acknowledged or the reality that Social Security frees younger family members to devote more resources to their children. This situation has allowed the bean counters to define social programs only in terms of immediate costs and to avoid looking at the distributional consequences of various proposed changes or at the consequences of change for community life. To emphasize such concerns

> is to ensure that the political response will be limited, driven by misunderstandings about the implications of population aging and by short range goals and void of values which respond to such basic issues as the meaning and purposes of life, individual and societal responsibilities, and even the kind of society the people of the country desire for people of all ages. (Cornman and Kingson 1996, p. 14)

There is a need for a more informed debate, one that extends beyond the question of how to fix Social Security and of whether the nation can afford the retirement of the baby boom cohorts. Policy makers should be challenged to think cross-generationally, to emphasize the need to invest in the education and advancement of all of today's young. Not only is it the right thing to do, but it is also the smart thing since they are the next generation of workers who will have to support the baby boom cohorts. Potential winners and losers from various Social Security and Medicare reform proposals should be identified, and the needs of those at greatest risk highlighted. If we can broaden the national dialogue to include concerns such as these, then the prospects of real Social Security reform leading to a more secure and meaningful old age will improve for most baby boomers and for those who follow them.

Discussion Questions

1. What are the implied messages in plans to privatize functions of government?

2. Will older men and women benefit equally from proposed changes in Social Security?

3. How would you like to see the Social Security Trust Fund used?

4. What steps could be taken to shore up the Trust Fund without investing in the stock market?

5. Whose interests are served through privatization?

References

Apgar, Jr., W. C., DiPasquale, D., McArdle, N., and Olson, N. 1990. *The State of the Nation's Housing 1989*. Cambridge, MA: Joint Center for Housing Studies, Harvard University.

Ball, R. M. 1997. "Bridging the Centuries: The Case for Traditional Social Security." In James H. Schulz and Eric R. Kingson, eds., *Social Security in the 21st Century*. New York: Oxford University Press.

Bechtel, William. 1994. "The Coming Entitlement Debate." *Perspective on Aging* 32: 4–9.

Bipartisan Commission on Entitlement and Tax Reform. 1995. *Final Report to the President*. Washington, DC: US GPO.

Board of Trustees, Federal Old-Age and Survivors Insurance and Disability Insurance Trust Funds. 1996. *Annual Report of the Federal Old-Age and Survivors Insurance and Disability Insurance Trust Funds*, Washington, D.C.: U.S. Government Printing Office.

Bouvier, Leon F., and De Vita, Carol J. 1991. "The Baby Boom—Entering Midlife." Washington, D.C.: Population Reference Bureau.

Brody, E. 1990. *Women in the Middle: Their Parent-care Years*. New York: Springer Publishing Company.

Burkhauser, Richard V. 1994. "Protecting the Most Vulnerable: A Proposal to Improve Social Security Insurance for Older Women." *The Gerontologist* 34: 148–149.

Cantor, Marjorie H. 1991. "Family and Community: Changing Roles in an Aging society." *The Gerontologist* 31(3): 337–346.

Concord Coalition. 1993. *The Zero Deficit Plan*. Washington, DC: Concord Coalition.

Congressional Budget Office. 1993. *Baby Boomers in Retirement: An Early Perspective*. Washington, D.C.: Congressional Budget Office.

Conner, Karen A. 1992. *Aging America: Issues Facing an Aging Society*. Englewood Cliffs, NJ: Prentice Hall.

Cornman, J. M., and Kingson, E. R. 1996. "Trends, Issues, Perspectives and Values for the Aging of the Baby Boom Cohorts." *The Gerontologist* 36(1): 15–26.

Crown, William H. 1985. "Some Thoughts on Reformulating the Dependency Ratio." *The Gerontoloigist* 24: 166–171.

Danziger, S., and Gottschalk, P. 1995. *America Unequal*. Cambridge, MA: Harvard University Press and New York: Russell Sage Foundation.

Grad, S. 1994. *Income of the Population 55 and Older, 1992*. Washington, D.C.: Social Security Administration, Office of Research and Statistics.

Gramlich, Ned. forthcoming. "Different Approaches for Dealing With Social Security." *Journal of Economic Perspectives*.

Hagestad, G. O. 1986. "The Family: Women and Grandparents as Kin-keepers." In A. Pifer and L. Bronte, eds., *Our Aging Society: Paradox and Promise*, pp. 141–160. New York: W. W. Norton.

Kingson, E. R. 1992. *The Diversity of the Baby Boom Generation: Implications for Their Retirement Years* (April). Washington, DC: American Association of Retired Persons, Forecasting and Environmental Scanning Division.

———. 1996. "A Broader Policy Discussion Is Needed to Plan for the Aging of the Baby Boom Cohorts and Those Who Follow." Paper presented at 42nd Annual Meeting of the American Society on Aging, Anaheim, CA.

Kingson, E. R., and Berkowitz, E. D. 1993. *Social Security and Medicare: A Policy Primer*. Westport, CT: Auburn House.

Kingson, E. R., and Quadagno, J. forthcoming. "Social Security: Marketing Radical Reform." In R. B. Hudson, ed., forthcoming. *The Future of Age-based Public Policy*. Baltimore, MD: Johns Hopkins University Press.

Kingson, Eric R., and Schulz, James H. 1997. "Should Social Security Be Means-Tested?" In James H. Schulz and Eric R. Kingson, eds., *Social Security in the 21st Century*. New York: Oxford University Press.

Lewin-VHI Inc. 1994. *Aging Baby Boomers: How Secure is Their Economic Future?* Washington, DC: American Association of Retired Persons, Forecasting and Environmental Scanning Division.

Light, P. C. 1988. *Baby Boomers*. New York: W. W. Norton & Company.

——. 1995. *Still Artful Work: The Politics of Social Security Reform*. New York: McGraw-Hill.

Luntz, F. 1995. "Memorandum to the Republican Conference." (Jan. 9) *New York Times*, (February 5).

Marmor, T. R., Mashaw, J. L., and Harvey, P. L. 1990. *Misunderstood Welfare State: Persistent Myths, Enduring Realities*. New York: Basic Books.

National Academy on Aging. 1994. *Old Age in the 21st Century*. Washington, DC: National Academy on Aging.

National Commission on Social Security Reform. 1983. *Report of the National Commission on Social Security Reform*. Washington, D.C.

Organisation for Economic Cooperation and Development (OECD). 1994. *New Orientations for Social Policy*. Paris, France.

Olson, Laura Katz. 1994. *The Graying of the World: Who Will Care for the Frail Elderly?* New York: Haworth Press.

Quadagno, J. 1996. "Social Security and the Myth of the Entitlement Crisis." *The Gerontologist* 36(2): 391–399.

Quinn, Joseph F., and Mitchell, Olivia S. 1996. "Social Security on the Table." *American Prospect*. (May–June), pp. 76–81.

Rix, S. E. 1996. "Chile's Experience With the Privatization of Social Security." *Public Policy Institute Issue Brief*. Washington, DC: American Association of Retired Persons.

Schorr, Alvin. 1996. Paper read at conference run by the Odyssey Forum, 27, January, Washington, D.C.

Siegel, Paul M. 1989. "Educational Attainment in the United States: March 1982 to 1985." *Current Population Reports*, U.S. Bureau of the Census, Series P-20, No. 415. Washington, D.C.: U.S. Government Printing Office.

Silverstone, Barbara. 1989. *You and Your Aging Parent: The Modern Family's Guide to Emotional, Physical, and Financial Problems*. New York: Pantheon Books.

Soldo, Beth J. and Agree, Emily M. 1988. "America's Elderly." *Population Bulletin*, 43(3). Washington, DC: Population Reference Bureau.

Torrey, Barbara Boyle. n.d. "Guns vs. Canes: The Fiscal Implications of an Aging Population." *AEA Papers and Proceedings* 72(2).

Trumka, R. 1995. "Statement of Commissioner Richard L. Trumka." In Bipartisan Commission on Entitlement and Tax Reform, *Final Report to the President*. Washington, DC: Bipartisan Commission on Entitlement and Tax Reform.

Eric R. Kingson, "Social Security and the Aging of the Baby Boom Cohorts: Disentangling the Policy Debates." 1996. Printed by permission of the author.

Future of SS in 21st century

6.

Chapter 46

Aging Population Will Broaden Our Understanding of Medicine

Charles F. Longino, Jr.

Not only are Americans living longer than in the past, but they are also living in better health. Nonetheless, most will eventually experience one or more chronic conditions. It is thus expected that the aging of the population will generate enormous pressure on a health-care system based on a model applicable to an earlier time. At one level, the traditional fee-for-service system is being replaced by corporate medicine in the shape of health maintenance organizations (HMOs) and other variations on managed care, with a subsequent loss of the physician's professional autonomy. At the same time, the medical establishment's monopoly over knowledge is threatened by laypersons' ready access to the Internet, as well as to mass media advertising by pharmaceutical companies, all of which empower the patient in relation to health-care professionals.

For Charles Longino, however, the major challenge to medicine-as-usual is the emergence of a model of health care by those who treat elderly patients, one based on a team approach, in which social and psychological factors are taken into account. Interdisciplinary assessment teams recognize that an older person's health is greatly affected by the social and physical resources in the immediate environment—an insight that Longino suggests should be applied to all patients. To see the patient in context, however, goes against the biologically centered worldview of physicians trained in this country since the 1920s, with

its emphasis on the body as source of illness and site of intervention.

As you read the following selection, think about the biophysical model of health care. Consider also the various other models discussed. What modifications to the organization and delivery of health care do you believe would most benefit the elderly?

The culture of medicine is changing and this change is likely to escalate because of the growth and aging of the U.S. retirement-age population. The amplification of chronic, rather than acute, illnesses that accompany aging, the broad range of non-institutional options for long-term care, and the interdisciplinary nature of geriatric assessment are all challenges to the curative, hospital-based, and physician-centered emphases of established medical culture. Furthermore, the emerging outline of a broader self-understanding of what scientific medicine is may be seen in the health needs of the elderly.

What we think and how we conduct our professional activities begin in the cultural context of ideas and values. These have evolved, often for centuries, and form the parameters within which academic structures emerge. However, when cultural paradigms harden into orthodoxies, they tend to stifle other approaches to the same concerns, even when the new approaches resolve problems left unsolved by the orthodox assumptions.

The existing paradigm of modern scientific medicine may be called the Western biomedical model. It relies on an essentially mechanical understanding of causation, one derived from science. Repairing a body, in this view, is analogous to fixing a machine. Furthermore, this view of causation leads to a remarkably optimistic expectation that each disease has a specific cause that is awaiting discovery by medical research. Finally, because the body is the appropriate subject of medical science and practice, it is also the appropriate subject of regimen and control. Although we may not consciously think of medicine in these terms, these are, nonetheless, the doctrines of the biomedical model and thus form the subconscious cultural context out of which our thinking, professional conduct, and medical education arise.

Because it has been so successful in dealing with the deadly diseases that have decimated human populations for centuries, medicine has worked itself out of much of its original job (the cure of diseases and relief of patients' sufferings) and now faces a large population of patients and potential patients that expect the same successes and advances in dealing with chronic conditions and the accumulated debilitations of advanced age. Unfortunately for physicians and their patients, scientific medicine cannot cure these conditions, and medicine will have to change its essential self-understanding if it is to be successful in the future.

The Challenge of a Growing and Aging Older Population

Consider, for example, the proportion of the whole U.S. population in different age categories in the decades since 1900 and those projected until 2050, when the baby-boomer generation will have begun to die off in appreciable numbers. During those 15 decades, the population 65 years of age and older will have increased from 4.1 to 20.4 percent of the total U.S. population, or by a multiple of five times. Even faster-growing will have been the population between 75 and 84 years of age, from 1.0 to 6.8 percent of the national population, an increase of 6.8 times. The fastest-growing of all will be the population 85 years of age and older, which will have increased from .2 to 4.8 percent—or 24 times its size in 1900. Not only will the older population have increased in the United States during this time period, but the older population will have also aged.[1] This is an impressive growth curve.

Population aging has a strong effect on medicine because health issues change during the life course. Epidemiologist Maurice Mittelmark made this point clearly when he asserted that "accident and injury are prominent concerns in childhood, adolescence and early adulthood, developing chronic diseases are a central feature of middle adulthood, morbidity and mortality from chronic diseases characterize the period around retirement, and deterioration in functioning, dis-

ability and dependency are concerns mainly of old and very old age."[2]

The aging of the population will increasingly bring into medical practice an ever-higher prevalence of chronic conditions and the deterioration of physiological functioning. But these health problems do not have a precise moment of onset, do not have a single and unambiguous cause, do not have an end that can be easily modified, and are implicated in a melange of factors related only indirectly to physiology. Accordingly, the incompatibility of the biomedical model with the chronic conditions of members of an aging population is undermining the efficacy of the model. This debilitating effect on current medical orthodoxy will accelerate in the future.

The Challenge of the Older Patient

The concentrated focus of scientific medicine on the body, and on more and more detailed levels of biology, often blocks the view of the environmental and contextual factors affecting health and health care. The biomedical model has encouraged and justified this body-centered view. The traditional solitary attention to basic biomedical science during the first two years of medical school and the relatively fleeting opportunities students are given to study patient care outside the hospital have produced this environmental blindness in our students. As responsible educators, we bear much of the blame.

Furthermore, medical students are usually even sheltered from interdisciplinary clinical experiences where nurses, social workers and others help to compensate for the blind spots fostered by traditional medical education. Diagnosis, in the orthodox view, is the doctor's job. Geriatric assessment teams provide a model to broaden the process of diagnosis. In geriatric medicine, treatment plans are routinely reviewed by interdisciplinary teams that look beyond the body, taking into account the social and physical environments of the patient and the support available in these contexts. In this way, geriatric medicine points the way to the emerging paradigm of scientific medicine, one that is more inclusive and sensitive to context.

To accommodate the emerging paradigm, medical education in the future will be strikingly different in some fundamental ways. Imagine a case conference in a medical school. The case presented by a professor of internal medicine is that of a man, age 78, found unconscious by a neighbor in his fifth-floor walk-up apartment in the inner city. When the man reached the emergency room, a quick chest examination pointed to pneumonia as the presenting illness. The attending physician expected that the pneumonia was caused by the pneumococcus, a belief later confirmed. The patient was thus treated with penicillin. Also, one of his knees was swollen, which turned out to be the result of osteoarthritis. The patient's pneumonia responded well to the drug therapy; his fever came down, his lungs cleared and he was released to go home. This appeared to be an example of the successful application of scientific medicine.

The interns and residents found the case uninteresting. The diagnosis had been quick and straightforward, the treatment was appropriate, and the patient got well without complications. "But there is more," said the professor. "It is artificial to stop at the boundaries of the body. There is a story here, and none of you discovered it because you did not ask all of the right questions." The man's grief at the loss of his wife caused him to be depressed. He was socially isolated, with no social support available to him. He lived alone and had kept to himself since his wife's death. The depression had caused a loss of appetite. The swollen knee made it very painful to go up and down the stairs, so he did not go out for groceries. He had become malnourished, which weakened his immune system and made him vulnerable to bacterial infections. Pneumonia took hold.

Yet, even this is only half of the case script. Later, in his "aloneness" and sorrow, the man began drinking one night, became intoxicated, vomited, aspirated the vomitus into his lungs, and developed a lung abscess or aspiration pneumonia, and he was brought back to the emergency room only two weeks after his release. The students again talked about diagnosis and treatment. The professor shook his head. "Don't you get it?" he said. "By lim-iting your view only to the disease state, you are missing the other factors in the story. His solitude, his bereavement, his living conditions, his bad knee, his nutrition *and* the pneumococcus infection, antibiotics and respirator, are *all* part of the story. The search for the cause of an illness is limited by the classic disease theory. It does not account for all of the facts, and until you understand this, you may be able to get a patient out of a hospital, but you cannot keep him out for very long." This hypothetical example, drawn largely from Cassel's[3] examination of human suffering and the goals of medicine, illustrates how the treatment of older patients calls attention to the ineffectiveness of the biomedical model and presses for a broader way of defining medicine.

Roots of the Biomedical Model

Medicine does not consist simply of the application of sophisticated procedures and techniques. Presupposed by the biomedical model are images of the individual, valid knowledge, the focus of intervention, causality, and so forth, which are preconditions for the prevailing practice of modern medicine. It adopts a rational view, with its advantages and its inherent limitations. Medicine has benefited greatly from its advantages but now is trapped by its limitations.

Understanding certain key ideas is essential for making sense of how medicine operates as a science. This constellation of ideas might be referred to as the silent side of biomedicine, the side that is so deeply accepted that physicians do not even think about, much less question it.

During earlier periods of Western history—from the early Greeks to the end of the medieval period—any complaint was considered to be the result of a combination of factors, both natural (biological) and spiritual. Health (often understood as "wholeness") included the whole person: body, mind, and spirit. Gradually, the theoretical bases of medicine moved away from religion and toward science. This change did not occur all at once, of course, and the admixture of spirit and nature continued as a dominant part of medicine. The ideas of René Descartes, however, introduced an important change. In the early 1600s, he developed a philosophical argument that allowed nature to be "rationalized"—nature, in other words, could be materialized and transformed into an inert object. The thrust of Descartes' position is that the mind (*res cogito*) could be severed from the body (*res extensa*). Matter is thus freed from subjectivity, and pristine matter is available for inspection. Like nature, the body becomes a material object to be observed, and factors such as mind, soul, consciousness, and spirit are unimportant and dismissed because they are intangible. Disease occurs in the body, which is envisioned to be nothing more than a physiological organism.

In keeping with Descartes' ideas, other changes began to take place that were vital to modern medicine. The belief that facts could be separated categorically from values took hold in a wide range of disciplines. This meant that facts were considered external, separate from the mind, or were thought to be associated with empirical indicators. Physicians could, thus, safely become empiricists and attend solely to physiological markers. The effects of non-empirical factors (related to culture or biography, for example) on illness became irrelevant. The experience of the person in the body was denigrated and treated as epiphenomenal, that is, the person's experience was considered a byproduct of the illness and therefore not relevant to understanding the illness itself. Only "objective" factors were considered real.

Consistent with this transformation in our understanding of nature—including the human body—was the change in how physicians reformulated their thinking about the role of causality in illness and health. Discussions revolved around "causal chains" and "webs of causation." This imagery enabled physicians to view events as structurally linked; accordingly, a sound rationale could be assigned to the advent of illness. Physicians could formulate propitious strategies because solitary causes are predictable and manipulable. Because the source of any health problem could be pinpointed through rigorous research, diagnostic activity became a scientific investigative process.

Sickness or pathology was understood to be a condition of disequilibrium, or of nature out of balance, and restoring the body to "normal" equilibrium became the goal of most interventions. Understanding and establishing such norms with respect to equilibrium was considered a significant improvement for biomedicine because the cause of imbalance was relatively easy to identify.

A final element of the rational worldview that grew from Descartes' ideas pertains to how knowledge should be acquired. We would all acknowledge that subjectivity or interpretation is a liability in the pursuit of valid data. In order to curtail the corrosive influence of bias and subjectivity, the use of quantitative measures is encouraged. Quantification is believed to be value-free and to give unimpeded (direct, clear, "true") access to reality. Quantitative methods are assumed to be divorced from interpretation, and truth and objective reality are seen as one.

The cornerstone of the biomedical model, then, is the "materialization" of life—specifically, humans are approached as if they are simply physiological organisms. But this view does not make much sense unless we accept several proposals: dualism (that mind and body can be separated), empiricism (that reality is limited only to what can be experienced by the senses and their aids), mechanical causality (that all causal relationships are linear), the equilibrium thesis (that normativeness is the goal, and stability is possible), and the neutrality of technique (scientific method removes interpretation and bias) constitute the philosophical underside of biomedicine.

The Doctrines of the Biomedical Model

As Freund and McGuire[4] have argued persuasively, the ways in which the body is understood are socially constructed. Just as societies conceive ideas of truth, justice, and beauty, they also develop philosophical conceptions of the human body, ideas that change from culture to culture and over time. The Western biomedical model is predicated on five related doctrines.

The first to arise was the doctrine of *mind-body dualism*. This formulation by Descartes may have been useful as a starting point for biomedical science, but it is increasingly difficult to affirm in the modern practice of medicine. This doctrine is a barrier to understanding the psychosocial component of medicine, including the placebo effect, the connection between stress and illness, the importance of support groups, and the more general relationships between social support and health. Although the doctrine is no longer strictly adhered to, psychosomatic phenomena (i.e., the interaction between the mind and body) are still often considered to be peripheral to scientific medicine.

In some contexts, this schism is actually an embarrassment, and many members of the medical science community seem ready for its reformulation. Behavioral medicine, for example, cannot affirm body-mind dualism. Furthermore, patient-centered interviewing is becoming common in medical school curricula. This style of interviewing attends explicitly to psychosocial consequences and the illness experience of the patient, alongside a review of systems, a history of current illness, and a family health history.

In the illustration of the older patient, the links between grief, isolation, depression, appetite, immune suppression, and infection demonstrate the mind-body connection that is essential in the medical care of the elderly. In the case study, an ideal treatment plan would alter the social, emotional, and housing context of the older patient, if possible, as well as the disease outcome of those interactive factors, to achieve the goal of reduced hospitalizations. Managed care, in attempting to reduce hospitalizations, may provide additional economic incentives in this direction. Such treatment plans require the physician to work closely with supportive elements of the family and community environments, within a network of services. This is the reason why geriatric assessment teams function well in such situations.

The second doctrine is that the body is a system of functionally interdependent parts. Usually, this thesis is referred to as the *mechanical analogy*, whereby the body is treated as though it operates like a machine. Further-more, the doctor is like a mechanic. The study of specific disease mechanisms—the clearest expression of this view—makes up a considerable block of the usual medical school curriculum. The diagnosis of disease is normally based on the belief that each bodily function reflects a particular structure (e.g., kidney function—the biochemistry and anatomy of the kidney). So when disease is present, the structure of an organ is the first place to look for a cause, microscopic or otherwise.

Thinking that a physician can repair one part of the body as if it were separate from others is, however, quite a simplistic view, and unfortunately one reinforced by academic medicine. Often students graduate without integrating their biomedical knowledge into an understanding of the human body as a whole, much less that of the total person. Curriculum committees have struggled with the issue of integration, which usually flies in the face of departmental structure, funding allocations, and decision-making power.

The mechanical analogy is very limited because its understanding has been constructed using linear models whose error terms contain many important, but unmeasured, variables. Non-linear models, derived from the study of turbulence, may eventually offer a more sophisticated way of understanding causal connections. Geriatric examples abound. The prevalence of co-morbidity (multiple chronic diseases), increases with age. Physicians, for example, may be called upon to help patients simultaneously to manage osteoarthritis, visual impairment, diabetes, and hypertension. To avoid the added problems of polypharmacy and iatrogenic outcomes requires a level of sophistication in integrating physiologic, psychological and social knowledge that goes considerably beyond the usual demands of medicine. But this is the direction of the emerging paradigm, and geriatric medicine is leading the way.

Third is the doctrine of *physical reductionism*. Simply put, disease is viewed as isomorphic with the malfunction of physiology. This focus excludes all non-material dimensions (social, psychological, and behavioral) in the search for causes and interventions and, therefore, obscures the social conditions or physical environments that contribute to pathology or promote healing. The context in which the disease occurs is denied, considered as irrelevant. The answers lie in the body alone. Reductionism is the tendency to look for answers at progressively more *basic* levels, and in biomedicine it takes its ultimate form in attempting to locate causes largely in the genes. Again, the relatively greater power of the basic sciences in academic medicine promotes this outcome, and concentrating the basic sciences in the first two years compounds the problem. Exposing students to behavioral and social medicine in the basic sciences curriculum would move toward alleviating the problem.

Treating older patients is forcing us in the opposite direction, into the larger world of the person, beyond the body, in search of answers. In the emerging paradigm these approaches are not viewed as mutually exclusive. The continued aging of the population in the United States, therefore, will accelerate the process of paradigm transformation.

The fourth doctrine is that the body is the appropriate focus of *regimen and control*. This principle is a logical corollary of physical reductionism—if disease exists in the body, then the body is the logical locus of treatment. Because of the emphasis that medicine places on physiology in the etiology of disease, the patient has the responsibility to follow the doctor's orders to get well, forming a power hierarchy with the doctor in control of the patient.

This doctrine is under great strain now because of the rise in medical consumerism, that is, the notion that the patient has autonomous rights and should be viewed as an equal partner in the doctor-patient relationship. This trend tends to empower patients at the expense of some professional autonomy for physicians. The effect of this view has spread from the realm of medical practice to the halls of academic medicine. In patient-centered interviewing courses, student doctors are encouraged to "negotiate" a treatment plan with the patient, an approach that violates the doctrine of regimen and control. Partnering with the patient, however, is good medical practice because by buying into the plan, the patient is far more likely to comply with it, and much less likely to blame the physician for any negative treatment outcomes.

One must consider the widespread independence and institutional skepticism found among members of the baby-boomer generation to appreciate the origin and growth of consumerism in medicine. It is that consumer-oriented generation that will give us a bumper crop of older patients in the future. Teaching medical students to negotiate treatment plans will become nearly universal in the future as the aging bodies of baby boomers increase the frequency of their medical encounters. The alternative is a dismal one, limited primarily to praying for radical medical tort reform.

Fifth, and finally, the doctrine of *specific etiology* relates to the idea that each disease has only one cause. This rendition of causality was strongly reinforced by germ theory and the invention of vaccines to attack the microbial origins of disease. This doctrine pushes medical research for "magic bullet" cures and promotes a form of medical optimism and over-promising that may have been useful in garnering funding support in the past but that has increasingly undermined credibility with the public today.

The eschatological hope of medical science today seems to lie in the promises of genetic research. However, even if infants eventually can be genetically engineered so that they bypass all inherited links to diseases during their lives, the chronic diseases and conditions that are nurtured by our lifestyles and environmental exposures, which finally come to plague us in old age, would still remain. And they will increase as the older population increases.

So far in this essay, the discussion of the biomedical model has remained at the theoretical level. Perhaps a better way to understand how philosophy has shaped medical practice is to examine briefly the rise of scientific medicine.

After Abraham Flexner of the Carnegie Foundation visited medical schools and wrote his famous *Bulletin Number Four*[5] in 1910, scientific medicine became the primary mode of investigating and treating disease. Flexner argued that all medical schools should be closed except those that trained the scientist-physician. Johns Hopkins and Harvard, which were already rooted in basic science and hospital medicine, were to be the models.

This reorganization of medical education had implications beyond the training of physicians because the entire edifice of professional medicine took shape around it. These changes were consistent with the rise of positivism in science (the belief that facts lay in observation of nature and in empirical verification) and the belief in medicine's ability to procure objectively valid knowledge. The result has been the cultural legitimization and dominance of scientific medicine, whose aim was to conquer disease. Doctors trained after 1920, on the whole, have a hard time distinguishing between science and medicine. Medicine's embrace of science has had profound and wonderful effects on human health, illness, and suffering. No one would want to give up the genuine benefits that scientific medicine has brought us. Nonetheless, by the end of the twentieth century, the biomedical model is increasingly seen as incomplete and deficient in the modern world that created it. The clinical demands posed by the growth of the older population in the United States—and other industrial and post-industrial societies—highlight these deficiencies.

The Emerging Paradigm

It is possible to point to some of the features of an emerging paradigm that will be responsive to the health of the growing elderly population. In some circles, this new philosophy is referred to as post-quantum theory, while in others, the term is postmodernism. At the core of either viewpoint, however, is the rejection of Cartesian dualism.

Broadening the biomedical model into a biopsychosocial model of medicine is to consider the patient as a social and emotional body interacting with physical and social environments in ways that affect the patient's health. This model moves away from the limiting focus of the biomedical model without losing its benefits. However, it significantly broadens the earlier model.

New paradigms grow out of old ones. This is ever the case. A new paradigm is always thought to be the result of tinkering around the edges with the old one until finally the new cultural system becomes very different from its ancestor. The process takes many decades. The decline in professional autonomy among physicians and the rise in corporate medicine may speed up the process. That is, if therapies from outside the Western biomedical model become popular among patients and are less costly to provide, corporate medicine may simply mandate them.

Major technological developments also can strain paradigms and increase the pace of change, just as rapid urbanization early in this century made hospital medicine viable for a mass public for the first time. The electronic communication revolution at hand may be one of these potentially profound influences. Because of the information highway, it may no longer be possible for professional medicine to monopolize its special knowledge. The control of knowledge reinforces power, as it did in recent communist totalitarian states, and it does to a lesser extent in all professions. By extension, it could be argued that the erosion of this monopoly of knowledge will speed the decline in the professional autonomy and social authority of physicians, making them less able, thereby, to defend their positions, including those embedded in the old paradigm.

To underscore this point, the world of Internet access to knowledge, for example, will increasingly pressure the academy to share medical knowledge, and not only with physicians. Could one imagine a Harvard-mednet or a Mayomednet, alongside those of alternative and complementary medicines, that would be widely available to millions of Internet patients? The equivalent of a medical Saint Jerome, translating medical Latin into a Vulgate version for the Internet is certainly imminent. And no one can stop her. Internet access is unimpeded. Unknown opportunities would open to academic medicine in a world where understandable medical knowledge is no longer confined to medical professionals. Furthermore, whereas physicians have tended in the past to shun computerized diagnoses, there is no assurance that a mass market does not await such technology in patient populations eager for second opinions or even self-care. Such a development would further complicate medical education. Will the emphasis now given in the basic sciences to teaching "the language" someday be given to "translating the language"? Consumerism may change yet again when physicians must match understandable medical knowledge with the patient. This possibility would create significant changes in medical education.

Where knowledge is so available, the new paradigm would encourage changes in academic medicine. These changes would place much greater emphasis upon integrated, interdisciplinary approaches to diagnosis, treatment, and the understanding of disease mechanisms. They would also place greater emphasis upon the empowered patient, the partner in healing.

Conclusions

Most of the diseases that will eventually afflict Americans as they age cannot be cured, but the impact of these maladies can be postponed through preventive medicine, lessened through skillful management, and often some degree of function can be restored through rehabilitation medicine.

Prevention, however, along with health promotion, is viewed in biomedicine as the province of public health, involving activities conducted primarily by nurses and social workers, and requiring resources that lie outside the bailiwick of the medical profession. The emerging paradigm would press for a merger of public health and medicine into an integrated health delivery system.

Such major changes cannot happen now because they would presuppose the existence of a broader perspective on health and healing. For this to occur, the biomedical model must be placed in a new context. Stated simply, the epistemology of medicine must be expanded, thereby fostering the development of a wider range of possible interventions. In this way, medicine can become more amenable to the complexity of chronic illness. Furthermore, medicine can meet the challenges of a new social environment, one with a rapidly multiplying older population. These adaptations cannot occur without major changes in academic medicine, many of which are not yet clearly discernable.

The academy is not ignorant about the problems that will be posed for medicine by the increase in chronic illness. It is a current topic of importance. Having to cope with chronic diseases has generated an uneasiness among physicians, however, because of the narrow approach that has traditionally been taken to complex medical problems. Many physicians feel trapped by the biomedical model and are aware of the advantages that the broader models used by holistic, environmental, and behavioral medicine have over their own.

There are four forces that drive social change: population, organization, environment and technology. Change is more rapid when these engines work in tandem. A friendly climate is being prepared for the future paradigm shift. Imminent changes in Internet access to medical information (and perhaps diagnostics) will broaden definitions of medicine. Public images of health and health care will then become more consistent with other elements of our convenience-oriented, personalized, economy. These changes will also become more parallel to the public health goals of health promotion and disease prevention.

In addition to technological change, we are in the vortex of organizational change, particularly, that of corporate medicine. Both technological and organizational changes will press to define health care more broadly and to use new, and less expensive, strategies to extend access and keep costs down. The central argument of this essay, however, is that the tidal wave of the older population in the first half of the next century, as it washes over American medicine, including its academy, will exert the final push for a new, broader paradigm.

Discussion Questions

1. Describe the origins and content of the biophysical model of medicine.

2. What are the negative and positive features of empowering patients?

3. How will medical education change in the twenty-first century?

4. Explain the costs and benefits of corporate medicine.

5. Define "holistic medicine."

References

1. U.S. Department of Commerce, Bureau of the Census. *Current Population Reports: 65+ in the United States*. Washington, DC: Government Printing Office, 1996.

2. Mittelmark M.B. "The epidemiology of aging." In: Hazzard W.L., Birman E.L., Blass J.P. et al (eds). *Principles of Geriatric Medical Gerontology*. New York: McGraw-Hill, 1993:135.

3. Cassel E.J. *The Nature of Suffering and the Goals of Medicine*. New York: Oxford University Press, 1991.

4. Freund P., McGuire M. *Health, Illness, and the Social Body: A Critical Sociology*. Englewood Cliffs, NJ: Prentice Hall, 1991.

5. Flexner A. *Medical Education in the United States and Canada*. A report to the Carnegie Foundation for the Advancement of Teaching. Bulletin No. 4. Boston, MA: Updyke, 1910.

Reprinted from: Charles F. Longino, Jr. "Pressure From Our Aging Population Will Broaden Our Understanding of Medicine." In *Academic Medicine*, 72:19, pp.341-347. Reprinted by permission.

Chapter 47

New Challenges for Gerontology

Meredith Minkler

[handwritten: Prof. of Public Health & Sociology Gerontology]

The postmodern outlook is one of doubt and questioning, taking little for granted; indeed, it sounds a lot like the definition of sociology. Sociologists today employ a number of different approaches to the study of social arrangements, those patterned regularities that lend a degree of predictability and normality to daily life. At the most abstract level, sociologists are concerned with how those with economic and political power determine the distribution of societal resources and produce rationales to justify inequality. Another strand of contemporary sociological analysis employs qualitative methods to understand how people perceive their experiences. At both levels of social reality, one's position in social hierarchies makes a difference: whether or not one is male or female, white or black, native-born or immigrant, Hispanic or Asian American, and so forth. In addition, the contribution of feminism to the social sciences is the recognition of social structures as innately gendered, that is, that entities such as businesses and schools are not gender-neutral but constructed along lines that favor the abilities and values of one sex or the other. Similarly, it can be argued that all American institutions are racist in the sense of being based on a white model of behavior.

When applied to the study of aging, these ways of knowing form what Meredith Minkler calls "critical gerontology," a challenge to the dominant model of aging as a biologically driven process, with universal transitions. Pay attention to how the diversity of the American population immediately suggests that they bring a diversity of experience to their old age. Notice how lifelong differences in resources will affect health and well-being. Think about the ways in which coping strategies will vary greatly by gender, race, ethnicity, and so forth.

Introduction

The epidemiologist Lois Verbrugge (1983) is fond of relating that when she was a child and used to lose fights with her brother, her mother would try to calm her down by saying 'it will all even out by the time you're 80'. As Lois points out, while this may well be true for minor matters like checker games and candy bars, it is certainly not true in terms of important things like health, mortality or social circumstances. The profound differences in life chances by race, ethnicity, gender and social class continue to operate in old age, and this simple fact has never had greater relevance than at the close of the 20th century.

As Linda Burton and her colleagues note:

> Current and future generations of the elderly are part of a quiet revolution—revolution of older individuals representing the broadest range of ethnic, racial . . . and [regional and class] diversity ever witnessed. . . . This diversity challenges us to evaluate the applicability of existing research, policy and programs to emerging elderly populations. And more important, it prods us to reassess the relevance of gerontological theories and perspectives. . . . (1992: 129)

Do concepts like caregiver burden, retirement and adjustment to old age apply equally across cultures, genders and social classes, what do theoretical notions like the double jeopardy hypothesis reveal about the minority ageing populations studied, but equally important, what do they miss, and what do they suggest about what gerontologists value—what they choose to study, and what is rendered invisible?

The last decade and a half has witnessed the emergence and growth of a set of diverse perspectives that would have us as gerontologists engage in precisely this sort of reassessment of some of the field's most cherished ways of thinking about and studying ageing and the elderly. Collectively referred to as 'critical gerontology', these alternative perspectives comprise, in Jan Baars' words, "a collection of questions, problems and analyses that have been excluded by the established mainstream" (1991: 220). As Chris Phillipson and Alan Walker suggest, what is proposed in critical gerontology is 'a more value committed approach to social gerontology—a commitment not just to understand the social construction of ageing but to change it' (1987: 12).

This paper will present two major paths in critical gerontology—approaches derived from the political economy of ageing and perspectives from the humanities—highlighting the special contributions of each to our understanding of ageing and growing old. Emergent feminist perspectives on ageing, and what Burton and her colleagues (1992) term 'culturally relevant ways of thinking' about ageing and diversity will be further presented as complementing and extending critical gerontology, with the concept of empowerment seen as linking all four of these conceptual approaches. Case studies and examples will be used to illustrate the relevance of these alternative perspectives for better understanding and to address the problems and challenges facing our field in the years ahead.

Two Paths in Critical Gerontology

Critical gerontology can be envisaged as evolving along two paths simultaneously—paths that sometimes intersect and move in common directions, but that have tended to remain distinct (Ovrebo and Minkler 1993). The first path embraces a broad political economy of ageing framework. Grounded in the work of such scholars as Peter Townsend (1981, 1986), Alan Walker (1981, 1987, 1990), Chris Phillipson (1991–2, 1994), Carroll Estes (1979, 1982, 1991), and Anne-Marie Guillemard (1986), critical gerontology in this sense views the 'problem' of ageing in structural, rather than individual terms. In the words of Carroll Estes and her colleagues (1982), it 'starts with the proposition that the status and resources of the elderly and even the trajectory, of the ageing process itself, are conditioned by one's location in the social structure and the economic and social factors that affect it'.

Although some political economy has been criticised for its over emphasis on social class, with a corresponding under emphasis on race, ethnicity, and gender, one of the strengths of a broad political economy framework lies in its ability to highlight the intersections between race, class, gender and ageing, (Minkler and Estes 1991). And in both North America and Europe, important movement in this direction is occurring. Feminist perspectives on ageing, for example, have integrated and enriched political economy by stressing the gendered nature of ageing and growing old, and 'the social construction of women's marginality in old age' (Walker, 1987: 9). Critical examinations of the gendered division of both formal and informal labour thus have helped illuminate why older women in Britain and the U.S. are twice as likely to live in poverty as men, and why in the U.S., fully three-fourths of the elderly poor are women (Arber and Ginn 1991; Bernard and Meade 1993; Porter 1995).

Explorations of the intersections of race, class and gender in caregiving similarly have demonstrated that while men and middle and upper class white women are most likely to be care *managers* for their disabled elderly parents, low income persons, and particularly low income minority women, are most likely to be hands-on *care givers*, who often have to quit their jobs or exhaust their meagre incomes in order to provide this care (Archibold 1983).

Finally, the political economy path in critical gerontology provides multidisciplinary lenses through which to examine such themes as the social creation of the dependent status of the elderly, and the management of that dependency through public policies and health and social services. To borrow John Myles's (1983) phrase, it helps bring to light the many ways in which 'politics, not demography', determines how old age is defined and approached in a society. It helps illuminate, for example, why in both the U.S. and the U.K., conservative policy makers are capitalising on what Ann Robertson (1991) calls 'apocalyptic demography' and what Alan Walker (1990) terms 'the alarmist demography of despair'. Relatedly, a political economy framework helps explicate the fact that in the U.S., the mass media and growing numbers of academics and policy makers have embraced concepts like inter-generational equity or justice between generations, arguing that the elderly are no longer poor and that Social Security and Medicare are directly responsible for the nation's economic woes and the fact that one in four pre-schoolers now lives in poverty (Minkler and Robertson 1991). Such arguments, of course, ignore the far more potent sources of inequities that lie at the base of these and other societal problems.

Critical gerontology in the tradition of political economy, in sum, offers a rich and multiperspectival framework within which to view and better understand old age as a 'problem' for societies 'characterized by major inequalities in the distribution of power, income and property' (Kart 1987: 79). As such, it provides a much needed supplement to the study of the biological and psychological aspects of ageing, which, for all their contributions, reveal little about the social construction of ageing in a broader sociopolitical context.

Despite its importance and richness, however, the political economy path in critical gerontology requires as a complement and supplement an approach to aging which puts a human face—and a human body and spirit—on ageing and growing old. And it is the second path in critical gerontology which helps us achieve this infusion of the human element into our craft. This second path emerges from a humanistic orientation and critiques, what Harry Moody describes as the ever more technical and 'instrumental' orientation of academic gerontology, within which 'the problems of later life are treated with scientific and managerial efficiency, but with no grasp of their larger political or existential significance. The last stage of life is progressively drained of meaning' (1988: 82).

Developed and embraced by such scholars as Thomas Cole (1988, 1992, 1993), Andrew Achenbaum (1986), Mike Featherstone and Mike Hepworth (1993), Martha Holstein (1994) and Harry Moody (1988, 1993), critical gerontology in this second sense is particularly focused on larger questions of meaning, or lack of meaning, in the lives of older people. It asks us to explore 'what makes a good life in old age and how a society can support multiple alternative visions of a good old age' (Holstein, 1995). In the words of British scholar Tom Kitwood, 'perhaps at bottom it is concerned with valuing persons in the full range of their capacity as sentient beings' (1990: 225).

Clearly, travelling this second path in critical gerontology shakes up some of our notions of what we can know, of what is 'true' and 'real' about ageing and being old. The kinds of questions asked, the way in which answers are sought, and the kinds of answers accepted become themselves areas ripe for rethinking as we are taught 'a more humble attitude toward epistemic certainty' (Holstein 1995).

Of special interest to some who travel and help carve this second path are the contributions of post modernism, with its sharp and piercing challenge to the notion that we can 'know truth' at all. Some, for example, resonate with the concept of the post modern life course—the notion that our 'multiplicity of lifestyles' and fluid movement throughout life has led to such a blurring of life stages that the very concepts of life course and life stages become somewhat artificial and irrelevant (Moody 1993; Johnson 1995; Kohli 1987; Cole *et al*. 1993).

Clearly, both the political economy path in critical gerontology and the humanistic path confront us with the *disempowerment* of the old—in the first instance, through the structural constraints in which ageing takes place, and in the second, by casting into sharper relief questions that have arisen since the Industrial Era about the loss of a sense of place and of meaning for the old in our societies. Yet as Chris Phillipson (1994) has pointed out, both the political economy of ageing and the perspectives offered from the humanities address as well issues of *empowerment*, whether through societal transformations in the redistribution of wealth and income or through the creation of new rituals and other means to facilitate transitions to and through later life.

Finally, as will be suggested below, emerging feminist perspectives on ageing, and perspectives reflecting what Linda Burton refers to as 'culturally relevant ways of thinking' about ageing and diversity place a heavy accent on empowerment, and particularly the empowerment of older women and blacks and other minorities. In a sense, then, empowerment may be the unifying concept bringing together diverse conceptualisations within critical gerontology, and the vehicle through which it may make its most significant contribution.

Perspectives on Empowerment and Their Applications in Ageing

In the United States, empowerment is a word many have grown to dislike, for it is a much used and abused term, and one that has been widely co-opted by conservative policy makers who use the rhetoric of empowering individuals and communities as a rationale for cutting back on needed health and social services. But if power is the ability to 'predict, control and participate in one's environment' (Kent 1971), then empowerment is a process by which individuals and communities are enabled to take such power and act effectively to transform their lives and their communities. As Chris Phillipson and Alan Walker point out, 'The task for a critical gerontology [is] to furnish both the theoretical and policy perspectives necessary' to create more equitable environments in which such empowerment can take place (1987: 11).

Some of the most exciting recent thinking about empowerment comes from the feminist literature. By moving from traditional notions of 'power over' to feminist notions of 'power with' and 'power to' (French 1986), and by stressing social relatedness, community good, and interdependence rather than individual good and independence (Browne 1995), feminist perspectives on empowerment have special relevance for gerontologists. This applies particularly as we think about older women, the poor, racial and ethnic minorities, older gays and lesbians, care recipients, and other neglected and marginalised groups.

These perspectives remind us as gerontologists to address the sociopolitical context in which ageing takes place, and the resultant profound disparities between subgroups within the elderly population. They prod us to look at 'the multiple roots of oppression' (Browne 1995: 363) in marginalised groups of older people, but would have us look also at their strengths including importantly how they construct maps of meaning on a journey through age that is often fraught with hardships (Ovrebo and Minkler 1993). With Miriam Bernard and her colleagues, they remind us to address the fact that 'older women know what it's like to be old, but contemporary society does not make it easy for their voices to be heard' (1993: 190). Finally, feminist approaches to empowerment would have us as gerontologists re-think some of the ways in which we formulate research questions and gather and analyse data, and indeed some of the underlying concepts and premises on which this research is based (Browne 1995). An example will illustrate this point.

In both Western Europe and North America, 'adding life to years', preventing disability and facilitating healthy or 'successful ageing' have achieved widespread popularity among gerontologists as representing what we should be striving for (Rowe and Kahn 1987; Schmidt 1994). Such ideals represent an important shift from earlier negative perceptions of ageing which focused on decline and loss and led one gerontologist to define our craft as 'the science of drawing downwardly sloping lines'.

At the same time, concepts like healthy or successful ageing, used uncritically, can contribute to the stigmatisation and disempowerment of those elders who fail to meet our criteria for ageing well. As Tom Cole (1988) suggests, we have seen the reemergence of a Victorian era notion that healthy old age is a just reward for a life of self control and 'right living'. In David Levin's (1987) words, 'good health has become a new ritual for patriotism, a marketplace for the public display of secular faith in the power of the will'. Within such a vision, where is there a place for the 85-year-old man with a disabling respiratory ailment or the diabetic and severely arthritic elderly woman in a wheel chair?

While we pursue the laudable aims of increasing and maintaining healthy functioning in the elderly, we must be sure that we don't in the process 'equate being ill with being guilty'(Becker 1986). And for those elders who already have substantial limitations, a real commitment to empowerment would mean recognising and reinforcing the essential meaning of old age which transcends the state of our bodies and involves the right to flourish and grow in whatever ways are possible, and whether one lives at home or in a residential care setting. In our preoccupation with healthy physical ageing, we often tend to forget, as Chuck Fahey and Martha Holstein remind us, that 'old age can be a time to enlarge one's sense of personal and communal history to forge ties in the intergenerational tapestry, to gain perspective in self knowledge about one's own relation to ageing and the end of life' (1993: 242–3).

The capacity for empowerment and growth in advanced old age, even in the face of frailty and death, and set against the backdrop of a lifetime of poverty and disappointments, is brought into sharp relief in the form of the character Maudie in Doris Lessing's (1983) *Diary of a Good Neighbour*. Dying, poor and alone in a cold water shack in a London slum, 90-year-old Maudie is a long-retired factory worker and the survivor of a lonely and abusive marriage. She has outlived her friends, and her social world.

Bitterly, alone, Maudie nevertheless is able to cross the divides of class and age to become friends with Janna, the quintessential modern successful woman, as each woman overcomes her own profound loneliness in becoming the other's 'good neighbour'. Through friendship with Janna, Maudie experiences her unconditional worth as a human being. Though her dying is painful,—she says at one point, 'dreadful, dreadful,'—Maudie's dignity is reclaimed. Janna helps Maudie die, and Maudie helps Janna live, by discovering her humanity and her possibilities (Ovrebo and Minkler 1993).

As Martha Holstein has pointed out, 'post modernism and deconstruction have stimulated sufficient intellectual unrest to make it difficult to approach literary texts' like this one 'with an easy innocence, for example, about their referential possibilities or their lack of ideological commitments' (1994: 823). At the same time, by engaging with such texts, we may be helped to appreciate the

empowerment that comes with the construction of maps of meaning in advanced old age, despite bodily decline, and in cases like Maudie's, despite the cumulative effects of a lifetime of social and economic hardship. Further, by engaging with such texts, we may ourselves be empowered as we accept their offer of 'a safe way to "try on" an aging body and make it more familiar through experiencing it in the bodies of those who have preceded us into old age' (Holstein 1994; Woodward 1991: 71).

This paper has addressed thus far the potentials within different streams of critical gerontology for better understanding both empowerment and disempowerment in the lives of elderly people. But applying an empowerment perspective to work in the field of ageing also has important implications for programme development and action research. For if gerontologists are serious about reframing old notions of 'power over' to embrace feminist concerns with 'power to' and 'power with', then elders themselves must be afforded a much greater role in deciding both the project agenda and the steps for achieving it. This is critical, in part simply to ensure that the issues addressed are the ones that really matter.

As sociologist Jon Mckinlay (in Labonte 1993) is fond of pointing out, professionals frequently suffer from an unfortunate malady known as 'terminal hardening of the categories'. They get the kinds of answers they are comfortable dealing with because they ask the kinds of questions that will provide those answers. Health professionals, for example, conduct health behaviour risk surveys that will carefully document heart disease as a major community health problem, but will in all likelihood miss the fact that very different sorts of issues, like drugs, violence, or inadequate income may be the major concerns of residents.

An empowering approach to working in partnership with older people would start where the people are in cases like this—shelving temporarily approaches such as blood pressure screening tests and lifestyle counselling to instead help residents address the health problems *they* have identified. The results can be dramatic, as illustrated in the following case study from work among isolated elderly people in San Francisco's lower income Tenderloin District.

The Tenderloin is a 45 block area adjacent to the downtown that for decades has been a poor, high crime neighbourhood that is home to large numbers of homeless people, ex-offenders, prostitutes and Indo Chinese refugees. But the neighbourhood is also home to some 8,000 elderly men and women of different races and ethnicities, who live in its many deteriorating single room occupancy hotels, often without cooking or private bathroom facilities. Sixteen years ago, students and a faculty member at the School of Public Health, University of California, Berkeley began what was to become the Tenderloin Senior Organizing Project, or TSOP. The project was designed to address the interrelated problems of poor health, social isolation and powerlessness that have been endemic among elders in this community.

The students began by offering informal coffee hours or discussion groups in hotel lobbies one morning a week. Gradually, as trust levels increased, they began asking resident participants what their major health problems were. In hotel after hotel, the residents responded, 'crime', and the students politely said, 'you misunderstood, we were asking about helath problems'. The residents held their ground, pointing out that they couldn't safely go outdoors without being mugged, and therefore couldn't get to the doctor's office, go for a walk or get an evening meal. Crime, they argued, was their biggest health problem.

The students and project staff listened. Then they helped the residents organise a community-wide meeting on the subject of crime, and enlist the support of the mass media. They helped garner resources so that the residents could start an inter-hotel coalition, 'Tenderloin Tenants for Safer Streets'. Members of this grassroots coalition met with the mayor and demanded and got increased beat patrol officers in the neighbourhood. The students and staff also helped, but always in the background, as residents began the Safehouse Project, recruiting 48 local merchants and agencies to be places of refuge where residents could go for immediate aid if they were being followed or just needed to sit down because of shortness of breath.

The organising of residents around crime prevention was given much of the credit for an 18 per cent drop in the crime rate that occurred in this neighbourhood in the first 12 months of their mobilisation (LA Times 1982). Their organising efforts also translated into some effective individual level behaviour change. For example, residents' newfound feelings of power, self efficacy and improved self esteem led some successfully to quit smoking and cut down on problem drinking (Minkler 1992).

From their initial focus on crime, the elderly residents went on to address malnutrition, creating resident-run mini markets in their hotel lobbies to provide access to fresh fruits and vegetables. They began a cooperative breakfast programme to qualify for participation in a food bank, and prepared a no cook cookbook, soliciting and testing recipes from the 49er football team and other local heroes, and later having the book published and widely distributed by the City's Department of Public Health. The residents also established a health-promotion resource centre, which contracted with a local theatre company to develop skits on health-related topics that could serve as triggers for discussion in the hotel support groups. Through TSOP, residents organised successfully to improve bus transportation; to seek compensation for a hotel elevator that had been out of service for five months; and to get hot water turned on in a building that had gone without for ten years. They organised around unfair rent hikes, and recently even won an out-of-court settlement against a prestigious and powerful local law school that owned senior housing in the neighbourhood and had reneged on promised security (Minkler in press).

The message behind this story is a simple one: had the students and staff of the Tenderloin Senior Orgranizing Project failed to pay attention to and support the elders' definition of need—had they not acknowledged, back in the beginning, that crime was indeed a health problem—they might still be running support groups in hotel lobbies one morning a week, if indeed they were still welcome at all. Instead, by trusting the elderly residents to determine and act on their own health agenda, they were able to contribute to something that has had a real and lasting impact on the health of this community.

The charge to start where the people are is difficult to live up to, for as Gail Siler-Wells (1989) points out, 'behind the euphemisms of community participation and empowerment lay the realities of power, control and ownership'. The very real structural distinctions that exist between professionals and elders, and the very location of professionals in health and social services bureaucracies and universities, confer a certain power that includes the power to set the health, social service, or research agenda. Consequently, even when older people are encouraged to set their own goals, they are, in reality, often asked to do so 'within the context of pre-existing goals' that outside experts have determined to be the important ones.

Peter Townsend (1981, 1986) and others (Estes 1979; Johnson 1993; Lloyd 1991 ; Phillipson *et al*. 1986) have written eloquently about the asymmetrical power relationships between older persons and professional care providers, and the dependency to which this gives rise. In *Democracy on Trial*, Jean Elshtain (1995) also makes this point, noting that 'When professionals solve problems, people grow weaker, not stronger, for their "needs" are authoritatively defined by people outside themselves'. A real commitment to empowerment of elderly people means more than incorporating the empowerment rhetoric-attempting, for example, to blur hierarchical distinctions by using the language of the market place, and talking about health care providers and consumers (Neysmith 1989). Rather, it means enabling elders to play a far greater role in determining the policies and programmes that affect them, and indeed the content of our community-based research efforts.

The Challenge of Increasing Racial/Ethnic Diversity

The challenge to take seriously the rhetoric of empowerment becomes even more difficult with the growing racial and ethnic diversity of our older populations, and the experi-

ence of the U.K provides a good case in point. For although only four per cent of ethnic minorities in the U.K. were older people in 1990, fully 16 per cent were in the age group immediately preceding pensionable age—45–64 for men, and 45–59 for women—suggesting a 4–5 fold increase in the older age group by the end of the decade. In many urban inner city areas, where blacks and Asians make up over half of the population, the implications of these demographic trends are particularly profound (Blakemore and Boneham 1994).

As Ken Blakemore and Margaret Boneham point out, 'Discussion of ageing, race and ethnicity in Britain has been almost entirely focused on the problem of social inequality and the additional disadvantages faced by older Asian and Afro Caribbean people' (1994: 38). Although research in the U.S. predates by almost two decades the emergent British scholarship in this area, American studies have tended to share this focus, and have reflected what Bond and Coleman describe as the 'theoretical barrenness' of much of our thinking about ageing (1993: 339).

There is, of course, much room for problem-focused descriptive research, conducted in the tradition of the double jeopardy hypothesis (Dowd and Bengtson 1978), which examines the additive negative effects of being old and a member of a racial or ethnic minority in terms of things like health and income. Recent British studies, for example, have shown a significantly greater drop in income at retirement among black and Asian elders than among whites, and the particular economic vulnerability of older minority women, who often do not receive the pension and welfare benefits to which they are entitled, nor, in the case of some East Asian groups, share in the property rights of male relatives (Blakemore and Boneham 1994).

Though certainly not as profound and entrenched as in the U.S., experiences of racism and discrimination based on one's race or ethnicity also are common in the UK, and must be the subject of intense research. Only a small fraction of epidemiological research in the U.S. has examined the effects of racism not simply on mental health and life satisfaction, but on exacerbating physical conditions like hypertension as well (Kreiger *et al.* 1995), and the results are indeed troubling.

This kind of research is critical, and never more so than in these politically conservative times. But as Jackson and his colleagues suggest, double jeopardy must be not simply 'a convenient label for the facts', but 'a concept for building hypotheses' and developing greater appreciation of the real heterogeneity of minority ageing populations (1982: 78). Moreover, gerontologists must go well beyond double jeopardy, since the heavy focus on social disadvantage in this research paradigm has inadvertently contributed to a 'deficit thinking mentality' that has been criticised by minority scholars as disempowering and ignoring the many strengths in their communities. As these critics have pointed out, researchers in the double jeopardy tradition have tended to pay little attention to 'the cultural meaning and dynamics of ageing' in specific racial or ethnic groups (Burton *et al.* 1992: 131; Jackson 1991). Further, when areas such as 'retirement' and 'adjustment to old age' are included in their studies, most researchers simply use standard measures of these concepts, derived from work with white middle class samples, without exploring their relevance in other cultural contexts. How meaningful is the concept of retirement for low income black men in either the U.S. or the U.K., for example, when many become redundant and permanently unemployed in their 40s and 50s, or take on the role Rose Gibson (1991) describes as 'unretired retired'?

In the U.S., African American scholars have similarly questioned the usefulness of the concept of adjustment to old age for blacks, among whom ageing may be perceived 'not as a series of adjustments, but rather as a process of survival' (Burton *et al.* 1992: 132). In support of this interpretation, they point to a rich legacy of music, poems and other art forms highlighting survival as 'an ethos of black American culture', and to the often pivotal role of black elders for the survival of the entire clan. Toni Morrison (1987) speaks eloquently to this theme, for example, in her novel, *Beloved*, whose central character, Baby Suggs, is the matriarch of a family broken by slavery, and race hatred. Like many of the older women characters in black novels, we meet in Baby Suggs a woman whose role was to preserve the clan, spiritually and physically, even while she deals with her own excruciating pain and sorrow.

On a lighter and more individualistic note, Maya Angelou (1986) also captures the spirit of survival in her popular poem *On Aging*. She reminds us:

> When my bones are still and aching
> And my feet won't climb the stair,
> I will only ask one favor:
> Don't bring me no rocking chair
> When you see me walking, stumbling,
> Don't study me and get it wrong
> 'Cause tired don't mean lazy,
> And every goodbye ain't gone.
> I'm the same person I was back then,
> A little less hair, a little less chin.
> A lot less lungs and much less wind.
> But ain't I lucky I can still breathe in.

If we as gerontologists are truly to understand racial and ethnic minority ageing, far more attention must be paid to poverty, racism, and other structural sources of oppression in these groups. But we must be open, as well, to travelling the second path in critical gerontology listening to themes that emerge in the poems and novels of a people, and allowing these to serve as crucibles on which we test the relevance of our accepted notions and constructs.

Developing a richer understanding of minority ageing also means embracing a life course perspective, which "highlights the way in which people's location in the social system, the historical period in which they live, and their unique personal biography shape the experience of old age" (Stoller and Gibson 1994: xxiii). Unlike earlier, rigid life stage theories, a life course perspective in this sense would, as Bernard and Meade suggest, pay particular attention to the 'social, environmental and cultural contexts' within which men and women live out their lives (1993: 8). Nor would it contradict the notion that ageing is in large part socially constructed. Rather, it would examine the multiple interacting levels on which this construction takes place.

A useful illustration may be found in relation to feminist theory, which has done much to illuminate the complexity of societal ambivalence around caregiving and its status as an activity that is at one and the same time 'sentimentalized and devalued' (Abel 1991). Central to much feminist thinking about caregiving is, of course, the notion of the dichotomy drawn in many advanced industrialised societies between the public world of work and the private world in which the largely invisible work of women in the home takes place. By focusing attention on society's differential valuing of the public and private spheres, feminist scholars have helped put into context the severe economic disadvantages faced by older women (Abel 1991; Baines *et al*. 1991; Bernard and Meade 1993).

But a closer look at the lived experience of black women in the U.S. and Britain suggests that this distinction between public and private spheres may not be a terribly meaningful one for many within these groups. The majority of Afro-Caribbean women who came to the U.K. in the 1950s and early 1960s, for example, share a life history of employment as cooks, cleaners and other ancillary workers in the public sector, performing for very low wages, many of the same chores commonly associated with women's work in the home (Blakemore and Boneham 1994). Across the Atlantic, their African American sisters disproportionately fill the ranks of domestic servants and other low level workers, and often experience a similar blurring of the line between the public and private spheres.

The irony confronted by black women who leave their own families at home in order to go and clean other people's houses and care for other people's children or disabled elderly relatives has not been lost on black feminist writers. Author June Jordan describes her anger and shame at watching, 'one black woman after another' trudge to the bus stop after a day of cleaning or caregiving in an affluent white neighbourhood, only to return home to the frequently thankless chores of their own loneliness, their own families (1985: 105).

The blurring of the line between the public and private spheres, and the added complexi-ties of caregiving within this context, were further underscored in a recent in-depth study of 71 African American grandmothers raising grandchildren because of the crack cocaine epidemic (Minkler and Roe 1993). Grandparent caregiving has increased dramatically in the U.S. over the last decade (US Census 1991), and while it cuts across racial and social class lines, it is particularly prevelent in inner city African American communities, where between 30 per cent and 50 per cent of children are often in the care of grandparents, and increasingly, great grandparents, because of the epidemics of drugs, AIDS, violence, and teen pregnancy (Minkler and Roe, 1993).

Many of the women in the Oakland, California-based Grandparent Caregiver Study were combining care for their grandchildren with low-paying jobs in which their responsibilities closely matched their work at home. One such grandmother, who worked the graveyard shift as a nurse's aide in a convalescent hospital, spoke poignantly about how she spent each night 'changing people's diapers', only to come home and do the same for her two-year-old grandson. Another older woman, raising four young grandchildren, worked as a bus driver for a local elementary school and said, 'it's kids at home and kids at work—everywhere I go it's kids'.

Finally, a number of the women in this study were combining care of grandchildren with the care of disabled elderly parents or other relatives. One of these women opened the interview by saying, 'I have three children—my nine-month-old grandchild who was born drug addicted, my 17-month-old who is HIV positive, and my 83-year-old mother with Alzheimer's. All three are in diapers'. Another woman was a carer across four generations. She was raising, several of her grandchildren, while her own youngest child, in his late teens, was still at home. She was doing all the errands, shopping, house cleaning, and other chores for her disabled mother, although her mother was able to reciprocate sometimes and help babysit the grandchildren. And she was responsible for bathing, feeding and providing all the other personal care for the elderly grandmother who had raised her during much of her own young life. Clearly, gerontologists' notions of carer, care recipient, and 'caregiver burden' take on a whole new meaning and complexity in this social and cultural context.

Critical Gerontology, Social Responsibility and Advocacy in 'Mean Spirited' Times: A Final Note

As Bond and Coleman point out, ageing into the 21st century ideally will see gerontology 'growing into a more truly liberating subject, less concerned with charting decline and predicting outcomes and more with outlining possibilities. . .' (1993: 339). For gerontology to reach its full potential, however, the important work that continues to take place in the biological and psychological aspects of ageing must be complemented by critical perspectives from political economy, feminist scholarship, and the humanities, coupled with newer, culturally relevant ways of thinking about ageing in multicultural societies. As this paper further has suggested, it is through its focus on empowerment of the elderly on multiple levels, as well as on structural constraints to empowerment, that critical gerontology may greatly enrich not only our appreciation of elderly people and their capacities, but indeed the very meaning of growing and being old in contemporary society.

Yet there is another crucial role which critical gerontology may play in this last decade of the 20th century, and that is in helping us place in clearer relief some of the dramatic, and in the U.S., the very frightening ideological and related policy shifts which are threatening some of the most basic moral and social underpinnings of our society.

The 1980s and 90s have seen dramatic changes in North America and parts of Western Europe in many fundamental areas of welfare state provision, with the politics of retrenchment resulting in reductions in the role of the state, privatisation of many health and social services, and increased calls for individual and family responsibility in health and human welfare (Arber and Ginn 1991; Goodin 1985). In the area of caregiving, for example, UK government policy in the early 1980s was explicit about the fact that 'care in

the community must increasingly mean care by the community', (DHSS 1981: 3, emphasis added). As Peter Lloyd has pointed out, although policy documents discussing such shifts continually refer to the 'independence' of elders, community care may often be seen as a euphemism for care by adult daughters, and as 'a somewhat more benign, but still dependency-creating paternalism' (1991: 130).

In the United States, this paternalism has been less than benign: One of Ronald Reagan's first acts as President was to repeal legislation that had banned the states from making it a criminal offence for adult children of means not to provide for the long-term care needs of their elderly parents! More recently, the unprecedented cutbacks in support for the elderly, the poor, women and children, and both legal and illegal immigrants embodied in the Republican Congress's 'Contract with America' have led critics to argue that this blueprint for action is in fact more a contract *on* America whose ramifications for the most vulnerable segments of our society we can only begin to imagine.

As Arber and Ginn have commented, 'many of these changes have been cast in the political rhetoric of increasing freedom and consumer choice. However, such a market ideology can only be a reality for those few elderly people who have the financial resources to exercise a choice' (1991: 187). For in the last analysis, increased individual responsibility for health and other matters must be accompanied by individual and community 'response-ability'. The latter may be defined as the capacity of individuals and communities for building on their strengths and responding to their own needs and the challenges posed by the environment (Minkler 1994). The contrasting stories of two older men in the U.S. are illustrative.

Jim Law was a recently retired college professor in a small town in Conn. when he decided really to take charge of his health. At the time, he was quite overweight, led a very sedentary life, had a cholesterol reading of over 300, and a two pack a day 49-year smoking habit. Jim lost weight, quit smoking, and began exercising with such tenacity that today, at age 69, he holds the U.S. and the world records for the l00, 200 and 400 metre runs in his age group. And when he is not running (and serving as a spokesperson for Total cereal) he is motivating other older people to follow his example. Jim is certainly to be admired, but it must also be recognised that as a retired professor with a nice income, a supportive wife and friends, who lived in a safe community, he was in an excellent position to take individual responsibility for his health.

Contrast Jim's situation with that of another man, Mr. Mario Hermoso. Like Jim, Mario was concerned about his health and wanted to do something about it. But he lived in the Tenderloin, in an area with no supermarkets and, until recently, almost no access to fresh fruits and vegetables. Mario could not afford to eat out, so he did what most of his fellow residents did and hooked up an illegal hot plate. In addition to the problem of rats and roaches, this behaviour posed a major fire hazard.

Mario wanted to get more exercise, but he was partially blind, and the crime rate in his neighbourhood was 70 crimes per person per year, so that taking a brisk walk or engaging in any other outdoor activity was ill advised. His small cramped quarters, however, made exercising in his room a near impossibility. Clearly someone like Mario Hermoso can't be expected to take individual responsibility for health unless the broader society is willing to increase his response-ability—his capacity to respond—by providing a decent income, a safe community in which to live, and access to nutritious foods, home-maker services, and other supports that, in the face of ideological shifts and budget cuts, have been so radically scaled back.

Public health leader Victor Sidel is fond of saying that 'statistics are people with the tears washed off'. One of the most vital roles that critical gerontology can play during this politically mean-spirited time in our history is to help our policy makers, the mass media, and the general public see the human faces behind the statistics. Our role as scholars, researchers and practitioners must be accompanied by a role as advocate. As Peter Townsend so eloquently put it, the attempted disassociation between social science research and policy making 'falsely neutralizes

scientific practice' and is a luxury we can ill afford (1986: 19). We, as gerontologists, must share what we have learned, in as personal a form as possible, and call out for policies and programmes that address poverty in old age, combat racism, sexism and ageism, and facilitate the empowerment of elderly people, not by calling upon them and their families to 'do more for themselnes' but by reclaiming the sense of community that would have us recognise that we are indeed all in this together.

Malcolm Johnson perhaps captured this sentiment best when he wrote:

> we have the global capacity to support all the world's people, but to do so will require a revolution in economic and political action which re-establishes human solidarity and reciprocity as central features of our social order. . . .

These transformations are essentially moral; but failure to address them puts at risk not only the contract between young and old, but society itself (1995: 262).

Discussion Questions

1. Apply the "political economy of aging" perspective to the Social Security debate.

2. What are the drawbacks to the critical perspective?

3. How would you describe the feminist perspective on old age?

4. In what ways does a critical approach empower individuals?

5. What is a "humanist" perspective?

Acknowledgments

This paper is based in part on a plenary presentation to the annual conference of the British Society for Gerontology in September 1995. The author gratefully acknowledges Chris Phillipson, Miriam Bernard, Malcolm Johnson and Alan Walker for their encouragement, inspiration and support. Deepest thanks also are due Martha Holstein for her valuable comments on an earlier draft of this paper.

References

Abel, E. 1991. *Who Cares for the Elderly? Public Policy and the Experience of Adult Daughters*. Temple University Press. Philadelphia.

Achenbaum, A., Jakobi, P. and Kastenbaum, R. 1993. *Voices and Visions of Aging: Towards a Critical Gerontology*. Springer Publishing Company, New York, 46–63.

Achenbaum, A. 1986. Aging of the first new nation. In Pifer, A. and Bronte, L. (eds.) *Our Aging Society: Paradox and Promise*. W. W. Norton Co., NY, 15–32.

Angelou, M. 1986. *And Still I Rise*. Virago Press.

Arber, S. and Ginn, J. 1991. *Gender and Later Life*. Sage Publications, London.

Archibold, P. G. 1983. An impact of parent-caring on women. *Family Relations* 32, 39–45.

Baars, J. 1991. The challenge of critical studies. *Journal of Aging Studies* 5, 219–243.

Baines, C., Evans. P. and Neysmith. S. (eds) *Women's Caring: Feminist Perspectives on Social Welfare*. McClelland and Stewart, Inc., Toronto.

Becker. M. 1986. The tyranny of health promotion. *Public Health Review* 14, 15–23.

Bernard, M. and Meade, K. (eds) 1993. *Women Come of Age*. Edward Arnold, London.

Blakemore, K. and Boneham. M. 1994. *Age, Race and Ethnicity: A Comparative Approach*. Open University, Philadelphia.

Bond, J. and Coleman, P. 1993. Ageing into the twenty first century. In Bond, J., Coleman, P. and Peace. S., (eds) 1993. *Ageing in Society: An Introduction to Social Gerontology*. 2nd Edition. Sage Publications, London, 333–350.

Browne, C. 1995. Empowerment in social work practice with older women. *Social Work*, 40, 358–364.

Burton, L., Dilworth-Anderson P. and Bengtson, V. 1992. Creating culturally relevant ways of thinking about aging and diversity: Theoretical challenges for the 21st century. In Stanford, E. P. and Torres-Gil, F. M. (eds) *Diversity: New Approaches to Ethnic Minority Aging*. Baywood Publishing Co., Amityville, New York, 129–140.

Cole, T. 1988. The specter of old age: History, politics and culture in an aging America. *Tikkun*, 3, 14–18 and 93–95.

Cole, T., Van Tassel, D. and Kastenbaum, R. (eds) 1992. *Handbook of Aging and the Humanities*. Springer Publishing Company, New York.

Cole, T., Achenbaum, A., Jakobi, P. and Kastenbaum, R. 1993. *Voices and Visions of Aging: Towards a Critical Gerontology*. Springer Publishing Company, New York.

Department of Health and Social Security. 1981. *Growing Older*. Cmnd 8173, HMSO, London.

Dowd, J. J. and Bengtson, V. L. 1978. Aging in minority populations: An examination of the double jeopardy hypothesis. *Journal of Gerontology*, 33, 338–355.

Elshtain, J. 1995. *Democracy on Trial*. Basic Books, New York.

Estes, C. L. 1979. *The Aging Enterprise*. Jossey Bass, California.

Estes, C. L. 1991. The new political economy of aging: introduction and critique. In Minkler, M. and Estes, C. L. (eds) *Critical Perspectives on Aging: The Political and Moral Economy of Growing Old*. Baywood Publishing Co., Amityville, New York, 19–36.

Estes, C. L., Swan, J. H. and Gerard, L. 1982. Dominant and competing paradigms in gerontology: Toward a political economy of ageing. *Ageing and Society*, 2 (Part 2), 151–164.

Fahey, C.J. and Holstein. M. 1993. Toward a philosophy of the third age. In Cole, T. R. *et al*. (eds) *Voices and Visions: Toward a Critical Gerontology*. Springer Publishing Co., New York, 241–256.

Featherstone, M. and Hepworth, M. 1993. Images of ageing. In Bond, J., Coleman, P. and Peace, S. (eds) 1993. *Ageing in Society: An Introduction to Social Gerontology*. Sage Publications, London.

French, M. 1986. *Beyond Power: On Women, Men and Morals*. Abacus, London.

Gibson, R. C. 1991. The subjective retirement of Black Americans. *Journal of Gerontology: Social Sciences* 46, S204–S209.

Goodin, R. E. 1985. *Protecting the Vulnerable*. The University of Chicago Press, Chicago.

Guillemard, A.M. 1986. *Old Age and the Welfare State*. Sage Publishing Company, California.

Holstein, M. 1994. Taking next steps: Gerontological education, research, and the literary imagination. *The Gerontologist* 34, 822–827.

Holstein, M. Personal communication, 16 June 1995.

Jackson, J., Kolody, B. and Wood, J. L. 1982. To be old and black: The case for double jeopardy in income and health. In Manuel, R. C. (ed) *Minority Aging*. Greenwood Press, Westport, Conn.

Jackson, J.J. 1991. The urrent status of ethnogerontology, and its complementary and conflicting social and cultural concerns for American minority and ethnic elders. Paper presented at the annual meeting of the American Society on Aging, New Orleans, LA.

Johnson, M. 1993. Dependency and interdependency. In Bond, J., Coleman, P. and Peace,

S. (eds) *Ageing and Society*. Sage Publications, London, 255–279.

Johnson, M. L. 1995. Interdependency and the generational compact. *Ageing and Society* 15, 2.

Jordan, J. 1985. *On Call*. South End Press, Boston, MA.

Kart, C. S. 1987. The end of conventional gerontology. *Sociology of Health and Illness* 9, 76–87.

Kent, J. 1971. A descriptive approach to community. Unpublished report, Denver, Colorado.

Kitwood, T. 1990. *Concern for Others: A New Psychology of Consciousness and Morality*. Routledge, London.

Kohli, M. 1987. Retirement and the moral economy. *Journal of Aging Studies* 1, 125–144.

Kreiger, N. *et al.* 1995. Racism, sexism, and social class: Implications for studies of health, disease and well being. *American Journal of Preventive Medicine*. (Special supplement on racial differences in preterm delivery) 9 (6): 82–122.

Labonte, R. 1993. Uniting for healthier communities. Keynote address to the 121st Annual Meeting of the American Public Health Association, San Francisco, CA. Oct. 24.

Lessing, D. 1983. *The Diary of a Good Neighbour/Jane Somers*. A. A. Knopf, New York.

Levin, D. 1987 Pathologies of The Modern Self. University Press, New York.

Lloyd, P. 1991. The empowerment of elderly people. *Journal of Ageing Studies*, 5(2): 125–35.

Los Angeles Times 1982. Safe houses now easing fears of elderly residents. 21.11.82: 1.

Minkler, M. 1992. Community organizing among the elderly poor in the U.S.: A case study. *International Journal of Health Services*, 22: 303–316.

Minkler, M. 1994. Challenges for health promotion in the 1990s: Social inequities, empowerment, negative consequences and the public good. *American Journal of Health Promotion*, 8 (6): 403-413.

Minkler, M (in press). Empowerment of the elderly in San Francisco's Tenderloin District. In Amick, B. and Rudd, R. (eds) *Society and Health: Case Studies*. Harvard University Press, Cambridge, Mass.

Minkler, M. and Estes, C. L. (eds.) 1991. *Critical Perspectives on Aging: The Political and Moral Economy of Growing Old*. Baywood Publishing Co., Amityville, New York.

Minkler, M. and Robertson, A. 1991. The ideology of age/race wars: Deconstructing a social problem. *Ageing and Society*, 11: 1–22.

Minkler, M. and Roe, K. M. 1993. *Grandmothers as Caregivers: Raising Children of the Crack Cocaine Epidemic*. Sage Publications, California.

Moody, H. 1988. *Abundance of Life: Human Development Policies for an Aging Society*. Columbia University Press, New York.

Moody, H. 1993. What is critical gerontology and why is it important? In Cole, T., Achenbaum, A., Jakobi, P. and Kastenbaum, R. *Voices and Visions of Aging: Towards a Critical Gerontology*. Springer Publishing Company, New York, xv–xvi.

Morrison, T. 1987. *Beloved*. New American Library, New York.

Myles, J. 1983. Conflict, crisis and the future of old age security. *Milbank Memorial Fund Quarterly/Health and Society*, 61, 462–472.

Neysmith, S. 1989. Closing the gap between health policy and the home-care needs of tomorrow's elderly. *Canadian Journal of Community Mental Health*, 8, 141–150.

Ovrebo, B. and Minkler, M. 1993. The lives of older women: Perspectives from political economy and the humanities. In Cole, T., Achenbaum, A., Jakobi, P. and Kastenbaum, R. *Voices and Visions of Aging: Towards a Critical Gerontology*. Springer Publishing Company, New York, 289–308.

Phillipson, C., Bernard, M. and Strang, P. (eds) 1986. *Dependency and Interdependency in Old Age: Theoretical Perspectives and Policy Alternatives*. Croom Helm, London, 30–45.

Phillipson, C. 1991. The social construction of old age: Perspectives from political economy. *Reviews in Clinical Gerontology*, 19, 27–36.

Phillipson, C. 1994. Modernity, post-modernity and the sociology of aging: Reformulating critical gerontology. Paper presented at the XII World of Congress of Sociology.

Phillipson, C. and Walker, A. 1987. The case for a critical gerontology. In De Gregorio, S. (ed.) *Social Gerontology: New Directions*. London: Croom Helm, 1–15.

Porter, D. 1995. *The Path to Poverty: An Analysis of Women's Retirement Income*. Older Women's League, Washington D.C.

Robertson, A. 1991. The politics of Alzheimer's Disease: A case study in apocalyptic demography. In Minkler, M. and Estes, C. L. *Critical Perspectives on Aging: The political and moral economy of growing old*. Baywood Publishing Co., New York.

Rowe, J. W. and Kahn, R. 1987. Human aging: Usual and successful. *Science*, 237 143–149.

Schmidt, R. M. 1994. Healthy aging into the 21st century. *Contemporary Gerontology*, 1, 3–6.

Siler-Wells, G. L. 1989. Challenges of the gordian knot: Community health in Canada. In *International Symposium on Community Participation and Empowerment Strategies in Health Promotion*. Bielefeld, Germany: Center for Interdisciplinary Studies, University of Bielefeld.

Stoller, E. P. and Gibson, R. C. 1994. *Worlds of Difference: Inequalities in the Aging Experience*. Pine Forge Press, California.

Townsend, P. 1981. The structured dependency of the elderly: A creation of social policy in the twentieth century. *Ageing and Society*, 1 (6).

Townsend, P. 1986. Ageism and social policy. In Phillipson, C. and Walker, A. (eds) *Ageing and Social Policy*. Gower, London, 15–44.

U.S. Bureau of the Census. 1991. Current population reports: Marital status and living arrangements: March 1990, Series P-20 No. 450. Government Printing Office, Washington, DC.

Verbrugge, L. 1983. Women and men: Mortality and health of older people. In Hess, B. B. and Bond, K. (eds) *Aging in Society: Selected Reviews of Recent Research*, Lawrence Erlbaum, New Jersey, 139–174.

Walker, A. 1981. Towards a political economy of old age. *Ageing and Society* 1, 73–94.

Walker, A. 1987. Ageing and the social sciences: The North American way. *Ageing and Society*, 7, 235–242.

Walker, A. 1990. The economic 'burden' of ageing and the prospect of intergenerational conflict. *Ageing and Society*, 10, 377–396.

Woodward, K. 1991. *Ageing and Its Discontents: Freud and Other Fictions*. Indiana University Press, Bloomington, Indiana.

Chapter 48
Aging in the Twenty-first Century

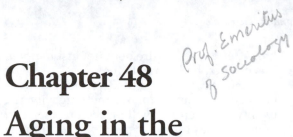

Matilda White Riley

If it is commonplace today to recognize that people born at different historical periods will have a very different experience of aging from that of people born only 10 years before or after, much of the credit goes to Matilda White Riley, who has spent much of her professional career explaining the interplay of cohort (birth date), age (chronological aging), and period (slice of history). For example, today's very old were young adults during the Great Depression and therefore know what it is like to lose one's job and life savings due to impersonal market forces. Their offspring, now the "young old," carry a less distinct memory of economic collapse but are very aware of the dislocations of wartime. In contrast, the baby boomers, who will enter old age in 2012 and after, grew up in an era of relative peace and prosperity. Thus, having undergone certain formative experiences at particular ages makes certain issues more salient than others, affecting values and voting behavior.

But individuals are only half the equation; they reach adulthood and age within specific social structures. The likelihood of one's having a college education, adequate health care, full-time employment, pension benefits, and access to a nursing home all vary historically. Health habits, such as smoking or being aware of cholesterol intake, vary from one birth cohort to another. As you read Riley's selection, pay attention to the point that she makes clear: aging has its chronological trajectory while social systems change at a different pace, creating a "structural lag" between the needs and capacities of older people and the social arrangements required to accommodate them.

Consider the types of interventions that might make structures more responsive in the century ahead. Think about Riley's statement: "For the first time in history people are aging in a society where most people will live to be old."

It would be no news, of course, if I observed that aging in the twenty-first century will predictably be different from aging in the twentieth. In the midst of all the other cataclysmic changes in the United States and throughout the world, I almost hesitate to address such a topic as changes in aging.

Yet the changes are daunting. I have no crystal ball to dust off as an aid in considering them, but I *do* have some important observations to make. Among other changes, the increase in human longevity and its enormous implications for the aging process have to rank high. For the first time in history people are aging in a society where *most* people live to be old. In addition, while nearly three decades have been added to individual lives during the twentieth century on the average, the entire world—and all familiar social structures and institutions—are changing around these lives. These social changes affect people in many dramatic ways, ways that are still hard for us to comprehend because we are part of them.

All this is well known. What *is* news is that social and behavioral scientists have begun to study these manifold changes and to anticipate and debate the consequences for the future of the aging process and for its potential. That is, scientific research is providing many clues not only to what aging *may* be like in the future but also to what aging *could* be like if the potential is fulfilled. These clues require a revision of traditional views as to what aging means.

Structural Lag

This selection is going to talk mainly about potentials. First, however, I want to tell you about a new insight that points to these potentials. This insight, recently forged from research, defines one of the most perplexing problems of our time, the problem "structural lag." This concerns the mismatch between two central changes: (1) changes in individual aging and (2) changes in the structure of society that influence the ways individuals age. While more and more people live longer than in the past and grow old in new ways, social structures have been slow to make room for them. These structures are still geared to the population of much younger people that characterized the nineteenth—certainly not the twenty-first, century.

Everyone can think of many personal anecdotes that illustrate this problem of structural lag, but I'll tell about one closest to my own experience. Because my husband reached age 65 in 1973, he was required to retire as a top executive of Equitable Life. He had to retire even though he was just reaching the peak of his vigor and his career. Jobs were for younger, not older, people. Of course, he is a special case, and over the intervening 17 years he has managed to create his own opportunities to be productive. But these opportunities were not ready-made for him in society.

The point of this anecdote is that societal institutions are generally failing to make room for those many workers who, as they age, continue to be capable and are not yet ready for full retirement. Similarly, health-care systems often fail to provide the supports necessary for the many older people who, even when frail, now want to function independently. Unlike roles for schoolchildren or for young entrants into the labor force, few roles have been developed to fit workers or students who have grown old. Nor does society accord esteem and prestige to the significant productivity of older people's unpaid roles as homemakers or caretakers of the disabled. So I speak of this current mismatch as "structural lag" because the structure of social opportunities has not kept pace with the rapid changes in the ways that people are now growing old.

Clearly this mismatch is fraught with problems. Yet within it lie untold promising potentials for the future. My message here is one of optimism. I shall argue that these potentials can become realities—that the mismatch can be reduced by diverse kinds of intervention. Intervention can occur through both public and private policies, changes in professional practice, and individual choices in everyday life. After all, the future does not just happen; it is created by human beings.

This is my vision: if the twentieth century has been the era of increasing longevity, the twenty-first century will be the era of social opportunities for older people to age in new and better ways.

To explain this prediction I am going to explore various kinds of intervention (both deliberate and "naturally" occurring social changes). First, I shall discuss the potentials for aging—that is, how to make the most of the already incredible strengths of people as they grow older. Second, and most critical for the twenty-first century, I shall consider the potentials for outdated social structures—how to make the most of the social opportunities for older people (and thereby to reduce the problem of structural lag). Third, I shall offer a conceptual framework that social scientists use as an aid to the understanding of individual aging, social opportunities, and the mismatch between them. Of course such understanding is essential to a scientifically grounded vision of aging in the future and to the changes needed for bringing this vision into reality.

Making the Most of Individual Aging

To begin with individual aging, let me call your attention to the unrecognized strengths and capacities of most older people. I shall destroy the myth that aging is exclusively a biological process. I shall ask you to think along with me that people do not grow up and grow old in laboratories but rather in rapidly changing societies. And I shall report evidence for the proposition that the aging process is not fixed; it is mutable and subject to intervention and improvement.

The Fallacy of Inevitable Decline

Much research has demonstrated that the doctrine of inevitable decline is a fallacy—a fallacy initiated by faulty interpretation of cross-sectional data. Nevertheless, despite all the evidence to the contrary, this fallacious doctrine is still blindly accepted by many government policy makers, corporate executives, professional practitioners, and the pub-

Figure 48.1
Increasing Number of Older People

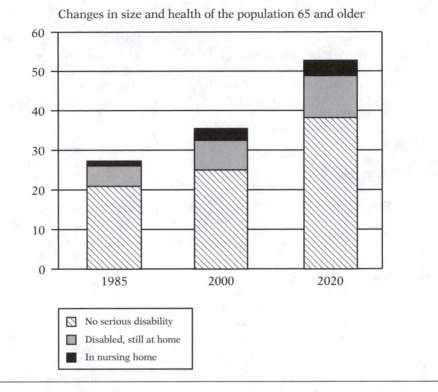

Changes in size and health of the population 65 and older

Legend:
- No serious disability
- Disabled, still at home
- In nursing home

Adapted from Kenneth Manton, Duke University

lic at large. The stereotype of inevitable decline remains stubborn; the very notion of aging seems to connote decrepitude, poverty, and misery ("afflicted with Alzheimer's disease," for example, or "imprisoned in a nursing home" or "dependent on medicine" as the only means of preventing either disease or institutionalization). Doctors are found to spend less time with older than with younger patients. Old people themselves take their aches and pains for granted and assume—falsely—that they cannot learn new skills or ways of thinking (such as use of computers or complicated technologies).

The 'Real' Aging Process: Neither Fixed nor Immutable

Yet those who listen to the evidence will realize that it is simply not true that, *because of age*, all older people are destined to be ill, impoverished, cut off from society, sexually incapacitated, despondent, or unable to reason or to remember. Of course, everyone dies. And some older people—a minority—are seriously disadvantaged and in need of personal and societal support. But the vast majority function independently and effectively (see Figure 48.1). The total number of people 65 and over will predictably multiply in the twenty-first century, as indicated by the rising heights of the bars in the figure; but the large number of the healthy (at the bottom of each bar) will heavily outweigh the number of disabled or institutionalized people (at the top). This chart underscores the first part of my message: that most older people are healthy and capable now and will continue to be in the twenty-first century.

In this selection I cannot focus directly on the critical problems of the minority who *are* irrevocably disabled or fatally ill. Rather I shall speak of "most" older people, who have even far greater and more diverse strengths and competence—in intellect, health, and interest in affairs— than are indicated in the chart or recognized generally.

Moreover, the research evidence demonstrates that the aging process is variable—so that still greater strengths are possible. Social scientists are showing how the aging process varies with social conditions: how individuals grow old in widely diverse ways depending on their family life, their socioeconomic status, and their work conditions. Social scientists are also showing how the aging process changes over time as society changes. My grandmother at 75 was very different from what I was at 75, and my granddaughters will be still different when they reach 75—because we were born at different times and grew older in different periods of history.

Entire cohorts of people already old differ markedly from cohorts not yet old as to education, work history and standard of living, attitudes and cultural tastes, diet and exercise, physical stature, age of menarche, experience with chronic rather than acute diseases, and so on.

Perhaps the most notable of all the historical alterations in the aging process spring from the unprecedented increases in longevity—which allow recent cohorts of young people to stay in school many years longer than their predecessors did, prolong retirement, postpone many diseases of old age, accumulate the experiences essential for wisdom, and extend family relationships, so that husbands and wives now typically survive together for four or even five decades or more. (For my husband and me next year will be our 60th year of marriage.) And it is these more recent cohorts who will be the old people of the twenty-first century.

Potentials for Intervention

In short, the aging process is mutable, and most older people are able to draw on widely diverse competencies—in health, intellect, and involvement in affairs. In addition (to reemphasize the point), there is significant potential for enhancing these strengths still further. Just consider what this means for the twenty-first century. Death is inevitable, but the nature of the aging process is not inevitable, and after all, it is the quality of the later years that counts.

What kinds of intervention, then, might sustain or even enhance this quality in the future? Social and behavioral research has been producing some spectacular findings:

- Among older workers intellectual functioning improves with age if the work situation is challenging and calls for self-direction.

- Very old people whose performance on intelligence tests has deteriorated can be brought back to their performance levels of 20 years earlier if the social environment affords incentives and opportunities for practicing and learning new strategies.

- Memory can be improved if the impoverished context that often characterizes retirement is altered to include the stimulation of a rich and complex environment.

- Even slowed reaction time, long attributed to irreversible aging losses in central nervous system functioning, can be speeded up if the social situation provides training and consistent feedback.

- Changing the social environment in nursing homes to increase the sense of personal control and independence in aging patients can result in greater social activity, changed immune functioning, and perhaps even lowered mortality.

Moreover, even when alterations in behavior, lifestyles, and social contacts are made late in life, such alterations can still reduce morbidity and mortality. To stop cigarette smoking at age 60, for example, can make a difference.

Social Opportunities

So much for the incredible strengths and potential capacities of older people. Please note, however, that all these and many similar instances of intervention in the ways people age are characterized by one common theme: the older person's functioning is contingent upon the social conditions. Bereft of social opportunities, resources, or incentives, older people cannot utilize or sustain their mental or physical strengths and capacities, and the doctrine of inevitable decline becomes a self-fulfilling prophecy. Thus the root of the mismatch lies not in people's capacities or in the aging process itself but in the lack of suitable social roles through which individuals can move as they grow older. Consequently, aging in the twenty-first century will depend upon changes in society: on reduction of the twentieth-century lag in social structures.

The Current Lag

Today's social structures and norms are the vestigial remains of the nineteenth century, when most people died before their work was finished or their last child had left home. Age 65 was established as the criterion for insurance eligibility in Germany back in the 1870s—yet age 65 is still used in many countries under today's utterly changed conditions of longevity. The older population is, of course, widely heterogeneous, but here are some examples of typical misfits between aging and social structures:

- For many decades now opportunities for older workers have been declining. Today less than half of men aged 55 and over are in the labor force, a fraction that could drop to only one-third by the start of the twenty-first century. For women, whose recent entry into the paid labor force will have untold consequences, the lag is even more pronounced. Yet survey after survey has indicated that large numbers of older workers wish to continue some kind of work—if the hours are flexible and the pay acceptable.

- In the family many older people are widows who live entirely alone. Those who are frail often lack social supports to maintain independent living in their own homes. Health-care facilities are inadequate and costly, and people who are disabled often lack caregivers; many live in fear of destitution.

- Older people's place in society generally has aptly been called a "roleless role."

In sum, modifications in the roles decreed by society have indeed lagged behind the rapid changes in the process of aging—changes in the strengths, as well as in the numbers, of older people themselves. So far these roles have largely failed to aid older people in developing or expressing their remarkable potentials.

Potentials for Intervention in the Twenty-first Century

Nevertheless, research on social structures is beginning to show that, like the aging process, they too are mutable. Here again intervention to correct structural lag is found to be possible, and the possibilities in the twenty-first century are predictably far-flung. Consider a few scattered attempts at improving roles for older people that are already under way and that give clear evidence of what is possible in the future.

In *education*, opportunities are being made for older people either to teach (teaching adults who cannot read, for example, or immigrants who can't speak English) or to go back to school. Nearly 1,000 colleges in the United States now accept students over age 65.

In *leisure*, opportunities are being made both for recreation and for more serious cultural pursuits. The Elderhostel movement is thriving worldwide, and retirement communities are increasingly located close to university facilities.

In the *household*, opportunities for frail older people to remain independent are being improved through supportive community services, injury-proof housing design, and elder-friendly tools older people can use.

Throughout the *health-care system* there are increasing demands for older people in the role of care*giver* (rather than care *receiver*).

At *work*, there is increasing provision of part-time work, job sharing, and flexible hours. Some companies have model programs for "unretirement," that is, for rehiring retired employees. There are untold opportunities for moonlighting in work that is not identified in official employment statistics. And there are increasingly varied and significant opportunities for many kinds of volunteer jobs.

This is the right moment to mention "financial gerontology," the focus of the Boettner Research Institute. Already we have begun to witness the development of increasingly flexible contracts: contracts that combine insurance and investment features, contracts that contain stop-and-go provisions, contracts that anticipate changing financial requirements over the life course, contracts that give people increasing control over the traditional problem of economic security. These changes are harbingers of a twenty-first-century array of new financial instruments and arrangements.

All such structural interventions are producing new and more flexible roles, and wider options, for older people. Whether or not particular older individuals wish to remain in the economic mainstream of society or to be productive in the many unpaid and volunteer roles, one thing is clear: older people do not wish now, nor will they wish in the next century, to be disregarded, denigrated, or dependent.

Implications for All Ages

There is another noteworthy point here. As such structural intervention develops in the next century, it will have implications for people of all ages: young and (as in the Boettner Research Institute emphasis) middle-aged, not just the old. Making room in a college classroom for older adults also affects the lives of traditional students who are younger. Any structural intervention, even though aimed at the old, will predictably have ramifications affecting how everyone grows older.

Indeed, I believe we can anticipate in practice in the twenty-first century what we once regarded as a purely visionary potential, the breakdown of the rigid age barriers that have traditionally divided societal roles into three parts: education in youth, work in middle age, and leisure in old age. Those "age-segregated" social roles may be giving way to more "age-integrated" roles—providing options for people over their lifetimes to intersperse periods of work with periods of education and leisure.

Furthermore, we can even begin to see signs of deliberate structural intervention to support this interspersing—to make it possible for people to move from school to work and later go from work back again to school; to change careers; and to spread leisure more evenly over the life course, rather than concentrating nearly all of it in retirement. For example, some organizations are providing educational leaves from work, more portable pensions, or retraining for older adults and preparation for new occupations; others are allowing employees over their work lives to take several years of leave, to be spent—according to choice—in family care, for travel, or in continuing education.

Unintended Consequences

All these signs are heady portents of aging in the twenty-first century. However, one critical question remains: how can social scientists ensure that changes and intervention undertaken today will increase (rather than diminish) older people's opportunities for the future? This question requires far-reaching vision and the knowledge base essential for intervention, because on the other hand, intervention can sometimes have unintended and undesired consequences. For example, encouraging everyone to engage in physical exercise, though intended for lifelong strengthening of joints and muscles, may injure them instead; tender loving care in nursing homes, though intended as emotional support for older patients, may instead reduce independence and effective functioning; and encouraging older people to work may result in abuse of older workers.

Even elaborately designed kinds of intervention can turn out to have very little effect. For example, legislation to abolish age as a basis for mandatory retirement has failed to slow the trend toward retiring early.

On the other hand, *failure* to intervene can exacerbate rather than reduce structural lag. For example, suppose the traditional trends are simply allowed to persist. A German scholar, Martin Kohli, has recently calculated the absurd outcome: sometime in the second half of the twenty-first century society could arrive at a point when people, at the age of about 38, will move from the university directly into retirement! An absurd idea, to be sure (but I am not being absurd when I pre-

Figure 48.2
Conceptual Framework: Aging and Social Change

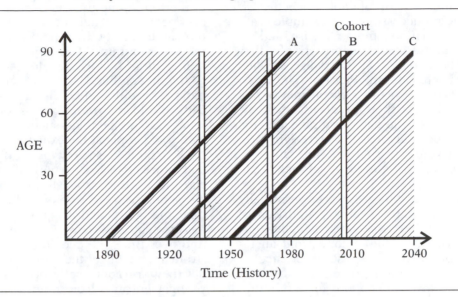

Source: Riley, M. W., Foner, A., and Waring, J. 1988. "Sociology of Age," in Neil J. Smelser, (ed.) *Handbook of Sociology.* Newbury Park, Calif.: Sage.

dict the end of nearly universal early retirement as we know it today).

The mission for social scientists, then, is to help guide intervention by providing not only a broad vision but also a firm scientific grounding for this vision.

A Conceptual View of Intervention

Toward this end a conceptual framework from the sociology of age is widely used for getting a handle on the future (as shown in Figure 48.2). It represents social space bounded by ages on the vertical axis and by dates on the horizontal axis. These dates indicate the course of history—past and future. Within this space two sets of lines crisscross each other. These refer to changes in aging and in social structures.

Aging

Consider first the diagonal lines, which refer to aging. They represent successive cohorts of people who were born in particular time periods and who are aging. As people age they move along the diagonal (see, for example, Cohort A), across time and upward through the social structure; they pass through the successive roles in family life, school grades and work careers, retirement, and ultimately death. As they age they change biologically, psychologically, and socially, and they develop their individual strengths and capacities.

Moreover, because successive cohorts (the series of diagonals) are born at different dates and live through different segments of historical time, their members age in different ways. Thus a man born in 1890 (Cohort A) could scarcely have looked ahead to retirement at all, but a man born in 1950 (Cohort C, now 40 years old) can expect to spend one-quarter of his adult lifetime in retirement.

The diagonals in the figure are not purely abstract. They are used to aid understanding of "growing old in the twenty-first century" because facts about the past lives of people now alive are already established. By tracing their lives into the future, social scientists can use these facts to forecast how they will grow old.

Many facts are now available as guideposts to the future. In some ways future cohorts of older people will predictably be better off than their predecessors. For example, with improved nutrition, more exercise, and reduced cigarette smoking in early life, they may well be less subject to heart disease when they reach later life. In other ways, however, the future cohorts of older people may be *less* advantaged than their predecessors: their lives will reflect the deteriorating economic conditions of today and the increasing proportion of young people who are failing to meet acceptable standards of academic achievement.

Two trends among women are especially provocative: an increasing proportion of young women in each successive cohort has participated in the labor force, and an increasing proportion has also experienced a divorce. Sociologists sometimes think of these as negative indications for the future. But do they perhaps mean instead that, as these young women become the older women of the future, they will have acquired more skills than their predecessors for living independently? Will their early work experience have increased the future economic security of the many who will predictably live alone in the next century?

Given this wide variety of early life experiences, one point about the older people of the future seems certain: they will be widely heterogeneous (as indicated by their heterogeneity in health status, shown in Figure 48.1). Their needs for role opportunities will be increasingly varied, and different types of people will call for different types of intervention.

Structural Change

In short, precisely what these older people will be like, how they will grow old, and what their needs will be will depend in part on their past lives. But in large part they will also depend on the changing structure of society. The perpendicular lines in Figure 48.2 schematize this structure and its changes. Consider a past year, such as 1980. Here the vertical line is a cross-section slice through all the diagonal lines. This slice denotes the age structure at a single moment in history. It indicates how both the people and their social

roles are organized roughly in age groupings, from the youngest at the bottom to the oldest at the top. Along this slice one can imagine how people of all ages coexist and interact in the same society. In a family, for example, members of four different generations interrelate, either by forming close ties or by engaging in conflict. Or, in another example, a nation's wealth can be distributed equitably between old and young, or—as some contend is already happening—so inequitably as to favor old people at the expense of children.

Over time, as society moves through past and future historical events and changes, one can imagine this vertical line moving—across tile space from one date to the next. Over time, the age-related structures of opportunities are subject to social and cultural changes. And over time, the people in particular age strata are no longer the same people; inevitably they are continually being replaced by younger entrants from more recent cohorts with more recent life experiences.

It is from these changes that the phenomenon of structural lag has been emerging. Today older people have become more numerous, better educated, and more vigorous than their predecessors back in 1940 or 1970; but so far few structural changes in society have been made for them. They are still generally treated as a disadvantaged minority; that is, they are handicapped by the lag. It is here that intervention will be especially crucial for the twenty-first century.

Asynchrony

One last—and I think intriguing—feature of Figure 48.2 is the inherent paradox of timing. Aging individuals are moving along the axis of the life course, the diagonal lines. But change in the structures of society (the moving vertical line) moves along its own axis of historical time. These two sets of lines are continually crisscrossing each other. Hence they can never be perfectly synchronized. And it is this asynchrony that accounts for the recurring mismatch between them—a mismatch that creates continuing pressures for intervention.

To return now to the critical question with which I began: How can the current lag be adjusted? How will roles change (or be changed) to foster the growing numbers, strengths, and heterogeneity of older people in the twenty-first century? The details are still dim; but our conceptual diagram opens up glimpses into the future.

My view of the future can now be quickly summarized. We can discern a vision of a future society in which older people's lives are more varied, more open to choice, more rewarding. We can glimpse aging in a possible future society where lifelong learning will replace the lockstep of traditional education; a society where ageist discrimination will no longer be a dominant force; a society where entirely new arrangements for financial security will characterize the life course; a society where retirement as we know it today will disappear and will be replaced by periods of leisure interspersed throughout life with periods of education and work; a society where the values of kinship and intimacy are matters of choice, not duty.

At this point the vision fades, to be replaced by the reality that these kinds of interventions have yet to be invented. I can, however, conclude with one sure prediction, theoretically grounded and empirically demonstrable: capable older people and empty roles cannot long coexist. Aging in the twenty-first century, in which the tension between the two must be continuously adjusted, will bear little resemblance to aging as we have known it in the twentieth century.

Discussion Questions

1. How does Riley envisage the life course of the twenty-first century?

2. Describe the ways cohort effects and aging effects interact.

3. Describe what you think will be the formative events of your birth cohort.

4. What kind of society do you foresee when you reach age 65?

5. How likely are the interventions mentioned by Riley?

Reprinted from: Matilda White Riley, "Aging in the Twenty-first Century." From Boettner Lecture, 1990. Byrn Mawr, PA: Boettner Research Institute. Reprinted by permission.